VATICAN II
Assessment
and Perspectives

VATICAN II
Assessment
and Perspectives

Twenty-Five Years After
(1962–1987)

VOLUME ONE

Edited by RENÉ LATOURELLE

PAULIST PRESS/ NEW YORK/ MAHWAH

The publication of this project has been helped immensely by generous gifts from trustees of the Gregorian University Foundation and other friends. Specific contributions were made by Mr. John Brogan, Mr. and Mrs. Cyril Nigg, and Mr. and Mrs. John T. Ryan, Jr. To them and all others whose assistance made possible this publication—in French, German, and Italian as well as English—warmest thanks from the writer and editor.

Library of Congress Cataloging-in-Publication Data

Vatican II: Assessment and perspectives: twenty-five years after
    (1962–1987)/edited by René Latourelle.
        p.   cm.
    ISBN 0–8091–0412–1 (v. 1)
    1. Vatican Council (2nd: 1962–1965)   2. Catholic Church—
    Doctrines—History—20th century.   3. Catholic Church—
    History—20th century.   I. Latourelle, René
    BX830 1962.V322 1988
    262'.52—dc19   87–35972
                                                                 CIP

Published by Paulist Press
997 Macarthur Blvd.
Mahwah, NJ 07430

Printed and bound in the
United States of America

A Note on the English Translation

Except where the author of a given article is making his own translation (in which case the English translation is based on this), or in quotations found in already published English translations of works cited by the various authors, the translation of the Holy Scriptures used is *The Holy Bible,* Revised Standard Version, Catholic Edition (London: Catholic Truth Society, 1966). However, in some cases, the Jerusalem Bible and the New American Bible have been consulted.

Except where the author of a given article is making his own translation (in which case the English translation is based on this), the translation of the Council documents used is that found in A. Flannery (gen. ed.), *Vatican Council II: The Conciliar and Post Conciliar Documents* (Collegeville, MN: Liturgical Press, revised edition 1984). However, on some occasions, the translation found in W.M. Abbott (gen. ed.), *The Documents of Vatican II* (New York: Guild Press, 1966), has been consulted.

Except where the author of a given article is making his own translation (in which case the English translation is based on this), the translation of the 1983 Code of Canon Law used is that produced by the Canon Law Society of America (Washington, DC, 1983). However, on some occasions, the translation produced by the Canon Law Society of Great Britain and Ireland (London, 1983) has also been consulted.

Works quoted in the text of articles: If an already published English translation could be found, this has been used—as will be seen from the relative notes. However, if no English translation could be found, the present translators translated such quotations from the original-language version of the works in question—again, as will be seen from the relative notes.

Works quoted in notes: All such quotations have been left in the original language, and have not been translated into English.

Apart from the various people whose names appear at the end of the different articles as translators or cotranslators, the following have assisted with library research and/or advice: Philip Gillespie and Rev. Father Robert Hagan, S.J.

Leslie Wearne

Acknowledgments

The English edition of the present work has been made possible thanks to the generosity and large-scale contributions of a group of benefactors in the United States and Canada. We wish to express our deep gratitude to all these persons.

We should also like to address our sincere thanks to Miss Leslie Wearne, who is responsible for coordinating the English translation, and also to the whole team of translators.

René Latourelle, S.J.
Editor

Abbreviations

1. Abbreviations of the books of the Bible are those used in A. Flannery (gen. ed.), *Vatican Council II: The Conciliar and Post Conciliar Documents.*

2. *Abbreviations of Council Documents:*

AA   *Apostolicam actuositatem,* Decree on the Apostolate of the Laity

AG   *Ad gentes,* Decree on the Missionary Activity of the Church

CD   *Christus Dominus,* Decree on the Pastoral Office of Bishops in the Church

DH   *Dignitatis humanae,* Declaration on Religious Freedom

DV   *Dei Verbum,* Dogmatic Constitution on Divine Revelation

GE   *Gravissimum Educationis,* Declaration on Christian Education

GS   *Gaudium et spes,* Pastoral Constitution on the Church in the Modern World

IM   *Inter mirifica,* Decree on the Means of Social Communication

LG   *Lumen gentium,* Dogmatic Constitution on the Church

NA   *Nostra aetate,* Declaration on the Relation of the Church to Nonchristian Religions

OE   *Orientalium Ecclesiarum,* Decree on the Catholic Eastern Churches

OT   *Optatam totius*, Decree on the Training of Priests
PC   *Perfectae caritatis*, Decree on the Up-to-Date
          Renewal of Religious Life
PO   *Presbyterorum ordinis*, Decree on the Ministry and
          Life of Priests
SC   *Sacrosanctam concilium*, Constitution on the Sacred
          Liturgy
UR   *Unitatis redintegratio*, Decree on Ecumenism

3. *Other abbreviations:*

AAS   *Acta Apostolicae Sedis* (Rome, 1909–   )
AS   *Acta Synodalia S. Concilii Oecumenici Vaticani II*, 26
          vols. (Vatican City, 1970–1980)
ASS   *Acta Sanctae Sedis* (Rome, 1865–1908)
CIC   *Codex Juris Canonici* (The Code of Canon Law)
DS   H. Denzinger and A. Schönmetzter, *Enchiridion
          Symbolorum, Definitionum et Declarationum de rebus
          fidei et morum* (Freiburg im Breisgau, 1965)
Mansi   J.D. Mansi, *Sacrorum Conciliorum nova et
          amplissima collectio* (Florence, 1759)
PG   *Patrologia Graeca*, ed. J.P. Migne (Paris, 1857–
          1866)
PL   *Patrologia Latina*, ed. J.P. Migne (Paris, 1844–
          1855)

Apart from this, the authors of certain articles use a system of
abbreviations generally accepted in their specific fields of study
when citing specialized publications dealing with their own disciplines.

Contents

Introduction

The Second Vatican Council undoubtedly constitutes the greatest reform operation ever carried out in the Church, not only in view of the number of Council Fathers (2,540 at the beginning, as compared with 750 at the First Vatican Council and 258 at the Council of Trent), and the unanimity of the voting, which often exceeded all previous records (for example, there were only six negative votes out of a total of 2,350 on the Constitution on Divine Revelation, and only five on the Constitution on the Church), but above all in view of the vast scope of the subjects treated: revelation, the Church (its nature, constitution, members, and pastoral and missionary activity), the liturgy and the sacraments, other Christian communities and other religions, the laity, the consecrated life, Christian education, the reform of ecclesiastical studies, religious freedom, relations between faith and culture, and the means of social communication. When the sixteen conciliar documents are printed in a single paperback volume, we can tend to forget the vastness of the work carried out during this exuberant chapter in the Church's history, which was inaugurated on 11 October 1962 by John XXIII and came to a close on 8 December 1965 under Paul VI. However, the twenty-six volumes of the *Acta Synodalia*—the Acts of the Council—attest to the mammoth dimension of the undertaking.

The year 1987 represents the twenty-fifth anniversary of the opening of the Council, and 1988 that of the promulgation of the first conciliar documents. The Church has moved from a past that has not yet completely vanished to a future that is only just beginning. The Council of Trent gave its name to a period of more than four hundred years. And Vatican II represents a much deeper change. Even so, for today's students, who had only just been born in 1962, or had not yet been born, the Council already belongs to history. This phenomenon cannot be attributed solely to the slowness of the transition and the breadth of the operation, but also to the fact that we are now living at an accelerated pace. All over the world, through the mass media, we experienced the Council in the universal present. Although Vatican II was indeed a planetary and "simultaneous" event, we should not forget that it is also a *great sign* within history; and here again the rapid succession of events as conveyed by the mass media threatens to obscure our view of the great sign and reduce it to the dimension of the other facts that are reported by press, radio, and television, and immediately buried.

Further, in view of the frenetic rhythm at which life is lived in the contemporary world, we feel that the interval of twenty-five years that has elapsed since the opening of the Council is sufficient reason to pause a moment and reflect on the results already attained and those still to be achieved. Similar reflection has already been carried out by other theologians (for example, Cardinal J. Ratzinger, in his *Report*, published in 1985), other publications (the *Osservatore Romano*; the *Nouvelle Revue théologique*; the 1984 *Festschrift* in honor of Karl Rahner; the collection of articles, *La Réception de Vatican II*, edited by G. Alberigo and J.-P. Jossua in 1985; or *El Vaticano II, veinte años después*, edited by C. Floristán and J.J. Tamajo in 1985); and even the official Church at the Extraordinary Synod held in November–December 1985.

The present work represents a project conceived and carried out by the three university institutions of the Society of Jesus in Rome: the Gregorian University, the Biblical Institute, and the Oriental Institute. This work, which comprises three volumes and is being published in various languages, is the fruit of collaboration on the part of a team of sixty-seven professors from these three institutions—an international team made up of men from close on twenty different countries. The selection of the contributors was carried out by a steering committee made up of specialists from the three institutions, representing different disciplines: Professors Juan Alfaro (dogmatic theology, Gregorian University), René Latourelle (fundamental theology, Gregorian University), Jean Beyer (canon law, Gregorian University), Peter Henrici (philosophy, Gregorian University), José O'Callaghan (textual criticism, Biblical Institute), Maurice Gilbert (exegesis, Biblical Institute), and Gilles Pelland (patristics, Gregorian University and Oriental Institute).

We are well aware of the limits inevitably entailed in a project of this sort as regards the number of pages, the number of contributors, and the choice of subjects treated. The contributors were chosen on the basis of the two criteria of active participation in the work of the Council or its implementation, and longstanding familiarity with the subjects dealt with at the Council, as demonstrated in their teaching, research, and published work. We would have liked to include many other scholars of undeniable worth, and omission is certainly not the expression of any sort of judgment.

We feel that the phrase "assessment and perspectives" in the title gives a clear idea of the orientation of the project. It is not simply the celebration of an anniversary, in other words purely retrospective, but is pro-spective, inasmuch as the Council is seen as a starting point, a promised land, and the context of achievements still to come. Nor is it an unadulterated hymn of praise—although each one of the contributors does express appreciation of the remarkable advances made by the Council.

The term "assessment" balances that of "perspectives." In practical terms, it means a critical evaluation of the work of the Council, with emphasis on the positive contributions, but also noting the uncertainties, omissions, ambiguities and limitations, and the extra attention given to certain subjects at the expense of others. It also means rereading the texts twenty-five years on, and grasping the underlying harmonics and perceiving depths that were unsuspected at the time of the event itself. It means noting the changes in attitude that express the metanoia or conversion hoped for and brought about by the Council itself, for example, attitudes of dialogue, service, interiority, the search for content rather than form, and attention to the spirit rather than the letter. It means noting not only the points achieved, but also those that are still hoped for—a difficult task, since some of the fruits of the Council, such as the new Code of Canon Law, the Apostolic Constitution on Ecclesiastical Universities and Faculties, and certain liturgical texts of the new Ritual, came to maturity in the late seventies or in the eighties. Lastly, it means pinpointing certain problems, the seeds of which were contained in the conciliar texts, but which came to light and developed in

the postconciliar period, under the onslaught of very recent historical factors: problems of justice, famine, peace, human rights,
violence, nuclear and space war, general technological growth,
computer technology, and cultural interaction.

We hesitated before deciding on the present structure of the
work, although we realized very early on that any division that
followed the chronological order of the sixteen conciliar documents would be impracticable, due both to differences in importance and breadth of the various documents, and also to the
greater or lesser impact of the texts in question. We soon agreed
to divide the work according to subject, which, even so, allowed
us to take account of all the important conciliar texts. Thus, the
work is divided into three volumes, comprising ten parts in all.

After this introduction on the aim and structure of the work,
Volume One, *Part I* gives the historical framework of the Council and considers methodological questions and conciliar attitudes. *Part II* is dedicated wholly to the Constitution *Dei
Verbum;* the implications, potential, and basic power of this
document have yet to make themselves fully felt. *Part III*, on the
Church, covers subjects dealt with in *Lumen gentium,* the Decree
on the Apostolate of Lay People, and the new Code of Canon
Law. In Volume Two, *Part IV* examines the subjects dealt with
in the Constitution *Sacrosanctum concilium:* the liturgy and its
relationship to the Church; the sacraments, particularly Baptism, Reconcilation, the Eucharist, and Matrimony; and the Divine Office. *Part V*, on the Church and the churches, defines the
position of the Catholic Church with regard to other Christian
churches, takes stock of ecumenical dialogue (*Unitatis redintegratio*), and describes the special character and contribution of
the eastern churches (*Orientalum ecclesiarum*). *Part VI* covers the
various aspects of anthropology dealt with mainly in *Gaudium et
spes,* such as human dignity and rights, the Christian conception
of the human person, various ethical questions, the human person's relationship to God, and the person's origin and ultimate
goal. In Volume Three, *Part VII* studies the Decree *Perfectae
caritatis*, which has enjoyed a remarkable degree of success, undoubtedly because of the revision of the statutes and constitutions of religious communities throughout the world. *Part VIII*
considers certain questions dealt with in the Decree *Ad gentes,*
the Declaration *Nostra aetate,* and the Constitution *Gaudium et
spes:* atheism, evangelization, interreligious dialogue, and the

monotheistic religions (i.e., Judaism and Islam). *Part IX* gathers together the various aspects of the theological training of the clergy, specifically exegesis and biblical theology, patristic theology, and fundamental theology, as these are found in the Decree *Optatam totius* on the training of priests, and the Declaration *Gravissimum educationis* on Christian education. *Part X*, which is the last in the work, focuses on certain problems that were considered by the Council, particularly in *Gaudium et spes*, *Lumen gentium*, and *Inter mirifica*, but that have come unexpectedly to the forefront in the course of the past decade.

The work thus covers almost all conciliar documents, although it does not claim to be exhaustive—for this is not its principal aim. Its primary objective is to be of service to the Church, both to academic circles and to all Christians. It is offered as a study on conciliar and postconciliar theology at a decisive turning point in the history of the Church. It also represents an act of homage both to Pope John XXIII, who received the inspiration for the Council, convened it, and bequeathed it his spirit, and to Pope Paul VI, who was the main craftsman of the Council and effectively fostered its application in the renewal of the structures of the Church.

We said at the outset that Vatican II is a *great sign* addressed to men and women of our times. This sign has been given, but will we be able to read and interpret it? A great breath of new life has roused the Church, but is this breath going to die away? What would become of the inanimate texts without the Spirit who gives them life and opens our hearts to hear them? The sign of the Council appears at the same time as threats of death for all humanity, and when it presents us again with Christ as Life and the Church as sacrament of life and universal salvation, it can help people triumph over death, on condition that it becomes the life of our life. Above all, the Council must give birth to saints to bear witness to its fruitfulness, for the world looks for the presence of saints, and if there are none to be seen, people live shrouded in fog and die of cold.

René Latourelle, S.J.
Editor

PART I

HISTORICAL CONTEXT
AND
METHODOLOGICAL
PROBLEMS

CHAPTER 1

The Historical Context in Which the Idea of a New Ecumenical Council Was Born

Giacomo Martina, S.J.

Summary

The general situation of society and the Church in the period between 1945 and 1959 was marked by two elements: first, a very strong and rapid evolution in various fields; and, second, within the Church itself, a clash between more open orientations and more conservative ones. The aforesaid evolution appeared at the end of the colonial era, when the peoples of Africa and Asia were gaining their independence, and in the context of rapid industrialization and of the influence of television on outlooks and behavior. The conservative tendencies of the Church, which were especially strong at its center, were expressed in the Spanish concordat of 1953, the "excommunication" of communists in 1949, and frequent interventions on the part of Rome, culminating in the Encyclical *Humani generis*. The orientations toward openness were defended by various representative figures in Italy and France, by the worker priests, and by the "new theology." However, the conservative wing prevailed in the suspension and suppression of the worker priests (1954–1959) and in the disciplinary measures taken against Daniélou, de Lubac, Chenu, Congar, and Murray. The situation would be reversed with Vatican II, in which the "guilty parties" would play an important role, with the promotion of Daniélou (1969) and de Lubac (1983) as cardinals, the reestablishment of the worker priests

(1965), and a new policy with regard to concordats (1976/79 with Spain, and 1984 with Italy). This deep underlying change can be seen clearly in the following pages: a change in mentality and pastoral practice, a change that is the result of Vatican II.

———————
———————

Other Councils were held with the clear aim of refuting and condemning doctrinal or practical trends that were clearly identified as to their formulation, if not equally so as to their authors. Vatican II, on the other hand, was planned and convened at a time when there was no specific trend in society and the Church that required a clearly expressed stand on the part of the magisterium. A great many biblical, dogmatic, and moral points were being discussed—for example, the new moral attitudes (partly as influenced by existentialist philosophy), new methods being used in interpreting the Bible, and the significance of Tradition—but all this did not seem to justify the convocation of a Council. Even so, when John XXIII announced the decision on 25 January 1959, with full awareness that he was committing all his own authority and all the prestige of the Roman papacy to it, it represented a response to an objective need and a malaise that was very widely felt in vast sectors of the clerical and lay world. At that time, very few people, among them the future Cardinal Costantini, had been imagining the possibility of an ecumenical assembly, and Pius XII had shelved the idea after some reflection. John XXIII had been reflecting on the matter for many years, and after only ten weeks as Pope, he struck off boldly along this path. For a long time to come, people will discuss the question of the extent to which Pope John was aware of the almost radical consequences of his action, and in this connection, we should not forget the statement contained in his Exhortation *Sacrae laudes* of 6 January 1962, that the Council represents a new epiphany, awaited not only by Catholics but by people throughout the world, and that the Church is on the threshold of a new era. Apart from this, from a strictly historical viewpoint, it must be recognized not only that the convocation of a Council represented a personal, considered, and lucid action on the part of the Pope, but also that it responded to the deeper needs of contemporary Christianity, and also to a large extent to the yearnings of all mankind.[1]

Many people were aware of the urgent need for the Church to respond adequately to a situation that was in many ways new and that had developed fairly rapidly over the past decades; they saw that the Church needed to move away from its severe cloistering, its suspicion of the modern world, its slowness of movement, and its reluctance in the face of any truly open dialogue—characteristics that had marked many pages in the history of the Church after the repression of Modernism, a move that was effective and undoubtedly positive from one viewpoint, but one-sided and negative from another.

In the present article, I should like to sketch some of the essential aspects of this ecclesial situation. The aim is not to give a detailed picture of these complex circumstances, but simply to recall some of the more significant points and episodes. By its very nature, this brief summary is destined soon to be rendered obsolete by broader and deeper studies, and my hope is that it will act as a spur to new research and as a reference point that will be useful even if not vital.

There are a number of paths to choose from. It would be useful to carry out a full examination of the "votes" of the bishops throughout the world in response to the request formulated by Secretary of State Cardinal Tardini on 18 June 1959 on the instructions of John XXIII.[2] This material undoubtedly deserves careful examination, but such a study has yet to be carried out. Certain observations can be seen that reveal the need for a change of course: the calm but prudent criticism of the authoritarian methods of the Holy Office, the wish for a clearer distinction between religion and politics (a clear reference to the very strong and possibly overenthusiastic involvement of many Italian priests in election campaigns), the request for a recognition of greater authority for bishops, the desire for the introduction of the vernacular in the liturgy.[3] However, it cannot be denied that on the whole the bishops could not see the whole situation objectively, and that their votes are fragmentary and unable to provide an overall picture—and, moreover, influenced by timidity, fear, and a strong streak of conservativism. I would, therefore, prefer to approach the subject from another angle, examining one by one the questions that seem to me most serious and decisive.

Toward a Different Type of Society:
The End of Christianity?

There are three major factors moving contemporary society—
with accelerating speed after 1945—toward a global structure
and toward a mentality, a way of life, habits, and general atmosphere very different from those that prevailed from the end of
the nineteenth century until the period between the two World
Wars. These three factors are as follows: first, the rise of the
Third World, which, freeing itself of colonial domination, is
tending to impose its own culture and values—often different
from those of Europe; second, the rapid and very intensive industrialization that is transforming agricultural countries into industrial ones, with all that this entails, including the predominance
of a market economy and policies based on economic reasoning;
and, third, the spread of television, with its effect on habits
already tending toward strongly consumeristic attitudes. Other
factors should also be recalled, such as the new industrial revolution (a result of automation), and postindustrialization. However, this would make our frame of reference too broad, entailing
the inevitable danger of blurring the basic outlines and the various chronological stages, some of which took place later than the
period with which we are dealing.

The End of Colonialism

At the beginning of the nineteenth century, when the ex-
Spanish colonies of South America gained their independence,
the Holy See dragged its feet in recognizing these new states, in its
wish not to offend Spain. The same happened in Asia and Africa,
with a similar but more violent resistance on the part of the colonial powers, and the same prudent hesitation on the part of the
Holy See, in its anxiety not to provoke anticlerical reactions in
countries that were only slowly and with difficulty moving away
from a strongly rooted past. The African and Asian process at the
second half of the twentieth century has broader consequences for
world civilization than the nineteenth-century South-American
one, due to the overwhelming rise of new young forces that destroy
previous equilibriums and that, as a result, involve the Church to
a greater extent. Further, although the countries of South America did develop their own culture after they had gained their

independence, this did not constitute a break with the traditional culture of Latin America, which had arisen through the now long-past superimposition of European culture on native culture; on the other hand, the very pressing urge to create a new culture was felt in Africa. Until the end of the fifties, the most that had been done were sporadic and unconnected attempts to turn local cultural elements to good account by integrating them into a European context. The Missa Luba is an example of this meeting of two cultures,[4] which was attempted not only in Africa but also in other places, for example, in Indonesia in the thirties. In the Missa Luba, the Latin of the old missal of Pius V is accompanied by the purest of Congolese rhythms, sometimes with Kyondo and Kikomvi drums and sometimes without. It was a successful attempt to harmonize the Roman liturgy with the wealth and beauty of Congolese music. Even so, this same Missa Luba, produced in about 1955, would soon be overtaken by other initiatives. It in fact represented a transitional stage, and, for the historian, it calls to mind that concordism so dear to exegesis at the turn of the century; this concordism was found in various authors, but maybe Vigouroux can be credited with expressing it most clearly and spreading it most effectively. It was hoped that paleontology and the book of Genesis could be reconciled by interpreting the six days of the biblical account as six geological ages. However, such concordism was soon outdated. In the same way, the Missa Luba was soon outdated as authentic inculturation began. For the moment, people were faced with the Africanization of the names of places and people, and of customs, thus presenting serious problems for the Church.

"Decolonization" moved through various stages in the different countries, sometimes with a peaceful hand-over of power, but sometimes with a long and bloody struggle.[5] Indonesia gained its independence early (1945), but only after initial resistance on the part of the Netherlands, which sent strong fighting forces to the Far East. The independence of the Philippines (1946) was much easier, and almost taken for granted. However, the independence of India had more far-reaching consequences. Aspirations for independence had been alive in India since the midnineteenth century. The nonviolent strategy of Gandhi triumphed, marking the end of an empire that had for decades been a source of pride in Great Britain and inspired a wealth of literary works. Despite Gandhi's assassination, and also despite the inevitable partition of India and Pakistan, the true victory lay with the Mahatma. An irresistible movement now gathered speed.

The state of Israel was born in 1948, and three years later Libya broke away from its recent status as a British protectorate. The harsh struggle for Algerian independence took place between 1954 and 1962, culminating, in the first nine months of 1957, with the "Battle of Algiers," which was fought by the parachutists of General Massu and followed in France with the slogan "Algérie française." The Archbishop of Algiers, Mgr. Duval, was respected by both sides due to his moderation and openness. In 1956, Moroccan independence put an end to the last effective, not symbolic, remains of Spanish power in Africa—that power that Pius IX had been moved to salute a century earlier (14 February 1860) when he congratulated Isabella II "on the glorious victories of the Spanish army" and because "the standard of our most holy religion, the cross, has been raised in place of the (sad) banners of Mohammed in that part of Africa." Almost at the same time the independence of the Sudan (1956) and that of Ghana (1957) were proclaimed, and a short time later (about 1960) that of the Congo (today's Zaire), Kenya, Uganda, and Madagascar. Portugal held out longer, only giving in after 1970 with the end of Portuguese domination in Angola and Mozambique. In Asia, the focal point of the political struggle was Vietnam (ex-Indochina, where St. Theresa of Lisieux had dreamt of spending her life as a Carmelite nun). After the harsh French defeats in the immediate postwar period, in 1954 the country was divided along the seventeenth parallel into the two states of North Vietnam, to all intents and purposes under the control of the Marxist powers, and South Vietnam, under the protection of the United States. And the war waged by the French after 1945 was followed by that waged by the United States between 1954 and 1975, with the deployment of large numbers of fighting troops. This conflict entered its most intense phase with the presidency of John Kennedy, and came to a close with the victory of North Vietnam over the great power of the United States.

It is not possible here to go into much detail on all the elements and problems, or to give space to all the historical debates between the declared opponents of the colonial system and those who tried to be more balanced in their appraisals, sometimes tending to attitudes that are overly indulgent toward regimes that may have had many positive aspects but that ignored historical evolution and did nothing to educate the peoples under their care with a view to eventual self-government. Even so, the main points of these judgments can be accepted. Colonialism is a complex phenomenon that has had varying effects, not all of them negative, on the peoples of Africa and Asia. It would appear that British domination has left deeper traces than that of France or Belgium. Great Britain once again showed her political maturity when, albeit it reluctantly, she accepted the already inevitable end of that illustrious age that had begun with Pitt the Elder in the eighteenth century, and gradually gave up her colonies without too much of a struggle. France entrenched herself firmly in the defense of her Algerian possessions and, for a long time, retained the utopian dream of coexistence between the European and overseas territories. The hand-over entailed inevitable problems in almost all countries with difficult moments for the new and almost untrained rulers, and for the general population. One age was coming to an end and another was beginning, in which the Third World would hold an increasingly important position, partly due to its very great demographic growth, which would bring the proportion between its population and that of the developed countries from 2 to 1 in 1950 to 3 to 1 in 1970, and, with further growth, to a predicted 5 to 1 in the year 2000.[6]

In the same period, but at clearly distinct chronological moments in the various states, although always along the same basic lines, a process of deep transformation was set in motion, which could be seen even by the most distracted and superficial onlooker. New discoveries in almost every scientific area and their rapid technical applications meant that industry received a strong boost, with a proliferation of manufacturing plants and production and a rise in national revenues. In turn, agriculture, which had until then been strongly conditioned by the scarcity of mechanical aids, underwent a radical change in methods, accepting previously almost unknown pesticides, new fertilizers, and new machinery (tractors, combine-harvesters, and so on). The size of the work force needed was reduced, so that certain traditional classes (such as rice weeders and many shepherds) died out. This phenomenon took place at first in Great Britain, Germany, France, and the Netherlands, a little later in Italy, and much later in Spain. Let us pause a moment and consider these last two countries, while always bearing in mind that their development is only one part—and a secondary one—of a much greater and more complex phenomenon, marked by a 10-percent reduction in the agricultural work force.

In Italy until 1950, 42 percent of the population worked in the agricultural sector; the average annual income was 305,900 lire (the rough equivalent of US$800 today); 12.9 percent of the population over six years of age were illiterate; and only 10 percent lived in urban centers of more than 100,000 inhabitants. From 1950 to 1960 (in Pius XII's last years as Pope), Italian society underwent rapid and far-reaching transformations, and this process continued at an ever-accelerating pace in the following years. In 1952, agricultural workers still accounted for 41.5 percent of the population, but in 1961, this figure had sunk to 30.8 percent, and would sink still further to 17.2 percent in 1971 and 11.1 percent in 1981. In the same period, industrial workers rose from 5,610,000 in 1952 (31.04 percent) to 7,646,000 in 1961 (37.9 percent) and 8,350,000 in 1971 (44.4 percent), a figure remaining much the same in 1981; due to automation and the increase in the numbers of white-collar workers, no further rise took place.[7] The consequences of all these factors were varied: an increase in the average annual income, which more than doubled in actual figures, and also increased purchasing power; the large increase in the inactive population, in other words, a rise in the average age of the Italian population (63 percent of the inactive population in 1971, 60 percent in 1981); widespread emigration, now more within the country than abroad, from the still predominantly agricultural regions to the more industrialized ones; the gradual birth of the megalopolises of Turin, Milan, Rome, and Naples; the change from a slower and more considerative mentality, as linked to an agricultural economy, to one that is more dynamic, often restless, and certainly more open to innovation, as linked to an industrial economy.

Spain went through the same process a few years later. The agricultural work force decreased from 48.8 percent in 1950 to 39.74 percent in 1960, 24.85 percent in 1970, and 14.49 percent in 1981; the industrial work force rose from 19.78 percent in 1950 to 22.31 percent in 1960, 27.14 percent in 1970, and 26.06 percent in 1981; the numbers of those involved in the white-collar sector (service industries, commerce, communications, information) rose even more sharply. The inactive population rose from 61.42 percent in 1950 to 66.04 percent in 1981.[8]

It is difficult to provide a global picture, due to differences in circumstances (the rise of the rich countries as against the persistent poverty of the underprivileged countries in Latin America as well as in Africa), the different criteria used in producing statistics, and also the varying chronological order of events in different continents and different countries. Nor should it be forgotten that this deep transformation had hardly begun in 1950 and only started to make itself felt in some countries between 1955 and 1960—although it should immediately be added that even in the early fifties, the circumstances already existed that in due course led to these consequences; in other words, the foundations of the forthcoming development and relative social changes had already been laid. Various almost identical, or at least parallel, aspects can be seen even in the different situations, with the birth or development of megalopolises in every part of the world. Here again, the results we can observe today are the outcome of a long process, which began to make itself strongly felt in about 1950. Today, we have Mexico City with over 15 million inhabitants out of Mexico's 75 million (so that 20 percent of the total population is found in the capital), Saõ Paolo with 12 million, Shanghai and Tokyo with 11 million each, Cairo with 10 million, Buenos Aires with just under 10 million, and Calcutta, Peking and Rio de Janiero with 9 million each.[9] Moreover, the speed of data transmission has eliminated the effects of distance, so that the political, economic, and social consequences of what is happening in far-off countries is today felt in every continent in the world.

Amidst stops and starts, sometimes moving forward but sometimes backward, and in a "continuous and tumultuous manner,"[10] the whole world is taking on a new face. Industrialization and urbanization were juxtaposed with the effect of television, which should not be underestimated:

It started in Italy in 1953, and spread rapidly at the same time that the transformation from agricultural society to industrial society was at its peak, so that the changes in mentality and life-style that are normally brought about by industrialization were magnified and broadened. Television acted as a multiplying factor in a process of transformation that was in itself dramatic.[11]

In this way, the life of the individual, of the family, and of society as a whole changed. A new rhythm of life came into

being, with the evening being extended until much later through
the viewing of television shows. Needs grew, in accordance with
the elementary principle of any economy as regards the relativity
and mutability of the concept of need. The traditional model of
the family has been eclipsed; the family has decreased in size, as
more people have tended to leave it, whether through the difficulties or increased ease of urban transport, while dialogue
within the family has been reduced. And in the economic field,
the concentration of vast anonymous sums of capital, the concentration of industrial undertakings, and the presence of power
groups have led to the predominant criteria being taken as individual utility, the well being of the greatest number of people,
and the quest for quantitatively less and qualitatively greater
performance. A period of the application of economic criteria
(the Beveridge Plan) that favored the development of less-
privileged countries and sectors (full occupation, social security,
etc.) later gave way to a different tendency that favored the
stronger and more capable. What is basically sought is a policy
that fulfills the requirements of the present moment, in other
words, something that "works." The day has gone in which people listened to the Church when it gave instructions in the
economic, political, and social fields. Altruism, commitment,
and a religious attitude are today seen as concepts that can only
be applied on the individual level, where a choice can be made
that is free of any outside pressure.

In these circumstances, various historians have on different
occasions raised the question of whether we can still speak of
Christianity or whether it should in fact be viewed as an outmoded concept.[12] What is the sense in speaking of a State religion in a pluralistic religious society that recognizes freedom of
conscience as a fundamental value? Can the Church continue to
be seen as possessing universally valid solutions for every problem? Can the Catholic world still be seen as a beleaguered for-
tress, sufficient unto itself and closed to influence from the outside world? Is it a positive thing to continue to ask the State—
which was once seen as the secular, supporting branch of the
Church—for civil juridical sanctions of ecclesiastical decisions?[13]
In more practical terms, while the earlier Christian inspiration of
the "Catholic parties" is growing weaker, and the number of
different trends and different practical opinions within these parties is growing, is it still reasonable to demand the political unity

of Catholics and expect unanimous practical choices in the name of the same faith? These are not theoretical questions being developed in academic circles today, but questions that have been asked since the end of the fifties, and that have played a part in certain dramatic cases of conscience.[14] They provide an indication of the situation of a Church on the defensive, immobile, in the face of a rapidly changing world. This was the Church of October 1958.

A Firm Defense of "Christianity"

Almost thirty years later, in a calmer historical perspective, after the inevitable enthusiastic eulogies and very harsh negative criticisms, we can now approach serene evaluation of the papacy of Pius XII.[15] The importance of his magisterium is clear, with the great Encyclicals that appeared between 1943 and 1947 (*Mystici Corporis*, which emphasized the sacramental aspect of the Church, thus moving beyond the ecclesiology predominant in the nineteenth century and at Vatican I; *Divino afflante Spiritu*, which recognized the validity of the methods that had been championed by Lagrange and his followers at the beginning of the twentieth century and that had long been viewed with suspicion; and *Mediator Dei*, which, although following traditional lines, represented a step forward and laid the groundwork for the great progress that was to come[16]); with the definition of the Assumption in 1950, which was the fruit of a great deal of study and fostered a pastoral renewal comparable to that following the definition of the Immaculate Conception; with *Summi pontificatus* in 1939; and with his Christmas radio messages in the war and postwar periods, which show a clear condemnation of any type of totalitarianism, affirm the dignity of the human person, and provide orientations for a new international order. Some of his discourses are still rightly remembered, such as that to Catholic Jurists on 7 December 1953, on the foundations of tolerance, and that of 7 September 1955 to those taking part in the Tenth Congress of the Historical Sciences, on various decisive moments in history in its relationship with the Church. His discourse to obstetricians on 29 October 1951 had even broader echoes, with its recognition of the Ogino-Knaus Method of periodic abstinence. Some of his initiatives were to prove very positive, whether in the cultural field (excavations around the tomb of St. Peter in the Vatican between 1940 and 1950) or in the pastoral field (the introduction of evening masses, the reduction and practical abolition of the eucharist fast, the revival after almost two thousand years of the Easter vigil, a definite openness in instructions on seminary formation in *Menti nostrae* in 1950, and the encouragement shown to secular institutes). Right at the beginning of his papacy, in December 1939, Pius XII explicitly recognized the legitimacy of the Chinese rites, definitively putting an end to a controversy that had been going on since the eighteenth century and that had for a long time acted as a brake on evangelization in the Far East. Following the orientations provided by Benedict XV and Pius XI, Pius XII personally consecrated various native bishops in 1939, and then with the 1951 document *Evangelii praecones* he stated that he was in favor of setting up of local hierarchies in all mission territories; at the time of his death, there were thus 139 sees entrusted to African or Asian bishops, and the first Chinese cardinal had been created. The radio message of Christmas 1955 recognized for the first time the legitimacy of the yearnings of old colonies for independence.[17] In the war, Pius XII avoided the solemn gestures that would have met with the enthusiastic approval of those who were far from the battle zone and maybe would have increased his own prestige, but which would most probably have provoked very harsh reactions from the Nazis at the expense of the Jews; even so, his effective but silent activity ensured saving the greatest possible number of lives of those who were being persecuted for their race and religion.[18]

These and many other positive aspects cannot make us forget the inevitable limitations of this papacy, despite its overall greatness. For fourteen years, from the death of Cardinal Maglione (an expert in French affairs) in 1944 until the death of Pius XII, the position of Secretary of State of the Vatican remained vacant. This situation had no parallel since the seventeenth century, but it reflected a clear choice on the part of the Pope, who was a tireless worker but also a great centralizer, and who, as he once said to the future Cardinal Tardini, did not want collaborators but simply executors.[19] The work of the office was carried out by two strong personalities, Montini and Tardini, who to start with had the titles of Secretary for Extraordinary Affairs and Substitute for Ordinary Affairs, and then, from 1953, that of Pro-Secretaries of State. Because they were neither cardinals nor bishops, they both remained in a clearly subordinate position as executors, not advisers or collaborators, although they gave precise instructions (in other words, orders) to those who, as bishops, could in fact claim a certain seniority to them. In the latter years, and at least from 1951 onward, the apostolic letters granting a particular title to a church or constituting a patron for a city, institute, or other such organization, previously signed by Montini, were signed by a prelate of the third or fourth rank, Gildo Brunola, who was described in these documents with the following words: "De speciali mandato Sanctissimi, pro Domino Cardinali a publicis Ecclesiae negotiis, Gildo Brugnola a Brevibus Apostolics." Nominations of cardinals were few and far between. There was a great stir in 1946 at the nomination of twenty-one cardinals from a wide variety of countries, including, for the first time, China. There was less interest over the nomination in January 1953 of twenty-three other cardinals, who, although they included men of great merit such as Roncalli and Stepinac, basically followed the traditional line. Contacts with bishops became fairly rare and somewhat impersonal. One of his closest collaborators, Cardinal Tardini, expressly states:

> During his papacy direct personal contact between the Supreme Pontiff and the bishops of the various dioceses was considerably reduced. . . . Thus the Roman curia suffered a certain stagnation, rather like the situation in the body when some irregularity in the circulation of blood sets in. We old people stayed on, standing in the way and preventing fresher and more robust forces than our own from moving forward. . . . [20]

The situation deteriorated in the last years, due to the banishing of the Substitute Montini, who was "promoted" Archbishop of Milan and who was never nominated cardinal and was never once received in private audience by the Pope (which whom he had been in daily contact for many years),[21] to the dismissal of Father Cordovani, who had previously been influential in the curia as Master of the Sacred Palaces, and, lastly, to the advanced age of the Pope himself. A group of Jesuits, most of them Germans, but also a few Dutchmen, always remained close to Pius XII; they were professors at the Gregorian University or the Biblicum, and they served the Pope in drafting his more important discourses and documents. Father Bea, who was at that time

Rector of the Biblicum, played an important role in the drafting of *Divino afflante Spiritu;* Father Tromp was the main draftsman of *Mystici Corporis;* Father Hürth wrote many addresses on moral questions; Father Leiber, Secretary for German Affairs, was the immediate author of many of the Pope's letters to the German bishops both during and after the war, most of which have now been published; while Father Gundlach, a great sociologist, produced the first drafts of a number of important documents and also of certain radio messages on international affairs.[22] These facts are well known in Roman ecclesiastical circles and are based on very solid oral tradition, although only research in the archives (which is impossible at the present time) will provide conclusive proof. It is, therefore, difficult to overstate the important influence of this group on the government of the Church in those years, although there were obviously serious drawbacks to the system. It favored the unified orientation and firmness of decisions, but also fostered Pius XII's tendency toward a wholly personal rule. Because the Pope did not have any effective, living contact with the base and was assisted only by a group of specialists, whose competence was undeniable but who were declared exponents of a very specific orientation, he ended up in splendid isolation. For this reason, his attitudes were not always as effective as he had hoped, and some of them were sooner or later seen as outmoded. This tendency was also influenced by his innate awareness of the deep crisis in contemporary society, which seemed to him to be dominated by opposing ideologies; this led him to an immobility that some historians have described as "disconcerting."[23]

Although I will deal with those episodes that concern the history of theology more specifically in later pages, I feel it will be helpful to emphasize here two events in the line of government pursued by Pius XII that can be interpreted in different ways. On 27 August 1953, the concordat with Spain was signed, thus bringing to a close the series of partial agreements drawn up in 1941, 1946, and 1950.[24] "The Catholic, Apostolic, Roman religion continues to be the sole religion of the Spanish nation, and will benefit from the rights and prerogatives to which it is entitled in accordance with divine law and Canon Law" (Article 1). Once again, after a space of several decades and in very different circumstances, a principle was reaffirmed for which the Holy See had always sought recognition wherever possible in the various cordats of the nineteenth and twentieth centuries and which had appeared almost word for word in the 1851 concordat with Spain and in the 1929 agreement with Italy. The character of the Church as "perfect society" was recognized, in those words so dear to nineteenth-century ecclesiology, which was concerned to ensure the independence of the society founded by Christ and thus to compare it to the State in the most explicit and direct manner as equal to equal. However, so far as I know, the Spanish concordat is the only one to use this precise wording. There were various consequences of this principle, and of particular importance among these were the following: the stringent restrictions on non-Catholic worship, in accordance with the provisions of Article 6 of the *Fuero de los Españoles* (only private freedom of worship in metropolitan territories, but public freedom in the territories "of Spanish sovereignty in Africa"); freedom of ecclesiastical worship and jurisdiction; the support of the Church by the State, including civil support for ecclesiastical sentences imposed for infractions of the laws of the Church (Article 16); and conformity of education to Catholic doctrine and the right of bishops to make sure that this stipulation is observed (Article 31). Once canonical matrimony has been registered, it is recognized in civil law. Ecclesiastical tribunals have exclusive authority in cases of nullity, separation, and dispensation from ratified and nonconsummated marriages, apart from the judgment of civil courts as regards the relative civil effects (Articles 23–24). Within certain limits, the traditional forms of immunity are recognized, at least for bishops and for major superiors of religious institutes, who are subject only to ecclesiastical courts, whereas in civil and criminal trials of clerics, the Ordinary is to be informed of the beginning of the trial and of the sentence, and priests and religious who are arrested are to receive treatment in conformity with "the respect due to their state and to their hierarchical position" (Article 17). As regards the nomination of bishops, the 1953 concordat makes implicit reference back to the 1941 agreements, which envisaged the exchange of lists of candidates between Madrid and Rome and thus ensured the government the major role. The 1953 concordat was then followed by agreements signed in July 1976 and January 1979 between Juan Carlos and the Vatican. Spain and the Holy See viewed the principle of a State religion as no longer relevant to the times, the Holy See for the most part renounced its privilege of conducting legal proceedings (which, as we have seen, was still

being claimed in 1953), and the State in turn gave up its traditional role in the nomination of bishops.[25]

This is not the place to carry out an in-depth study of all the
complex questions regarding the Spanish concordat.[26] Here I
shall confine myself to three observations. First, the 1953 agreement undoubtedly corresponded to the hopes of the two sides; in
other words, it reflected to a large extent the shared mentality
found at that time in the Vatican and in Madrid. It demonstrates
the ideas so keenly pursued by Pius XII, who was anxious to
ensure that the State gave official recognition to the prerogatives
of the Church, which in practice meant its own particular juridical system and special support from the government. Thus, the
aim was not only to protect Christian matrimony as the basis of
the family, but also to mold the whole of society, with special
authority for bishops in the sphere of education, and mere tolerance of private non-Catholic worship. In turn, the Spanish rulers
of the time were concerned to preserve what they saw as one of
the main elements of Spanish civilization and history, and as an
essential component of *hispanidad:* fidelity to Catholic tradition.
In historical terms, the concordat could be seen as the response
to the anticlericalism and the antiecclesiastical laws of the thirties, and it certainly becomes comprehensible in this perspective.
Second, history never stands still, and even the 1953 agreements
are simply one of the many moments in relations between
Church and State in Spain: thus, after 1953, we have 1976, with
a State that is now more aware of its lay nature (and therefore
does not allow the privilege of jurisdiction, but remains within its
own sphere and does not concern itself in the nomination of
bishops) and a Church that is freer. Third, it is hard to imagine
that the evolution observable in 1976 did not have deeper roots.
It is probable that even in 1953, a sector of Spanish public
opinion was not reflected in the concordat and viewed the defense of Christianity as carried out with the close support of the
State as outmoded. Be that as it may, the agreement is a good
expression of the ecclesial and political path followed by Pius
XII, and its history corresponds to the general evolution of society and Church before and after the Council.

Another event of the same period can be taken as symbolic:
the proclamation issued by the Holy See on 30 June 1949, refusing the sacraments to those who voted communist and excommu-
nicating those who professed its "materialistic and antichristian"

teaching.[27] This move was a response to the concern of many of the Italian clergy who wanted clear instructions to follow in dealing with "practicing communists." It was also a response to the aspirations of many bishops—aspirations that would be seen again in the votes expressed for the Council—and to the mentality at that time predominating in many parts of the Vatican curia, which had Alfredo Ottaviani (not yet a cardinal, but already in an important position as Assessor of the Holy Office) as its most notable exponent. However, it was also a response to the historical and political situation of the time, with the cold war and the Russian advance in eastern Europe. In 1947, the Kominform was set up and was seen as Moscow's effective control over communism in the different countries, in other words, as a reincarnation of the Third International. The crucial year is 1948: Mao Tse-tung's advance left the whole of mainland China in communist hands, a coup d'état brought the communists to power in Czechoslovakia under Gottwald, and the Berlin blockade and airlift took place. In Rumania, Catholics (especially those of the Byzantine-Slavonic rite) were being harshly persecuted. Between 1945 and 1953, Monsignor Slipy, the Ruthenian Metropolitan, was arrested and tried, as were Archbishop Stepinac of Zagreb, Cardinal Mindszenty, Archbishop of Budapest, Bishop Beran of Prague, Bishop Trotcha of Litomerice in Czechoslovakia, and the Polish Primate, Bishop Wyszinski. In Italy, the 1948 elections took on dramatic tones, becoming a direct struggle between the two sides, with the Christian Democratic Party and its lesser allies on one side and the Communist and Socialist parties on the other. The heavy victory of the Christian Democrats only broadened the ideological and practical gulf.

The decision of the Vatican puzzled even some well-known Vatican figures. Monsignor Tardini confided to Federico Alessandrini, Vice-Director of the *Osservatore Romano*, that if the threat of excommunication for communists (as the provision was then and later, rightly or wrongly, referred to) was not heeded, seven million people would be excommunicated in Italy. What a wonderful result![28]

The provision of the Holy Office was almost immediately officially interpreted by the same Holy Office in a restricted sense and communists were allowed to be married in church.[29] Even so, almost forty years later, its consequences are clear. The decree did not have any positive result because it did not cause many members to leave the party—members who included a number of frontline intellectual figures and sincere Catholics, such as Franco Rodano—just as it did not have any effect on the general masses, who were by now solidly bound to communism and were untouched by any threat or any international event. No fall in communist and socialist votes was observed in that period. Even so, the provision of 30 June 1949 did have a considerable effect, inasmuch as it contributed to an even deeper division in Italy and to a rise in the numbers of those whom contemporary history refers to, with an expression very familiar and dear to politicians such as De Gasperi, as a "historical stockade" (a very solid counterforce or a type of Berlin Wall set up between Catholics who follow the Pope and his instructions in both the religious and political fields and those who do not feel obliged to respect these instructions in the political sphere). It also reaffirmed the working masses in their conviction that the Church is on the side of the powerful and that religion does not understand rightful social claims. The pastoral ministry was strongly affected by this situation, and it was not rare to see the text of the instruction pinned up over confessionals. (For example, in the church of St. Mary of the Angels in Assisi, the sheet was clearly exhibited on both sides of the twelve confessionals in the church. This was also true of various churches in Rome, such as St. Agatha in the working-class area of Trastevere, where the percentage of party members was probably very high.) Preaching was often very harsh and almost threatening in tone. Thus, the whole ecclesial and religious life of Italy became strongly "politicized." It may be going too far to describe all this is an abuse of power, as a use of the penal code of the Church in a way that was really not in harmony with its purpose, and as an implicit political choice between the two blocs into which the world was divided at that time; even so, it cannot be denied that the decree did not have the desired effects. The historian is reminded of the many documents in which Pius IX excommunicated those who had in one way or another contributed to the decline of the Church's temporal power, although excommunication of half of Italy did not prevent the new regime from taking root and developing.

The division—or historical stockade—continued to stand firm, and a number of relatively important episodes helped strengthen it. In the spring of 1952, the Holy See tried to impose a unified list on De Gasperi for the Rome city elections; this list would have included both fascists and antifascists in opposition to communism. This proposal was entrusted to Sturzo, now in his eighties (1871–1959), and did not meet with success for a number of reasons. However, the "Sturzo operation," as it came to be called, highlighted once again the politicization of Italian religious life. It also embittered De Gasperi, who was willing to obey, although with infinite reluctance, and irritated the Pope, who refused the statesman's request for an audience a few weeks later on the occasion of the solemn profession of his daughter as a Sister of the Assumption. Further, it made relations between Church and State even more strained, and disturbed the Italian public at large. Meanwhile, Pius XII continued to emphasize the role of the Church in the political and social sphere, insisting that Catholics must obey in this area (2 November 1954). Bishop Fiordelli of Prato had a letter read in church in which he referred to two Catholics who had been married civilly as "public concubines." This led to a widely publicized trial for slander, which ended on 1 March 1958 with a finding of guilty by the Florence Court, although this judgment was overturned by the Court of Appeal of the same city on 25 October 1958 at the time of the conclave that had opened on the death of Pius XII. [30]

These few episodes, representative of many others, will suffice to demonstrate the tension of those years, the bitter nature of the controversies, the harshness of the struggle carried on in defense of Christianity, the more-than-doubtful outcome of this struggle, and the general atmosphere in the Vatican, which came to affect the whole Church—just as at the time the Roman Question had come to affect the whole Church and not only the life of the Italian Church.

Theological and Pastoral Orientations
Between 1940 and 1960:
Roman Intervention

It is difficult to give a summary of the more important orientations in theology and pastoral affairs for the period between 1940 and 1960. The difficulty springs from a variety of factors: the breadth and also the delicate nature of the material, the lack of access (even if only temporarily) to many important archives, and the lack of historical detachment (although this latter factor is overemphasized by certain scholars, who must in any case agree on the need for research that helps us understand so far as possible the contemporary situation, and also the need to balance partial and one-sided information with objective overviews). Here again I shall confine myself to some basic points. Three things are absolutely certain. Catholic thinking in the war and postwar years was not some unified whole, but included a wide range of attitudes in which we can, in very general terms, distinguish a more open attitude in various outlying sectors and a more cautious line at the center (i.e., in the Vatican and the great Roman theological institutions). The different positions and resulting reactions to these have been examined from a number of viewpoints: some people feel that certain theologians ran the risk of undervaluing the very essence of the supernatural, while others feel that these same theologians were simply concerned to emphasize the harmony between the natural and supernatural orders and to highlight existence as it in fact is, and that this is why they kept away from distinctions they considered to be overly abstract, distinctions dear to sixteenth- and seventeenth-century Scholasticism (e.g., the concept of "pure nature," which may have been helpful in understanding the supernatural, but which is still an abstract concept). Lastly, although we certainly cannot speak of excommunications and later canonizations (for there were neither), in those years, certain great theologians were subjected to a number of restrictive measures, but were then later among the main *periti* at the Council and had a great deal of influence on the drafting of the conciliar documents. After the Council, certain authors whose books had been banned from libraries in 1950 were made cardinals (de Lubac and Daniélou). Certain pastoral movements (e.g., that of worker priests) had been condemned and banned, but were then taken up again during and after the Council. We can thus see a certain evolution, which will seem less or more dramatic according to our viewpoint, but which cannot be denied; indeed, it is an example of a phenomenon with which historians are not unfamiliar. People who are at first isolated, if not actually rejected, take on a new role and come to have wide influence; or ideas that are for a while viewed with suspicion are reconsidered for a whole complex of different reasons.

The liveliness of French Catholicism in both the pre- and postwar years is well-known. French Catholics had taken up the challenge offered to the Church in the 1905 Law of Separation.

After the confiscation of ecclesiastical property and the disper-
sion of religious, there was the peculiar practical situation of
parishes and places of worship that were tolerated by the State
even if this was not in accordance with the 1905 law. Then, with
the recognition of religious associations dependent on the hierarchy and with the practical return of religious to their houses, the
Church moved toward normalization. Many initiatives and movements sprang up, from the Little Brothers and Little Sisters of
Father Charles de Foucauld to the Jeunesse Ouvrière Chrétienne
and the Scouts, while a number of major intellectuals and thinkers were active, and various new journals were issued: *Vie
spirituelle*, *Vie intellectuelle*, *Esprit*, and *Sept* (the latter raised a
good deal of controversy due to its antifascist and antifranco
attitudes).[31]

It was against this background that on 24 July 1941 the "La
Mission de France" Seminary was opened at Lisieux with the aim
of training priests who would exercise their ministry among the
working classes. September 1943 saw the publication of the book
France, pays de mission by Henri Godin and Yves Daniel. And, in
the same year, the assembly of the cardinals and archbishops of
France decided to send priest volunteers dressed as workers into
German labor camps. The experience gained from this project,
and also the resulting growth in psychological and pastoral maturity, gradually led to the birth of the movement of worker priests,
the earliest moments of which date back to the beginning of
1944 in Paris. The movement was watched carefully and fearfully
by the Vatican, which sent the French bishops repeated calls for
prudence. By 1953, it could claim about ninety secular and religious priests, and had gained the sympathy of the general public,
partly as a result of G. Cesbron's 1952 book, *Les saints vont en
enfer*. Between July 1953 and January 1954, Roman fears over
the attitudes of certain worker priests who were involved in
union struggles and in predominantly political demonstrations
(against the Atlantic Alliance), and who were calling for the
complete autonomy of Catholics in political and union activity,
led to various actions on the part of Rome, various French attempts at clarification, and three decisive documents: the letter
of 29 August 1953 from the Congregation for Religious, ordering
that religious should be withdrawn from working in factories;
Cardinal Pizzardo's letter of 27 July, forbidding all seminarians,
without exception, from serving as apprentices in any type of

work; and the letter of 19 January 1954 from those bishops who had worker priests, ordering all such priests to resign from any type of organization, join a team of priests, and reduce their working hours to a maximum of three hours per day. While the first of these measures condemned the active participation of priests in union activity, the third in practice reduced, and indeed prevented, the true integration of priests into the labor sector. Especially in a broader historical perspective, the meaning is clear: the measure represented a first step toward the definitive end of this experiment. Most of those concerned obeyed, although with a good deal of anguish, and some of them suffered true crises. Despite the general French shift toward the right in recent times, due both to the last-stand attempt to defend French rule in Indochina and to various other political events, public opinion in France was largely on the side of the worker priests. Between March 1953 and March 1954, nine hundred articles on this subject appeared, and this eventually worked to the detriment of the very people they were trying to defend because certain harsh criticisms of the Vatican tended to cause a hardening of the attitudes of the latter. However, the movement did continue in a watered-down form that was fully obedient to the instructions received from Rome. (Among those who continued the operation under these difficult conditions was the Auxiliary Bishop of Lyons, Ancel.) Then, in 1959, a fourth document—a new letter from Cardinal Pizzardo—proclaimed the theoretical and practical imcompatibility of extended manual labor with the nature of the priesthood. This led to the suspension of the whole project, which was already in dire straits. It would be taken up again some years later with the declaration of 23 October 1965 from the French cardinals and archbishops.

Cardinal Pizzardo's two letters of July 1953 and July 1959 certainly did not resolve all the problems. On the contrary, they raised a number of questions as to the nature of the priesthood, its mission, and its incompatibility with physical work or with any profession that is not directly pastoral. A good many people wondered why the existence of astronomer priests or priests who were professors of mathematics or science had been accepted for many centuries if the legitimacy of worker priests was now denied. Moreover, the second letter was ratified by John XXIII, who was perfectly familiar with the movement, having been present at its birth in 1945 and having seen its gradual development between then and 1952. Time alone would make it possible to reach a more balanced judgment on this series of apparently contradictory events and actions. In history, it is not unusual for movements to be condemned at the outset because of their teething problems, the lack of a sense of proportion on the part of those involved, the raising of doctrinal questions, and a generally unfavorable historical context; and then, later, once these problems have been ironed out and the context has changed, the idea is taken up again and eventually becomes accepted as normal. However, at the time, the restrictive measures, the two letters from the cardinal, the crisis of some of the worker priests, and the dramatic obedience of the majority made a strong impression on public opinion both in France and abroad, so that a numerically minor episode (there were less than one hundred worker priests in France) was seen as symbolic; it was transformed into a problem involving the whole of the Church in France and was felt to touch on the country's national pride. The end result was an increased malaise in many circles, both ecclesiastical and lay—a malaise that had already been roused by other factors.[32]

This atmosphere and malaise can also be seen in other episodes. Roger Aubert's book, *Le Pontificat de Pie IX*, published in Paris in 1952, was a masterly study, giving an objective picture of the various aspects of the life of the Church in the second half of the nineteenth century and of its clash with the modern world. It was very favorably received by history critics, who saw in it first and foremost confirmation that apologetic history, with its concern to defend the Church even if this meant disguising certain facts, had now been superseded; however, it was viewed coldly and somewhat disapprovingly by various members of the curia. Fortunately, the idea of condemning it and placing it on the Index was immediately discarded—although the fact that the possibility was even considered is significant. Monsignor Paschini, who had for several decades been Rector of the Lateran University and who was a conscientious historian, was not so fortunate with his *Vita di Galileo*. This work, which had originally been called for by the Pontifical Academy of Sciences to mark the third centenary of the death of Galileo, contained nothing particularly new, partly, of course, because the author was more familiar with the sixteenth century than the seventeenth, and also because he was not sufficiently familiar with the history of science and of modern thinking. However, the pedantic, fault-finding observations of a modest official of the Academy—the lay secretary—and the stubbornness of the author, who refused to agree to any changes, led to a dramatic episode. The work was examined by the Holy Office, who suspended publication for un unspecified period. Only much later, during the papacy of Paul VI, did the work see the light of day, following requests to the Pope by an old disciple of Paschini, Monsignor Maccarrone, whom Paschini had set on the path of scientific research. Its publication took place just in time for it to be cited in *Gaudium et spes* in connection with the rightful autonomy of the sciences. Here again, we see a move from a virtual veto on publication in 1942 to implicit praise of the work on the part of the Council in 1965.[33]

In the same period in Italy, great suspicion and harsh measures were directed against Father Primo Mazzolari (1890–1959), who had for many decades been parish priest of Bozzolo, a tiny and poor village in the Po Valley near Cremona. Father Mazzolari was a fiery and effective preacher, and his writings attracted people because of their simplicity and the sincerity of feeling they transmitted. His love for his region and for his poor parishioners led him to make ringing denunciations of every type of injustice, and, although these criticisms were in themselves just, they were often expressed in overexcited and radical tones. He also felt called to make bitter declarations deploring the real or assumed involvement of the Church with those in power in every age— who at that time (prior to 1943), the parish priest identified with the fascist regime, with which the Vatican had signed a concordat—and to express strong criticism of the smug respectability of the average Christian, who was strongly conservative and was deaf to calls for social justice. In 1934, the Holy Office ordered the withdrawal from circulation of the book *La più bella avventura*, an original commentary on the parable of the prodigal son, which concentrated mainly on the elder brother, a figure in whom too many Christians could recognize themselves. *Anch'io voglio bene al papa* (1942) did not find favor in high Vatican circles, and *Impegno con Cristo* (1943), which emphasized individual responsibility, led to a warning from the Holy Office. *Impegni cristiani e istanze comuniste* cost the priest of Bozzolo a five-day retreat and suspension from the right to say Mass for that period. After 1948, and partly through his contributions to the periodical *Adesso*, of which he was at least cofounder, Mazzolari stepped up his sharp criticism of the Catholic laity and hierarchy, with calls for a return to the social teachings of the gospel. This was the period of Christian Democratic rule in Italy and of the Holy See's support for this party, although this support was sometimes only general and was not unmixed with reservations of an anti-communist nature. Mazzolari was a pastor and a writer, not a politician, but he called for a more courageous social policy and longed for an episcopate that would provide a spur and not simply support in elections. On 14 February 1951, Cardinal Schuster banned any member of the clergy from contributing to *Adesso*, and Mazzolari was forbidden to preach outside his diocese, and also came in for very specific censure. His bishop, Cazzani, tried unsuccessfully to defend him to the Holy Office, writing a number of beautiful letters between 1946 and 1951, emphasizing the ineffectiveness "of the Roman form of apologetics and polemics" in some areas, and basically approving the methods of his priest. The suspicion continued even after Mazzolari's death, and led to a further instruction from the Holy Office to the Bishop of Cremona, preventing the republication of *La più bella avventura*. Paradoxically, criticism of the elder son, which was the central theme of the book, would later be taken up by John Paul II in his Encyclical *Dives in misericordia*.[34]

Lorenzo Milano (1923–1967) was younger than Mazzolari. He had been ordained to the priesthood early in life, but after considerable heart searching and suffering. He was assistant and then parish priest near Florence, and from his tiny parish in the Apennine Hills, to which he had been virtually exiled, he awoke lively interest in a great deal of Italy with his statements, open letters, and challenging declarations. His books, *Esperienze pastorali* (1957) and *Lettere a una professoressa* (1967), caused a particular stir. The first of these works, which appeared with the "Imprimatur" of Cardinal Elia Della Costa and a preface by Archbishop D'Avack of Camerino, was read with great interest and approval by Luigi Einaudi, an outstanding economist who was at that time President of Italy. However, one of the most lively books to come from the Italian Church in those last years of Pius XII's papacy once again elicited a reaction from the Holy Office, which ordered its withdrawal for reasons of timeliness. It was then harshly attacked by *Civiltà Cattolica*, which criticized Father Milani for not paying enough attention to supernatural education and for aiming at the formation of men rather than Christians. (The journal was unaware of a letter in that period, but only published at a later date, in which the fiery Tuscan priest warned a young parishioner: "You're wrong. Blessed are the poor, for theirs is the kingdom of God," and said that if the boy were to become rich he would turn against him.) The second volume was a real accusation against the public schools, which cared more for the children of the rich than those of the poor. Relations between Father Milani and Cardinal Florit, who had succeeded Cardinal Della Costa in Florence, were tense and difficult to the end, and it cannot be denied that Father Milani was not an easy person. The Florentine priest lacked the moderation of Father Mazzolari, and ended up by exaggerating concepts and views that were basically just, presenting them in such one-sided and inaccurate ways, and using such aggressive and violent tones, that he lost the sympathy of many ordinary Catholics, as well as the benevolence of his ecclesiastical superiors (an example being his statement that the rich man per se always remained bad, just as the wolf always remained a wolf).[35]

Father Mazzolari acted on the literary and pastoral level, whereas Father Milano's witness was very personal, as the parish priest speaking from the midst of his community. Giorgio La Pira, however, was a professor of Roman law, a member of the Italian Congress, Under-Secretary for Labor and Social Security from 1948 to 1950, and Mayor of Florence from 1951 to 1957 and again from 1961 to 1965. He became one of the best-known and controversial figures in Italy in the fifties with his very individual way of acting and administering a city: requisitioning private housing, confiscating the Pignone industries (which were on the brink of collapse, but which he managed to save), and organizing international meetings on peace with no ideological discrimination. Even so, Pius XII was most probably referring to him in his Christmas radio message in 1953, which branded "the political figure who has almost changed himself into a sort of charismatic preacher of a new social theory, thus contributing to an increase in the sense of disorientation."[36]

However, the stand taken by certain important Vatican figures against Jacques Maritain was much harsher, despite the latter's orthodox Thomism and his unquestionable Catholic faith. The philosopher claimed that lay Catholics should be independent in their temporal and political activity, and expressed the wish to see a society founded not on any explicit profession of the Catholic faith, but rather on shared agreement on underlying values—such as the dignity of the human person—that were upheld by Christianity but also accepted by adherents of other ideologies. His work, *Le primat du spirituel* (1927), marked the final eclipse of *Action Française*—a movement in favor of a strong, militaristic State, which saw the Church above all as an indispensable instrument of social order. *Humanisme intégral* (1936) represented a further step, with the proposal of a system that would be characterized by its religious conception and its pluralism and that would move beyond right-wing or left-wing totalitarianism, or the agnostic liberal State, or the old-fashioned sectarian-run State. If Church and State have different objectives, the Christian can and should act in the political sphere not as a Christian or a member of the Church, but as a member of the temporal city. This concept became famous with the expression "the distinction of levels of human activity" and obviously entails considerable autonomy for Catholics in the political sphere. Moreover, if there are certain values that are shared by Christianity and other ideologies, and that are necessary and sufficient to provide a basis for a humanly viable social life, cooperation between Catholics and non-Catholics becomes normal. Independence of action and cooperation with non-Catholic elements, even in the quest for a society based on solid moral foundations, were ideas that ran counter to any traditional way of thinking. It is easy to understand the positive way in which Maritain was viewed in the fifties, particularly among many relatively young Catholics who were just starting on their professional and political lives, and also the strong suspicions that predominated in ecclesiastical circles, with the almost sole exception of Monsignor Montini. The first criticism, relatively indirect, was launched against Maritain by Cardinal Ottaviani on 2 March 1953 in an address to the Lateran University in which he confirmed the duty of the rulers of a State made up almost totally of Catholics to base legislation on Christian principles, with religion being manifested even in social terms, and to protect the religious heritage of the people from any attack or danger. The reaction of *Civiltà Cattolica* was harsher in an article by Father Messineo in 1956. Maritain's integral humanism was judged to be an "integral naturalism," tinged with historicism and strangely similar to certain writings of Benedetto Croce. It was easy to recognize at the basis of all these criticisms a conception of reality that was somewhat abstract and pessimistic, and far removed from a healthy historical sensitivity such as that of Maritain. The strong criticism was not followed up, although we do not know if this was due to instructions from high up or to some other reasons, such as the reactions of various surprised and embittered groups.[37]

John Courtney Murray (1905–1967), an American Jesuit born in New York, was viewed with similar suspicion for many years. He distinguished between State and civil society, and considered that the former had the duty to defend individual and social rights (in a view that moved beyond the paternalism to which Leo XIII remained bound, and was closer to Pius XII and the vision of a rightful State), although he did not consider that the State had the duty to protect Catholics in any special way, and did not view religious freedom as a now inevitable situation, but as a basic right essential to the human person. Here again, the new ideas ran broadly counter to traditional views as these were defended not so much by Pius XII as by Ottaviani. Murray's comment on the previously mentioned address given by Ottaviani in March 1953 caused considerable irritation in Rome. Murray pointed out the difference in thought and expression between the Pope and the Secretary of the Holy Office, while Rome emphasized their complete agreement. The American theologian was subjected to special censure from Rome, which was implemented by the general curia of the Society with remarkable fairness. Even so, the publication of certain of his writings was banned and a number of addresses and lectures were forbidden. Murray was to all intents and purposes reduced to silence for about ten years, but was heard again at Vatican II, where he managed to gain acceptance for his ideas.[38]

The controversy concerning the new theological trends that appeared in France had more far-reaching consequences. Between 1945 and 1950, a lively debate developed between a number of Jesuits, most of them French, who were professors at the Fourvière Theologate near Lyons, and the most outstanding theologians from the Angelicum in Rome, who could count on a number of allies in France (e.g., the theological faculty at Angers). In the forefront of the Jesuit group were Henri Bouillard, Jean Daniélou, Henri de Lubac, and Vedast Fessard, who in turn had the support of Maurice Blondel and who expressed their views not only in individual works (such as de Lubac's *Le surnaturel* and Daniélou's *Dialogues*), but also in the journals *Etudes* and *Recherches de science religieuse*. Against them were ranged the Dominican group from the Angelicum in Rome, with

Father René Garrigou-Lagrange as their main adversary, along with Father Labourdette and the more moderate Father Cordovani, Master of the Sacred Palaces, and with the support of the Angers' theological faculty and one or two Jesuits from the Gregorian University (although the latter institution did not necessarily share de Lubac's line of reasoning in its totality, it by and large tried to maintain a certain balance in its attitude). The vehicles of the Dominican group's thought were the journals *Angelicum, Revue Thomiste, L'année théologique,* and *Pensée catholique.* Subjects that had already been seen in the Modernist crisis emerged again in the ensuing debate: the need for a theological renewal (a concern that provided the name, "the new theology," by which the trend was known, especially among its adversaries); the need to move closer to the contemporary world; the need to move beyond Scholasticism, which has often dried out into stereotyped forms—not genuine Thomism, which is always fresh and relevant; and the concern for a major return to the Fathers of the Church. St. Thomas should remain a beacon, but should not be seen as a Berlin Wall. There were, of course, other aspects, both psychological and political, to the debate. The innovators were viewed sympathetically in more open circles and by the leaders of the resistance (de Lubac had been one of those who inspired this movement, developing the theory of the lawfulness of resistance to an unjust power) and those who defended the worker priests, while they were viewed with suspicion in conservative circles and by supporters of the Vichy regime. Nor should we underestimate the very fiery temperament of Father Garrigou-Lagrange, who excelled at launching indictments, so that, in the words of his adversaries, he "spread terror wherever he passed." Even so, the discussion remained on the theological level and never descended to other levels.[39]

As early as 1946, Pius XII expressed his concern to the representatives of the Jesuits and the Dominicans who had gathered in Rome to elect their respective superiors general. On 17 September 1946, after recalling the need to adapt our methods to the mentalities of different ages, the Pope reminded the Jesuits:

Let no one seek to change what cannot be changed. Much has been said about "the new theology," which, along with everything that evolves, is itself in evolution, always on the way but never arriving. If such an opinion were to be embraced, what would become of never-to-be-changed Catholic dogmas, what would happen to unity and stability?

On 22 September, after recalling the danger of any attack on the fundamental elements of Catholic thought, the Pope told the Dominicans:

> It is a question of science and faith, their nature, and their mutual relationship. It is a question of the very basis of faith, which no mere judgment of human opinion can shake. Concerning this matter, it is being asked whether indeed what St. Thomas Aquinas constructed rests on a solid foundation and remains firm and valid for ever. [40]

In this atmosphere of general controversy, and of suspicion on the part of the Holy See for lines of thinking that appeared radically new, the Encyclical *Humani generis* was produced. Published on 12 August 1950, it confirmed the immutability of dogma, the importance of the papal magisterium, the inerrancy of Scripture, the validity of Scholasticism, and the didactic value of the first chapters of Genesis, which, although they are not an historical account in the normal meaning of the expression, do state the fundamental truth about the origins of the human race. The Encyclical is prudent and cautious toward evolutionism, seeing it, within certain limits, as the object of legitimate research and discussion. However, it declares that at this time it cannot be seen how polygenism could ever be reconciled with what the sources of revelation teach us about original sin. According to reliable witnesses, the drafting process of the Encyclical was particularly difficult, with the elimination of various rather harsh expressions against the proponents of the new theology, and an orientation toward a calmer tone and more moderate declarations. It basically confirmed the central elements of Catholic thinking, avoiding explicit individual condemnation or extreme positions. Even so, although the juridical significance of the document may have been limited, its historical importance—in other words, its effective influence and practical consequences—was broad, and taken all in all may have been prevalently negative. It is true that the position taken up by Cardinal Gerlier was moderate; as Archbishop of Lyons, where the foremost exponents of the new theology lived, he was directly involved in the matter. In a calm note that appeared in *La Croix* on 11 September of that year, the cardinal expressed his loyal and sincere acceptance of *Humani generis*, but recommended that full brotherly charity should not be lost, that any harsh or polemical expressions should be avoided, and that people should remember the merits of those who have tried to carry out their research with sincerity. The cardinal concluded by saying that the Pope did not want to be discouraging but merely to protect them from dangerous deviations from orthodoxy. A similar opinion was expressed by Monsignor Montini (at that time Substitute) to Jean Guitton, who had told him of his concern. In the cardinal's opinion, the Encyclical simply sought to point out dangers that should be avoided, so that the path already started could be followed without fear; the tone of the document was quite different from that of *Pascendi*. Montini was relatively close to Cordovani. However, his attempt at putting the papal intervention in proportion did not apparently meet with the approval of Pius XII, who complained to the head of *Civiltà Cattolica* about the efforts being made to minimize his document, which was not meant simply as a warning; the Pope also complained that although he had spoken to the representatives of the Society of Jesus in September 1946, there appeared to be a lack of concern over the faithful following of papal instructions. [41]

The effects of all this were soon felt. Father Janssens, the General of the Jesuits, immediately ordered that various books and articles by Fathers Bouillard, Daniélou, le Blond, de Lubac, and de Montcheuil should be withdrawn from libraries. [42] He carried out important changes in the French Provincials, and removed Fathers de Lubac and Bouillard, and another three Lyons professors from their teaching positions. The Jesuits obeyed faithfully, but not without some bitterness. [43] Later, in February 1954, the Dominican General, Father Suárez, personally visited Paris in order to announce the removal of the three Dominican Provincials of Paris, Lyons, and Toulouse, and of four other well-known Dominicans: Father Boisselot, Editor of *Actualité religieuse* and *Vie intellectuelle*, Father Féret, author of a work on obedience, and the two "great ones"—Fathers Chenu and Congar. However, this action was due not so much to theological suspicions as to pastoral considerations, in view of the progressive attitude of the four representatives of the vanguard of French Catholicism. [44]

Thus, the main French theologians who were the subject of these measures were the Dominicans Chenu and Congar, and the Jesuits de Lubac and Daniélou, although a figure who should also be remembered is another Jesuit, Father Teilhard de Chardin, a paleontologist who was led by his discoveries to try to produce a new approach, and who was also closely watched. The first four later had a great deal of influence on the Council, whereas Teilhard, who died earlier, attracted wide admiration in many circles.

From 1920, Father Chenu[45] was Professor of the History of Doctrine (a title preferred to that of "History of Theology") at the Dominican House of Studies of Le Saulchoir, near Lille in Belgium, close to the French frontier. The Dominicans had taken refuge in Belgium in 1903 when, like all other religious, they were expelled from France. About 1935, hopes began to be raised of a possible return to France, and this in fact took place between 1937 and 1939. The French Dominican school in exile in Belgium looked optimistically and hopefully to this forthcoming return, which was seen as a new exodus from Egypt toward the promised land; the members were convinced that theology still had a great role to play in the contemporary world, on condition that it was able to set stereotyped formulas aside and face modern-day problems with courage. This was Chenu's view, and he had a decisive influence on the Le Saulchoir school. With his lively mind and depth of thought, he showed the slow and laborious development of ideas, from the imperfect intuitions of Aristotle to the splendid syntheses of St. Thomas. However, the theologian was also critical of those who did not share his own passion for a return to the sources and for a living theology. His little book, *Une école de théologie: Le Saulchoir*, came under suspicion from the time it was first published in 1937; then, after a controversy that took place away from the public eye, and after a "visitation" entrusted to the Dominican T. Philippe, which resulted in Chenu's removal from his teaching position, and in a warning to *La vie intellectuelle* to pay less attention to contemporary matters, the book was placed on the Index in February 1942. A large part of the progressive section of the Dominicans was affected. Chenu did not stop writing, and his influence in the French Church continued, including his work as theoretician and inspirer of the worker priest movement. His basic orientation can be seen clearly in the titles of two of his works: *La Foi dans l'intelligence* and *L'Evangile dans le temps*, both published in Paris in 1964. In this way, Chenu linked research into the great historical tradition with analysis of contemporary questions, seeing the solution of these problems as a constant incarnation of the word of God. Much later, however, when the question of worker priests came to the forefront, Chenu was hit: in 1954 he was removed from Paris and sent into semiexile in Le Havre. The situation would be reversed by the Council.

Congar was a close eyewitness of what happened to Chenu.[46] He was a Le Saulchoir professor, but at the time that his colleague's work on this theological school was being placed on the Index, he was a prisoner of war, and paradoxically this is what saved him from any censure for the time being. He returned to his teaching and writing immediately after the war, and in 1950 published Vraie et fausse réforme dans l'Eglise. In this book, he used great historical vigor and lively psychological sensitivity to emphasize the need for constant reform in the Church, giving a picture of the true reformer (St. Francis, for example) as clearly distinguished from that of the false reformer (Luther or Calvin, for example). As he himself notes in the preface to the second edition, the Church in France was in a state of ferment and was searching for new forms of apostolate that would be of help in approaching those who were alienated from the Church (by now a majority). Certain experiments disturbed Roman circles. Pius XII was not against change, so long as it took place on his initiative and under his supervision, and in full fidelity to traditional theological methods, with particular prudence over contacts with Protestants and Orthodox[47]; he was prepared to adapt the Church to new requirements, but without any thought of change to be carried out from within. Congar went further than this by accepting a distinction that was unusual and tended to be frowned upon at that time: the distinction between Christianity and Christian world. He wrote as follows:

> It was a question of freeing the gospel from more or less outmoded sociological, pastoral and liturgical forms, in order to restore to it its full dynamic force in a world that was calling for new forms, new expressions, and the invention of new structures.[48]

This orientation was bound to upset the Holy See, which was already very concerned over what was happening to France and was also involved in drafting Humani generis. The Italian translation of this book (which a keen disciple of Congar described as "a work that, through the many corrections, has lost its original purity, becoming like a great, unintegrated mosaic"[49]) and the new French editions were banned.[50] The book would be reissued in France in 1968 and in Italy in 1972 in a very different atmosphere, so that proposals that had seemed dangerous in 1950 now seemed quite normal and moderate: ". . . it was no longer a question of adapting Catholicism and the Church to a modern society that had sprung up outside these cultural forms," but of "rethinking and reformulating the Christian truths."[51] However, worse was yet to come. In 1954, in connection with the question of worker priests, Congar was removed from Paris and sent to Jerusalem, and then, in 1955, to Cambridge, where on his own initiative a local superior tightened the restrictions with unkind limitations on pastoral activity and on study visits to other places. Congar himself compared what he underwent to the experience described with such intensity by Carlo Levi in *Cristo si è fermato ad Eboli*. However, in 1955, the Dominican was allowed to move back to France and settle in Strasbourg, and to continue his scholarly work in the areas of ecclesiology (*Jalons pour une théologie du laïcat*, 1952, and *La Tradition et les traditions*, 1960) and ecumenism (*Neuf cents ans après, Note sur le schisme oriental*, 1954). The man who had been exiled to Cambridge and Strasbourg would later become a member of the theological commission and various other conciliar commissions.

The story of Father Henri de Lubac is very similar.[52] He was a Professor at the Lyons campus of Fourbière from 1929 and the author of an impressive number of works (we would recall particularly *Catholicisme*, 1938, *Le drame de l'humanisme athée*, 1944, *Surnaturel*, 1946, and *Méditation sur l'Eglise*, 1953). The meditation on the Church, which combines a remarkable erudition, a sure knowledge of the Fathers, and a deep *sensus Ecclesiae*, together with an impassioned description of the *aner ecclesiasticos*, was very dear to Monsignor Montini, whose copy of the work eventually became dog-eared. Here we would simply quote from the biographical sketch of the Jesuit made by G. Chantraine:

> His theology was not new except inasmuch as it was less recent than a certain so-called commonly held theology or than that of certain of his critics. It simply returned to the sources. . . .
> Thus it was not new except inasmuch as it was traditional and

dialogical. However, the error in perspective that led to the use of the word "new" as a criticism is not simply an accident affecting the life of one man or a single group. It was again used of those who laid the groundwork for Vatican II. And it weighed on those who had the apparently healthy and legitimate reaction of rejecting this preparatory work. Lastly, it gave weight to the idea . . . that Vatican II is some sort of absolutely new beginning.[53]

Humani generis did not contain anything against de Lubac. Indeed, in connection with the gratuitousness of the supernatural—which de Lubac totally accepted, although he emphasized the need not to contrast nature and grace too violently in a dualistic or separatistic way—the document used expressions that appeared to be drawn from one of his articles, with which it chimed perfectly.[54] However, the General of the Society ordered the father to refrain from teaching and took other steps as has already been recalled.[55] His suspension from teaching was diplomatically disguised as a leave of absence. Thus, de Lubac moved from Lyons to work as spiritual father and to write in a Jesuit house in Paris. At the Third International Thomistic Congress, which was organized by the Pontifical University of St. Thomas Aquinas and took place in Rome shortly after the publication of *Humani generis*, Father Boyer declared that *Surnaturel* should have been placed on the Index.[56] Pius XII was told of this remark by Father Bea, and through the same Father Bea sent de Lubac assurance of his trust and encouragement.[57] However, de Lubac's books were still banned from the libraries of Jesuit theologates, and he was only able to return to teaching in 1954. Then, in 1960, he was nominated as a member of the preconciliar theological commission, and, in 1983, he was made cardinal.

Father Jean Daniélou, a great patristic scholar, was also caught up in the wave of repression. Coeditor with de Lubac of the *Sources chrétiennes* series and a writer with wide-ranging interests, he was capable of moving with ease from the biblical sphere to that of liturgy and also of discussing the burning issues of the day.[58] He was generally speaking a moderate, but on a number of occasions he had taken up clear and decided positions on various subjects. His article, "Les orientations présentes de la pensée religieuse," which appeared in 1946 in the journal *Etudes*, was seen by some people as a programmatic manifesto for the new

line of thought—the new theology. His 1948 work, *Dialogues
avec les marxistes, les existentialistes, les Protestants, les Juifs,
l'Hindouisme,* sought to launch dialogue with other religions in a
more popular than scientific manner, so that it would be accessible to the masses; this slant was based on his vast knowledge and
on the gift of reaching out to a wide readership. The article and
books were eliminated from Jesuit libraries immediately after
Humani generis. At the same time, the theologian was relieved
from his editorship of *Sources chrétiennes,* which had come under
suspicion due to its insistence on the need for a return to study of
the sources, which some people saw as an indication of less
respect for the magisterium. Daniélou was, however, permitted
to continue teaching. Later, in 1969, after a great deal of work at
the Council, he would be made cardinal.

The Jesuit Pierre Teilhard de Chardin was not a member of
the Lyons group, having followed a very individual path, with
long periods spent in China and journeys to many parts of the
world. He was a great expert in geology and paleontology, but his
particular bent, and his work itself, led him to attempt to produce a more general synthesis within a strictly theological framework.[59] And this attempt at a theological synthesis by a scientist
who was not a theologian and who went so far as to present
theories on human evolution and original sin that were very
different from the traditional views alarmed the Jesuit authorities
in Rome. In 1933, Teilhard was forbidden to accept a professorship in Paris, and, in 1947, he was instructed to limit himself to
the field of natural science and not to write anything of a philosophical nature. He was called to Rome in 1948 by the General,
Father Janssens, and told that he was forbidden to teach at the
Collège de France in Paris. His works *Le phenomène humain* and
Le milieu divin were subjected to lengthy examination, which
ended with a negative judgment. Teilhard was neither to publish
nor to teach. However, on 25 September 1947, the Jesuit had
already assured his General: "You should never doubt that for a
long time now my only concern has been the glory and the
spread of knowledge of Christ Jesus, and in any circumstances
you can always depend on my very respectful and total devotion
in Him." Cyclostyled copies of his writings were circulated in
Jesuit houses and among his friends in a semiclandestine way,
with the tacit tolerance of superiors, but the ban was not lifted.
Shortly before his death, thanks to a broad interpretation of the

vow of poverty he received from a canonist, the Jesuit scientist bequeathed his manuscripts to his secretary. Thus, after his death in April 1955, his writings began to appear in France, quite independently of the Society. However, on 6 December 1957, the Holy Office confidentially ordered the withdrawal of these books from seminary libraries and forbade their translation into Italian. On 30 June 1962, three months prior to the opening of the Council, the same office issued a public warning, indicating the weak points in Teilhard's synthesis and in his theory on original sin. Many years would pass before the works of this Jesuit scientist would appear in Italian, although his fame had been spreading in the meantime.

In 1957, a French historian, Bedarida, came to Italy to take part in a congress. During his visit, he was received by Pius XII, who expressed to him his concern over certain trends in French Catholicism that the Pope viewed in a negative light. The scholar was upset by this and was quick to share his distress with some Italian Catholic historians.[60] He felt that the Pope did not understand the great vitality of the Church in France, which was so keen to meet and exchange views with that world that had hitherto shown itself so hostile. This was an example of the heavy atmosphere of the last years of a great papacy.

However, the intransigence of Rome was not due solely to the character and mentality of Pius XII, but also to pressure from theologians living in Rome who were professors at the Angelicum or Lateran. Some people have even spoken of a Roman school of theology (without making the necessary distinctions) and of agreement between this school and the Roman curia. Monsignor—later Cardinal—Parente spoke of "old professors, who were dyed-in-the-wool conservatives, attached to their traditional patterns, and opposed to any critical revision," and who saw "heretical modernism in any attempt at rejuvenation and updating."[61] Such views could not be expected simply to disappear immediately on the day of Pius XII's death, and, in the first months of John XXIII's papacy, they made another sortie, this time against the professors of the Biblical Institute, whom they accused of using a type of exegesis that was tinged with rationalistic tendencies. The ensuing controversy involved a combination of theological concern, conservatism, and a reaction that was to some extent natural to the broad influence exercised by the group of Rome-based German and Dutch Jesuits during Pius XII's papacy. Certain excellent professors from the Biblical Institute (i.e., Father Zerwick, author of a number of works, including a most useful *Analysis Philologica Novi Testamenti Graeci,* and Father Lyonnet, a specialist in St. Paul) were suspended from teaching for the sake of prudence. Everything calmed down in due course because of the deliberate detachment maintained by John XXIII, who, although he did not intervene in defense of the Biblical Institute, did not support its opponents—and also because of the clear stand taken by Paul VI.[62]

This clash of the two opposing currents of traditionalism and innovation was a feature of the general atmosphere of the years preceding the announcement of the Council and played a part in the immediate preparations for the Council itself. I shall refrain from giving further details of the situation and confine myself to noting three different witnesses, all of whom can be of great help for an understanding of the historical context of that time.

In 1961, while the work of the preparatory conciliar commissions was in full swing, the Dominican Father Ciappi, who was later made cardinal, gave a summary in the following terms of the votes of the Italian theological faculties in response to the questionnaire sent out by Cardinal Tardini on 18 June 1969: "Action was needed for the conservation, defense and interpretation of doctrines in the fields of dogma and morals"; there was also need for "confirmation of the tokens of regard and encouragement for theology . . . which were found in profusion in the earlier ecclesiastical magisterium," and also for recognition of St. Thomas "as the primary witness of theological tradition—indeed, as the fullest, clearest and most dependable exponent of the very doctrine of the Church."[63] The expressions and concepts used are in the traditional line and purposely remain on a generalized level, without going into specific problems or details, even if only in tacit acknowledgment of *Humani generis,* inasmuch as the brief mention of recognition by the magisterium of the function of theology touched on an ever-present question, and one that had become more pressing during the papacy of Pius XII, who seemed to emphasize the role of the magisterium as against that of theology.

A different impression is given by Roger Aubert's study, *La théologie catholique au milieu du XXe siècle.* This short but effective summary, which reveals the hand of an expert historian of Catholic thinking and theology, was published in 1954, but re-

produced three talks given in Brussels at the beginning of 1953.[64]
Parallels with the subjects dealt with and orientations given by
Vatican II, and later to a great extent absorbed by theology,
might lead an unwary reader to imagine that it is a picture of
postconciliar theology. However, Aubert was writing during the
papacy of Pius XII, only shortly after the appearance of *Humani
generis*. Even then there were movements in the direction of a
renewal. Three factors appear even as early as the Introduction.
Aubert acknowledges his debt to two studies, one by Daniélou
and the other by Congar, both of which deal with the same
question of the present orientations in religious thought.[65] Even
then these two theologians constituted a reference point, if only
because of their ability to summarize and integrate different aspirations. However, it is above all the following lines from pages 7
to 8 of the Introduction that give pause for thought:

It will mean . . . trying to discern the *trends* that appear to be
predominant at present and that give an indication of the orientation of the years to come. Whether we like it or not, it must be
admitted that since the end of the Second World War it is
France that has been setting the pace in this field. We shall
therefore be directing our attention especially toward this country, while not ignoring what has been taking place in Germany,
where the source of more than one present-day trend is to be
found—nor indeed what has been happening in Belgium, the
influence of which has been growing in European Catholicism
in recent years. Present-day theology is marked by two main
concerns: first, the desire for closer contact with Tradition,
and, second, the concern for better adaptation to the modern
world. . . . The desire for theology to draw fresh strength from
the ever-flowing spring that is the Word of God, as proclaimed
and commented on in the Church, is seen in a threefold—
biblical, liturgical, and patristic—renewal. As regards the efforts of theologians to provide a fresh response which is still in
conformity with the eternal principles to the new questions
raised by contemporary lines of thought, this is seen in *the
formulation of new chapters in a science that had long been considered immobile*: the theology of the laity, the theology of earthly
things, the theology of history. It is also seen in a concern to
rethink ancient views, whether in function of marxist or existentialist thought, or in function of the irresistible thought, or

in function of the irresistible aspiration toward Christian unity that is sweeping through Christianity today.

There is no need at this point to examine Aubert's splendid, effective summary in further detail. It is sufficient to recall the continuity between various preconciliar theological trends and the basic ideas of the documents of Vatican II. The Ecumenical Council does not represent a break with the past, but a development and fulfillment of aspirations that were already widespread, even if not at the center but only in the outlying areas.

We are led to almost identical conclusions on reading the reports of the foremost Catholic information agencies, which provide a relatively full and objective overview of the hopes expressed by the different countries. We shall take a look at just one of these many publications, the October 1962 bulletin of the *Katholische Naxhrichten-Agentur*, [66] which summarizes articles that appeared in that animated waiting period, together with declarations of the episcopal conferences. In most quarters, there was a hope for a wide-ranging liturgical reform, with the introduction of the vernacular and the direct full participation of the faithful in the eucharistic sacrifice. In Italy, too, at least the more open bishops insisted on asking why practices long permitted in northern Europe were not permitted in their own country (the administration of baptism, extreme unction, and matrimony in the vernacular). The demands were now centered on the use of the language of the people in the Mass, but they did not stop here. Most of the requests were of a practical, disciplinary, or pastoral order. In countries where Catholics were in the minority, or where there were many Protestants, there was a desire, not for reunification but for dialogue—for a more friendly attitude on both sides. The talks given by Cardinal Bea between 1960 and 1962 in Berne, Basel, Fribourg, and Zurich had been real "events," and a good number of professors from the Evangelical theological institutions had also attended. There was, of course, great concern over the question of mixed marriages, and there was a call for an easing of existing discipline, at least with regard to the marriage rite itself. [67] Some other questions discussed, on which there was felt to be a need for reform, were: the Index of forbidden books, ecclesiastical censorship of the press, the internationalization of the Vatican curia, the simplification of ecclesiastical customs and behavior, with the abolition of titles and positions that were by now anachronistic, the introduction of the permanent diaconate for married men, improvement in the formation of the clergy, an easing of laws on fasting and abstinence, and the speeding up of marriage cases. In Scandinavian countries, there was concern over any further increase in Marian devotions because this could be an obstacle in relations between Catholics and Protestants, and, in any case, it ran counter to more sober northern tastes. Lastly, various countries strongly criticized the Vatican measures regarding the behavior of Catholics in political elections. Without going into the question of whether such interference was legitimate in Italy or not, the Dutch Catholics firmly asked the Holy See to respect the political freedom of Catholics in the Netherlands and complained of the lack of understanding Rome had shown toward them.[68] Many people were equally strong in their calls for greater participation of lay people in the government of the Church and for greater attention to be paid to public opinion. Nor were more sensitive contemporary problems forgotten, such as the questions of birth control, war, and atomic armaments. A number of questions that came to the fore during and after the Council were not voiced by public opinion between 1959 and 1962: in that period, no voice was raised against the celibacy of the priesthood or, on the other hand, in favor of the admission of women to the priesthood; and, strangely enough, nobody called for the proclamation of freedom of religion—or, in other words, for clarification of one of the vital elements in relations between Church and modern civilization, which had been the subject of lively debate in the fifties.

Most of these pastoral questions would, however, be faced and solved by the Council and by Paul VI in his courageous albeit gradual application of the conciliar decrees and spirit. Liturgical reform in particular represented an event that had been longed for and begged for; it was the fulfillment of the hopes of many centuries and was the most keenly desired—and at least potentially the most fruitful—pastoral reform.

The Preconciliar Ecclesiastical Atmosphere in Rome: Some Specific Episodes and Memories

The picture I have sought to paint would be even less complete without some references to what we might refer to as "the preconciliar ecclesiastical atmosphere in Rome." This expression is somewhat generic and refers to a certain style, a certain mentality, and certain trends observable in philosophical and theological teaching and in discipline in religious institutes and seminaries. Clearly, in this article, I am speaking of the Roman Church and world, which form a part of the universal Church but are distinct from the latter, even though its special position means that the Roman Church has an influence on the whole Church. I am basing myself both on recent publications and on personal recollections of the postwar years when I studied philosophy and theology at the Gregorian University (from 1945 to 1947 and from 1951 to 1954). This section of the article will have a different slant from the others, abandoning a strictly historical approach in order to give room to recollections. This may mean running the risk of breaking the unity of the whole work, apart from that of projecting what may be a restricted experience into a broader dimension. Even so, I feel that it is worth running these risks.

In the immediate postwar period in Rome, the basic aim of the religious life was to protect and transmit intact the basic underlying values, such as total consecration to the Lord, a striking austerity, an intense and personal prayer life, authentic and sincere fidelity to the Church, a spirit of service devoid of any career-minded ambition, burning pastoral zeal, and a strong cultural grounding, which tended to be predominantly if not exclusively philosophical and theological, although it was also open to other aspects. And I remember with warmth and gratitude various superiors and professors from those years of my priestly youth who, despite all their limitations, contributed to the building up within all of us of the evangelical house based on rock and capable of withstanding winds and tempests (or so we hope!). However, it cannot be denied that these values were often presented in a contingent historical form that was already outmoded. No distinctions were ever drawn between value and historical form, and even the slightest criticism of the latter was taken as an attack on the former and, therefore, immediately rejected by those in authority without any calm discussion. Today, having for almost twenty years listened to lines of reasoning that tried, not very successfully, to present given customs as logical, just, and almost necessary, and then having listened in the following twenty-five years to the overturning of these positions and to efforts to present diametrically opposite customs as logical, just, and almost necessary, I look with a certain detachment on many factors and observe certain lines of government with an attitude of prudent watchfulness; I tend instinctively to lay hold of the essential values—with consecration to God as foremost among these—and to view many things as relative. However, I must admit that the evolution the Lord has permitted me to witness has undoubtedly been positive, stripping away worn coverings and emphasizing the essentials.

In other words, I think that considerable ground has been covered, that we have not yet reached the end of the journey, that certain problems (as history teaches us) are never totally solved, and that progress (or, if we prefer, the historical process) always operates on many levels and is never definitively over and done with. I am equally sure that certain aspirations expressed in various quarters today and still viewed with ironical skepticism as unattainable and dangerous utopian dreams (e.g., true dialogue between ecclesiastical superiors and lay people or religious, an ever-growing sharing of responsibility by all those who make up the people of God, and greater trust in the laity) will in fact be well on their way to being resolved in a few decades. The contribution of the younger churches and other cultures will receive ever greater space, but here, too, any excessive swing in one direction or the other, with the attendant dangers, is to be avoided. Above all, I am thinking of the need for a healthy critical attitude that will not be swayed by passing fashions, and that is always able to distinguish between essence and appearance, and retains its own independence of judgment and a healthy openness that is untainted by extremism, naïve overtrustfulness, or antihistorical pessimism. However, although these reflections would be easy to develop and would throw light on the mind-set of the generation that has taken part in this evolution—the generation of the Exodus—they are not really germane to the central subject of this article to which I now return.

The points I remember most from my parish of St. Rocco in downtown Rome, which I attended throughout the thirties, are the solid eucharistic piety we were taught there, linked to a certain emphasis on the severity of God. I am not sure why, but the latter aspect did not make a great impression on me: I absorbed the love for the Eucharist, but remained more or less indifferent to the thought of hell. I reacted in the same way to the catechetical booklets illustrated by Alceste Grandori, one hundred thousand copies of which were at that time distributed throughout Italy: I was struck by the large biblical illustrations, some of which were taken from eighteenth-century German publications, and did not really notice how mannered or how harsh much of it was. In the same spirit, I read the *Piccoli martiri* of D. Pilla, which went through fourteen editions between 1929 and 1953, and which presented a terrifying picture of Masonry. There was also *Una vocazione tradita* (I do not recall the name of the author), which— with scant theological foundation—described the terrible vicissitudes of a young man who had not had the courage to persevere in the seminary. Probably, a pinch of Roman common sense and above all the healthy lay atmosphere at home balanced any excesses in the teaching I was receiving from the parish. In this connection, I have a clear memory of my mother's efforts to persuade me that a person who entered a Protestant church was not excommunicated, as I had learned "down at St. Rocco."

In the novitiate, which I made at Ariccia, near Rome, from 1940 to 1941, I fortunately did not experience the unbending harshness that Monsignor Bettazzi, who is now Bishop of Ivrea, experienced at about the same time. I came into indirect contact with those methods when I went as a professor to the regional seminary of Anagni in 1956, and learned that this type of discipline had ruled the lives of the students for decades: "The individual cells were locked from outside for the whole night, and the light was automatically switched off ten minutes after we had all retired."[69] At Anagni, the only thing that had forced them to leave the doors unlocked at night had been the air-raid sirens in the war, but even in 1956, the lights were switched off in the seminarians' rooms a few minutes after the end of night prayers. Even so, in the novitiate, a phobia for what were referred to as "particular friendships" was inculcated; indeed, I heard a great deal of talk about such friendships, without actually understanding what was meant by the expression. This attitude inevitably suffocated the normal tendency of young people toward comradeship and friendship, and this was aggravated by the fact that we were absolutely forbidden to address one another with the familiar "tu" form, but had to use the formal "lei." "The 'tu' form," insisted Father Janssens, "ignores the special nature of the consecrated person." The day was marked by the ringing of bells, and the daily timetable was rigid, taking place under constant supervision: for instance, an officially appointed "visitator" checked on the novices' full fidelity to their meditation, which took place in their rooms and not in chapel. (This use of a visitator continued until the time of Vatican II, and Father Janssens considered it a good idea and in line with healthy educational principles.) Correspondence— even that of older fathers—was carefully watched, although some superiors kindly left envelopes only partly opened, thus observing the principle but mitigating the practice. We were forbidden to stay with our families, even for short visits, except in the case of serious illness of a parent. (As someone put it, "I'll only be able to see my father again when he's on his deathbed," but fortunately this did not apply to those like me who had their family in Rome.) Normal reading for the two years of the novitiate was *The Exercise of Christian Perfection and Virtue* by Father Alfonso Rodriguez, S.J., a classic that helped form generations of religious, but which reflected a typically counterreformation mentality.[70] The cassock was worn at all times, even on strenuous mountain hikes; thus, toward the end of the fifties, I climbed to the top of the Gran Sasso Mountain clad in a cassock. Although we were convinced of the uselessness and anachronism of these rules, we accepted them calmly and somewhat stoically—maybe because we were trained on the principle of the "dry stick," in other words, we had to be willing to water a dry stick "for a whole year and with a great deal of hard work."[71]

At the Gregorian University, we were forbidden to talk with students who were not Jesuits, following a rule dating from the sixteenth or seventeenth century.[72] This was a cause of such embarrassment to us young people that between one lesson and another we all used to hide together in a small room that is now the office of the Dean of History. The rule was not dropped until the beginning of 1951, and then partly because of my personal requests, which were accepted by the then Provincial without enthusiasm or conviction. I was wise enough not to tell anyone about this battle and the ensuing victory. The relaxation of the rule meant that I could speak German with a student from the German College: now Auxiliary Bishop of Munster, I am happy to be able to send him my greetings in these pages.

At the Gregorian, I did not only meet austere and exemplary religious, but above all excellent professors and scholars who never paused in their task of research, and who were often able to combine intense scientific activity with direct and fruitful pastoral work (especially through spiritual retreats and high-level conferences). Apart from this, they often labored free and in absolute silence in difficult and demanding work for the Holy See. But, above all, I found a very solid education, which taught us to base ourselves on the sources (Scripture, Fathers, magisterium), discern the underlying problems, respect the historical dimension of theology, and strike a balance between traditional orientations and the new paths that were opened—and, in moral theology, between the great principles and the inevitable individual applications. In those four years (seven if we include my philosophy studies), I certainly received a solid, systematic forma mentis, and learned to instinctively shun any superficial unprofessionality. The overall picture is undoubtedly positive, and it would take too much space to recall the individual professors and their specific contributions. Here, I would like to point out certain less positive aspects, although I would not wish this emphasis to make the reader forget the solid character of the institution and its apostolic and scientific fruitfulness.

The Gregorian University was at that time witnessing the normal hand-over between generations. They were the last years of such great figures as Galtier, Cappello, Hürth, Lennerz, Filograssi, and Tromp, and the first of professors who would later become very well-known, such as Flick, Alfaro, and Alszeghy. The university was anxious to follow papal instructions to the letter, and I remember how the then Rector, Father Abellán, told us, with great satisfaction, that Pius XII had had no fault to find with "his" university. Only today, looking back with more detached hindsight, do I recognize the implications of this statement, which was made at the height of the so-called "new theology" crisis, shortly after the promulgation of *Humani generis.* The Gregorian held itself aloof from the controversy, ensuring its students a solid and "safe" education, at the cost of keeping them relatively isolated from contemporary discussions and problems.

During my first lessons in moral theology, I heard the following thesis. A Catholic doctor who is treating a dying Protestant or Orthodox, or a follower of some other religion (although at that time we used the word "sect"), could not call the sick person's minister so that he might receive religious comfort in accordance with his own rites, inasmuch as one cannot formally call for an action that is formally illicit. The doctor can only tell the minister that a certain person wants to talk to him (". . . but who can know why?"). This line of teaching was explicitly given in the old, classic Noldin, which reached its thirty-fourth edition right at the beginning of the second phase of Vatican II.[73] It did not satisfy me, so I went to see Father Hürth in his room to ask for further explanation. However, the old professor was immovable: any non-Catholic cult is contrary to the objective order willed by God, and any direct cooperation with it is intrinsically wrong. I kept my own ideas, but was unable at the time to integrate them rationally. What I felt dimly as a barely twenty-year-old aspirant to the priesthood became a clearer conviction over the following thirty years: when the dying non-Catholic asks for the comforts of his religion, he is carrying out the will of God as this has been manifested to him—maybe inadequately and incompletely, but in a way sufficient for salvation—and when the Catholic doctor calls his priest to administer the rites of his religion to him, he is helping him to fulfill the will of God in the way possible in view of his background and the actual historical circumstances of his upbringing. The objective order cannot ignore subjective aspects (to use the terms that seem to us most suitable). I felt that I was faced here with one of the crucial points in the struggle between the Church and modern civilization, and I could not blindly accept the position held for centuries by the hierarchy and the official magisterium.

What I did not know was that I was in fact witnessing the final throes of an old school, which would see its definitive closure with Vatican II and the papacies of Paul VI and John Paul II (just consider Assisi, 1986!). In other ways Hürth was a very great moral theologian, and his teachings on the whole still hold good, but on this point he was one of the last representatives of a whole series: Tarquini begot Cavagnis, Cavagnis begot Cappello and Ottaviani, and so on. It was Tarquini, a professor of public ecclesiastical law at the Roman College in the mid-nineteenth century, a notable jurist but an abstract man far removed from reality, who taught:

Whatever may be true concerning the internal good faith of the heterodox, it is certain that no one from outside can judge it fairly. For either they seriously direct their attention with an

upright will to the reasons for credibility of the Catholic
Church and to the false features of their sect, or else they do
not direct their attention to them. If . . . they do not give
these matters due consideration, their ignorance . . . is incompatible with good faith. But if they do accord them due consideration, it is much less easily admissible that they can in good
faith persist in their error. . . .[74]

Cappello himself followed a similar line. I shall always remember with warmth that apparently fragile little man, who was such
a great jurist and professor, and a very great confessor. His weekly
"moral cases" were a joy for everybody: "I have confessed thieves,
murderers, bandits, people of every type. Any problem can be
solved in five minutes, or ten at the most. In all my life I have
only refused absolution two or three times. Absolution should
never be refused to anyone." This did not mean granting absolution mechanically, but carefully and gently eliciting at least the
minimum of the required disposition in the penitent, and being
satisfied with the present state of spirit, without bothering too
much about the future. However, although Cappello was such a
great exegete of the canonical text and such a great pastor ("Principles are one thing, people quite another"), he lacked any true
historical sensitivity. In his *Summa Juris publici ecclesiastici,* published in Rome in 1954, he followed opinions that were by then
overly traditionalistic and that even Popes Pius IX and Pius XII
had interpreted with considerable elasticity. Ignoring certain
statements of Pius IX,[75] Cappello maintained with assurance that
the deposing of certain sovereigns, as called for by various Popes
in the Middle Ages and at the beginning of the modern period,
was an application of indirect power.[76] As regards religious freedom, Cappello accepted the idea of tolerance, which "was to last
for a limited time, according to the circumstances, that is, as
long as grave reasons of public order persisted."[77] It was an evil,
and Cappello accepted it in an even more restricted manner and
in even more hostile tones than Pius XII, a jurist with a totally
different degree of historical sensitivity.

It is easy to imagine the uneasiness caused by hearing such
statements from people who were excellent religious, very experienced confessors, and famous teachers. And this uneasiness grew
when one heard close confidants of Pius XII (Jesuits, but not
teachers at the Gregorian) describe the Pope's harsh judgments

on Alcide De Gasperi, one of the greatest Italian statesmen, considered by the Pope to be "dangerous, and far from true Catholic principles." I clung for dear life to the classic distinction between *thesis* and *hypothesis*. A consequence of this was that my first, very modest, historical study met with serious difficulties from the Roman censor, and only escaped by the skin of its teeth—although it was then praised by R. Aubert in the *Revue d'Histoire ecclésiastique* for its rare moderation.[78] In any case, this distinction was itself already becoming outdated, and a professor of history from the Gregorian did not meet with much success when he tried to explain the Syllabus to a congress of historians of all schools by confidently basing himself on another similar distinction: that between *contrary* propositions ("Freedom must always be condemned," "Freedom is always a good") and *contradictory* propositions ("Freedom is always a good," "Freedom can in some cases be limited or withheld"). In condemning the proposition that "Freedom is always a good," the Syllabus affirmed the contradictory "Freedom can in some cases be limited or withheld." Although the distinction was in itself valid, it was too subtle, and seemed to be an overly scholastic concept invented to avoid the underlying problems. He was lucky that the listening historians, Catholics included, did not answer him back with the words of the Athenians to St. Paul: "We will hear you again about this" (Acts 17:32).

Thus, we left the Gregorian in the fifties with a strong feeling of the difference between certain classic, traditional Catholic positions, and the principles commonly accepted by the modern world. This sense of uneasiness was felt all the more by people like me who wanted to pursue historical studies, and floundered around in the difficult attempt to integrate two opposing trends (which the aforementioned professor would maybe have called "contradictory," that is, apparently irreconcilable).

Although in itself rich and fruitful, the ecumenism of Father Boyer, who was for years director of the *Unitas* movement, did not have much relevance in many areas in which I was most interested. Nobody any longer treated Protestants with the proud certainty of former times. There was recognition of their good faith and the partial truths they held that brought them closer to us, but we were still a long way from accepting a universal right for each person to practice in public and to spread the religion he or she held to be true (or, to be more exact, the right to immunity from any individual or social coercion in acting according to one's own conscience).

Nor was I helped by such authors as Chenu, Congar, and Maritain, whom I discovered relatively late, and whom I had been taught to view with suspicion. I was helped more by de Lubac's *Méditation sur l'Eglise,* which I devoured enthusiastically toward the end of my theological studies. Even so, I had to go through a laborious process of clarification, which took place slowly and almost independently, partly because for years I had been cut off from much living contact. I was helped in this journey (or exodus) by some fortunate reading, such as the rediscovery of Pascal's *Provincial Letters,* which I would recommend to all theology students, Newman's writings, from *Tracts for the Times* to his *Apologia pro Vita Sua,* and the even more joyful discovery of Rosmini's *The Five Wounds,* and of Aubert, John Courtney Murray, and Congar. I also benefited from meetings with Catholic scholars who had been trained in other schools, and here I should especially like to recall Arturo Carlo Jemolo, a first-rate jurist and historian. I was equally helped by the serious encounter and comparison with non-Catholic positions that took place at high-level, nonconfessional congresses. Thus, I was able to retain what was valid in the teaching I had received in the theological field, examine certain principles in greater depth and in other frameworks, and drop some positions that were by now obsolete.

I was not exactly like a waterless desert when Vatican II came, although I was certainly thirsty for an opportunity to organize and integrate my ideas in a clear and systematic manner. The day of the promulgation of *Dignitatis humanae* was certainly a happy one for me. The distinction between thesis and hypothesis had been abandoned, and religious freedom now had its true foundation. Even prior to this, however, the serious limitations of the pastoral program proclaimed by Father Lombardi had become clear. For years, Father Lombardi had been viewed with great admiration by many Italian Jesuits, young and old alike, and he was seen as a model, or a sort of beacon, partly because he enjoyed the confidence of Pius XII. We imagined him to be greater than he in fact was, and indeed we only really came to see him in perspective after 1980,[79] when we came to understand the weakness of a plan that aimed at building a wholly Catholic society in the twentieth century, with a great deal of State support (even of a financial nature) for the Church, and with broad recognition of Catholic culture and principles; a program flawed with a certain amount of integrism, it was far removed from the integral humanism of Maritain, and did not have the support of a solid historical knowledge and sensitivity. It was just another of the stages in the evolution that took place in the preconciliar period.

My theological formation had different results, both in dogma and in ecclesiology, but certain shortcomings could already be discerned. The revelation professor, the great Tromp, brought even the usually undiscerning to see the difficulty in certain scholastic formulas, criticizing those who were happy to recite them without understanding their essence, and in this way, with his caustic wit, he trained us to have a healthy critical spirit. Even so, the underlying attitude was still too atemporal, without any historical study of the knowledge of revelation through the centuries— unlike the view we find expressed in such lively terms in the manual of his successor, Father Latourelle. In ecclesiology, the whole section on the episcopate was omitted, and the professor was not really aware how closely he followed in the footsteps of his predecessor, Father Palmieri, who called his treatise *De Romano Pontifice cum prolegomenis de Ecclesia.* Nor do I know if he would have dared state, with Paul VI, that "All those who are baptized, even if they are separated from Catholic unity, are in the true Church, in the one Church. . . . This is one of the greatest truths of the Catholic tradition. . . ."[80] I should add in connection with the sacraments that, despite the fact that I clearly understood the great historical evolution of penitential doctrine and practice, and listened to long *excursus* on sacramental causality, even so I did not receive any historical picture of other basic questions (for instance, the development of teaching on matrimony, clarification of the inner essence of orders, the slow historical distinction of its various levels, or the ultimate basis of episcopal jurisdiction). In Scripture lessons, which were in many ways extremely good, I never heard a word about the theory of Wellhausen, or about the different sources of the Pentateuch (Elohistic, Yahwistic, etc.) and its real value; indeed, the question was more or less ignored. And I have regretted ever since that we were never taught how to use Merk, or to practice interpreting his very useful critical apparatus, which remained a closed book to us, and which I only deciphered on my own, with a great deal of difficulty. In the same way,

I only learned the characteristics of the different recensions on my own: Hesychiana, Lucianea ("the worst of all, but common throughout the Christian world"), Caesarensis, Occidentalis D. Fortunately, an understanding of the religious significance of the Scriptures was already creeping in, although this was still very far removed from the deeply spiritual exegesis taught by Father Mollat in the sixties.

However, I would be being totally unfair if I forgot the clarity of the teaching methods of many professors, the emphasis given to the treatise *De gratia* (which has ever since represented one of the firm foundations of my spiritual and apostolic life, and helped reverse many of my views that were maybe a little semipelagian), the development of the relationship between nature and grace, and between natural order and supernatural order (these were the years of the "new theology" and of *Humani generis*), and the interest shown in fairly lively discussions on the personality and consciousness of Christ. In this latter connection, some Italian theologians, such as the future Cardinal Parente, emphasized particularly the unity of the person, while the old, but great and unforgettable, Father Galtier, together with Father Flick, highlighted the effective reality of his human nature, with its own consciousness as distinct from his divine consciousness. Nor should we forget the patient and fruitful efforts of many teachers—Flick, Alfaro, and Alszeghy, to name just three—to build a bridge between theology and modern culture, to develop in us an awareness of the historical dimension of dogma, and to bring us to see Modernism not as an exclusively negative phenomenon, or as a parenthesis that had been definitively closed and was best forgotten.

I must also admit something that my own experience (and not only my own!) as a teacher and scholar has shown me every day: it is impossible to emerge from any university training, however good, with a complete command of the subject studied and with clear ideas on every aspect, not even on those so far discussed. We are often tempted to ignore positive aspects in order to highlight the inevitable shortcomings. It is not only in adolescence that people often go through a phase of blaming and judging their parents, and they get over it only slowly and with time. I must admit that the Gregorian University provided me with very solid foundations on which I have then tried to build something, and now, years later, I become increasingly aware that the later development was also due to the principles I received there. It is, however, undeniable, and was maybe inevitable, that however solid the teaching I received was, it was in many ways linked to a relatively traditional view of the past, and lacked all the sensitivity needed in order to discern the full significance of the "signs of the times." Such sensitivity was maybe more alive in other theological centers of that period.

Even so, some noteworthy contributors to Vatican II came from the Gregorian. Those very men who might have seemed somewhat traditionalist devoted the best of their energies to drawing up the great conciliar documents. The Gregorian did not provide this new ecumenical assembly with a decisive contribution such as that given to the 1867–1870 gathering by Franzelin, Fleutgen, Perrone, and Schrader; nor was it the source of such experts as Daniélou, de Lubac, Rahner, Murray, Congar, and Chenu. Even so, Father Bertrams and Father Tromp were among its professors: Father Bertrams was responsible for the first draft of the *Nota praevia* for *Lumen gentium,* intended by Paul VI to overcome the last-stand resistance of a minority, and in order to obtain greater clarity; Father Tromp was secretary first of the preparatory theological commission and then of the doctrinal commission, and it was this elderly professor, who was already nearing the close of his activity, who drew up the minutes of all the meetings of the two commissions, produced numerous reports that are for the most part still unpublished, and helped in the drafting of many documents; his work was not restricted to purely executive aspects, but often involved the genuinely laborious task of writing—which was always carried out with an open and conciliatory attitude. The work of other experts, such as Fathers Dhanis and Grasso, was maybe less well-known and far-reaching. Be that as it may, the Gregorian provided Vatican II with a useful, direct, and effective contribution.

In all faculties, there is a great difference between programs and the content of courses before and after the Council. From philosophy to theology, the historical dimension is now given more space, as also is the examination of contemporary problems in every discipline. At the same time, study of the sources, both scriptural and patristic, is more strongly emphasized. Certain vital elements of modern thought have been accepted, first among these respect for the human person, and for his or her dignity, and search for truth and good, free from any outside coercion. And some of the unbending positions of previous days that we have sketched in the foregoing pages have been abandoned.[81]

This change does not mean a break with the past. As is always the case in history, progress does not preclude continuity. However, continuity does not mean monotonous, mechanical repetition, and should be seen more as a movement beyond many aspects typical of the immediate postwar period. Structures, habitats, and methods that were by then anachronistic and linked to a different society from that in which we live, have now been given up without regret.

Thus, we have a new policy with regard to concordats (the specific dates in Italy, 1929 and 1984, and in Spain, 1953 and 1976/79, are significant); a new presence in the world, including that of worker priests (again the dates: 1954 and 1965); ecumenical dialogue and closely shared prayer meetings with all religions (from Noldin in 1965 to Assisi in 1986); broad cooperation with different ideological groups, with the end of the political unity of Catholics as imposed from above on the basis of the shared faith, and with broad independence being recognized for the laity (from "excommunication" for those who voted communist in 1949, to the first center–left government in Italy in 1963); the abandoning of any claim to have solutions that are universally valid for every social problem (from *Quadragesimo anno* in 1931 to *Octogesima adveniens* in 1971); wide recognition of the necessary freedom of scientific research. It has been a tiring journey from the posttridentine Church to the Church of Vatican II, one that necessarily presumed a more open and objective ecclesiology (*Lumen gentium*), a view of revelation that was more sensitive to the historical dimension (*Dei Verbum*), and greater understanding of the true presence of the Church in the world (*Gaudium et spes*). These documents are in fact the outcome of a difficult journey, and its extent can only be understood by looking back for a moment to the distant starting point: the historical context of the fifties, with the general atmosphere of society in the immediate postwar period, and the contrast between a society in rapid evolution and a Church that in many ways stood immobile in defense of threadbare and outdated positions. We have made a definitive move from condemnation to dialogue, from ghetto to presence, from defense of Christianity to the building of a Church that is based on the strength of truth and the effectiveness of grace, a Church that is seen as a reminder, as the guardian of unchanging values even for a society that seems to forget or deny them, as a city built on a high place, as a lamp placed on a lampstand, as the spring of living water at which all can drink.

Translated from the Italian by Leslie Wearne.

Notes

1. Cf. the concluding address of G. Alberigo to the meeting held in Bergamo, 3–7 June 1986, on *L'età di Roncalli;* Alberigo spoke on "Giovanni XXIII e il concilio," but the text has not yet been published. The Exhortation *Sacrae laudes* is found in AAS, 54 (1962), 66–75; the document speaks with poetic warmth of the beauty of the Office of the Hours, calling on the clergy to recite it with fervor, if possible before the altar, but also refers to the importance and breadth of the Council; cf. p. 67, and especially p. 69: "Asseverare possumus . . . nos omnes jam aetatem ingressos esse novam, quae . . . miram portendit rerum . . . progressionem."

2. *Acta et documenta Concilio Oecumenico Vaticano II apparanda,* series I, antepraeparatorio II/I, "Consilia et vota episcoporum" (Vatican City, 1960), IX.

3. *Ibid.,* series I, II/III, "Europa, I, alia." Cf. pp. 346–347, where Bishop Benedetti of Lodi writes: "Novo examini subiciatur disciplina S. Officii, Refero heic ad verbum epistolam sacerdotis cuiuisdam a S. Officio damnati"; this is followed by the priest's dramatic story, taken by the bishop as evidence against the Holy Office. As regards the liturgy, a number of bishops hope that Latin will be retained (Del Signore of Fano, p. 252), but a considerably larger number advisedly suggest the language of the people (Piazzi of Bergamo, Stoppa of Alba, Cannonero of Asti, Rizzo of Rossano, pp. 29, 79, 103, 570). Many hope for a strengthening of the authority of the bishop in his own diocese (Boiardi of Apuania, Jannucci of Penne-Pescara, Santin of Trieste and Capodistria, pp. 62, 595, 695). There is a very generalized complaint over the problems of the abuses caused by the exemption of religious. Very few emphasize the need for greater separation between religion and politics (Mazzocco of Adria, Marchisano of Chiavari, Pullano of Patti, pp. 25, 207, 511). It would be helpful if this study were extended to other countries.

4. *Missa Luba,* conducted by Father Guido Haazen (Philips Records, 428 138 PE). On the cover of the record, we read: "It is sung by . . . a choir of boys trained by Father Guido Haazen when he went to the Congo in 1953."

5. For an overall picture of old-style colonialism and its consequences, cf. D.K. Fieldhouse, "Colonialismo," *Enciclopedia del*

Novecento, 1 (1975), 766–790, especially 885ff.: "Le consequenze economiche del colonialism; Conclusioni: a) conseguenze dovute a sistemi politici estranei; b) ripercussioni del dominio straniero sulla psicologia della società coloniale; c) le conseguenze economiche del colonialismo." For the facts, cf. R. Cornevin, *Histoire de l'Afrique*, III: *Colonisation, Décolonisation, Indépendance* (Paris, 1975); this is the work of a specialist who spent many years in Africa and has written a number of works on African history, the main points of which are summarized here; the book is very detailed, and there will inevitably be imprecisions and the expression of judgments not necessarily shared by others, but it does represent an honest and basically successful effort to produce a difficult but well-based overview. With regard to Vietnam, cf. S. Bordone, "Vietnam," *Enciclopedia Italiana, Appendice IV, 1961–1978* (Rome, 1981), 821–824, especially 822–823, "Storia," which provides a clear and detailed summary of events from 1954 to 1979. For the previous period, cf. *Appendice II* and *Appendice III*. The various appendices of this encyclopedia also contain excellent articles on the other countries mentioned above; as an example, I would note only the article on "Zaire" in the same appendix; this article is signed by S. Bono, and refers to the years 1961 to 1979 (including the difficulties met with by Cardinal Malula).

6. ONU, "World population prospects as assessed in 1963," *Population studies*, 41 (1966), 1–49; ONU, "The world population in 1970," *Population studies*, 49 (1971), 1–78. Cf. F. W. Notestein, "Demografia," *Enciclopedia del Novecento*, 2 (Rome, 1977), 89–101; A. Sauvy, "Populazione," *Enciclopedia del Novecento*, 5 (Rome, 1980), 489–508. In 1950, out of a world population of 2,500 million, 858 million belonged to the developed countries, and 1,642 million to the underdeveloped countries. In 1970, the picture was as follows: world population, 3,632 million; developed countries, 1,090 million; underdeveloped countries, 2,542 million. For the year 2000, the following figures are predicted: world population, 6,500 million; developed countries, 1,454 million; underdeveloped countries, 5,046 million.

7. Cf. Instituto Centrale di Statistica, *Annuario statistico italiano* (1953), 330–331; (1985), 41; *Annuario di statistiche del lavoro*, 12 (1971), 41. The percentages refer to the occupied population, not to residents. There can obviously be slight variations in these data according to the sources used, due to the different methods adopted, but the overall picture remains the same. The increase in industrial workers, for example, stops at a certain date, while the fall in agricultural workers continues.

8. Instituto Nacionale de Statistica, *Annuario* (1985).

9. We would indicate two sources. (a) Instituto Geografico De Agostini, *Calendario atlante De Agostini* (Novara, 1986); this might

superficially appear to be an extremely modest work instrument, but it is much appreciated by experts because of the wealth, precision, and fullness of its data; for the sake of simplicity, I have not distinguished between the two sets of statistics that are in fact separate in this work with regard to administrative circumscription and urban agglomeration, and have chosen the latter. (b) ONU, *Growth of the world's urban and rural population, 1920–2000* (New York, 1973).

10. From the Apostolic Constitution of Paul VI, *Vicariae potestatis* (6 January 1977), AAS, 69 (1977), 5–18. The document refers specifically to Rome, but some statements are valid for many other parts of the world, for example: ". . . the continuous and tumultuous growth of the city has given rise to a considerable number of people in a situation of hardship, who need attentive care for their spiritual and material necessities. Among other things, the phenomenon of a migration of vast proportions towards the city, uprooting so many persons from their native environment, threatens to endanger the faith" (English translation, *L'Osservatore Romano*, English edition [27 January 1977], 4).

11. In the tidal wave of publications on secularization, its precise meaning, its evolution, and its radicalization in the years before, during, and after the Council, the following can be helpful for general and bibliographical orientation: H. Raab, "Secolarizzazione (giuridico-politico)," *Sacramentum mundi*, 7 (Brescia, 1977), 578–586; A. Keller, "Secolarizzazione e secolarismo (in senso ideologico)," *Sacramentum mundi*, 7 (Brescia, 1977), 586–600; and the short article by A. Auer, "Säkularisierung," *Lexicon für Theologie und Kirche*, 6 (1964), 253–254. Cf. also: J.A. Schumpetere, *Capitalismo, socialismo e democrazia* (Milan, 1955); A.E. Loen, *Säkularisation. Von der wahren Voraussetzung und angeblichen Gottlosigkeit der Wissenschaft* (Munich, 1965); H. Lubbe, *Säkularisierung. Geschichte eines ideenpolitischen Begriffs* (Munich, 1965); A. Del Noce, *L'epoca della secolarizzazione* (Milan, 1971); G. Marramao, *Potere e secolarizzazione. Le categorie del tempo* (Rome, 1983); the series of articles contained in the volume *Pro Oriente. Ökumenische Hoffnungen. Neun Pro oriente symposien 1965 bis 1970* (Innsbruck/Vienna, 1984): E. Wenzierl, "Das historische Phänomen der Säkularisation," 48–61; F.M. Schmolz, "Die Säkularisierung des europäischen Geistes," 62–71; M. Geiger, "Säkularismus als historisch-theologisches Problem," 72–93; K. Luthi, "Glaube im Dialog mit der säkularisierten Welt," 94–103. The following works also contain further indications: P. Scoppola, *La nuova cristianità perduta* (Rome, 1985), esp. 143; G. Guizzardi and R. Stella, "Teorie della secolarizzazione," in D. Pizzuti (ed.), *Sociologia della secolarizzazione* (Rome, 1985), 173–212 (with a concluding bibliography, which notes works by Acquaviva, Berger, Dobbelaere, Fenn, Ferrarotti, etc.).

12. *L'idea di un progetto storico. Dagli anni trenta agli anni ottanta*

(Rome, 1982); G. Miccoli, *Fra mita della cristianità e secolarizzazione* (Casale Monferrato, 1982) (a collection of articles written over a period of twenty years); D. Menozzi, "La Chiesa e la storia. Una dimensione della cristianità da Leone XIII al Vaticano II," *Cristianesimo nella storia*, 5 (1984), 69–106.

13. Cf. article 23 of the Lateran Treaty (not "Concordat"), which assures full civil juridical effect in Italy to ecclesiastical measures transmitted to the civil authorities concerning ecclesiastical persons on spiritual matters.

14. Cf. the third section of our article.

15. After the portraits written only a short time after his death by N. Padellaro (Turin, 1949), P. Bargellini (Florence, 1959), and I. Giordani (Rome, 1961), and after the lively discussions provoked by the controversial play *Der Stellvertreter* by Rudolf Hochhuth, a calmer, more reflective, historical phase has set in. A sign of this is the recent collection edited by A. Riccardi, *Pio XII* (Bari, 1984); cf. the review of this work by G. Martina, *RivStChIt*, 39 (1984), 160–169; in the volume itself, cf. especially F. Traniello, "Pio XII dal mito alla storia," 5–29, which gives a broad historical overview.

16. I. Lengeling, *Die neue Ordnung der Eucharistiefeier* (Munster, 1970), which was reworked and summarized in *Rivista liturgica*, 58 (1971), 496–503.

17. A. Giovagnoli, "Pio XII e la decolonizzazione," in Riccardi (ed.), *Pio XII*, 179–209.

18. Cf. the eleven volumes of *Actes et documents du Saint-Siège pendant la deuxième guerre mondiale* (Vatican City, 1965–1981), and the ensuing historical discussions, including the contributions of G. Miccoli and D. Veneruso, mentioned by Traniello, "Pio XII dal mito alla storia," 29, and that of A. Pincherle, "Intorno a Pio XII," *Rivista di storia e letteratura religiosa*, 4 (1968), 55–133.

19. D. Tardini, *Pio XII* (Vatican City, 1960), 79.

20. *Ibid.*, 72–74.

21. This significant episode has not yet been fully clarified. Various factors were involved in the decision for this removal: the unpopularity of Monsignor Montini with the Secretariat of State, Pius XII's irritation over a certain independence of judgment on the part of his collaborator, and Montini's delay in reporting certain events to the Pope in the hope that in the meantime the situation would have calmed down. Cf., among other works, the debatable and debated work of M. Rossi, *I giorni dell'onnipotenza, Memorie di una esperienza cattolica* (Rome, 1975), 109–120; and G. De Luca, *Letteratura di pietà a Venezia dal '300 al '600* (Florence, 1963), 27–42 (an address given by Monsignor De Luca in Venice on 5 September 1956, in which he makes clear reference to the removal).

22. Apart from the solid oral tradition already recalled, it will suffice to recall some of Pius XII's discourses with Father Hürth's moral texts in order to realize how much the former depended on the latter.

23. G. Alberigo, "La condition chrétienne après Vatican II," in G. Alberigo and J.P. Jossua (eds.), *La réception de Vatican II* (Paris, 1985), 28, n. 49; Alberigo compares the immobility he attributes to Pius XII with the theological optimism of Cardinal Suhard, and in this connection he cites J. Vinatier, *Le cardinal Suhard, L'évêque du renouveau missionnaire 1874-1949* (Paris, 1983).

24. The text is found at A. Mercati, *Raccolta di concordati* (Vatican City, 1954), 271-294, as taken from AAS, 45 (1953), 625-656. Cf. Facultad de Derecho de la Universidad de Madrid, *El concordato de 1953* (Madrid, 1956); and E.F. Regatillo, *El concordato español de 1953* (Madrid, 1961).

25. The texts of the agreements of 26 July 1976 and 3 January 1979 are found in R. Garcia Villoslada (ed.), *Historia da la Iglesia en España*, 5 (Madrid, 1979), 771-786; that of 26 July 1976 is also found in AAS, 68 (1976), 509-512. The text and comments are also found in J.G.M. De Carvajal and C. Corral (eds.), *Iglesia y Estado en España, Régimen jurídico y sus relaciones* (Madrid, 1980), 285-327; C. Corral and L. de Echeverria (eds.), *Los acuerdos entre la Iglesia y España* (Madrid, 1980); and C. Corral and J.G.M. Carvajal, *Concordatos vigentes*, 2 vols. (Madrid, 1981).

26. Cf. the complex judgments of J. Lortega, in Garcia Villoslada (ed.), *Historia de la Iglesia en España*, 669 (Franco's tenacity in defending the government's presentation of candidates to the episcopate, and Paul VI's pressure to obtain the abandonment of this practice), and 676-678 (overall judgment). After recalling the euphoria induced by the agreement, the author goes on to say: "Era . . . la cumbre de un proceso. Pero lo años y los acontecimientos posteriores se encargarían de demostrar que, al tocar la cumbre, se había llegado tambien al final. El concordato recibido a la hora de su nacimiento con tantos aplausos, iba a tener . . . una existencia poco brillante. Juzgar ya anacrónico, primero por la Iglesia y luego por el proprio Estado español, arrastaría una vida lánguida, sin que durante muchos años . . . ni Roma ni Madrid se dicidiesen a reconoscer su muerte histórica." C. Corral, an expert in this field, wrote very clearly, in *Peridocia de re morali, canonica, liturgica*, 85 (1986), 492: "Hispanum [concordatum] totaliter abrogatum est novis conventionibus." The same reservations are expressed by A. Marquina Barrio, "La Iglesia de España y el régimen de Franco (1939–1975)," in Q. Aldea and E. Cardenas (eds.), *Manual de Historia de la Iglesia, X: La Iglesia del siglo XX en España, Portugal y América Latina* (Barcelona, 1987), 343-380, esp. 368-370. The author quotes some phrases from the memoirs of the new Nuncio Antoniutti, which we give here in their Spanish translation: "Reflejaba una mentalidad y un modo de concetir las cosas que habían de ser superadas a corto plazo. . . . La Iglesia había salida favorecida y podia dirse, en cierto sentido, que privilegiada. . . . El concordato resultária poco constructivo y signo de contradicíon."

27. The decree, which was approved by the Holy Office on 28 June 1949, and ratified by Pius XII two days later, was published on 1 July; *AAS*, 41 (1950), 334. Cf. A. Rava, "L'atteggiamento della Chiesa di fronte al comunismo dal 1848 al 1949," *Raccolta di scritti in onore di A.C. Jemolo*, 1/2 (Milan, 1963), 1077–1119; G. De Rosa, *Chiesa e comunismo in Italia* (Rome, 1970), 137 (a basically negative judgment); L. Milani, *Lettere alla mamma*, edited by A. Milani Comparetti (Milan, 1973), 81–82; and G. Alberigo, "La condanna dei comunisti nel 1949," *Concilium*, 11/7 (1975), 145–158, where Alberigo recalls the frequently embarrassed comments in Catholic reviews, and expresses a strongly negative judgment on the decree. Cf. also the positions of two Italian bishops, Nasalli Rocca of Bologna, and Della Costa of Florence, who tried to apply the decree more elastically: G. Battelli, "Vescovi, diocesi e città a Bologna dal 1939 al 1958," in A. Riccardi (ed.), *Le Chiese di Pio XII* (Bari, 1986), 259; and B. Bocchini Camaiani, "La Chiesa di Firenze tra La Pira e Della Costa," in *ibid.*, 273, 289.

28. G. Allessandrini, "Federico Alessandrini: una testimonianza," *Studium*, 31 (1985), 726–737, esp. 735: "Se la scomunica attacca, abbiamo in Italia sette milioni di scomunicati, se poi non attacca me lo dice a che serve?"

29. Interpretation of the Holy Office of 11 August, published in *AAS*, 41 (1949), 427–428.

30. With regard to these episodes and the history of those years, cf. the summary and bibliographical notes in G. Martina, *La Chiesa in Italia negli ultimi trent'anni* (Rome, 1976), 29–41, 200–202. Cf. also note 68 that follows.

31. A. Dansette, *Histoire religieuse de la France contemporaine* (Paris, 1965[2]); A. Latreille, J.R. Palanque, and R. Remond, *Histoire du catholicisme en France*, III: *La période contemporaine* (Paris, 1962); the latter work is later than the first edition of Dansette, and more synthetic; although Dansette's work is earlier, it is more analytical, but pays more attention to literary, political, and religious aspects than to institutional and juridical ones. For the period between 1930 and 1940, cf. R. Remond, *Les catholiques dans la France des années 30* (Paris, 1979[2]). For the postwar years, cf. Y.M.-J. Congar, *Chrétiens en dialogue* (Paris, 1964), XLIII: "Qui n'a pas vécu les années 46–47 du catholicisme français a manqué l'un des plus beaux moments de la vie de l'Eglise. A travers une lente sortie de la misère, on cherchait, dans la grande liberté d'une fidélité aussi profonde que la vie, à rejoindre évangeliquement un monde auquel on venait d'être mêlé comme on ne l'avait pas été depuis des siècles. . . ."

32. A. Dansette, *Destin du catholicisme français, 1926–1956* (Paris, 1957), 165–306; *Les prêtres ouvriers* (Paris, 1954) contains important documents; G. Siefer, *Die mission der Arbeitpriester* (Essen, 1960), with the chronology, and various documents; E. Poulat, *Naissance des prêtres ouvriers* (Tournai, 1965); G. Barra and M. Guasco, *Chiesa e mondo operaio, Le tappe di un'evoluzione: da don Godin ai preti operai, ai "preti al lavoro"* (Turin, 1967). The essential documents are found as follows: Cardinal Pizzardo's letter of 27 July 1953, in *Documentation Catholique* (18 October 1953), and in *Civiltà Cattolica* (1954/1), 391; the letter of 19 January 1954 from the French bishops to the worker priests, in *Les prêtres ouvriers*, 244–249; the letter of July 1959 from Cardinal Pizzardo, in *Le Monde* (15 September 1959), and the essential extracts in Siefer, *Die mission der Arbeitpriester*, and in Barra and Guasco, *Chiesa e mondo operaio*, 229–234; the declaration of the French bishops of 23 October 1965, in Barra and Guasco, *Chiesa e mondo operaio*, 234.

33. M. Maccarrone, "Mons. Paschini e la Roma ecclesiastica," *Lateranum*, 45 (1979), 158–218, esp. 194–207, 208–218 (extremely well documented); P. Bertolla, "Le vicende del 'Galilei' di Paschini, dall'epistolario Paschini-Viale," *Atti del convegno di studio su Pio Paschini nel centenario della nascita, 1878–1978 (Pubblicazioni della deputazione di storia patria per il Friuli*, 10 [n.c., n.d.]); F. Miccoli, "Metodo critico, rinnovamento religioso e modernismo. A proposito di Pio Paschini," in F. Miccoli (ed.), *Fra mito della cristianità e secolarizzazione* (Casal Monferrato, 1985), 93–111.

34. Apart from the recent new edition of the complete works, with regard to Mazzolari, cf. G. Barra (1966), L. Bedeschi (1966 and 1974), S. Ravera (1967), A. Bergamaschi (1968), G. Fanello Marcucci (1972), and N. Fabbretti (1962). See also F. Molinari (ed.), *P. Mazzolari, La più bella avventura e le sua "disavventure" 50 anni dopo* (Bozzolo, 1984), with Vatican documents of 1934–1935 and 1960 against *La più bella avventura*; G. Miccoli, "Don P.M.: Una presenza cristiana nella storia," *Cristianesimo nella storia*, 6 (1985), 561–598; and *DizSt di MovCattItal*, 2 (Casal Monferrato, 1982), 349–353.

35. On Milani, cf. the biographies of R. Mazzetti (1982), G. Lentini (1973), G. Bruni (1974), and N. Fallaci (1974); the various collections of letters (1970, 1973); *Don Lorenzo Milani: Atti del convegno di studi* (Florence, 1981); *Don Lorenzo Milani fra Chiesa, cultura e scuola* (Milan, 1983); *DizSt de MovCattItal*, 2 (Casal Monferrato, 1982), 384–388. The attack by *Civiltà Cattolica* was in the form of an article by A. Perego, "Le esperienze pastorali di don Lorenzo Milani," *Civiltà Cattolica* (1958/3), 627–640.

36. As regards La Pira, cf. the article in *DizSt di MovCattItal*, 2,

285–290, which also gives a full bibliography up to 1982. Cf. also *La Pira oggi* (Florence, 1983) (the acts of a congress).

37. As regards Maritain, for a preliminary view, see the articles in *Lessico universale italiano*, 13 (Rome, 1974), 87, and *Enciclopedia Filosofica*, 5 (Rome, 1979), 436–442 (with a good bibliography). For the attack by *Civiltà Cattolica:* A. Messineo, "L'umanesimo integrale," *Civiltà Cattolica* (1956/3), 449–463. For the implicit criticism of Ottaviani: *Chiesa e Stato. Alcuni problemi presenti nel Magistero di Pio XII*, which was very fully summarized in *L'Osservatore Romano* (4 March 1953). For the full Spanish text: A. Ottaviani, *Deberes del estado-católico con la religión*, Preface by F. Martin-Sanchez Julia, "Sobre el tema Iglesia y Estado, según palabras de Roma" (Madrid, 1953). As regards Ottaviani, cf. the very moderately toned article by A. Riccardi in *DizSt di MovCattItal*, 2, 435–439 (including a bibliography). Some important details of the whole episode (the move against Maritain was apparently due to fears of the influence of the philosopher's ideas on the political choices of Italian Catholics, fears that were strongly felt in the Vatican and shared by the Pope; it was also due to fears of similar influence in other countries in Europe and Latin America; the halt to the debate, with the order not to publish the second article—which was now ready—was brought about by the strong reaction of the French Ambassador to the Holy See) in R. Sani, *Da De Gasperi a Fanfani. "La Civiltà Cattolica" e il mondo cattolico italiano nel secondo dopoguerra (1945–1962)* (Brescia, 1986), 137–139.

38. D.E. Pelotte, *John Courtney Murray, Theologian in conflict* (New York, 1976), which is very well documented; R. Sebott, *Religionsfreiheit und Verhältnis von Kirche und Statt. Der Beitrag J.C. Murrays zu eider Modernen Frage* (Rome, 1977), which gives no biographical information, but provides a broad analysis of his thought, and a full bibliography of his works (pp. XIX–XXVI) and references to works on him (p. XXVII).

39. For contemporary summaries of the debate, cf.: M. Labourdette, "La théologie et ses sources," *Revue Thomiste*, 56 (1946), 354–371; R. Garrigou-Lagrange, "La nouvelle théologie où va-t-elle?" *Angelicum*, 23 (1946), 126–145; Anon., "Neue Theologie?" *Schweizerische Kirchenzeitung*, 115 (1947), 133ff.; Anon., "La théologie et ses sources, Réponse aux Etudes critiques de Revue Thomiste," *Recherches de science religieuse*, 33 (1946), 385–402; B. de Solage, "Autour d'une controverse," *Bulletin de Littérature ecclésiastique*, 48 (1947), 3–17; idem, "Pour l'honneur de la théologie, Les contre-sens du R.P. R. Garrigou-Lagrange," *Bulletin de Littérature ecclésiastique*, 48 (1947), 65–84; R. Garrigou-Lagrange, "Variété et immutabilité des dogmes," *Angelicum*, 24 (1947), 124–139; correspondence between R. Garrigou-Lagrange and M. Blondel, *Angelicum*, 24 (1947), 210–214; M. Labourdette, "Fermes propos," *Re-*

vue Thomiste, 56 (1947), 5–19; *Dialogue Théologique, Pièces du débat entre la Revue Thomiste d'une part et les RR.PP. de Lubac, Daniélou, Bouillard, Fessard et von Balthasar S.J. d'autre part* (Paris, 1947); Cardinal Suhard, *Essor ou déclin de l'Eglise* (Paris, 1947); H. Rahner, "Wege zu einer 'neuen' Theologie?" *Orientierung*, 11/23–24 (1947), 213–217; A. Perego, "La teología nueva," *Ciencia y Fé* (Argentina), 5 (1949), 7–30; C. Frey, *Mysterium der Kirche. Öffnung zur Welt, Zwei Aspekte der Erneuerung französischer katholischer Theologie* (Gottingen, 1969). There is no need in the present summary to cite all the relative articles in the *Revue Thomiste, Angelicum, L'Année théologique, Etudes,* and *Recherches de science religieuse.* As regards Father René Garrigou-Lagrange (1877–1964), cf. the sufficient bibliography provided by H. de Lubac in *Lettres de M. Etienne Gilson adressées au p. Henri de Lubac* (Paris, 1986), 84–85, the obituaries recalled by him (*Revue Thomiste*, 1964; *Vie spirituelle*, 1964; and *Angelicum*, 1965, with an entire issue dedicated to the deceased), and the brief biographical portrait by de Lubac himself, in *ibid.*, 85–86, where the Jesuit, who was the object of attacks by the Dominican, repeated the opinion of a French scholar (who was not a theologian), Stanislas Fumet: "Il y avait chez ce grand théologien une delicieuse pointe d'infantilisme."

40. *AAS*, 38 (1946), 384–385, 387.

41. *La Croix* (10–11 September 1950). For the interpretation of Montini and Pius XII, cf. J. Guitton, *Paolo VI segreto* (Rome, 1981), 40–47; A. Riccardi, "Une école de théologie fra la Francia e Roma," *Cristianesimo nella storia*, 5 (1984), 11–28, esp. 27–28. Cf. also the following comments on the Encyclical: M. Flick, "L'enciclica 'Humani Generis.' Vero e falso progresso del pensiero cattolico," *Civiltà Cattolica* (1950/3), 577–590; F. Morandini, "Filosofia ed apostolato nell'enciclica 'Humani Generis,' " *Civiltà Cattolica* (1950/4), 159–172; A. Bea, "L'enciclica 'Humani Generis' e gli studi biblici," *Civiltà Cattolica* (1950/ 4), 417–430; *Documentation Catholique* (1950), 1298, 1299, 1305–1307 (extracts from the French press); R. Garrigou-Lagrange, "Le relativisme et l'immutabilité des dogmes," *Angelicum*, 27 (1950), 219–246; *idem,* "La structure de l'encyclique 'Humani Generis,' " *Angelicum*, 28 (1951), 3–17; *Revue Nouvelle*, 2 (1950), 302–309; *Etudes*, 267 (1950), 353–373; H. Marrou, " 'Humani Generis': du bon usage d'une encyclique," *Esprit*, 18 (1950), 562–570; Marrou very objectively distinguishes the "orthodox" orientation of authors such as de Lubac and Daniélou, who were not affected by *Humani generis*, from the exaggerated interpretations of those who do not understand the fine points of the two theologians, so that they misrepresent their thought ("Des idées justes, des directions valables, servaient, en fait, de prodromes à l'erreur, à l'hérésie"). This view is also accepted by Aubert, *La théologie catholique au milieu du XXe siècle*, 84–86. Cf. also Frey, *Mysterium der Kirche*, 90–106; and Congar,

Chrétiens en dialogue, L: "Je ne note ces choses . . . que pour suggérer ce que c'était le climat de méfiance qui régnait au moment de la publication de *Humani Generis*" (fear of some new restrictive measures on the part of the Holy See and superiors).

42. *Acta Romana Societatis Jesu,* 11 (1946–1950), 882–883. The frequency of similar actions on the part of the General of the Society of Jesus in the years prior to the Council is striking, and a considerable number of such documents can be found. In the vast majority of these cases, however, the Father General was merely passing on the precise orders of the Holy See. There is a certain similarity to the severe antimodernist repression, during which Father Wernz, the then General, passed on identical instructions on a number of occasions. Proper study of the books and articles involved—a long and delicate task— would be needed before an adequate judgment could be reached. In the present case, Father Janssens was not passing on orders received from above, but was acting on his own initiative, although it is always possible that advice and pressure from higher authorities were involved. Referring back again to what was said about the removal of Daniélou's works from libraries, and about de Lubac's *Surnaturel* (which I have always claimed is in full conformity with the principles of *Humani generis*), here I note only that *Surnaturel* was made up of a combination of four previous studies: "Deux Augustiniens fourvoyés, Bajus et Jansenius," *Recherches de Science Religieuse* (1931); "Remarques sur l'histoire du mot 'surnaturel,' " *Nouvelle Revue Théologique* (1934); "Esprit e liberté dans la tradition théologique," *BullLittEccl* (1939); and "La recontre de 'superadditum' et de 'supernaturale' dans la théologie médiévale," *Revue du Moyen Age Latin* (1945). Only the first part was reissued in 1965, in a considerably expanded form, under the title *Augustinisme et bajanisme.* Lastly, it is helpful to compare the measures taken by Father Janssens, who purposely avoided making any judgment on the matter, but who implicitly admitted that the books indicated were not in line with the principles of *Humani generis,* and the comments made on the Encyclical by the Cardinal Archbishop of Lyons, Montini, Marrou, and Aubert, as cited above.

43. From the catalogues of the French provinces of the Society of Jesus. As early as 1949, Father E. Dhanis, a Belgian who enjoyed the confidence of Father Janssens, had carried out a "visitation" to the scholasticates of the Society of Jesus in Belgium and France.

44. Dansette, *Destin du catholicisme français, 1926–1956,* 286–288; Congar, *Chrétiens en dialogue, LIV–LVI.*

45. As regards Father Marie-Dominique Chenu, born in 1895, cf. Frey, *Mysterium der Kirche,* 37–40, 62–63, 287–290 (an exhaustive bibliography); O. de la Brosse, *Le Père Chenu, La liberté dans la foi* (Paris, 1970); Y.M.-J. Congar, "M.D. Chenu," in R. Vander Gucht and H.

Vorgrimmler (eds.), *Bilancio della teologia del secolo XX*, 4 (Rome, 1972), 103–122. Cf. Congar, *Chrétiens en dialogue*, XL: "J'apprenais . . . avec stupeur, au printemps de 1942, que Le Saulchoir était frappé en la personne de son animateur, le Père Chenu. Le maigre courrier qui nous arrivait en Silésie [where he was a prisoner of war] nous laissait sans précision sur des mésures dont nous ne saisissions ni l'ampleur, ni la nature exacte, ni surtout les motifs. Aujourd'hui encore, d'ailleurs, après avoir interrogé, cherché, après avoir appris bien des détails, je me heurte à tant de contresens et d'incompréhensible que je ne puis voir en cet affaire qu'une erreur ou un mauvais coup sans justification. . . . Mais les résultats étaient là: un homme iniquement désigné à la suspicion, les institutions plus vivantes d'une Province ébranlées, déséquilibrés pour vingt ans, l'élan et la confiance à demi brisés." However, today cf. M.-D. Chenu (ed.), *Une école de théologie: Le Saulchoir*, with studies by G. Alberigo, E. Fouilloux, J. Ladrière, and J.-P. Jossua (Paris, 1985); from our point of view, of special interest are the contributions of G. Alberigo, "Christianisme en tant qu'histoire et 'théologie confessante,' " 9–34 (which also appeared in the Italian edition of the book; Casale Monferrato, 1982), and of E. Fouilloux, "Le Saulchoir en procés (1937–1942)." See also Riccardi, "Une école de théologie fra la Francia e Roma" (on which Fouilloux partly based his study). The condemnation of 6 February 1942 is found in *AAS*, 34 (1942), 37; together with Chenu's *Le Saulchoir*, Charlier's work, *Essai sur le problème théologique*, is also condemned. Thus, we have the history of the condemnation, the condemnation itself, and the later rehabilitation (for it certainly cannot be said that the new 1985 edition of the book that was condemned in 1942 has been subject to censorship). Cf. also R. Guelluy, "Les antécédents de l'encyclique *Humani Generis* dans les sanctions romaines de 1942: Chenu, Charlier, Draguet," *Revue d'Histoire ecclésiastique*, 81 (1986), 421–497.

46. As regards Y.M.-J. Congar, born in 1904 at Sedan, cf. his autobiographical notes in the Preface to *Chrétiens en dialogue*, IX–LXIV, under the title "Appels et chéminements 1929–1963." See the studies of Frey, *Mysterium der Kirche*, 31–34 (with a sufficient bibliography of his works), 290–296 (a full bibliography), 135–238; and M.J. Le Guillou, "Y.M.-J. Congar," *Bilancio della teologia del secolo XX*, 4 (Rome, 1972), 188–205. Of very great help is the Preface to the Italian edition of *Vraie et fausse réforme de l'Eglise* (Milan, 1972), where we find the following, not in strictly chronological order (although the latter would have been preferable): the Introduction from 1950 (pp. 23–51), the Preface from 1967 (pp. 9–21), the final note dating from July 1968 (pp. 437–441), all by Congar, and an Introduction by the Italian editor, Marcello Camisasca, (pp. I–III) entitled "Esposizioni approfondite della situazione della Chiesa e della società contemporanea."

47. Cf. Congar, *Chrétiens en dialogue*, LX–LXI: "Relativement ouverte *ad intra*, l'Eglise est demeuré, sous Pie XII, en situation de citadelle *ad extra*. Le pape . . . est demeuré, non seulement monolitique-ment opposé au communisme, mais très méfiant envers l'oecuménisme. Le mot même était suspecte; on ne devait pas employer le titre d'"Orthodoxes' pour les Orientaux. Il semble bien qu'il ait existé, en 1948–49, un projet de réduction et de contrôle assez étroit du travail oecuménique des catholiques."

48. From the 1967 Preface, 12, where we also find the following words: "La différence entre la situation de 1947–50 et celle de 1967–68 est très bien exprimée par les titres que la revue *Esprit* a donné . . . à ses fascicules d'août-septembre 1946, *Monde chrétien, Monde moderne*, et d'octobre 1967, *Nouveau monde et parole de Dieu*. Les interrogations apparues dans les milieux chrétiens vont beaucoup plus loin. D'où la nécessité d'élaborer des réponses."

49. Le Guillou, "Y.M.-J. Congar," 191.

50. Congar, *Chrétiens en dialogue*, LII. Apart from the prohibition on an Italian translation and the ban on a new French edition, he was ordered to submit all writings, even modest reviews, to the censorship of Rome, which was exercised by the far-off censors with "incroyables étroitesses." A number of writings did not pass the censor, which be-came "plus méfiante et plus étroite après février 1954." See Y.M.-J. Congar, "Remarques générales," in *Paul VI et la modernité dans l'Eglise* (Rome, 1984), 852: "L'on voulait que je dis 'le soi-disant évêque' (angli-can)."

51. 1967 Preface, p. 12.

52. Cf. K. Neufeld and M. Sales, *Bibliographie Henri de Lubac S.I., 1925–1974* (Einsiedeln, 1974²), which is the only true complete bibliog-raphy. As regards de Lubac, who was born in 1896, cf. Frey, *Mysterium der Kirche* (see index of names); H. Vorgrimmler, "Henri de Lubac," in *Bilancio della teologia del XX secolo*, 4, 207–223; H. von Balthasar and G. Chantraine, *Le cardinal de Lubac. L'homme et son oeuvre* (Paris, 1983); *Lettres de M. Etienne Gilson addressées au P. Henri de Lubac et commentées par celui-ci* (Paris, 1986), which is helpful for the reconstruc-tion of certain details, especially as found in de Lubac's notes to the letters.

53. Chantraine, *Le cardinal de Lubac*, 21–22.

54. This is stated by de Lubac himself in *Lettres de M. Etienne Gilson*, 78–80, note 1: "On a cru de voir dans le livre de 1965 [the new, partial, edition of *Surnaturel*] un effort pour corriger, ou du moins pour défendre en l'expliquant celui de 1946, en vue de le rendre plus conforme à une phrase de l'encyclique *Humani generis*. . . . Or c'est au contraire cette encyclique qui s'inspirait habilement de mon article de 1949, pour éviter la théorie dite de la 'nature pure' que plusieurs théologiens voulaient lui faire canoniser. . . ." De Lubac had written: "Dieu . . . ne puet être contraint par rien d'imprimer à mon être une finalité surnaturelle." The Encyclical condemns the thesis according to which "God cannot create intelligent beings without ordering them and calling them to the beatific vision."

55. Cf. note 42 above.

56. Note by de Lubac, *Lettres de M. Etienne Gilson*, 87.

57. According to de Lubac, *ibid.*, the letter was sent "aussitôt," in other words, in 1950. Others (cf. Vorgrimmler, "Henri de Lubac," 219) date the letter to 1957.

58. As regards Jean Daniélou (1905–1974), who was created cardinal in 1969, cf. Frey, *Mysterium der Kirche*, 296–299 (bibliography of Daniélou's writings), 49–50 (basic information), and *passim* (see index of names).

59. I am not concerned to provide bibliographical information on a figure who provoked a whole series of writings both for and against. I recall only his dates—1891–1955—and two good, complementary bibliographies: C. Cuenot, *Pierre Teilhard de Chardin, les grandes étapes de son évolution* (Paris, 1966); and D. Pulin, *Teilhard de Chardin, Essai de bibliographie (1955–1966)* (Quebec, 1966).

60. The information comes from another Italian professor, to whom Bedarida spoke about this.

61. R. Spiazzi, *P. Mariano Cordovani dei Frati Predicatori*, 2 vols. (Rome, 1954), with a Preface by G.B. Montini; Parente's discourse is found in 2, 102 (the citation is taken from the article of Riccardi, "Une école de théologie fra la Francia e Roma," 49). As regards Father Cordovani, who was a moderate, cf. also the article by A. Riccardi in *DizSt di MovCattIt*, 2, 124–138.

62. Cf. A. Romeo, "L'enciclica 'Divino Afflante Spiritu' e le 'Opiniones novae,'" *Divinitas*, 4 (1960), 387–456 (also printed as a separate leaflet). The *monitum* of the Holy Office, of 20 June 1961, is found in *AAS*, 53 (1961), 507 (the attack of *Divinitas* had caused concern in high Roman offices); Associazione Biblica Italiana, *Chiarificazioni sul convegno di Padova (a proposito di un recente articolo)*, edited by the President of the Association, an Appendix to the volume *Atti e conferenze della settimana Biblica 1960* (Rome, 1961), but also printed separately under the name of the author, S. Zedda; "Pontificium Institutum Biblicum et recens libellus R.mi D.ni Romeo," *Verbum Domini*, 39 (1962), 3–17, speaks of "gravissimas accusationes" made against the professors of the Biblical Institute "inaudita vehementia"; Paul VI, "Discorso alla Pont. Univ. Lat." (31 October 1963), *Insegnamenti*, 1/1 (Vatican City, 1965), 273: "I nostri voti . . . auspicano . . . che la sua [the Pontifical Lateran University's] affermazione nel concerto dei grandi, celebri e benemeriti istituti romani di alta cultura

ecclesiastica sia quella della sincera riconoscenza, della fraterna collaborazione, della leale emulazione, della mutua riverenza e dell'amica concordia, non mai d'una gelosa concorrenza, o d'una fastidiosa polemica; non mai!"

63. L. Ciappi, "Le attese della teologia di fronte al Concilio Vaticano II," *Divinitas*, 5 (1961), 494–502; it is worth considering the extent to which the title of the article actually corresponds to the content; maybe it would have been more precise to speak of the "attese di determinate correnti teologiche." A fuller and more objective picture can be obtained not only from the three-volume work, edited by Vander Gucht and Vorgrimmler, *Bilancio della teologia del XX secolo*, but also from the votes of the theological faculties expressed in response to the request of Cardinal Tardini, of 18 June 1959, and published in *Acta et documenta Concilio Oecumenico Vaticano II apparando*, I, antepraeparatorio, II/I, "Consilia et vota episcoporum" (Vatican City, 1960).

64. Tournai/Paris, 1954. It should be remembered that Aubert started with theology (his first study was on one of the vital points of theology, *Le problème de l'acte de foi* [Louvain, 1945]), and that he then moved toward history, although he always retained a perspective that was not sociological and political, but theological and doctrinal. However, his study has a serious and most significant limitation, inasmuch as he completely ignores all theologians, whether Italian or otherwise, who worked in Rome (including Bea, Garofalo, Ricciotti, and so on).

65. J. Daniélou, "Les orientations présentes de la pensée religieuse," *Etudes*, 249 (1946), 5–21; and Y.M.-J. Congar, "Tendances actuelles de la pensée religieuse," *Cahiers du Monde Nouveau* (1948/4), 33–50.

66. Bonn/Munich/Berlin/Frankfurt/Rome. The issue mentioned cites as its sources: *Etudes* (October 1961), *La Croix*, and *Informations Catholiques Internationales*, but also *Kirchens Verden* (Copenhagen), *Znak* (Poland), and *Vaterland* (Switzerland).

67. Italian bulletin of *Katholische Nachrichten-Agentur*, 8 (Switzerland): "Es sollte alles vermieden werden was den nicht-katholischen Ehepartner verletzen und sich in der Folge als verhängnisvoll für die Ehe auswirken könnte. Die Brautmessen un der Brautsegen sollen auch in der Trauung einer Mischehe gestatt werden." *Ibid.*, 12 (Great Britain): "Auch eine Mischehe zwischen gwei Getauften sei ein Sakrament, und sollte einer gewissen Frierlichkeit und Würde nicht entbehren, sagt man in England: eine Mischehe die ohne Blumen und ohne Kerzen geschlossen wird, zeige gewisse Abwertungstendenzen."

68. *Ibid.*, 6 (Netherlands): "Vor zwei Jahren erschien in 'Osservatore Romano' ein Artikel, der einem hohen Kurienprälaten zugeschrieben wird [Parente and Ottaviani: cf. A. Riccardi, 'Ottaviani,' DizSt di MovCattIt, 2, 438], und worin dargelegt wurde, dass die Bischöfe das Recht hätten, bestimmte politische Koalitionen zu verbieten. Man hat

später—nachdem auch anderswo in der Welt der Artikel auf Wider-
stand gestossen ward—gesagt, dass sich diese Ausführungen lediglich
auf italienische Zustände bezogen. Das ist zwar möglich, aber die
allgemeine und autoritäte Manier einer Verkünding, verbunden mit
einem Seitenhieb auf die niederländische Katholiken, hat dem Gefühl
'Im Rom begriefen sie uns nicht' feste Nahrung gegeben. Und diese
Gefühl ist niemals durche eine Loyale Richtigstellung petilgt worden."

69. L. Bettazzi, *Farsi uomo. Confessioni di un vescovo* (Turin, 1977),
21–22.

70. On various occasions, I have suggested to professors at the
Gregorian University that someone should write a thesis on "Rodriguez:
Reasons and Limitations of a Success Story," but they have all said that
such a work goes beyond the limits of a thesis, and indeed it would
mean examining the whole religious education in novitiates and houses
of study from the seventeenth century until Vatican II. Rodriguez does
defend authentic values, but he has no true historical sensitivity. He
sees religious life more as a flight from the world than as an apostolic life
consecrated wholly to God, and follows an ascetical orientation rather
than a mystical one (a result of the controversy of the period). Moreover, he tends unwittingly toward a sort of semipelaganianism. Even so,
formation in many institutes was based on Rodriguez; and even a
Discalced Carmelite confided to me that in her novitiate (in about
1970!) Rodriguez was preferred to the works of St. Teresa of Avila,
which tended to be viewed as dangerous.

71. From St. Ignatius' letter to the fathers and brothers of Portugal,
on the virtue of obedience, Rome, 27 March 1553. The validity and
effectiveness of these principles could be discussed at length.

72. *Regulae Scholasticorum*, 9: "Eorum colloquia qui cum Scholas-
ticis externis loquendi facultatem habuerint, sint solum re rebus ad
studia vel profectum spiritus pertinentibus, prout ad maiorem Dei
gloriam omnibus utilius fore judicabitur."

73. H. Noldin (A. Schmitt and G. Heinzel), *Summa theologiae
moralis*, 2 (Innsbruck, 1963[34]), 114: "Advocare ministrum haereticum
ad moribundum. . . ." The exposition summarized in our text then
follows, concluding with the following words: ". . . si ministro nil aliud
dicatur, nisi adesse infirmum, qui visitationem petit, est res indifferens,
sed tamen cooperatio propinqua, quae ex adiunctis facile perperam
intelligi potest: ideoque solum ex causa gravis necessitatis excusari
videtur." On Father Franz Hürth (1880–1963), cf. the necrology and
list of his writings (mostly articles written between 1916 and 1961);
necrology appearing in *Liber annualis* of the Gregorian University
(Rome, 1964), 141–149. He was professor at Valkenburg (Netherlands) from 1915 to 1935, and then at the Gregorian from 1935 to
1960, succeeding the well-known Father Vermeersch. From 1936, he

was consultant to the Holy See, and in the review *Periodica,* he illustrated the most important decisions of the Holy See, many of which he
had in fact helped prepare. Among his numerous articles, we would
recall only those on various aspects of the conscience, the Nazi
sterilization laws, and the killing of the innocent as carried out on the
orders of civil authorities. Father Hürth also had time to draw up an in-
depth paper in view of Vatican II, on the purposes of marriage as seen
from the classical perspective—which he had already defended against
the opinions of Doms—and on some of its other aspects (nature, origin,
essential properties, celebration); this paper was published together
with the votes of the Gregorian University in *Acta et documenta Concilio
Oecumenico Vaticano II apparanda,* I, antepraeparatorio, I, "Studia et
vota Universitatum et facultatum Ecclesiasticarum et catholicarum," I,
"Universitates et Facultates in urbe," I (Vatican City, 1961), 90–119.
Despite the criticisms I have expressed of some aspects of his teaching, I
must admit that Father Hürth belongs to the ranks of the great masters
of the Gregorian.

74. C. Tarquini, *Juris publici ecclesiastici institutiones* (Rome, 1973),
76–77; this work went through more than thirty editions. As regards
Tarquini, cf. the classic work of C. Weber, *Kardinäle und Prälaten in den
letzten Jahren des Kirchenstaates. Elite Rekrutierung, Karriere-Muster und
soziale zusammensetzung der kurialen Führungschicht zur Zeit Pius IX,
1846–1878* (Stuttgart, 1878), esp. 524.

75. Discourse of 20 July 1871 to the members of the Academy of
Catholic Religion, *Civiltà Cattolica,* 8/3 (1871), 485: "Il diritto di
deporre i sovrani . . . la di lui fonte [era] secondo il diritto pubblico
allora vigente e per l'accordo delle nazioni cristiane . . . stendeasi a
giudicare anche civilmente dei Principi."

76. Cappello, *Summa juris publici ecclesiastici,* 197–198: "Jus historicum per se solum . . . adaequatam non exhibet explicationem declara-
tionum, quas ipsi dederunt. . . . Inde liquido patet, systema historicum
falsum esse."

77. *Ibid.,* 227–231.

78. *Revue d'histoire ecclésiastique,* 57 (1962), 1159–1160; a review of
my "youthful" work, *Il liberalismo cattolico e il Sillabo* (Rome, 1959).
Without going into too much detail (the judgment of the Roman
censor, unsuccessful attempts to gain access to confidential archives
that I was able to consult only thirty years later, etc.), I reproduce here
some of Aubert's opinions because they give a good picture of the
sincere but only partially successful effort in the direction of a certain
openness as made by a person who was reflecting on the formation
received at the Gregorian University in the fifties: "Il présente sur la
signification du mouvement catholique libéral européen du s. XIXe une
interpretation nuancée et modérée encore trop rare dans les milieux
ecclésiastiques italiens. Sans doubte son appréciation doctrinale du Syl-

labus demeure-t-elle encore trop dans la perspective des ces mêmes milieux, généralement très réticents à l'égard des progrès récents de la théologie en la matière. . . ." Once again, I thank Professor Aubert for his kind words, which he repeated in the same publication more than twenty years later, in 1986.

79. As regards Father Lombardi, cf. John XXIII, *Giornale dell'anima* (Rome, 1967⁵), 342 (notes from 1955); Angelo Roncalli to Monsignor Dell'Acqua, Substitute, 6 November 1955, in John XXIII, *Lettere 1958–1963* (Rome, 1978), 143–144; V. Rotondi, "P. Riccardo Lombardi. Una vita conquistata da Cristo," *Civiltà Cattolica* (1980/1), 220–236, gives some interesting information on the disagreements between Father Lombardi and Pius XII, although the Pope in fact respected and supported the Jesuit.

80. Cited by Y.M.-J. Congar, "L'oecumenisme de Paul VI," in *Paul VI et la modernité dans l'Eglise* (Rome, 1984), 810; according to *Documentation catholique*, 1474, this is a report of the audience of 1 January 1966. For the situation of ecclesiology at the Gregorian University in the fifties, cf. two complementary reviews of T. Zapelena, *De Ecclesia Christi, pars altera apologetica dogmatica* (Rome, 1954); C. Crevola, in *Gregorianum*, 36 (1955), 124–128, praises the breadth of the treatment, the profound analysis of the texts, the boldness of the speculation, the calm discussion of contemporary problems, and the love of the Church; on the other hand, G. Dejaifve, in *Nouvelle Revue Théologique*, 80 (1958), 1116–1117, emphasizes the excessively polemical thrust, caused by a rather aggressive attitude, and also the harping on subjects that are no longer relevant (maybe a reference to the discussion of the recognition of the primacy on the part of Cyprian?), and the review concludes that the work reflects the situation of a theology moving toward a new ecclesiology ("une théologie en travail vers l'édification d'un traité systematique sur l'Eglise").

81. For an overview of the currents in the Gregorian University in the preconciliar period, cf. the votes formulated for the Council, in *Acta et documenta Concilio oecumenico Vaticano II apparando*, I, antepraeparatoria, IV/I, "Studia et vota universitatum et facultatum ecclesiasticarum et catholicarum," I, "Universitates et facultates in Urbe" (Vatican City, 1961), 1–119. An in-depth study would be too time consuming here. Even so, a sincere effort to combine prudence and openness can be seen. Emphasis is thus given to the need to accept dogmatic progress, the place of lay people in the Church, the transcendental value also of external union within the Church (in connection with missionary activity), it is suggested that the possibility should be studied of introducing the vernacular into the liturgy in all or some countries, and the traditional purposes of marriage are pointed out. Many of the proposals made by the faculty of canon law were more suited to a revision of the Code than to a Council.

CHAPTER 2

In the Service of the Council

Bishops and Theologians at the Second Vatican Council (for Cardinal Henri de Lubac on His Ninetieth Birthday)

Karl Heinz Neufeld, S.J.

Summary

The article begins with a general presentation of how theologians contributed to the Council and its results, and of the meaning of theology for its dealings and decisions. The author then illustrates this collaboration with the specific example of the contribution made by Henri de Lubac to Vatican II. This should throw a little more light on the as-yet largely obscure field of the collaboration between magisterium and theology.

———

———

"Council" is usually taken to mean the texts of decisions and declarations of such a gathering. If we wish to find out more precisely how these pronouncements are arrived at, we can find a great deal in the published Acts, concerning drafts, debates, and discussions by the bishops who were assembled at the Council. Thus, we can follow the path of a document from its first draft, through criticisms and redrafting, corrections and voting, to its final text. This path may be more or less direct, but the Acts show us all these steps linked with the names of the bishops, the actual members of the Council, where they had seats, and votes.

However, in the case of many Councils, and especially that of Vatican II, it is well known that there was a great deal of work by theologians behind the drafts, proposals, and recommendations, without their contribution ever being clearly acknowledged in the official documents. Of course, occasionally some theological influence of a particular stamp cannot be missed, but this remains more or less a matter of chance. The task of grasping the interplay of bishops' and theologians' collaboration at the Council would appear to require a great deal of detailed work, and it may be asked how reliable the results may be. This does not mean it is superfluous, as there are excellent reasons to support the opinion that, on the one hand, a decisive element in forming a Council in general is to be found in this collaboration that takes place prior to the conciliar documentation, and, on the other hand, it is at this very point that the problem of the much-discussed relationship between magisterium and theology arises in specific terms. The example of Vatican II permits us to say certain things today, from the theologians' point of view, which will bring our appointed task a step forward. This sheds light not only on the history of the importance of theologians and theologies for the Council, important as this may be, because it is still hard to grasp and to survey: it also throws a little theological light on how the collaboration of magisterium and the science of faith must be organized so that their common and respective specific services for belief and the Church may be realized.

However decisive the influence of theologians on the work of the Second Vatican Council may have been, their work nevertheless remained outside the Council Hall, and thus outside the event itself. It was an essentially hidden service,[1] despite all the sensational journalistic reports. Indeed, this hidden quality prompted considerable speculation during the sessions, and this continued after the Council. With varying degrees of justification, specific theologians were credited with this or that formulation of a conciliar text, whereas others, it was said, were to be thanked for presenting certain perspectives, and yet others for a viewpoint, a question, or a criticism. But what does it all come down to? Who were these theologians? What were the bases for assigning to them the task of collaborating at the Council? And how, specifically, was their contribution to be made? Lastly, the most vital question: What in the fruits of the Council can be traced back to them?

These and similar questions contain some very varied aspects, which cannot all be dealt with exhaustively and in proper order in an article of the present proportions. This does not prevent us from giving an overview that bundles them all together just as the reality of the Council's work did. It will be sketched out here in both a general and a specific fashion: first, in a picture of the engagement of the conciliar theologians in general, and then in a report of how one of them placed himself at the service of the Council, and what he came up against by doing so. This will permit us to make comparisons and clarifications by contrasting the more general description with the more personal one, and should help us to distinguish at least the problems and also, in part, the possible meaning of theological collaboration at the Council.

At first, neither the composition nor the role of the circle of *periti*,[2] as the theological specialists were also called at the Second Vatican Council, were very clearly defined, and to the present day we search in vain for information about them—if by this we mean a coherent, reasoned presentation. Although there is a wealth of the most varied indications, they must be gleaned here and there, and they can usually be discovered only as marginal observations in connection with different questions. This also points up the role of service as embodied by these men who were called to help the progress of an undertaking, and who also, by and large, understood their contributions in these terms. For the sake of this undertaking, their work often developed independently, so that both their actual role and also their personal weight at the Council acquired their own history. Naturally, this cannot all be adequately described in this general outline of the *periti*. Thus, the very varied information concerning the engagement of Henri de Lubac[3] at the Council will supplement and illustrate our account. Both should then show what the conditions, difficulties, and possibilities were for a theologian collaborating with the bishops in the work of the Council.

Theologians of the Council

It was only during the third session of Vatican II in 1964 that closer public attention was given to the circle of theological experts. It may be that Pope Paul VI gave the impetus for this with his Apostolic Letter *Ecclesiam Suam*, [4] by directly addressing the *periti* of the Council near the end of this text. He speaks of them as men outstanding for their lives and their wisdom, stating that he expects them to be aware of their obligation in fulfilling their task. They must work in the interests of the Council—an event surpassing personal interests. In their life-style, words, and writings, they must collaborate with those responsible for the Council in such a way that—insofar as it depends on them—it may have a successful outcome.

At the end of the same year, the *Osservatore Romano*[5] also carried an article of its own concerning the unobtrusive, effective work of the conciliar theologians. And G. Caprile, one of the most important chroniclers of the Council, observes, looking back at the third session:

> This year there are 434 *periti*, although they are not always all present in the Council Hall. Outstanding names are to be noted among them, men who are well-known for their teaching and activity, for their experience in action and leadership. They have made a constant, effective, disinterested and unobtrusive contribution to the Council. It is on their shoulders that the major part of the tiring burden of drafting, revising, correcting and redrafting of the texts has fallen. They have merited being called to remembrance all the more, since their daily work has received very little outside recognition—indeed, they have sometimes been the object of attack as a group in excessively sweeping criticism: they have been viewed with distrust, suspected of obscure machinations, and held solely or at least mainly responsible for certain delays, comments and tendencies. We would prefer, by contrast, to see in them an example of tireless work and true dedication to the Church, as well as an example of courage in opening up new paths in order to spread the gospel throughout the world. In a word: they are the fearless pioneers of the Council. [6]

This judgment summarizes nicely what had become clear up to that date. Originally, it had not appeared feasible for the theologians ever to play such a role. Their contribution was conceived of as being different, but following the tasks that were set them, it developed notwithstanding numerous difficulties.

Invitation

How did one become a conciliar theologian in the first place? In the summer of 1962, Pope John XXIII promulgated the procedure for the Council that was then imminent, in his Motu Proprio *Appropinquante Concilio.*[7] The following year, Pope Paul VI confirmed this *Ordo Concilii Oecumenici Vaticani II* with certain supplementary points. What was at stake with these rules for procedure can have been understood by few as clearly as the Church historian H. Jedin,[8] in whose *Lebensbericht*[9] (or *Diary*) we find a note to the effect that "a subcommittee presided over by Cardinal Roberti, accompanied by his secretary, Professor of Dogmatic Theology at the Viterbo Seminary, Vincenzo Carbone,"[10] drew up the order of procedure promulgated on 6 August 1962. The *Osservatore Romano* published a summary of the principal points a month later. The first part of this document deals with those taking part in the Council, as well as with the *periti,* concerning whom article 1, paragraph 3, states: "These Fathers are assisted by theologians, canonists and other experts."[11] Thus, the group of specialists was in no way limited to theologians. In the fifth chapter of the same document, we find closer treatment "concerning the theologians, canonists, and other experts as well as the observers." This account comprises articles 9, 10, and 11, dealing respectively with the conciliar *periti,* the private *periti,* and the (lay) observers.[12] We need not occupy ourselves with the latter here, nor with the private *periti,* the bishops' personal advisors, the circle of whom would, only naturally, be hard to grasp and describe. However, we may note that they too are called *periti,* a word which seems to make its earliest appearance at this point. It is clearly a general term for theologians, canon lawyers, and other experts, that is, an expression with a rather vague content. The conciliar *periti* are distinguished from the private advisors by certain important points: they are officially called by the Pope, and they may be present at the discussions in the Council Hall, although they normally do not have the right to speak there. At the discretion of the chairman of the committee, they can be brought in on the work of the conciliar committees. By way of an exception, it is specified that lay experts may also participate in the work of the committees; this ruling makes it clear that the conciliar *periti* are normally priests.

Thus, the committees are the conciliar theologians' real field of work. From now on, we must accord their engagement our full attention. They are totally dependent on the mandate and judgment of the chairman of the committee in question, although the chairman must ask the specific opinion of his delegates. *Periti* can be engaged on all committees, where their work consists "in drawing up and revising drafts and composing reports."[13] This means that it is their task to compose the actual phrasing of the declarations of the Council: the first drafts of the texts, their revision and correction are mostly the work of the theologians. Consequently, they are bound, like the other members of the Council, by the obligation to secrecy (GO, II, 27, 1). We also find certain general rules for their collaboration on the committees (GO, II, 65, 2 and 3).

These few indications to be found in the document on conciliar procedure nevertheless make it clear what idea of the expert was prevalent at the beginning of the Council, and how his participation in the general effort was envisaged. The chairmen of the committees were to be cardinals, and it was clearly expected that they would run their work groups after the model of the Roman Congregations. The theologians were correspondingly attributed the precise role of the consultants of such Congregations. However, this also tells us how it was imagined that the Council and its results would turn out: a confirmation, extension, and reinforcement of what was already known and familiar. There was no room for a serious, unfamiliar task, for a true decision and the weight of genuine responsibility in the face of something completely new in the framework of this project—an attitude that was more automatic than considered.

Today, it is evident that such a description of roles specified the Council in terms that were too narrow, failing to recognize its actual potential. And this expression concealed what was already the most important source of the controversies that were soon to break out in the Council itself and that led first to a self-awareness on the part of the Council as such, then to a self-awareness on the part of the bishops that they were Fathers of the Council, and lastly to a self-awareness on the part of the theologians of the Council. It was only this awareness, which became gradually clearer, that could correspond to the set task of an *aggiornamento*, as Pope John XXIII had called it. However, close inspection reveals that this new perspective already contained everything that was later—for the most part with difficulty—to take shape. This is because, from the very beginning, it stood out in contrast to otherwise prevalent ideas, yet by this very fact did much greater justice to the nature of a Council than ideas that envisaged merely temporarily extending the life and work of the Roman Curia to a gathering of bishops. According to another observation by Jedin, who could base himself on his historical studies, the conciliar order of procedure "reflected the structural relations of the Church at that time."[14] He then adds an observation made by an Italian friend of his to the effect that the present Council did not have

> . . . a bi-polar structure like the last two General Councils (Pope–Council), but a triangular structure . . .: Pope–Curia–Council. This point of view was based on certain private confidences on the part of Pope John. He in no way saw eye to eye with the curial viewpoint.[15]

Thus, we can say that the original description of the Council's task was not at all clear. As work progressed, it rapidly became evident that the version given by the Order of Procedure was insufficient, at least as concerns the contribution of the theologians: the questions they were faced with required thorough study, an alert sense of the spiritual situation of the period and of the Church's potential within this context, courage and insight in developing new perspectives and in formulating concepts in a comprehensible fashion, the gift of discernment, and the strength to withstand the seduction of certain tendencies. These demands were of a considerably different nature from questions of applying already established principles and resisting ordinary or periodically reemerging dangers. The openness the Pope had called for included, first of all, listening to the difficulties and needs of today's world (later the now-established expression of being attentive to the "signs of the times" was employed, although not without a certain amount of ambiguity on some occasions), in other words, an acceptance of the actual situation in which the Church must also live and proclaim its message. Without doubt, the next goal was the Church's consideration of its own nature, and this was, in the presence of its own task, to become newly conscious, and deeper, more lively, and more challenging than the customary course of events had permitted. This was to find its expression in testimonies that pointed to a time beyond the present day and that could give the Church a kind of guidance, as it were, for the steps it must take in the future. This, in turn, rendered necessary certain gestures in order to impart courage and to render comprehensible what cannot be stated and expressed solely in words and declarations.

The theologians of the Council could not contribute to the solution of this problem without at the same time presenting with greater insight than had previously been done the collaboration of magisterium and theology in the process of clarification of Christian truth. In other words, it was indispensable that the ecclesial society gain a clear conception of itself from within, thus corresponding to its actual action and the effort accomplished. Nonetheless, this was achieved marginally, gradually. The point of departure for this process was the indications mentioned from the Order of Procedure[16] and the nominations of official conciliar specialists made by the Holy See on the basis of these.

As the *Osservatore Romano* announced on 28 September 1962, on that occasion 201 conciliar *periti* were called. Their number increased over the following months, reaching 348 by April 1963. After the Council was concluded, all the names of these collaborators were given in a list published at the end of the Acts of the Council.[17] This list and the formula of the oath sworn by these collaborators[18] constitute the only direct indications in the official documents of the work of the theologians behind the scenes. The list gives 480 names. In each case, it is also stated for which sessions each individual was at the Council's disposal. Analysis of this information shows that 281 took part in the whole Council, 95 at three sessions, 63 at two sessions, and 41 at one session. The differences derive from various factors. Many theologians were coopted only when work was already in course for specific questions, or left after the relative subject was concluded. Certain of them became bishops, and from then on took part in Vatican II as Fathers of the Council with full rights. And some died.

A first glance at this list shows at once that here experts with multiple specialities were gathered together. They were far from being solely theologians—the principal subject of the present contribution. Although the specialities are not mentioned specifically, the well-known names oblige us to draw this conclusion. It is hardly surprising that in this broad circle a considerable num-

ber of unknown names is to be found. It was not only leading
lights who were summoned, for alongside them we find many
who were only locally known and who provoked little or no
subsequent interest, not even during the Council or in the
postconciliar period. This means, of course, that the contribution of the various *periti* requires different evaluation; indeed, it
could hardly be otherwise in a context involving the collaboration of so many representatives. Lastly, the group of specialists
was not assembled in a unified manner, and so it must also be
broken down into the objectionable and questionable yet so generally employed terms of "conservative" and "progressive" wings.
Thus, when they began work, their tendencies suggested to them
various, sometimes opposed and contradictory, aims. Soon the
new paths taken by the Council, as well as delays and obstacles,
were connected with specific names; whether this was always
justified is another question. Thus, although this division remains inevitable when discussing Vatican II, it is equally delicate
because attributions of this nature often serve quite different
interests.

Work

Our first overview of the conciliar theologians was based on the
document on conciliar procedure and the list of those who were
summoned. The document on conciliar procedure also specified
certain measures concerning the work of the specialists, stipulat-
ing that the theologians were to collaborate in drafting the documents to be discussed, in the process of their subsequent improvement, and in preparing their presentation to the Council. This
contribution was already expected in the committees set up to
prepare for the Council, for which Pope John XXIII had summoned consultant theologians since July 1960. Closely modeled
on the corresponding Congregations of the Roman Curia, these
work groups had drafted the texts that the Council was to examine
and vote on as the basis of their discussions. It was not imagined
that the bishops could reject these texts or make other proposals in
place of them. At the very beginning of the sessions, this produced
the difficulties related in detail in the chronicle. Many Fathers had
the impression that the texts as prepared were one-sided and left
no space for really taking into account the problems of today's

world. This rapidly provoked an energetic attack on the part of certain well-known bishops against the debates being established by the drafts. Thereby, they defended a living consciousness of themselves on the part of the participants in a Council, that is, their own responsibility. What is more, the choice of consultants actually coopted for the work by the preparatory committee met with criticism. On 17 November 1962, Cardinal Döpfner expressed these objections strikingly during the Twenty-First General Congregation, when he stated that he wished "that among the *periti* nominated by the Pope those might also be called who were particularly competent in the various problems that had presented difficulties."[19] This remark shows that by no means all the theologians who had been summoned to date had actually been invited to collaborate by the committee chairmen. On the contrary, a selection had been made, from which a whole series of well-known specialists had been excluded. Nor was this contested by those accused, who did, however, reply in defense of the criticism made of them that they had composed one-sided work groups whose products were not a representative witness to Catholic awareness of belief.[20] However, the opponents were no doubt talking about different things and at cross-purposes. The matter at stake is expressed more clearly still by the proposal made by French bishops at the end of November 1962, to the effect that, in order to reduce the workload, the right to choose *periti* be ceded to the Council as such, to receive subsequent confirmation from the Pope.[21] This offensive had no success, but must have contributed to improving the actual situation and to increasing readiness to also invite certain theologians to collaborate who had not previously been invited to participate in the work, despite the fact that they had been officially nominated.

Although each bishop was able to engage private specialists of his choice, their status at the Council was fundamentally different from that of the official *periti*, who had attached themselves to the Council Fathers known to them, when the Council gathered. One group, who had contributed to establishing the preparations, furthermore, remained close to the committee presidents. The other group was soon invited by those bishops who were dissatisfied with the texts that had been prepared and who were set on giving the Council its own living awareness of itself, which would then make it possible for it to act on its own initiative. The following event recalled by Father Yves Congar,

O.P., in his memoirs may be seen in the context of this search for the Council's independence:

> Friday, 19 October 1962, 4 P.M., in the "Mater Dei" House, Via delle Mura Aurelie 10: meeting of certain German and French bishops and certain German and French theologians, assembled at the initiative of Bishop Volk. The following were present: Bishops Volk, Reuss, Bengsch (Berlin), Elchinger, Weber, Schmitt, Garrone, Guerry and Ancel, Fathers Rahner, de Lubac, Daniélou, Grillmeier, Semmelroth, Rondet, Labourdette, Congar, Chenu, Schillebeeckx, Professors Feiner and Ratzinger, Mgr. Philips, Father Fransen and Professor Küng.
> Object of the discussion: it is necessary to elaborate and establish tactics concerning our attitude in reaction to the theological schemata. Naturally, during a discussion lasting almost three hours, all possible nuances were given an airing. . . .[22]

By gatherings of this sort, bishops and theologians were seeking to understand their own situation and possibilities, but also, and no less so, their responsibility and duty in response to the proposed texts and the existing order of conciliar procedure. They had had no opportunity to exercise any influence on these decisive premises. Those taking part in these gatherings found them to be helpful, and thus throughout the Council groups of bishops repeatedly asked for theological explanations of individual points or broader contexts. Conversely, during such meetings, theologians gave their view of the questions being dealt with at the Council or of the background of certain themes. This exchange was, however, observed by certain circles with distrust and, in part, with heavy suspicion. Yet, because there were no other possibilities for conciliar Fathers and theologians to make each other's acquaintance, to gather information, and to form an opinion, such initiatives on the margin of the sessions in St. Peter's became of ever greater importance.

Such meetings brought about more intensive personal collaboration and ever-growing confidence. Doubtless, this contributed to surprising proposals and solutions, even though others may have viewed this more as plotting and machination. An attempt to regularize the exchange between bishops and theologians can be discerned in the norms of behavior for the activity of the *periti,* as promulgated in the name of the Pope on 28 December 1963 by the coordinating committee for conciliar work:

1. In conformity with the collaboration requested of them, the specialists must reply to the best of their knowledge, and with all their insight and objectivity, to the questions submitted to them for examination by the committees;
2. they are requested not to form any groups of opinion, to give interviews, or to represent publicly private ideas concerning the Council;
3. they are not to criticize the Council, they are not to pass outside any information concerning the work in the committees, and on this point they are to keep strictly to what the Holy Father has stipulated concerning respect for the secrecy of the conciliar work.[23]

The norms reveal the reproaches that had meanwhile been expressed aloud and how it was proposed to respond to them. It never became completely clear how far such reproaches against the specialists were justified, but it is certain that there were forces at the Council that wanted, with the help of these norms, to steer the work of the official theologians on to paths that suited them. Above all, the task of the *periti* is strongly emphasized as service of the Council. This corresponded to the general concept that Vatican Radio had already recalled prior to the 1963 session: "The *periti* nominated by the Holy Father and present in Rome during the conciliar session are at the disposition of the Fathers of the Council."[24] Thus, the offer was free, and bishops, episcopal conferences, or groups of conciliar Fathers could make use of it as they saw fit. In the meantime, the cooperation had become so regular that the important role of the conciliar theologians could no longer be ignored. On 30 November 1963, Pope Paul VI granted the *periti* a special audience,[25] which was also intended as a sign of esteem for their work. Those involved then began to think more thoroughly themselves about their role and also to speak about it publicly. An example is a program broadcast at that time by Vatican Radio during which Father H. Hirschmann spoke on "The *Periti* of the Second Vatican Ecumenical Council."[26] The question was posed as such, even though a rather more detailed reply might have been expected. The opinions and actions as mentioned demonstrate the interest that had been evoked; nevertheless, the difficulties and struggles concerning the problem of the conciliar theologians had not been overcome.

On 21 September 1964, at the Eighty-Fourth General Congregation, Cardinal Tisserant made himself the spokesman of certain bishops who "had complained about the fact that certain *periti* had given talks with the purpose of expressing and spreading their own ideas."[27] This was one side of the question. The other was such that in the meantime Cardinal Alfrink, Mgr. Heenan, and others had thrown public light on the collaboration of the conciliar theologians and had praised it highly.[28] It must be admitted that H. Fesquet, in his Conciliar Diary for 5 November 1964, says something that seems rather to contradict the foregoing and that gives the impression of a journalistically pointed picture of well-known content. Nevertheless, he too documents the continuing difficulties of one part of the Council with the growing importance of the theologians' work. He writes:

> The experts of Vatican II . . . have become dangerous men . . . for certain Fathers of the Council. This can readily be understood, as they prepare the bishops' declarations and influence the development of opinions. Who are they? Several hundred theologians. . . . For France, the following are experts, for example: Fathers de Lubac, Daniélou; Mr. René Luarentin; without counting the bishops' private theological counselors such as Fathers Chenu and Liégé.[29]

It is a fact that many conciliar theologians, especially those who were the most renowned, had meanwhile played key roles in conciliar history, and this could not fail to arouse and nurture opposition, which expressed itself unpleasantly and objectionably because it could often act only indirectly, with recourse to means against which defensive tactics were scarcely possible. It was often the case that everything was avoided that might have permitted genuine, open debate. The Pope himself was not unaware of this. On repeated occasions, he let it be known that he did not desire such intrigues. We would include here his repeated references praising individual theologians in his speeches from spring 1965 onwards.[30] The meaning of these references becomes clear only when we recall the covert attacks to which these men were subjected at that time. In the concluding phase of the

Council, however, those concerned were also so overloaded with theological work that they themselves hardly had enough time, strength, and opportunity to defend themselves and to clarify misunderstandings, deliberate or otherwise. These papal encomia appear to have had little influence on the public criticism, however. During the last period of sessions, particularly energetic defamations were heard in Rome once again, and there was no mistaking who they were aimed at, even though no names were mentioned.[31] The Pope was sensitive to this situation, and reacted in the following manner: on 13 November 1965, he had the Council informed that "in order to show his benevolence towards the *periti*, many of whom had worked with the greatest love for the Church and with true zeal, albeit sometimes in a totally hidden fashion,"[32] he was inviting some of them to concelebrate at the Mass he was to celebrate with the Council in St. Peter's in five days' time on the occasion of the promulgation of the Dogmatic Constitution on Divine Revelation and the Decree on the Apostolate of the Laity.[33] This gesture made it clear to all that the Pope held the work of the conciliar theologians in very high esteem, that he had confidence in them— including the very ones under attack—and that he desired a new kind of collaboration with Catholic theologians throughout the world. They had shown their value by their work at the Council through their selfless, competent, and courageous contribution in the interests of the Church. This progress was later to be preserved for the Church and Church leaders by the setting up of the International Papal Theology Commission.[34]

Thus, through the work they had done, the image of the theologians and that of their role had developed well beyond all ideas still obtaining at the outset of the Council. With the bishops who, through the Council, had come to a new experience of their own task, the *periti* had also grown into a new kind of collaboration that did greater justice to the complexity of the tasks at hand and the need for competent, diligent, and persuasive theological updating. Yet, all this came spontaneously into life, just as it had grown in the enthusiastic atmosphere of the Council. No clear-cut formulations were as yet available for this. What is more, nobody even considered actually fixing this in writing, although this state of affairs, as later became evident, provided many an opportunity for further conflicts, inasmuch as the earlier forms of coexistence between bishops and theologians remained prevalent—and perfectly justifiably so—alongside the new kind of collaboration. The models should be understood as being complementary, provided both sides have the necessary mutual openness. However, neither on the theoretical nor on the practical levels does this possibility appear so far to have been exploited seriously. By all appearances, conceptions seem rather to be categorized into contrast and competition, along with all the undesirable consequences of such an approach.

These general observations concerning the theologians at the Council, their contribution, and the transformation in the understanding of their role do not yet, however, give us any specific picture of the varied conditions, the personal commitment and influence, and the actual fruit of the efforts of an individual specialist. This general outline needs to be filled out with an example, so that from an individual viewpoint light may be thrown on collaboration at the Council.

Henri de Lubac as a Conciliar Theologian

Within the throng of *periti* at Vatican II, Henri de Lubac was one of the best-known and most outstanding from the very beginning.[35] In this respect, he is not a typical example—although there really can be no "average expert." By the importance of his theological production,[36] de Lubac had acquired a worldwide reputation. The discreet manner in which he reacted to the difficulties that had prevented him from teaching since 1950 and that imposed weighty restrictions on his publications had strengthened and enhanced this reputation.

By contrast, in Roman circles he was viewed with deep suspicion. Nevertheless, surprisingly, he was summoned in summer 1960 as consultant to the Papal Theology Commission for the preparation of Vatican II.[37] In his *Bilan du Concile*, René Laurentin[38] has given an explanation for this. According to him, the consultants for the preparatory commission were named in part by those directly responsible, but in part by the Pope himself. It was in this latter manner that "Fathers Congar and de Lubac were named for the theology commission."[39] This is a plausible explanation, even though a series of accusations had passed over the desk of the former Nuncio in Paris, resulting in the suspension of these religious from their teaching positions.

Now, as Pope John XXIII, he felt it was right to summon them for the preparation of the Council.

Nevertheless, the actual invitiations were sent to the consultants by the respective chairmen of the commissions, who enjoyed complete freedom in conducting their work. Thus, the nomination of de Lubac appears to have had no practical consequences: the theological preparatory commission was closely linked with the Holy Office as concerned subject matter and the persons participating, and the Holy Office harbored clear reserves against the French Jesuit. On the other hand, a consultant summoned by the Pope could not simply be ignored as the Council gradually approached. It is in this context that we should see the admonition published by the Holy Office on 30 June 1962, only a few months prior to the opening of the Council. This was an attack on "the work of Father Teilhard de Chardin."[40] The *Osservatore Romano* of 1 July gave the text with a commentary that left no doubt that this was first and foremost a determined rejection of the newly published work, *La pensée religieuse du Père Teilhard de Chardin*,[41] which Henri de Lubac had written at the request of the French bishops and on commission from his superiors.[42] The above-mentioned commentary rather bluntly called into question de Lubac's judgment, his knowledge, and even his sense of faith. This declaration was therefore bound to attract attention and cause debate, and this consequence would appear to have been neither undesired nor coincidental. In this way, the full light of publicity was thrown on profound dissent within the group charged with the theological preparation of the Council. The controversy concerning the precise significance to be attributed to the writings and person of Teilhard de Chardin overshadowed the entire conciliar period for Henri de Lubac. He himself sought to support his point of view and to present it convincingly by editing texts and carrying out further investigations.[43] When he was in Rome, he was again and again obliged during meetings to rectify misunderstandings and misrepresentations concerning the religious position of his confrère, who had in the meantime become famous.[44]

Nonetheless, neither Pope John XXIII nor Pope Paul VI let themselves be misled by these attacks, which were dragged out into the open—often by dubious means. In September 1962, Henri de Lubac was nominated an official conciliar expert. This meant that he was requested to place his knowledge and his efforts at the disposal of the Council. The question was only how this would be able to take place, for at the beginning, those responsible appear to have taken little notice of him. Thus, it was not a matter of chance that Henri de Lubac accepted Bishop Volk's invitation to the above-mentioned meeting on 19 October 1962. He was also certainly in Cardinal Döpfner's mind when the latter drew attention on 17 November to particularly competent theologians who should surely be coopted for difficult questions. An indirect piece of evidence showing that the French theologian was at first rarely invited to take part in the work of the Council is to be found in his bibliography. The first volume of Part II of his long study on *Exégège médiévale*[45] had been published in 1961. Work continued without any significant delay, and the final volume was published in 1964. This was all achieved when the author was not far from his seventies, but despite this, he showed an astonishing activity as regards both his theological research and also the contemporary problems affecting him. By contrast, in the daily information referring to this journalistically very active year, he was almost entirely reserved. He did not, unlike many *periti,* write regular reports from the Council, and he gave neither interviews nor talks on his own initiative, unless an explanation on an individual controversial point was indispensable. Henri de Lubac did not avail himself of the various opportunities and offers of publicity presented during the conciliar period. At the same time, he was fully aware of the value and necessity of proper information. However, he left this to others, so as to be able to devote himself systematically to difficult theological tasks.

At the beginning of the Council, he was often mentioned. However, the other *periti* soon moved much more strongly into the limelight, and his work remained largely hidden, only rarely attracting attention. He influenced the Council first of all by his works, which had long since been available in printed form. Many Fathers of the Council had studied books by him, from which they had adopted ideas that, during debates, were repeatedly referred to, positively or negatively.

Influence in the Council Hall

According to the Order of Procedure, a theologian could speak at the Council only if expressly invited to do so. This was rarely enough the case. Thus, the Acts of the last Council report no declaration by de Lubac. However, the bishops as speakers in St. Peter's repeatedly drew direct or indirect inspiration from contributions by de Lubac. In this way, he himself played a role in the debates of the Council. Naturally, many allusions are hard to prove. Thus, we can attempt only a preliminary overview here, taking into account points that are immediately striking.

Already at the first session of the Council, de Lubac's name was mentioned during the debates concerning the draft on the Church. He had spoken of the duty of the Church to proclaim the gospel to all peoples and to the whole world in his *Le fondement théologique des Missions*.[46] In general, the teaching on the Church would be clarified on several further points from his works. His *Méditation sur l'Eglise* (1963) proposes the idea of Mary as "type of the Church."[47] Furthermore, at least certain fundamental features of the view of the Church contained in the Dogmatic Constitution *Lumen gentium*[48] are due to the contributions of the French theologian, who had long before begun to use the term "the mystery of the Church,"[49] and who had been one of the first to point out its sacramental character.

However, the Fathers of the Council did not refer back to his theology in a positive sense only. The attacks from outside the Council Hall also found an echo within. So it was that during the third session in 1964, two extremely weighty attacks were made on positions to which he himself attached a great deal of importance. During the One Hundred Nineth General Congregation, the discussions on the hotly debated Draft 13 on the Church in our times offered a first opportunity. A speaker launched into an offensive against ideas that he attributed to de Lubac in *Surnaturel* concerning the relationship between nature and the supernatural, or, more precisely, against the signification he gave to the "natural desire"[50] of man for God. What was at stake here was nothing less than the basic idea underlying the subsequent text of *Gaudium et spes*[51]: the question of the correct understanding of being a Christian in the world. The second criticism was aimed at a point of no less importance, and was, moreover, connected with the subject of the first attack: the image of God's revelation. During the debates on divine revelation, de Lubac's name was mentioned explicitly, and the objection was formulated as an unmistakable refutation.[52] At that time, practically no attention was given to the fact that in the same weeks during the discussion on the Decree on the Church's Missionary Activity de Lubac's name also received positive mention in the hall.[53]

In his reaction, de Lubac showed himself not indifferent to the severity of the reproaches directed against him, especially as, in part, there had evidently been gross misunderstandings. He let the first attack prompt him to resume his twenty-year-old studies on *Surnaturel* and to revise them in the light of the objections that had since been raised. This led to two new volumes, which appeared in 1965 and which attempted to give a clearer presentation of his position: *Augustinisme et Théologie moderne*[54] and *Le Mystère du Surnaturel.*[55] Had these two works been read attentively, there should have been no further misunderstandings concerning this question. Naturally, de Lubac also did what he could to exclude such misunderstandings as far as possible from the drafted text of *Gaudium et spes.* He was able to counter the criticism of his idea of revelation by his intensive collaboration on the text of the Constitution *Dei Verbum.*[56] His basic concern convinced not only the commission charged with preparing the Constitution, but also the Council itself. The French theologian already recorded his principal preoccupation at that time in his first commentary, "La Révélation divine," in 1966[57], and again in 1968 in a large composite work with the same title.[58] This text was subsequently twice published alone.[59] The proof that de Lubac's work and his basic concept concerning divine revelation were considered highly even by the Pope is found in Pope Paul VI's nomination of de Lubac as one of the eleven conciliar theologians who concelebrated with him at the Mass preceding the solemn promulgation of the Constitution on Revelation on 18 November 1965, in St. Peter's Basilica.

In the final discussion of this important text during the last session, de Lubac was once again named as a man of confidence.[60] In a similar manner, his influence was brought to bear, by means of his book *Le Drame de l'Humanisme athée,*[61] for a thorough study of the problem of atheism, which was dealt with in the framework of the Pastoral Constitution.[62] These positive mentions were not devoid of importance. They proved once again how much his major publications had been taken up by the Fathers of the Council.

Influence on Decisions

For the results of the Council, it is not so much the discussions and the Acts as the texts as promulgated that count. When, in these texts, the French theologian appears here and there as a direct source, this shows that the Council adopted his thought, even though he may not always have been the only one to develop and represent the conviction in question. Nevertheless, it was not infrequently the case that it was his contributions that made known and transmitted specific new approaches. He had often dug out the decisive arguments from the Fathers of the Church and from later theology that demonstrated that such ideas had already been at home in the early Church.

In his voluminous historical studies, de Lubac developed several apparently new insights from the tradition of the Church. He had devoted himself to this tradition to an remarkable extent, not only in the Church Fathers, but also in the early and central Middle Ages, in baroque theology, and the modern period of the most recent centuries. He was rarely to be shaken in his demonstrations. Hence, his opponents preferred to apply themselves to a different interpretation and commentary. But he had also turned his attention to the rules of interpretation and due acquaintance with the witnesses of faith. He had studied premises, conditions and criteria, and investigated the influence of mentality and spirituality. The school of Blondel[63] had had its effect on his ideas, especially as concerns the question of correct interpretation. With great sensitivity, he had noticed and recorded the imperceptible shifts that had, for example, in the works of M. Baius and C. Jansen, more or less of necessity led to offbeat and false results. He had shown, as concerns the history of modern Augustinianism, how serious could be the consequences of certain changes of emphasis that at first might appear negligible. It was now his concern to see that these insights be also taken into account in the decisions of Vatican II. Nevertheless, it is difficult to find evidence of this point of view that, by its very nature, involves an indirect approach and thus always depends on the reader's open readiness to apprehend it.

In the foreground of the conciliar texts, we find statements that are theological in content. It is possible to recognize the influence contributed by de Lubac to the formation of several of these. J.A. Jungmann recalls, for example, in his commentary on the Constitution on the Liturgy, the unity of the many in Christ, which becomes reality in the celebration of the Eucharist.[64] De Lubac's expression, "The Church makes the Eucharist, but the Eucharist makes the Church,"[65] was much quoted in this connection. Jungmann is not the only one to recall this expression, nor does he do so by chance: Pope Paul VI had cited it on 2 February 1965[66] in order to give special prominence and honor to the author.

Lumen gentium also shows signs of de Lubac's influence. G. Philips mentions that the French Jesuit had already in 1963 described the Church as the sacrament of Jesus Christ, just as Jesus Christ as Man is for us the sacrament of God.[67] This is the expression of one of the principles of the Council's view of the Church. De Lubac developed this from his idea of the Church as mystery, which he had used as a title in his *Méditation sur l'Eglise*[68] and which he was to discuss in detail after the Council in his *Paradoxe et Mystère de l'Eglise*.[69] But *Catholicisme*[70] and *Corpus Mysticum*[71] had already taken important preparatory steps in this direction. However, it was above all the *Méditation sur l'Eglise* with which the Council Fathers were familiar as a source of theological ideas and as inspiration for the spiritual life. Thus, this book played a striking role in the composite work *De Ecclesia*,[72] which was planned and composed under the inspiration of *Lumen gentium*. Henri de Lubac wrote the introductory essay to this volume. The other contributors then made such frequent reference to his *Méditation* that close comparison of this contribution with the conciliar text promises many discoveries.

De Lubac's influence is clearly perceptible in specific questions, such as that of the relation of the Church with non-Catholic religions,[73] where we see ideas derived from *Catholicisme*.[74] In the same context, reference was made to his works on Buddhism,[75] and this contribution also partially influenced the Decree on the Church's Missionary Activity.[76] But most important for him was the text on divine revelation. In his investigations on the sacred Scriptures and their meaning for theology, on medieval exegesis and the spiritual change that had led to the historical-critical analyses of Scripture in modern times, he had laid the foundations for a more comprehensive and lively conception of the very event of revelation. This conception was now in need of defense. It can be quite generally described as the idea of the history of salvation. E. Stakemeier observed in his report on the Constitution on Divine Revelation that there was "a close connection between the reading from Scripture and the whole of the Liturgy of the Word . . . and this also derives from a well-documented patristic tradition"[77]; his guarantor for this statement was Henri de Lubac. Likewise, J. Ratzinger refers to de Lubac and his book *L'Ecriture dans la Tradition*[78] on two occasions in his introduction and commentary on the Decree, and B. Rigaux refers to the "spiritual meaning of the Scriptures,"[79] as restored to honor by de Lubac, when dealing with the question of the relationship between the Old and New Testaments. A whole series of other such references could be given, but here it will suffice at least to have shown the continued influence of the French theologian's contributions, affecting even the decisions of Vatican ii. A more detailed presentation must be made elsewhere.

Around the Council

The actual field of activity of a conciliar theologian was situated outside the hall. A few details need to be given in this connection as concerns Henri de Lubac, even though only a few points can be recalled here. One of the conciliar theologians' most fruitful opportunities was occasioned by the bishops' need in the context to be informed of the theologians' point of view concerning particular questions. They soon began to invite theologians to give informative talks. This also gave the bishops an opportunity to meet each other, and they made use of it for sharing and exchanging information. In this way, they gained experience that was to be important for bishops' conferences. In his entry in his conciliar diary for 27 October 1962, H. Fesquet speaks of such a study conference of the French bishops, fixed for the following day: "Tomorrow there will be Father de Lubac, whose recent and new works have won him undoubted respect"[80]; thus, de Lubac was to address the bishops. X. Rynne must also have been referring to this talk, which he also dates 27 October.[81] Henri de Lubac did not refuse if bishops invited him to clarify a problem or fundamental question by presenting it in a talk.

We have already stated that, alongside the tasks connected with the Council, he continued to pursue his own theological work. He was not among the younger experts, for in 1963 he was able to celebrate the fiftieth anniversary of his joining the Society of Jesus. This occasion produced the Festschrift in three volumes, *L'Homme devant Dieu.* [82] The editors explained:

> The title given to this collection of articles would no doubt fit the whole of Father de Lubac's works rather well; at least it can be said that it expresses what those who render him this homage today have tried to say. [83]

These voices expressed themselves on a series of contentious points that were also of significance for the work of the Council. Along with esteem for the person of de Lubac, this was an effective aid for his work as a conciliar theologian, although this may not always have been stated explicitly or directly. This is seen clearly in the contributions concerning the interpretation of the religious view of Teilhard de Chardin or in M. Villain's considerations on the meaning of *Catholicisme* for the Council. [84] The absolute necessity of such contributions can be seen from X. Rynne's note during the second session of the Council, to the effect that the Vicariate of Rome had attempted to block the sale in the eternal city of books by various authors, including Henri de Lubac. [85] Tension was evidently high and must have led the French theologian himself to favor the greatest of reticence.

At the same time, he kept on the lookout for a change and made the effort to come more closely to grips with the significance of the conciliar event and to understand it more deeply. He was particularly helped in this respect by Pope Paul VI's planned journey to the Holy Land and to Jerusalem. This journey was prompted entirely by motives of faith. In his small article, "Paul VI, pèlerin de Jérusalem," [86] de Lubac situated the projected journey fully in the context of his own experience of the Council. The text was already completed one month prior to the papal journey, and thus is to be considered as quite different from a report concerning the pilgrimage to the Lord's own country. In point of fact, the conciliar theologian's principal concern was the theological meaning of this return to the origins of Christianity for the Council, and for a deepening of the *aggiornamento* entrusted to it, so that all the external reforms might be connected back to the inner nucleus of the gospel and of faith. The text betrays new hope nurtured by de Lubac: "The third session of the Council will not be simply grafted on to the final declarations of the second one, but on to the new situation created by this pilgrimage,"[87] as its meaning was summarized by a commentator at the time.

We may leave open the question of whether this actually came to pass. What is certain is that the Council took a turning, even though it is difficult to specify when this set in and to what extent it influenced the individual participants. Seen from the outside, the work continued in the forms that had been developed previously; the entirely new atmosphere is, by contrast, rather hard to grasp, apart from the fact that it did not dominate the whole field. During the 1964 session, the so-called "Schema 13" was also dealt with and discussed. At that time, several initiatives were taken, including the setting up of a subcommission to examine questions related to contemporary atheism. This subcommission was under the guidance of Cardinals König and Šeper; the *periti* involved were Fathers de Lubac and Daniélou, while Bishops Aufderbeck, Hnilica, and Kominek were coopted as members along with Fathers Miano and Girardi to represent the Secretariat for Unbelievers.[88] There can be no doubt that de Lubac was the outstanding expert on this problem.[89] His contribution here throws light on a particular form of collaboration between bishops and theologians. Alongside the major commissions, smaller subcommissions were more effective in reaching formulations and clarifications. This experience was made use of above all toward the end of the Council. Here, too, Henri de Lubac contributed his knowledge and willingness.

Prior to this, he had already collaborated intensively in work on the problems discussed. Unfortunately, there is only very little documentation available to show this. It can, however, be demonstrated that in 1965 he was a member of subcommission II, "De condicione hodierna,"[90] which had the task of preparing part of the Constitution *Gaudium et spes*. The new definition of the relationship of the Church and the world also profited from the results of de Lubac's research on the relation of nature and grace,[91] as well as from his theology of catholicity, which was used for the theological justification and definition of the "dialogue" with the world.[92] It is clear that readiness to adopt de Lubac's ideas had increased. Yet, this did not bring about the simple disappearance of the resistance. On the contrary, around the final session, it flared up fiercely once again, forcing de Lubac to react, and publicly. This was because two further talks were

delivered in Rome in October 1965, containing attacks and expressing doubts concerning the memory of Teilhard de Chardin,
owing to false interpretations.[93] Following this, de Lubac addressed an unusually large number of listeners in the Domus
Mariae, without dealing directly with what had been said during
these talks. Nevertheless, a brief statement was unavoidable.
The approval of the audience gave the theologian the assurance
that the general public was also not in agreement with methods
of suspicion and machination, and was prepared to state this
emphatically. Something had changed through the experience of
the Council.

After the Council was concluded, and after the ecumenical
celebration of closure in St. Paul's without-the-Walls with the
non-Catholic observers of the Council, the Pope added one further personal gesture of special esteem by inviting Henri de
Lubac, along with Oscar Cullmann and Jean Guitton, to dine
with him the following Sunday.[94] This gesture was both personal
and official. In any case, it shows the special common feeling
that had come about through work and service at the Council.

Recapitulation

To recapitulate briefly once more the significance of the collaboration of theological experts at Vatican II, we can take as
certain that it was not limited to helping the bishops to formulate
their awareness of their faith. They themselves had animated,
deepened, and strengthened this awareness of faith, so that the
Church represented at the Council could go out toward the
world without fear and with a new confidence in the Lord living
within her. She needed first to be reminded once more of many
things that had long since been forgotten or had been left inactive in the background. The theologians helped with these discoveries. This produced a new awareness of themselves, that is to
say, a knowledge of their own strengths and limits, a mutual
association that bore the seal of openness and responsibility.
Naturally, it is difficult to produce evidence of this development,
but the numerous isolated pointers should convey a certain corporate impression.

As far as Henri de Lubac is concerned, the Council as a
Church event can best be elucidated by referring to his first

book, *Catholicisme*. This theology of what is Catholic has in common with Vatican II the fact that it was provoked and produced from problematic encounters on the fringe of Christianity: with the missions, with social questions, and with the search for true community. It was specific needs and dire difficulties that these succinct theological considerations attempted to examine in a genuine *aggiornamento*, and that produced the book when assembled. It had its unity, despite the varied multiplicity of the individual questions, because de Lubac found it necessary on each occasion to return once more to the nucleus of faith, in order to be able to give a response. The intellectual movement of a genuine *reductio in mysterium* is characteristic of his book and should have guaranteed it persistent success and relevance, against fashionable deductions, for times beyond the immediate moment. From the very beginning, de Lubac took "the present situation"[95] seriously—not, however, in unreal isolation and artificial separation, but as a whole, as a unified reality, which subsequently permits and demands differentiation precisely because it is not exclusively a question of *one* principle and *one* necessity.

All this means that the Christian and the Church are called to seek. Indeed, they have a task that must be accomplished, for the people of God are on a journey and have not yet reached their goal. The Church is not the world, yet Church and world are inseparably interrelated. Even where explicit Christianity is lacking, God and the redemption wrought by his Son are at work.[96] Because this is the case, there are points of contact, there is a basis for dialogue, and the possibility of finding a common conviction. This view of what is Catholic claims a certain tension that must be experienced and that can be experienced only in common. Diversity is here an a priori, but without prejudice. It is seen not as a threat, but as a fullness of points of departure that all lead to God in the last analysis, but to him as the mystery in whom all things live and have their being.

Translated from the German by Ronald Sway.

Notes

1. Cf. Memorandum to the Council, 13 November 1965, AS, IV/ VI, 413. On the hidden character of the conciliar theologians, cf. also

G. Caprile, "Aspetti positivi della terza sessione del Concilio," *Civiltà Cattolica*, 116/I (1965), 317–341. There appears to have been no previous investigation of the theme as such, maybe because it is so difficult to trace and assemble the relevant material.

2. On the expression and the task, cf. *Ordo Concilii Oecumenici Vaticani II celebrandi* (Vatican City, 1963²), 2. This is a collective designation for theologians, canon lawyers, and other experts, which is not devoid of ambiguity. In any case, the persons in question were to collaborate on the specialized questions of the Council and were distinguished from the technical assistants.

3. Tributes to the person and work of Henri de Lubac composed up to the present date hardly touch on his work as a conciliar theologian.

4. *AAS*, 56 (1964), 352–356.

5. Cf. G. De Rosa, "I periti conciliari: umile e feconda collaborazione," *Osservatore Romano*, 104 (21/22 December 1964), 18.

6. Caprile, "Aspetti positivi della terza sessione del Concilio," 322.

7. Cf. *ibid.*, note 2, 7–11.

8. G. Caprile, *Kirche des Glaubens—Kirche der Geschichte* (Freiburg im Breisgau, 1966), 577–588 (the orders of procedure of the last two Ecumenical Councils from an ecclesiological viewpoint). Cf. *ibid.*, 582, note 17: the concept of "conciliar theologian" was more closely defined only in the order of procedure for the congregation of theologians, published on 20 July 1962.

9. (Mainz, 1984) (Veroffentlichungen der Kommission fur Zeitgeschichte, Series A, Quellen, no. 35).

10. *Ibid.*, 203. On the discussion, cf. *ibid.*, 205ff.

11. *Ordo Concilii*, 17.

12. *Ibid.*, 22ff.

13. *Ibid.*, 22 (No. 3).

14. Jedin, *Lebensbericht*, 209.

15. *Ibid.*

16. Cf. *Ordo Concilii.*

17. *AS*, Indices, 937–949.

18. *Ibid.*, I/I, 103.

19. *Ibid.*, I/III, 124–126 (quotation, 125).

20. Cf. *ibid.*, 131–132 (Ottaviani's reply).

21. Cf. G. Caprile, *Il Concilio Vaticano II—Il primo periodo 1962–1963*, 2 (Rome, 1968), 265. This work contains the reports of the Council published in *Civiltà Cattolica;* hereinafter referred to as Caprile, *Concilio.*

22. Y.M.-J. Congar, "Erinnerungen an eine Episode auf dem II. Vatikanischen Konzil," in E. Klinger and K. Wittstadt (eds.), *Glaube im Prozess (Festschrift K. Rahner)* (Freiburg im Breisgau, 1983), 23.

23. *Kipa-Concile,* 10 March 1964, according to Caprile, *Concilio,* 3, 364.

24. Caprile, *Concilio,* 3, 18.

25. *Ibid.,* 187. Apart from the conciliar theologians, the bishops' secretaries and drivers were also received by the Pope in private audience.

26. *Ibid.,* 364, note 2.

27. Cf. *ibid.,* 4, 32ff.

28. Cf. *ibid.,* 32, note 4, where the Archbishop of Westminster is mentioned as one of the bishops who publicly drew attention to the service of the *periti* and expressed his thanks to them.

29. *Diario del Concilio* (Milan, 1967), 661. The well-known reporter of *Le Monde* (Paris) is no doubt mistaken here, when he presents the Archbishop of Westminster as a critic of the conciliar theologians; there is no other evidence for this.

30. Cf. "La SS.ma Eucaristia centro e vertice della liturgia e della vita cristiana" (15 September 1965), in *Insegnamenti di Paolo VI,* 3 (Vatican City, 1965), 1036: "Un valente studioso moderno (non forse sconosciuto ad alcuni di voi) ha enunciato tale relazione in un bel capitolo d'un suo bel libro con queste due proposizioni: la Chiesa fa l'Eucaristia; e l'Eucaristia fa la Chiesa! Provate ad esplorare queste due affermazioni, e vedrete quale ricchezza di dottrina ne risulta." On 2 February 1965, Pope Paul VI had already employed a quotation from *Méditation sur l'Eglise;* cf. Fesquet, *Diario,* 975. See also *ibid.,* 980, where a laudatory mention of Father Yves Congar, O.P., by the Pope is recorded on 22 October 1965.

31. Cf. Fesquet, *Diario,* 949, 974ff; and René Laurentin, *Bilan du Concile* (Paris, 1966), 391.

32. Caprile, *Concilio,* 5 (for 15 November 1965).

33. Cf. Fesquet, *Diario,* 1057; and G.F. Svideroschi, *Storia del Concilio* (Milan, 1967), 550.

34. This commission was not set up until 1969: *AAS,* 61 (1969), 432, 540ff., 713–716. Cf. *Herder-Korrespondenz,* 23 (1969), 256ff., where the names of the members are also given.

35. Cf. Fesquet, *Diario,* 55, 599; H. Vorgrimler, "Henri de Lubac," in R. van der Gucht and H. Vorgrimler (eds.), *Bilanz der Theologie im 20. Jahrhundert,* IV: *Bahnbrechende Theologen* (Freiburg im Breisgau, 1970), 199–214.

36. Cf. K.H. Neufeld and M. Sales, *Bibliographie Henri de Lubac, S.J., 1925–1974* (Einsiedeln, 1974²).

37. Cf. *AAS,* 52 (1960), 841.

38. Laurentin, *Bilan du Concile,* 11.

39. *Ibid.*

40. *Documentation Catholique,* 59 (1962), 950–956.

41. Paris, 1962.

42. Cf. M. Sales, "Préface," in H. de Lubac, *Teilhard Posthume* (Paris, 1977), 2.

43. During the Council period, he published: P. Teilhard de Chardin, *Lettres d'Egypte* (Paris, 1963); *La Prière du P. Teilhard de Chardin* (Paris, 1964); "Autour de 'teilhardogenèse'?" *EphemCarmel*, 15 (1964), 190–199; "Le P. Teilhard, homme de prière," *La Croix*, 85 (12–13 April 1964), 4; *H. Blondel and P. Teilhard de Chardin* (Paris, 1965); P. Teilhard de Chardin, *Ecrits du temps de la guerre* (Paris, 1965); P. Teilhard de Chardin, *Lettres d'Hastings et de Paris* (Paris, 1965); "L'épreuve de la foi," in P. Teilhard de Chardin, *Lettres à Léontine Zanta* (Paris, 1965); "Envergue et limites du Père Teilhard," *Choisir*, 6/66 (1965), 19–20.

44. Cf. "Le R.P. de Lubac a fait une conférence sur le P. Teilhard de Chardin à Rome," *La Croix*, 82 (4 December 1963), 5; and "Controverses autour du P. Teilhard de Chardin. Le P. de Lubac a critiqueé une conférence de M.H. Rambaud," *La Croix*, 85 (13 October 1965), 4. Here also Fesquet, *Diario*, 949, 974, 975; and Laurentin, *Bilan du Concile*, 391.

45. The work is in two parts, the first of which was published in 1959 in two volumes, and the second, also in two volumes, was published in 1961 and 1964. Thus, the work on the final volume extended over a considerable part of the conciliar period.

46. Cf. AS, I/IV, 79. This book was published in Paris in 1946, but originated as a talk given in 1941.

47. Cf. AS, II/III, 715, following a question in writing from Mgr. D. Sengemon Fukahori.

48. On the conciliar Constitution on the Church, cf. "L'Eglise, salut de l'homme," *Catho-Journal*, 8 (special number), 37–42; and *Paradoxe et Mystère de l'Eglise* (Paris, 1967).

49. This is the title of the first chapter of his well-known work, *Méditation sur l'Eglise*, which has been reprinted twice since the first edition in 1953. K. Kasper had already referred to the renewal of "the sacramental view of the Church," in "Catholicisme," in Klinger and Wittstadt (eds.), *Glaube im Prozess*, 224; and likewise G. Philips, *L'Eglise et son Mystère au IIe Concile du Vatican*, 1 (Paris, 1967), 74.

50. Cf. AS, III/V, 519ff. See also here Fesquet, *Diario*, 621.

51. In this connection, later on, H. de Lubac, *Athéisme et sens de l'homme. Une double requête de "Gaudium et Spes,"* Foi Vivante 67 (Paris, 1968).

52. Cf. AS, III/III, 808ff.: question in writing from Mgr. M.A. Builes with the reproach of the danger of dogmatic and theological relativism.

53. Cf. AS, III/VI, 792: comment by Patriarch P.P.Méouchi on the bases of Christian mission.

54. This historical investigation covers the first part of *Surnaturel*

(1946), the essential part of which had already been composed and published in 1931.

55. This more systematic presentation is based on the fourth part of *Surnaturel* (1946) and on the concluding remarks, which had been what had given rise to the criticisms and difficulties suffered by de Lubac since 1950.

56. Henri de Lubac considers this text to be the most important and decisive pronouncement of the whole Council. Evidence of de Lubac's influence can be found in the introduction to the text by J. Ratzinger, in *Das II. Vatikanische Konzil*, 2, LThK Supplementary Volumes (Freiburg im Breisgau, 1967), 501, and in the commentary, *ibid.*, 562 (B. Rigaux, on the relationship of the Old Testament to the New), and 572 (the spiritual meaning of the Scriptures), as well as in his work *L'Ecriture dans la Tradition* (Paris, 1966).

57. Lyons, 1966.

58. "Commentaire du Préambule et du Chapitre I de la Constitution dogmatique *Dei Verbum*," in *La Révélation divine*, Unam Sanctam 70 (Paris, 1968), 159–302.

59. Cf. in the first place "Constitution *Dei Verbum*," in *Essor et permanence de la Révélation*, Le Point 14 (Paris, 1970), 263–320; and then *Dieu se dit dans l'histoire. La Révélation divine*, Foi Vivante 159 (Paris, 1974; and lastly *La Révélation divine* (*Traditions chrétiennes*) (Paris, 1984), which gives the full text once again with all the notes and certain additions.

60. Cf. *AS*, IV/V, 729, for a formulation in Chapter VI, "De S. Scriptura in vita Ecclesiae," no. 21, referring to *Exégèse médiévale*, 1, 523.

61. From 1944 to 1984, this book was published in seven reprints and a paperback in France.

62. Concerning the subcommission in question, cf. G.F. Svideroschi, *Storia del Concilcio* (Milan, 1967), 601; Fosquet, *Diario*, 1050; and *Das II. Vatikanische Konzil*, 3, LThK Supplementary Volumes (Freiburg im Breisgau, 1968), 338.

63. De Lubac had studied him early on with G. Fessard. He was familiar with his work *Histoire et Dogme* (1904), which is now published as *Les Premiers Ecrits de Maurice Blondel* (Paris, 1956). The following are certain of his own works in the field of this problem: "Le problème du développment du dogme," *RSR*, 35 (1948), 130–160; "A propos de l'allégorie chrétienne," *RSR*, 47 (1959), 5–43; "Saint Grégoire et la Grammaire," *RSR*, 48 (1960), 185–226; "Les humanistes chrétiens du XVe–XVIe siècle et l'herméneutique traditionelle," in E. Castelli (ed.), *Ermeneutica e Tradizione* (Rome, 1963), 173–177; "P. Rousselot, Petite théorie du développement du dogme," in *Mémorial P. Rousselot (1878–1915)*, *RSR*, 53 (1965), 355–390.

64. Cf. *Das II. Vatikanische Konzil*, 1, LThK Supplementary Volumes (Freiburg im Breisgau, 1966), 51.

65. This corresponds to the titles of the third and fourth sections in Chapter IV of *Méditation sur l'Eglise* (1953).

66. Cf. *Insegnamenti di Paolo VI*, 3 (Vatican City, 1965), 1036.

67. *L'Eglise et son Mystère au IIe Concile du Vatican*, 1 (Paris, 1967), 74.

68. Cf. *ibid.*, the first chapter, with this title.

69. Paris, 1967.

70. Paris, 1938, 1941, 1947, 1952, 1965, 1984.

71. Paris, 1944, 1949.

72. Cf. G. Barauna (ed.), *L'Eglise de Vatican II* (Paris, 1966).

73. Cf. *Das II. Vatikanische Konzil*, 2, 422, 454, 483, 485.

74. Above all, he had here already formulated the idea that the redemptive grace of Jesus Christ was also effective for those living outside the official Church; he gave Irenaeus as his authority here. Cf. Chapter 7, on "The Church, the Sole Means of Salvation."

75. Because of his course on the history of religion and his personal acquaintance with J. Monchanin, Henri de Lubac began to take an interest in Buddhism at an early date. However, publications on this subject first appeared during his enforced rest period, starting in 1950. Thus: *Affrontements mystiques* (Paris, 1950); *Aspects du bouddhisme I* (Paris, 1951); *La rencontre du bouddhisme et de l'occident* (Paris, 1952); *Amida—Aspects du bouddhisme II* (Paris, 1955).

76. Cf. *Das II. Vatikanische Konzil*, 3, 40.

77. *Die Konzilskonstitution über die Göttliche Offenbarung* (Paderborn, 1966), 195, note 50.

78. Cf. *Das II. Vatikanische Konzil*, 2, 501, 562.

79. Cf. *ibid.*, 572.

80. *Diario*, 55.

81. *Letters from Vatican City* (London, 1963), 132.

82. Three vols. (Paris, 1963–1964): 1, *Exégèse et Patristique*; 2, *Du Moyen Age au Siècle des Lumières*; 3, *Perspectives d'aujourd'hui*.

83. *Ibid.*, 1, 7.

84. *Ibid.*, 3, 223–248; G. Fessard, "La vision religieuse et cosmique de Teilhard de Chardin," 331–346; R. d'Ouince, "L'épreuve de l'obéissance dans la vie du Père Teilhard de Chardin"; and M. Villan, "Un grand livre oecuménique: *Catholicism*," 319–329.

85. *The Second Session* (London, 1963–1964), 75.

86. *Christus*, 11/41 (1964), 97–192; the contribution is dated 9 December 1963. Contrary to the first impression given by the title, this is a consideration based on the experience of the Council concerning its task. Henri de Lubac can hardly be said to have expressed himself so directly about the Council elsewhere.

87. "Que penser de la deuxième session?" *Informations Catholiques Internationales*, 210 (1964), 24.

88. Cf. *Das II. Vatikanische Konzil*, 3, 338; Svideroschi, *Storia del Concilio*, 601; Fesquet, *Diario*, 1050.

89. Cf. *Le Drame de l'Humanisme athée* (Paris, 1944), cf. note 61, but also "L'idée chrétienne de l'homme et la recherche d'un homme nouveau," *Etudes*, 255 (1947), 3–25, 145–169.

90. Cf. *Das II. Vatikanische Konzil*, 3, 273.

91. Cf. *ibid.*, 402.

92. Cf. *ibid.*, 419.

93. Cf. Laurentin, *Bilan du Concile*, 391; Fesquet, *Diario*, 949, 974ff.; *La Croix*, 85 (13 October 1965), 4.

94. Cf. Fesquet, *Diario*, 1130.

95. Title of Chapter 10 of *Catholicisme* (1938); however, the ideas are already to be found in "Le caractère social du Dogme chrétien," *Chronique Sociale de France*, 45 (1936), 167–192, 259–283.

96. Cf. *Catholicisme*, Chapter 7.

CHAPTER 3

A Few Words on Triumphalism

Gilles Pelland, S.J.

Summary

A great deal has been said about "triumphalism" both during and since the Council—obviously with a view to condemning it! The subject of triumph or victory is often found in early Christian writings, but in a very specific sense, and this sense could not be lost to view (as in fact happened) without giving way to rhetoric. The Church will never know any other true triumph than that of the resurrection. However, the demands of this triumph should be enough to discourage any sort of complacency. On the other hand, the carping type of attitude that sees triumphalism in everything the Church does could very well be a sign of an impoverished understanding of its mystery.

On 1 December 1962, in an intervention that caused a considerable stir, Bishop de Smedt of Bruges pointed out three dangers of which the Council Fathers should beware: clericalism, legalism, and triumphalism. This triptych has enjoyed a great success, and has been repeated ad nauseam for more than twenty years to describe a style of theology or government: (1) viewing the Church as if it were the property of the clergy, and reducing the participation of lay people to a strict minimum on every level of its activity; (2) dealing with practical problems as if they could always be pigeonholed or fitted into ready-made frameworks or solutions; (3) celebrating the greatness of the Church with fanfares of trumpets blaring, as if it simply moved from one triumph to another, and as if, whatever the circumstances, the words and actions of its representatives could never be greeted with anything other than admiration. Of course, nobody would have wanted to confess to such a caricature attitude, and references were therefore confined to talk of "tendencies" or "risks." However, these threats were far from being imaginary. We know the debates that took place during the Council, and what the results were: since the Council, the Church has taken on a new style in its self-expression and acting.

It must be admitted that events themselves pushed it toward this change. Since the sixties, the appearance of most Christian communities has changed, due to the crisis in family life with all the moral and social consequences entailed, the vast increase in the remarriage of divorced people, the rise in the numbers of lapsed or alienated Catholics, the massive departures from seminaries and scholasticates, the very large number of reductions to the lay state, the rise in the average age of the clergy, and so on. In the context of the cultural revolution we have experienced, these phenomena reflect a new world view and a new approach to basic questions. In all these areas, people have tried hard to discern to what extent received ideas can be seen as relative to the fact that they are the expression of certain cultural attitudes and factors. The faith has not been immune to such examination or "suspicion." For this very reason, a large number of believers today may feel that the language of Christianity has become more and more foreign to them. Whereas in a relatively recent past, detachment from the Church tended to take the form of opposition or simple desertion, today it tends much more to take the form of "calm lack of interest."[1]

An unfortunate experience has led many people to this type of detachment. Having tried to adapt and to identify with the person in the street in his or her concerns and language, we have now started to doubt the wisdom of such an attitude:

We would seem to be simply repeating what everybody says: using religious names for the most mundane merchandise; speaking of "mystery," "revelation," "magisterium," and "tradition," in order to proclaim various truths regarding freedom, dialogue, or progress—truths which are already widespread and are often in fact hackneyed. In other words, we are simply acting as echoes (albeit in somewhat archaic language), and actually have nothing new to say. In this perspective, we would not be speaking in a vacuum, but emptily: the vacuum would not be merely before us, but within us.[2]

The vague malaise or uneasiness from which Christians in general have been suffering has affected the pastors themselves, often in proportion to how close they were to those it was their task to guide. In this connection, it is worth rereading the very clear analysis published by Father Congar in 1967 in the journal *Esprit*.[3] Priests who had been trained with a very hierarchical view of the ministry were repeatedly being told that they must change their outlook and pay more attention to the service of the Word, but at the very same time the Christian assembly was melting away like snow in the sun. The moment they had been "renewed" and "recycled," they found their position was one of harsh solitude, inasmuch as they were faced with a scattered flock who expected nothing from them or found nothing "meaningful" in what they had to say.[4] We may wonder how many departures can basically be laid at the door of this factor.

Such a situation could hardly be said to encourage us to put out the flags and sing hymns of victory! After May 1968, and in the early seventies, we tended to encounter more the very reverse of triumphalism, in the form of bitter criticism tinged with sadness. In the preconciliar period, the Church may have fallen victim to triumphalism, but after the Council, it became uneasy and troubled, if not downright uncertain.

The Faithfulness of God

It is of course true that the Church's oldest sources spoke to it of victories or triumphs, but this was in a very specific sense, which could not be lost to view without running the risk of foundering in rhetoric.

Even in the most difficult times, Israel is certain of the Lord:

> Yahweh God is my shepherd;
>   what can I lack if Yahweh protects me? . . .
> Thou preparest a table before me
>   in the presence of my enemies; . . .
>   and my cup overflows.
>
> Ps. 23:1–5

Whatever may happen, God's fidelity to the Covenant will have the final word. Despite the apostasy of a great number, a remnant will be saved: those who have been left in Israel or Judah after the fall of Samaria or the invasion of Sennacherib (Am. 5:15; Is. 37:31–32), the exiles in Babylon after the destruction of Jerusalem (Jer. 24:8), the community that returned to Palestine after the exile (Zech. 8:6, 11, 12; Ezra 9:8, 13–15). This remnant will grow and come to form a holy people, who will be heir to the promises:

> In that day the root of Jesse shall stand as an ensign to the peoples; him shall the nations seek, and his dwellings shall be glorious.
>
> Is. 11:10

> Arise, shine; for your light has come,
>   and the glory of the Lord has risen upon you. . . .
> And the nations shall come to your light,
>   and kings to the brightness of your rising.
>
> Is. 60:1–3

The worker of the final triumph assumes the features of the royal Messiah (see Ps. 2:1–9; 110:5), the Son of Man (Dan. 7), or the suffering Servant (Is. 52:13ff.; 53:11ff.). The wise already enjoy the fruits of his victory:

> Blessed is the man
>   who walks not in the counsel of the wicked,
> nor stands in the way of sinners,
>   nor sits in the seat of scoffers. . . .
> He is like a tree
>   planted by streams of water,
> that yields its fruit in its season,
>   and its leaf does not wither. . . .
> In all that he does, he prospers.
>
> Ps. 1:1–3

This theme runs through the whole of the New Testament like a thread. During Christ's public life, his miracles show that he is the victor over evil and death. Before entering into his Passion, he warns his followers not to fear the hatred that will follow them: ". . . be of good cheer, I have overcome the world" (Jn. 16:33). Even in his Passion, there are many elements that manifest his glory.[5] And his resurrection definitively shows that extent of his mystery. Conquering sin and death (1 Cor. 15:24ff.), he draws the vanquished powers behind his victor's chariot (Col. 2:15). The victory of the immolated lamb who is the Master of the world and of history (Rev. 5:12) is extended to those whom he has made his body. The martyrs who have been crushed by the Beast (Rev. 11:7; 13:7) have already conquered it in him and through him; the apostles follow him in his victory (2 Cor. 2:14); similarly, those who have been baptized, and have thus been born of God, have conquered the world (1 Jn. 5:4), and from now on nothing will be able to separate them from the love of Christ (Rom. 8:35ff.). They will receive the victor's prize, the imperishable crown of life (Jas. 1:12; Rev. 2:10) and of glory (1 Pet. 5:4). The ecclesial body lives because it is the body of the risen Christ, full of the presence and gifts of the Spirit, and can thus overcome all obstacles. The Book of Acts describes how the Church is brought to the center of the world through the very power of God. However, what is true of the Church as a whole is also in a sense true of each member insofar as he or she is in Christ: ". . . and your life is hid with Christ in God. When Christ who is our life appears, then you also will appear with him in glory" (Col. 3:4). "I will all the more gladly boast of my weaknesses, that the power of Christ may rest upon me . . . for when I am weak, then I am strong" (2 Cor. 12:9–10), strong with a strength that comes wholly from God. "But we have this treasure in earthen vessels, to show that the transcendent power belongs to God and not to us" (2 Cor. 4:7).

The early Church took up this theology and developed it, despite persecution: "Sanguis martyrum, semen christianorum."[6] Nor was the scorn of the ruling classes an obstacle. Pliny the Younger, who did not yet know the Christians of Bythiny at all well, viewed their beliefs simply as an *amentia,* a *superstitio prava et immodica,* and said they were riddled with *obstinantio* and *pertinacia.* Tacitus had much the same opinion, and said that those known as *chrestianos* were members of a sect of people *per flagitia invisos,* and that their belief was an *exitiabilis superstitio* that united criminals deserving of the harshest type of punishment. Similarly, Suetonius described them as *genus hominum superstitionis novae et maleficae.* St. Paul's experience in Athens was repeated again and again, and what the Christians preached was considered ridiculous. This was the world to which the apologists persisted in bringing the gospel. In this context, the Letter to Diognetus sounds like a sort of provocation. Who are the Christians?

> They love all men, but are persecuted by all. . . . They are put to death, but it is life that they receive. They are poor, and enrich many; destitute of everything, they abound in everything. They are dishonored, and in their dishonor find their glory. . . . What the soul is in the body, that the Christians are in the world. . . . The soul is locked up in the body, yet is the very thing that holds the body together; so, too, Christians are shut up in the world as in a prison, yet it is precisely they that hold the world together.[7]

The author of the letter is clearly borrowing from the traditions of Platonism and Stoicism, but his main source of inspiration is the Sermon on the Mount,[8] which he transposes into hellenistic categories. Christians are the salt of the earth and the light of the world. In a sense, they sustain the world, acting as the principle through which it holds together. Without them, the avenging arm of God would wipe it out. Hence, in Vatican I's adaptation of the words of Isaiah 11:12 and 49:22,[9] the Church is like "a standard raised up in the midst of the nations." This is a classic theme, and Cardinal de Lubac listed a certain number of its fundamental expressions:

> It is this "mountain," visible from afar to the eyes of all, this shining "city," this light placed on a stand to give light to the whole house (St. Gregory of Nazianzus). It is this building of cedar and incorruptible cypress (Origen), the majestic solidity of which defies the passage of time, . . . this shining vault in which the saints, like so many stars, sing the Redeemer's glory (Alan of Lille). . . . Thus, through a thousand converging paths it leads us to Christ. . . . To those who live its mystery, it always appears—as it did to the seer of Patmos—as the city of precious stones, the heavenly Jerusalem, the Bride of the Lamb. . . . "When I speak of her, I can never say enough" (Augustine).[10]

And how could it be otherwise, when the Church has its whole life and being from Christ himself? Since before the beginning of time, the Father, who knew his chosen ones by name (Is. 43:1), has called them to be *one* in his Son, entrusting them to him in advance; generation after generation the Son comes to them, takes them with him in his Exodus, and brings them back to the Father.[11] What we are witnessing is the time of the ripening of this mystery. In the hiddenness of God's ways, the Son is gradually making ready for his final victory over evil and death—for the day when he will restore the Kingdom to his Father and when "God will be all in all" (2 Cor. 15:24–28). In reality, nothing is of any significance except to the extent that it is in relation to the divine *economy*. The Pastor of Hermas uses the image of the "ancient lady" to illustrate this fact:

> "Who do you think that the ancient lady was from whom you received the little book? . . . The Church." "Why then is she old?" I said to him. "Because," he said, "she was created the first of all things. . . . For her sake was the world established."[12]

Thus, the Church can already be seen as triumphant, because it is the very Spirit of the Lord who binds it together into one single body and gives it the very strength of God in the concrete circumstances of our human history. In a few magnificent lines, Rupert of Deutz gives the essential elements of this theology, which comes straight from St. Paul and has been taken up in so many different ways by tradition:

> All the members of the body, all those who have been received into the faith of this mystery and the fullness of this love, are joined to the one and only Son of God and Son of Man, as their head. Thus, it is a single body, a single person, a single Christ, made up of the head and the members, which is raised up to heaven. And in its gratitude it cries out, showing God the Church in its glory: "Here is the bone of my bones and the flesh of my flesh!" . . . The flesh of Christ, which prior to his Passion was the flesh of the Word of God alone, has grown and spread so much through his Passion, and has filled the universe to such an extent, that he has united into one single Church all the chosen ones who have been since the beginning of the world or who will be until the end, and in this Church God and man are bound in an eternal embrace;

he has done this through the action of this sacrament, which has formed the Church into a new dough.[13]

It is interesting to consider these themes in the perspective of the theological method of the Fathers, and especially their exegesis, inasmuch as all early theology was done within the framework of the relationship between the two Testaments. "Baptism, Eucharist, Church, etc. were only considered for the first time— at least when it came to reflecting on them—in function of Melchezedech, the official Passover, the passage through the Red Sea, manna, the assembly in the desert, the Jerusalem Temple."[14] If we confine ourselves strictly to the mystery of the Church, we often find images such as these: "She [the Church] is Paradise in the midst of which Christ, the tree of life, is planted, whence spring the four rivers of the Gospel. She is Noah's ark; . . . the holy place whereon Jacob or Moses trod. . . ."[15]

Clearly this theology has not always been equally successful. There was a danger that the use of Old Testament images to translate the mysteries of the New Testament would in the long run come to be exploited as a fixed formula, and this is in fact what happened. Father Congar has noted the consequences this had for the concrete life of the Church in the Middle Ages.[16] Old Testament institutions and legal dispositions were appealed to not only in support of respect for the established order, but also in support of the rules of morality imposed on the clergy or the use of force to suppress disagreement. Bishops and Councils looked to the Old Testament for examples not only to establish the organized ritual character of the Christian priesthood, but also its correct tithe or proper sexual conduct. The observance of Sunday is easily compared to that of the Sabbath, for example. And it was also easy to impose the sacred character of public power as a revealed fact. In a famous text from the end of the fifth century, Pope Gelasius still spoke of two powers: "Twofold are the powers by which the world is governed: the sacred authority of the [Roman] Pontiff, and the power of the monarch."[17] If imperial power is subordinated to priestly power, this is only so in the order of *res divinae*. The State is clearly seen as independent of the Church. However, after Charlemagne there was a tendency to see the two powers as two functions of the Church, which was viewed as a single organism.[18] In the fourth and fifth centuries, the Fathers still saw the Church as within the Empire,

but in the Middle Ages, the State came to be viewed as within
the Church:

> Just as in heaven Jesus Christ is the sovereign priest who
> presides over all the earthly celebrations of the Church, in the
> same way, from heaven, he rules over and governs this
> Church, which under his eternal rule holds councils and pro-
> mulgates laws through the combined authority of his pontiffs
> and princes. [19]

As Father Congar also notes, the density of eschatology already
fulfilled within time ended up by being absorbed by the Church
and turned to the purposes of immediate performance of its temporal activities. [20] And we know the extreme consequences this
has sometimes had; indeed, history has often been written by
these. Similarly, the terminology of glory and triumph has
tended to be applied somewhat indiscriminately to the men and
institutions of the Church, who have too often or too easily been
happy to have the benefit of this without sharing in the reservations of St. Augustine: "One must not say that the Church is
glorious because kings serve it, which is a very dangerous and
great temptation." [21] These misunderstandings or ambiguities persisted long after the Middle Ages, into times when the Church
had lost all temporal power. Even after it had lost its temporal
influence, it sometimes retained at least the illusion that this was
not so by an abundant use of rhetoric. However, we should not
be overly severe in our judgment on its behavior in this regard.
As Montalembert very rightly says, "To be able to judge the past,
one would have to have lived it; and in order to condemn it, one
would have to be sure of owing it nothing!"

The Glory of the Risen One

Although the Church needs to be brought to see that
triumphalism represents a threat to it, it equally needs to recognize the vast importance of Christ's victory.

The resurrection of the Lord is more than a personal victory
over death. What was accomplished on that first Easter morning
will be communicated to each member of the chosen. [22] This is
how the *firstborn from the dead* will form the kingdom, so that it is
finally enabled to become what Love—in the measureless mea-

sure of God—wanted it to be. But this is also how his function as *firstborn of all creation* will be seen in all its significance and light (Col. 1:15–20) because this is what everything was ordered to "from before the foundation of the world." Early theology often explained the relationship between the two mysteries on the basis of the Genesis narrative. Man was created in the image and likeness of God—as Irenaeus and Tertullian explained as early as the second century, in the image and likeness of the incarnate Word.[23] Through a long growth process, man was destined to share in the glorious condition of the Lord. If he has been "blessed in Christ with every spiritual blessing in the heavenly places" (Eph. 1:3–4), this means that Christ must one day "change our lowly body to be like his glorious body, by the power which enables him even to subject all things to himself" (Phil. 3:21). In the beautiful words of Maximus the Confessor, "he who has been initiated into the hidden power of the resurrection, knows the destiny in view of which God brought about the beginning of everything."[24] Left to his own devices, man could expect nothing but aging and death, but he is rescued from his radical destitution by and in Christ, not only at the end but already now. Any other triumph is so ephemeral and ambiguous as to appear laughable.

However, it is a triumph that should also discourage any complacency. Christ's resurrection can only invest our existence if we are plunged into the mystery of his death (Rom. 6:4) and our lives are hidden with Christ in God (Col. 3:3). This is not just some beautiful formula. Our participation in Christ's death takes place throughout our life, before finding its fulfillment in our definitive passage from this world to the Father. As Karl Rahner writes, baptism is the sacramentally manifested beginning of this mystery.[25] Similarly, if what we work in the Eucharist is the sacramental celebration of the death of Christ, and if what we receive in this mystery is the grace that became ours in his death, this sacrament must also bring about Christ's death in us, bringing it into our lives, drawing us into it, and making us subject to its unfathomable laws.[26] Do we have the courage to repeat as often as the Council calls us to do, that no Christian existence can avoid this element, and that the new law entails formidable demands? In this connection, it is striking to see the reaction of Jesus' disciples when he spoke about the indissolubility of marriage: "If such is the case of a man with his wife, it is not expedient to marry" (Mt. 19:10). It was as if they saw some unattainable ideal in his words. We can easily have the same reaction when we read St. Paul: "Husbands, love your wives, as Christ loved the church" (Eph. 5:25). The same applies to what Jesus had to say about riches: " 'How hard it is for those who have riches to enter the kingdom of God! For it is easier for a camel to go through the eye of a needle than for a rich man to enter the kingdom of God.' Those who heard it said, 'Then who can be saved?' " (Lk. 18:24–26). This is only possible with God, who has chosen to give the full measure of his strength in our weakness (2 Cor. 12:9). What is true here of the individual is all the truer of the Church as a whole: its victories and triumphs, if such there be, can only be in the Spirit, who works within it to conform it in every way to the Passover of the Lord's resurrection.

"The Lord Has Done Great Things in Me"

A passage from Exodus tells us how Moses comes down from the mountain, having spent forty days in the presence of God. His face reflects the glory of what he has seen so strongly that nobody can approach him or look directly at him, and he has to wear a veil in order to speak to the children of Israel (Ex. 34:29–35). St. Paul comments on this episode as follows: "Now if the dispensation of death, carved in letters on stone, came with such splendor, . . . will not the dispensation of the Spirit be attended with greater splendor?" (2 Cor. 3:7–8). As in a mirror the Church today reflects "the knowledge of the glory of God in the face of Christ" (2 Cor. 4:6),[27] and this is particularly so in the life of charity of the saints, because the Spirit mysteriously conforms the Church to its Lord, including the mystery of his death. Hence its confidence and strength, and hence also its *parrèsia,* which is just as great today as in the days of the first disciples (Acts 2:29; 4:13, 29; Eph. 3:12; Phil. 1:20; 1 Tim. 3:13; etc.).

It is hardly surprising that the Church feels the need to say this—as the Eastern Church (which is so wonderfully sensitive to the epiphany of glory, and to the mystery of the beauty of God as this is revealed precisely in the act of pouring himself out[28]) does in a perception that is inextricably bound up with a sort of rapture and seeks to express itself in praise.[29] In more restrained style, the Latin liturgy offers us the same theology in the *Vexilla Regis* sung in Holy Week.[30] However, we could cite a good many other texts that celebrate the multiple manifestations of God in Jesus Christ. He shows himself in so many signs that it may seem difficult not to reduce the *mysterium velatum* to the *mysterii velamen!*[31] We still need eyes in order to see the burning bush as permeated by the divine light. We have to enter into the midst of the cloud on Tabor, and dare to live "in the shadow of the Spirit," in faith. Only then can we see "the joyous light of the holy glory in which God reveals himself as Trinity, at the same time as he reveals the twofold, divine and human, beauty of the incarnate Word."[32]

> Jesus without wealth or any outward show of knowledge has his own order of holiness. . . . With what great pomp and marvelously magnificent array he came in the eyes of the heart, which perceive wisdom! It would have been pointless for Archimedes to play the prince in his mathematical books, prince though he was. It would have been pointless for our Lord Jesus Christ to come as a king with splendor in his reign of holiness, but he truly came in splendor in his own order. . . . If we consider his greatness in his life, his passion, his obscurity, his death, in the way he chose his disciples, in their desertion, in his secret resurrection and all the rest, we shall see that it is so great. . . .[33]

The Church does not only see this, but it also knows that its prayer is answered because the Son makes it his own: "Father, I desire that they also, whom thou hast given me, may be with me where I am." This prayer is taken up every day at the anaphora. And we can already see it expressed in the beautiful words of the *Didache*: "As this broken bread was scattered over the hills and then, when gathered, became one mass, so may thy Church be gathered from the ends of the earth into thy kingdom."[34] The Church will never have any other triumph, but what else could it need once it has found the one thing necessary? As always, we must be able to say this to the contemporary world. This means returning to the essence.

> This world will not expect psychological or sociological or biological contributions from us Christians: it produces

enough of its own. What then is the specifically Christian task? . . . Truths derived from the center.[35]

What can the specific contribution of the Christian world be in the face of the burning problems of the life of society, with a view to gaining mastery over the forces that cause the upheavals of history? It is simply a question of knowing if it can help in some way in solving a problem that no science or politics can avoid, although they may not even be able to pinpoint it—the problem that springs from the fact that whatever is in man's power depends on the power who alone can give him certainty, and that disregard or neglect of this power is the source of all uncertainty.[36]

At the time of the Council, people quite rightly criticized the pompous style of some of the Church's ministers or feasts, and the irritating and excessively smug tones in which "the glories" of the Church tended to be celebrated. We cannot now be sure that since the Council we have not often fallen prey to the opposite excess. Although it is true that the Church must remain modest, as history and experience have taught,[37] it must also be able to repeat the words of the *Magnificat* daily, and in burning, heartfelt tones: ". . . he who is mighty has done great things in me." But how can it say this without often expressing it in terms of celebration? And how can it sing its joy without doing so in beauty—in particular on the liturgical level—even, and indeed especially, when speaking to the poor? It would not be serving them well if it tried to tell them as little as possible about the vast horizon of Christian hope. A certain type of carping attitude that sees triumphalism in everything the Church does could very well in practice be an indication of an impoverished understanding of its mystery, in the very full sense given to this word in the letters of St. Paul. One thing is certain: neither the texts nor the spirit of Vatican II provide even the slightest support for such an attitude.

Translated from the French by Leslie Wearne.

Notes

1. F. Roustang, "Le troisième homme," *Christus*, 13 (1966), 567.

2. M. de Certeau, "La parole du croyant dans le language de l'homme," *Esprit*, 35 (1967), 463–464.

3. *Esprit*, 35 (1967), 556–557.

4. *Ibid.*

5. See especially D. Mollat, "Nous avons vu sa gloire," *Christus*, 3 (1956), 310–327.

6. Tertullian, *Apol.* 50, 13.

7. Letter to Diognetus, 5, 11–6, 7, in J.A. Kleist (trans.), *Ancient Christian Writers*, 6 (New York, 1985), 139–140.

8. See the analysis of H.I. Marrou, in *S.Chr.*, 65, 119–176, together with what can be drawn from the caustic criticism of R. Joly, *Christianisme et philosophie. Etudes sur Justin et les Apologistes grecs du IIe siècle* (Brussels, 1973), 210–220.

9. *Const. de fide cath.*, 3, in DS, 3014.

10. H. de Lubac, *Méditations sur l'Eglise*, Coll. Théologie 27 (Paris, 1954), 36–37.

11. Y. Congar, "Ecclesia ab Abel," in *Abhandlungen über Theologie und Kirche, Festschrift für Karl Adam* (Dusseldorf, 1952), 80: "La pensée chrétienne a toujours reconnu que l'Eglise, bien qu'elle s'affirme dans le temps, n'est pas une réalité du temps. Avouons qu'il n'était pas nécessaire que le milieu fût saturé d'inspiration platonicienne ou 'essentialiste' pour que ces idées s'y formulassent dans des termes de réalité céleste ou même de prêexistence éternelle. . . . Sous une catégorie ou sous une autre, l'Eglise ancienne s'est comprise elle'même comme une réalité supra-temporalle et dont les origines, antérieures au fait historique de l'Incarnation, coincidaient avec celles du monde ou tout au moins de l'humanité." Y. Congar, *L'Ecclésiologie du Haut Moyen Age* (Paris, 1968), 107: "[Dans la catéchèse ancienne] l'Eglise terrestre est une descente dans le temps et dans le monde corporel d'une réalité préexistante mais d'abord cachée et qui se dévoile en elle."

12. Pastor of Hermas, *Vis.*, 2, 4, 1, in K. Lake, *The Apostolic Fathers*, 2 (London, 1976), 25. Cf. *ibid.*, 1, 1, 6.

13. Rupert of Deutz, *De div. off.*, 2, 11, in *PL*, 170, 43, cited in H. de Lubac, *Corpus mysticum. L'Eucharistie et l'Eglise au Moyen Age*, Coll. Théologie 3 (Paris, 1944), 300.

14. H. de Lubac, *L'Écriture dans la Tradition* (Paris, 1966), 21.

15. H. de Lubac, *Catholicism. A Study of Dogma in relation to the Corporate Destiny of Mankind* (London, 1950), 92.

16. Y. Congar, "Deux facteurs de la sacralisation de la vie sociale au Moyen Age," *Concilium*, 47 (1969), 53–63. Cf. also Congar, *L'Ecclésiologie du Haut Moyen Age*; E. Rieber, *Die Bedeutung alttestamentlicher Vorstellungen für das Herrsherbild d. Gr. und seins Hofkreises* (Freiburg, 1949).

17. Cf. Congar, *L'Ecclésiologie du Haut Moyen Age*, 254.

18. *Ibid.*, 257–258.

19. *Ibid.*, 261.

20. *Ibid.*, 127.

21. *De perf. just.*, 15, 35, in *PL*, 44, 310.

22. Cf. this beautiful text of Origen, *Commentary on John*, X, 35 (20), in *The Ante-Nicene Fathers*, 10 (Grand Rapids, MI, 1978), 400–401: ". . . the resurrection of the Savior from the passion of the cross contains the mystery of the resurrection of the whole body of Christ. But as that material body of Jesus was sacrificed for Christ, and was buried, and was afterwards raised, so the whole body of Christ's saints is crucified along with him, and now lives no longer; for each of them, like Paul, glories in nothing but the cross of our Lord Jesus Christ, through which he is crucified to the world and the world to him. Not only, therefore, is he crucified with Christ, and crucified to the world. . . . And then he says, as if enjoying some earnest of the resurrection, 'We rose with him.' "

23. Tertullian, *De res. carnis*, 6, 3–5: "Quodcumque enim limus exprimebatur, Christus cogitabatur homo futurus. . . . Ad imaginem Dei fecit [hominem], scilicet Christi. . . . Ita limus ille jam tunc imaginem induens Christi futuri in carne, non tantum Dei opus erat sed et pignus." Cf. *Adv. Marc.*, 5, 8, 1, and *Adv. Prax.*, 12, 3–4. As regards Irenaeus, cf. A. Orbe, *Antropologia de San Ireneo* (Madrid, 1969), 96–107; "El hombre ideal en la teologia de San Ireneo," *Gregorianum*, 43 (1962), 449–491; "Supergrediens angelos," *Gregorianum*, 54 (1973), 5–59. We would also cite Prudentius, *Apotheosis*, 302–311, 1039–1041:

Nimirum meminit scriptor doctissimus illo
Orbis principio non solum nec sine Christo
Informasse Patrem facturae plasma novellae. . . .
Christus forma Patris, nos Christi forma et imago
Condimur in faciem Domini bonitate paterna
Venturo in nostram faciem post saecula Christo. . . .
Decrerat quoniam Christum Deus incorrupto
Admiscere solo, sanctis quod fingere vellet
Dignum habuit digitis et carum condere pignus.

See L. Padovese, *La cristologia di Aurelio Clemente Prudenzio* (Rome, 1980), 224.

24. Maximus the Confessor, *Cap. theol. et oec. Cent.*, 1, 66, in *PG*, 90, 1107.

25. Karl Rahner, *Theological Investigations*, 3, 165–168.

26. *Ibid.*, 167. Compare with the vigorous formula of St. Leo, *De Passione Domini*, XII, in *SC*, 74, 84: "Non enim aliud agit participatio corporis et sanguinis Christi ut in id quod sumimus transeamus et in quo commortui et consepulti sumus, ipsum per omnia et spiritu et carne gestemus. . . ."

27. Cf. *Lumen gentium* 1: "Christ is the light of humanity; and it is, accordingly, the heart-felt desire of this sacred Council, being gathered together in the Holy Spirit, that, by proclaiming his Gospel to every creature (cf. Mk. 16:15), it may bring to all men that light of Christ which shines out visibly from the Church."

28. See, for example, O. Clément, "La beauté comme Révélation," *Vie spirituelle*, 637 (1980), 251–270; H. Urs von Balthasar, "Religion et esthétique," *ScEccl*, 12 (1960), 299–305.

29. Myrrha Lot-Borodine, *La déification de l'homme* (Paris, 1970), 59–61: "Dans la théologie grecque, plus particulièrement dans la tradition alexandrine qui domine toujours chez nos contemplatifs, l'élément humain est à tel point pénétré, saturé—non résorbé—par ledivin qu'il paraît déjà comme nimbé de gloire. . . . Avec quelle munificence l'Église grecque célèbre l'Epiphanie dans le Baptême de Jésus par le Précurseur, et sa Transfiguration en la lumière surnaturelle du Thabor! Quelle poésie liturgique, hymnes d'une joie sans pareille, déverse-t-elle à flots sur la nuit claire comme 'le jour sans déclin,' la nuit de Pâques. . . . L'Orient chrétien se prosterne, lui aussi, devant la victime sans tache, il baise non le bois du supplice, mais, sur l'epitaphios, le Corps sacré veillé par les Séraphins, le linceul de Celui qui a 'aimé jusqu'à la mort.' L'Orient n'égrène pas toutes les stations du chemin de la croix qu'il embrasse d'un seul regard: dans le sommeil même de la mort, il sent l'incorruptible vie divine et ne s'attarde pas à la pleurer humainement. A travers les ombres tragiques de Gethsémani et du Calvaire, il épie l'approche du radieux miracle dans le sépulcre scellé. Du Golgotha où tout est consommé, il tourne ses regards vers le jardin d'Arimathie, jardin de la Résurrection, prototype elle-même de la Transfiguration finale, qui découvre à ses yeux fascinés la Jérusalem céleste. . . . Du haut de sa croix, le Christ-Roi ne laisse tomber aucune plainte et ne paraît contempler, au loin, que la moisson de la vie éternelle qui lève, en confiant sa Mère et fille, l'Ecclesia, au disciple bien-aimé. . . ." *Ibid.*, 63–64: "L'Orient byzantin a suivi, lui aussi, son Kyrios, plié sous le faix de la Croix, par la voie étroite du renoncement total, mais en cherchant toujours du regard, jusque dans l'abîme de l'abaissement, de la kénose, les éclatants vestiges divins. Jamais l'idée de la *Basileia* ne le quitte. En même temps, pareil à l'âme platonicienne tombée, il se souvient éternellement de sa propre origine surnaturelle, cierge solitaire brûlant devant le Seigneur des Béatitudes. . . . La soif du cerf altéré, courant à la fontaine, la soif de la Contemplation qui déjà ne paraît plus de ce monde, l'apatheia ou 'sainte indifférence' préparant l'âme à l'union déifiante. . . ."

30. Vexilla Regis prodeunt
Pulget crucis mysterium. . . .
Arbor decora et sanguine
ornata regis purpura. . . .
Beata cujus brachiis

> Saecli pependit pretium.
> Salve, ara . . . de
> Passionis gloria. . . .

See P. Jounel, "Le culte de la croix dans la liturgie romaine," *Maison-Dieu*, 75 (1963), 68–91. Jounel notes (p. 90) that the temptation to triumphalism has not spared the East: "La croix du Christ n'est pas un talisman qu'il suffirait de graver au fronton des édifices publics pour assurer la pérennité d'une civilisation: 'Réjouissez dans votre puissance nos rois croyants en leur accordant la victoire contre leurs ennemis; qu'ils jouissent de votre alliance, arme et paix, trophée invincible,' chante la liturgie byzantine. Et pourtant Constantinople est tombé. . . ."

31. St. Bernard, *In Cant. s.*, 73, 2, in *PL*, 183, 1134D.

32. J. Rousse, 'La beauté sauvera le monde," *Vie spirituelle*, 604 (1974), 705–706.

33. Pascal, *Pensées*, 308 (Harmondsworth, England, 1966), 124.

34. *The Didache*, 9, in J. Quasten (ed.), *Ancient Christian Writers* (New York, 1948), 20.

35. H. Urs von Balthasar, *Love Alone: The Way of Revelation* (London, 1968), 125.

36. G. Abeling, *Wort und Glaube*, II, 183, cited by R. Marle, *Parler de Dieu aujourd'hui. La théologie herméneutique de Gerhard Ebeling* (Paris, 1975), 145.

37. *Gaudium et spes* 43.

PART II

THE WORD
OF
GOD

CHAPTER 4

Revelation Past and Present

Gerald O'Collins, S.J.

Summary

Dei Verbum, other documents of Vatican II and some post-conciliar documents of the magisterium speak of the divine self-revelation as both a past reality (which reached its complete fullness with Christ) and a present reality. Present revelation actualizes the living event of the divine self-revelation without adding to its content. The definitive revelation of God communicated through Christ and his apostles can be appropriately called "foundational" revelation. The present revelation that we receive now can be called "dependent" revelation, inasmuch as it depends on the foundational figures of Christ and his apostles.

The Second Vatican Council's Constitution on Divine Revelation (*Dei Verbum*) speaks of the divine self-disclosure in both the past and the present tense. On the one hand, Jesus

> completed and perfected Revelation and confirmed it with divine guarantees. He did this by the total fact of his presence and self-manifestation—by words and works, signs and miracles, but above all by his death and glorious resurrection from the dead, and finally by sending the Spirit of truth (No. 4).[1]

On the other hand, *Dei Verbum* also portrays revelation as a present event that invites human faith: " 'The obedience of faith' (Rom. 16:26; cf. Rom. 1:5; 2 Cor. 10:5–6) must be given to God

as he reveals himself" (No. 5). The Constitution associates revelation as it happened then and as it happens now (in the
Church) in these terms: "God, who spoke in the past, continues
to converse with the spouse of his beloved Son" (No. 8).

Other documents of the Council likewise use both the past
and the present tense in talking of the divine self-revelation. In
preaching the gospel, bishops draw "from the storehouse of revelation" (*Lumen gentium*, No. 25)—that is to say, from the "deposit
of faith" or the definitive revelation of God given once and for all
through Christ and entrusted to the Church to be proclaimed
and preserved with fidelity. The Pastoral Constitution on the
Church in the Modern World (*Gaudium et spes*) notes the cultural pedagogy in God's revelation that reached (past tense) its
complete climax with Christ: "In his self-revelation to his people
culminating in the fullness of manifestation in his incarnate Son,
God spoke according to the culture proper to each age" (No. 58).

At the same time, those other documents from the Second
Vatican Council also recognize the divine revelation to be a
present reality. Apropos of the various liturgical presences of
Christ, the Constitution on the Sacred Liturgy acknowledges
that "it is he himself who speaks when the holy scriptures are
read in the Church" (*Sacrosanctum Concilium*, No. 7). In the
context of the community's worship, "Christ is still proclaiming
his Gospel" (*ibid.*, No. 33). The Decree on the Church's Missionary Activity (*Ad gentes*) properly highlights the actual nature of
revelation: "In manifesting Christ, the Church reveals to men
their true situation and calling" (No. 8). In the mystery of
Christ, "the charity of God is revealed" (No. 12). Finally,
Gaudium et spes describes the Church as "the universal sacrament
of salvation" that is both "manifesting and actualizing the mystery of God's love for man" (No. 45).

The same approach to revelation as being both a past and a
present reality turns up in the teaching of John Paul II. In his
1979 Apostolic Exhortation on Catechesis in Our Time
(*Catechesi tradendae*), the Pope wrote of

> the revelation that God has given of himself to humanity in
> Christ Jesus, a revelation stored in the depths of the Church's
> memory and in Sacred Scripture, and constantly communi-
> cated from one generation to the next by a living active *traditio*
> (No. 22).

A "simple revelation of a good and provident Father" is something, however, that happens now when "the very young child receives the first elements of catechesis from its parents and the family surroundings" (No. 36). In a telling passage about catechesis for the young, Pope John Paul II presents divine revelation as something that has happened and that should continue to happen:

> In our pastoral concern we ask ourselves: How are we to reveal Jesus Christ, God made man, to this multitude of children and young people, reveal him not just in the fascination of a first fleeting encounter but through an acquaintance, growing deeper and clearer daily, with him, his message, the plan of God that he has revealed, the call he addresses to each person, and the Kingdom that he wishes to establish in this world . . .? (No. 35)

In 1980, the Pope published *Dives in misericordia,* an Encyclical that took as its theme "the revelation of the mystery of the Father and his love" (No. 1). Here again this divine revelation was portrayed as something completed in the past: "It is 'God who is rich in mercy' whom Jesus Christ has revealed to us as Father: it is his very Son who, in himself, has manifested him and made him known to us" (No. 1). Yet the same Encyclical repeatedly proclaims the present nature of this revelation: "The Cross . . . speaks and never ceases to speak of God the Father" (No. 7); "the genuine face of mercy has to be ever revealed anew" (No. 6). John Paul II names the reason for the Church's ongoing existence as being "to reveal God, that Father who allows us to 'see' him in Christ" (No. 15). Through Mary the love of God "continues to be revealed in the history of the Church and of humanity" (No. 9). The Pope himself prays that "the Love which is in the Father may once again be revealed at this stage in history" (No. 15).

To sum up this sketch of recent Church teaching, both the documents of the Second Vatican Council and in important postconciliar statements, revelation is understood to have been a complete, definitive, and unrepeatable self-communication of God through Jesus Christ. Almost in the same breath, however, this official Church teaching also calls revelation a present reality that is repeatedly actualized here and now. How can we relate these two sets of affirmations that at first sight could seem to be mutually exclusive? If revelation was definitively completed in the past, how can it happen today? If revelation is a present event, how can we speak of it as having reached its final and perfect culmination two thousand years ago?

Some False Moves

It could be tempting here to allege that present revelation is not revelation in the proper sense but only a growth in the collective understanding of the biblical revelation completed and closed once and for all with Christ and his apostles. Undoubtedly, such a growth in true understanding can and does take place. *Dei Verbum* takes up this theme:

> The Tradition that comes from the apostles makes progress in the Church, with the help of the Holy Spirit. There is a growth in insight into the realities and words that are being passed on. . . . Thus, as the centuries go by, the Church is always advancing towards the plenitude of divine truth (No. 8).[2]

Nevertheless, we would not do justice to tradition if we credited it only with the development in understanding of a closed and past revelation, but denied that it brings about an actual revelation of God. *Dei Verbum* offers no such low version of Tradition. It sees in the following terms the results of Tradition as guided by the Holy Spirit:

> By means of the same Tradition . . . the holy Scriptures themselves are more thoroughly understood and constantly actualized. Thus God, who spoke in the past, continues to converse with the spouse of his beloved Son. And the Holy Spirit, through whom the living voice of the Gospel rings out in the Church—and through her in the world—leads believers to the full truth, and makes the Word of God dwell in them in all its richness (*ibid.*).

Here the Council expresses its conviction that through the force of Tradition, the divine self-revelation recorded by the Scriptures is not only "more thoroughly understood" but also "actualized" as a living revelation of God to Christ's Church and through her to the world.

To deny present revelation is to doubt the active power here and now of the Holy Spirit as guiding the Tradition and mediating the presence of the risen Christ. In effect, this also means reducing faith to the acceptance of some revealed truths coming from the past rather than taking faith in its integral sense—as the full obedience given to God revealed here and now through the living voice of the gospel. In brief, to deny the present revelation of God is also to sell short its human correlative, faith.

Of course, if one persists in thinking that revelation entails *primarily* the communication of revealed truths, it becomes easier to relegate revelation to the past. As soon as the whole set of revealed doctrines is complete, revelation ends or is "closed." For this way of thinking, later believers cannot immediately and directly experience revelation. All they can do is remember, interpret, and apply truths revealed long ago to the apostolic Church.

Dei Verbum and the other conciliar and postconciliar documents do, of course, describe revelation as something that reached its full and definitive climax in the past—through "the total fact" of Christ's "presence and self-manifestation" (*Dei Verbum*, No. 4). There was content to this personal revelation, so that *Dei Verbum* could refer to "the things he [God] had once revealed for the salvation of all peoples" (No. 7), "the divinely revealed realities" (No. 11) and the "deposit of faith" entrusted to the Church at the beginning and to be maintained faithfully through the Tradition (No. 10). Nevertheless, these official Church documents do not hesitate to portray the divine self-revelation as something happening now through the liturgy (*Sacrosanctum Concilium*, Nos. 7, 33), the prayerful reading of the scriptures (*Dei Verbum*, No. 25), missionary activity (*Ad gentes*, No. 8), the signs of the times (*Gaudium et spes*, Nos. 4, 11), the Christian education of very young children (*Catechesi tradendae*, No. 36), the lives of saintly persons (*Lumen gentium*, No. 50) and so forth.

One could sum up this magisterial teaching on revelation as follows. Present revelation *actualizes* the living event of the divine self-manifestation, but it *does not add* to the "content" of what was completely and fully revealed through Christ's life, death, resurrection, and sending of the Holy Spirit. Revelation continues to be an actual encounter, but this living dialogue adds nothing to "the divinely revealed realities" (which essentially amount to Jesus Christ crucified and risen from the dead).

A Choice of Terminology

The double "time-sign" of revelation leaves open the invitation to find an appropriate terminology for naming (1) revelation inasmuch as it reached an unsurpassable climax with Christ, and (2) revelation inasmuch as it remains a living, interpersonal event. In one sense, revelation is past; in another sense, it is always present. How can we best describe (1) the history of revelation that found once and for all its perfect fulfillment with Christ and (2) the history of revelation that continues and will continue to the end of time?

1. The National Catechetical Directory for Catholics of the United States, *Sharing the Light of Faith* (Washington, DC, 1979) used "revelation" and "manifestation" or "communication" to contrast what happened *then* with Christ and what happens *now* in the Church and the world (No. 50). An earlier draft of the Directory had tried out another terminology: "Revelation" (uppercase) then and "revelation" (lowercase) now. After noting (No. 42) the various "signs" of God's self-communication (for instance, biblical and liturgical signs), the final text contrasted the "revelation" that was concluded and completed nearly two thousand years ago with the self-manifestation of God that continues today (Nos. 54–55). It insisted that this manifestation is a genuine, actual communication and not merely "the memory of something that happened long ago" (No. 53).

This terminology of "revelation" then and "manifestation" now does not, however, serve too well for distinguishing the past and the present. In many contexts, "revelation" (whether in uppercase or lowercase), "manifestation," and "communication" prove synonymous or practically synonymous. The same goes for the verbs "reveal," "manifest," and "communicate." In particular, the Second Vatican Council often enough uses these terms more or less interchangeably. For instance, *Ad gentes* describes missionary activity as follows: "In manifesting [*manifestando*] Christ, the Church reveals [*revelat*] to men their true situation and calling" (No. 8). The verbs could be switched without altering the meaning: "In revealing [*revelando*] Christ, the Church manifests [*manifestat*] to men their true situation and calling." In translating *Lumen gentium*, the Flannery version in one place uses "is revealed" rather than "is manifested" or "is disclosed" to render *manifestatur*: ". . . the kingdom is revealed in the person of Christ himself" (No. 5).

Appealing to the Pauline notion of "the new man," *Ad gentes* observes that all Christians "have an obligation to manifest [*manifestare*] the new man which they put on in baptism" (No. 11). A little later, the same document presents "the mystery of Christ" in which "the new man created in the likeness of God has appeared . . . and in which the charity of God is revealed [*revelatur*]" (No. 12). With these two passages about the witness of Christian life, we would hardly tamper with the sense if we made the first talk of the "obligation to reveal [*revelare*] the new man" and the second speak of "the mystery of Christ" in which "the charity of God is manifested [*manifestatur*]." Another example. Apropos of the gospel and various human cultures, *Gaudium et spes* recalls the history of Old Testament revelation: "In his self-revelation [*sese revelans*] to his people culminating in the fullness of manifestation [*manifestationem*] in his incarnate Son, God spoke according to the culture proper to each age" (No. 58). No real alteration of meaning would occur if, instead of the given text, we read: "In his self-manifestation or self-disclosure [*sese manifestans*] to his people culminating in the fullness of revelation [*revelationem*] in his incarnate Son," etc. A final example, which involves "communicate." Toward the end of Chapter One, *Dei Verbum* sums up what has been stated about revelation: "By divine Revelation [*divina revelatione*] God wished to manifest [*manifestare*] and communicate [*communicare*] both himself and the eternal decrees of his will concerning the salvation of mankind" (No. 6). Here "revelation," "self-manifestation," and "self-communication" largely coincide. In this context, all three terms refer to what happened through the past history of God's people, which climaxed with the events involving Jesus Christ. This passage would not support the linguistic decision to reserve "revelation" for the past and apply "self-manifestation" and "self-communication" to God's present activity.

To sum up, *Sharing the Light of Faith* wishes to contrast the "revelation" that happened back there and then with the divine "self-manifestation" and "self-communication" that continues now. The distinction does not seem very serviceable. In ordinary usage, the three expressions seem to be largely synonymous. The documents of the Second Vatican Council often apply the terms interchangeably.

2. In his *Revelation and Its Interpretation* (London, 1983), Aylward Shorter proposes to alter my terminology of "foundational" and "dependent" revelation (of which more shortly) by speaking of "foundational" and "participant" revelation (pp. 139–143). Shorter prefers "participant revelation" because of "the participatory character of all reality." In particular,

> our experience of Jesus Christ in the events and relationships of our own life really participates in the foundational revelation bestowed on the apostles and living on effectively in the tradition (p. 141).

The "participatory character of all reality" raises a problem, however, for Shorter's choice of terms. The apostles themselves participated in the final stage of Israel's history and in the events that climactically embodied God's self-revelation—the life, death, and resurrection of Christ and the sending of the Holy Spirit. Hence, one could properly talk of the participant revelation bestowed on the apostles. In these terms, we participate in a participation. One might then contrast the "Participant" (uppercase) revelation communicated at the time of Christ with the "participant" (lowercase) revelation available now.

Ultimately, however, it is a question of explaining more fully the terminology I first suggested in the aftermath of the Council: "foundational" and "dependent" revelation.[3] As regards God's self-communication, where the apostles participated in a foundational way, later Christians participate in a dependent way—that is to say, in dependence upon those apostolic witnesses.

3. According to Ephesians, "the household of God" is "built upon the foundation of the apostles and prophets, Christ Jesus himself being the corner-stone" (2:19–20). Revelation's account of the new Jerusalem includes a similar image to describe the foundational role of the apostles: "The wall of the city had twelve foundations, and on them the twelve names of the twelve apostles of the Lamb" (21:14).

This foundational role of the apostles and the apostolic generation included the following functions. (1) The kerygmatic formulas recorded in Paul's letters (e.g., 1 Cor. 15:3–5), the Acts of the Apostles (2:22–24, 32f., 36; 3:13–15; 4:10–12; 5:30–32) and elsewhere in the New Testament (e.g., Lk. 24:34) reflect a primary function of Peter and the other apostles. Their basic message ("the crucified Jesus has been raised from the dead and of that we are witnesses") gathered the first Christians. Those who had not seen and yet believed (Jn. 20:29) depended upon the testimony of the Easter witnesses for their faith in and experience of Jesus crucified and risen from the dead.[4] (2) Believers entered the community through being baptized "into" Jesus' death and resurrection (Rom. 6:3–11). Together, they celebrated eucharistically the death of the risen Lord in the hope of his final coming (1 Cor. 11:26). Thus, the post-Easter apostolic proclamation initiated the essential liturgical life of the Christian Church. (3) The apostolic leaders made the normative decision not to impose on gentile converts the observance of the Mosaic law (Acts 15:1–30; Gal.; Rom.). The resurrection of the crucified Jesus brought the new covenant that both confirmed God's promises to the chosen people (Rom. 9:4; 11:29; 2 Cor. 1:20) and liberated believers from the obligation of circumcision and other burdens of the law (Gal. 5:1). (4) The apostles and "others of the apostolic age" left in writing "the fourfold gospel" and the other New Testament writings (*Dei Verbum*, Nos. 18–20). Together these inspired books "stand as a perpetual and divine witness" to the definitive revelation of God in Christ and the origins of the Church (*ibid.*, No. 17).

In short, the apostles and others in the apostolic age shaped once and for all the essential sacramental (2) and moral (3) life of the Church. Through the New Testament books (4), they left for all subsequent ages of believers a divinely inspired record of the definitive revelation and its reception in the first decades of Christianity. Right from the birth of Christianity, through their Easter kerygma (1) the apostles witnessed to the absolute climax of God's self-revelation, which they had experienced in the crucified and risen Christ.

I sum up these apostolic functions by speaking of those who witnessed to that "foundational" revelation that took place normatively through a specific series of events and the experiences of a specific set of people. God's saving word came through the history of Israel, the prophets, and then—in a definitive fashion—through Jesus of Nazareth and the experiences in which he and his first followers were immediately involved. Christians experience now God's self-communication reaching them through preaching, sacraments, the scriptures, and other things that recall and reenact those past experiences and events. Thus, the mediation of revelation (and grace) by means of the sacramental life, the Scriptures, the preached word, and other means essentially depends upon our acceptance of authoritative testimony about certain past acts of God on our behalf. In that sense, revelation as we experience it and accept it now is "dependent" revelation. The apostolic witness to foundational revelation remains determinative for the postapostolic history of the Church.

We saw how documents of the magisterium speak of the divine self-revelation in the past and the present tense. We may appropriately add that revelation in the past tense is "foundational" and revelation in the present tense is "dependent." The history of revelation goes on and will go on till the end of time, as God continues to speak and invite people to the life of faith. In equivalent terms, *Dei Verbum* talks of "the Christian economy" that "will never pass away" while we wait for "the glorious manifestation of our Lord, Jesus Christ" (No. 4). But all this postapostolic history of revelation takes place in dependence on that irrevocably valid revelation that reached its unsurpassable climax with Jesus Christ and his apostles.

The End of Foundational Revelation

To complete this reflection on past (foundational) revelation and ongoing (dependent) revelation, it is worth asking: When did foundational revelation end and the period of dependent revelation begin?

Without using my terminology, one traditional response (a) has in effect stated that foundational revelation ended with the apostolic age—that is to say, around the close of the first century. Thus, the antimodernist decree of 3 July 1907, *Lamentabili*, condemned the proposition that "revelation, which constitutes the object of Catholic faith, was not completed with the apostles" (DS, 3421). Obviously, this document understood divine revelation primarily in terms of its content, the various truths or mysteries disclosed by God. Theological manuals often expressed

Lamentabili's view by declaring that revelation closed at the death of the last apostle.[5]

Karl Rahner and others have suggested that (foundational) revelation ended much earlier—with the resurrection of the crucified Christ, his appearances to the official witnesses, and the coming of the Holy Spirit. Rahner wrote:

> While textbook theology usually says that revelation was closed with the death of the last apostle, it would be better and more exact to say that revelation closed with the achievement of the death of Jesus, crucified and risen.[6]

This second view (b) highlights the revealing events themselves without paying much attention to the way the apostolic witnesses fully assimilated and expressed those events. It underplays the fact that, as a reciprocal affair, revelation is not properly there before being adequately accepted and lived out by the recipients.

Provided that it is adjusted to allow that revelation consists primarily in a personal encounter and then secondarily means some revealed "content," view (a) seems preferable. It can allow for the full reception of revelation by respecting the fact that the apostles' experience of Christ included also the phase of discernment, interpretation, and expression of that experience. Peter, Paul, and the other founding fathers and mothers of the Church spent a lifetime expressing and proclaiming their experience of the crucified and risen Jesus. Collectively and personally, they gave themselves to interpreting and applying the meaning, truth, and value of their total experience of Jesus. That experience lodged itself profoundly in their memories to live on powerfully and productively till the end of their lives. They could not interpret once and for all what they had directly known of Jesus' ministry, death, and resurrection, so as to be finished with their experience of those events.

Understood that way, the period of foundational revelation covered not merely the climactic events (the life, death, and resurrection of Jesus and the gift of the Spirit), but also the decades when the apostles and their associates assimilated those events, fully founded the Church for all peoples, and wrote the inspired books of the New Testament. During those years, the apostles were not receiving new truths as if Christ had failed to complete revelation by all that he did, said, and suffered. Rather, they were being led by the Holy Spirit to interpret normatively and apply what they had directly experienced of the fullness of revelation in the person of Christ. In these terms, the activity of the Spirit through the apostolic age also entered into foundational revelation—in its phase of immediate assimilation. Thus, that age belonged to the revealing and redemptive Christ event, and did so in a way that would not be true of any later stage of Christian history.

When the apostolic age closed—roughly speaking at the end of the first century—there would be no more founding of the Church and writing of inspired scriptures. The period of foundational revelation, in which the activity of the original witnesses brought about the visible Church and completed the written word of God, was finished. Through that community and its scriptures, later generations could share independently in the saving self-communication of God mediated through unrepeatable events surrounding Jesus and his apostles. As the prologue of *Dei Verbum* indicates by citing 1 John 1:2–3, till the end of time all later generations will be invited to accept the witness of those who could announce what they had personally experienced of the full divine revelation in Christ: "We proclaim to you the eternal life which was with the Father and was made manifest to us."

Notes

1. I follow the translation of A. Flannery (ed.), *Vatican Council II. The Conciliar and Postconciliar Documents* (Tenbury Wells, 1975).

2. Apropos of this growth in understanding, *Gaudium et Spes* talks rather of a task: the Church (aided by the Holy Spirit) should reflect on and "in the light of the divine Word" interpret "the many voices of our times," so that "the revealed truth may be more deeply penetrated, better understood and more suitably presented" (No. 44).

3. See G. O'Collins, *Theology and Revelation* (Cork, 1968), pp. 45–47, 49f., and *Fundamental Theology* (New York and London, 1981), 101–102. P. Tillich speaks of "original and dependent Revelation" (rather than "foundational and dependent revelation") and uses that language with the nuances of his own system (*Systematic Theology* 1 [London: SCM Press ed., 1978], 126–128). In *Der apostolische Abschluss*

der Offenbarung Gottes (Freiburg im Breisgau, 1979), pp. 144 and 146f., J. Schumacher contrasts revelation "in actu primo" (the revelation that reached its complete fullness with Christ and his apostles) and revelation "in actu secundo" (revelation as it happens in the postapostolic Church).

4. On this dependence from the apostolic witnesses, see K. Rahner, *Foundations of Christian Faith* (New York, 1978), pp. 274–276.

5. See J. Schumacher, *Der apostolische Abschluss*, 121–136.

6. "The Death of Jesus and the Closure of Revelation," *Theological Investigations* 18, 132–142, at 140–141. In *Der apostolische Abschluss*, Schumacher reports a number of others who propose similar views and then marshals the arguments of those who hold that the apostolic age also belonged to what Schumacher calls the constitutive period of revelation or "revelatio in actu primo" (pp. 153–169).

CHAPTER 5

The *Sensus Fidei* and
the Development of Dogma

Zoltán Alszeghy, S.J.

Summary

The Second Vatican Council lists three factors in dogmatic development: study, the teaching of the magisterium, and the *sensus
fidei*. If we compare it with the two former and better known
elements, the meaning of the *sensus fidei* becomes clearer. This
article tries to describe the *sensus fidei*, discerning the epistemological paths along which it moves and the criteria in the light of
which it can be verified, and then attempts an explanation of
how it operates.

———
———

In recent decades and under various aspects, the *sensus fidei*
has been the subject of theological reflection, from the context
of the marian dogmas to that of the theology of revelation.[1] As
we know, on a number of occasions, the Second Vatican Council had recourse to this concept and similar notions.[2] Here we
shall be concerned with a text that does not use these words but
that speaks of the same thing, including it among the factors
involved in the development of Catholic dogma. We give the
phrase here in its surrounding context:

> The Tradition that comes from the apostles makes progress in
> the Church, with the help of the Holy Spirit. There is a

growth in insight into the realities and words that are being passed on. This comes about in various ways. It comes through the contemplation and study of believers who ponder these things in their hearts (cf. Lk. 2:19 and 51). It comes from *the intimate sense of spiritual realities which they experience.* And it comes from the preaching of those who have received, along with their right of succession in the episcopate, the sure charism of truth. Thus, as the centuries go by, the Church is always advancing towards the plenitude of divine truth, until eventually the words of God are fulfilled in her. [3]

We would note immediately that the variety in translation of the phrase in question demonstrates the difficulty in interpretation. The translation given above is from the A. Flannery edition of the documents of Vatican II, whereas the W.M. Abbott edition reads: ". . . through the intimate understanding of spiritual things they experience. . . . " The original phrase, "ex intima spiritualium rerum quam experiuntur intelligentia," is not speaking of an experience that comes from the intelligence (which is the sense indicated, for instance, in the official Italian translation), but of an experiential knowledge based on what has been lived. The phrase has been examined a number of times. [4] However, we return to examination of the text because, among other things, wide use has been made of it in regard to the relationship between two factors of progress, theology and magisterium, [5] and it is thus to be hoped that a comparison of what we know of these two factors with the *sensus fidei* will lead to a better understanding of the latter.

Our reflection will be divided into four parts. The first will throw light on the concept of progress in knowledge of the faith, which is the common horizon in which theology, *sensus fidei,* and ecclesiastical magisterium are viewed. The second will try to pinpoint the phenomenology of the *sensus fidei,* as compared with the other factors in development. The object of the third will be the epistemology of the *sensus fidei,* and it will consider how much certainty the believer obtains through it. The fourth will examine the psychology of the *sensus fidei,* reflecting on the way in which the Holy Spirit and the created intellect develop that understanding that represents at least one of the aspects of the evolution of dogma.

The Development of Dogma

The conciliar text speaks of the progress of Tradition, but this is nothing other than the development of dogma. The magisterium teaches:

> . . . only what has been handed down to it. At the divine command and with the help of the Holy Spirit, it listens to this devotedly, guards it with dedication and expounds it faithfully. All that it proposes for belief as being divinely revealed is drawn from this single deposit of faith.[6]

The two expressions, "progress of the deposit of faith" and "dogmatic development," indicate the same thing, but viewed under two different aspects. When we speak of the progress of revelation, we are considering this progress from its starting point; and when we speak of dogmatic development, we are considering it from the viewpoint of its result. It is a single process inasmuch as the whole of revelation, until the end of time, is being recalled and better understood. Thus, the evolution of dogma is not only the history of some isolated formulas. The formulas proclaimed as dogmas are therefore not some definitive point of arrival, because even partial truths proclaimed as dogmas can always be better understood and better formulated, through comparison between the various dogmas, between the dogma in question and empirical truth, and between the dogma and the objective of the whole history of salvation, which is God.

According to the Council, the Church moves "unceasingly" toward the fullness of the divine truth. This means that in the life of the Church, there is a constant attempt—never completely satisfied—to gain a better understanding of the meaning of revelation, although this does not mean that at any given moment in history our understanding of the faith is always necessarily greater than at any other previous moment. Understanding of the faith is influenced by many factors, both natural and supernatural, for example, the intellectual level of the society in which the community of believers lives, the fidelity of the community to the promptings of the Spirit, and the extent to which the community uses the gifts and charisms it has received. There are, therefore, ups and downs in the development of dogma, with moments of greater and lesser splendor; there are even moments when it may be somewhat dimmed, although even at such moments, the Word is never completely extinguished in the community of believers.

The progressive understanding of revelation on the part of believers—that is, the evolution of dogma—is a homogeneous or integrated process. We are not using "homogeneous" in the sense given it by Father Marin-Sola, because we do not believe that all dogma can be drawn, by a process of deductive reasoning, from the explicit faith of the apostolic community.[7] However, the evolution of dogma unfolds "within the perspective of the truth."[8] In positive terms, this means that, even if we do not always see it, God sees that the supernatural life of the apostolic community cannot be authentically continued if the results of dogmatic development are rejected as false, and that the faith life of the apostolic community would not be reasonable if the results of dogmatic development were not true. In other words, God sees that the result of the evolution of dogma corresponds to an objective interior need of the faith life of the apostolic community, and it is thus based on this. The same truth can be expressed negatively by saying that in order to move from revelation to dogma, the influence of the Holy Spirit is needed, recalling the word of God, which has entered once and for all into the consciousness and preaching of the community of believers, and bringing about an improved understanding of that word. However, no new (that is, no constitutive and not simply explanatory) revelation is needed, adding to the word once spoken something that is not objectively contained therein, and nor is any new direct experience of objective supernatural reality needed, through which the human intellect would learn something that until now it has not known in any way. In the work just cited, we indicated two ways in which the faith life of the apostolic community developed toward the explicit recognition of dogma. The first way is that of conceptualization, in which a truth known in a preconceptual manner is thought out in constantly new conceptual systems; the second way is that of objective understanding, in which the community judges that the overall revealed image of the economy of salvation cannot be reconciled with some statement that has emerged later in the history of thinking, or is inseparable from that statement.

This homogeneous process, which continues ceaselessly and is never complete, transmits its specific character to all its parts: to the overall doctrinal development of a given period, to the development of a specific partial doctrine, to the development of the theology of a particular school, and to the intellectual maturation of the faith in each individual believer. The evolution of a dogma is not some exceptional event; it is not expressed only in the solemn declarations of the magisterium, or in the great scientific works of famous thinkers. Rather, it is an aspect of everyday faith-life, in the same way that salvation history takes place both within general history as a whole, within the history of peoples, and within the events of the life of the individual person who moves from sin, through justification, to glory.

What Is the *Sensus Fidei*?

According to the conciliar text, the evolution of Catholic dogma is brought about through three factors. The first, "the contemplation and study of believers," is *theology*, understood as an activity inspired by faith and organized by science, which tries, with all the resources of human reasoning, to understand and explain the mystery of salvation as this emerges from Scripture and is interpreted by the Church.[9] The third factor obviously refers to what has been called the *magisterium* in the last century, in other words, the exercise of the mission given to the apostles and their successors, under the guidance of the Spirit, of faithfully guarding and infallibly declaring the deposit of faith.[10] The second factor clearly refers to the *sensus fidei*, and it is this element that we are trying to understand better. For the moment, we must be satisfied with the description found in another conciliar text, where the *sensus fidei* is described as an "appreciation of the faith, aroused and sustained by the Spirit of truth," through which the people of God "unfailingly adheres to . . . the faith once for all delivered to the saints, . . . penetrates it more deeply with right judgment, and applies it more fully in daily life."[11]

Here we have three functions, which are innate to the people of God. These different functions are not distinguished according to the different persons who exercise them. It is true that one can be a theologian without being a bishop, and that one can have and exercise the teaching office without having studied theology; indeed, the administrative demands of a diocese are so heavy and theological research is so broad and progresses so fast, that it is practically impossible for a bishop personally to follow every development in contemporary theological work, even from afar.[12] In the patristic era, however, the three functions were often found in the same people; thus, there were bishops who were both theologians and mystics, and the coexistence of these functions produced a golden age for the understanding of the faith! It is particularly absurd to imagine that the *sensus fidei* cannot be reconciled with study, or that it is extinguished with episcopal ordination. The Council explicitly states that the *sensus fidei* is extended with its full vigor when "the whole people, . . . from the bishops to the last of the faithful, . . . manifest a universal consent in matters of faith and morals."[13]

Nor are the three functions distinguished on the basis of the *object* that is known in them, as if there were truths accessible only to one or another cognitive function. On the contrary, theology and the *sensus fidei* of the faithful often pave the way for and develop statements of the magisterium. On the other hand, the three functions are not infrequently in conflict, inasmuch as theologians, bishops, and ordinary practicing lay people have different opinions on the same truths.[14] Such agreement and disagreement would not be possible if each of the three functions had its own specific object or objects, different from those of the other two.

The distinction between the three paths becomes clearer if we take into account the *three functions of any human discourse.* When a person speaks, he or she *observes* some aspect of reality, *calls for* suitable behavior on the part of the listener, and *expresses* some aspect of his or her interior being. The specific nature of the discourse depends on the predominance of one function and on the subordination of the other two.

In *scientific* discourse, the observational function predominates, almost absorbing the other two. If we say that "every living being has the capacity to reconstruct its own structures," the main meaning is that living creatures do in fact have such a capacity; the phrase is true if they really do have it. The call to the listener to accept the truth of the statement is barely perceptible, and the same applies to the manifestation of the views of the speaker.

In the *fulfilling* language of exhortation—laws and administrative acts—pride of place is given to the call for a specific attitude on the part of the listener, or the creative effectiveness that brings about a new juridical situation. In such phrases as "Entry forbidden," "The meeting is closed," or the military command "Attention!" observation has a role only in function of the creative call, which does not primarily describe reality, but brings about a new state of things.

Lastly, in *poetical* discourse, the decisive element is communication of one's own interiority. The phrase, "calmness reigns over all the peaks, and a faint breath passes over the tops of the trees," is just as valid during a hurricane, because the intention is simply to manifest and communicate the sweet melancholy of the evening, with no claim to be providing a meteorological bulletin or casting some sort of spell to produce good weather.

The observational sense predominates in *theological* language. The positive theologian states that certain sources have a specific meaning (for example, "Col. 1:15–20 reveals the cosmic role of Christ"), whereas the systematic theologian says something about the revealed reality itself ("Christ is the center and apex of the universe").

In *magisterial* discourse, the head of the community effectively proclaims the mystery. The model for such speech is the summary of the proclamation of Jesus: "The time is fulfilled, and the kingdom of God is at hand; repent, and believe in the gospel" (Mk. 1:15). The center of the statement is the call to conversion. The call changes the circumstances of the listener, "binding" him, so that he cannot live in righteousness if he does not obey it; henceforth, whoever does not believe and is not converted will die in his or her sins (cf. Jn. 8:24). The call to faith and conversion is motivated by an observation: "The kingdom of God is at hand." However, this presence of the kingdom is not a fact existing prior to the call: the kingdom is present to the listeners because Jesus proclaims it and makes it present with his words.

This linguistic form is found in every "magisterial" statement. It is no coincidence that the traditional form of the most binding use of the teaching office is the anathematization of those who do not accept a given statement as true. The very action of the hierarchy is of a creative, fulfilling nature, and anyone who is no longer within the interior union of faith is also cut off from the exterior life of the Church. Of course, this act of "authority" also entails the declaration of the truths that are the object of faith, but this teaching is proposed in function of the creative act, as its basis, its legitimation, or its explanation and application. This can be seen very clearly in the relationship between the canons and certain chapters in the Council of Trent and the First Vatican Council. A similar "operational" concern can be seen in the formula often used by the organs of the magisterium, which prefer to declare whether a doctrine is (or is not) "able to be safely taught." It is, of course, a question of the truth or falsity of certain statements, but this question is considered under the aspect of the function of statements in the perspective of Christian life and salvation. However, the orientation of the declarations of truths toward the fulfillment of values is also found in those statements of the magisterium that are purely explanatory in their linguistic form. This is the basis of truth in the controversial book of P. Thibauld on the restoration of thomism as desired by Leo XIII.[15] The Pope who promulgated *Aeterni Patris* makes theological and also philosophical statements, but does so in the perspective of the establishment of the kingdom of Christ in the world. Despite this, his teaching does not become some irrational ideology that subordinates truth to value (and theory to practice), because the objective for which the proclamation is made—the accomplishment of the kingdom of God through the development of the Church—has an absolute validity, which can also be legitimized in theory, inasmuch as the theoretical presuppositions that are what make it possible cannot but be true. In this sense, we can say that in the case of the recommendation of "the eternal philosophy," the faith postulates a line of behavior, and this behavior implies the acceptance of a certain indpendence in reasoning.

A comparison between the form of expression of theology and the magisterium makes it possible to discern the specific way in which the *sensus fidei* proclaims the truth of Christianity.

The *sensus fidei* does not directly declare truths as such, and does not aim at bringing about some state of affairs by proclaiming certain truths; rather, it expresses an *experience*. Here again, we are not using the word "experience" to indicate the perception of a previously unknown aspect of truth—the type of knowledge acquired, for instance, when one travels and comes to know certain countries, or when one carries out some experiment and discovers a law of nature (*Erfahrung*). Rather, it means something "lived" (*Erlebnis*), through which a personality is enriched and through which certain imprecisions are clarified. The new

state of being can also, of course, entail an awareness, can become the object of reflection, and can, therefore, enrich the
knowledge of new notions; however, this is a secondary aspect of
the experience and does not constitute its essence. Meeting others in friendship, a hard-fought struggle, and suffering are all
"experiences," even leaving aside the fact that after the experience, the person has a better understanding of what meeting,
struggling, or suffering means.

The specific experience with which we are concerned here is
the "Christian experience," which takes place in those who accept the word of God that rings in their ears, and accept the
grace that knocks at the door of their hearts. Such specifically
Christian events are the "theological" life of faith, hope, and
charity, with the ensuing virtues, gifts, and attitudes through
which we accept the word of God with the joy of the Spirit in
much affliction (cf. 1 Thess. 1:6).

As a lived event, this experience is not in itself a *doctrine.*
Fides qua is not *fides quae.* Even so, the experience is not independent of the doctrinal content that is accepted as true in it.

There is above all a psychological relationship between the
two. The experience is supported by certain convictions, even
though these may not always have been reflectively thought out
in advance but are only implicitly and preconsciously accepted.
Nobody can have trust in God if he or she does not believe that
God is powerful and good. However, there is also another relationship. The experience is valid and reasonable only if certain
assumptions are true. The whole Christian experience would be
vain—a baseless deception—if a personal God did not exist. The
"eternal religion" that certain thinkers have tried to construct on
the basis of an "atheistic theology" does not correspond to the
Christian experience, and its authors themselves view it as a
"post-Christian" religiosity.[16] The relationship between experience and doctrinal conviction is not, however, confined to such
extreme cases, but also encompasses the whole gamut of the two
terms. A theology highlights certain truths and leaves others in
shadow, develops certain notions analytically and treats others
superficially, structuring its assertions on the basis of one specific
viewpoint. A specific emphasis of this type inspires a corresponding spirituality. However, it can also be said that a specific supernatural experience, as developed in a corresponding spirituality,
directs the attention toward certain concepts, emphasizes certain

truths, and pays greater attention to certain structurizing principles, thus giving rise to a theology. In other words, if a theology
is thought out and lived in depth, it creates a spirituality; and if a
spirituality is also developed in subjective intellectual life, it
orientates us toward a particular school of theology.

And this is the point at which our reflection on the *sensus fidei*
comes in.

The believer is grafted into Christ like shoots into the vine,
and thus shares in Christ's thoughts (*nous*, 1 Cor. 2:16) and
sentiments (*ennoia*, 1 Pet. 4:1), and all this entails a structure of
beliefs, opinions, affective attractions, and behavioral tendencies that he or she considers valid because it is testified to by the
Spirit as a requirement and way of following Christ. When the
believer meets outside elements or doctrines, he or she measures
them against this interior picture, and "judges" them (1 Cor.
2:15) with a spontaneous, intuitive, and analytical judgment,
brought about and accompanied by strong affective elements, as
a necessity for the life of faith, or as reconcilable with faith or
irreconcilable with it.

In my opinion, the *sensus fidei* is precisely this *capacity to
recognize the intimate experience of adherence to Christ and to judge
everything on the basis of this knowledge.* In this conception, we
find all the elements of the conciliar phrase. Intimate participation in the life of Christ constitutes the "spiritual realities." The
believer "experiences" a "sense" of the mystery in which he
shares. This sense is "intimate"; it is not some reasoning, maybe
carried out with the help of external elements, but is a basic
intuition, a view of lived reality. On the basis of this understanding or intuition, the believer judges the possible interpretations
of the mystery, and also the conformity or lack of conformity
between, on the one hand, the lived and understood mystery,
and, on the other, the realities and respective theories coming
from outside.

The three functions of Christian discourse on the mysteries do
not indicate three fully distinct types of religious discourse
because—at least to a small degree—all three are always present.
When a Catholic thinks and speaks about his or her faith, this is
done on the basis of the proclamation through which Christ, his
apostles, and their successors announce the mystery of salvation.
Whenever we have a religious discussion, there is also a certain
theological echo, inasmuch as we are aware of the meaning our

words have within the community in which we are speaking, and we have a certain legitimation for what we are saying. In every case, we are guided by the *sensus fidei* at least insofar as it proposes hypothetical models for our verification, just as the scientist always bears in mind natural common sense. The three functions of language do, however, correspond to and provide a distinction between three *types* of discourse, according to the predominance of one or another emphasis. The same person's speech is different according to whether he is speaking as bishop, writing as theologian, or, before God, founding, regulating, explaining, judging, and communicating his own inner life and that of the community in which he participates.

Epistemological Models

H. Hammans' excellent book[17] introduced some rather unfortunate terminology when it placed "theological" explanations of the development of dogma in opposition to "intellectualistic" explanations. Those systems that can rightly be criticized for trying to explain the evolutionary process by the exclusive use of deductive models (Schultes, Tuyaerts, Marin-Sola) are in fact "theological," despite their interest in the epistemological connection between the various stages in this development, inasmuch as they try to use the light of faith to solve questions that spring from the sources of faith.

The *sensus fidei* neither invents new truths nor deduces only new conclusions from explicitly known truths. As we have said before, in our opinion its epistemological operation can be explained by the use of two models.

The first is that of "transconceptualization." If the believer compares certain truths expressed in symbolical and imaginary representations with formulas expressing these truths in conceptual systems to be found in different cultures, he or she "sees," or "intuitively perceives," the correspondence or incompatibility of the old formulas and the new ones. In this way, new christologies come into being within the one unique faith in Jesus Christ the Lord.

The second model is that of "objective comprehension." The believer does not only know analytical assertions, but on the basis of these conceives an objective and synthetic view of the whole order of salvation. When ideas not previously contemplated are compared with this overall picture, he or she again "sees," or intuitively perceives, that this idea can or cannot be integrated into the picture. This is the path taken in the birth of the marian dogmas, and this is the way in which the Church is at present evaluating the Christian validity of technical development, economic and social progress, revolution, and so on, in the perspective of liberation theology.[18]

Although magisterial, theological, and experiential discourse do not each have some sort of exclusive competence in certain areas, each of them does have preferential areas with regard to which it is more at ease.

The *sensus fidei* rarely takes up positions on abstract and marginal theological questions; its voice is stronger with regard to questions that have a more direct connection with the basis of the Christian faith and on which personal behavior depends more directly. Thus, there was a more lively reception in the Church in general for the christological doctrines of the first great Councils and for the teaching of Vatican II on human activity in the world, whereas the declarations of the Council of Trent on the use of the term *transsubstantiatio*[19] and the teaching of Vatican II on the sacramentality of the episcopate[20] only attracted attention in specialized theological circles.

When we have to evaluate the compatibility of a given doctrine with the faith, the *sensus fidei* does not consider this doctrine in its abstract essence (as a theologian can do), but in the actual form in which it enters the common awareness within history. For example, in the last century, the theory of the evolution of the species was judged by the Christian sense of the faithful to be in clear opposition to Christianity. However, people understood evolution as it was explained in popular literature of the period, that is, a theory that rejected creation and denied the essential difference between human beings and lower forms of life. On the other hand, as regards the doctrine of the faith, they assumed that the Genesis account of the creation must be taken in a strictly historical sense. These two concepts were quite rightly seen as incompatible. When the members of the faithful eventually reached a more purely scientific understanding of evolution, free of any philosophical implications and thus compatible with a theistic and spiritualistic view of the world, and when the predominantly sapiential interpretation of the creation narrative moved into the realm of common knowledge, the violently negative reaction was eliminated, and indeed gave way to an openness toward the idea of an evolution that was willed, directed, and brought about by God.

Even so, it should be noted that the dictates of the *sensus fidei* can change even in cases when the terms of the comparison remain basically unchanged. This, of course, also goes for the two other types of theological discourse. Because theology is a science, the principle of fallibility is part of its very essence; in other words, there is a constant openness, so that when results have been obtained, they are reexamined, and can become obsolete or be corrected. The teaching of the magisterium is irreformable and infallible only when the hierarchy commits its authority in a definitive way, that is, in the proclamation of dogmas of the faith. The dictates of the *sensus fidei*, which are more closely connected with the sentiments, are especially prone to revision. However, there are criteria according to which we can reach a practically certain validity even on the basis of the *sensus fidei*.

The first criterion is found in St. Paul's admonition in Romans 12:6: "Having gifts that differ according to the grace given to us, let us use them: if prophecy, in proportion to our faith."[21] The apostle is speaking of the way in which Christians must use the gifts God has granted them, according to the measure of their faith (v. 3). One of these gifts is prophecy, which Paul appreciates greatly, because it is very helpful in building up the community. It does not mean the foretelling of future events, but an unveiling of the secrets of hearts, or of the will of God. Now, if a number of the faithful has a prophecy to make, they must examine it to make sure it is true, because there are also false "prophecies." We can check the truth of a prophecy by comparing it with the rule of faith. The apostle is thinking of formulas that were then emerging from the life of the community, and that were the yardstick for discerning whether words really came from the Spirit. If an apparent prophecy is not in harmony with the objective content of the evangelical proclamation, it must be rejected as not genuine (cf. Gal. 1:8–9). If this criterion is applied to the *sensus fidei*, we can say that if a spontaneous inclination or aversion to some doctrine is not compatible with what has been clearly proclaimed as the word of God, this inclination or aversion does not come from the spirit and is not genuine. It can be added that the more easily an inclination can be integrated into the system of the faith as a whole, the more it can be assumed to be a true sense or understanding of the "spiritual things" that God brings about in his Church.

We find another criterion in the Lord's advice regarding presumed prophets: "You will know them by their fruits" (Mt. 7:16).[22] Not all those who proclaim prophecies are true prophets and authentic members of the faith community. There are some who may seem to be disciples, but who are in fact outsiders—or even enemies of the kingdom. If the person who speaks does the will of God, and if the words of the presumed prophet encourage others to do the will of God, in other words, to observe the law of Christ, then conformity with the rules of Christian behavior becomes a criterion of orthodoxy. The more the dictates of the Christian intuition bear the charismatic fruit of the love of God and neighbor, the more we can assume that we are dealing with a true understanding of the order of salvation.

However, the Second Vatican Council indicates how these two criteria are to be used. "The whole body of the faithful who have an anointing that comes from the holy one (cf. 1 Jn. 2:20 and 27) cannot err in matters of belief." A true *sensus fidei* is fully shown when "*the whole people,* from the bishops to the last of the faithful, . . . manifests a *universal* consent in matters of faith and morals."[23] The *sensus fidei,* therefore, offers an absolute certainty only when the whole Church consents. Consent may be fuller or less full, so that we can say that the more universal the consent, the closer we are to a definitive certainty. The enthusiastic support of one group does not automatically represent a criterion of truth. The community of Carthaginian Montanists around Tertullian or the convinced audience who heard Calvin in Geneva cannot be seen as a reliable criterion for the validity of the doctrine accepted by these groups. The history of Arianism is also a warning that the claim to a consensus does not concern only the number of adherents, but also the length of time of such adherence. Moreover, intuitive judgment does not come like a flash of lightning, but grows and matures with time. Consent becomes a sure criterion of truth when the community of believers perseveres in its spontaneous inclination toward a doctrine, becomes aware of all its aspects, considers the objections raised against it, and examines all its consequences. We can, therefore, say that the *sensus fidei* is sure when, presuming the other two criteria are met, a sufficiently large community of believers perseveres for an extended period in the spontaneous, affectively experienced, conviction that a doctrine is inseparably linked to the experience in which the believer freely and wholly entrusts himself to God, who is the source of salvation.

How the *Sensus Fidei* Works

Over the past twenty-five years, M. Seckler[24] and others have provided considerable help toward reaching an understanding of the supernatural instinct through which a person is drawn to the faith and to the development of the faith with a view to building up the Christian personality of the person. Here we take their contribution as a presupposition for our study, and try to apply it to the psychological explanation of the *sensus fidei*.

The doctrinal context of this understanding is found in the conciliar teaching on the act of faith as:

> . . . the full submission of . . . intellect and will to God who reveals. . . . Before this faith can be exercised, man must have the grace of God to move and assist him; he must have the interior helps of the Holy Spirit, who moves the heart and converts it to God, who opens the eyes of the mind and "makes it easy for all to accept and believe the truth." The same Holy Spirit constantly perfects faith by his gifts, so that revelation may be more and more profoundly understood.[25]

The last phrase explains that the "mechanism" through which faith is formed is the same as that through which faith develops in a progressive understanding, in other words, in dogmatic development, including the operation of the *sensus fidei*.

This whole process represents a psychological fact that the psychologist can describe with his methods—without, of course, being able to approach the transcendental (indeed, supernatural) nucleus of the process.

The inspiration of grace brings about an inclination that is both intellective and affective, and these two aspects are so intermingled that there is no use asking whether a given factor concerns the intellect or the will; it all takes place at a very deep level of human existence, on which there is no point in applying distinctions between the different components of the human psyche.

The inspiration to faith and to the development of the under-standing of the faith can also be described in terms of the relation-ship between the various successive experiences. It is unlikely that a teetotal and unpolished person will understand the dithyrambs of Anacreon; a deeply felt bereavement makes it easier to share in the pain of a person who is mourning the death of a dear one; and the memory of a passionate love enables a person to grasp the meaning of the images used in love poetry. And this law also applies in the supernatural life. The acts that lay the groundwork for justification (faith, fear, hope), psycho-logically predispose the soul to the act with which, accepting God's grace, he or she moves from unrighteousness to righteous-ness, and from enemy to friend of God.[26] The same thing takes place in the progress of faith. Free, intense, and long-lasting participation in the sentiments of Christ (the "spiritual realities" of *DV* 8) enables us to gain a better understanding of the mean-ing of the message of Christ in which we believe, hope, and love.

However, the wealth of the gift of the Spirit is not limited to this objective assistance of previous experiences. A child can have a natural bent for mathematics even before he or she comes across the first notions of this discipline, and this bent only becomes operative when he or she goes to school and finds the solution of mathematical problems enjoyable and easy. In the same way, the Spirit gives each person (though not necessarily in equal measure) an "ease to accept and believe the truth." This "ease" basically lies in the nature of the human person, to whom it is natural to accept grace when it is offered, and who advances in the sensitivity infused by God through exterior and interior graces, according to the measure of the gift of the Spirit and of the faithfulness of cooperation with the graces offered. This doc-trine is simply the practical application of the antisemipelagian teaching of the Second Council of Orange[27] and the first Vatican Council,[28] and hence of the normal doctrine of actual graces.[29]

Concluding Observations

Now, at the conclusion of our observations, it would be a good idea to eliminate a misunderstanding that often creeps into dis-cussions of this subject.

When people speak of the *sensus fidei*, they often refer to "the simple people" who are, even so, guided by its light. With this term they mean that the believer has a capacity for discernment, even if he has neither the knowledge of a theologian nor the charism of a bishop. However, sometimes they also imply that the *sensus fidei* has no connection at all with cultural gifts, since the famous "old woman" of whom St. Bonaventure spoke consoling words is equally endowed with such a capacity to judge.

Now, we must steer clear of the exaggeration that attributes to the "old woman," precisely because of her simplicity, a privileged capacity to "prove what is the will of God, what is good and acceptable and perfect" (Rom. 12:2). Of course, if our old woman lives a purer and more elevated spiritual life, she will participate in the *sensus fidei* to a greater degree. However, if two people are equally open to grace, the one who is less illuminated by the declarations of the magisterium and the teaching of theology, and who is less culturally gifted, will be at a disadvantage with regard to the *sensus fidei*. The "simple old woman" uses her own experience as the yardstick for facts and words as she understands them. The Holy Spirit helps her to reach a good judgment on what she understands, but does not miraculously make up for any lack of precise understanding of the facts and words that are the object of this judgment. The "scandal of the simple" frequently comes from the fact that simple people are not really aware of what is involved. This means that their first reaction to any religious innovations tends to be negative. They experience the relationship between the usual state of things and their Christian experience as positive, and have not yet discovered the validity there can be in impulses to innovation.

Thus, the efforts the Church is making at the present time to foster the religious education of the laity will hone the *sensus fidei*, because, although we are not always able to give them a complete theological training, the "simple ones" will gain an ever-growing understanding of what is to be judged in the light of the Spirit.

Translated from the Italian by Leslie Wearne.

Notes

1. M. Fernández de Troconiz y Sasigain, "Sensus fidei": lógica connatural de la existencia christiana. Un estudio del recurso al "sensus fidei" en la teología católica de 1950 a 1970 (Vitoria, 1976); Foi populaire, foi

savante: Actes du Ve Colloque du Centre d'études d'histoire des religions populaires, tenu à Ottawa (Paris, 1976).

2. *Sensus fidei:* LG 12; PO, 9. *Sensus catholicus:* AA 30. *Sensus christianus fidelium:* GS 52. *Sensus christianus:* GS 62. *Sensus religiosus:* NA 2; DH 4; GS 59. *Sensus Dei:* DV 15; GS 7. *Sensus Christi et Ecclesiae:* AG 19. *Instinctus:* SC 24; PC 12; GS 18.

3. DV 8.

4. J. Ratzinger, *Das zweite Vatikanische Konzil, Dokumente und Kommentare,* 2 (Freiburg, 1967), 518–523. The most penetrating analysis is that of M. Kothgasser, "Dogmenentwicklung und die Funktion des Geist-Parakleten nach den Aussagen des Zweiten Vatikanischen Konzils," *Salesianum,* 31 (1969), 379–460 (on our text, 431–457).

5. Y.M.-J. Congar, "Bref historique des formes du 'magistère' et de ses relations avec les docteurs," *RevScPhilThéol,* 60 (1975), 99–112; Commissio theologica internationalis, "Theses de Magisterii Ecclesiastici et Theologiae ad invicem relatione," *Gregorianum,* 57 (1976), 549–563; A. Descamps, "Théologie et magistère," *EThL,* 52 (1976), 82–133; K. Rahner, "Lehramt und Theologie," *Schriften zur Theologie,* 13 (Einsiedeln, 1978), 69–92; Y.M.-J. Congar et al., "Le témoignage des théologiens et le Magistère," *Les quatre fleuves,* 12 (1980), 7–134; J. Alfaro, "La teologia di fronte al magistero," in R. Latourelle and G. O'Collins (eds.), *Problemi e prospettive di Teologia fondamentale* (Brescia, 1980), 413–432; W. Kern (ed.), *Die theologie und das Lehramt* (Freiburg, 1982); F. Sullivan, *Magisterium, Teaching Authority in the Catholic Church* (Dublin, 1983), 174–218; W.J. Hoye, "Lehramtliche Aussagen und wissenschaftliche Wahrheit in der katholischen Theologie," *ZKT,* 105 (1983), 156–167; R. Franco, "Teología y Magisterio: dos modelos de relación," *EstEcl,* 59 (1984), 3–25.

6. DV 10.

7. With regard to this debate, we would refer to H. Hammans, *Die neueren katholischen Erklärungen der Dogmenentwicklung* (Essen, 1965).

8. With regard to the meaning and verification of this expression, cf. our *Lo sviluppo del dogma cattolico* (Brescia, 1967).

9. Cf. Y.M.-J. Congar, "Le théologien dans l'église aujourd'hui," *Les quatre fleuves,* 12 (1980), 7.

10. Cf. Y.M.-J. Congar, "Pour une histoire sémantique du terme 'magisterium,' " *RevScPhTh,* 60 (1976), 95–97.

11. LG 12.

12. D. Pézeril, "Evêques, théologiens et peuple de Dieu," *Les quatre fleuves,* 12 (1980), 60.

13. LG 12.

14. This conflictual situation has been pointed out by J.-M. Tillard, "Le 'sensus fidelium,' réflexion théologique," in *Foi populaire, foi savante,* 11–12.

15. P. Thibault, *Savoir et pouvoir. Philosophie thomiste et polique cléricale au XIXe siècle* (Quebec, 1972). Similar opinions have been noted also in Hoye, "Lahramtliche Aussagen und wissenschaftliche Wahrheit," 157–158.

16. Cf., for example, F. Ferrarotti, *Una teologia per atei, La religione perenne* (Rome/Bari, 1983).

17. H. Hammans, *Die neueren katholischen Erklärungen der Dogmenentwicklung.*

18. Cf. M. Flick and Z. Alszeghy, *Metologia per una teologia dello sviluppo* (Brescia, 1975²)

19. DS, 1641, 1652, 1866; cf. 2629.

20. LG 21.

21. For the interpretation, cf. H. Schlier, *Der Römerbrief* (Frieburg, 1977), 369–370.

22. On the interpretation of the text, cf. W. Grundmann, *Das Evangelium nach Matthäus* (Berlin, 1971²), 233.

23. LG 12.

24. M. Seckler, *Instinkt und Glaubenswille nach Thomas von Aquin* (Mainz, 1961); T. Horváth, *Caritas est in ratione. Die Lehre des hl. Thomas über die Einheit der intellektiven und affectiven Begnadung des Menschen* (Munster, 1966).

25. DV 5.

26. Council of Trent, sess. VI, cap. 5–7; in DS, 1525–1527.

27. Can. 7; in DS, 377.

28. Constitution *Dei Filius,* 3; in DS, 3010.

29. Cf. M. Flick and Z. Alszeghy, *Il vangelo della grazia* (Florence, 1964), 364–371.

CHAPTER 6

A Word on Chapters IV and VI of *Dei Verbum*

The Amazing Journey Involved in the Process of Drafting the Conciliar Text

Stanislas Lyonnet, S.J. *

Summary

The first draft of the Constitution *Dei Verbum* was presented in 1962, and it had a long and difficult path to follow before it was eventually promulgated on 18 November 1965. However, this journey was not in vain, for the successive drafts made it possible to provide a final text that was brief, but of exceptional richness. It is one of the most beautiful fruits of the Council. The history of the drafting of the conciliar text of Chapters IV and VI gives an excellent picture of this constant progress from one version to the text. The choice of Chapters IV and VI was not arbitrary. Chapter IV points out that, far from rendering them obsolete, the fact that "the books of the Old Testament [are] all of them caught up into the Gospel message" gives them new importance: that of "shedding light on it and explaining it." In bringing Chapters IV and VI together, the author emphasizes how the holy Scriptures, taken in their totality (both Old and New Testa-

*Father Stanislas Lyonnet, who died in June 1986, submitted his manuscript a few months before his last illness. In publishing it, we should like to render homage to a man who was an outstanding exegete, who was "in love" with the Word of God, and whose passion for holy Scripture was contagious. All those, both colleagues and students, who knew him during his long years of teaching at the Pontifical Biblical Institute in Rome, will be happy to hear once again, through this text, the warm, moving, interior voice that made him a living witness as well as a professor.—*Editor*

ments), nourish the spiritual life of the Christian. The Church draws the bread of life as much from the table of the word of God as from that of the body of the Lord in the Eucharist.

The Old Testament (Chapter IV)

It is already significant that the conciliar Constitution chose to devote a whole chapter to the Old Testament and to emphasize its "lasting value" for Christians themselves. And there is a valid question here. If a person has Christ—who is fulfillment and perfection—what interest is left in the rough draft, the simple promise, the imperfection? If "the books of the Old Testament [are] all of them caught up into the Gospel message," as number 16 explicitly states (from as early as Text 2), why should they still be read and studied? And this is quite apart from the fact that people today are often very aware that "they contain matters imperfect and provisional" (No. 15).

The three short numbers of the chapter set out to answer this question. It would seem that this was the first time that a Council or official Church document had dealt with the question *ex professo*. The great Encyclicals of Leo XIII, Benedict XV, and Pius XII on biblical studies make no mention of the subject. *Divino afflante Spiritu* of Pius XII is widely used in Chapter III, but is nowhere to be found in the notes to Chapter IV. Moreover, secondary or marginal questions have purposely been left aside in order to deal with the one problem under consideration.

The Silence of the Constitution on Questions of Authenticity

This fact can be seen in the first place from the silence of the Constitution on a certain number of problems that had in the past, due to the circumstances that had given rise to them, concerned practically all official documents dealing with the Old Testament, and that often took up most of the space in theological teaching on study of this part of the Scriptures. Text 1, which was considerably longer than the definitive text, did in fact explicitly consider the question of "the human authors of the Old Testament," even if this was done at the end and in the form of an appendix.

Even while declaring that the authenticity of the books of the Old Testament "does not as such directly concern the dogma regarding their divine inspiration," this text did refer to the two-source theory, calling on the interpreter to "carefully retain all that both sources of revelation contain as certain on this point." And it added that "inasmuch as such a question concerns faith, it is the prerogative of the Church alone to make a definitive judgment on this point." This amounted to suggesting that the faith can be concerned in the question of whether the various books of the Old Testament, which are recognized as inspired and as the word of God, do or do not have as their origin the authors to whom they are attributed. It was above all difficult, in this case, to decide "what Scripture and Tradition contain as certain," when (to take what is undoubtedly the most typical case) until relatively recently, it was generally accepted that both taught that Moses was the author of the whole of the Pentateuch.

Be that as it may, the question is no longer considered in Text 2 and the successive drafts. Everything is centered on the value of the Old Testament and on its significance for Christians themselves.

The Old Testament Ushers in the History of Salvation

The permanent value of the Old Testament comes firstly from the fact that it relates a "history of salvation." The title of number 14 states this explicitly from Text 3 onward: ". . . the history of salvation recorded in the books of the Old Testament"—a clearer formula than that of Text 2, which reads: " . . . the history of the chosen people recounted in the books of the Old Testament." Even so, both versions make a clear distinction between the economy itself and the books that tell of it. The Old Testament is firstly this economy, the implementation of God's plan as proposing "the salvation of the whole human race," as is stated right from the first words (Text 2). Text 1 rightly stated, with regard to "the character of the Old Testament," that "the books of the Old Testament . . . describe the supernatural path followed by the one divine revelation and the divine plan of salvation," but it saw it mainly as the means by which God had "taught his people." On the other hand, Texts 2 and 3 set out to describe this economy, as number 3 of Chapter I did (especially in Texts 3 and 4), by describing "gradually accomplished revelation" (Text 2) or "the preparation for the Gospel revelation," except that number 3 also considers "the constant evidence that God gives of himself to men through his Word" (Text 3). It is no longer just a question of a teaching concerning the "bases of the Christian religion" (Text 1), but of God's revelation of himself "in words and deeds as the one, true, living God, so that Israel might be able to learn by experience the ways of God with men," and "understand them ever more profoundly and clearly, as God himself spoke through the mouths of the Prophets." Text 3 also mentions the mission of Israel with regard to other peoples, confirming what had been said from the beginning about the salvific plan as being for "the whole human race." This "series of events" (Text 2) is given its true name of "economy of salvation" (Text 3).

Only after this is mention made of the "books of the Old Testament," and the negative formulation of Text 1 is replaced by a positive one, stating that they "preserve in a lasting manner their power and their authority" (Texts 2 to 4) or rather "preserve a lasting value" (Text 5), because they "announce beforehand, recount and explain this economy of salvation," because they are "the true word of God" and "divinely inspired books."

Despite Its Imperfections, the Old Testament Offers Precious Teaching on God and Mankind

Like the foregoing consideration, and unlike the following one, what is said here views the Old Testament in itself, so to speak, and is therefore addressed not only to Christians, but is equally valid for those who do not recognize the New Testament.

It is true that Text 1 spoke only of "the incomplete character of the old economy, especially as regards morals," and therefore confined itself to stating that it "must finally be compared with the Gospel of Christ preached by the Apostles," adding that its "correct interpretation must be duly submitted to the living magisterium of the Church," which is the sole "guarantee of truth according to the good pleasure of the Father." However, this negative presentation disappears in successive versions. While still mentioning the "still imperfect" manner in which the books of the Old Testament "provide believers with a knowledge of God and man" (Text 2) or saying that they "contain matter imperfect and provisional" (Text 3), they mainly emphasize their positive contribution.

Even Text 2 states that they "provide believers [and it would seem that these "believers" could not yet be "Christians"] with a knowledge of God and man" and teaches them "how God in his mercy is wont to deal with man." Text 3 finally identifies a positive aspect in this very imperfection. Drawing its inspiration from Pius XI's Encyclical against Nazism, it states that it is the witness of "authentic divine teaching." Revelation, which was unfolded in history in a human way, had to develop slowly and progressively. This aspect of "progressive revelation" would also be found in the New Testament. Christ would explain to his apostles that he had "many things to say to you, but you cannot bear them now"; it would be the task of "the Spirit of truth" to "guide you into all truth" (Jn. 16:12–13). The still incomplete manner in which God reveals himself in the Old Testament certainly should not disconcert us; rather, we should see it as demonstrating the marvelous "condescension" referred to at the end of Chapter III.

From Text 2 onward, each redaction adds new details as to the riches presented by the books of the Old Testament.

As we have seen, Text 2 speaks of the "knowledge of God and man" and of "how God in his mercy is wont to deal with man"; in number 14, it speaks of "the ways of God with men," which Israel "learned by experience" and "understood ever more profoundly and clearly," thanks to the prophetic preaching of which it was in fact the principal object. Now these "ways" have not changed, and (to give only one example from among many others) when St. Paul wants to illustrate the scandal of the "folly of the cross," he points to God's behavior with his people in the Old Testament, referring explicitly to Isaiah and Jeremiah (1 Cor. 1:18–31).

Text 2 also adds that these "ways of God with men" must "be taken as models for all men in their behavior towards God." This concept is behind the whole morality of the Old Testament: "Be holy, for I am holy" (Lev. 11:44, cited in 1 Pet. 1:16). Because God is by definition "he who executes justice for the fatherless and the widow, and loves the sojourner, giving him food and clothing," the Israelites must also "love the sojourner," as they were loved by God when they were "sojourners in the land of Egypt" (Deut. 10:18–19). And Christ will simply take up this idea in the Sermon on the Mount: "Be merciful, even as your Father is merciful" (Lk. 6:36). This addition disappeared from later drafts, but I do not know why.

Text 3 points out that while God is merciful in his actions with men, he is also "just," but in particular it adds that the books of the Old Testament do not simply show us the existence of a just and merciful God, as well as his way of behaving toward men: they also "splendidly express a rich sense of God as most holy and merciful," a view of God that is seen particularly clearly in the whole of Jewish literature—and also in Islamic literature, insofar as it depends on it.

Text 4 expands the list of these "riches," with a certain amount of repetition, inasmuch as it returns to what was said when speaking of the "sublime teachings of God." However, with the clear intention of defending wisdom literature and the psalms, it adds the words: ". . . a sound wisdom on human life as well as a wonderful treasury of prayer."

It would be left to Text 5 to complete the list by noting the element that constitutes, at least for Christians, the main wealth of the books of the Old Testament, in other words, the fact that in them "is hidden, too, the mystery of our salvation [in other words, Christ]." And this leads us to the next point.

The Unity of the Two Testaments

For Christians, this point is undoubtedly the most important one, and in fact is peculiar to them, inasmuch as it is supported by the evangelical and apostolic teaching (Text 1), in other words, on the declarations of Christ and the apostles, some of which are then noted in later versions.

It was practically the only one clearly stated and in any way developed in Text 1: "The *raison d'être* and the importance of the whole of the Old Testament are to be found in the fact that the Old leads to the New and is unveiled in the New," a statement supported by a long citation from St. Leo the Great, who compares the promise with the fulfillment, the law with grace. Text 1 goes on to emphasize the preparatory nature of the Old Testament: "God . . . , the author and inspirer of both cove-

nants, . . . wisely established the old covenant in order to prepare for the new, . . . to announce it prophetically, . . . and to
indicate it by various types."

Even in its title, Text 2 distinguishes "the old covenant" from
"its books" that narrate it, and it also states that "the old covenant was disposed . . . in order to prepare for the coming of
Christ, the universal redeemer, and of his kingdom, to announce
this event prophetically, . . . and to indicate it by different
types." Above all, it adds a whole number entitled "Interrelation
of the New and the Old Testaments." It replaces the citation
from St. Leo with a reference to the famous formula of St. Augustine: "The New Testament should be hidden in the Old, and the
Old should be made manifest in the New." This formula not only
points out what the New Testament brings to the Old, but also
indicates the positive value of the Old Testament itself, in which
the New is found in hidden form. It recognizes that "certain
institutions of the old covenant . . . were abolished by the new,"
but states that henceforth the Old Testament has "become part
of the one revelation," and that as a result it "acquires and shows
forth its full meaning in the New."

Text 3 makes three slight changes: from now on the title
becomes "The unity of the two Testaments"; instead of speaking
of "certain institutions of the old covenant" as being "abolished"
by the new, it simply says that "the old covenant has ceased with
the new by virtue of the death of Christ"; and, above all, it
avoids any suggestion that the Old Testament only "became part
of the one revelation" with the New Testament, because it was
always so.

Text 4 does not confine itself to replacing the negative formulation of the previous versions regarding the abolition of the old
covenant with the positive formulation, "Christ founded the new
covenant in his blood." It also introduces a new and very important element, which will then be emphasized in Text 5: the
contribution of the Old Testament to an understanding of the
New. Not only does the New Testament give the books of the
Old Testament "their full meaning" (the term "meaning" is purposely used instead of "sense" in order to avoid canonizing what
many exegetes call the "plenary sense"), but—a point that had
not yet been clearly stated anywhere—the books of the Old
Testament "in their turn shed light on" the New Testament, and
Text 5 then adds: ". . . they shed light on it and explain it."

This point is less frequently developed than the previous ones, but is maybe the one that makes it easiest for Christians today to understand the permanent interest of these books, bearing in mind the fact that many people tend to think that they could with impunity be left to the scholars, and are amazed that the Church gives them so much space in its liturgy and is so concerned to familiarize ordinary members of the faithful with them. It is therefore a good idea to emphasize this point.

The Old Testament Sheds Light on and Explains the New

The statement that "the books of the Old Testament shed light on and explain the New" does not in fact go far enough. Contemporary exegesis is increasingly discovering how indispensable they are for a precise and deep understanding—and even more so for a scientific one—of the New Testament. It has been said that "a commentary on the Gospels that does not take account of the Old Testament as the intellectual ambient in which the New was produced, dates itself and nothing more."[1]

1. The New Testament does not presuppose the Old simply because it is the fulfillment of the latter. It presupposes knowledge of the Old Testament, and is addressed to people who were brought up on the Old Testament, rather as the Moslem of today is brought up on the Koran; it assumes that it is unnecessary to repeat what went without saying for them.

Thus the Constitution speaks of the "lively sense of God" expressed in the Old Testament (No. 15) and describes it as "a storehouse of sublime teaching on God" (*ibid.*). A person who is unaware of this will find it difficult to understand exactly what an author such as St. Paul means when he speaks of God, a name which recurs again and again in his letters—indeed, much more frequently than that of Christ, although it has been said that the latter recurs in every sentence. Paul's prayer is always addressed to God, with Jesus Christ as Mediator. Now, this God is the loving God of the Old Testament who long ago appeared to Moses in the burning bush and whose name is "I Am": ". . . he who was with Israel in her tribulations, who is today with her, and who will always in the future be faithful to his people," as the Targum explains, foreshadowing the definition of the Book of

Revelation (1:4, 8, etc.), the God who dares compare his love to that of the husband who, despite the infidelity of his wife, cannot leave the one he loves because he knows that he alone can bring her happiness (Hos.), and whose love is celebrated in the burning accents of the Song of Songs. The New Testament only speaks of God in rapid allusions because these are enough to conjure up all these texts and many others with which its readers will be familiar.

The same applies to references to man's response to this love, which is summed up in the single word "faith." If we had gradually ceased considering the aspect of faith represented by trust and self-abandonment—an aspect restored to its proper position by the Constitution in its first chapter—and come to consider only the intellectual aspect of assent to truths, the reason is that we were not paying sufficient attention to the teaching of the Old Testament, although St. Paul, for example, refers explicitly to the faith of Abraham. The description of this faith found in the book of Genesis undoubtedly explains better than many definitions can, what faith really is and why the New Testament attributes it such a role in man's justification.

2. Further, the New Testament will often remain incomprehensible to the person who does not have the necessary knowledge of the Old.

Not only does the New Testament constantly base itself on the Old, but even where it does not refer to it explicitly, it borrows its categories and even its language. It is hardly surprising, therefore, that these categories and language very often provide an indispensable key for any proper understanding of those of the New Testament; this is so, for example, for the concept of the "justice of God," which is very different from what we normally understand by this term, and for the redemptive activity of Christ, as this is described in Titus 2:14 with the threefold reference to the Servant of Yahweh, the Exodus, and the Sinai covenant.

Many such examples could be given. Let us choose one or two that are rather more familiar.

The words of Christ as "founding the New Covenant in his blood," which are recalled by the Constitution in number 16, will be practically incomprehensible to anybody who does not know what God's covenant with Israel was for the Old Testament, how this covenant had been sealed by Moses through a special rite of the sprinkling of blood on the two parties to the contract, making of the two one single living being in which the same blood and the same life were found, and, lastly, what the expression "new covenant" meant in the eyes of the Jews, with its explicit reference to the prophecy in which Jeremiah foretold that it would consist of the gift of a law carved on the heart and no longer on stone (Jer. 31:31–33—the only Old Testament passage in which the term "new covenant" is found).

Similarly, only a reader who has some familiarity with the Old Testament will grasp what St. John understood in the blood and water he saw flowing from the pierced side of Christ, to which he attached so much importance (Jn. 19:35) and which he explains precisely by referring to two Old Testament texts. The first (Ex. 12:46) recalls the paschal lamb: Jesus dies on this "day of preparation" (Jn. 19:31) before the setting of the sun, marking the beginning of the sabbath, at the precise moment when the paschal lambs were sacrificed in the Jerusalem Temple. On the first passover, each family had to sacrifice a lamb, "taking some of the blood and putting it on the two doorposts and the lintel of the houses in which they eat them," so as to mark the house for the exterminating angel as a dwelling of Israel, "firstborn son of God" (Ex. 12:7—13:13). The second citation refers to the vision of Zechariah contemplating the death of the mysterious figure of "him whom they have pierced" (Zech. 12:10), over whom "they shall mourn . . . as one mourns for an only child, and weep bitterly over him as one weeps over a firstborn"; this death seemed to be a catastrophe similar to the one Israel suffered in the Plain of Megiddo, but we are also told that "on that day there shall be a fountain opened for the house of David and the inhabitants of Jerusalem to cleanse them from sin and uncleanness" (Zech. 13:1). St. John, for whom water clearly indicates the Holy Spirit (cf. Jn. 7:39), sees the fulfillment of what John the Baptist had foretold at the beginning of his gospel: Christ was truly "the Lamb of God who takes away the sin of the world" by baptizing "with the Holy Spirit" (Jn. 1:29, 33).

3. Lastly, only by comparing the New Testament with the Old can we understand the radically new contribution of the New Testament although it still remains in true continuity with the Old.

Here again, one or two examples will provide more clarification than any long explanation. There are wonderful passages in which the Old Testament recalls the fatherhood of God with regard to his people: "Is Ephram my dear son? Is he my darling child? For as often as I speak against him, I do remember him still. Therefore my heart yearns for him; I will surely have mercy on him" (Jer. 31:20). And there is also his "motherhood": "As one whom his mother comforts, so I will comfort you" (Is. 66:13); or, again: "But Zion said, 'The Lord has forsaken me, my Lord has forgotten me.' 'Can a woman forget her sucking child, that she should have no compassion on the son of her womb? Even these may forget, yet I will not forget you' " (Is. 49:14–15). In the Old Testament, however, Israel never, unlike the surrounding peoples, invokes God by calling him "Father" in the vocative case. Nor did Aramaic, the language spoken by Jesus, use the term "Abba" in this case; it was the word Jewish children used when addressing their earthly fathers, and it did in fact indicate paternity in the normal sense. Now this is the only term we find on the lips of Jesus in the gospels, and St. Mark was careful to give us the original Aramaic form of "Abba" (Mk. 14:36). It even seems that the term scandalized the apostles when Jesus used it in their presence for the first time: "I thank thee, Father. . . . Yea, Father, for such was thy gracious will" (Mt. 11:25–26). He apparently thought it a good thing to explain such a use on his part: "All things have been delivered to me by my Father; and no one knows the Son except the Father, and no one knows the Father except the Son" (v. 27). However, an even more extraordinary element is the term the Holy Spirit puts in the mouth of every Christian, as St. Paul tells us: "And because you are sons, God has sent the Spirit of his Son into our hearts, crying, 'Abba! Father!' " (Gal. 4:6). The novelty of the gospel is not that God is Father, but that he is so in a sense that the Old Testament, however marvelous its statements on the divine fatherhood, had never even dreamed of: God is "the father of our Lord Jesus Christ" (Eph. 1:3), and in him our Father too (v. 5). In Christ we are, through grace, what he himself is through nature. This is also why the Fathers and the liturgy tend to see the gospel statement about the filiation of Jesus, at his baptism or transfiguration, as confirmation of our own filiation: ". . . in the transfigured glory of Christ your Son, you . . . show us the splendor of your beloved sons and daughters" (Prayer of the Feast).

Similarly, the parable of the good shepherd in St. John (10:1–21) and that of the lost sheep in the Synoptics (Mt. 18:12–13;

Lk. 15:3–7) are clearly inspired by what Ezekiel said about the "bad shepherds" of Israel and about Yahweh who would himself become the shepherd of his people: "I myself will be the shepherd of my sheep, and I will make them lie down. . . . I will seek the lost, and I will bring back the strayed, and I will bind up the crippled, and I will strengthen the weak" (Ez. 34:15–16). But only Christ could say: "The good shepherd lays down his life for his sheep" (Jn. 10:11). God had to be made man in order to be able to die for us.

The fact that "the books of the Old Testament have all of them been caught up into the gospel message" certainly does not make them obsolete. On the contrary, it gives them the new role of "shedding light on it and explaining it." No Christian who wants to understand the New Testament in all its depth can avoid the necessity of gaining a similar knowledge of the Old.

For this reason, as well as for all the others recalled by the Constitution, the Old Testament retains a "lasting value" even for Christians—or *especially* for Christians. And in the text cited by the Constitution in number 14 (from as early as Text 1), St. Paul was thinking of the Old Testament when he spoke of the "Scriptures" as giving "steadfastness and encouragement" (Rom. 15:4), or again of the "sacred writings" as "profitable for teaching . . . so that the man of God may be complete, equipped for every good work" (2 Tim. 3:16–17, cited in No. 11).

Successive Drafts of Chapter IV

NUMBER 14

Text 1	*Text 2*
[The authority of the Old Testament in the Church.] Through the Holy Scriptures of the Old Testament, already since the earliest of times, God set himself the task of teaching a people he had acquired in a particular fashion and to whom he bound himself by a covenant of friendship in view of the plans of salvation he was to carry out amongst men. This is why, especially as concerns the	[The history of the chosen people recounted in the books of the Old Testament.] God, in his great love, ever concerned, in a hidden manner, for the salvation of the whole of the human race, was particularly concerned for the people he had chosen. Indeed, having established a covenant with Abraham and with Moses, he revealed himself to this people he had acquired for himself in words and

bases of the Christian religion, neither in the words, nor in the historical events up to the end of time, are the power, the authority and the importance of the Old Testament to be in any way diminished: "For whatever was written in former days was written for our instruction, that by steadfastness and the encouragement of the Scriptures we might have hope" (Rom. 15:4).

deeds in such a way that Israel might learn by experience the ways of God with men, and might understand them ever more profoundly and clearly, as God Himself spoke through the mouths of the Prophets. This series of events announced, recounted and explained by the sacred authors under the inspiration of the divine Spirit, is still to be found in the books of the Old Testament, as the true word of God; this is why these books preserve their power and their authority: "For whatever was written in former days was written for our instruction, that by steadfastness and the encouragement of the Scriptures we might have hope" (Rom. 15:4).

Text 4 (and 3)

[The history of salvation recorded in the books of the Old Testament.] God in his great love planning carefully the salvation of the whole of the human race, chose for himself, by a particular dispensation, a people to whom he would entrust his promises. By his covenant with Abraham (cf. Gen. 15:18) and, through Moses, with the people of Israel (cf. Ex. 24:8), he revealed himself in words and deeds as the one, true living God, so that Israel might be able to learn by experience the ways of God with men, understand them even more profoundly and clearly, as God himself spoke through the mouths of the Prophets, and make them more widely known among the nations (cf. Ps. 21:28–29; 95:1–3; Is. 2:1–4; Jer. 3:17). This

Text 5

. . . planning and preparing

. . . might experience what were the ways of God with men,

economy of salvation, announced beforehand, recounted and explained by the sacred authors, appears in the books of the Old Testament as the true word of God; this is why these divinely inspired books preserve in a lasting manner their power and their authority: "For whatever was written in former days was written for our instruction, that by steadfastness and the encouragement of the Scriptures we might have hope"(Rom. 15:4).

. . . preserve a lasting value.

NUMBER 15

Text 1

[Relation between the Old and the New Testaments.] The relations of God with man since Adam's act of disobedience, through promises made to our fathers, through prophetic oracles concerning the Redeemer, and also through announcements which became ever clearer, were aimed towards access to the hoped-for salvation being opened to every human being: "The prophets who prophesied of the grace that was to be yours searched and inquired about this salvation" (1 Pet. 1:10). Indeed, the Holy Scriptures of the Old Testament bear witness to Christ (cf. Jn. 5:39) and, by the will of the almighty and most merciful God, it was necessary that all that had been said concerning the promised Savior be fulfilled, according to the teaching of Jesus our Lord to his apostles, whose spirit he had at last opened to understand the Scriptures (cf. Lk. 22:44–45).

Text 2

[The character of the old covenant and its books.] The old covenant was disposed principally, strongly and tenderly, in order to prepare for the coming of Christ, the universal redeemer, and of his kingdom, to announce this event prophetically in various ways (cf. 1 Pet. 1:10) and to indicate it by different types (cf. 1 Cor. 10:11). Furthermore, although the books of the Old Testament are still imperfect, they provide believers with a knowledge of God and man, and teach them how God in his mercy is wont to deal with man, and they must be taken as models for all men in their behavior towards God and their neighbor.

Thus, the *raison d'être* and the importance of the whole of the Old Testament are to be found in the fact that the Old leads to the New and is unveiled in the New. [There follows a long quotation from St. Leo the Great.]

[The character of the New Testament.] This is why the holy Vatican Council, based on the doctrine of the Gospels and of the Apostles, solemnly teaches that God is the author and the inspirer of both covenants, that he wisely established the old covenant in order to prepare for the new by his tender providence, to announce it prophetically in various ways and to indicate it by various types, in such a way that the books of the Old Testament might also describe the supernatural path followed by the one divine revelation and the divine plan of salvation. As regards their content, granted the incomplete character of the old economy, especially as regards morals, it must finally be compared with the Gospel of Christ preached by the Apostles, and its correct interpretation must be duly submitted to the living magisterium of the Church, i.e., to the judgment of those who "with the apostolic succession have received the sure charism, the guarantee of truth according to the good pleasure of the Father" (Irenaeus).

[The human authors of the Old Testament.] Lastly, as regards the

human authors of the books of the
Old Testament, although this authenticity does not as such directly concern the dogma regarding their divine inspiration,
Catholic interpreters of the Holy
Scriptures should carefully retain
all that both sources of revelation
contain as certain on this point.
But inasmuch as such a question
concerns faith, it is the prerogative of the Church alone to make
a definitive judgment on this
point.

Text 4 (and 3)

[The importance of the Old Testament for Christians.] The economy [of salvation] of the Old Testament was principally disposed
in order to prepare for the coming of Christ, the universal redeemer, and of the Messianic
Kingdom, and to announce this
event prophetically (Lk. 24:44;
Jn. 5:39; 1 Pet. 1:10), and to indicate it by means of different types
(cf. 1 Cor. 10:11). For the books
of the Old Testament, in the context of the human situation before the era of salvation established by Christ, make clear to all
the knowledge of God and man,
as well as how a just and merciful
God deals with mankind. Although these books contain matter imperfect and provisional,
they nevertheless show authentic
divine teaching. Hence, these
same books, which give expression to a lively sense of God,
[and] which contain sublime
teaching on God and sound wisdom on human life as well as a

Text 5

wonderful treasury of prayers, are to be accepted with veneration by Christians.

. . . and in which, too, is hidden the mystery of our salvation, are to be accepted with veneration by Christians.

NUMBER 16

Text 1

The *raison d'être* and the importance of the whole of the Old Testament are to be found in the fact that the Old leads to the New and is unveiled in the New.

Text 2

[Interrelation of the New and the Old Testaments.] Thus God, the inspirer and author of both Testaments, in his wisdom has so brought it about that the New should be hidden in the Old and that the Old should be made manifest in the New. For, although certain institutions of the old covenant, which were suitable only for the time of preparation, were abolished by the new, still, the Old Testament in its entirety, caught up into the Gospel message, has become part of the one Revelation, and acquires and shows forth its full meaning in the New. Hence the Church recognizes with veneration the canonical books of the Old Testament and accepts them as its own Scriptures.

Text 3

[The unity of the two Testaments.] And thus, God, the inspirer and author of the books of both Testaments, in his wisdom has so brought it about that the New should be hidden in the Old and that the Old should be made manifest in the New. For, although the Old Covenant ceased with the New by virtue of the death of Christ (Rom. 7:4; Col. 2:14), still the books of the Old Testament, all of them caught up

Text 4

For, although Christ founded the New Covenant in his blood (cf. Lk. 22:20; 1 Cor. 11:25), still the books of the Old Testament, all of them caught up into the Gospel message . . .

as part of the one revelation into the Gospel message, acquire and show forth their full meaning in the New (cf. Mt. 5:17ff; Rom. 8:2–3).

. . . their full meaning in the New (2 Cor. 3:14), and, in their turn, shed light on it.

Text 4 (and 3)

[The unity of the two Testaments.] Thus God, the inspirer and author of the books of both Testaments, in his wisdom has so brought it about that the New should be hidden in the Old and that the Old should be made manifest in the New. For, although Christ founded the New Covenant in his blood (cf. Lk. 22:20; 1 Cor. 11:25), still the books of the Old Testament, all of them caught up into the Gospel message, acquire and show forth their full meaning in the New (2 Cor. 3:14), and, in their turn, shed light on it.

Text 5

(cf. Mt. 5:17; Lk. 24:27; Rom. 25–26; 2 Cor. 3:14–15) and, in their turn, shed light on it and explain it.

Final Text of Chapter IV as Promulgated

14. [The history of salvation recorded in the books of the Old Testament.] God, in his great love planning *and preparing* carefully the salvation of the whole of the human race, chose for himself, by a particular dispensation, a people to whom he would entrust his promises. By his covenant with Abraham (cf. Gen. 15:18) and, through Moses, with the people of Israel (cf. Ex. 24:8), he revealed himself to this people he had acquired for himself in words and deeds as the one, true, living God, so that Israel *might experience what were* the ways of God with men, might understand them ever more profoundly and clearly, as God himself spoke through the mouths of the Prophets, and might make them more widely known among the nations (cf. Ps. 21:28–29; 95:1–3; Is. 2:1–4; Jer. 3:17). This economy of salvation, announced beforehand, recounted and explained

by the sacred authors, appears in the books of the Old Testament as the true word of God; this is why these divinely inspired books preserve *a lasting value*. "For whatever was written in former days was written for our instruction, that by steadfastness and the encouragement of the Scriptures we might have hope" (Rom. 15:4).

15. [The importance of the Old Testament for Christians.] The economy [of salvation] of the Old Testament was principally disposed in order to prepare for the coming of Christ, the universal redeemer, and of the Messianic Kingdom, and to announce this event prophetically (Lk. 24:44; Jn. 5:39; 1 Pet. 1:10) and to indicate it by means of different types (cf. 1 Cor. 10:11). For the books of the Old Testament, in the context of the human situation before the era of salvation established by Christ, make clear to all the knowledge of God and man, as well as how a just and merciful God deals with mankind. Although these books contain matters imperfect and provisional, they nevertheless show authentic divine teaching. Hence, *these same books*, which give expression to a lively sense of God, which contain sublime teaching on God and sound wisdom on human life as well as a wonderful treasury of prayers, *and in which, too, is hidden the mystery of our salvation*, are to be accepted with veneration *by Christians*.

16. [The unity of the two Testaments.] Thus God, the inspirer and author of the books of both Testaments, in his wisdom has so brought it about that the New should be hidden in the Old and that the Old should be made manifest in the New. For, although Christ founded the New Covenant in his blood (cf. Lk 22:20; 1 Cor. 11:25), still the books of the Old Testament, all of them caught up into the Gospel message, acquire and show forth their full meaning in the New *Testament* (cf. *Mt. 5:17; Lk. 24:27; Rom. 16:25–26; 2 Cor. 3:14–16*), and, in their turn, shed light on it *and explain it*.

Sacred Scripture in the Life of the Church (Chapter VI)

This concluding chapter of the Constitution might seem of minor importance when compared with the previous ones and their wealth of doctrinal content. However, Pastor Max Thurian sees it as "a key for the understanding of the whole Constitution,"[2] and another observer at the Council, Pastor Lukas Voscher, considers it "perhaps the most important part of the text." In the official report that he presented to the Central Committee of the World Council of Churches at Enugu in January 1965, not only did Vischer declare that "the texts adopted and promulgated by Vatican II [referring to the Constitutions on the Liturgy, 1963, and the Church, 1964, as well as the Decrees on Ecumenism and the Eastern Church, in particular 1964] go far beyond what even the boldest forecasts would have dared hope for from the Council"; referring to the schema on revelation, which was then in the process of being drafted, he added that it was "one of the richest in promise," particularly because of the "last chapter," which "deals with the use of the Bible in the life of the Church."[3]

Although it was not the subject of so much discussion and although the original text may have undergone fewer radical changes, the slow evolution of the definitive text is just as instructive concerning the orientations provided by the Council. It is worth examining this process, pausing a moment over certain points that may be of major interest.

What the Church Owes to Scripture (No. 21)

The accent in the original draft of this text was shifted by the Council, as can be seen in the first number, and indeed in the title, which was changed from "The Church's Care Concerning Holy Scripture" to "The Church's Veneration of Holy Scripture" (Text 2). Text 1 wanted to answer an objection, and therefore declared: "The heavenly treasure of the holy books . . . has never been hidden in the Church," adding that the Church "has preserved [it] with the greatest of veneration and earnestness, . . . has defended [it] against all false interpretations, [and] has used [it] with care for the salvation of souls," especially in "preaching" and the "liturgy." In short, Text 1 considers mainly what the Church has done for Scripture, whereas the successive versions consider exclusively what the Church owes to Scripture.

The "veneration" of the Church for Scripture, which was merely noted in passing in Text 1, becomes the central element in Text 2: "From the beginning, the Church has surrounded the heavenly treasure of the holy books of the Old and New Testaments with the greatest of veneration"; they are the "precious gift which God has entrusted to her" and which she "recommends [to the faithful] to receive with extreme piety as a precious gift from God."

In particular, however, two reasons for such veneration are

briefly indicated in two qualities that belong to Scripture as such. The first will be taken up by Text 3 in Chapter I, number 2, with regard to revelation itself, which is described as the "conversation of God with men."[4] Here it is stated that "in the holy books the Father who is in heaven comes with great love to meet his children, and almost talks with them"; even the "almost" will disappear from Text 3, which reads, "and talks with them."

The second reason for which Scripture holds such a position in the Church is "the strength and power" found in the "word of God." Catholic theology has tended to neglect this feature, and to consider the word of God almost exclusively from the viewpoint of the truth it revealed; however, it was dear to Scripture itself as also to the Fathers of the Church, and Protestant theology restored it to its proper position. If Scripture is received by believers with faith, it will "truly serve the Church as her support and vigor, and the children of the Church as a solid basis for their faith, food for their souls, and the fount of spiritual life."

It will then be left to Text 3 to add the two citations from Hebrews 4:12 and Acts 20:32, where the "word of God" does not in fact really mean the Scriptures, but either the personified Word (Heb. 4:12) or the apostolic teaching (Acts 20:32), so that Text 5 will thus explain that the two statements apply "in a most excellent way . . . to holy Scripture." The same can be said of 1 Thessalonians 2:13, where St. Paul is referring directly to his own preaching, which is "accepted" by the Thessalonians "not as the word of men, but as what it really is, the word of God, which is at work in you believers."

Above all, Text 3 enriches the number with two entirely new points.

The first is the parallelism between Scripture and Eucharist. The Council could not have expressed the veneration in which the Church holds Scripture more strongly than it does by placing it parallel with the worship it offers to the "body of the Lord" as present in the Eucharist. This was certainly not done, as certain Fathers feared, in order to reduce the eucharistic presence to pure symbolism, nor with any intention of saying that the two presences are the same (for it is an analogy), but more in order to emphasize the reality of Christ's presence in Scripture as inspired word. Pastor Thurian notes "the considerable ecumenical importance" of this "close link between word and Eucharist."[5]

In the conclusion of the chapter, Text 2 undoubtedly already

paralleled the benefit brought to the Church by "progress in
worship of the holy Eucharist" with what we have the right to
hope for from progress in "the esteem and cult . . . of the word of
God" (No. 26). However, the statement in number 21 of Text 3
is much more precise.

The Constitution on the Liturgy spoke of "the table of the
Lord's Body" and "the table of God's word" in two different
paragraphs (SC 48 and 51). Here we no longer have two tables
but a single one: "The Church . . . never ceases to take the
bread of life upon the table both of the word of God and of the
Body of the Lord, and to offer it to the faithful." The Decree on
the Renewal of Religious Life will also refer to "the table of the
divine law and of the sacred altar" (PC 6), and the Decree on the
Ministry and Life of Priests of "the double table of Holy Scripture
and the Eucharist" (PO 18).

There is in fact a tradition of such parallelism. It is found in
The Imitation of Christ with the formula of the "two tables" (IV,
11d), and is based on the interpretation the Fathers and many
exegetes give to the passage in Chapter 6 of St. John's Gospel,
where Jesus is called "the bread of life" both through the teaching
of the Father that can be absorbed through faith (vv. 32–50) and
through his flesh and blood, which he gives as food and drink
(vv. 51–58). The Fathers were familiar with this parallelism.
Thus, Origen writes: "You know with what respectful care you
look after the body of the Lord when it is given to you. . . . Why
would you expect neglect of the word of God to receive less
severe punishment than that of his body?"[6] St. Hilary speaks of
the two tables: "We receive our nourishment, the bread of life,
from the table of the Lord . . ., and we are nourished with the
teaching of the Lord at the table of the Sunday readings."[7] For
St. Augustine, the daily bread we ask for in the Lord's Prayer is
both the eucharistic bread and the bread of the word of God.[8]
And St. Jerome is equally categoric: "Knowledge of the Scriptures is a true food and true drink."[9]

The second point is of equal ecumenical interest, as O.
Cullmann noted at a press conference after the promulgation of
the Constitution.[10]

It is not merely said of the Scriptures that "taken together with
sacred Tradition" they constitute "the supreme rule of the
Church's faith," but a reason is given that applies only to the
Scriptures: ". . . as they are inspired by God and committed to

writing once and for all time, they present God's own Word in an unalterable form, and make the voice of the Holy Spirit sound again and again in the words of the Prophets and Apostles." As will be said in number 24, "The holy Scriptures contain the word of God; and they truly are this word." Above all, it is added that "the preaching of the Church, as indeed the Christian religion itself, should always take the Scriptures as the norm and the authority which rules and judges them" (Text 3). This is a bold statement, and because certain Fathers found it exaggerated, it was toned down in Text 4: ". . . all the preaching of the Church, as indeed the Christian religion itself, should be nourished by sacred Scripture." However, it was to all intents and purposes resurrected in Text 5, which reunited the two aspects of nourishment and rule as of equal importance: ". . . all the preaching of the Church, as indeed the Christian religion itself, should be nourished and ruled by sacred Scripture." On the other hand, there is nothing surprising in this if it is true that the Scriptures "communicate" and "are" this "word of God," of which previous chapters have said that "the sacred Synod hears it with reverence and proclaims it with faith" (No. 1), and that, far from considering itself "superior to it," the magisterium, to which "it has been entrusted," "is its servant, . . . listens to it devotedly, guards it with dedication and expounds it faithfully" (No. 10).

It will be recalled that in the Church only Scripture, unlike the documents of Tradition and the magisterium, receives the honor of liturgical reading, and that it presided over the reflections of the Council, which was itself conceived as a liturgical function.

The Different Versions of the Scriptures (No. 22)

As regards the different versions of the Scriptures, Text 1 simply notes the preference of the Latin Church for the Vulgate, and upholds the "authority" of this version against its opponents. The perspective is strictly apologetic. The text states that "without calling into question the preeminent authority of the original texts," the Vulgate is "an authentic witness to the faith" and is "absolutely free from all errors as concerns matters of faith and morals." In other words, it must "be conceded the authority of Tradition."

Even so, a fleeting reference to other versions shows that the non-Latin branches of the Church are not forgotten: "Neverthe-less, at the same time, this holy Vatican Council receives with deference the other venerable versions in use in the Eastern Churches, particularly the ancient Greek version of the Old Testament, known as the Septuagint, approved by the use of the Apostles themselves."

Text 2 is no longer concerned with ancient versions, whether Vulgate or Septuagint, or with their greater or lesser authority. Everything is centered on the concern of the Church "that access to sacred Scripture may be opened wide to Christians," and thus "that vernacular translations be carefully made . . . based on the original texts, the authority of which is preeminent."

Although Text 3 brings back the reference to the Septuagint and the Vulgate, this is because they are privileged witnesses of this concern of the Church. We should also note the position given to the Septuagint version: in Text 1 it seemed to belong only to the Eastern Churches, even though it was "approved by the use of the Apostles themselves," whereas here it is placed first as a version that the Church "from her very beginning made her own," while the Vulgate is mentioned among "the other transla-tions" that the Church also "honors."

Similarly, Text 3 emphasizes more strongly than Text 2 the need to establish translations that are not only "carefully made" but are also "suitable and correct," stating that this should be done "into various languages," "from the original texts." How-ever, in order not to condemn the present usage of the Latin liturgy, which generally employs translations made on the basis of the Vulgate, Text 4 will tone down this latter statement, adding an *etiam:* ". . . preferably from the original texts."

The Church had not of course waited for the Council before concerning itself with the spread of the sacred Scriptures, and various recent documents of the magisterium had contained press-ing exhortations in this regard. In his Encyclical on biblical studies, Pius XII recalled the encouragement given by Pius X and Benedict XV to the Society of St. Jerome, which had the aim of "distributing the Gospels and the Acts of the Apostles to every Christian family" (*EB* 544; cf. 478). However, it must be admit-ted that such emphasis on establishing translations of the whole Bible "in various languages" and preferably on the basis of the original texts had tended in the past to be more the concern of our separated brethren.

The Council went even further. For the first time an official document approved the idea—indeed, discreetly suggested it— that such translations should be "made in a joint effort with the separated brethren" (Text 3).

In the seventeenth century, Richard Simon, followed at the end of the nineteenth century by three other Frenchmen—a Protestant pastor, a Catholic priest, and a rabbi—had in fact tried to produce an "ecumenical" translation before the term was even being used. However, these were completely unofficial undertakings, and, in any case, they were not followed up. On the other hand, the wish of the Council would be fulfilled in a shorter time than could reasonably have been foreseen. In France, the undertaking began with the Letter to the Romans, which was to be a sort of test. "It was felt that the ecumenical translation of the Bible would not come up against insuperable obstacles if the Letter to the Romans could be presented in a French version accepted to all parties."[11] This version appeared as early as January 1967, and the notes provided were so abundant that they constituted a real commentary. Here again, in the words of Pastor Lukas Vischer, "the fulfillment went far beyond what even the boldest of forecasts could have dared hope."

Scripture and the Pastoral Ministry (No. 23)

In Text 1, there is a number toward the end of the chapter reminding exegetes of certain rules for the interpretation of the Scriptures. These are the same rules that the Constitution lists in Chapter III (No. 12), which is in fact a more suitable place for them: the need for the help of the Holy Spirit, and the attention given to the analogy of faith, to Tradition, and to the magisterium. Added to these elements is a reference to the pastoral orientation to be given to exegesis: "scientific research" and "scholarship" are to "foster holiness in life of all the faithful." Further, exegetes must be "greatly concerned with the theological teaching of the sacred texts," and knowledge should be combined with "the subtle language in which the ancient Fathers and Doctors of old excelled, motivated as they were exclusively by love for the Church and the salvation of souls."

This early draft had the form more of a warning, but those that followed replaced the warning tone with a wholly positive exposition, entitling it "The Apostolic Task of Catholic Teachers."

This task consists of assisting the Church, as she is "taught by the Holy Spirit," in her efforts to "reach day by day a more profound understanding of the holy Scriptures in order to feed her children without failing from the divine words" (Text 3, and already substantially Text 2). The work of theologians is linked to that of exegetes: they must "combine their forces." There is a research task to be carried out, "so that the divine Scriptures may be examined more profoundly," and also a "pastoral" task, "so that as many as possible of those who are ministers of the divine word may distribute fruitfully to the people of God the nourishment of the Scriptures." These tasks must, of course, be carried out "guided by the Magisterium of the Church" (Text 2), or, to use a formula that Text 3 tones down slightly in order to reserve a supervisory role for it, "under the watchful eye of the Magisterium."

Text 4 notes that in this research, we must make use of all "appropriate techniques," in other words, those listed by Pius XII in his Encyclical and recalled in Chapter III of the Constitution; and Text 5 also adds a reference to "the study of the holy Fathers, both Eastern and Western, and of the sacred Liturgies."

First and foremost, however, from Text 3 onward, the Council is keen to reproduce explicitly and literally the encouragement that Pius XII addressed at the end of his Encyclical "to the experts in biblical sciences," to all those who are devoted sons of the Church and who faithfully follow her doctrine and rules," calling on them to "pursue with all the energy at their command the work they have so happily undertaken with strength that is renewed each day" (*EB*, 569). Text 4 even slightly modifies Pius XII's expression so as to avoid any impression of blaming non-Catholic exegetes; it now speaks simply of "sons of the Church who are expert in biblical studies," and they are now all assumed to be "devoted sons . . . who faithfully follow her doctrine and rules." Text 5 will use the same phrase, adding: ". . . in accordance with the mind of the Church."

Scripture and Theology (No. 24)

In Text 1, the corresponding number closes the chapter and the Constitution. It sets itself the task of studying "The Relation of Theology with Holy Scripture" (title). Here again, we can see a clear apologetic concern, inasmuch as the main objective was

that of defending Catholic doctrine against incorrect interpretations of the Scriptures. Those responsible for producing the text
did undoubtedly state at the outset, with an explicit allusion to
the "two-source theory," that "Scripture, together with Tradition, are as it were the soul of theology," and that "the study of
these two sources is for sacred science the source of constant
rejuvenation." The allusion to the two sources will disappear
naturally, particularly in view of the fact that the formula "the
soul of theology" is borrowed from Leo XIII and Benedict VI,
who were not speaking about Tradition: "It is very desirable and
necessary that the use of divine Scripture should exercise its
influence on the whole of theological science and be as it were its
soul."[12]

However, with the fear that Scripture will not be correctly
interpreted, the main concern of the redactors is immediately to
be seen: that of showing "the perfect agreement of Catholic
doctrine as handed down from the beginning until our era with
the divine word," an agreement that theologians have the task of
"illustrating and confirming," by virtue of the knowledge they
possess." The reason for this is that because "the same God is the
author of the holy books and of the doctrine entrusted to the
Church as a deposit, . . . it is impossible that an official interpretation should read into the holy books a meaning divergent from
this doctrine in any way whatsoever."

Text 2 and successive texts, on the other hand, abandon any
apologetic aim, and set about the direct and exclusive task of
describing the role of Scripture in theology instead of that of
theology with regard to Scripture. This is emphasized by the title
of Text 2, "Theology Relies on the Word of God," and even
more clearly by that of Text 3, "The Importance of Holy Scripture for Theology."

In reaction against the two-source theory, Text 2 eliminates
anything in Text 1 that concerned Tradition, and at the same
time suppresses Leo XIII's beautiful description of Scripture as
"the soul of theology," which was linked to this reference. It
states first that Scripture is "the basic, unshakable foundation of
theology," which furnishes its "arguments." Long before this, St.
Thomas explained that only the arguments provided by "canonical Scripture" are "holy teaching's own proper authorities," and
that those of "other doctors of the Church" "carry no more than
probability." He also added that "our faith rests on the revelation

made to the Prophets and Apostles who wrote the canonical books, not on a revelation, if such there be, made to any other teacher."[13]

Text 2 then gives the reason for this unique position of the Scriptures: they "do not simply contain the word of God [as Tradition and the documents of the Magisterium can also contain it], but they truly are this word." And Text 4 will explain that this is because only the Scriptures are "inspired."

This is also the basis of their role in "the ministry of the word of God," that is to say, in "pastoral preaching in which the liturgical homily should hold pride of place." And Text 4 will explain that this preaching also includes "catechetics" and, in a general way, "all forms of Christian instruction."

Text 3 and the ensuing texts will reintroduce the mention of Tradition in connection with Scripture as the foundation of theology, but will avoid making it a "second source" of revelation, in some way independent of Scripture. The expressions vary from one text to another so as to reproduce as faithfully as possible the teaching given in Chapter II, in particular in number 9. Text 3 confines itself to placing Scripture and Tradition side by side: "the word of God, . . . written and transmitted." Text 4 is more precise: "the written word of God, which must be explained in the light of Tradition," together "forming one thing, and moving towards the same goal" (No. 9). Text 3 also brings back Leo XII's description of Scripture as the soul of theology, but is more faithful this time to the original meaning, so that, as in Leo XIII and Benedict XV, what is involved is "study of the sacred page." The expression will be found again in the Decree on the Formation of Priests (published a month before the Constitution on Revelation) in a paragraph describing the privileged position that Scripture must have in the theological studies of seminarians (*OP* 16).

The Reading of the Bible (No. 25)

The first draft gives two long numbers, especially the second, studying first the duty of priests, and then that of the faithful. The exhortation is entirely positive for priests, recalling St. Paul's admonition to his disciple Timothy in 2 Timothy 3:15–17, which was then inserted into the definitive text of Chapter III (No. 11). This is followed by a series of patristic citations on the need for preachers to devote themselves to study of the Scriptures; in particular, St. Augustine is cited on "an empty preacher of the Word of God to others, not being a hearer of the Word in his own heart."

However, as regards the faithful, although Text 1 rejoices that "the reading of holy Scripture has spread amongst numerous members of the faithful" and that translations into the vernacular have been made on the basis of the original texts, and above all over "the love with which the New Testament in particular is spread every day more widely," it warns the faithful even more strongly against the dangers of imprudent reading of the Bible, saying that such reading requires first of all a good knowledge of "the doctrine of the Church," and a basis of "serious preparation"; this goes especially for the Old Testament, but also for the New, which contains some difficult passages, as St. Peter recognized (2 Pet. 3:16). Text 1 therefore states that this reading should be carried out in translations that have been approved by the bishops and are equipped with necessary and really adequate explanations. It recalls that for the faithful, the living magisterium is the supreme law of faith, inasmuch as the task of interpreting Scripture has been entrusted to the magisterium alone. Lastly, it is the task of the bishops, whose "authority" is invoked, to approve "every incipient activity aimed at spreading holy Scripture among the faithful."

Text 2 is considerably shorter, but retains the two separate numbers regarding priests and faithful. Although the exhortation to priests is more restrained, it is no less emphatic. However, the tone changes completely with regard to the laity. All Christians are called to "go gladly to the sacred text itself, whether by means of the sacred liturgy, which is full of the divine words, or by the other institutions suitable for this purpose,[14] which, with the approval of the authority of the Church, are happily spreading everywhere in our day."

As regards bishops, their role is no longer simply that of watching over "every incipient activity" with a view to providing Christians with a biblical education, but that of "suitably instructing the faithful . . . in the correct use of the divine books." They must, therefore, encourage and no longer simply "approve" translations; these are aimed at educating Christians and will, therefore, be "equipped with necessary and really adequate explanations."

In Text 3, a single exhortation addressed first to all clerics and then to all Christians is combined into one number. The difference that was so clear in the original text between clergy and laity disappears completely, except that the clergy have a more serious obligation than ordinary Christians to read and study the Bible.

"All clerics," because apart from "priests" explicit mention is made of "others who, as deacons or catechisets, are officially engaged in the ministry of the word." Text 4 will describe this reading as "spiritual" (*sacra*) in order to recall that it is a "meditation" and not simply some ordinary reading.

The exhortation is much stronger for ordinary Christians than in Text 2: ". . . the sacred Synod forcefully and specifically exhorts all the Chrsitian faithful. . . ." Although special mention is made of "members of religious Institutes," the exhortation is addressed to everybody. It speaks of "frequent reading" of the Scriptures, which will enable everybody to learn what St. Paul called "the surpassing knowledge of Jesus Christ" (Phil. 3:8), as is also recalled in the Decree on the Renewal of Religious Life with the same Pauline citation (*PC* 6), although in the Constitution on Revelation, the Council also repeats the words of St. Jerome that had already been quoted by Benedict XV and Pius XII: "Ignorance of the Scriptures is ignorance of Christ."[15]

Text 3 adds a paragraph of great importance, in which the Council declares that non-Christians should also read the Bible, and with this in view it asks that "editions . . . provided with suitable notes" should be prepared, and calls on all Christians, whether priests or laity, to "circulate" these "prudently."

Lastly, Text 4 is careful to indicate the role of "prayer," which Pius XII had also mentioned in passing, calling on priests not only to "examine the sacred pages with diligent study," but also to "assimilate them through prayer and meditation" (*EB*, 566). ". . . in the sacred books the Father who is in heaven comes with great love to meet his children, and talks with them" (No. 21), and it is therefore prayer, man's response, that will establish "the dialogue between God and man" evoked in a beautiful citation from St. Ambrose.

A New Spirit

We have already seen, in connection with translations of the Scriptures into different languages, and even translations produced in collaboration with our separated brethren,[16] that this concern to spread the word of God everywhere, even among ordinary Christians, is an indication of a "new spirit" in the Church. And comparison of the successive versions of number 25 make it easier to see the extent and precise manner in which this spirit was truly "new."

The text prepared by the theological commission reflected a wary attitude to Scripture, at least where ordinary Christians were concerned. It is true that this attitude was already tending to disappear, as can be seen in the references in notes to the Encyclicals of Pius XII and Benedict XV,[17] but it had not yet wholly vanished, as Text 1 itself goes to prove, and had in any case previously been relatively common in the Church.

Of course, the Church has never "hidden the heavenly treasure of the holy books" (No. 21, Text 1). It transmitted it not only to priests but to all Christians in its liturgy—although in a liturgy that, at least in the Latin Church, the people did not understand and of which no translation had even been allowed for a long time.[18] Apart from the encouragement given to the Society of St. Jerome, which was concerned only with the gospels and the Acts of the Apostles, and a few sporadic references, the exhortations of the supreme pontiffs mentioned were really only addressed to theologians and "preachers of the word of God," and not directly to simple members of the faithful.[19] Today, we may find it embarrassing, or indeed scandalous, to read the restrictions the hierarchy imposed on the reading of the Bible by all Christians in the past. To give only one or two examples, we wonder how on earth Clement XI, in 1711, could condemn propositions such as the following: "The reading of sacred Scripture is for everybody," or "Forbidding Christians to read the Scriptures and particularly the Gospel means forbidding the use of light to the children of the light and making them suffer a type of excommunication."[20] A modern-day Christian may be even more amazed at the retraction Pius VII imposed on Bishop Stanislas of Mohilev in 1816. The bishop had recommended that everybody read the Bible, and he did not only have to "declare that his intention had not been that of recommending, from among the versions of the Bible in the vernacular, those that are not in conformity with the holy canons and constitutions of the Church," but Pius VII also added: "You will explain and declare that when you recommended the reading of the holy books, you in no way intended all the members of the faithful without distinction, but only the clergy and those among the laity who have, in the opinion of their pastors, received sufficient instruction."[21] Such an attitude must, of course, be interpreted in the perspective of the circumstances. Even so, it is precisely by comparing the past and present attitudes of the Church with regard both to translations of the Scriptures into the vernacular, and to the reading of the Bible by ordinary Christians, that we can see the extent to which the atmosphere has changed, and the sense in which we can speak of a "new spirit."

As regards the circulation of versions of the Bible even among non-Christians, I do not think that any official document had ever before mentioned such a thing—and, as noted, the same applies to translations produced in collaboration with non-Catholics. Until then, any such concern had been confined to Protestant Bible societies, and although their versions did not generally include notes, certain other Protestant editions, such as the *Bible du Centenaire* in France, were also "equipped with necessary and really adequate explanations." When Cardinal Bea welcomed the representatives of these Bible societies in Rome in January 1967, where they had come to discuss the possibilities of collaboration with Catholics with a view to producing translations of the Bible and distributing them, he could state that this was "a task that is fundamental and vital for the future of Christianity," and did not hesitate to add: "I do not think it would be an exaggeration to say that such cooperation constitutes one of the most important factors in the history of contemporary Christianity."[22]

Here again we can recognize "the new spirit" that is revealed not only in Chapter VI but, as this study has tried to show, in the whole of the Dogmatic Constitution *Dei Verbum* on Divine Revelation.

Successive Drafts of Chapter VI

NUMBER 21

Text 1	*Text 2*
[The Church's care concerning Holy Scripture.] The heavenly treasure of the holy books, which	[The Church's veneration of Holy Scripture.] From the beginning, the Church has surrounded the

the Holy Spirit in his extreme charity and generosity has transmitted to men through the Church, has never been hidden in the Church; indeed, from the beginning, the Church of Christ has preserved the divine oracles with the greatest of veneration and earnestness; she has defended them against all false interpretations, she has used them with care for the salvation of souls, especially in sacred preaching, and she has unceasingly offered them to all day by day in her liturgy.

heavenly treasure of the holy books of the Old and the New Testaments with the greatest of veneration, and has never ceased to distribute this precious gift which God has entrusted to her to the faithful, above all in the holy liturgy, and to recommend them to receive it with extreme piety as a precious gift from God.

In the holy books the Father who is in heaven comes with great love to meet his children, and almost talks with them; and the strength and power found in the Word of God are so great that it can truly serve the church as her support and vigor, and the children of the Church as a solid basis for their faith, food for their souls, and the fount of spiritual life.

Text 3

[The Church's veneration of the holy Scriptures.] "We have known the economy of our salvation solely by means of those who brought us the Gospel; first, they preached this Gospel, and then, according to the will of God, they transmitted it to us in the Scriptures so that it might become the foundation and pillar of our faith" (St. Irenaeus). Thus the holy Scriptures are an excellent witness to the preaching of the Gospel. The Church has always venerated them as she also venerates the very Body of the Lord, for she never ceases to take the bread of life upon the table both of the Word of God and of the Body of the Lord, and to offer it to the faithful. She has always considered them, taken together with

Text 4

OMITS: "We have known . . . to the preaching of the Gospel.

The Church has always venerated the divine Scriptures as she also venerates . . .

sacred Tradition, as the supreme
rule of her faith, since they are not
only inspired by God in such a way
that they present the very Word of
God, but what is more, they offer
the character of immutability as be-
fits a rule, and they make the voice
of the Holy Spirit sound again and
again in the words of the Prophets
and Apostles.

. . . offer the character of immutability and make the voice of the
Holy Spirit sound again and
again . . .

It follows that all the preaching
of the Church, as indeed the Christian religion itself, should always
take the Scriptures as their point of
reference as the norm and authority which rules and judges them.
For in the sacred books the Father
who is in heaven comes with great
love to meet his children, and talks
with them; and the strength and
power found in the Word of God
are so great that it can truly serve
the Church as her support and
vigor, and the children of the
Church as a solid basis for their
faith, food for their souls, and the
source of their spiritual life. "The
Word of God is living and active"
(Heb. 4:12), and "is able to build
you up and to give you the inheritance among all those who are sanctified" (Acts 20:32; 1 Thess. 2:13).

It follows that all the preaching of
the Church, as indeed the Christian religion itself, should be nourished by sacred Scripture. For . . .

Text 4 (and 3)

[The Church's veneration of the
Holy Scriptures.] The Church has
always venerated the divine Scriptures as [she] also [venerates] the
very Body of the Lord, insofar as
she never ceases to take the bread
of life upon the table both of the
Word of God and of the Body of
the Lord and to offer it to the faithful. She has always considered

Text 5

. . . never ceases, above all in the
holy Liturgy, to take the bread of
life . . .

them, taken together with sacred Tradition, as the supreme rule of her faith, since they are not only inspired by God in such a way that they present the very Word of God, but what is more, they offer the character of immutability and make the voice of the Holy Spirit sound again and again in the words of the Prophets and Apostles.

. . . since, as they are inspired by God and committed to writing once and for all time, they present God's own word in an unalterable form, and . . .

It follows that all the preaching of the Church, as indeed the Christian religion itself, should be nourished by sacred Scripture. For in the sacred books the Father who is in heaven comes with great love to meet his children, and talks with them; and the strength and power found in the Word of God are so great that it can truly serve the Church as her support and vigor, and the children of the Church as a solid basis for their faith, food for their souls, and the source of their spiritual life. "The Word of God is living and active" (Heb. 4:12), and "is able to build you up and to give you the inheritance among all those who are sanctified" (Acts 20:32; 1 Thess. 2:13).

. . . should be nourished and ruled by sacred Scripture.

. . . and a pure and lasting fount of spiritual life. Thus, in a most excellent way, the following words are applied to holy Scripture: "The Word of God is living. . ./

NUMBER 22

Text 1

[The Vulgate Latin version.] Without calling into question the preeminent authority of the original texts of Holy Scripture, over the course of time the Latin Church preferred one of the various Latin versions then in current use, the Vulgate, which she considers to be an authentic witness to the faith. For by virtue of the

Text 2

[Carefully translated versions are recommended.] In order that access to Sacred Scripture may be opened wide to Christians, the Church of God recommends authoritatively and is concerned, with motherly care, that vernacular translations be carefully made, for a deeper understanding and richer knowledge of the Word of

official use of this version over so many centuries in the Church, it is clear that it is absolutely free from all error as concerns matters of faith and morals, in the manner in which it has been understood and continues to be understood by the Church, and that, in arguments, lessons or talks, it can be quoted in all safety and without risk of errors. Indeed, the Vulgate has been so closely bound to the very Magisterium of the Church that it must be conceded the authority of Tradition.

Nevertheless, at the same time, this holy Vatican Council receives with deference the other venerable versions in use in the Eastern Churches, particularly the ancient Greek version of the Old Testament known as the Septuagint, approved by the use of the Apostles.

God, based on the original texts, the authority of which is preeminent.

Text 3

[Carefully translated versions are recommended.] Access to sacred Scripture ought to be open wide to the Christian faithful. For this reason the Church, from her very beginning, made her own the ancient Greek translation of the Old Testament called the Septuagint, which she continues to honor along with the other Eastern translations, and the Latin translation which is called the Vulgate. However, since the Word of God must be made available to men of all times, the Church attaches her authority, with motherly concern, to her desire that translations be carefully made into various languages, for use in the liturgy, in catechetics

Text 4

. . . called the Septuagint; but she also continues to honor the other Eastern translations . . .

. . . the Church, with motherly concern, sees to it that suitable and correct translations are made into various languages, preferably from the original texts of the holy

and spiritual reading, from the original texts of the holy books. If it should happen that these translations are made in a joint effort with the separated brethren, they could be used by all Christians.

books. If it should happen that, with the approval of the authorities of the Church, according to opportunity, these translations are made in a joint effort with the separated brethren, they may be used by all Christians.

Text 4 (and 3)

[Carefully translated versions are recommended.] Access to sacred Scripture ought to be open wide to the Christian faithful. For this reason the Church, from her very beginning, made her own the ancient Greek translation of the Old Testament called the Septuagint; but she also continues to honor the other Eastern translations, and the Latin translation which is called the Vulgate. However, since the Word of God must be made available to all men of all times, the Church, with motherly concern, sees to it that suitable and correct translations are made into various languages, preferably from the original texts of the holy books. If it should happen that, with the approval of the authorities of the Church, according to opportunity, these translations are made in a joint effort with the separated brethren, they may be used by all Christians.

Text 5

. . . and the Latin translations, principally that which is called the Vulgate.

. . . when the opportunity presents itself and the authorities of the Church agree . . .

NUMBER 23

Text 1

[Catholic exegetes.] Since today recent discoveries supply numerous points which are of use in order to understand more deeply the literal meaning which must be the object of particular consid-

Text 2

[The apostolic task of Catholic teachers.] The spouse of the incarnate Word, which is the Church, is taught by the Holy Spirit of God and of Christ. She reaches day by day a more profound understand-

eration in the divine Scriptures, nonetheless, those who, in the Church and for the profit of the Church, are so happily engaged in research work to clarify the divine oracles by their knowledge, must recall that they always need the help of God's Holy Spirit to explain the Holy Scriptures, and that Scripture cannot be understood otherwise than "as is required by the meaning of the Holy Spirit with whose help it was composed." For God did not give men the Holy Scriptures so that they might exercise their talents, but for their spiritual good; and thus it is necessary that the greatest scholarship of contemporary interpreters be combined in their research and presentation of spiritual doctrine with the subtle language in which the ancient Fathers and Doctors excelled, motivated as they were exclusively by love for the Church and salvation of souls. Thus Catholic exegetes should be greatly concerned with the theological teaching of the sacred texts, so that not only they themselves and all those devoted to the study of theology may offer each other mutual aid, but also that they may help priests to explain to the people in the most suitable fashion the Catholic teaching, and that they may foster holiness of life in all the faithful.

All this may be achieved only if, when they explain the Bible with due deference and obedience, they give constant attention to the analogy of faith, to the Tradition of the Church, and to the ing of the Holy Scriptures, in order to feed her children without falling from the divine words. For their part, Catholic exegetes and all those who are devoted to the study of sacred theology should work, combining their forces, guided by the Magisterium of the Church, so that the divine Scriptures may be examined more profoundly, so that as many as possible of those who are ministers of the divine Word may distribute faithfully to the people of God the nourishment of the Scriptures, which enlightens the mind, strengthens the will and fires the hearts of men with the love of God.

rules promulgated on this point by
the apostolic See.

Text 3   *Text 4*

[The apostolic task of Catholic
teachers.] The spouse of the incarnate Word, which is the Church,
is taught by the Holy Spirit. She
strives to reach day by day a more
profound understanding of the
holy Scriptures, in order to feed
her children without failing from
the divine words. For their part,
Catholic exegetes and all those
who are devoted to the study of
sacred theology should work, zealously combining their efforts, fol-
lowing the Fathers, guided by the   . . . under the watchful eye of the
Magisterium, to examine the di-   Magisterium, at examining the divine Scriptures more profoundly,   vine Scriptures using appropriate
so that as many as possible of   techniques so that as many as pos-
those who are ministers of the di-   sible . . .
vine Word may distribute fruit-
fully to the people of God the
nourishment of the Scriptures,
which enlightens the mind,
strengthens the will and fires the
hearts of men with the love of
God. The sacred Synod encour-   The sacred Synod encourages
ages those who are expert in bibli-   those sons of the Church who are
cal studies, those who are de-   expert in biblical studies to renew
voted sons of the Church and   their efforts in order to con-
who faithfully follow her doctrine   tinue . . .
and rules, constantly to renew
their efforts in order to continue
the work they have so happily begun, with complete dedication.

Text 4 (and 3)   *Text 5*

[The apostolic task of Catholic
teachers.] The spouse of the incarnate Word, which is the Church,
is taught by the Holy Spirit. She
strives to reach day by day a more
profound understanding of the

holy Scriptures, in order to feed
her children without failing from
the divine words. For their part,
Catholic exegetes and all those
who are devoted to the study of
sacred theology should work, zealously combining their efforts, following the Fathers, under the
watchful eye of the Magisterium,
at examining the divine Scriptures
using appropriate techniques, so
that as many as possible of those
who are ministers of the divine
Word may distribute fruitfully to
the people of God the nourishment of the Scriptures, which enlightens the mind, strengthens the
will and fires the hearts of men
with the love of God. The sacred
Synod encourages those sons of the
Church who are expert in biblical
studies constantly to renew their
efforts in order to continue the
work they have so happily begun,
with complete dedication.

. . . from the divine words. For
this reason also she duly fosters
the study of the holy Fathers, both
Eastern and Western, and of the
sacred Liturgies.

. . . and at explaining them in
such a way that as many as possible . . .

. . . constantly to renew their efforts, in order to carry on the
work they have so happily begun,
with complete dedication and in
accordance with the mind of the
Church.

NUMBER 24

Text 1

[The relation of theology with
Holy Scripture.] Given that Holy
Scripture together with Tradition
is as it were the soul of theology,
and that the study of these two
sources is for sacred science the
source of constant rejuvenation,
theological experts must hold the
progress of their discipline in the
highest esteem; this is achieved by
the correct interpretation of the
holy books. For the same God is
the author of the holy books and

Text 2

[Theology relies on the Word of
God.] The science of theology
rests on the Word of God as on a
basic, unshakable foundation, and
it derives from it the arguments in
which it finds the firmest guarantee of its strength and is constantly
rejuvenated. For the Holy Scriptures do not simply contain the
Word of God, but they truly are
this Word, from which the ministry of the Word of God too—
pastoral preaching, in which the

of the doctrine entrusted to the Church as a deposit, and thus it is impossible that an official interpretation should read into the holy books a meaning diverging from this doctrine in any way whatsoever. Our theologians, by virtue of the knowledge they possess, should thus take care to illustrate and confirm the perfect agreement of Catholic doctrine as handed down from the beginning until our era with the divine Word which the wonderful action and plan of the Holy Spirit have put into writing for the Church in view of the salvation of all men.

liturgical homily should hold pride of place—is healthily nourished and thrives in holiness.

Text 3

[The importance of holy Scripture for theology.] Sacred theology relies on the Word of God as it is revealed, written and transmitted, as on a permanent foundation. In it, it finds the firmest guarantee of its strength and is constantly rejuvenated, as it searches out, under the light of faith, the full truth stored up in the mystery of Christ. The holy Scriptures contain the Word of God and they truly are this Word. Therefore, the study of the sacred page should be as it were the soul of sacred theology. The ministry of the Word too—pastoral preaching, catechetics and all forms of Christian instruction, among which the liturgical homily should hold pride of place—is healthily nourished and thrives in holiness through the Word of Scripture, and the faith of the believers recognizes in it the truth of God as he reveals himself.

Text 4

Sacred theology relies on the Word of God, which must be explained in the light of Tradition, as on a permanent foundation.

The holy Scriptures contain the Word of God and, because they are inspired, they truly are this Word.

OMIT: and the faith . . . as he reveals himself.

Text 4 (and 3)	*Text 5*

[The importance of holy Scripture for theology.] Sacred theology relies on the written Word of God, which must be explained in the light of Tradition, as on a permanent foundation. In it, it finds the firmest guarantee of its strength and is constantly rejuvenated, as it searches out, under the light of faith, the full truth stored up in the mystery of Christ. The holy Scriptures contain the Word of God and, because they are inspired, they truly are this Word. Therefore, the study of the sacred page should be as it were the soul of sacred Theology. The ministry of the Word too—pastoral preaching, catechetics and all forms of Christian instruction, among which the liturgical homily should hold pride of place—is healthily nourished and thrives in holiness through the Word of Scripture.

. . . taken together with sacred Tradition, . . .

NUMBER 25

Text 1 (résumé)

[The reading of Holy Scripture by priests.] The text recalls St. Paul's admonition in 1 Timothy 3:16–17, and quotes the Fathers on the need for preachers never to abandon the reading of the Scriptures, especially the text of St. Augustine on "an empty preacher of the Word of God to others, not being a hearer of the Word in his own heart."

[The reading of Holy Scripture by the faithful.] The text expresses joy that the reading of Holy Scripture has spread amongst numerous

Text 2

[The reading of Holy Scripture is recommended to priests.] Therefore priests of Christ must immerse themselves in the Holy Scriptures by assiduous reading and diligent study, lest it happen that anyone become "an empty preacher of the Word of God to others, not being a hearer of the Word in his own heart," when he ought to be able to transmit to his flock the immense riches of the divine Word, particularly in liturgical worship.

[Likewise to the faithful.] Let

members of the faithful and that vernacular translations have been made from the original texts, and even greater joy at the love with which the New Testament in particular is spread every day more widely.

Nonetheless, it admonishes the faithful to approach the sacred text itself bearing in mind the doctrine of the Church and following serious preparation. This applies especially to the Old Testament, but also to the New, which contains difficult passages (2 Pet. 3:16). Thus the translations intended for the use of the faithful must receive the approval of the Bishops and be equipped with necessary and really adequate explanations, according to the mind of the Church, whose living Magisterium is for the faithful the first rule of faith. It is this Magisterium alone to which has been entrusted the task of interpreting Scripture.

To the authority of the Bishops must likewise be submitted every incipient activity aimed at spreading Holy Scripture among the faithful.

Christians too go gladly to the sacred text itself, whether by means of the sacred liturgy, which is full of the divine words, or by the other institutions suitable for this purpose which, with the approval of the authority of the Church, are happily spreading everywhere in our day.

It is for the Bishops, "with whom the apostolic doctrine resides," suitably to instruct the faithful entrusted to them in the correct use of the divine books, which should be equipped with necessary and really adequate explanations, so that the children of the Church may familiarize themselves safely and profitably with the sacred Scriptures.

Text 3

[The reading of holy Scripture is recommended.] Therefore, all clerics, particularly priests of Christ and others who, as deacons or catechists, are officially engaged in the ministry of the Word, should immerse themselves in the Scriptures by constant reading and diligent study, lest it happen that anyone become "an empty preacher of the Word of God to others, not being a hearer of the Word in his own

Text 4

. . . should immerse themselves in the Scriptures by constant spiritual reading . . .

heart" (St. Augustine), when he ought to be sharing the boundless riches of the divine Word with the faithful committed to his care, especially in the sacred Liturgy.

Likewise, the sacred Synod forcefully and specifically exhorts all the Christian faithful, especially the members of religious Institutes, to avoid "ignorance of Christ because they are ignorant of the Scriptures," but rather to learn by frequent reading of the divine Scriptures "the surpassing knowledge of Jesus Christ" (Phil. 3:8). Therefore, let them go gladly to the sacred text itself, whether in the sacred liturgy, which is full of the divine words, or in devout reading, or in such suitable exercises and various other helps which, with the approval and guidance of the Church, are happily spreading everywhere in our day.

It is for the Bishops, "with whom the apostolic doctrine resides" (St. Irenaeus), suitably to instruct the faithful entrusted to them in the correct use of the divine books, especially of the New Testament, and in particular of the Gospels. They do this by giving them translations of the sacred texts which are equipped with necessary and really adequate explanations, so that the children of the Church may familiarize themselves with the sacred Scriptures, and become steeped in their spirit.

Moreover, editions of sacred Scripture, provided with suitable notes, should also be prepared for the use of non-Christians, and

. . . the members of religious institutes, to learn "the surpassing knowledge of Jesus Christ" (Phil. 3:8) by frequent reading of the divine Scriptures. "Ignorance of the Scriptures is ignorance of Christ" (St. Jerome). Therefore, let them go gladly . . .

Let them remember, however, that prayer should accompany the reading of sacred Scripture, so that a dialogue may take place between God and man. For "we speak to him when we pray; we listen to him when we read the divine oracles" (St. Ambrose).

adapted to their circumstances; these should be prudently circulated, either by pastors of souls, or by Christians of every rank.

Text 4 (and 3)	*Text 5*

[The reading of Holy Scripture is recommended.] Therefore, all clerics, particularly priests of Christ and others who, as deacons or catechists, are officially engaged in the ministry of the Word, should immerse themselves in the Scriptures by constant spiritual reading and diligent study, lest it happen that anyone become "an empty preacher of the Word of God to others, not being a hearer of the Word in his own heart" (St. Augustine), when he ought to be sharing the boundless riches of the divine Word with the faithful committed to his care, especially in the sacred Liturgy.

Likewise, the sacred Synod forcefully and specifically exhorts all the Christian faithful, especially the members of religious Institutes, to learn the "surpassing knowledge of Jesus Christ" (Phil. 3:8) by frequent reading of the divine Scriptures. "Ignorance of the Scriptures is ignorance of Christ" (St. Jerome). Therefore, let them go gladly to the sacred text itself, whether in the sacred liturgy, which is full of the divine words, or in such suitable exercises and various other helps which, with the approval and guidance of the pastors of the Church, are happily spreading everywhere in our day. Let them remember, however, that prayer should accompany the reading of sacred Scripture, so

that a dialogue may take place between God and man. For "we
speak to him when we pray: we
listen to him when we read the
divine oracles" (St. Ambrose).

It is for the Bishops, "with
whom the apostolic doctrine resides" (St. Irenaeus), suitably to
instruct the faithful entrusted to
them in the correct use of the divine books, especially of the New
Testament, and in particular of
the Gospels. They do this by giving them translations of the sacred
texts which are equipped with necessary and really adequate explanations, so that the children of the
Church may familiarize themselves safely and profitably with
the sacred Scriptures, and become
steeped in their spirit.

Moreover, editions of sacred
Scripture, provided with suitable
notes, should also be prepared for
the use of non-Christians, and
adapted to their circumstances;
these should be prudently circulated, either by pastors of souls, or
by Christians of any rank.

NUMBER 26

Text 1

Text 2

For just as the life of the Church
draws increase from progress in
worship of the holy Eucharist, so a
new impulse of spiritual life may
be expected if the Word of God
which "stands forever" is accorded
the esteem and cult it deserves.

Text 3

Text 4

[Epilogue.] So may it come about
that, by the reading and study of
the sacred books, "the Word of

God may speed on and triumph" (2 Thess. 3:1) and the treasure of Revelation entrusted to the Church may more and more fill the hearts of men. Just as the life of the Chruch draws increase from progress in worship of the holy Eucharist, so a new impulse of spiritual life may be expected if the Word of God which "stands forever" (Is. 40:8; 1 Pet. 1:23–25) is accorded the esteem and cult it deserves.

Just as the Church draws increase from constant attendance at the eucharistic mystery, so a new impulse of spiritual life may be expected from increased veneration of the Word of God which "stands forever" (Is. 40:8; cf. 1 Pet. 1:23–25).

Text 4 (and 3)

Text 5

[Epilogue.] So may it come about that, by reading and study of the sacred books, "the Word of God may speed on and triumph" (2 Thess. 3:1) and the treasure of Revelation entrusted to the Church may more and more fill the hearts of men. Just as the life of the Church draws increase from constant attendance at the eucharistic mystery, so a new impulse of spiritual life may be expected from increased veneration of the Word of God which "stands forever" (Is. 40:8; cf. 1 Pet. 1:23–25).

Final Text of Chapter VI as Promulgated

21. [The Church's veneration of the Holy Scriptures.] The Church has always venerated the divine Scriptures as [she] also [venerates] the very Body of the Lord, insofar as she never ceases, *above all in the holy liturgy*, to take the Bread of life upon the table both of the Word of God and of the Body of the Lord and to offer it to the faithful. She has always considered them, *and continues to consider them*, taken together with sacred Tradition, as the supreme rule of her faith, since, as they are inspired by God and *committed to writing once and for all time*, they present God's own word *in an unalterable form*, and they make the voice of the Holy Spirit sound again and again in the words of the Prophets and Apostles.

It follows that all the preaching of the Church, as indeed the Christian religion itself, should be nourished *and ruled* by sacred Scripture. For in the sacred books the Father who is in heaven comes with great love to meet his children, and talks with them; and the strength and power found in the Word of God are so great that it can truly serve the Church as her support and vigor, and the children of the Church as a solid basis for their faith, food for their souls, and a *pure and lasting* fount of spiritual life. *Thus, in a most excellent way, the following words are applied to holy Scripture:* "The Word of God is living and active" (Heb. 4:12), and "is able to build you up and to give you the inheritance among all those who are sanctified" (Acts 20:32; 1 Thess. 2:13).

22. [Carefully translated versions are recommended.] Access to sacred Scripture ought to be open wide to the Christian faithful. For this reason the Church, from her very beginning, made her own the ancient Greek translation of the Old Testament called the Septuagint; but she also continues to honor the other Eastern translations, and *the Latin translations, principally that* which is called the Vulgate. However, since the Word of God must be made available to all men of all times, the Church, with motherly concern, sees to it that suitable and correct translations are made into various languages, preferably from the original texts of the holy books. If it should happen that, when the opportunity presents itself and the authorities of the Church agree, these translations are made in a joint effort with the separated brethren, they may be used by all Christians.

23. [The apostolic task of Catholic teachers.] The spouse of the incarnate Word, which is the Church, is taught by the Holy Spirit. She strives to reach day by day a more profound understanding of the holy Scriptures, in order to feed her children without failing from the divine words. *For this reason also she duly fosters the study of the holy Fathers, both Eastern and Western, and of the sacred Liturgies.* For their part, Catholic exegetes and all those who are devoted to the study of sacred theology should work, zealously combining their efforts, under the watchful eye of the *sacred* Magisterium, at examining the divine Scriptures using appropriate techniques, and *at explaining them in such a way* that as many as possible of those who are ministers of the divine Word *may be able to distribute* fruitfully to the people of God the nourishment of the Scriptures, which enlightens the mind, strengthens the will and fires the hearts of men with the love of God. The sacred Synod encourages those sons of the Church who are engaged in biblical studies constantly to renew their efforts, in order to carry on the work they have so happily begun, with complete dedication and in accordance with the mind of the Church.

24. [The importance of holy Scripture for theology.] Sacred theology relies on the written word of God, *taken together with sacred Tradition,* as on a permanent foundation. In it, it finds the firmest guarantee of its strength and is constantly rejuvenated, as it searches out, under the light of faith, the full truth stored up in the mystery of Christ. The holy Scriptures contain the Word of God and, because they are inspired, they truly are this Word. Therefore, the study of the sacred page should be as it were the soul of sacred theology. The ministry of the Word too—pastoral preaching, catechetics and all forms of Christian instruction, among which the liturgical homily should hold pride of place—is healthily nourished and thrives in holiness through the word of Scripture.

25. [The reading of holy Scripture is recommended.] Therefore, all clerics, particularly priests of Christ and others who, as deacons or catechists, are officially engaged in the ministry of the Word, should immerse themselves in the Scriptures by constant spiritual reading and diligent study, lest it happen that anyone become "an empty preacher of the Word of God to others, not being a hearer of the Word in his own heart," when he ought to be sharing the boundless riches of the divine Word with the faithful committed to his care, especially in the sacred Liturgy.

Likewise, the sacred Synod forcefully and specifically exhorts all the Christian faithful, especially the members of religious institutes, to learn "the surpassing knowledge of Jesus Christ" (Phil. 3:8) by frequent reading of the divine Scriptures. "Ignorance of the Scriptures is ignorance of Christ." Therefore, let them go gladly to the sacred text itself, whether in the sacred Liturgy, which is full of the divine words, or in devout reading, or in such suitable exercises and various other helps which, with the approval and guidance of *the pastors* of the Church, are happily spreading everywhere in our day. Let them remember, however, that prayer should accompany the reading of sacred Scripture, so that a dialogue may take place between God and man. For "we speak to him when we pray; we listen to him when we read the divine oracles."

It is for the Bishops, "with whom the apostolic doctrine resides," suitably to instruct the faithful entrusted to them in the correct use of the divine books, especially of the New Testament, and in particular of the Gospels. They do this by giving them translations of the sacred texts which are equipped with necessary and really adequate explanations, so that the children of the Church may familiarize themselves safely and profitably with the sacred Scriptures, and become steeped in their spirit.

Moreover, editions of sacred Scripture, provided with suitable notes, should also be prepared for the use of non-Christians, and adapted to their circumstances; these should be prudently circulated, either by pastors of souls, or by Christians of any rank.

26. [Epilogue.] So may it come about that, by the reading and study of the sacred books, "the Word of God may speed on and triumph" (2 Thess. 3:1) and the treasure of Revelation entrusted to the Church may more and more fill the hearts of men. Just as from constant attendance at the eucharistic mystery the life of the Church draws increase, so a new impulse of spiritual life may be expected from increased veneration of the word of God which "stands forever" (Is. 40:8; cf. 1 Pet. 1:23–25).

Translated from the French and Latin by Leslie Wearne and Ronald Sway.

Notes

1. X. Léon-Dufour, "Brève histoire de l'interpretation 1ère partie: Les évangiles synoptiques," in A. Robert and A. Fueillet (eds.), *Introduction à la Bible*, 2 (Tournai, 1959), 156.

2. R. Schutz and M. Thurian, *La Parole vivante au Concile* (Taizé, 1966), 165.

3. *La Documentation Catholique*, 62 (1966), 353–370 (see 354 and 362).

4. See Chapter I.

5. Schutz and Thurian, *La Parole vivante au Concile*, 167.

6. Origen, *Homily on Exodus*, 13, 3, in *SC*, 16.

7. St. Hilary, *Commentary on Psalm 127:10*, in *PL*, 9, 709.

8. St. Augustine, *Sermons 56*, 20; 57, 7; 58, 4(5); 59, 3(6); in *PL*, 38, cols. 381, 389, 395, 401.

9. St. Jerome, *Commentary on Ecclesiastes 3:13*, in *PL*, 23, 1092.

10. O. Cullmann, press conference of 2 December 1965; see *La Documentation Catholique*.

11. *Traduction Oecuménique de la Bible. Epître aux Romains* (Paris, 1967), 23.

12. Leo XIII, *Providentissimus Deus*, in *EB*, 114; cited by Benedict XV, *Spiritus Paraclitus*, in *EB*, 483.

13. St. Thomas Aquinas, *Summa Theologiae*, I, q. 1, a. 8, ad 2; cited by Pius XII, "Allocutio ad Moderatioribus, Docentibus atque alumnis Pontificii Athenaei, quod 'Angelicum' nuncupatur" (14 January 1958), in *L'Osservatore Romano* (15 January 1958), and *AAS*, 50 (1958), 150–161.

14. The Decree on the Apostolate of Lay People lists some of these: "sessions, congresses, recollections, retreats, frequent meetings, conferences, books and periodicals" (*AA* 32).

15. St. Jerome, Prologue to the *Commentary on Isaiah*, in *PL*, 24, 17; Benedict XV, *Spiritus Paraclitus*, in *EB*, 491; Pius XII, *Divino afflante Spiritu*, in *EB*, 568.

16. See Chapter VI, no. 22.

17. Pius XII, *Divino afflante Spiritu*, in *EB*, 544, recalls the encouragement given by Pius X and Benedict XV to the Society of St. Jerome (cf. p. 180); it would have been a good idea to add *EB*, 566. Benedict XV, *Spiritus Paraclitus*, in *EB*, 475–480, groups together a series of texts of St. Jerome on the need to know the Bible.

18. Ban on translating the Missal.

19. Thus Benedict XV in various passages in his Encyclical, in *EB*, 444, 482, 484, to which Pius XII refers, *Divino afflante Spiritu*, in *EB*, 544.

20. Pascal Quesnel, Propositions 80 and 85. See DS, 2480 and 2485.

21. See J.B. Malou, *La lecture de la Sainte Bible en langue vulgaire* (Louvain, 1946), II, 531; similar statements can be found, for example, on pp. 520, 523, and 526.

22. Cf. W.M. Abbott, "Alla ricerca di una Bibbia comune," *Civiltà Cattolica* (1967/I), 338.

Chapter 7

Interpreting the Scriptures
(*Dei Verbum* 12)
Affinities Between the Popular Koiné
and the Neotestamentary

José O'Callaghan

Summary

This article first considers the question of interdependence between the neotestamentary Greek and the popular Greek of the era, by trying to avoid two extremes: exaggerating this dependence or, on the contrary, denying it. Various examples of syntactic similarity are cited. Finally, the possibility of a new Pauline exegesis, based on the language of Christian Greek letters of the early centuries, is examined.

———————
———————

Regarding the divine inspiration of Scripture and its interpretation (*DV* III 12), Vatican II insists on the necessity of grasping the exact meaning that the sacred writers wanted to convey to us. God made use of human instruments; therefore, we have to find out what they meant and what God wanted to communicate to us. To do this, we must keep in mind the literary genres employed, situate the texts in the historical and cultural atmosphere of the era, and, of course, take into account the whole of Scripture, the Tradition, and the analogy of faith. As regards the topic of this article, the Council states:

Rightly to understand what the sacred author wanted to affirm in his work, due attention must be paid both to the customary and characteristic patterns of perception, speech and narrative which prevailed at the age of the sacred writer, and to the conventions which the people of his time followed in their dealings with one another.[1]

This assertion is in general not new. Pius XII, in his Encyclical *Divino afflante Spiritu* of 30 September 1943, had affirmed: "And it is just as important to employ and to search for papyri which frequently have been useful in comprehending the writings and the institutions, both public and private, which existed especially at the time of our Saviour."[2]

Vatican II does not explicitly mention papyrology, as Pius XII had done before, but it reminds us that the biblical scholar must be very well acquainted with the prevailing ways of speaking at a particular time, so as to grasp the complex meaning of Scripture. Now, the popular phrasings and expressions are preserved in the manuscripts, that is, in the papyri that have survived. Thus, it appears that Vatican II indirectly encourages the study of papyri in order to determine the characteristic ways of speaking employed by the people when the Bible was written. This is true of the New Testament as well, the particular subject of this article.

Philologically speaking, the popular koiné and the neotestamentary koiné have already been contrasted. It is understandable that similar elements have been pointed out, because after all the Greek of the New Testament is not a linguistic island, isolated from its environment, but is immersed in the Hellenistic world of the time.

This is what A. Deissmann[3] has decidedly claimed by juxtaposing "greco-biblical" language to classic Greek, and by relating it to the vividness of popular speech. This comparison, "als epochemachend,"[4] opened up new directions for many specialists and researchers who have recently[5] studied neotestamentary Greek.[6]

We must admit that the grammatical analyses of Deissmann are generally still authoritative,[7] and are confirmed by the opinion of many philologists. But it would be exaggerated to reduce neotestamentary Greek to a mere instance of the popular koiné.[8] Such an attitude was, not without reason, rejected by representative scholars of both the biblical and the strictly papyrological disciplines.[9] One cannot deny that the neotestamentary Greek has its own personality: it possesses both biblical and popular traits. It is a literary Greek, characterized by the direct and semitic diction of the people who received the Lord's heritage.

herefore, one can easily note the correspondences and analogies between the Greek of the New Testament and that of the content of the papyri.[10] We shall, therefore, provide some examples in which this expressive quality evidently clashes, or at least, is in dissonance with the rules of atticism. Of course, we intend here neither to offer a complete list of these particularities, nor to furnish a comparative grammar of these two styles of expression. This would go far beyond the limits of this article. But, by means of a few examples, we will point out at least some syntactic analogies.

For instance, we have noticed in the neotestamentary language the discordance between the genitive absolute and its pronoun, while in classic Greek the participle would invariably agree with this pronoun. See, e.g., Matthew 8:1:[11] Καταβάντος δὲ αὐτοῦ ἀπὸ τοῦ ὄρους ἠκολούθησαν αὐτῷ ὄχλοι πολλοί. Among the papyri, we can mention POxy. X 1298, 16–18 [IVp]: καὶ ἐμοῦ παραγεναμένου ἐν τῷ Ὀξυρεχίτῃ ὑπελόγησέ μοι ἑκάστου σπαθίου (τάλαντα) ζ.

Instead of using a subordinate infinitive-form clause, or one with ἵνα, neotestamentary language sometimes employs a simple coordinate clause: thus, in Luke 14:18: ἐρωτῶ σε, ἔχε με παρῃτημένον. The same thing can be confirmed in BGU II 423, 11–12 [IIp]: ἐρωτῶ σε οὖν ηὑριέ μου πατήρ, γράψον μοι ἐπιστόλιον πρῶτον.

In Acts 14:18, we find the articulated infinitive subordinate to a verb equivalent to "prevent": μόλις κατέπαυσαν τοὺς ὄχλους τοῦ μὴ θύειν αὐτοῖς. The same construction can also be noticed, for instance, in PCol. Zen. I 6, 3 [257a]: ἐκώλυσεν τοῦ μὴ ἰδεῖν σε.[12]

In the story of Emmaus, the disciples say (Lk. 24:21): ἡμεῖς δὲ ἠλπίζομεν ὅτι αὐτός ἐστιν ὁ μέλλων λυτροῦσθαι τὸν Ἰσραήλ, where we see that ἐλπίζω requires ὅτι with the indicative.[13] This type of construction is also found in PIand. II 11, 2–2 [IIIp]: ἐλπίδω γὰρ εἰς θεὸν ὅτι παρακληθῆναι [βούλεται ὁ κύριός ?] μου ὁ Ἐ[πίμα]χος καὶ τάχα παραχωρεῖ πὴν συνωνήν.

In 1 Corinthians 16:10, we notice the use of a completive clause, introduced by ἵνα with correspondence of tenses in the subordinate clause: βλέπετε ἵνα ἀφόβως γένηται τρὸς ὑμᾶς. In PTebt. I 33, 2 [112a], we find the same usage: [φρόν]τισον οὖν ἵνα γένη(ται) ἀκολούθως.

In Romans 1:11, Paul expresses his desire to go to Rome: ἐπιποθῶ γὰρ ἰδεῖν ὑμᾶς, ἵνα τι μεταδῶ χάρισμα ὑμῖν πνευματικὸν εἰς τὸ στηριχθῆναι ὑμᾶς. This verse contains two final clauses: the first has a regular form, whereas the second has an infinitive with an article preceded by εἰς. An example of this usage can also be found in BGU III 747 II 20 [139p]: εἰς τὸ μήτε τ[ὴ]ν ἀπαίτησιν τῶν δημοσίων ἐμ[ποδ]ί[ζ]ε[σ]θαι.

In Revelation 8:3, we read καὶ ἐδόθη αὐτῷ θυμιάματα πολλά, ἵνα δώσει ταῖς προσευχαῖς τῶν ἁγίων πάντων. We notice here a final clause with the verb in the future indicative. As a proof of this particularity,[14] one can quote PAmh. II 144, 19–21 [Vp]: Ἐλπείδα δὲ ἔχομεν εἰς τὸν θ(εὸ)ν ἵνα αὐτὸς πρόνοιαν ἡμῶν ποι(ή)σει.

Jesus, when referring to his life (Jn. 10:18) emphasizes the power he has over it, says: ἐξουσίαν ἔχω θεῖναι αὐτήν, καὶ ἐξουσίαν ἔχω πάλιν λαβεῖν αὐτήν; one notices that the infinitive used is not preceded by τοῦ. In like manner, this usage is recorded in the papyri: e.g., in PTor. 1 VIII 25–26 [117a]: μηδεμίαν ἔχειν τινὰ ἐξουσίαν, μηδὲ τὸν Ἑρμίαν, ἐφάπτεσθαί τινος αὐτῶν ἐνγαίου.

In Ephesians 5:33, his well-known text on the duties of parents, Paul says to the husband and wife: πλὴν καὶ ὑμεῖς οἱ καθ᾽ ἕνα ἕκαστος τὴν ἑαυτοῦ γυναῖκα οὕτως ἀγαπάτω ὡς ἑαυτόν, ἡ δὲ γυνὴ ἵνα φοβῆται τὸν ἄνδρα. According to grammatical rules, the second member of this sentence, which clearly should be a final clause, is in fact an imperative clause.[15] To confirm this peculiar usage, one can quote PBrux 4, 17–21 [IV/Vp]: τὰ μέγιστά μοι δὲ χαριζόμενος εἴνα μετὰ πολλῆς σπουδῆς 'τοῦτο' ποιήσις καὶ ἀπόστιλε. Interestingly, we notice here the conjunction of two imperative verbal forms: one enunciated in its normal form, and the other with the subjunctive and ἵνα.[16]

Finally, we want to examine another case that is just as interesting, and has attracted the attention of specialists. At the present time, we do not claim to be able to offer a final solution to it, because we think it is difficult to do so *vi formae*,[17] and because the authors consulted were unable to provide us with an adequate explanation. In Mark 4:12, which concerns the reason for the use of parables, Isaiah is quoted (vv. 6, 9–10): ἵνα βλέποντες βλέπωσιν καὶ μὴ ἴδωσιν, καὶ ἀκούοντες ἀκούωσιν καὶ μὴ συνιῶσιν, νή ποτε ἐπιστρέψωσςιν καὶ ἀψεθῇ αὐτοῖς. We shall neither begin with the intrinsic exegetic discussion of this verse, nor recall that in Mark 4:33 Jesus is said to have spoken in parables in order to adapt himself to the capacity of his listeners; nor shall we lose sight of the parallel passage in Matthew 13:13, where the ὅτι causal is used. Nor do we mention that the causal use of ἵνα with the subjunctive is attested in Apolonio Discolo (IIp).[18] But, from the papyri (cf. Mandilaras § 590), one can put forward the unquestionable example found in PGiss 17, 5–6 [IIp]: Ἠγωνίασα, κύριε, οὐ μετρίως, ἵνα ἀκούσω ὅτι ἐνώθρευσας.

Having briefly examined some of the grammatical analogies between neotestamentary and then current popular Greek, we now intend to find out if these insights can also aid the exegesis of the New Testament. More precisely, we shall concentrate on the original text of 1 Thessalonians 5:23: Αὐτὸς δὲ ὁ θεὸς τῆς εἰρήνης ἁγιάσαι ὑμᾶς ὁλοτελεῖς, καὶ ὁλόκληρον τὸ πνεῦμα καὶ ἡ ψυχὴ καὶ τὸ σῶμα ἀμέμπτως ἐν τῇ παρουσίᾳ τοῦ κυρίου ἡμῶν Ἰησοῦ Χριστοῦ τηρηθείη. In this Pauline passage, there are three key words (σῶμα, ψυχή, and πνεῦμα) that have given rise to two interpretations: that of C. Masson and that of P.A. van Sempvoort.

Masson,[19] taking into account the liturgical character of the text and its link with other similar Pauline passages, says that the expression μετὰ τοῦ πνεύματος ὑμῶν ("with your spirit") is just a more solemn way of saying μεθ᾽ὑμῶν ("with you"). Therefore, in the text we are discussing, ὑμῶν τὸ πνεῦμα ("your spirit") is equivalent to ὑμεῖς ("you, your person"). And the words καὶ ἡ ψυχὴ καὶ τὸ σῶμα ("and the soul and the body") unfold the content of ὁλόκληρον τὸ πνεῦμα ("your whole person"). If we take into consideration that ὁλόκληρον refers more exactly to ὑμῶν τὸ πνεῦμα than to ψυχή and σῶμα because of the chiasmus resulting with the previous ὑμεῖς ὁλοτελεῖς, we could suggest the following translation: "que Dieu . . . vous sanctifie tout entiers, et que toute votre personne, . . . soit gardée!"

P.A. van Sempvoort[20] also relies on the datum "dass ὑμῶν τὸ πνεῦμα in den Briefen Pauli die Ich-Bedeutung haben kann." According to this datum, along with the fact that this pericope conveys a chain of Jewish thoughts consonant with a mold of Jewish diction, he also admits the existence of the chiasmus, which includes an alliteration (ὁλοτελεῖς and ὁλόκληρον). The first paragraph ends with ὁλόκληρον τὸ πνεῦμα, and the following begins with καὶ ἡ ψυχὴ, etc. He insists on the semantic strength of ὁλοτελεῖς and ὁλόκληρον, and gives them an adverbial meaning, thus translating the whole pericope: "Und der Gott des Friedens heilige euch gänzlich und in allen Teilen. Sowohl Seele als Leib sei beim Kommen unseres Jesu Christi untadelig bewahrt."

Even though I acknowledge the merit and the degree of progress of these new interpretations, I repeat that it might be of positive interest to find some traces of the Pauline trichotomy in the popular Greek of the time.[21]

Indeed, after examining the private Greek letters of the early Christian centuries, I can produce two texts proving the existence of this trichotomy. The first is the only one that proves without further declarations the existence of the Pauline elements to which reference is made. In POxy. VIII 1161 [Ivp], we find a brief and simple missive written by a poor sick woman on her bed of pain. The first and last words were mutilated. The fragment preserved thus begins (lines 1–7): . . . ας καὶ τῷ ἀγαθ[ῷ ἡμῶ]ν σωτῆρι καὶ τῷ οι[ἱ]ῷ αὐτοῦ τῷ ἠγαπημένῳ ὅπως οὗτοι πάντες β[ο]ηθήσωσιν ἡμῶν τῷ σώματι, τῇ ψυχῇ, τῷ [πν(εύματ)ι] πν(εύματι). The editor, A.S. Hunt (p. 265), translated the fragment as follows: ". . . [to our God] and gracious savior and to his beloved son, that they all may succour our body, soul, and spirit."

We find another letter in the papyrus PHarr. 107, which the editor, J. Enoch Powell, attributes to the third century, but which M. Naldini,[22] like H. Idris Bell, prefers to date from the beginning of that century, that is to say, around 200. This missive has no particular significance. A man named Besas writes to his mother, Mary, inquiring about her health and begging her not to forget to send him his garment for Easter day. The content of the letter is trivial, but its first lines (4–12) are quite important: Πρὸ μὲν πάντων εὔχωμαι τῷ πατρὶ θεῷ τῆς ἀληθείας καὶ τῷ παρακλήτῳ πνεύματι ὅς σὲ διαφυλάξωσιν καιτά τε ψυχὴν κα(ὶ) σῶμα καὶ πνεῦμα· τῷ μὲν σώματι ὑιγίαν, τῷ δὲ πνεύματι εὐθυμία(ν), τῇ δὲ ψυχῇ ζωὴν αἰώνιον. The editor translated these lines according to their traditional meaning: "Before all things I pray to our Father, the God of truth, and the Holy Ghost, the Comforter, that they may preserve you, in both soul and body and spirit, and give to your body health, to your spirit gladness, and to your soul life everlasting."

This opening salutation gave rise to various interpretations. G. Ghedini at first thought it was Gnostic,[23] but then definitely considered it Christian.[24] This opinion was shared, until H. Crouzel suggested an Origenian interpretation.[25] I do not personally share this view,[26] but think that this letter is authentically Christian, "senza tinta ereticale," as Ghedini would say.

Having said this, it is advisable to examine the word that is without doubt one of the New Testament words having a quite polyvalent meaning.[27] According to the lexicons, the use of the word πνεῦμα with a more specific meaning than the ordinary one "spirit," is not unfamiliar to neotestamentary language. Thus, F. Zorell[28] accepts the meaning: "*animus certo modo dispositus, sic vel aliter sentiens, animi dispositio, sensus, mens: Gesinnung.*" J.H. Thayer[29] also attributes to πνεῦμα a kind of disposition of the mind with a view to action and a certain dynamic tension: "*the disposition or influence which fills and governs the soul of any one; the efficient source of any power, affection, emotion, desire, etc.*"

W. Bauer[30] agrees with Zorell: "*d. geistige Haltung, d. Gesinnung.*" In addition to the biblical dictionaries, let us mention that L. Rocci[31] admits the meaning of a particular disposition of mind: "*spirito,* nel senso di *ardore, forza, veemenza.*" We therefore can assign to πνεῦμα the meaning "disposition of the mind in a given form, practical criteria, *moral attitude*" along with the corresponding way of behaving.

After this philological preamble, we return to PHarr. 107, and notice that, by taking into consideration the accumulated data, we can give a perfect interpretation of it. Indeed, in accordance with what we have just said, it would be translated as: ". . . may they keep you in [your] soul, [your] body and [your] moral attitude, [by giving] health to your body, strength to your moral attitude, and to your soul eternal life." Notice how perfectly the thought in the second part of the sentence is conjoined, because the practical moral attitude is good, due to the comfort received from above; and the soul will receive eternal life as a reward for its behavior. On the contrary, the two interpretations discussed do not seem to offer an adequate explanation of this text.[32]

Let us now examine the Pauline text, leaving aside the already mentioned possibility of dividing it into two parts, although such a division would not complicate our interpretation. I think, however, that it is advisable to recall the context that immediately precedes the pericope we are now studying. In verses 21 and 22, Paul gives some final advice concerning putting into practice precise norms of moral conduct: πάντα δὲ δοκιμάζετε, τὸ καλὸν κατέχετε· ἀπὸ παντὸς εἴδους πονεροῦ ἀπέχεσθε.

Thus, by including these verses, the literal translation of the text would read as follows: "Put all things to the test: keep what is good and avoid every kind of evil. May the God of peace make you holy in every way and keep your whole being—moral attitude, soul and body—free from every fault until the coming of our Lord Jesus Christ." On the basis of this literal translation, we could render Paul's thought in a freer form: "Take a course of action which, while allowing you to put all things to the test, urges you to keep what is good and to refrain from what is evil. And may the God of peace himself totally sanctify you. And may your whole behavior, which manifests itself both in the activities of your soul and in those of your body, remain beyond reproach until the coming of our Lord Jesus Christ."

The interpretation we suggest fits well into the *immediate* context of the epistle. And with respect to the thematic, we can say that it also is in harmony with its *mediate* context. We should recall Paul's concern for his beloved community at Thessalonica: he did not want it to be influenced by the sly insinuations of Jesus and the gentiles. That is why, despite the joy brought to him by the good report of Timothy concerning the Christians there, the apostle exhorts them to chastity, work, Christian living, overcoming anxiety about the coming of the Lord, and fulfilling God's will. Therefore, it is a *normative* letter, marked by orientation and advice about moral behavior. For this reason, this final exhortation on the upright conduct of his dear Thessalonians appears to be consonant with the tone of the epistle.

Finally, we find in a letter of Saint Jerome[33] a confirmation of the relevance of our interpretation. After presenting the text according to the traditional doctrine and mentioning as well the resurrection, Jerome adds: "Sunt qui ex anima tantum, et corpore subsistere hominem disserentes, spiritum in eo tertium, no substantiam velint intellegi, sed efficientiam, per quam et mens in nobis et sensus, et cogitatio, et animus appellantur, utique non sunt tot substantiae quot nomina." Now, what is this "efficientia," thanks to which there is in us what we call mind, conscience, thought, or soul? Could not this text of Jerome, which reflects the opinion of a whole group of then current interpreters, correspond, in its dynamic content, to the meaning we have suggested as appropriate to πνεῦμα?[34]

As was mentioned, until now I have tried to highlight some of the numerous links that can be found between the neotestamentary and the popular koiné. This paper, because of the bounds imposed on it, could not be exhaustive. Nevertheless, I would say that it sheds enough light so as to admit that there is an interdependence between these two kinds of Greek. I conclude by recalling the wise statement of Vatican II in *DV* 12, which, as was noted in the beginning, insists on the necessity of knowing the speech patterns of the people whose culture influenced the Bible. These patterns are available to us in the papyri, and through them we can attain a far more correct and precise understanding of the Word of God.

Translated from Spanish by Louis-Bertrand Raymond.

Notes

1. *DV* 12.

2. AAS 35, 305: "Atque haud minoris momenti est inventio et inquisitio, adeo frequens aetate hac nostra, papyrorum, quae ad cognoscendas litteras, institutiones publicas et privatam, temporis praesertim Servatoris Nostri, tantopere valuere."

3. *Bibelstudien. Beiträge, zumeist aus den Papyri und Inschriften, zur Geschichte der Sprache, des Schriftums und der Religion des hellenistischen Judentum und der Urchristentums* (Marburg, 1895); *Neue Bibelstudien, Sprachgeschichtliche Beiträge, zumeist aus den Papyri und Inschriften, zur Erklärung des Neuen Testaments* (Marburg, 1897); *Licht vom Osten. Das Neue Testament und die neuentdeckten Texte der hellenistisch-römischen Welt* (Tübingen, 1923[4]).

4. L. Radermacher, *Neutestamentliche Grammatik. Das Griechisch des Neuen Testaments im Zusammenhang mit der Volkssprache* (Tübingen, 1925[2]), 18.

5. Cf., for example, F.-M. Abel, *Grammaire du grec biblique suivie d'un choix de papyrus* (Paris, 1927), XXXVII: "Le grec du N.T., jadis stigmatisé comme un monstre, surtout par des esprits ne jurant que par l'attique, a été tiré de son isolement depuis le dépouillement des papyrus et des inscriptions"; A.E. Springhetti, *Introductio historica-grammatica in graecitatem Novi Testamenti* (Rome, 1966), 52; etc.

6. F. Blass, A. Debrunner, and F. Rehkopf, *Grammatik des* *neutestamentlichen Griechisch* (Göttingen, 1976[14]), 3: "Das ntl Griechisch ist als nicht-literarische und nicht-klassizistische Fachprosa mit den unliterarischen Papyri und mit Schriftstellern wie etwa Epiktet (60–140[P]) zu vergleichen." Although he practically leaves aside the papyri, cf. also M. Reiser, *Syntax und Stil des Markus-evangeliums im Licht der hellenistischen Volksliteratur* (WUNT II 1; Tübingen, 1984).

    7. G.H.R. Horsley, "Divergent Views on the Nature of the Greek of the Bible," *Bib* 65 (1984), 403.

    8. One could perhaps blame the following assertions of J. López Facal for boasting in that sense, in "Diccionarios de papiros. Problemas, existencias, deficiencias," in F.R. Adrados, E. Gangutia, J. López Facal, and C. Serrano Aybar (eds.), *Introducción a la lexicografía griega* (Manuales y Anejos de "Emerita" 33, Madrid, 1977), 163: "Gracias a los papiros podemos conocer la koiné popular, reflejo más o menos fiel de la lengua hablada en la época. Después de su descubrimiento se han derrumbado una serie de mitos, como el de la existencia de un llamado griego bíblico, que, hoy sabemos, no es otra cosa que la koiné popular que reproducen los papiros documentales, con algún escaso semitismo." This study of López Facal corresponds to paragraph II 3 of the book quoted, which is a summary of the methodology used to publish the monumental Greek-Spanish dictionary. Since 1962, the latter has been underway at the *Antonio Nebrija* Institute of Madrid, under the direction of F. Rodríguez Adrados; the first fascicule has appeared: *Diccionario griego-español, volumen I* (Madrid, 1980).

    9. Cf., G. Bonaccorsi, *Primi saggi di Filologia neotestamentaria I* (Turin, 1933), XLVII; A.E. Springhetti, *Introductio historica-grammatica in graecitatem Novi Testamenti*, 53; C.F.D. Moule, *An Idiom Book of New Testament Greek* (Cambridge, 1953), 3–4; M. Naldini, *Il Cristianesimo in Eggito. Lettere private nei papiri dei secoli II–IV* (Florence, 1968), 48. By rejecting the terminology used to point out the characteristics of the Greek of that time, it has been recently defined in a far more radical sense by L. Rydbeck, *Fachprosa, vermeintliche Volkssprache und Neues Testament* (Acta Universitatis Upsaliensis, Studia Graeca Upsaliensia, Upsala, 1967). Despite the efforts of the author and the undeniable qualities of his book, serious objections can be raised against it, as did the review of H. Thesleff, *Gnomon* 42 (1970), 551–555.

    10. O. Montevecchi, *La Papirologia* (Turin, 1973), 77.

    11. Cf. J. O'Callaghan, "Mt 8,1: Discusión crítica," in *Palabra y Vida. Homenaje a José Alonso Díaz en su 70 cumpleaños* (Madrid, 1984), 133–134. Because from now on some papyri will be quoted, I must point out that the initials ordinarily found in the papyrological publications will be used in this article. One may consult, for instance, Montevecchi's book mentioned in the previous note. The Roman numeral in square brackets indicates the century of the papyrus, the arab numeral indicates the year, and the two small letters tell whether the era is pre-Christian or Christian: a ("ante Christum natum"), p ("post Christum natum"). This article is not a strictly specialized paper; I do not take into account the infralinear points found in the texts of the papyri; however, I do reproduce them in their original phonetics and spellings.

12. B.G. Mandilaras, *The Verb in the Greek Non-Literary Papyri* (Athens, 1973), 335: "The articular infinitive in the genitive is used . . . *with verbs of bearing, hindering, preventing*, etc. like ἀνέχομαι, κωλύω, ὀκνέω, and καταπαύω."

13. The classic Greek, instead of ὅτι and the indicative would require a future or aorist infinitive; cf. M. Naldini, *Il Cristianesimo in Egitto*, 87.

14. Strictly speaking, it would not be incongruous that here ποι-⟨ή⟩σει comes from ποι⟨ή⟩ση or more clearly from ποι⟨ή⟩ση, although the presumption is in favor of the future; cf. J. O'Callaghan, *Cartas cristianas griegas del siglo V* (Biblioteca Histórica de la Biblioteca Balmes II, XXV) (Barcelona, 1963), 88; and for other similar cases, G. Ghedini, *Lettere cristiane dai papiri greci del III e IV secolo* (Milan, 1923), 62, where the author is inclined to favor the indicative. Notwithstanding, for the changes η > ει, cf. F.T. Gignac, *A Grammar of the Greek Papyri of the Roman and Byzantine Periods I. Phonology* (Milan, 1976), 239–240.

15. M. Zerwick, *Graecitas biblica* (Rome, 1960[4]), 130: "ἵνα revera iam in NT interdum imperativo aequiparari ostenditur." Cf. F. Blass, A. Debrunner, and F. Rehkopf, *Grammatik des neutestamentlichen Griechisch*, 313.

16. This case of the presence of two imperatives (normal and in the subjunctive with ἵνα) has already been examined by grammarians ("the alternation of the ἵνα clause and the imperative"); cf. B.G. Mandilaras, *The Verb in the Greek Non-Literary Papyri*, 264.

17. I think this is a good reason for emphasizing the ambiguity of this usage. Let us compose, for instance, the following sentence: Δίδωμί σοι τοῦτο, ἵνα ἧς ἀγαθός. Because of its form, this sentence can thus be translated: "I give you this so that you be good," or "I give you this because you are good." Due to its form, this sentence is therefore ambiguous. *Grammatically* speaking, the donation can be considered as inciting to goodness, or, also, as rewarding goodness. I do not think we can resolve the question as to whether the clause is final or causal by taking into consideration only its syntactic form. Consequently, if we have at our disposal no other criteria coming from the characteristic meaning of the verbs used, from the context into which the sentence is inserted or from the particular circumstances that gave rise to it, this sentence by itself will not be able to decide which of the two meanings should prevail.

18. *Grammatici graeci* (ed. G. Uhlig, Teubner, Leipzig, 1910), II 2, 377, 4–5; 382, 3–4.

19. *Les deux épîtres de saint Paul aux Thessaloniciens* (Commentaire du Nouveau Testament XIa, Neuchâtel, 1957), 77–78.

20. "Eine stilistische Lösung einer alten Schwierigkeit in 1 Thess. V. 23," *NTS* 7 (1960–1961), 262–265.

21. Many interpreters deny that in this passage a true philosophical distinction is made between the elements making up the human person. Cf., for instance, J. Goitia, "Noción dinámica del ηνεῦμα en los libros sagrados," *EstBíb* 15 (1956), 170; S. Obiols, *Epístoles de sant Pau* (La Bíblia XXI, Montserrat, 1930), 261; J. Leal, "Cartas a los Tesalonicenses. Traducción y comentario," in *La Sagrada Escritura* (BAC 211, Madrid, 1962), 929–930.

22. *Il Cristianesimo in Egitto*, 76.

23. "Note a tre lettere cristiane in P.Har," *Aeg.* 17 (1937), 98–99.

24 "La lettera P.Har. 107," *Aeg.* 20 (1940), 209–211.

25. "La lettre du P.Har. 107 et la théologie d'Origène," *Aeg.* 49 (1969), 138–143.

26. J. O'Callaghan, "Sobre la interpretación de P.Har. 107," *Aeg.* 52 (1972), 152–157. Cf. B.F. Harris, "Biblical Echoes and Reminiscences in Christian Papyri, in *Proceedings of the XIV International Congress of Papyrologists, Oxford, 24–31 July 1974* (London, 1975), 157.

27. P. Gächter, "Zum Pneumabegriff des hl. Paulus," *ZKT* 53 (1920), 345–408; F. Puzo, "Significado de la palabra 'pneuma' en san Pablo," *EstBíb* 1 (1941), 437–460; C.H. Dodd, "Some problems of New Testament Translation," *ExpTim* 72 (1960–1961), 271–272.

28. *Lexicon graecum Novi Testamenti* (Paris, 1963³), col. 1084.

29. *A Greek-English Lexicon of the New Testament* (Edinburgh, 1908⁴), 523.

30. *Greichisch-deutsches Wörterbuch zu den Schriften des Neuen Testaments und der übrigen urchristlichen Literatur* (Berlin, 1958⁵), col. 1340.

31. *Vocabolario greco-italiano* (Milan/Città di Castello, 1970²²), 1516.

32. Cf. J. O'Callagahn, ¿"Una neuva interpretación de 1 Th 5,23?" *SPap* 4 (1965), 22–23.

33. *Epist. 120. Ad Hedibiam* 12; *PL* 22, 1006.

34. Cf. *Sagrada Biblia. Versión crítica sobre los textos hebreo, arameo y griego*, F. Cantera Burgos and M. Iglesias González (eds). (BAC Maior 10, Madrid, 1975). In the translation of the New Testament, M. Iglesias accepts the interpretation here proposed, and, in the corresponding footnote, he explains the translation adopted (p. 1360): "La traducción VUESTRA ACTITUD MORAL (o *vuestra disposición de ánimo*) se basa en la terminología de cartas cristianas de los primeros siglos conservadas en papiros" (J. O'Callaghan).

CHAPTER 8

Interpretation of Holy Scripture
in the Spirit in Which
It Was Written (*Dei Verbum* 12c)

Ignace de la Potterie, S.J.

Summary

The principle recommended by *Dei Verbum* 12c for a theological and ecclesial interpretation of Scripture has hardly received any study since the Council. The Constitution did not introduce anything new on this point, but simply returned to a principle often found in Tradition. The present article proposes a commentary on this principle: (1) starting with its patristic background (Origen, St. Jerome), and (2) carrying out a thorough analysis of the whole of *Dei Verbum* 12, which makes a clear distinction between technical work on the biblical text and its Christian and ecclesial interpretation. In the conclusion, the author considers why these conciliar recommendations on the Christian interpretation of holy Scripture have not yet been truly "received" into contemporary Catholic exegesis.

———
———

In Chapter III of the Dogmatic Constitution on Divine Revelation *Dei Verbum*, number 12 describes how Holy Scripture should be interpreted. In the various translations, the text is given in three paragraphs (the official text had four: see the following), the second of which recalls the requirements of critical exegesis (the study of literary forms and the historical circumstances of the texts), and the following paragraph describes the criteria for a Christian and ecclesial exegesis. This third paragraph is made up of three sentences, but only the first is concerned with the theological principle and specific norms that must guide the believing interpreter of the Scriptures. It reads as follows:

> But since sacred Scripture must be read and interpreted in the same Spirit in which it was written [*sed, cum Sacra Scriptura eodem Spiritu quo scripta est etiam leganda et interpretanda sit*], no less attention must be devoted to the content and unity of the whole of Scripture, taking into account the Tradition of the entire Church and the analogy of faith, if we are to derive their true meaning from the sacred texts.

Apart from the first proposition (the causal phrase beginning with "since"), this long sentence was already found in essence in the third schema, which was produced by the doctrinal commission prior to the third session of the Council, which opened on 14 September 1964. On the other hand, the general principle indicated at the outset ("cum Sacra Scriptura . . . interpretandi sit") was not introduced until the very end of the fourth and last session (October 1965). And it was with this important addition that the definitive text was promulgated shortly afterward, on 18 November of the same year.[1] We do not intend carrying out a detailed study of the circumstances leading up to the insertion of this phrase at the eleventh hour, only a few days before the official close of Vatican II (which took place on 8 December 1965), although we shall in due course give some details of these circumstances when we are trying to indicate its precise significance and consequences. However, our main aim is to study this great theological principle in itself and in its own context, and to show its full importance for the Christian interpretation of Scripture.

Such an analysis needs to be undertaken, for, strange to say, in the commentaries on the Constitution *Dei Verbum* that have appeared so far, the text in question has not received any very close study, and has in some cases been completely ignored.[2] In the course of the twenty years since the Council, the only author to have examined it in detail is Divo Barsotti, in his address to the Twentieth Italian Bible Week, which was consecrated to *Dei*

Verbum.[3] He then developed his text into a slim volume published later: La parola e lo spirito. Saggi sull'esegesi spirituale.[4] More
recently, however, this theological principle was the subject of
the doctrinal dissertation of M.A. Molina Palma, which was
presented at the Biblical Institute in 1985 under the title La
Interpetación de la Escritura en el Espíritu. Estudio historico y
teologico de un principio hermenéutico de la Constitución "Dei
Verbum" 12.[5] The importance of this work lies in the fact that for
the first time the detailed history of the theological principle
indicated by Vatican II (that "Scripture must be read and interpreted in the same Spirit in which it was written") has been
reconstructed. The ground covered by this historical investigation stretches from the beginning of the Church until the sixteenth century, and the documentation gathered together enables us to gain a clear picture of the variations this Christian
hermeneutic principle has seen, especially in two critical periods:
the twelfth to thirteenth centuries, with the challenging of the
dialectic system and the rise of the scholastic system,[6] and then
most especially in the sixteenth century, with the Reformation
and the Council of Trent.

However, the principle indicated by Vatican II aims at a direct
revival of the great patristic tradition. Indeed, in a note to the
passage under consideration here, the Council refers to the Encyclical Spiritus Paraclitus of Benedict XV (1920), but the latter is
itself based on a passage from St. Jerome's commentary on the
letter to the Galatians.[7] We shall examine this passage more
closely in due course. Here, however, we should note that in the
prologue to his commentary, Jerome recognized that he had followed that of Origen, which has since been lost.[8] We must
therefore examine the other works of the great Alexandrian to
see how he himself understood this norm for the interpretation of
Scripture. Origen and Jerome will therefore be the two main
witnesses whom we shall examine in order to gain a better understanding of the background of the conciliar text. This will constitute the first part of our study.

In the second part, we shall analyze the principle more carefully in the specific context of the Constitution. And we wish to
conclude by drawing some methodological consequences from
these data for the future development of Christian exegesis in the
present period that has been opened by Vatican II.

The Patristic Background of the Text

In a recent article, Y.M.-J. Congar writes: "It has constantly been stated within the Church that the Word of God—Scripture—can only be understood through the same Spirit who inspired it; thus there must always be unity between object and subject."[9] With a view to illustrating this principle, we shall, as we have said, cite the two main witnesses of the patristic era, one from the Greek world and the other from the Latin tradition.

Origen

1. The hermeneutical norm recalled by Father Congar was passed down in the West in the formulation given it by St. Jerome. However, Jerome most probably borrowed this formulation from Origen, and Origen was certainly the first to produce such clear expressions regarding the role of the Spirit in the interpretation of Scripture. In this sense, the Alexandrian Master is to be found right at the beginning of the whole tradition.

2. The fundamental principle on which he bases himself is that of the inspiration of the biblical text.[10] Unlike modern scholars who are most interested in the psychology of the inspired authors, Origen adopts a theological point of view. He sees the Bible itself as the work of the Spirit and as the place or sphere of the presence of the Spirit: "The Spirit dwells in the Scriptures; we can say that he is their basis."[11] It follows that Scripture contains a deeper meaning than its obvious one, and this is the meaning intended by the Holy Spirit—the spiritual meaning. Thus, Origen writes:

> The Scriptures were written under the action of the Spirit of God, and apart from their obvious sense [*qui in manifesto est*], they have another sense, which escapes most people. For what is described there is both the figure of certain mysteries and the image of the divine realities.[12]

The connection and relationship between the obvious sense and the spiritual meaning also depend closely on the work of the Spirit, for he acts on both of these two levels. This conception of Origen has been analyzed very well by M. Harl:

Origen's originality lies in the fact that he places himself, if we can put it like this, by the side of the Spirit as the latter inspires the Scriptures, and envisages the aims and method involved in the work of the Spirit in inspiring the writers of the sacred texts. With great assurance, he describes what he calls the two "aims" (σκοποί) that presided over the inspiration of the texts. The main "aim" was that of revealing to men the "mysteries" useful for their salvation; the secondary aim was to "hide" these mysteries under the guise of easily read texts, historical narratives, and collections of laws.[13]

The implications of such a conception for the task of interpreting Scripture can immediately be seen. When a person is faced with a biblical text and really wants to *understand* it in depth, he must realize that it not only has an historical, literal meaning, but also a deeper, hidden meaning—a spiritual sense intended by the Spirit. Origen supports this statement with a reference to the opening of Ezekiel's warning to false prophets: "Thus says the Lord: 'Woe to those who speak out of their own heart [ἀπὸ καρδίας αὐτῶν] and see absolutely nothing'" (Ez. 13:3, Septuagint). Speaking "out of one's own *heart*" (Septuagint) or "out of one's own *spirit*" (Hebrew) is what false prophets do, whereas, according to Ezekiel, the true prophet speaks from the Holy Spirit. Origen comments: "Just as the person who received the order to say these things needed the Holy Spirit, in the same way, the person who wants to explain what is secretly signified therein [*latenter significata*] needs the same Spirit [*sic eodem Spiritu opus est ei*]."[14]

He goes on to say that what was true for the words of the prophets in Israel applies equally to the words of Christ in the gospels and to those of the apostles.[15] Hence, those in the Church who teach the words of Christ must do so in conformity with the sense intended by Christ, for he too spoke under the inspiration of the Spirit.

If somebody says what the Lord Jesus Christ said and understood, and this person speaks from that place [*in eo loco*] in which he [Jesus] spoke when he taught, then he is not speaking from his own heart [*non de corde suo*]; it is from the Holy Spirit [*de Spiritu Sancto*] that he speaks the words of Jesus, the Son of God. If he is obedient to the will of the Holy Spirit,

who spoke in the apostles, then he speaks not from his own
heart but from the heart of the Holy Spirit [de corde Spiritus
sancti].[16]

Thus, we have a fundamental norm, which clearly expresses the
hermeneutical principle with which we are concerned:

He who reads Scripture and receives it *otherwise than as it was
written*, sees Scripture in a false way. But he who hears Scripture in conformity with the understanding of the truth and
interprets it, in this way, sees the truth.[17]

However, we would once again ask what the practical consequences of this are for the understanding of Scripture. We must
"consider in the spirit what was written by the Spirit."[18] The
twofold task of the pontiff and priest will thus be: "To learn of
God by reading the divine Scriptures and by meditating on them
with great frequency, or teach the people. But he must teach
what he has learned of God, not from his own heart or any
human sense, but what the Spirit teaches."[19] Origen's thought
with regard to biblical interpretation is therefore as follows:
"That which comes from the Spirit is fully understood only
through the action of the Spirit."[20]

3. How are we to evaluate this position of the Alexandrian
Master? The most striking aspect is that the hermeneutical principle he proposes in these different texts for understanding the
Scriptures is in most cases described from the subjective and
existential viewpoint of the people involved (first the figures of
biblical history, then the biblical authors, and lastly the interpreters of the Bible). The prophets, Christ, and the apostles—and
similarly the authors of the Old and New Testament writings
(but therefore also their texts, in other words the whole of
Scripture)—are all inhabited by the Spirit. Hence, the interpreter can only understand the Scriptures correctly if this same
Spirit in turn dwells in him.

In this connection, people have been led to speak of interior
illumination or mystical experience in Origen.[21] According to
M. Harl, the most individual and personal aspect of Origen is
"his religious faith, and, beyond his scientific work, *a mysticism of
exegesis.*"[22] But surely this is going too far, because in this case
Christian understanding of the Scriptures would be confined to

certain privileged people who had received special charisms?
However, one thing is certain: for Origen, true understanding of
the Scriptures requires conversion of heart, and therefore *faith*.
H. de Lubac puts it very well when he says:

> Only the Church understands the Scriptures: the Church, in
> other words, this portion of humanity that is converted to the
> Lord: "Ecclesiae ad Deum conversæ ablatum est velamen."[23]
> The spiritual interpretation of the Scriptures is the interpreta-
> tion "that the Spirit gives to the Church."[24] And each person
> can make this his own to the extent that he participates in this
> movement of conversion of the Church.[25]

True understanding of the Scriptures is therefore possible only for
the person who is converted to the Lord, in faith: "Far be it from
us to think," says Origen, "that an unbeliever may see the word
of God."[26] Such understanding calls for the interpreter to participate in the action of the Spirit, the sense of the Church. From
this point of view, we can say, with Origen, that it is reserved to
the saints,[27] because the word of God can be understood in all its
depths only by those who believe, who pray, and who have an
overall understanding of the mystery of salvation.

However, there is a second corollary in this teaching, and one
that is more objective and more easily verified. It concerns the
Bible itself, considered as a whole, and is the concept of the
unity of the whole of Scripture. Let us quote H. de Lubac once
again:

> The bond of all Scripture to the Spirit is a guarantee of its
> unity. And this unity should be understood in the simplest and
> deepest sense. It is not something that we bring about by
> collecting the inspired books together after we have recog-
> nized how they are linked to one another. Ontologically speak-
> ing, it comes first.[28]

The unity of Scripture is a result of something that is *interior* to
the writings: it is "the intention, the 'will,' the guiding thought,
which orients the word without suppressing it, and thus, whatever it may be individually, makes it part of a unified movement."[29]

There is yet another consequence of these principles: the

"truth" of the texts, their deep meaning, their spiritual significance, are always found "beyond what is written."[30] Origen expresses this by making free use of a saying cited by Paul in 1
Corinthians 4:6 about "not going beyond what is written." Human words are incapable of giving perfect expression to the divine mysteries. In support of this conviction, Origen also bases
himself on the concluding verse of St. John's Gospel (21:25),
where it is said that "the world itself could not contain" all the
books that would have to be written "to tell what the Lord has
done." However, for Origen and for many others after him, "this
impossibility applies not so much to the number of facts described as to their magnitude and spiritual depth: man cannot
understand and fully express the whole breadth of the significance of Christ's words and actions."[31]

Even so, there is no reason to conclude that this depth is to be
sought outside the Scriptures: "It is . . . *in the very text of the
Scriptures* that the reader who has 'the spirit of Christ' will discover 'what is beyond what is written' "[32] The spiritual meaning
of the sacred text must be sought in the *interiority* of the letter,
within the *depths* of the literal sense.

Most of these concepts, and especially the last, would be
found again in the Latin world of St. Jerome.

St. Jerome

When the Constitution *Dei Verbum* states the hermeneutical
principle that the Scriptures must be interpreted in the Spirit in
which they were written, it makes formal reference to St.
Jerome's commentary on Galatians 5:19–21.[33] However, the
principle is also found elsewhere in the same commentary and in
other of the great Latin Doctor's writings. We shall first present
these different passages, and then on their basis consider the
implications of this principle for the interpretation of the Scriptures, as this whole question appears in Jerome's perspective.

1. The first text to be cited is Jerome's interpretation of
Galatians 1:7. In this part of the epistle, Paul is polemicizing
against the Christians of the churches of Galatia who want to
turn "to a different gospel" (1:6). Certain agitators were stirring
things up, and trying to "pervert the gospel of Christ" (Gal. 1:7).
Jerome comments:

They want, he says, to alter, to overthrow, to pervert the gospel of Christ, but they cannot do so. . . . Whoever interprets the gospel in a spirit and mentality other than those in which it was written [*alio interpretatur spiritu et mente quam scriptum est*] disturbs believers and perverts the gospel of Christ; whatever is in front, he puts behind, and whatever is behind, he puts in front. If a person follows nothing but the letter [*tantum litteram sequitur*], he places what is in front, behind; if a person accepts the interpretations of the Jews, he places what was according to its nature made to be in front [*ex natura sua in faciem constituta sunt*], behind [*post tergum*].[34]

The imagery Jerome uses here is somewhat paradoxical, but evocative: the contrast behind/in front may have been suggested by the contrast in the history of salvation between what for us Christians is "behind" us (that is, the old law), and what is "in front of" us (the gospel). There is certainly the contrast between the obsolete elements of the law and its true spirit. The "behind" of the law (*tergum*) is the letter alone, and the true "face" (*facies*) it must show to the believer is the spirit in which it was written (here the Holy Spirit is not being referred to as such). This amounts to saying that the only true and definitive meaning of Scripture—the meaning it takes on in the light of the gospel—is its spiritual one.

The second passage in which the principle is expressly formulated is the one referred to in *Dei Verbum*, and is found in St. Jerome's commentary on Galatians 5:19–21. Here Paul is no longer concerned with the contrast between the law and the gospel, but with the moral behavior of Christians. He contrasts the works of the flesh with the fruit of the Spirit, which is one: the love that manifests itself in different forms (Gal. 5:22–23). Among the disorders of the flesh, the apostle draws special attention to the divisions that demonstrate the absence of love: "enmity, strife, jealousy, anger, rivalries, dissension, schisms" (v. 20). Jerome translates the last two words (διχοστασίαι and αἱρέσεις) as *dissensiones* and *haereses*, and then broadens the horizon to observe that dissension can sometimes arise in interpretation of the Scriptures, and this can lead to heresies, which are works of the flesh; αἱρεσις means "choice," in other words, each person opts for the teaching that seems best to him, whereas in fact he is choosing the worst. St. Jerome concludes:

Even if he does not stray from the Church, anyone who . . . understands Scripture otherwise than in the *sense* demanded by *the Holy Spirit in whom it was written* can be called a heretic; his choice belongs to the works of the flesh, for he has chosen the worst.[35]

A Christian's acceptance of a heretical teaching is a work of the flesh and not a fruit of the Spirit, and it cannot have been inspired by the Spirit who inspired the Scriptures.

In the two texts considered thus far, the principle is given in a negative form, with a view to warning against Judaicizing deviations in the Galatians. However, in his commentary on Mark's Gospel, Jerome gives a positive version, in his explanation of the account of the Transfiguration (Mk. 9:2): "*After six days.* Pray to the Lord that I may interpret these words in the same spirit [*eodem spiritu*] in which they were spoken."[36] A little earlier, he has warned his listeners how important it is, in this episode, to reach its theological and spiritual meaning: "*This is my beloved Son.* . . . These words describe an historical event. . . . We do not deny the history, but we prefer the spiritual understanding." He wants to follow the example of Paul who, for the episode of Sarah and Agar, "did not deny history, but showed its mystery."[37]

2. We must now try to discern precisely what interpretation of the Scriptures "in the Spirit in which they were written"—that is, their spiritual interpretation—means for Jerome.

a. He provides us with a first series of indications that enable us to see what this principle means in the *objective* perspective of the content of the Scriptures.

An image frequently found in Jerome (and also in most of the other Latin Fathers,[38] where it plays a very important role) is the contrast between the exterior and interior aspects of the biblical text:

According to Paul, the person who truly understands the law is not the one who sees its surface, but the one who perceives and penetrates its interior [*medullam ejus introspicit*]. Anyone who, like the Galatians, follows only the outer shell does not understand the law.[39]

This is also true of all heretics, such as Marcion and Basilides: "They do not possess the gospel of God, because they do not have the Holy Spirit, without whom even the gospel remains merely human." And here is the decisive text with regard to this first aspect of the question: "Let us not think that the gospel lies in the *words* of the Scriptures: it is in their *meaning;* not in the *surface,* but in the *marrow;* not in the *leaves* of words, but in the *root of understanding* [*in radice rationis*]."[40] For the Holy Spirit, and thus the meaning of the Scriptures, are hidden in the letter, and constitute its depth and its mystery.[41]

Like St. Paul before him (Gal. 2:5, 14; Col. 1:5), Jerome also refers to this hidden sense as the truth of the gospel or of the Scriptures. At Antioch, when Peter was influenced by the Judaicizing tendencies of certain people and wanted to follow the precepts of the law, he was not walking "according to the truth of the gospel."[42] It would be a mistake to think that this Pauline expression—which was taken up and commented on by Jerome, but which Paul himself had developed on the basis of the Jewish apocalyptic tradition (the unveiling of the mystery of God)[43]—could be interpreted solely on the conceptual level as a *doctrine* formulated in the gospel, like, for example, the doctrine of the abrogation of the law. The "truth" of the gospel is something different, something deeper, more interior, and more spiritual, which has been revealed to believers. St. Jerome explains very clearly that this "truth" is found "not in the letter but in the spirit [*non . . . in littera, sed in spiritu*], not in the fleshly sense but in the spiritual understanding, not in the Judaism that is visible but in that which is hidden (cf. Rom. 2:28–29)."[44] Thus, without the grace of the Holy Spirit people are not capable of finding the truth.[45] We must therefore leave behind us the prefigurations and "move to the *truth* of the Scriptures, to their *spirit.*"[46] The truly free man, says Jerome, following Origen, is the one who "in a deeper sense follows the spirit and the truth [*spiritum et veritatem sequitur*]."[47]

This truth and spirit, which are contrasted with the letter, are the spiritual meaning of the Scriptures. Jerome sees another image of this in the episode of the barren fig tree (Mk. 11:12–14): this fig tree bore "leaves, and not fruit; words, and not the sense; the Scriptures, but not *the understanding of the Scriptures.* . . . This fig tree represents the synagogue of the Jews: it has only the words, but not the understanding of the Scriptures."[48] We must also move beyond the historical and literal sense if we want to understand the healing of the blind man at Bethsaida (Mk. 8:22–

26) correctly: "The story is clear, and the literal sense obvious. Let us seek the spirit."[49] This is a general rule for Jerome in any interpretation of the words of the gospels: "To the letter we must join the *spirit;* everything that seems cold at first glance is warmed when it is touched."[50]

However, further explanation is required. What does this "truth" of the gospel and of the Scriptures—this interior sense of the texts, this spirit—basically lead us to? The answer cannot be in any doubt, even if Jerome does not very often express it as such: the spiritual meaning of the Scriptures is their hidden relationship to the *mystery* of Christ.[51] Here we might quote the famous saying: "Ignorance of the Scriptures is ignorance of Christ."[52] We are not concerned with some simple historical knowledge of Jesus, but with a spiritual knowledge, in other words, knowledge of his mystery. And only "the spiritual man" (1 Cor. 2:15) possesses this type of knowledge:

> For us, the spiritual man, who judges all things and is judged by no man, is the one who knows all the mysteries of the Scriptures and understands them in a sublime manner: *he sees Christ [Christum . . . videns]* in the divine books and takes no account of Jewish tradition.[53]

Jerome also sees this teaching in the episode of the Transfiguration, where Moses and Elijah (the law and the prophets) spoke with Jesus. He goes on to say that in the splendor of this sun, which is Christ, the light of the two lamps on either side of him—the law and the prophets—faded away to nothing.

> I am not speaking against the law and the prophets. Indeed, I praise them, for they announce Christ. I read the law and the prophets in such a way that I do not remain in the law and the prophets, but come to Christ through them.[54]

b. However, interpretation of the Bible "in the Spirit in which it was written" also entails *subjective* requirements, presupposing an inferior disposition and openness on the part of the person who is interpreting the Scriptures.

In one of his letters, Jerome explains this in connection with the interpretation of the Letter to the Romans: "The whole of the Letter to the Romans needs interpretation. It is enveloped in so much obscurity that in order to understand it we need the help of the Holy Spirit, who made use of the Apostle in order to dictate [*dictavit*] all these things."[55] Without the grace of the Spirit, we cannot reach the truth of the Scriptures and of the gospel. Elsewhere, in a text already cited above, Jerome bases what he is saying on the text of 1 Corinthians 4:6, and insists that the interpreter of the Scriptures must be a spiritual person.[56] It will be remembered that Origen also placed great emphasis on this requirement.

Conclusion

At the outset of this first section, we quoted an expression of Father Congar with regard to the theological principle that must govern any Christian interpretation of the Scriptures: ". . . there must always be unity between object and subject."[57] However, the texts we have collected from Origen and Jerome indicate that this expression needs to be expanded on and nuanced. The relationship between the "object" of the *Scriptures* and the "subject" of the *intepreter* is not the only one, for there is also another "subject" on the Scripture side: the figure of the sacred writer. Further, the action of the Spirit is exercised in both. And, lastly, there is a special relationship between the word of God in the *text* of the Scriptures, and the personal Word of God incarnated within history, that is, Christ, the Word made flesh. We must, of course, speak of "the unity of object and subject," but this also entails the unity of christology and pneumatology, the unity of sacred writer and interpreter, the unity of the persons of the sacred writer or the interpreter or the Spirit, but also of the letter of the Scriptures and the Spirit. Thus, we can see that here we are faced with various complex relations and tensions between exteriority and interiority, and the fact that they operate through these different elements means that any analysis is particularly difficult.

Origen places the main emphasis on the role of the Spirit and the "subjective" aspect of the norm of intepretation. In all cases, it is thus the Spirit who is the principle of interiority, and this applies equally to the prophets and to the biblical authors, to Jesus and to the apostles, and also to the very text of the Bible and to the interpreter of the Scriptures. The same Spirit, who is present everywhere, is thus the principle of unity for the whole Bible, but he is equally (or should be) a principle of communion between the authors of the Scriptures and those who at a later date interpret them.[58]

In Jerome, the emphasis is somewhat different, and the relationships are also seen differently. We find the same principles in his writings as in those of Origen, but the Latin Doctor places greater emphasis on what we have called the "objective" aspects of interpretation—those aspects that are linked to the actual text of the Scriptures and that express the truth of the gospel. He always emphasizes the interior dimension of the Scriptures themselves (and not only of the person who is reading them!): the truth of the gospel and of the Scriptures is the Spirit within the letter; the Scriptures cannot be interpreted heretically except by those who have not entered into their inner depths; the spiritual sense of the gospel, as has been observed recently, is only understood truly if we seek an *"interior penetration of the text, as it was written for believers, by inspired believers, in accordance with their experience of God."*[59]

The material gathered together in this first part will help us to gain a better understanding of everything entailed and implied by the hermeneutic principle indicated by the Council. However, it will also make it possible for us to describe it more precisely and develop it further.

The Conciliar Text

After introductory sentence (para. a), the Latin text of number 12 of the Constitution *Dei Verbum* gives the norms for interpreting the Bible in three separate paragraphs: first, the norms for critical exegesis (paras. b and c), and then those for theological interpretation (para. d).

What relationship should we see between these two aspects? The first word of the last paragraph is the adversative conjunction "but" (*sed*), indicating the introduction of a certain opposition. But in what sense? The question has been examined by M.A. Molina Palma,[60] and we shall base ourselves on his analysis.

The Relationship of the Paragraphs on Interpretation

At first glance, we might think that historical-critical exegesis and theological interpretation should be clearly separate and distinct. It is a fact that they are all too often kept apart today, and such a separation is quite rightly deplored by D. Barsotti.[61] It certainly does not correspond in any way to the intention of the conciliar text, as this is stated in the short introductory paragraph with all the clarity that could be desired: ". . . the interpreter of sacred Scriptures . . . should carefully search out the meaning which the sacred writers really had in mind, that meaning which *God has wished to manifest* through the medium of their words." This *sensus divinus* must therefore be sought in the *sensus humanus* itself."[62] But does this mean, on the other hand, that the sense intended by God *is identified* purely and simply with the sense of the human author? J. Gnilka holds that it does, and says that the only scientific way of understanding Scripture is to extract its *theological* sense by use of the historical-critical method,[63] and that it would not be "scientific" to go any further than this. This position seems untenable to us, for it implies that *theological* science can only be an *historical* science. It is also clearly contrary to number 12 of the Constitution, which is constructed precisely on the distinction between the two approaches to the text (the second being introduced by *sed*). The traditional analogy between the biblical word (which is both *human* word and word of God) and the Word of God (who is God and Man) can help clarify things here. A sort of monophysism (but in reverse!) can arise in exegesis, according to which only historical-critical exegesis would be considered truly valid for Christians.

The twofold request made of them by the Council is emphasized by two adverbs: on the one hand, they must carefully (*attente*, 12a) search out what the sacred writers really meant, but they must also, on the other hand, and with no less care (*non minus diligenter*, 12d), bear in mind the three principles of theological exegesis, which we shall discuss in due course. Here we are clearly moving beyond the previous stage.

We must consider whether, on this basis, we can agree with M.A. Molina, and speak of two *levels* of exegetical work. To our way of thinking, this image tends to conjure up to too great an extent the static idea of a separation of levels. If we wanted to use a metaphor, we would prefer to use that of two concentric circles: although the work of criticism certainly obeys its own laws, the Christian exegete practices such work within a larger context (the second circle) and in a broader perspective, toward which he remains constantly open. His orientation is always within this perspective, and through the interior dynamism of a deep under-lying intention—that of faith—he is always oriented in this direc-tion. This will appear even more clearly from the literary struc-ture of the text, which we shall now consider.

The Literary Structure of Number 12

We said at the outset that in the official edition, *Dei Verbum* 12 is made up of four paragraphs. However, it seems helpful to combine the second and third into a single one, inasmuch as the third paragraph is simply a development of what is an-nounced in the second, which is composed of a single sentence (*Sed hagiographorum . . . respicienda sunt*), and there is no rea-son to separate this sentence from what it introduces; moreover, the latter begins with "Hence. . . ." On the other hand, in 12d (which, in our structure is going to become 12c), the text begins with "But" (*Sed*), marking a very definite break, so that it has quite correctly been made the beginning of a new para-graph. However, in this case, the four last lines of the para-graph are to be separated from what goes before them, inas-much as they are a general conclusion to everything that has been said since the beginning of number 12 (*Cuncta enim haec . . .*). We, too, therefore end up with four paragraphs, although, except for the first, they do not correspond to those of the official text.

From the viewpoint of vocabulary and subject matter, these four paragraphs form a clear chiasmus (A B B′ A′), and this arrangement will help in interpreting the text. Figure 1 shows this structure. (To our knowledge this is the first time that a similar analysis of *Dei Verbum* 12 has been made.)

The Rational Work of the Interpreter

The aim of our study is to provide a commentary on the formula that opens the third paragraph (the one concerned with *theological* interpretation: B′). Even so, it will be helpful to start with a few remarks on the preceding paragraph (B) in order to gain a better understanding of the substance of the technical work carried out on the text on the level of critical exegesis.

A regular movement can be seen in this paragraph B from the interior to the exterior, and from the exterior to the interior, of

A:
Announcement of the subject

Cum autem DEUS on Sacra Scriptura per homines more hominum locutus sit, **INTERPRES SACRAE SCRIPTURAE,**

(*a*)   ut perspiciat quid IPSE (DEUS) nobiscum communicare voluerit,

   (*b*)   attente investigare debet quid HAGIOGRAPHI reapse significare intenderint

(*a'*)   et eorum verbis manifestare DEO placuerit.

B (= b):
Hagiographus

Ad HAGIOGRAPHORUM *intentionem eruendam inter alia etiam genera litteraria respicienda sunt.*
Aliter enim atque aliter veritas in textibus vario modo historicis, vel propheticis, vel poeticis, vel *in* aliis dicendi generibus proponitur et exprimitur. Oportet porro ut **INTERPRES** *sensum inquirat,* quem in determinatis adiunctis HAGIOGRAPHUS, pro sui temporis et suae culturae condicione, ope generum litterariorum illo tempore adhibitorum exprimere *intenderit* et *expresserit.* Ad recte enim *intelligendum* id quod sacer auctor scripto asserere *voluerit,* rite attendendum est tum ad suetos illos nativos sentiendi, dicendi, narrandive modos, qui temporibus HAGIOGRAPHI vigebant, tum ad illos qui illo aevo in mutuo hominum commercio passim adhiberi solebant.

B' (=a,a'):
Spiritus (Deus)

SED,
cum Sacra Scriptura EODEM SPIRITU quo scripta est etiam legenda
et **INTERPRETANDA** sit,
ad recte sacrorum textuum sensum eruendum,
non minus diligenter respiciendum est ad
• contentum et unitatem totius Scripturae,
• ratione habita vivae totius Ecclesiae Traditionis
• et analogiae fidei.
Exegetarum autem est secundum has regulas adlaborare *ad* Sacrae Scripturae *sensum penitius intelligendum* et exponendum, ut quasi praeparato studio, iudicium Ecclesiae maturetur.

A':
Conclusion

Cuncta enim haec, de ratione **INTERPRETANDI SCRIPTURAM,** Ecclesiae iudicio ultime subsunt, quae verbi Dei servandi et **INTERPRETANDI** divino fungitur mandato et ministerio.

Figure 1

the text, both for the original ancient author of the text, and for the contemporary interpreter of the same text. In the structure of Figure 1, the "interiority" is noted with italics and the "exteriority" with boldface type. The aim of the interpreter is to "release" or illuminate (*eruere*) the hidden intention (*intentionem*) of the sacred writer. The truth (*veritas*) of his text is found in this ("interior") intention of the ancient author, but it can only be discovered by today's interpreter "in" (*in*) the texts themselves; this is done through the study of literary forms (*genera litteraria*) and modes of expression (*dicendi narrandive modos*) used by the sacred writer to express himself (*expresserit*). Through such study, the interpreter hopes to "understand rightly" (*recte intelligendum*, from *intus-legere*) what the author wanted to state in his writing (*scripto asserere voluerit*). As can be seen, the verbs defining the interpreter's task describe two complementary movements: first, a "penetration" (cf. the use of verbs in *in-* and *inter-*: *investigare, inquirere, interpretari, intelligere*); second, a reverse task of "explanation" (*sensus eruere*). The "sense" was hidden in the intention of the ancient author, in the "truth" of his text, in its interiority. It is striking how close these expressions of the Council are to those of St. Jerome, who made a distinction in the Scriptures between *verba* and *sensus, superficies* and *medulla*, preaching of the gospel (*praedicatio*) and *veritas evangelii, littera* and *spiritus*.[64] And it is equally striking that it is also in tune with the language of contemporary hermeneutics: "Understanding," writes L. Pareyson, "therefore means interpreting, in other words, delving into what is *explicit* in order to discover this infinity of the *implicit* that is announced and contained therein."[65] "Understanding" the text means that we grasp its "truth," returning to the intention of the author; "interpreting" this text therefore means speaking the "unspoken" in what it says, extracting its meaning and significance, explicating what is implicit in it.

Let us take a look at another detail here. It is interesting to group the three terms used in B to describe the interior dimension of the texts to be studied: *intentio* (that of the sacred writer), *veritas* (that of his text), and *sensus* (what he wanted to express therein). The ancient author tried to express his thought, his "intention"; he wanted to give a "sense" to his text; and this sense of the text is its "truth." Today's interpreter follows the same path in reverse order. Thus, starting from the exterior aspect of the texts he has before him, he tries to enter into the intention of the sacred writer of long ago, so as to discover the "sense," the "truth," of his text. However, so far there has been nothing permitting us to move beyond the simply human, existential, and historical level in studying these ancient texts.

The perspective will change radically in the following paragraph (B'). Hence, the opening *Sed.* Even so, we shall find the same dialectic of exterior and interior, although with striking modifications and new perspectives, which will be constantly expanded on and will gain even greater depth.

Christian and Ecclesial Interpretation (B')

1. *Where Does the Real "Interpretation" of the Sacred Scriptures Begin?* In the two previous paragraphs (A and B), there were two separate references to the work to be undertaken by the person (in the Church) who is called to be an "interpreter" (*interpres*) of the holy Scriptures (12a and b: A and B), in other words, the exegete. However, the technical work of the exegete as described in B is not yet indicated with the active verbal form "to interpret" (*interpretari*).

This verb—and thus what constitutes interpretation strictly speaking, according to the Council—appears for the first time at the beginning of the third paragraph (B'), in the very phrase we are studying (*cum Sacra Scriptura eodem spiritu . . . interpretanda sit . . .*), where it introduces the specific principles of Christian interpretation; consequently, the true work of "interpreting" the Scriptures only begins here. We should not find this surprising: the verb "to interpret" will be used twice more in the last paragraph (A'), where the *interpretation* of the Scriptures will be presented as the task proper to the Church (cf. 10b, where it was reserved to the magisterium of the Church). The theological explanation of this view is found at the beginning of our section. It will be sufficient to compare our two paragraphs on the work of interpretation (B and B') with the opening paragraph (A), which announced the general subject matter of *Dei Verbum* 12, and where the task of "the interpreter of sacred Scriptures" is briefly indicated in a phrase made up of three elements arranged as a chiasmus (*a, b, a'*).

The immediate technical task assigned to the exegete was indicated in the center (*b*)—"carefully searching out the meaning which the *sacred writers* really had in mind"—and this would then be developed in the second paragraph, which we have already discussed ("determining the intention of the *sacred writers*," B).

However, this technical work of the exegete is still not what the Council means by "interpretation" of the sacred Scriptures, but is simply presented as a *means* toward this end. In the chiasmus of the long sentence of paragraph A, the aim is indicated twice: first, in the final proposition (*ut perspiciat quid . . .*), which means that we must seek the intention of God (*a*); and then in the indication of the goal the exegete hopes to reach when, apart from his technical work (*b*), he will consider what God wanted to manifest through the words of the sacred writers (*a'*). Let us transcribe the two parallel texts:

(a)　"*to* ascertain [*ut perspiciat*] what [God] *himself* has wished to communicate to us";

(a')　"that which God had thought well to manifest through the medium of their words."

This search for the divine meaning of sacred Scripture will be described more fully in the third paragraph (B'), which we shall now analyze with care. Authentic "interpretation" of sacred Scripture is formally constituted of this search for what "God *himself* has wished to communicate to us," and is carried out "in the same Spirit in which they were written." These preliminary remarks fully confirm what we said at the start of this second part of our study: the "divine" and specifically Christian meaning of the Scriptures represents something *beyond* the "human" meaning that is revealed by simple technical exegesis; true "interpretation" of Scripture must be carried out "*in the Spirit* in which it was written." This echoes what Origen said when he stated that *beyond* their obvious meaning, the Scriptures contain a deep underlying meaning, which comes about through the action of the *Spirit of God,* and is found "*beyond* what is written." Although it puts it less starkly, the text of the Constitution therefore returns to what an eastern bishop, Monsignor N. Edelby, stated very explicitly at the Council (during the third session, on 5 October 1964), in an intervention that received a great deal of attention:

The mission of the *Holy Spirit* cannot be separated from the mission of the incarnate Word. This is the first theological principle of any interpretation of the sacred Scriptures whatever. And it should not be forgotten that, *apart from* auxiliary sciences of all kinds, the final *aim* of Christian exegesis is the *spiritual understanding of sacred Scripture,* in the light of the risen Christ. . . . [66]

These words of a representative of the eastern Churches were most important, for Bishop Edelby's intervention (with the convincing theological reasons he gave) was in fact the starting point of the efforts made right at the end of the Council to introduce the theological principle of which we are going to speak at the beginning of *Dei Verbum* 12c: ". . . sacred Scripture must be *read and interpreted in the Spirit in which it was written.* . . ."[67]

Examination of the principle of interpretation "in the Spirit" (B') will confront us with the dialectic of exterior and interior to an even more marked degree than was the case with examination of critical study (B). However, the perspective is much more complex here, because this is where we find a new term, the *Spirit,* which comes from a totally different frame of reference, and which is used here both in connection with the human persons in question (the sacred writer, the reader, the interpreter) and in connection with the actual scriptural text—as we shall see. However, in order to demonstrate this, we must first resolve a philological question.[68]

The grammatical subject of the verbs is something inanimate, a book: *Sacra Scriptura.* Despite this, the three verbs describe human actions (writing, reading, interpreting) that are performed by three persons (the author, the reader, the interpreter of the book). However, the conciliar text does not use the verbs in the active mood: it does *not* say that the sacred writer wrote, that the believer reads, and that the exegete interprets, although this would be strictly correct. This simple observation leaves us or brings us back to the horizontal level of the previous paragraph (B), where the actions of the sacred writer and the interpreter were in fact expressed by verbs in the active mood, and they were being considered purely as *human* activities. On the other hand, in our case (in B'), the three verbal forms are in the passive: the text *has been written,* it must *be read,* it must *be interpreted.* Why is this so? The clear reason for this reversal of perspective (in other words, for this move from the active to the passive) is that here there is a sudden opening to an influence that comes *from above,* and to which the sacred writer, the reader, and the interpreter are subject. This influence is that of the *Spirit,* or of God (the two words are structurally parallel), and in the face of the action of the Holy Spirit and of God, although the three *agents* of the human actions do truly perform these actions, they cannot be other than passive; or, rather, we can say that their attitude must be one of submission, acceptance, openness. And this is the new element presented in paragraph B′.

What is the role of the Spirit here? He is certainly not the direct agent of the three actions because he does not take the place of human beings: the Spirit is neither he who "reads," nor he who "interprets," nor even he who "has written" (in which case the *quo* would have had to be replaced by *a quo scripta est*). His role is added to that of these three human persons; he does not replace them. However, another noteworthy factor is that neither the Spirit nor any of these three people is the subject of the three verbs. The role of the Spirit is indicated each time by the same grammatical form: a Latin ablative (*eodem Spiritu* and *quo*). It is important to be clear about the type of ablative involved, for the fact that the grammatical forms are identical indicates that the functions attributed to the Spirit in each case are also identical. Thus, in order to understand these functions, we must define the significance of the expressions used. In our view, there is only one possible answer: *eodem Spiritu quo* is not an ablative of place (in which case we would have had *in Spiritu,* as in Jn. 4:23 in the Vulgate), but an ablative of manner, with a nuance of cause (because the Spirit is a personal being), or, in other words, "an instrumental marking the cause."[69] This means that a true causality of the Spirit is exercised on the sacred writer, the reader, and the interpreter of the Scriptures, and this causality determines the *manner* in which they perform their respective actions. The three verbs are in the passive because these three persons are subject to the action of the Spirit in the very exercise of their human activities.

However, it is significant that the *grammatical subject* of the three passive verbs is not the group of these persons, but an inanimate object: "sacred Scripture." It is Scripture that is presented as the subject of *scripta est, legenda* (*est*), and *interpretanda* (*est*), and for each of the actions thus envisaged, Scripture (the subject) is presented as also being *subject* to this causality of the Spirit (indicated in the ablative).

This means that we can now conclude that the causality of the Spirit (first cause) through his action on the sacred writer (secondary cause) is equally exercised on the *actual text* of Scripture, which the ancient writer has *written,* and which believers today *read* and *interpret.* This amounts to saying that there is an indwelling of the Spirit in Scripture itself, that the text that has been written is the bearer of the Spirit, and that it must then be read and interpreted in the Spirit.

This detailed analysis has enabled us to reach the following very important observation, the theological significance of which will appear in due course: according to this theological principle of the Council, the action of the Holy Spirit is exercised just as much on the *persons* involved (the writer and the interpreter of the Bible) as on the actual *text* of the sacred Scriptures. Let us now try to visualize these multiple relationships in the integrated diagram of Figure 2.

This action of the Spirit, which is exercised just as much on the sacred writer, the reader, and the interpreter as on the text of the Scriptures, gives these people on the one hand, and the Scriptures on the other, a hitherto unsuspected dimension of interiority. We shall now examine these two elements one by one, for if interpretation of the text "in the Spirit" is the only true interpretation according to the Council, it will not be truly achieved unless, in the case of the *interpreter,* it springs from those innermost depths where the Holy Spirit acts in his faith life, and unless, in the case of the *text,* it reaches those depths that transform the book of the Bible into sacred Scripture, into the word of God.

2. *Subjective Interiority: That of the Sacred Writer, the Reader, and the Interpreter.* Let us return to a detail concerning vocabulary. The three verbs of the proposition are used in a passive form, so that it is said of Scripture: *scripta est, legenda* (*est*), *interpretanda* (*est*).

However, writing, reading, and interpretation are, regardless, three human activities. These verbs therefore draw attention not only to the book itself, but to the actions performed and to their agents. Despite this, these verbs are in the passive.

The three agents have in common the fact that they are all

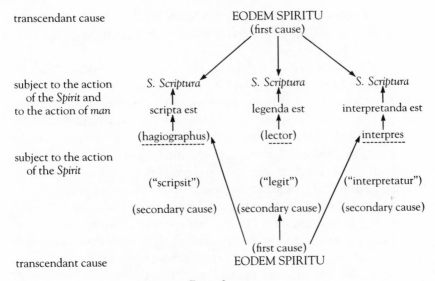

transcendant cause

EODEM SPIRITU
(first cause)

subject to the action
of the *Spirit* and
to the action of *man*

S. *Scriptura*   S. *Scriptura*   S. *Scriptura*

scripta est   legenda est   interpretanda est

(hagiographus)   (lector)   interpres

subject to the action
of the *Spirit*

("scripsit")   ("legit")   ("interpretatur")

(secondary cause)   (secondary cause)   (secondary cause)

(first cause)

transcendant cause   EODEM SPIRITU

Figure 2

moved "by the same Spirit." Here, the fact that these three persons live in completely different periods and circumstances is of no interest whatsoever (although this was not so for the previous paragraph!). The important thing is that "the same Spirit" dwells in them for the accomplishment of their task.

The decisive word is obviously "Spirit" (*Spiritu*), which appears here for the first time in number 12, but which clearly refers back to number 11, where "the Holy Spirit" (*Spiritu Sancto*) was mentioned three times in connection with the inspiration of the books of "sacred Scripture." The first two of these references in *Dei Verbum* 11a are as follows:

> The divinely revealed truth which is contained and presented in the books of sacred Scripture has been committed to writing [*consignata*] under the inspiration of the *Holy Spirit*. For Holy Mother Church . . . accepts as sacred and canonical the books of the Old and the New Testaments, whole and entire, with all their parts, on the grounds that, composed [*conscripti*] under the inspiration of the *Holy Spirit*, . . . they have God as their author. . . .

Our text of *Dei Verbum* 12 (B′) clearly refers back to this because here too what is being discussed is the role of the *Spirit* in the *writing down* of the sacred Scriptures by the sacred writer (*eodem Spiritu quo scripta est*): they were written under the inspiration of the Holy Spirit.

There is a further detail concerning the transcendant "agents" at work here. In the second sentence of *De Verbum* 11a that we have quoted above, there was a correspondence between two subjects: the "Holy Spirit" (who *inspires* all the books of Scripture) and "God" (who is their *author*). The same correspondence is found in number 12, if we take a careful look at the structure given above: "God" (A: *a* and *a'*) corresponds to "Spirit" (B': taken up from *a* and *a'*), which justifies the parallelism we indicated—a parallelism that might at first glance seem paradoxical.

Let us now move on to the horizontal and human level, and examine more closely the movement here from the ancient period of the composition of "sacred Scripture" by the writers to that of its present-day readers and interpreters. The two groups have in common the fact that they are in an identical relationship to the same transcendant subject, the Holy Spirit. But here again, as in the previous case (B), we find a dialectic of exteriority and interiority between them. However, here it is more complex, and is found on a deeper level; it is no longer simply a case for the modern *interpreter* to discover the intention of the *authors,* and thus a human intention, in the ancient texts. The Council makes a further demand here: the text of "sacred Scripture must be read and interpreted in the same *Spirit* in which it was written [by the sacred writers]," in other words, "in the Holy Spirit." Thus, we move from the human intention of the ancient writer to the *Holy Spirit* who inspired him, and a similar interiorization—or, better, a spiritualization—is required of today's interpreter, who must also read and interpret sacred Scripture "in the Spirit," that is, spiritually. However, the text specifically states that it is "the *same* Spirit" in both cases. Outwardly, the writer of old and the interpreter of today are unacquainted, and are very far removed from one another in space and time; even so, the conciliar text emphasizes the fact that for both of them it is "the *same* Spirit" (*eodem Spiritu*) who is at work, which must obviously create a deep communion, a mysterious unity, between them, going far beyond the barriers of their respective characters and cultural milieu, and the very different historical circumstances in which the two of them move. The Spirit undoubtedly brings them together, and unites them.

The question then, of course, arises of the precise implications of this strange parallelism between the sacred writer and the interpreter, and also that of how we are to understand the phrase "*reading* and *interpreting* sacred Scripture in the *same* Spirit." The Council repeated the traditional teaching on inspiration but did not offer any theological explanation. The parallelism indicated in *Dei Verbum* 12c, according to our hermeneutic principle, certainly does not mean that the sacred writer's charism of inspiration is renewed in the reader and in the interpreter of Scripture. But if they have "the same Spirit," there must be something the three have in common, some deep analogy in their way of approaching Scripture. Several Fathers of the Council independently offered a very simple explanation of the words *eodem Spiritu . . . interpretanda,* saying that they mean that this reading of sacred Scripture, this interpretation must be done "in the light of *faith.* "[70] The faith of the author of old must be the faith of the reader and interpreter of today, and any work of interpretation must be imbued with this *same faith.* Here we find again the idea of Origen that true understanding of the Scriptures is possible only if we are converted to the Lord *in faith,*[71] of that of St. Jerome that only the *spiritual man* (cf. 1 Cor. 2:15) can discover Christ in the divine writings.[72] This is the underlying requirement for any truly Christian reading or interpretation of the sacred Scriptures.

If we take the trouble to see how this principle has been understood in the course of Tradition, we are left in no doubt that this is one of the two fundamental implications of the theological principle under consideration. We shall speak of the other in the following subsection. The element we have called "the *subjective* aspect" of the principle (the *faith life* of the interpreter) is always present in this tradition. We have already seen it in Origen and St. Jerome—and this is important because they are the source of the conciliar text—and we could also find it in other texts of these same authors.[73] While people have gone so far as to speak of a "*mysticism* of exegesis" in Origen, they have also discovered in his disciple Gregory Thaumaturgus the conviction that it is not possible to interpret Scripture without an interpreter's *spirituality.*[74] However, the interpretation of Scripture tends to be linked even more closely to "spiritual *experience*" in the Latin world than in that of the Greeks.[75] Here we could cite St. Hilary and St. Ambrose,[76] but we want to consider most

especially the two authors in whom the concept is clearest and in
whom it is found very precisely linked to our theological principle: St. Gregory the Great and St. Bernard. St. Gregory is one of
the great Doctors of Christian interiority.[77] For him, "the words
of God cannot in any way be penetrated without his wisdom; for
if a person has not *received the Spirit of God,* he can in no way
understand the words of God."[78] We emphasize the parallelism
here between the Spirit and the word. Later the same conviction
is found in St. Bernard. In the words of J. Leclerq:

> . . . in him, the first conviction is that *the same Spirit* who
> inspired the sacred writers acts in those who *read* them, . . .
> inasmuch as the wisdom, . . . which is that of God, unceas-
> ingly communicates itself through the same texts that it
> caused to be written; in these texts, the *reader* must reach
> God, and continue within himself the *experience* that was at
> the outset that of the *sacred author.*[79]

We move from the exteriority of the text to the interiority of the
spiritual experience of those involved.

However, it would be a great mistake to imagine that the
action of the Holy Spirit is applied only to the persons themselves (the "subjects"), eliciting and fostering faith and spiritual
experience within them. It is just as important to recognize that
it is equally exercised on the object of their activity—the *text* of
Scripture, its content—which thus acquires an interior dimension that other texts lack. We must now take a closer look at this
point.

3. *Objective Interiority: The Letter and the Spirit.* Here again,
our starting point will be an observation on vocabulary. The
common element between *Dei Verbum* 12c (B') and the preceding paragraph (B) is that they both deal with the same texts.
Nevertheless, the Council changes its way of speaking of them
between one paragraph and another. In B, it simply calls them
"texts" (*textibus*), whereas in B', when it wants to indicate the
object of Christian interpretation, the Constitution twice uses
the more theological expression "sacred Scripture" (*sacra Scriptura*), and when it again uses the word "text," it now places the
adjective "sacred" before it (*sacrorum textuum*).[80]

Here (in B') the distinction between the exteriority and the
interiority of the texts is even more eloquently expressed than in

the discussion of their technical analysis (in B). Here we are no longer concerned simply with the interiority of the *people* who wrote these texts and with that of those who later read and interpret them, but with that of the *actual texts* with which the three groups are concerned. These texts, taken as a whole, also have an exterior aspect and in interior dimension. The exterior aspect is obviously that of being texts that were written at a specific date and in a specific language, and that can be and are the object of an infinite number of studies from the philological, literary, and historical viewpoints. However, when the Council now calls them "the sacred texts" or "sacred Scripture," its intention is to invite us to recognize that they have a permanent religious value because of *another* dimension they possess—an invisible and interior, divine and spiritual dimension. This other dimension is their relationship to the Holy spirit (B') and to God (A), although neither God nor the Spirit is any longer a direct object of philological analysis or historical investigation.

Does this mean that this "interior" dimension or inspired character of Scripture remains beyond our reach? Obviously not. As we have already said, the reader and the interpreter of Scripture must have faith in order to understand it properly. However, this faith is not empty, but has as its object God who reveals himself. We should remember that the subject of the whole Constitution *Dei Verbum* is "divine revelation." And in the immediate context of number 12, the subject is God as he reveals himself in Scripture. Thus, the interpreter of sacred Scripture must seek to ascertain "what God has wished to *manifest*" through the *words* of the sacred writers (A). This is what number 11 referred to as the truth of the Scriptures—"the truth which God, for the sake of our salvation, wished to see confided to the sacred Scriptures." This "truth" of salvation, which is referred to elsewhere as *veritas salutaris* (LG 17; GS 28; cf. DV 7), is not simply the historical truth, but is the actual *revelation* that took place within history and that "shines forth for us in Christ, who is himself both the mediator and the sum total of revelation" (DV 2).

But let us return to the formula found in *Dei Verbum* 12c. The Christian who, in conformity with the orientations of the Council, wants to read and interpret the Scriptures "in the Spirit" is, of course, the one who, subjectively speaking, seeks to interpret them "in the light of faith," but is also the one who objectively tries to discover this truth of salvation—"what God has wished to communicate to us, . . . what God has wished to manifest [to us] (12a)—within the sacred Scriptures themselves. This "truth" of the Scriptures should not be understood as meaning that all the statements in the Bible are true. It means, rather, that the Scriptures have an interior dimension, an underlying "sense," a value as revelation; that they reveal the salvific plan of God; that they are the word of God, the word that rang out of old, but that is still present among us in the Scriptures, thanks to the Spirit who dwells within them (cf. *DV* 8c). It is basically the spiritual sense of the Scriptures, the presence of the Spirit *in the letter.*

We are thus called to interpret the sacred Scriptures while bearing in mind the fact that they are inspired. We must seek an underlying sense, which is "spirit and life," within the words of the Scriptures, in line with Jesus' statement that "the words that I have spoken to you are spirit and life" (Jn. 6:63), which has been referred to as "one of the most important biblical foundations of spiritual exegesis."[81] This concept of the *objective interiority of the text,* in other words, the presence of the Spirit in the letter,[82] and hence also the spiritual depth of the sacred Scriptures, is completely traditional—indeed, even more so than the previous aspect of subjective interiority. Here we would recall the Jewish and patristic symbolism of the well and the living water.[83] The depth of the word of God is symbolized by the well, and its fruitfulness by the living water that springs from it. Origen, for example, writes:

> Thus, according to the already cited Proverbs, where a well—or a spring—is mentioned, it must be understood to concern the word of God: a well, if it hides a deep mystery; and a spring, if it flows out over the peoples and waters them.[84]

St. Jerome uses other metaphors to describe this "interiority" of the word of God, which is due specifically to the presence of the Spirit in the letter, and in this connection we can take another look at two basic texts already cited above: "Let us not think that the gospel lies in the words of the Scriptures: it is in their meaning; not in the surface, but in the marrow; not in the leaves of words, but in the root of understanding."[85] "The truth of the gospel is not found in the letter, but in the spirit; not in the fleshly sense, but in the spiritual understanding."[86] St. Gregory says that anyone who reads the sacred Scripture with the grace of contemplation and love from on high will discover the whole strength of the word of God, because it has its life from the Spirit of life: ". . . the wonderful and ineffable *power* of the sacred word."[87] We must, therefore, return to the conviction common to the Fathers, which is expressed so well by St. Augustine: "O wonderful depth of your words. . . . O wonderful depth, my God, O wonderful depth!"[88] According to the Council, it is precisely the search for these depths of the Scriptures, for the presence of the Spirit in the letter, for the interior dimension of revelation of the word of God, that constitutes Christian interpretation of the Scriptures, or interpretation "in the Spirit."

As we have said, this underlying sense of the biblical words is what the Council calls the "truth" of the Scriptures (*DV* 11) or the "saving truth" (*DV* 7). The concept of these inner depths of Scripture can be understood even better through reference to the term "mystery," to the idea of revelation of the mystery of salvation. According to *Dei Verbum* 24, theology rests on the word of God, and is "constantly rejuvenated as it searches out, in the light of faith, the full truth *hidden* in the *mystery* of Christ." This mystery that is revealed to us by the Scriptures is the revelation that they bring us and that finds its fullness of Christ. However, it is "hidden" in the mystery of Christ, and must therefore be "searched out" and uncovered. This means that we must move beyond history—a movement that is made "in the light of faith"—in order to enter into the "interior dimension" of the mystery hidden in the words of God, for "in them . . . the *mystery* of our salvation is present in a *hidden* way" (*DV* 15).

Here again the expressions used by the Council could be traced back to numerous patristic texts, but we shall merely cite three examples. After recalling what the law laid down with regard to the functions of the Levites in the tent of the meeting (Num. 4:1–20), Origen moves on to the spiritual meaning: "If you have understood the historical repercussions, move upwards now toward the *splendor of the mystery,* and contemplate the light of the spiritual law."[89] In a similar way, St. Gregory the Great uses the contrast between "history" and "mystery" to indicate the hidden meaning of the story told in Genesis 27:1–40 of Jacob's guile in usurping Esau's blessing: "But if a person understands the episode more deeply and wants to explain it by recourse to the hidden elements of allegory, he immediately rises from history to mystery [*ab historia in mysterium surgit*]."[90] Although it cannot be denied that in order to reach their aim Gregory and Origen make use of all sorts of allegorizations of details that seem factitious and arbitrary to us, the central concept is still valid: that of seeking the *underlying meaning* of history. And this applies also to the gospel history, as we find in St. Augustine's interpretation of the Johannine account of the marriage feast of Cana. After explaining the literal meaning, Augustine sets out to show "that which pertains to the mystery underlying this event."[91] The mystery expressed in this "the first of his signs" (Jn. 2:11)—in other words, the underlying meaning of the episode—is that the marriage feast of Cana is the *symbol* of the messianic marriage feast, the *sign* of the New Covenant.[92] The *true sense* of the episode is hidden in the story.

To conclude this subsection, we would say that the very synthetic formula, "Cum Sacra Scriptura eodem Spiritu quo scripta est etiam legenda et interpretanda sit," contains many implicit elements that will be unsuspected on a first reading. It implies that the Holy spirit is present and constantly active in the very letter of the words of God, which were inspired by the Spirit; thus, the believer is made capable of discovering the underlying meaning of the text, or its truth. "Interpreting" the word of God, therefore, means discovering the Spirit in the letter, extracting the *underlying spiritual meaning* from the sacred Scriptures, and bringing out the mystery that is revealed within history.

4. *The Means and the End.* After its reference to St. Jerome's principle (*cum . . . interpretanda sit*), which forms the first proposition in paragraph B′, and in which the gerundive is used to indicate a task that is to be performed, the Council then gives exegetes three practical recommendations for the Christian interpretation of sacred Scripture. However, it prefaces these recommendations with a second circumstantial proposition, "AD recte sacrorum textuum SENSUM eruendum," which also indicates the aim. Further, this turn of phrase is repeated a little later in a similar construction: "AD Sacrae Scripturae SENSUM penitius intelligendum." These three propositions are parallel with one another:

a. "search out the exact meaning of the sacred texts";
b. "to understand more deeply the meaning of the sacred Scriptures";
c. "to interpret [the sacred Scriptures] in the Spirit. . . . "

Interpretation "in the Spirit"—or the spiritual understanding of the Scriptures—is therefore the true way of discovering the "meaning" of the sacred Scriptures. It is an "in-depth" (*penitius*) interpretation.

The central proposition of our long sentence then lists the three practical *means* that exegetes must use in order to attain this aim: ". . . no less attention must be devoted to the content and unity of the *whole of Scripture*, taking into account the *living Tradition* of the entire Church and the *analogy of faith*."

What exact relationship should be seen between this three-fold exegetical norm and the three-fold mention of the aim given above? M.A. Molina Palma rightly asks this question,[93] and says that from the purely grammatical viewpoint, the fundamental recommendation made in the first sentence of *Dei Verbum* 12c is undoubtedly found in the *principal* proposition (*respiciendum est ad . . .*), and would, therefore, at first glance seem the most important. However, if this were so, St. Jerome's principle given at the beginning would merely serve as justification of these three rules of interpretation. He adds that such a reading would be *reductionistic*. And indeed, such an approach, which is based solely on the grammatical construction, assumes that the objection given at the beginning remains totally extrinsic to the use of the norms. However, this is impossible, precisely because what is involved is an *aim*, and through its very nature, an aim or a true intentionality (*ad . . .*) is immanent in the action concerned, informing this action ("The end coincides with the exemplary form"), and imprinting the whole unfolding of the action with a specific orientation, a movement, a definite dynamics. Inasmuch as the end is the moving force behind the whole action, it is its first cause.[94]

A diachronic reading of the text (in other words, a survey of its origins and of its progressive development until the end of the Council) is very helpful at this point.[95] The three exegetical norms that we now find in the main proposition (paying attention to the unity of the whole of Scripture, and taking into account the living tradition and the analogy of faith) were also found in the previous schema, although not prefaced by St. Jerome's principle of interpreting "in the Spirit," which is now found at the beginning of the paragraph; this principle was added specifically in order to provide the application of these norms of interpretation with a new, more general, *objective*, and hence with a new *significance*.

What was the orientation of the three norms (paying attention to the unity of Scripture, to Tradition, and to the analogy of
faith) *before* this theological principle of interpreting "in the
Spirit" was added? In the penultimate draft, these were the only
recommendations given by the Council for a Christian and
ecclesial reading of the Scriptures. These rules are of course
important, and would be retained in the definitive text. However, in the previous schema, they were still seen basically as
norms of an historical and rational type (investigation of other
texts, and doctrinal consistency), and did not aim at discovering
the *spiritual meaning* of the Scriptures. Not without justification,
Bishop Edelby deplored the "timidness" of this text, which he
saw as still overly influenced by the posttridentine perspective,
and too strongly tinged with a legalistic mentality. He called for
a return "to the totality of the *mystery* of the Church," and thus
for a reference to the mission of the *Holy Spirit.*

But let us now take a look at the significance of the three
means in the definitive text. The Council says that in the first
place, we must be attentive "to the *content* and *unity* of the whole
of Scripture." We can say that this is an absolutely fundamental
rule of interpretation, and it is found throughout Tradition, both
patristic and medieval.[96] The whole of Scripture was inspired by
the Holy Spirit, and thus it forms one single book, with Christ as
its center and the Holy Spirit as its unifying principle. This is the
gist of the famous saying of Hugh of St. Victor: "All of sacred
Scripture is one single book, and that one book is Christ."[97] But
what is the relationship between the means ("the unity of the
whole of Scripture") and the end ("interpretation in the Spirit")?
The answer to this question is indicated by the structure: *eodem
Spiritu* (B′) is an echo of *Deo* and *Deus* (A); the *Spirit* who
inspired Scripture also acts in the interpreter, to enable him to
discover "what God himself has wished to communicate to us," in
other words, "what God thought well to manifest through their
[the sacred writers'] words." Interpreting Scripture "in the Spirit"
means discovering the *secret plan* of God, the divine intention,
within it; and it is this plan of salvation that forms "the unity of
the whole of Scripture." As we saw earlier,[98] this was Origen's
basic reasoning when he said that we must seek to extract the
main "objective" or the divine intention that informed the
source of the inspiration of the texts. Carefully examining "the
content and unity of the whole of Scripture" therefore no longer

means the simple material task of collecting the texts of the different authors. Following Jerome's principle, it now means assembling these materials in order to discover a new "form,"[99] a divine intention—that of the Spirit—within them. The aim of the work carried out on the *surface* and in breadth (on the *letter* of the biblical text) is thus that of entering into its *depth,* and discovering the *Spirit,* or the spiritual sense, in it. This is the completely traditional method of explaining the New Testament in the light of the Old, and the Old in the perspective of the New, following St. Augustine's great principle,[100] which is repeated in *Dei Verbum* 16: "God, the inspirer and author of the books of both Testaments, in his wisdom has so brought it about that the New should be hidden in the Old, and that the Old should be made manifest in the New." Now the main purpose of the Old Testament was to "prepare for and declare in prophecy the coming of *Christ,* . . . and . . . indicate it by means of different types" (*DV* 15). Interpreting the Scriptures "in the Spirit" and paying attention to the unity of the whole of Scripture, therefore, means discovering the Word "condensed" therein: "God's speech is the Word of God, and the Word of God is the Son of God."[101]

A similar observation must be made with regard to the next means: attention to the "living Tradition of the whole Church." These words simply sum up the classical principle of Catholic exegesis, which was explained at greater length in the previous chapter, that is, the mutual relationship between Tradition and Scripture (*DV* 9; cf. also *DV* 10). From the viewpoint—which is ours as exegetes—of comprehension of the biblical text, this means first of all that true Christian interpretation of the Scriptures cannot be carried out except in a living continuity with the Tradition of the Church, and it is in this way that the exegete in fact is able to interpret the sacred Scriptures "in the Spirit." This constitutes a call to maintain (or rediscover) the unity and continuity between present-day exegesis and patristic exegesis,[102] inasmuch as what the Fathers sought in the Scriptures was, as we have seen, their spiritual meaning. This principle of the indissoluble unity between Scripture and Tradition was already found in the Fathers themselves. St. Cyril of Alexandria, for example, expresses it in the succinct formulation, "The Fathers and the Scriptures."[103] In his mind, the Fathers and the Scriptures are one, and the scriptural line of reasoning and the patristic line together enable us to see the *unity* of God's plan and to carry out "a unifying reading of the many scriptural writings that are gathered together in the one Bible, with a view to discovering the one and only Christ within them."[104]

Lastly, we have the analogy of faith.[105] This third norm, which has Pauline origins (Rom. 12:6), can be seen here as a combination of the two previous ones. Paul spoke of it in connection with the gift of prophecy, stating that when this gift is manifested within the community, it must always be used "according to the analogy of faith," in other words, according to a received interpretation, and in harmony with the whole Christian faith. In *Dei Verbum* 12c, the interpretation of Scripture "taking into account the analogy of faith" means that it must be integrated into the overall movement of the Old and New Testaments, but also into the movement that unifies Scripture and Tradition. In this way, the "meaning" it takes on within the orientation of the whole of revelation will be seen, beyond any difficulties that may be involved in interpreting an isolated text. And this is where its "truth" lies. The reader or interpreter must, therefore, become aware of this vast movement of salvation history, and of the constant expectations and sometimes contrasting aspirations of the people of God: "The reader [or interpreter] who abandons himself therein in faith breathes in harmony with the Spirit who guides this *history*, fosters this expectation and these aspirations, and grants understanding of the *letter inspired* by him."[106]

Let us conclude this second part by highlighting a paradox. More than once in the foregoing pages, we have drawn attention to the tension between the exteriority of texts or persons and their interiority, and we said that true interpretation means "saying what is not said," or making explicit what is implicit in the text. In the case of Scripture, this means seeking the Spirit in the letter, which in turn means that the interpreter himself must be imbued with the Spirit who inspired the sacred writer. And this is what the Council calls for in the final version of *Dei Verbum* 12c when it says that we must interpret Scripture "in the Spirit." Now this "Spirit" is found in the *interiority* of the sacred writer, and also in that of the Scriptures and that of the interpreter (cf. above), so how are we to explain the fact that in order to discover the "Spirit" of the Scriptures, the conciliar text proposes three steps for the exegete that again concern the *exteriority* of the different texts (those of the whole of Scripture to start with, and then those of Tradition)? This is the paradox of the hermeneutic circle of the dialectic between exteriority and interiority, inasmuch as the interiority of the *interpreter* (his subjectively, his understanding as a believer) has the aim of exploring the texts in order to reach their *interiority* or depths. However, in his objective work, he only has a direct grasp of the *exterior dimension* of the texts, whether of Scripture or of Tradition. Nevertheless, through this whole investigation, which broadens and spreads outward as it moves progressively forward, his final aim is always that of reaching their *interior depths*—or what St. Jerome called "the root of understanding,"[107] and St. Hilary and St. Gregory "the interior intelligibility."[108] The exterior dimension of the texts is undeniably a detour, but it is a necessary one of their *objective* interior dimension (the Spirit *in* the letter) is to be opened up to the interpreter and to his *subjective* interiority, in other words to his faith. And this is how he will finally reach "the spiritual understanding of Scripture, as the Christian ages have understood it."[109]

Toward a Conclusion

At the end of this already overlong study, it will be most illuminating to compare the principles of interpretation studied in the foregoing pages with the present-day practice of exegesis in Catholic circles.

1. Can we speak of a "reception" of the principle of Vatican II according to which we should "interpret sacred Scripture *in the Spirit* in which it was written"? Are exegetes today truly concerned (if we may repeat the expression of Cardinal de Lubac cited before) to reach "the spiritual understanding of Scripture, as the Christian ages have understood it"?[110] To a great extent, we must answer in the negative.[111] In support of this statement, it should be enough to observe that St. Jerome's principle, which was studied before with the whole paragraph it introduces (*DV* 12c), has received almost no echo in the years since the Council.[112] On the other hand, the previous paragraph (*DV* 12b) has been accepted with the most heartfelt satisfaction.

2. For this reason, we should like to call on exegetes to carry out a critical reflection as to what Christian exegesis should be

today, and, with this in mind, we would suggest a number of questions:

a. What role is played in Bible interpretation of believing exegetes today by the theological principle of the inspiration of the Scriptures? We could recall that for the Fathers this was the fundamental principle: because the Scriptures are inspired, they considered that the interpreter must seek the meaning intended by the Spirit, the spiritual sense of the Scriptures.[113] According to the New Testament itself, the presence and action of the Spirit of truth is indispensable if we are to understand the words of Jesus (Jn. 6:63; 16:7, 13). But what is the hermeneutic function assigned to the role of the Spirit in actual practice?

b. Should we not give further consideration to the historical origins of what today goes under the name of "the historical-critical method"? It would be a good idea to remember that according to a number of recent authors, it is basically derived from the Enlightenment.[114] A purely historical, and therefore secularized, manner of reading the Scriptures predominates today.

c. Are exegetes sufficiently aware of what M. Blondel referred to as "the philosophical deficiencies in modern exegesis"?[115] Now the two distortions he was speaking against were extrinsicism and historicism. The latter danger is still with us today: the historical method is too often seen as the only possible exegetical method, so that there is a risk either of stifling any interest in the theological and spiritual significance of the Scriptures, or of fostering a sort of fear, or even contempt, of this significance.

d. Another philosophical or more specifically hermeneutical question is as follows: In contemporary exegesis, is sufficient concern shown over the *meaning*—the *whole* meaning—of the biblical text? And this question applies even more especially to the interior aspect of the Scriptures themselves (*contentum et unitatem totius Scripturae—DV* 12c) than to the aspect of their sources or the milieu in which they originated. Is exegesis sufficiently sensitive to the challenge of hermeneutics, which asks this specific question of *meaning*? The question is all the more relevant in that this is the precise perspective of our paragraph (*DV* 12c), which repeatedly uses the words *sensus* and *interpretari* (both of which appear three times).

e. What is the epistemological status of exegesis today? Is the exegetical method used exclusively that of philology and history? Or again: Are scientific exegesis and faith incompatible? Exegesis belongs to what J. Ladrière calls "the hermeneutical sciences,"[116] and on this basis the answer is obvious: exegesis, like theology, seeks to *interpret* the Christian message, but it does so according to its own methods, seeking the meaning of the inspired words, which were written by believers and for believers. Exegesis too is therefore a *fides quaerens intellectum* and must be carried out in faith. And this is maybe the precise point on which one of the greatest ambiguities or misunderstandings exists today.

3. We would conclude by simply recalling a famous saying of Luther, which is echoed to such a large extent in contemporary hermeneutics: "Qui non intelligit res, non potest ex verbis sensum elicere."[117]

A foreunderstanding (of faith) is needed by anyone who truly wants to "understand" the meaning of the words of sacred Scripture.

Translated from the French by Leslie Wearne.

Notes

1. For this historical information, we are using especially the work of U. Betti, "Storia della Costituzione dogmatica 'Dei Verbum,' " in U. Betti (ed.), *La Costituzione dogmatica sulla divina Rivelazione* (Turin, 1967³), 11–152.

2. See the following commentaries on *Dei Verbum* (and especially on Chapter III): L. Alonso Schökel (ed.), *Comentarios a la constitución Dei Verbum sobre la divina revelaciòn*, BAC 284 (Madrid, 1969), 420–480 (L. Alonso Schökel); Betti (ed.), *La Costituzione dogmatica sulla divina Rivelazione*, 265–322 (P. Dacquino); B.-D. Dupuy (ed.), *La révélation divine. Constitution dogmatique "Dei Verbum,"* 2 vols. Unam Sanctam 70 a and b (Paris, 1968), 2, 369–378 (P. Grelot); B. Rigaux, "L'interprétation de l'Écriture selon la Constitution 'Dei Verbum,' " in *Au service de la Parole de Dieu. Mélanges offerts à Mgr. André-Marie Charue* (Gembloux, 1969), 262–289 (although there is nothing on number 12).

A particularly significant case is the recent study of D.J. Harrington, "Catholic Interpretation of Scripture," in K. Hagen et al., *The Bible in the Churches. How Different Christians Interpret the Scripture* (New York, 1985). In this chapter, which is written in an ecumenical perspective (cf. the title of the whole work), the author emphasizes with satisfaction "the freedom of research" in the Catholic Church since the Encyclical *Divino afflante Spiritu* and the Constitution *Dei Verbum*, pointing out that critical exegesis is not merely permitted, but is officially called for.

This is correct. But why does the author make so little mention of *Dei Verbum* 10 (on Scripture and Tradition), and no mention at all of *Dei Verbum* 12c (on specifically Christian and ecclesial exegesis)? Is this what he should have told his non-Catholic fellow contributors to this volume when he came to tell them about what is (or should be) "the *Catholic* interpretation of the Scriptures"? The essential element is not mentioned. We may assume that the author himself finds the above-mentioned passage of *Dei Verbum* 12c an embarrassment; in any case, whatever the reason, he ignores it.

3. "Sacra Scriptura eodem Spiritu quo scripta est etiam legenda et interpretanda (*Dei Verbum* 12)," in *Costituzione conciliare Dei verbum* (*Atti della* XX *Settimana Biblica*) (Brescia, 1970), 301–320.

4. *La parola e lo spirito* (Milan, 1971).

5. *La Interpretación*, Facultad de Teología del Norte de Spagña, Sede de Burgos, 52 (Burgos, 1987).

6. See below, the end of note 9.

7. *In Gal.*, 5, 19–21; in *PL*, 26, 417A.

8. *In Gal.*, prol. (*PL*, 26, 332–333): "Origenis commentarios sum secutus. Scripsit enim ille vir in Epistolam Pauli ad Galatas, quinque proprie volumina."

9. Y.M.-J. Congar, "Aimer Dieu et les hommes par l'amour dont Dieu aime?" *REtAug*, 28 (1982), 86–99 (cf. p. 96). See also *id.*, *La Tradition et les traditions*, I, "Essai historique" (Paris, 1969), 236, and 269, note 20, where he cites various witnesses, but only for the Middle Ages (and it is to be regretted that, even among the authors cited, there is none earlier than Abelard, that is to say, the beginning of scholasticism).

10. In this connection, see the excellent analysis of M. Harl in his edition of the *Philocalia* of Origen, *Philocalie, 1–20: Sur les Ecritures*, SC 302 (Paris, 1983), 59–74 ("La théorie de l'inspiration divine des Ecritures"). See also H. de Lubac, *Histoire et Esprit. L'intelligence de l'Ecriture d'après Origène*, Théólogie 16 (Paris, 1950), 294–335 ("Inspiration et intelligence").

11. De Lubac, *Histoire et Esprit*, 296.

12. *De principiis*, I, Praef. 8 (GCS, V, 14; SC, 252, 84–86).

13. Harl, *Origène. Philocalie, 1–20*, 75–76.

14. *In Ezech. hom.*, 2, 2 (GCS, VIII, 341–342).

15. *De Principiis*, IV, 2, 9 (GCS, V, 322; SC, 268, 340).

16. *In Ezech. hom.*, 2, 2 (GCS, VIII, 342).

17. *In Ezech. hom.*, 2, 5 (GCS, VIII, 347). See also *In Lev. hom.*, 92 (GCS, VI, 419): the danger which always exists of "legem Dei in alium sensum quam scripta est violenter inflectere."

18. *In Num. hom.*, 16, 9 (GCS, VII, 153): ". . . ut in spiritu considerantes quae per Spiritum scripta sunt. . . ." In this connection, see de Lubac, *Histoire et Esprit*, 297.

19. *In Lev. hom.*, 6, 6 (*GCS*, VI, 369; *SC*, 286, 297).

20. *In Exod. hom.*, 4, 5 (*GCS*, VI, 176–177; *SC*, 16, 124–125). The remark we have cited is that of the editor, J. Fortier, with regard to this passage from the homily on Exodus (*SC*, 16, 125, note 1).

21. Molina Palma, *La interpretación*, 52.

22. Harl, *Origène. Philocalie, 1–20*, 147. Cf. also de Lubac, *Histoire et Esprit*, 193: "La mystique d'Origène, a-t-on dit encore, 'est la mystique d'un exégète.' Elle l'est en effet, par tout un aspect d'elle-même. On dirait toutefois aussi bien, et peut-être avec plus de vérité, de son exégèse qu'elle est l'exégèse d'un mystique."

23. *In Cant.*, 3 (*GCS*, VIII, 204–205); *In Lev. hom.*, 1, 1 (*GCS*, VI, 281): ". . . ut veritatem verbi Dei sub litterae tegmine coopertam ad Christum jam dominum conversa cognoscat Ecclesia."

24. *In Lev. hom.*, 5, 5 (*GCS*, VI, 343): "Secundum spiritalem sensum quem Spiritus donat Ecclesiae."

25. De Lubac, *Histoire et Esprit*, 303–304.

26. *In Luc. hom.*, 1 (*GCS*, IX, 8). See Harl, *Origène. Philocalie, 1–20*, 147: "Le rôle de la foir: 'cherchez et vous trouverez.' " This is the principle found in *Phil.*, 1, 28 (*SC*, 302, 202).

27. *De principiis*, I, 3, 7 (*GCS*, V, 59; *SC*, 252, 158): ". . . Spiritus vero sancti participationem a sanctis tantummodo invenimus."

28. De Lubac, *Histoire et Esprit*, 301.

29. *Ibid.*; and the many texts of Origen, cited in note 44, on this dynamism, and this ever-present and sole orientation, which are imprinted in the various passages of the Bible; the words that recur are *intentio, voluntas*—βούλημα, σκοπός.

30. See Harl, *Origène. Philocalie, 1–20*, 145–157.

31. See the note of H. Crouzel and M. Simonetti in their edition of *Traité des principes* (*SC*, 253, 273). We intend publishing a more detailed analysis of this conclusion of John's Gospel in a forthcoming issue of *Biblica*.

32. Harl, *Origène. Philocalie, 1–20*, 153 (italics ours).

33. The reference given in the official text of the conciliar Constitution is as follows: "St. Jerome, *In Gal.*, 5, 19–21 (*PL*, 26, 417A)." The Council follows the first edition of Migne for citations of the works of St. Jerome. However, we shall always cite the second edition, in which the pagination is different. In the second edition, Jerome's commentary on Galatians 5:19–21 is found in *PL*, 26, 445A.

34. *In Gal.*, 1, 7 (*PL*, 26, 343C).

35. *In Gal.*, 5, 19–21 (*PL*, 26, 445A–B): "Quicumque igitur aliter Scripturam intelligit, quam sensus Spiritus sancti flagitat, quo conscripta est, licet de Ecclesia non recesserit, tamen haereticus appellari potest, et de carnis operibus est, eligens quae pejora sunt." See also *In Gal.*, 5,13 (*PL*, 26, 435A). And a little later (435C): "Multo quippe labore et sudore, et digno cultu in Scripturis fructus spiritus invenitur. . . . Quod si relictis typis, ad *veritatem* Scripturae transeamus et *spiritum*, statim nobis prima charitas panditur" (the *truth* of Scripture is in its *spirit*). Cf. also *Dial. contra Luciferianos*, 28 (*PL*, 23, 190D–191A), in a similar context of antiheretical polemic: "Scripturae non in legendo consistunt, sed in intelligendo" (the *sense* or *understanding* goes beyond the text we read). Cf. what was said above concerning Origen.

36. *In Mc.*, 9,1–7 (*CCL*, 78, 480, 87ff).

37. *In Mc.*, 9,1–7 (*CCL*, 78, 479, 71–76, 84f).

38. St. Hilary, *In Mt.*, 14, 3 (*PL*, 9, 997B): ". . . in his, quae gesta narrantur, subesse interioris intelligentiae ratio reperiatur." St. Gregory, *In Cant.*, 2 (*CCL*, 144, 4): "Dum recognoscimus exteriora verba, pervenimus ad interiorem intelligentiam." Cf. C. Dagens, *Saint Grégoire le Grand* (Paris, 1977), 205–244 ("La théorie grégorienne de la connaissance: l'"interna intelligentia' ").

39. *In Gal.*, 4, 21 (*PL*, 26, 414B).

40. *In Gal.*, 1, 11 (*PL*, 26, 347A). As regards the Pauline distinction between "receiving" and "learning" the gospel, Jerome explains that the first verb describes the first acceptance of the gospel, or the beginning of the life of faith, and the second concerns deeper understanding, which is possible only through a revelation of Christ. See also *In Eccle.*, 12, 9s (*PL*, 23, 1169B): ". . . divinum sensum altius perscrutandum . . . "; *In Ezech.*, 47, 6 (*CCL*, 75, 718, 1255–1257): "Ut verba simplicia intellegamus in foliis, in fructibus vero sensum latentem."

41. *In Gal.*, 3, 8 (*PL*, 26, 378C). *Ep. 29 (ad Marcellam)*, 1, 3 (*CSEL*, 54, 233): ". . . de scripturis sanctis disputanti non tam necessaria sunt verba quam sensus." *In Ezech.*, 1, 3 (*PL*, 25, 35A): ". . . foris, in historiae littera; intus, intelligentia spirituali." *Ep. 58 (ad Paulinum)*, 9, 1 (*CSEL*, 54, 538): "Totum quod legimus in divinis libris, nitet et fulget etiam in cortice, sed dulcius in medulla est. Qui esse [= edere] vult nuculeum, frangit nucem." *Dial. contra Lucifer.*, 11 (*PL*, 23, 174B–C). *In Mt. II*, 13, 55 (*CCL*, 77, 111, 953ff): ". . . nec manifestam tantum sonare litteram, sed et abscondita mysteria." *In Mc.*, 1, 13–21 (*CCL*, 78, 460, 24–29): ". . . ut nobis aperiat evangelica adyta . . . ; non intrinsecus, id est in spiritu: sed foris, in littera. Et . . . introducat nos in mysteria sua." *In Mc.*, 11, 1–10 (*CCL*, 78, 486, 52.56): ". . . omne quod fecit Iesus, sacramenta sunt, salus nostra est . . . ; nostra sunt sacramenta." *Ep. 18A*, 12, 2 (*CSEL*, 54, 88).

42. *In Gal.*, 2, 14 (*PL*, 26, 367A).

43. Cf. Dan. 10:21: "But I will tell you what is inscribed in the Book of Truth"; Bar. Syr. 44:14: "the truth of the Law."

44. *In Gal.*, 2, 3–5 (*PL*, 26, 359B–C).

45. *In Gal.*, 5, 17 (*PL*, 26, 440A).

46. In Gal., 5, 13 (PL, 26, 435C); the text is quoted above in note 35.

47. In Gal., 5, 13 (PL, 26, 434A). See also the distinction Jerome makes between the *preaching* of the gospel and the word of *truth:* the first can remain the simple object of outward hearing, but the second is perceived only in faith, due to the gift of the Spirit: In Ep., 1, 13 (PL, 26, 486B).

48. In Mc., 11, 11–14 (CCL, 489, 45–52). The same image recurs in In Ezech., 47, 6 (CCL, 75, 718, 1253–1257), partially quoted in note 40 above.

49. In Mc., 8, 22–26 (CCL, 78, 474, 10–11). See also In Is., prol. (PL, 24, 20B): "Post historiae veritatem spiritualiter accipienda sunt omnia." In Am., 9, 6 (CCL, 76, 341, 185f.): "Et cum historiae habuerint fundamenta, tunc spiritalis intelligentiae culmen accipiant." In Am., 1, 9–10 (CCL, 76, 225, 421f.).

50. In Mt., 14,14 (CCL, 77, 121, 1215ff.).

51. Compare with what H. Crouzel, *Origène* (Namur/Paris, 1985), 120, has to say with regard to Origen: "L'exégèse littérale, selon sa définition moderne, vise à retrouver ce qu'a voulu dire l'auteur sacré. Ceci établi, l'exégèse spirituelle le situe dans le mystère du Christ."

52. In Is., prol. (PL, 24, 17B). See also Ep., 53, 5 (CSEL, 54, 452–453).

53. In Gal., 4, 24 (PL, 26, 417A).

54. In Mc., 9, 1–7 (CCL, 78, 484, 280–285).

55. Ep. 120, 10, 1 (CSEL, 55, 500).

56. In Gal., 4, 24 (PL, 26, 416D–417A). See above.

57. See above.

58. Here we could use the image so dear to Gadamer of the "fusion of horizons" between biblical writers and modern commentators.

59. R. Laurentin, *Comment réconcilier l'exégèse et la foi?* (Paris, 1985), 17.

60. *La interpretación,* 65.

61. *La parola e lo spirito. Saggi sull'esegesi spirituale* (Milan, 1971), 10: "Una pura interpretazione letterale difficilmente può sottrarsi, come l'esegesi guidaica, alla tentazione di impoverire i testi delle Scritture."

62. A. Grillmeier, "Commentar zum III. Kapitel," in *Das Zweite Vatikanische Konzil,* LThK 2 (Freiburg im Breisgau, 1967), 555.

63. Cf. J. Gnilka, "Die biblische Exegese im Lichte des Dekretes über die göttliche Offenbarung (Dei Verbum," *MüTZ,* 36 (1985), 5–19 (esp. 14–15). It is amazing to note that in his commentary on *Dei Verbum* 12, the author finds nothing at all to say regarding the Spirit, the unity of the whole of Scripture, the living Tradition of the whole Church, and the analogy of faith, which are the principles of theological interpretation of Scripture explicitly mentioned in the conciliar text.

64. See above.

65. Cf. L. Pareyson, *Verità e interpretazione* (Milan, 1971), 22.

66. AS, III/4, 306; italics ours. The Latin text reads: ". . . intelligentia spiritualis Sacrae Scripturae. . . . "

67. The following chronological information enables us to see in practical terms how our formula came to be introduced at the beginning of *Dei Verbum* 12c, right at the end of the Council:

a. Bishop Edelby's intervention was given during the third session (which lasted from 14 September to 21 November 1964) in the course of General Congregation 94, on 5 October 1964.

b. In the interval between the third and fourth sessions, at the beginning of 1965, the Biblical Institute presented four *modi* on Chapter III of the Constitution to various conferences of bishops and individual bishops. In the *textus emendatus*, which had been distributed to the Fathers on 20 November 1964 (at the end of the third session), the text began as follows: "Sed ad recte sacrorum textuum sensum eruendum . . ." (*AS*, III/3, 90). The following is one of the amendments proposed in the following months by the Biblical Institute, with three reasons in support:

Ad n. 12, lin. 22: "Sed ad recte. . . . " Inseratur: "Sed, *cum S. Scriptura eodem Spiritu quo scripta est etiam legenda et interpretanda sit,* ad recte sacrorum textuum sensum eruendum. . . . " Ratio: (*a*) Hoc propositum est in aula conciliari ab E.D. Edelby; (*b*) repraesentat doctrinam quae in tota traditione antiqua Ecclesiae vigebat, et apud Orientales usque in praesentem diem viva mansit; (*c*) opportunum esset mentionem facere de Spiritu Sancto etiam relate ad interpetationem S. Scripturae.

c. During this intermediary period (the fourth session would not open until 14 September 1965,) a number of bishops accepted this amendment and proposed it in their written recommendation to the doctrinal commission (see their names in *AS*, IV/2, 983 and 996).

d. At the start of the fourth session, the amendment was accepted by the doctrinal commission, which simply asked for the addition in a note of the two references now found in the official text: to the Encyclical *Spiritus Paraclitus* of Benedict XV, and to St. Jerome, *In Gal.*, 5,19–31 (read: 5, 19–21). The text was approved by a vote in General Congregation 132, on 21 September 1965.

e. In General Congregation 155, on 29 October 1965, it was officially stated that the addition had been definitively accepted (*AS*, IV/5, 712).

68. With regard to the principle of St. Jerome at present being analyzed, it is helpful to realize how exceptionally pregnant a formulation it received at the Council. Although the principle itself was of course traditional, the expression it received in *Dei Verbum* 12c is really not traditional. There are many patristic and medieval texts we could cite as examples, but we shall choose two that are particularly close to the formula found in *Dei Verbum* 12c. The first, already cited in note 35, is that of St. Jerome, *In Gal.*, 5, 19–21 (*PL*, 26, 445A–B), and is the text to which the Constitution itself refers: "Quicumque igitur aliter Scripturam intelligit, quam sensus Spiritus sancti flagitat *quo* conscripta est: . . . haereticus appellari potest"; here, as in the conciliar text, we have the ablative *quo* (referring to *Spiritus sancti*), but the norm indicated by Jerome for understanding Scripture is not the Spirit, but the "sense" intended by the Spirit, whereas the Council calls directly for interpretation "in the Spirit." The other text, which is closer to ours, is from William of St. Thierry, *Epist. ad fratres de monte Dei*, I, 10,31 (*PL*, 189, 327C; *SC*, 223, 238): "Quo enim spiritu Scripturae factae sunt, eo spiritu legi desiderant: ipso etiam intelligendae sunt"; here, the construction with two ablatives is the same as that of *Dei Verbum* 12c (*quo spiritu*), but *spiritu* is written with a small "s"; in order to understand David or Paul, we must have the "spirit" of David or the "spirit" of Paul (although this "spirit" is permeated by the action of the Holy Spirit). See Molina Palma, *La interpretación*, 131–133. The same remark applies to the passage in *The Imitation of Christ* in which this principle is cited (I, 5). On the other hand, in *Dei Verbum* 12c, the word is written with a capital "S" and indicates the Holy Spirit.

69. Cf. A. Ernout and F. Thomas, *Syntax latine* (Paris, 1953²), 206–207, §228: "Le complément [du passif] à l'ablatif seul est un instrumental marquant la cause." An example is found in Cicero, *Pro Sestio*, 95: "Qui stipatus semper sicariis, saeptus armatis, munitus indicibus fuit." In the words "always escorted by assassins," the ablative *sicariis* indicates both the *cause* (they are assassins who escort) and the shameful *manner* of being escorted (by assassins).

70. Cf. the *modus* presented by various Fathers between the third and fourth sessions. At the end of the formula indicated above (note 67), they add: ". . . nam facienda est *sub lumine fidei*" (*AS*, IV/2, 996).

71. See above.

72. See above.

73. For Origen: *In Lev. hom.*, 6, 6 (*SC*, 286, 297); *In Num. hom.*, 16,9 (*GCS*, VII, 153); *In Ez. hom.*, 2, 2 (*GCS*, VIII, 341–342). For St. Jerome, we would recall that according to him, neither Jew nor heretic is capable of understanding the Scriptures (see above).

74. As regards Origen, see above. For Gregory Thaumaturgus, cf. Molina Palma, *La interpretación*, 53: ". . . la idoneidad para la tarea de exégeta tiene su punto de apoyo en la propria espiritualidad del intérprete."

75. Cf. Molina Palma, *La interpretación*, 114–119 ("La interpretación como experiencia espiritual").

76. St. Hilary, *In Mt.*, 13, 2, 2 (*PL*, 9, 993D; *SC*, 254, 296): "Regni mysteria fides percipit." For St. Ambrose, cf. G. Francesconi, *Mysterium in figura. La simbolica storico-sacramentale nel linguaggio e nella teologia di Ambrogio di Milano* (Brescia, 1981), 325 ("Le condizione soggettive").

77. See Dagens, *Saint Grégoire le Grand*, 133–244 ("Intériorité").

78. *Moralia*, XVIII, 39, 60 (*PL*, 76, 72A; *CCL*, 143A, 927). ". . . *dicta Dei* nullatenus sine eius sapientia penetrantur; nisi enim quis *spiritum eius* acceperit, *eius* nullo modo *verba* cognoscit."

79. J. Leclercq, *Opere di San Bernardo*, I, "Trattati. Introduzione generale" (Milan, 1984), XL–LXI. For further development, cf. D. Farkasfalvy, *L'inspiration de l'Ecriture Sainte dans la théologie de saint Bernard* (Rome, 1964); cf., for example, p. 92: ". . . Bernard souligne à chaque pas les analogies entre l'expérience de l'auteur et celle de l'exégète . . ."; see also the whole of Chapter II, " 'Inspiratio': expérience 'in Spiritu' " (pp. 42–58), and Chapter III, "L'expression de l'expérience spirituelle" (pp. 59–93).

80. However, it is true that the adjective "sacred" had already been used once in B (*sacer auctor*).

81. Farkasfalvy, *L'inspiration de l'Ecriture Sainte dans la théologie de saint Bernard,* 96.

82. Cf. H. de Lubac, *Exégèse médiévale*, I/1, Théologie 41 (Paris, 1959), 128: "Ce ne sont pas seulement les écrivains qui furent inspirés un jour: les livres sacrés eux-mêmes sont et demeurent inspirés. . . . L'Esprit ne l'a pas seulement dictée: il s'est comme enfermé en elle. Il y habite. Son souffle l'anime toujours. . . . Elle est pleine de l'Esprit." As St. Anselm said, *De concordia*, III, 6 (*PL*, 158, 528B), Scripture is "Spiritus sancti miraculo fecundata."

83. On the subject of the living water of the word, as linked to the theme of the well, see our work *La vérité dans saint Jean*, II (Rome, 1977), 688–692.

84. *In Num. hom.*, 12, 1 (*GCS*, VII, 94; *SC*, 29, 236). Other texts of Origen are referred to in de la Potterie, *La vérité dans saint Jean*, II, 691, note 137.

85. *In Gal.*, 1, 11–12 (*PL*, 26, 347A). "Nec putemus in verbis Scripturarum esse Evangelium, sed in sensu: non in superficie, sed in medulla; non in sermonum foliis, sed in radice rationis."

86. *In Gal.*, 2, 3–5 (*PL*, 26, 359B–C).

87. *In Ez.* I, 7,8 (*PL*, 76, 844A). The same is found in Origen; cf. Harl, *Origéne. Philocalie, 1–20*, 148–151.

88. St. Augustine, *Confess.*, XII, 14, 17 (*PL*, 32, 832). In this connection, see the very beautiful pages of de Lubac, *Exégèse médiévale*, I/1, 119–128 ("Mira profunditas").

89. *In Num.*, 5, 1 (*GCS*, VII, 25; *SC*, 29, 111). In this regard, see

H. Urs von Balthasar, "Le 'mysterion' d'Origène," *RSR*, 26 (1936), 513–562.

90. *In Ez. I*, 6, 3 (*PL*, 76, 829C). See also Mor. *in Iob*, XX, 1,1 (*PL*, 76, 135C; *CCL*, 243, 1003): "Scriptura sacra . . . uno eodemque sermone dum narrat textum prodit *mysterium.*"

91. *Tract. in Ioan.*, 8, 13 (*PL*, 35, 1458); and, a little earlier (*ibid.*), ". . . quid mater Iesu in mysterio"; or (*PL*, 35, 1460) "His ex Evangelio quae certe manifesta sunt, intellectis, patebunt illa omnia mysteria quae in isto miraculo Domini latent." On the contrast between *historia* (or *littera*) and *mysterium*, see also St. Jerome, *In Mc.*, 9, 1–7 (cited above); *In Mt. II*, 13–35 (cited in note 41 above). See also Barsotti, *La parola e lo spirito*, 64–76 (Chapter 3, "La parola e il mistero").

92. Cf. our article, "Le nozze messianiche," in *Lo Sposo e la Sposa*, Parola, Spirito e vita 13 (Bologna, 1981), 87–104. Similar remarks could be made for most of the great Johannine symbols.

93. Molina Palma, *La interpretación*, 275–277.

94. Cf. the scholastic sayings: "Finis, etsi sit postremus in executione, est tamen primus in intentione agentis" (*Summa Theologiae*, II, q. 1, a. 1, ad 1); ". . . finis . . . est . . . causa principalissima, inquantum movet ad agendum" (*ibid.*, q. 7, a. 4, ad 2).

95. See note 67 above.

96. Cf. de Lubac, *Histoire et Esprit*, 166–178 ("Les deux testaments"); *idem*, *Exégèse médiévale*, I/1, 305–363 ("L'unité des deux testaments"); Barsotti, *La parola e lo spirito*, 38–42 ("L'unità di tutta la Bibbia").

97. *De arca Noe morali*, II, 8 (*PL*, 176, 642).

98. See above.

99. See above.

100. St. Augustine, *Quaest. in Hept.*, 2, 73 (*PL*, 34, 623).

101. Adam of Persenia, *Fragmenta mariana* (*PL*, 211, 750D), cited by de Lubac, *Exégèse médiévale*, II (Paris, 1961), 189.

102. In this connection, cf. our article, "La lecture de l'Écriture Sainte 'dans l'Esprit': la manière patristique de lire la Bible est-elle possible aujourd'hui?" *Revue Catholique Internationale, Communio*, XI/4 (1986), 11–27.

103. See B. de Margerie, *Introduction à l'histoire de l'exégèse*, I, "Les Pères Grecs et orientaux (Paris, 1980), 281, in Chapter X, regarding the exegesis of St. Cyril of Alexandria.

104. *Ibid.*, 282.

105. See E. Przywara, "Analogia Fidei," *LThK*, I (Freiburg im Breisgau, 1957), 473–476.

106. J. de Finance, "De l'indicible à l'Indicible," *Gregorianum*, 65 (1984), 657–694 (cf. 681); italics ours.

107. *In Gal.*, 1, 11 (*PL*, 26, 347A); see note 40 above.

108. St. Hilary, *In Mt.*, 14, 3 (*PL*, 9, 997B): "interioris intelligentiae ratio." St. Gregory, *In Cant.*, 2 (*CCL*, 144, 4): "interiorem intelligentiam." See note 38 above.

109. H. de Lubac, *L'Ecriture dans la Tradition* (Paris, 1966), 7.

110. In this connection, see what we say in our article, "La lecture de l'Ecriture Sainte 'dans l'Esprit,' " cited in note 102 above.

111. Cf. P. Toinet, *Pour une théologie de l'exégèse* (Paris, 1983); and the general conclusions of the 1985 Extraordinary Synod of Bishops.

112. See above. Cf. particularly the studies of Rigaux and Harrington, cited in note 2 above.

113. See also what we said above when discussing the actual text of *Dei Verbum* (p. 248 above).

114. R. Guardini, *Auf dem Wege. Versuch* (Mainz, 1923), 59f.; H. Urs von Balthasar, *La gloire et la croix*, I (Paris, 1965), 450; H.-G. Gadamer, *Truth and Method* (London, 1979²), 155–156.

115. Subtitle of *Histoire et dogme*.

116. J. Ladrière, "Postface," to T. Tshibangu, *La théologie comme science au XXe siècle* (Kinshasa, 1980), 224–229.

117. *Tischreden*, WAT 5, 26, n. 5246. This phrase is cited as an epigraph at the beginning of the second part of Gadamer's work *Truth and Method*, 151.

CHAPTER 9

Old and New Testament

Participation and Analogy

Horacio Simian-Yofre, S.J.

Summary

Taking its inspiration from some texts of St. Irenaeus, particularly Book IV of the *Adversus Haereses,* the present study tries to show how one can conceive the relationship between the Old and the New Testament, starting with the idea of a full salvation present in the Old and in the New Testament, in which both historical periods share, and which manifests itself equally in both Testaments.

Introduction

The relationship between the Christian Church and the Old Testament has not been an easy one.

The modest place given for centuries to the Old Testament in the Catholic eucharistic liturgy before the reform inspired by Vatican Council II, its rare use in homilies, its notable absence as a constructive element in dogmatic theology, the widespread lack of knowledge of the Old Testament, which most of the Christian faithful and not a few of their pastors suffer from, and the lack of personal motivation for the study of the Old Testament, which effects the average student in theology, are only some of the eloquent signs of the uncertain place of the Old Testament in the theology and the life of the Church.[1]

267

With clear spiritual intuition, the Church has always rejected
the temptation to get rid of this difficulty that is constitutive of
her existence, though she has not always found the most apt
formulas to express the importance of the Old Testament, the
reasons that demand its presence, and the type of relationship
that exists between the Old Testament and the New Testament.

Non-Catholic Christian confessions have shown a special sensitivity to this problem, and have contributed, with many successful
efforts, to an adequate formulation of this difficult relationship.[2]

The Dogmatic Constitution *Dei Verbum* devoted its fourth
chapter to the Old Testament.[3]

In number 14, the "permanent value" of the Old Testament is
founded on its character as witness to the *oeconomia salutis*, in
which we find her "praenuntiata, enarrata atque explicata."

In number 15, there is a step forward in relation to number 14 in
two ways. On the one hand, it makes clear the meaning of economy in the Old Testament, i.e., to prepare for the coming of
Christ, announce him prophetically, and indicate him through
various figures. On the other hand, the description of the function
of the Old Testament *books* is more generic than the earlier formulation. The terms *praeparare, nuntiare,* and *significare* are not used.
The Old Testament books, it is affirmed, manifest men's knowledge of God, and God's way of working with them. This manifestation is characterized as in accordance with "the state of mankind
before the time of salvation established by Christ." Because of
this, the books of the Old Testament may contain some things
that are imperfect and transitory.

Finally, number 16 describes the relationship between the Old
Testament and the New Testament in St. Augustine's proverbial
phrase: "The New Testament is hidden in the Old Testament,
and the Old is made manifest in the New." The books of the Old
Testament "acquire and manifest their full meaning in the New
Testament . . . illustrating it and explaining it at the same
time."

Notwithstanding the depth of the doctrine proposed, it is
possible for the Christian reader or, for that matter, the Jewish
reader of these documents, the theologian, and the exegete of
the Old Testament to feel uneasy. Lastly, the central expressions
of this chapter of *Dei Verbum* seem to consider the Old Testament as a poor relative of the New Testament, a habitual guest
yet an unwelcome one.

Nonetheless, it affirms the perennial value of the Old Testament; however, the description of its function as "to prepare, to announce, and to indicate" suggests a subordinate and temporary function. Why should the Old Testament continue to prepare and announce with figures what is already a present reality and which is evident?

If the Old Testament as economy of salvation has an exclusively propaedeutic function, it is legitimate and necessary that the proclamation of the definitive salvation brought about by Jesus Christ replaces the narrative of that economy of salvation.

If these objections were irresistible, one would have to conceive the Old Testament like a pedagogue who has to leave the house when the son has reached adulthood. Perhaps one can still accept him in the house, as a recompense for the role he has played, and one can even consult him, but his services are basically terminated.

At any rate, the formulations of *Dei Verbum* (and also the majority of the studies in both Catholic and Protestant circles) justify the possibility and the right of the Christian community to preserve and use the Old Testament, but they rarely refer to the *necessity* of such use, to the reasons on which it is founded, or to the fruits derived from it.

An expression of *Dei Verbum* states the essential permanence of this "pedagogue" even more decisively than the others. The Old Testament, it says, "sheds light on and explains the New Testament" (No. 16). If this shedding of light is permanent and necessary, one can never renounce the Old Testament in principle or in practice.

But in what does this shedding of light and explanation that the Old Testament brings consist? Is it purely technical, i.e., to inform, as a dictionary does, about the meaning of some words, or, as an encyclopedia does, to clarify the cultural background of personalities and institutions of the New Testament? If this were the principal contribution, the Old Testament would have no more intrinsic value for the Christian than the documents of Qumran or any other writing related to the times of the New Testament.

Or is the contribution of the Old Testament essential, that is to say, to explain and illuminate the New Testament *inasmuch as* it witnesses the salvation that we have received in Christ?

The following reflections are the tentative contribution of an exegete, who, faced with the wealth of patristic writings, and basing himself on some of Irenaeus' insights, is trying to clarify the problem, bringing together certain elements that Book IV of *Adversus Haereses*[4] provides about the relationship between the Old and the New Testament.

Nothwithstanding the privileged place that other conciliar documents give to the writings of Irenaeus[5], this is a source that has been relatively little used in dealing with this problem.

Irenaeus did not deal explicitly with the relationship of the Old to the New Testament. As is well known, his concern was to reject gnostic doctrines, showing "the continuity of the economy of salvation, the progressive development of the redemptive work."[6]

The need to show, when faced with the heresy, that one and the same God is the origin of creation and the source of salvation enables him to emphasize the strict unity existing between the Old and the New Testament.[7]

Our study presents the texts of Irenaeus in four short sections: the first is dedicated to the continuous action of God for the salvation of man; the second considers the function of Abraham in relation to the Christian; the third studies the relation of the prophets to the word of God; the fourth reflects upon the presence of Christ "inseminatus" in the Old Testament.

The concluding part of the study tries to identify the principle of unity existing between the Old and the New Testament and draws some conclusions that follow from this unity.

The Uninterrupted Salvific Action of God

1. *Adver. Haer.* IV, 14, 1 treats at length of the pèrfection of God, who, not being in need of anybody, and out of his love and generosity, creates man in Adam to bestow his favors on him and so demands our service in order to grant us salvation.

Irenaeus renders this thought explicit in IV, 14, 2, describing the way God acts:

> Thus God, from the beginning modeled *man*
>   because of his own bounty;
> and chose the *Patriarchs*
>   *propter illorum salutem;*

He formed his *people* beforehand
   teaching the ignorant to follow God;
again He prepared the *prophets*
   accustoming *man* to carry his Spirit on earth
   and to have communion with God.

The inclusive structure of this paragraph through the use of the word "man" suggests that this modeling does not refer exclusively to the formation of Adam. In this text, "to model" includes the totality of men and the ensemble of the gifts granted to them. The election of the patriarchs, the anticipated formation of the people, and the preparation of the prophets are three aspects of this modeling.

The text does not have a gradually ascending classification either in mentioning the stages of the modeling (patriarchs, people, prophets), or in the actions that characterize each of them (to elect, to form, to prepare), or in the aim of such actions (*propter salutem*, to teach, to accustom), or, finally, to the addresses of such actions (*illorum*, the ignorant, man).

Still, *illorum* can hardly refer to the patriarchs themselves. In neither of the other two members of the text does the instrument of God's action identify itself with the addressee of the action. Thus, *illorum* must take into account as antecedent *man*, who in this case, as we have already suggested, must be understood complexively: man, including comprehensively Adam and the patriarchs, the people and the ignorant, and the prophets.[8]

Irenaeus thus presents us not with a sketch of the progressive history of humanity, but with a portrait of humanity valid for all times. Looking at humanity from different angles, Irenaeus explains to us who is man, and how God works with him at every moment.

This reading of the text finds confirmation in the expressions that sum up God's action and its aim. God bestows his *koinonia* to (all) those who need him, and sketches the building of salvation for whoever pleases him.

Irenaeus exemplifies the salvific action of God with three events in the history of Israel (the guidance of the people in Egypt, the bestowal of the law in the desert, and the gift of the land). He then completely changes the type of affirmation and mentions the gift of the better garment for he who returns to the house of the Father (cf. Lk. 15:22–23).

The meaning of the examples is evident: even the history of Israel in Egypt and the desert contribute to the participation in the *koinonia* of God. Irenaeus can rightly conclude his demonstration:

> . . . multis modis componens humanum genus ad consonatiam salutis. ("Thus [God] disposed mankind in many modes blending it into a 'harmony' of salvation.")

The image of the symphony of salvation (evoked perhaps by Lk. 15:25 in the passage just cited) suggests the chant of thanksgiving of those who receive the salvation, but much more the several melodies of salvation that the Father composed, for those who know how to listen to them, using the vast scale of tones and semitones that constitute the human race.[9]

The image calls to mind like a paraphrase the mention of the multiple waters of the Spirit, "For the Father is rich and multiple (in his way of acting)."[10]

2. In his demonstration of the parable of the wicked husbandmen (IV, 36, 1–2). Irenaeus expresses yet again this continuous, multiple, untiring salvific action of the Father by means of the prophets and the Son in favor of all men.

It is not necessary here to repeat the careful and rich exegesis of the text that has been presented by A. Orbe.[11] It is enough to note how the concept of the vine confirms the proposition of IV, 14, 2.

The vine is the human race that "God planted . . . fashioning Adam and electing the fathers (= patriarchs)." God did not fashion man only to abandon him later, but he has elected him in the person of the patriarchs.[12]

This statement, on the one hand, restricts the meaning of the vine to the teaching at which the parable aims, but on the other hand, it amplifies it: the human race is affected as a totality through the election of the patriarchs.

If from a historic point of view, one must affirm that a section of the "human substance"[13] was leased to the people of Israel, or more precisely, to each Israelite, to make it bear fruit in the presence of God (and the parable refers to this "section" when it talks of the vine handed over to new tenants), it is no less legitimate to conclude that other sections of this large vineyard have been entrusted to other vinedressers, of whose administration nothing is said.

The words of A. Orbe[14] express with the necessary exactitude and conciseness the results of the interpretation of this parable that concern our study more directly:

> The symbolism of the vine in Irenaeus . . . is always centered on the *only* human lineage, the mold common to all men, Jews and Gentiles, first chosen among the descendants of Abraham to give fruits of justice (in the Old Testament) and *extended* after . . . to all the believers of the New Testament. . . .
>
> The change from one vinedresser to others in the possession of the vine does not indicate a radical mutation of the economy. . . .
>
> St. Irenaeus condemns the distinction of justices, one of the Old and another of the New Testament.
>
> God always seeks the same works: equal in both Testaments, because they are animated by the love for the one God and for man.

There can be no doubt about the importance Irenaeus attaches to the salvific action of the Father toward the whole of humanity from the beginning of time and to the presence of the word. The word reveals the Creator through creation; by means of the Son (made flesh), the Father who has engendered him; and announces himself and the Father through the Law and the prophets (cfr. IV, 6, 6).

There is no foundation in Irenaus for an adequate distinction, still less an opposition, between preparation and realization of the salvific work that could coincide with the Old and New Testament, respectively.

Abraham and the Word of God

1. In *Adver. Haer.* IV, 5, 1–2, Irenaeus had affirmed the unicity of God, creator and savior, who was announced by the Law and the prophets, and was recognized by Christ as his Father.

In IV, 5, 3–5, he affirms the unity that exists between the Father, the God of the living, and Christ, the resurrection and the life.

We must now show that "Christ therefore himself, with the

Father, is the God of the living, who spoke unto Moses, who was also manifested to the Fathers" (IV, 5, 2).

The argument starts with the affirmation of Jesus: "Abraham saw my day and he was glad" (Jn. 8:56).

Irenaeus identifies "to see the day of Jesus" with the faith of Abraham, of which Romans 4:3 speaks. What was the content of Abraham's faith? To believe that the one God was the author of heaven and earth, and believe in the posterity that had been promised to him.

There are three implications to this belief, emphasized and linked by a triple *juste* ("justly," IV, 5, 3–4).

It was just and reasonable that Abraham should leave his earthly kin, to follow the word of God, becoming a foreigner along with the word in order to become its fellow citizen. In some way, Irenaeus tells us, Abraham perceives the command to leave his kin and follow as an expression of the word.

The way the text continues requires our attention even more. Rightly did the apostles also, having their birth from Abraham, leave their boats and their father, and follow the word. And finally: rightly then likewise do "we," having the same faith as Abraham, take up our Cross, as Isaac did his Wood, and follow the same word.

The apostles are united to Abraham through a triple link: as descendants according to the flesh, renouncing their fathers and their possessions, and following the word. Even "we" are tied to Abraham through a triple bond: the same faith, submission to suffering, and following the word.

Following the word then implies a strict relation to Abraham, which is made explicit in the renouncing of possessions (fatherland, family, possessions) to make oneself a cocitizen of the word.

Juste ("to be reasonable") suggests more than to appreciate the convenience of certain means to reach determined aims. It is the perception of the will of the word, a logic that derives from the nature of things. Abraham having believed in God and in his promises, accepted the consequences: abandoning his family and following the word.

In a similar manner, whoever recognizes himself as belonging to the family of Abraham, like the apostles, must set out to follow the word. And, on the contrary, whoever follows the word (like "us") recognizes his consanguinity with Abraham.

Thus, one arrives at the exxtraordinary conclusion that Irenaeus proposes: *in* Abraham, *man* had learnt beforehand and had grown accustomed to follow the word of God (IV, 5, 4).[15]

Two affirmations in this paragraph are beyond dispute; they belong to the content of Christian faith: the unicity of God (as against the gnostic theory of the difference between the God of the Old Testament and the "Father" of Jesus), and the presence and activity of the word united to the Father from all eternity.

But the relation between Abraham and the believer includes other points of view whose richness has not yet been definitely incorporated into Christian spirituality.

To affirm that *in* Abraham *man* (as such) had learnt in anticipation to follow the word of God is to affirm an almost mediatory role on the part of Abraham for all believers. Abraham is presented not only as a religious *model* for the believer, whom one must imitate, nor solely as a "figure" of the believer (as an historic anticipation), but—in some way—as an efficient cause for the faith of the believer.

In like manner, to the Pauline affirmation that in Adam we have all sinned and in Christ we have all been saved, it is affirmed here that in Abraham we have *all* received the faith. Abraham thus acquires the stature not only of a far away and dignified ancestor who believed "before," but of an authentic father of the believer, whom one must recognize so in order to participate in the faith.

This also seems to be the implication of the reference to the apostles. They left their father's boat (as Abraham had left his father Terah) and followed the word not only *like* Abraham but *because* Abraham had already followed the same word. The faith of Abraham made the faith of the apostles possible, and the faith of the apostles, in following Abraham, made that of all believers possible.

Abraham foreshadows by justification obtained through faith without circumcision, and by the alliance of circumcision, all believers, both the circumcised and the uncircumcised, and so he firmly establishes all believers on the cornerstone that is Christ (cfr. IV, 25, 1).

2. In IV, 21, 1, Irenaeus comes back to the centrality of Abraham in the process of the faith of the believer, stating that in him our faith is "prefigured," that Abraham is patriarch and prophet of our faith, and also father of those among the gentiles

who believe in Christ. And he concludes with the admirable affirmation: "his faith and ours are one and the same faith." This statement refers not only to the subjective act of faith, but to its object: "He indeed believed in things to come as already being accomplished, because of the promise of God, and we in like manner by faith contemplate the inheritance which is in the Kingdom."

Like Abraham, we are set on our way toward the future by faith, which we see as already realized; we follow the word as he did in so far as we renounce our security (our paternal family, our fatherland, our possessions, and our very descendance), and imitate the word, who in Christ had renounced even his father and his fatherland to be able to arrive at possessing them anew and definitvely.

The faith of Abraham is not only a suggestive mirror of our faith, on which we can meditate to our own profit. It is as constitutive and as irrevocable to the Christian faith as that of the apostles.

The consequences that follow from this for the relation between the Old and the New Testament are not without importance.

Because the Old Testament is the witness of the faith of Abraham, which is constitutive of our faith as an efficient cause and archetype, the Old Testament cannot be reduced to a mere preparation for, or figure of, the New Testament, but it must be received as truly constitutive of the New Testament. Obviously, a thematic ignorance of the Old Testament does not make the Christian faith impossible, nor can a thematic ignorance of the New Testament make the paths of God with men impossible. And it is also evident that the Old Testament, because it belongs as an entity to the process of faith, must also belong thematically to the content of this same faith.

The Prophets and the Word of God

1. The rich vision of the prophetic mission that Irenaeus presents has a fundamental nucleus, i.e., the action of the prophets does not consist solely in the announcing of the message received.

By means of the prophets, the Spirit indicates the future. To indicate is to establish a system of signs that points toward the future. These signs are not only the words that the prophets utter, but also the visions, behavior, and gestures that they perform:

> quae quidem videnda erant visibiliter videntes,
> quae vero audienda erant, sermone praeconantes,
> quae vero agenda erant, operatione perficientes
> universa vero prophetice annuntiantes (IV, 20, 8).

It is difficult to decide if the verbal forms should be translated simply as future ("that which will be seen," as the edition of *Sources Chrétiennes* translates them) or rather with a sense of obligation ("they performed with acts what [also] was to be achieved in the future").

This interpretation insists on the continuity between the performance of the sign by the prophet, and that in which all participate.

The prophetic action appears as an active and anticipatory gesture in history that introduces a change and calls for the gesture of others, who must continue it.

The prophet is not only an announcer or preacher of salvation, but plays an active part in it; he makes efficient gestures under the guidance of the Spirit, although such gestures must be continued and completed.

A close relation then exists between what the prophet transmits, and the way it comes to his knowledge.

Because an essential element of the prophetic task is to witness to the future vision of God, it is necessary that the prophets have an experience of such a vision. Only this vision enables the prophet to announce God as he who one day will be contemplated by those who remain faithful to the announcement. Moses (Ex. 33:20–22), conceived as a prophet, had only seen "the back of Yahweh." This event manifests two things: that it is not possible to see God face to face, but also that a divine manifestation adapted to men is possible. Such will be the concrete manifestation of Jesus.

In a similar manner, the presence of Yahweh to Elias in the breeze and not in the wind, or the earthquake or in the fire (IV, 19, 11–12), expresses the pacific character of the Kingdom of God in Christ, which has yet to be manipulated.

Contrary to the first impression that the reader might have, these texts do not read allegorically the manifestation of Yahweh in the Old Testament, starting from the manifestation of Jesus in the New Testament.

Yahweh's manifestation to Moses is the ontological figure of that of God in Jesus. The relationship between Yahweh and the people through Moses is equivalent (one can say analogically proportional) to the relationship between God and the Christian community through Jesus. Whoever meditates from the New Testament the accounts of the visions of Moses and Elias will recognize this analogy quite clearly. But the foundation of this analogy does not remain hidden to those who have access only to the Old Testament texts. Behind the manifestations of God (to Moses, to Elias, in Jesus), there is the word that reveals the Father, manifold and rich like him, and that manifests him not only under one form, nor solely under one aspect, but "according to the working of His several economies" (IV, 20, 11).

In IV, 20, 5, Irenaeus distinguishes three different modes of vision.

God, invisible in his power and his glory, makes himself visible by means of the Spirit in a prophetic way, by means of the Son according to adoption, and in the kingdom of heaven according to the fatherhood. The Spirit prepares man for the Son, the Son leads him to the Father, and the Father grants him the incorruptibility that this vision produces.

But the time of the prophetic vision according to the Spirit does not differ from the salvific nature of the time of the vision by means of the Son.[16]

The prophetic vision that is talked about in IV, 20, 8 extends not only to the prophets, but to "all His members, sanctified and taught the things which belong unto God." This vision allows "man" to be formed and exercised beforehand "in appropriating to himself that glory which shall be hereafter revealed unto them that love God."

Here again there appears the insistence on "man" as the universal addressee of the action of the patriarchs and the prophets, which we have underlined and commented on in IV, 14, 2 and IV, 5, 4.

2. That the prophet takes an active part in salvation is also affirmed in IV, 33, 10:

The Prophets typified all these things in themselves, for the love of God, and for his Word's sake.

"All these things" are persecutions and sufferings. They who are more identified with the word, like the prophets and the early Church, must also share the destiny prepared for the followers of the word by those who reject it.

The sufferings of the prophets are a kind of prefiguration in their own flesh of the sufferings of the word. This helps Irenaeus to extend his doctrine to other prophetic actions, taking up once again the Pauline metaphor of the body and its members.

In a well-structured paragraph (IV, 33, 10), Irenaeus thus presents his doctrine. The prophets, because they were already members of Christ:

> uniusquisque eorum . . . et prophetationem manifestabat
> omnes et multi *unum* praeformantes
>   et ea quae sunt *unius*
>   annuntiantes
> omnes quidem *unum* praefigurabant
> unusquisque autem eorum
>   et dispositionem adimplebat
>   et . . . operationem Christi
>   prophetabat

The presupposition of the text is that the body manifests itself by the action of all its members, and not by that of only one of them, but in conformity to the proper nature of each member. The prophets are considered in two ways, individually (*unusquisque*) and as a whole (*omnes*); the actions of the prophets fall into two groups: *manifesting, announcing* and *prophesying* refer to the proclamation. The other three verbs differ from the first three. They do not express the announcement or proclamation but the performance. This is evident in the case of *adimplere dispositionem* (to accomplish the economy) if we take into account that "salvific economies" are the salvific action of God. The prophet completes in some measure the salvific action of God. This meaning is confirmed by the other uses of *adimplere* that Irenaeus presents in book IV;

- accomplishment of Scripture: IV, 23, 1; 26, 1; 29, 1
- Christ confirms and *adimplet* that which had been announced of him: IV, 24, 2; 34, 2
- Christ accomplishes the Pasch that long before Moses *figuratim praenuntiavit*: IV, 10, 1

- the accomplishment of the paths of the Lord enables Israel *adimplere amicitiam Dei:* IV, 16, 4

The structure of the paragraph also suggests that *praeformare* and *praefigurare* belong to the same area of meaning as "to perform."

Besides, the way of expressing the object of the two verbs is also curious: "unum." It is not evident that this "unum" is "the only personality" (Christ) as proposed by the edition in *Sources Chrétiennes*.

The infrequent use of *praeformare* in *Adver. Haer.* confirms our suspicion. In III, 22, 3, the word *praeformat* in Adam the "economy" of humanity; IV, 14, 2: *Deus . . . populum . . . praeformabat;* IV, 20, 8: *Spiritus Dei . . . futura significavit, praeformans nos . . . ut homo praeformaretur;* in II, 3, 1–2, it is God who *praeformavit creationem in semetipso;* in V, 13, 1, the cures of Jesus *per temporalia praeformant aeterna;* in IV, 26, 1, the "Law" as read by Christians, *Christi regnum praeformat.*

In each of these texts, where usually one of the persons of the Trinity or actions closely connected with them (cures, the Law) is the subject, there is not simply an announcement of a future action. In each of the indicated actions, God performs his salvific work.

Praeformare also indicates that the action with which it is concerned is not confined to the present; its meaning goes well beyond itself. But to understand *praeformare* as a synonym of *praefigurare,* giving the latter verb the weak meaning of *annuntiare,* does not do justice to the texts.

Nor does *praefigurare* in Irenaeus seem to have primarily the cognitive meaning of "to announce beforehand," or outline the drawing of a reality that will be verified later (even if this meaning is not completely excluded, cfr. IV, 32, 2, *imagines praefigurans;* and IV, 21, 3, Rachel prefigures the Church). The use of *praefigurare* in opposition to *praenuntiare* (IV, 21, 3; 22, 2; cfr. IV, 25, 3) suggests that the two verbs do not overlap completely. This impression is reinforced by the texts where *praefigurare* appears in relation to Abraham (IV, 25, 1: *ut praefigurarentur in eo utraque testamenta;* IV, 21, 1: *in Abraham praefigurabatur fides nostra*), whose ontological relation with the Christian we have considered in the second part of this study.

The conclusion is that in IV, 33, 10, Irenaeus proposes two ways of seeing the action of the prophets. The prophets announce a work of salvation because it is not yet concluded and because Christ must set his seal on it; but, at the same time, they participate actively in the achievement of the unique act of salvation (*unum?*), which is already being accomplished and is already producing its fruits.

This rich way of conceiving prophetic activity does not prevent Irenaeus, in IV, 33, 11–13, from making a lengthy explanation of the relation between the texts and the events of the Old and the New Testament in an allegorical way, which became the usual way of reading the Scriptures.

The relation is established by means of introductory terms that echo each other. Irenaeus relates what the prophets "saw" with what they "contemplated" or wished to "signify," and what they "said" with what they "indicated, made known, announced, prophesied, explained and proclaimed." In these correspondences, the verbs of the second group, which we have discussed with regard to IV, 33, 10, do not figure!

Some of the correlations established are the classic ones already suggested by the New Testament itself: the Suffering Servant of Isaiah is the figure of Jesus (IV, 33, 12); Isaiah 7 refers to the birth of Jesus (IV, 33, 11). Other correlations are due to Irenaeus' creativity: e.g., the coming of Yahweh and the coming of the word made flesh, his birth in Bethlehem, and the entry into Jerusalem (IV, 33, 11–12).

Even more subtle are the correspondences that Irenaeus sees between the motivations of Yahweh and those of Jesus (IV, 33, 12), between the darkness of the Day of Yahweh and those of the hour of the crucifixion (*ibid.*), between the poetic expressions of the psalms and the mysteries of the resurrection, ascension, and the Church (IV, 33, 13).

If some of these allegorical relationships seem strange and even unacceptable to the modern mind, which is reared in another type of exegesis, nevertheless the general principle established by Irenaeus continues to be valid and suggestive: each one of the prophets, with his words and his own life, has achieved one of the "economies" of salvation that the Father achieves in humanity.

The Son "Inseminatus" in the Scriptures

1. Irenaeus deduces the proof of the presence of the Christ-Logos in the Old Testament from the words of Jesus in Matthew

13:17: "many prophets and holy men longed to see what you see. . . ."

His argument here once again has a Pauline flavor: the desire presupposes the knowledge of what one desires. This knowledge, not being of things present, and thus acquirable through experience of reality, must have been received beforehand. Thus, it is the same word who revealed himself in multiple ways to those who believed, who at one time converses with Adam, at another time gives the Law, sometimes exhorts, frees the slave and adopts him as son, and in due time bestows the inheritance of incorruption upon man (IV, 11, 1).[17]

In this text, the action of the word is not exercised in favor of individual personalities known in the Old Testament. In compliance with the expression of Matthew, "many prophets and holy men," Irenaeus uses universal formulations that allow him simply to include all men.[18]

2. The Son is not only revealer of the Father since the beginning, inspirer of prophetic visions and bestower of graces and ministries (IV, 20, 7), he is at the same time, already in the Old Testament, the object of this revelation: "The Son of God is as seed scattered everywhere in His Scriptures" (IV, 10, 1).

The presence of the Son ". . . sown" in the Scriptures has a pedagogical function. The patriarchs and the prophets:

> also prefigured our faith, and announced throughout the earth the coming of the Son of God; who and of what sort he shall be, so that men who were to come . . . might easily receive the coming of Christ . . . (IV, 23, 1).

The purpose of this sowing, according to the following examples, is to offer to the personalities of the New Testament witness (of the Old Testament) that will help them to accept the paths of God. Joseph can accept the imcomprehensible pregnancy of Mary through the mediation of Isaiah 7:14; the contemporaries of Jesus are prepared to accept him on the strength witness of Isaiah 61, which Jesus himself cites in the synagogue at Capharnaum, and the Ethiopian in Acts 8 finds himself prepared for the preaching of Philip through Isaiah 53 (IV, 23, 2).

On the contrary, Paul's activity among the gentiles is rendered more difficult because these are not prepared, and for them Paul must preach "to the Gentiles in discourse without scriptures" (IV, 24, 2).

3. But it is in IV, 25, 3 that Irenaeus takes a decisive step in his doctrine of the patriarchs and the prophets as "sowers" of the word that concerns Christ:

> For it was meet that some things should be foretold (*praenunti-ari*) in a fatherly way by the Fathers; others should be typified (*praefigurari*) in a legal way by the Prophets; others again should be fully traced (*deformari*) after the delineation of Christ, by those who have received adoption" (IV, 25, 3).

Which is the way proper to the patriarchs of announcing beforehand? An answer should be offered in IV, 21, 1–3, which considers the stories of Abraham, Isaac, and Jacob, searching for their "Christian meaning."

It is said of Abraham (IV, 21, 1) that in him our faith was prefigured.[19]

In the story of Isaac (IV, 21, 2), not only "the actions of the patriarchs," but above all the birth of Esau and Jacob as the origin of two peoples, one a slave the other free, constitutes the prophetic action.

In the story of Jacob (IV, 21, 3), Irenaeus states that "his acts" are "full of providential turns" (*plenos dispositionum*).

There is a progressive allegorization of the interpretation of the "acts of the patriarchs." In the Scriptures, Abraham is truly the starting point of Israel's faith and consequently of the Church, by means of the apostolic community; Isaac is—according to the patriarchal tradition—effectively the origin of two peoples, which represent freedom and slavery according to their relationship to Yahweh's will.

But to find in Jacob's birth a figure of the birth of Jesus, according to the text in the book of Revelation, "he comes out as a winner and to win"; or to compare the salary received by Jacob, the many-colored sheep, with Christ, who has as "salary" men of different nations reunited under the same reign of faith, is to enter decidedly into allegorical elaboration.

The general conclusion holds nevertheless in the solidly theological line we have already followed in other passages:

> And so far indeed He (the Logos?) was through His Patriarchs and Prophets prefiguring and foretelling (*praefigurans et prae-nuntians*) things to come, exercising beforehand His part in

God's ordained ways, and training His heritage to obey God, and to be strangers in the world, and to follow His Word, and to presignify (*praesignificare*) what is to come. For with God nothing is void, nor without significance (IV, 21, 3).

On these theological premises and with a different exegetical mentality, Irenaeus could easily have shown how Jacob performs in a paradigmatic way (prefigures) the path of man enclosed in himself and used to dispose of all things, who must learn through a painful process of guilt and suffering to follow "the word of God", from injustice to reconciliation.

The affirmation that the acts themselves of the lives of the patriarchs have an objective connection with the mystery of salvation (which is always achieved through Christ), and from this point of view such acts "announce" Christ, is then always valid.

Other things, continues Irenaeus in IV, 25, 3, were prefigured by the prophets in the way proper to the Law.

"To announce" and "prefigure"[20] do not seem to be applied in this paragraph more specifically to one subject rather than to another. In IV, 20, 1, the acts of the patriarchs (and not of a prophet) are those that "prefigure"; in IV, 21, 3, to prefigure and foretell are applied both to the prophets and to the patriarchs. The prophets therefore prefigure the teaching of Jesus and also the exhortation to the accomplishment of the Law.

But it is above all the third way of "the sowing of Christ" in the Scriptures to which IV, 25, 3 alludes that is the most difficult to comprehend.[21]

Oportebat enim . . . quaedam vero deformari secundum formationem Christi ab his qui adoptionem perceperunt.

Several times in *Adver. Haer.*, "adoption" refers to divine filiation obtained in Christ.[22] But of particular interest for our context is IV, 8, 1: God has introduced into the Kingdom of heaven:

Abraham et semen eius quod est Ecclesia, per Christum Jesum cui et adoptio redditur et hereditas quae Abrahae promissa est.

As careful comparison between V, 32, 2 and IV, 8, 1 would show, this is not an adoptive divine filiation, but "the adoptive filiation in relation to Abraham: through Christ the gentiles were converted into adoptive sons of Abraham (cf. IV, 25, 1) and have a part in his inheritance."[23]

In the Latin text *cui* refers not to Jesus, but to *Ecclesia*. The latin translator of the text invariabily introduces the relative pronoun into the proposition governed by it, instead of putting it before it.

It is likely that Irenaeus used the concept of filiation in relation to Abraham to refer not only to the gentiles but also to the Hebrews who obtain it through blood, even though partially. The full adherence to the faith of Abraham enables one to be a true son of Abraham.

Whoever wishes to arrive at adoptive filiation in the fullness of times (cfr. III, 21, 4) must pass through the Abrahamic filiation, which the Hebrew receives through his adherence to the faith of Abraham, and the gentile in Christ Jesus.

With these presuppositions, *qui adoptionem perceperunt* in IV, 25, 3 will mean whoever by his faithfulness to Abraham has agreed to belong to his people, and not simply was born into it. Because this group comes immediately after the patriarchs and the prophets, and because its function is "to conform certain things to Christ," one can conclude that the Hebrews are this anonymous group, before Christ, who had "conformed the things to Christ," that is to say, had interpreted and lived the laws, the institutions, and the events of history in such a way that through them one day the figure of Christ would be recognized.

This interpretation corresponds to the general drift of the paragraph (IV, 25, 3). After the references to the three groups (patriarchs, prophets, *qui adoptionem perceperunt*), which from the Old Testament "announce" Christ, and only after mention of Abraham—who is the synthesis of the two alliances—and in opposition to those who have sown are those who have "reaped" (that is to say, the Church) introduced. The Church as such cannot be identified in the paragraph with *qui adoptionem perceperunt* because the function assigned to the latter is not to "reap."

If our painstaking interpretation is correct, with IV, 25, 3, the number and the function of those who even in the Old Testament have "sown" Christ without having known, it is extended.[24]

Participation and Analogy

1. The reading of the texts of Irenaeus leaves us with a hand-ful of rich theological suggestions, and numerous questions and worries.

We have already stated the importance that the unity of the Father's, the word's, and the Spirit's action from all times has for Irenaeus.

The richness and multiplicity of the divine action is expressed adequately with the images of the symphony and of the multiple waters.

This action is carried to completion in the first Testament by the patriarchs and the prophets, as well as by means of the whole people, and always to the benefit of all men.

The patriarchs and the prophets do not carry on a merely didactic or kerygmatic activity, proclaiming a message or an-nouncing events that will have to be verified later on. There is an ontological continuity between the faith of Abraham and our own, just as there is a continuity between the action of the prophets and that of those who receive the message. The proph-ets and patriarchs (particularly Abraham) appear as actively en-gaged in a salvation that at every moment is fully achieved.

It does not seem that Irenaeus had attained the complete synthesis of the two tendencies that appear in his writings, i.e., consideration of the prophetic, patriarchal, and "popular" activ-ity as announcement, and consideration of this same activity as participation in the salvific activity of the Father and of the word. At times, the expressions *praeformare* and *praefigurare* sug-gest the synthesis between *annuntiare* and *adimplere*.

The outline "prefiguration–accomplishment" to express the relationship Old Testament–New Testament is so dominant among Christian theologians, and, particularly, among Catho-lics, that we run the risk of reading only this approach to the problem in the writings of Irenaeus, and overlooking what may be his true and rich contribution to its solution.[25]

2. *Adver. Haer.* IV, 33, 15, the text that probably best synthe-sizes what we can call the Trinitarian structure of the relation-ship between the Old and New Testament can serve as a point of departure for our conclusive reflections.[26]

The importance of this text is also underlined by its place in Chapter 33, which has as its general theme: "The truly spiritual disciple judges all men, and is not judged by anybody" (1 Cor. 2:15).

In the first section of the chapter (paragraphs 1 to 7), Irenaeus looks back upon the errors of the heretics who did not understand the Scriptures. In numbers 8 to 10, he describes the spiritual disciple who participates in the true gnosis. Finally, in numbers 11 to 14, he exposes the meaning of certain texts of the Scriptures that only the spiritual disciple is capable of understanding adequately. He concludes with paragraph 15, the words of the prophets:

he who is truly spiritual will interpret, pointing out to which aspect of the Lord's providential work each one of the things which have been said belongs, and exhibiting the entire Body of the work of the Son of God:
always knowing the same God;
and always acknowledging the same Word of God, though He be but now made manifest unto us;
and always recognizing the same Spirit of God, though in the last times He be newly poured out upon us, and upon mankind itself from the creation to the end of the World:
from whom such as believe in God, and follow His Word, obtain the salvation which is from Him.

The text is structured with the precision of the paragraphs where Irenaeus synthesizes an important doctrine with complete clarity.

The recognition at every moment (*semper*) in history, of the same Father, word, and Spirit, even if they manifest themselves in different ways, belongs to the nucleus of Irenaeus' antignostic thought. This affirmation is taken up by Irenaeus several times.[27] Peculiar to this text are, on the other hand, the first and the last affirmation.

God exercises his salvific activity on the whole of the human race from the beginning till the end of time. Man is the place of revelation, and where there is humanity there is salvific action. The function of the truly spiritual man is then to recognize the modality of this salvific action in each period of history and in each man.[28]

In this context, the first paragraph does not refer to the capac-

ity of the spiritual man to discover correspondences either material or allegorical between the action of Jesus and the prophetic
texts. Irenaeus demands true spiritual discernment to discover in
each prophetic action which aspect of the economy of salvation
is achieved (not forgetting that even the patriarchs, the judges,
and the kings are prophets), that is to say, in each act and word
of the Old Testament. The salvific economy of God includes not
only the works that the word performs, starting with his presence
in mortal flesh in the world, but also those that the word accomplished before the incarnation, and those that he continues in
the resurrected Christ.

Hence, to discover which feature of the economy of salvation
corresponds to an action or prophetic word does not mean establishing a correspondence between the thing foretold and what
has been fulfilled, but between the whole structure of salvation
and a particular fulfillment, independently of whether such fulfillment happened in the time of the Old New Testament.[29]

This thought is well brought out by the expression *integrum
corpus operis Filii Dei ostendens*. But how is the whole structure of
salvation discovered?

By means of particular fulfillments. The action of God on
individuals and peoples presents us each time with an aspect of
salvific action, which we integrate into our total vision of salvation. There is a process that goes from the particular to the
whole, which at the same time recognizes an aspect of the totality in the particular. The relationship that is established between
the Old and New Testament cannot then be conceived as a
temporal one of before and after, but more correctly through the
category of participation. The full salvation that the Triune God
carries out at each moment of history, at an ontological level, is
part of the whole action of salvation.

The "degree" of salvation included in the consoling word of a
prophet is no less than that which is encountered in the word of
Jesus; God's being present to Isaiah is no less effective than his
being present in Jesus to the disciples; the suffering of the "saints
of the Old Testament" is truly redemptive, although its efficacy is
part of Christ's redemptive action; the divine indwelling in the
temple of Jerusalem is as real as the eucharistic presence.

If salvation in the order of acts must be understood through
the category of participation (the salvation exercized in the Old
and New Testament participates in the whole single plan of

salvation), the knowledge we have of such salvation is best expressed through the category of analogy.

Our act of faith, the only way in which one can "verify" the
salvific action of God—"here is salvation!" in a particular case
(Jesus' encounter with the Samaritan woman by Jacob's well)—
leads us to discover salvation in other acts (God's encounter with
the people through Moses who grants living water to the people)
and thus to recognize progressively the "whole plan" of salvation.

But this process is not effected solely in one direction (from
the New to Old Testament). The adequate comprehension of
the salvation granted to us in Christ is only fully comprehensible
through the Old Testament. The discovery of the analogy of
salvation is not confined solely to the events in the Old Testament or in the New Testament. Even contemporary events, the
"signs of the times," can and should be read in relation to salvation arising out of either the Old or New Testament, or both
taken together organically.

The conception of the structural analogy of salvation in the
Old and the New Testament, to which the study of the texts of
Irenaeus has led us, seems to fill in the gaps that we discover in
the terms announcement–promise/accomplishment, in particular those that refer to the provisional character of, and consequent nonnecessity of, the Old Testament, which follows from
this.

The analogical outline has already been presented by G. von
Rad in his *Theology of the Old Testament.*[30] Von Rad's critics have
over a period of thirty years diagnosed serious flaws in his concept
of *heilsgeschichtlich* (historical-salvific). *Heilsgeschichte* apparently
implied empiricism and fundamentalism in the interpretation of
the history of Israel, illegitimate identification between the history of Israel and *Heilsgeschichte*, ambiguity in the treatment of
the concepts of "traditions" and history, linearity in the concept
of history, theological rationalism on the pretext of clearly discerning "God's plan," neglecting the proclaimed word in favor of
the "history" contained in such word, disrespectful Christian
manipulation of the Hebrew Scriptures.[31]

It is possible that the depth of the concept has prevented von
Rad from obtaining a perfectly balanced formulation. It is no less
true that his fundamental intuition of the structural analogy of
salvation is present in his work and compensates for the excesses
of "historization," which in some pages might have escaped him.

3. With the help of the concept of the structural analogy of salvation, the concept of typology is freed from its negative elements and can finally be made a full citizen in the domain of scholarly exegesis. Typological exegesis does not try to identify a type starting from an antitype, or bestow a value on the former inasmuch as it helps to put the latter into evidence.

On the basis of the identity of being in a different time[32] or, put in the more striking words of Irenaeus, with the conscience that one and the same God readily offers his salvation to the same humankind, typology discovers with joy that God is in fact faithful to his continual salvation. It thus discovers that persons, institutions, and words, but above all events[33] (without which persons, institutions, and words lose their identity) in one or other Testament reflect each other mutually, and together reflect the symphony of salvation that the Father, the Son, and the Holy Spirit carry to completion, without any distinction of time or persons.[34]

This concept of typology enables us to recover in a reasonable measure allegory as the analytical–imaginative method at the service of the symbol or of the analogy. "An exuberant allegory can be indicative of a dead thought."[35] If the reader of allegory is aware that it provides a possible arrangement of the multiple meanings of the text, allegory can be accepted as a possible didactic explanation that discovers (but at the same time creates!) the community of being between apparently diverse entities.

4. The presence of a "full salvation" in the Old Testament undoubtedly presents some difficulties. The first is that the New Testament seems to lose its absolute character of indispensability. Is not Christ thus transformed merely into another instrument of the salvific action of the Father?

Irenaeus has already posed the difficulty, which was that of the Marcionites:

Quid igitur Dominus attulit veniens? (IV, 34, 1)

Answer:

Cognoscite quod omnem novitatem attulit, semetipsum afferens (*ibid.*)

The great novelty is the presence of Christ himself, of the king who fills his subjects with joy. His subjects benefit from seeing him, listen to his words, and are filled with joy through his gifts (*ibid.*)

The meaning of the comparison between the coming of Christ and that of the king hoped for by his subjects leaves no room for doubt if one thinks of a victorious king whose subjects already enjoy the effects of victory. All that is left now is to see him personally. Irenaeus does not explain the comparison in so much detail, but it is legitimate to understand it, on the basis of his doctrine as a whole having this meaning.[36]

Between the time of the Old Testament and the time of the New Testament there exists the same distance as between the time of the New Testament, which we have already started to live, and the time of the full vision. Redemption is complete, but we do not contemplate it as yet.

This difficulty is theoretical and has a concrete counterpart: if the Old Testament expresses the fullness of salvation, is it legitimate for the Christian to do without the New Testament?

Taking his comparison further, Irenaeus would have answered: To whom it is conceded to see the triumphant entry of the king into the city, it is not conceded to turn his head to ignore him out of arrogance. But who does not live in the city of the New Testament, even he benefits from the king's victory.

The third difficulty concerns the reading of the Old Testament done in the light of the New Testament—does it give it a richer understanding? The question posed in more general terms: Is it hermeneutically acceptable that a text be fully comprehensible if one starts from a particular moment, for example, with the appearance in history of a particular person?

The answer seems to have to be positive. A constitutive element of a literary masterpiece is its capacity to reflect the profound structure of reality.

But when the cultural world has changed radically, a masterpiece can no longer be recognized as such because the circumstances on which its understanding of reality rested have changed beyond recognition. (How much of the *Divine Comedy* does the cultured reader manage to understand today?) The absence of the historical, political, and ideological background on which such a work is built enables one to capture only individual aspects, isolated rich thoughts, poetical aspects, but it does not give access to the totality of the work.

If, by some freak of history, we were to return to the times of the *Divine Comedy*, it would take on its full expression.

Something similar happens to the Old Testament.

This masterly work expresses the religious experience of a people. (Therefore, the Old Testament can be described thus inasmuch as it is a literary work.) Its manifold richness is at hand to anybody who approaches it with respect. Whoever approaches the Old Testament, even without faith, obtains a share in its benefits. Whoever approaches the Old Testament as word of God will receive much more. But it is also possible that the point of view of someone who reads only the Old Testament remains incomplete, inarticulate, and inorganic, and that he gets lost in the multiplicity without getting an insight into the unity, in the secondary without grasping the central point, in the transitory without discovering what is permanent.

Whoever approaches the Old Testament through the New Testament, accepting the authoritative interpretation of Jesus and the community that united to him, accepts his interpretation, arrives at the totality of the richness of the Old Testament. Jesus and his community are the historic circumstances that make the full salvation of the Old Testament fully comprehensible. Obviously, this is a valid affirmation only within the Christian faith. The ultimate foundations of all interpretation are cultural a priori and injustifiable existentials. Thus, one must understand Irenaeus sentence:

> Because every prophesy, before the event, is just a riddle and a question mark unto men: but when the time is come, and the thing foretold takes place, then it admits the most exact interpretation (IV, 26, 1).

Whoever does not have the key to the interpretation of the whole, i.e., the coming of the Son of God as man, cannot arrive at an exegesis of the whole.

A rigorous and unprejudiced reader must close the Old Testament overwhelmed by a magnificent work of inexhaustible wealth and depth, of which the last chapter is obviously missing.

Notes

1. Lack of clear knowledge of the function of the Old Testament in revelation has made Christian theologians coming from cultures rich with non-Christian religious literature (e.g., in India) wonder whether such literatures could play the "propaedeutic" function in the local Church, and not the Old Testament, which is a foreign reality to these cultures.

2. Cfr., e.g., C. Westermann (Hrsg.), *Probleme alttestamentlicher Hermeneutik*, Theologische Bücherei 11 (München, 1960), which brings together various contributions by the most important German exegetes of our time; B.W. Anderson (ed.), *The Old Testament and Christian Faith. Essays by Rudolf Bultmann and Others* (London, 1964), which includes contributions from English-speaking exegetes. Other important studies are J. Barr, *Old and New in Interpretation, a Study of the Two Testaments* (London, 1966); P. Beauchamp, *L'un et l'autre Testament. Essai de lecture* (Paris, 1976); and A.H.J. Gunneweg, *Vom Verstehen des Alten Testaments. Eine Hermeneutik* (Göttingen, 1977). D.L. Baker, *Two Testaments, One Bible* (Leicester, UK, 1976), presents a wide and useful (though necessarily general) review of opinions on the theme, where only a small part treats of Catholic exegetes. The most recent *status questionis* presented by M. Oeming, *Gesamtbiblischen Theologien der Gegenwart. Das Verhältnis von AT und NT in der hermeneutischen Diskussion seit Gerhard von Rad* (Stuttgart, 1985), which omits non-German bibliography, adds very little to what Gunneweg had already said. His own brief reflections are more interesting (pp. 232–241).

3. On the abundant bibliography on *Dei Verbum*, see U. Betti et al., *Commento alla Costituzione Dogmatica sulla Divina Rivelazione "Dei Verbum"* (Milan, 1967). The commentary on Chapter IV is by A. Kerrigan (pp. 155–185): U. Betti et al., *La Costituzione Dogmatica sulla Divina Rivelazione* (Turin, 1967). The commentary on Chapter IV is by A. Penna. Of particular interest is L. Alonso Schökel, *Comentarios a la constitución Dei Verbum sobre la divina revelación*, BAC 284 (Madrid, 1969), particularly pp. 495–532. Here one finds a multifaceted exposition of the terms on which we have briefly commented here.

4. Within the limits of this study, it is impossible to deal with all the problems that in some way concern the relationship between the Old and New Testament in *Adversus Haereses*. We have, therefore, limited ourselves to establish—in the good company of St. Irenaeus—the basis for conceiving this relationship in a different way from the scheme preparation–accomplishment, apparently favored by *Dei Verbum*. This conception of Irenaeus enables us better to expound the theoretical and practical need of the Old Testament for the Christian.

Adversus Haereses is here quoted according to the excellent edition of *Sources Chrétiennes*, Volume 100, I–II (Paris, 1965). IV, 1, 1, means, therefore, Book IV, Chapter 1, paragraph 1. In the absence of the original complete Greek text of Book IV, the Latin translation is the most faithful witness. The English translation generally follows that of J. Keble, *Five Books of S. Irenaeus Bishop of Lyon Against Heresies* (London, Oxford, and Cambridge, 1872), corrected when necessary according to the text and translation in the *Sources Chrétiennes* edition.

5. B. de Margerie, *Introduction à l'histoire de l'exégèse* (Paris, 1980), I, 93–94: *Dei Verbum* mentions Irenaeus four times (Nos. 7, 16, 18, 25). On the relation between the Old and New Testament, number 16 mentions *Adver. Haer.* III, 21, 3: "the books of the Old Testament with all their parts were received in their entirety in the proclamation of the gospel."

6. P. Evieux, "Théologie de l'accoutumance chez Saint Irénée," *RechSR* 55 (1967) 5.

7. The close relationship between the Old and New Testament has already been pointed out, of course, being a central theme in Irenaeus—in numerous studies. Nevertheless, the type of relationship that exists has not been made sufficiently explicit. The classic study by A. Benoit, *Saint Irénée. Introduction à l'étude de sa théologie* (Paris, 1960), for example, only states that "L'Ancien Testament est le livre qui rend un témoignage prophétique au Christ. En effet, les citations sont essentiellement consacrées à montrer comment le Christ est prédit dans l'Ancien Testament" (pp. 101–102). Other studies consider the way in that Irenaeus interprets the Old Testament (e.g., N. Brox, *Offenbarung, Gnosis und gnosticher Mythos bei Irenäus von Lyon* [Salzburg, 1966], particularly pp. 86–87 on the use of allegory), and above all the theological interpretation that Irenaeus makes of the Old and New Testament texts (e.g., A. Houssiau, *La Christologie de Saint Irénée* [Louvain/Gembloux, 1955]). On the interpretation of the Old Testament by Irenaeus, see pp. 79–92. Although primarily interested in the inspired character and the authority of the biblical texts in the theology of St. Irenaeus (p. 319), D. Farkasfalvi, "Theology of Scripture in St. Irenaeus," *Revue Bénédictine* 78 (1969), 319–333, contains some significant observations on the relationship between the Old and New Testament: "This uniqueness of the source of all revelations establishes the unity of the two Testaments" (p. 321); "the roles of the 'apostles' and of the 'prophets' appear to be parallel" (p. 322); "the Logos was there (in the Old Testament) already revealing himself to the prophets" (p. 324); "Scriptural texts of the Old Testament, says Irenaeus, should be equated with the words of Christ" (p. 326). His next affirmation seems to me less consistent with the preceding statements and not evident in the doctrine of Irenaeus: "Revelation is said to be gradual; the Old

Testament is an imperfect initiation, necessarily partial and incomplete" (p. 327).

A.H.J. Gunneweg, *Vom Verstehen des Alten testaments*, has disqualified too generally Irenaeus' conception of the Old Testament that "keineswegs dem ursprünglichen, urgemeindlichen Umgang mit der Schrift, entsprach" (p. 165). Irenaeus' conception, notwithstanding its amplitude and richness (p. 148), cannot be maintained, because he is the father of a concept *heilsgeschichtlich* (historical-salvific) of the Scriptures, which for Gunneweg is completely unacceptable (pp. 164–175). See the section beginning on p. 286 in this study. Unfortunately, it has not been possible to consult P. Bacq, *De l'ancienne à la Nouvelle Alliance selon St. Irénée* (Paris, 1978).

8. A slightly different interpretation of *illorum* is proposed by P. Evieux, "Théologie de l'accoutumance," 19: *illorum* seems to include the patriarchs and "ceux dont ils sont les pères dans la Foi. Le choix divin porte sur des individus, mais ces individualités sont des figures universelles."

9. Cfr. also IV, 20, 7: The Son unfolds before men "les visions prophétiques, la diversité des grâces, ses ministères, la glorification du Père *consequenter et composite*" ("à la façon d'une mélodie bien composée et harmonieuse"). Some translations do not bring out the musical image (cfr., e.g., A. Houssiau, *Le Christologie de Saint Irénée*, 112). If the image is not evident at first, it becomes very clear immediately after:

où il y a composition, il y a mélodie
où il y a mélodie, il y a temps voulu
où il y a temps voulu, il y a profit (A. Rousseau).

"Composition" refers to the action of the Son, "mélodie" to the result obtained. The concept of *consonantia* naturally suggests the opportune time (= rhythm). The musical methaphor thus expresses the multiplicity of salvation by the multiplicity of "author," of the means used, the result obtained (the melody), and of the rhythm that the author gives to the melody.

10. However the thought recurs in other texts: IV, 20, 11, the word in all its manifold richness manifests itself and makes itself known not only under one form only nor under one aspect only; III, 10, 6, one God manifests himself and actuates in manifold rich ways; III, 16, 17 mentions the wealth and multiplicity of the Father's will. Cf. also A. Rousseau, *Irénée de Lyon. Contre les Hérésies*, IV, I, Sources Chrétiennes 100/I (Paris, 1965), 236.

11. A. Orbe. *Parábolas Evangélicas en San Ireneo*, I (Madrid, 1972), 243–270.

12. *Ibid.*, 251. Italicized by the author.

13. *Ibid.*, 252.

14. *Ibid.*, 268–270. Italicized by the author.

15. In this study, we emphasize the identification of the believer with Abraham. On the aim of this identification, to "accustom oneself to follow the Word," see the excellent article, quoted above, by P. Evieux, "Theologie de l'accoutumance," 9–12.

16. The affirmation that this unique vision is achieved "selon trois modes successifs de plus en plus élevés" (cfr. A. Rousseau, *Irénée de Lyon. Contre les Hérésies*, IV/I, 251) seems to rely more on the general precomprehension that the New Testament and the realities contained in it must overcome the Old Testament always and in all, than on the text itself. This insists on the unity of vision, only alludes to the succession, and does not touch in any way the quality of the vision, even though it states its entitative difference.

17. The subject of the actions in this text is not clear. Does it refer to the Father or to the word? It seems correct to hold with A. Rousseau, *ibid.*, 227, the ambiguity suggested by the Greek: the participles can refer to God or to the Logos, or to both at the same time. In fact, Irenaeus attributes the different actions here mentioned both to the Father and to the Son.

18. Cfr. supra p.

19. Cfr. supra p.

20. Cfr. supra p.

21. A. Orbe, *Parábolas Evangélicas*, I, 22, mentions this text but does not discuss the meaning of the expression. The affirmation that only a few (the patriarchs and the prophets) had divine knowledge before the coming of the word leads one to suppose an interpretation of "qui adoptionem perceperunt" different from the one we propose.

22. Cfr., e.g., III, 11, 1; 16, 3; 18, 7; 19, 1; 20, 2; IV, 16, 5; 33, 4; 36, 2; V, 12, 2.

23. Cfr. A. Rousseau, *ibid.*, 220.

24. In this context, it would be interesting to discuss III, 6, 1 and III, 19, 1, where Irenaeus comments on Ps. 81:6–7 and identifies the assembly of the gods with those who have received filial adoption (*huiosezia* = the nature of gods), where the Son presides. Does not the way in which Irenaeus reads this Psalm lead us to suppose that the ecclesial community of those who have received filial adoption is also extended to the Old Testament?

25. We do not deny that the scheme prefiguration–accomplishment may be present in Irenaeus. See, for example: "Thus in each instance the Word of God hath a sort of outline of things to come (*lineamenta rerum futurarum*) and hath manifested unto men as it were the special features of the Father's providences (*species dispositionum*) . . ." (IV, 20, 11). In IV, 22, 2, we read: "For as in those who come first we were prefigured (*praefigurabamur*) and foretold (*praenuntiabamur*), so they in their turn are completely drawn out in us; (*in nobis illi deformantur*), i.e., in the

Church. . . ." The note of A. Rousseau, *Irénée de Lyon. Contre les Hérésies*, IV, I, 256, insists on this scheme. The concept of reciprocal immanence, which is also used to explain the text, is nearer to the scheme of salvific analogy than to that of prefiguration–accomplishment; they do not seem to coincide strictly. In the same text, Irenaeus starts out with his fundamental thought of the one God who leads the patriarchs in their "economies," and who justifies the circumcised *ex fide*, and the uncircumcised *per fidem*. In fact, the whole paragraph is dedicated to the salvation that the Father and Christ exercise in favor of "all men altogether who from the beginning, because of their excellence in their generation, have both feared and loved God, and conversed justly and piously with their neighbors, and desired to see Christ and to hear His Voice." The text also establishes a relationship between the "first" (the men who came before the coming of Christ?) and "us." The problem goes further than the relation between the Old and New Testament.

26. Among contemporary authors, J. Barr, *Old and New in Interpretation. A Study of the Two Testaments*, 153–154, has emphasized (without reference to Irenaeus) the importance of the Trinitarian structure of this relationship: ". . . Our approach to the Old Testament is Trinitarian rather than Christological. The direction of thought is from God to Christ, from Father to Son, and not from Christ to God . . . ; where we have a Trinitarian structure we can proceed to a Christological one . . . ; it is less clear that we can begin from a Christological approach." D. Farkasfalvy, "Theology of Scripture in St. Irenaeus," speaks of the Trinitarian structure of Revelation: "the unity of the two Testaments is affirmed . . . by showing in both Testaments the similarity of structure with regard to the future" (p. 324).

27. See, for example, IV, 6, 6; 20, 4; 20, 11.

28. See, for example, the parable of the vinedressers (IV, 36, 7) and the exegesis of A. Orbe, *Parábolas Evangélicas* I, 439–441, on the "cinco horas" of the call: "De los cinco tiempos, cuatro pertenecen al AT; uno al Nuevo. Eso basta para urgir contra los herejes la unicidad de vocación (resp. salud) y de Amo en los dos Testamentos" (p. 441).

29. Texts like IV, 32, 2, which even seem to give a theoretical precedence to the scheme announcement–accomplishment, should be discussed in more detail. We simply observe how the two Testaments are put in *parallel* (not subordinate one to the other), addressed to two peoples at different times, to accomplish both the work of faith in both; the "first Testament" is designed to bring about the service of God in men for the benefit of men; it is the figure of "divine things" (not necessarily of those of the New Testament); it prefigures realities of the Church (a function that it partially shares with the New Testament); and contains a prophecy for the future in a less-precise sense. Here Irenaeus proposes an apologetic aim for this function: "that man might learn God's universal foreknowledge."

30. G. von Rad, *Theologie des Alten Testament,* II (München, 1961; 1968[5]), 376–396. The study of A.H.J. Gunneweg, *Vom Verstehen des Alten Testaments* (Göttingen, 1977), which devotes much space to von Rad and his concept of *heilsgeschichtlich,* has not explicitly recognized his contribution to this discussion. One notes his absence in pp. 178–180.

31. These are the fundamental chapters containing criticism of von Rad. This is not the place to evaluate his contributions nor the value of the criticism. The above-mentioned study of M. Oeming, *Gesamtbiblischen Theologien der Gegenwart,* can serve as a starting point for such an assessment.

32. A.H.J. Gunneweg, *Vom Verstehen des Alten Testaments,* 159–180, quoting E. Fuchs, *Hermeneutik* (1954), 201.

33. D.L. Baker, *Two Testaments, One Bible,* 251–272, presents a documented and useful *status questionis* on the typology, as well as some opportune remarks.

34. A brief but important study (often overlooked) on typology is the article by P. Beauchamp, "La figure dans l'un et l'autre Testament," *RechSR* 59 (1971), 209–224. Beauchamp tries to explain the structure of the "activité figurante," of which typological exegesis (even if it is not completely identical with it) is at least one form. Here are two of his enlightening points of view: "la visée de l'activité figurante est de donner un réel à cette totalité passée, dont elle ne supporte pas qu'elle soit passée" (p. 214); "Il y a un compte à régler entre la parole qui reste, et le fait infirme qui s'évanouit" (p. 218). My thanks are due J.-M Carrière, who called my attention to this article.

35. H. de Lubac, *Exégèse Médiévale. Les quatre sens de l'Ecriture,* Seconde Partie, II (Paris, 1964), 179. See the scholarly exposition in this volume on the use of allegory by the Fathers, pp. 125–181. On allegory, see also the important study by R.P. Hanson, *Allegory and Event* (London, 1959). It does not seem that, among the majority of exegetes, there has been a clear assimilation of the distinction between allegory as literary *tropos,* and typology as a theological presupposition. There is no graduation between the two concepts of "more" to "less," or of the "reasonable" to the "exaggerated." Allegory as such does not allow a positive or negative evaluation. A typological concept can be developed on the basis of historical premises, as well as by means of allegorical elaborations. Neither one nor the other development jeopardizes the value of the typological concept.

36. A different interpretation of this image is proposed by G. Wingren, *Man and the Incarnation. A Study in the Biblical Theology of Irenaeus,* trans. R. Mackenzie (Edinburgh/London, 1959), 73–74. In IV, 34, 3, Irenaeus adds another answer that corresponds to the scheme announcement–accomplishment: what has been announced by the prophets is fully verified only in Christ.

CHAPTER 10

Historicity of the Gospels
(*Dei Verbum* 19)
Genesis and Fruits of the Conciliar Text

José Caba, S.J.

Summary

The present article endeavors to study the conciliar text on the historicity of the gospels (*Die Verbum* 19) as regards its origins in the past and its fruits in the present. Following a long historical account of the previous declarations of the Church, the conciliar text was developed and brought to a conclusion in the course of the evolution of the five drafts through which the Dogmatic Constitution on Divine Revelation passed. The main influence it was subject to was the document *Sancta Mater Ecclesia* of the Pontifical Biblical Commission. The fruits of the conciliar text can be seen in the principal directions taken in the abundant exegetical literature on the theme, which, while examining tradition in the gospels, anchors itself in Jesus, who is their original source, and goes on from there to the writings of the authors. The future of the conciliar text is promising, especially if to the historical-critical study of the text of the gospels, we add the vision of faith that recognizes it to be the word of God; and if the exegete, instead of being locked into the "pure primitive text" of the gospel, uses it to reach the riches of its theological context, as manifested in the very life of the Church.

Introduction

On 18 November 1965, His Holiness Pope Paul VI, in a public session, solemnly promulgated the Dogmatic Constitution on Divine Revelation. In number 19 of this document, the Council summarized the attitude of the Church toward the historicity of the gospels, while on its part synopsizing the whole process these books followed during their formation. The conciliar text is as follows:

> Holy Mother Church has firmly and with absolute constancy maintained and continues to maintain, that the four Gospels just named, whose historicity she unhesitatingly affirms, faithfully hand on what Jesus, the Son of God, while he lived among men, really did and taught for their eternal salvation, until the day when he was taken up (cf. Acts 1:1–2). For, after the ascension of the Lord, the apostles handed on to their hearers what he had said and done, but with that fuller understanding which they, instructed by the glorious events of Christ and enlightened by the Spirit of truth, now enjoyed. The sacred authors, in writing the four Gospels, selected certain of the many elements which had been handed on, either orally or already in written form, others they synthesized or explained with an eye to the situation of the churches, the while sustaining the form of preaching, but always in such a fashion that they have told us the honest truth about Jesus. Whether they relied on their own memory and recollections or on the testimony of those who "from the beginning were eyewitnesses and ministers of the Word," their purpose in writing was that we might know the "truth" concerning the things of which we have been informed (cf. Lk. 1:2–4).[1]

This text, in its definitive redaction, represents the last stage of a long, hard effort. Its development was painful. But the efforts made to work it out are amply compensated for by the exegetical fecundity it has generated during the years that followed its promulgation. The vast horizon it then opened up still makes new realizations possible today.

In joyful recollection of that great ecclesial event that was Vatican II, we want to offer, with the past in mind, some thoughts on the development of the section concerned with the historicity of the gospels. Looking at the postconciliar present, we shall endeavor to present a summary evaluation of the fruits produced. Regarding the future, we shall try to see what possible avenues we might take to be in a position to continue on the path now opened up with increasing profit, while remaining faithful to the heritage we have received.

Genesis of the Conciliar Text

The attitude of the Council toward the historicity of the gospels subsumes, as the most recent stage of development, a series of prior actions of the Church. In fact, because of various attacks against the historicity of the gospels having been made over a period of time, various condemnatory or clarifying documents had already come to its defense in the century before Vatican II.

1. *Declarations prior to Vatican II,* dealing more or less explicitly with the problem of the historicity of the gospels, go back to exactly a century before the constitution *Dei Verbum.* Indeed, in 1864, the *Syllabus* mentioned, in its seventh proposition, the opinion of those who consider the books of the New Testament to be mythical, and Jesus Christ himself a mere fiction.[2] Shortly afterwards, in 1870, Vatican Council I ratified this proposition of the *Syllabus,* by including it to a degree in the canons on the faith of the third session.[3] In a practical application regarding the fourth Gospel, the Pontifical Biblical Commission held, in a response dated 29 May 1907, in favor of historicity, defending it against merely symbolic interpretations or mystic speculations.[4] A few days later, on 3 June 1907, the decree *Lamentabili* mentioned a series of modernist propositions, about six of which allude to the problem of the historicity of the gospels.[5] The Encyclical *Pascendi,* a few months later, on 8 September 1907, undertook to systematize the modernist errors, including those alluding to the transfiguration, or disfiguration for the faith, of the very historical figure of Jesus.[6] The problem of historicity of the gospels does not confine itself to the fourth Gospel, but also concerns the three Synoptics, and in their defense the Pontifical Biblical Commission once more was heard from. First, on 19 June 1911, it supported the historicity of Matthew's Gospel,[7] then, on 12 June 1912, it dealt with the two remaining evangelists, Mark and Luke.[8] After that, the four evangelists were

treated as a whole under the same heading of historicity by Pope Benedict XV in his Encyclical *Spiritus Paraclitus* of 15 September 1920, which celebrated the fifteenth centenary of St. Jerome's death. His Holiness contrasted the teaching of the venerable doctor on "the historical authority of the Gospels" with the doctrine of those who "in their exposition of Gospels diminish the human faith owed to them and destroy the divine."[9]

All the documents hitherto mentioned have in common that they suggest a sense of opposition to or condemnation of incompletely understood attitudes toward the historicity of the gospels. On 30 September 1943, Pius XII published the Encyclical *Divino Afflante Spiritu,* on the occasion of the fiftieth anniversary of Leo XIII's Encyclical *Providentissimus Deus,* "the chief law of biblical studies."[10] In the Encyclical of Pius XII, one breathes the fresh air of biblical renewal. The Encyclical did not tackle the specific problem of the historicity of the gospels, but it gave an impulse to scholars to study the thorniest questions, among them those "dealing with history."[11] The pontiff set forth as the main rule of interpretation the precise verification and definition of "what the writer meant."[12] The publication of the Encyclical was the cause of a rapid growth in biblical studies in general and of the gospels in particular. But very different attitudes developed, as Cardinal Bea complained in his remarks on 24 September 1960, at the Italian Bible Week commemorating the nineteenth centenary of the arrival of St. Paul in Rome. Some, declared Cardinal Bea, deplore the boldness of exegetes "who adopt the theories of non-Catholic authors, for instance, relative to literary criticism, and of 'history of the forms' in its application in a particular way to the Gospels," while others oppose them, basing themselves on previous documents like the Encyclical *Divino Afflante Spiritu* in their anxiety "to develop a more critical biblical science" and "to take into consideration the intentions of the sacred writer."[13] Cardinal Bea complained that he found "in lectures and publications, dealing especially with the New Testament, assertions which sometimes border almost on heresy."[14] These judgments of Cardinal Bea were supported a few months later by a *Monitum* of the Holy Office, dated 20 June 1961, which sounded an alarm concerning "opinions which jeopardize the authentic and objective historical truth of Holy Scripture, not only of the Old Testament . . . , but also of the New, and even of the words and deeds of Jesus Christ."[15] Six days later, on 26 June 1961, the

Sacred Congregation of the Holy Office put a life of Jesus on the Index of Prohibited Books.[16]

2. *The development of the conciliar text* on the historicity of the gospels began its first stage in this tense and not very open atmosphere. The present Dogmatic Constitution on Divine Revelation, in which the theme of the historicity of the gospels (*Dei Verbum* 19) is incorporated, is the outcome of a laborious gestation. The definitive text of *Dei Verbum* is the fifth of a series of schemas. Number 19, dealing with the historicity of the gospels, was among the most difficult, having been continuously altered until it ultimately reached its present formulation.

a. *Schema I*, written by a theological commission presided over by Cardinal Ottaviani, was brought up for discussion in the Council assembly on 14 November 1962. This first document was entitled *De Fontibus Revelationis*. Chapter IV was dedicated to the New Testament, and in number 20, the historical value of the gospels was discussed. There, at the very beginning, the attitude of the Church toward the gospels was presented in these words: "With firm and most constant faith, she has believed and still believes that the four Gospels referred to faithfully communicate what Jesus, Son of God, living among men, really did and taught."[17] Subsequently, in number 21, the draft went on to condemn "those errors through which by whatever manner or reason the genuine historical and objective truth of the facts of our Lord Jesus Christ's life, as reported by the gospels, are denied or diminished."[18] Lastly, in number 22, there were condemned "the errors which maintain that the words of Christ, just as the Evangelists attribute them to the Lord, at least as regards the meaning they express, are not, most of the time, of Christ, but rather reveal to us the Evangelist's thought or, which is still more serious, the thought of the early Christian community."[19]

All these sections of Schema I had the same outcome as the whole document. When the latter was subjected to a vote in the assembly of the Council, out of 2,209 votes, 1,368 were opposed to the discussion of the schema, 822 approved it, and 19 votes were null. Although debate on the schema was approved, because the opponents did not reach two-thirds (1,473 votes would have been required), on the following day the Secretary-General of the Council, Monsignor Felici, read an announcement that declared that the Holy Father considered it useful to have a special commission study the schema before pursuing debate on it. This commission was to include various cardinals and members of the Theological Commission and of the Secretariat for the Unity of Christians.[20] A few days later, Cardinals Ottaviani and Bea were appointed copresidents of this commission, and Monsignor Willebrands and Father Tromp, secretaries.

b. *Schema II*, written by the joint commission, was sent to the Council Fathers on 23 April 1963. The new title of the document, *De Divina Revelatione,*[21] itself indicated a change of orientation in comparison with the first schema with regard to the two sources of revelation. On the particular theme of the historicity of the gospels, there were also notable changes.[22] The new schema left out the condemnation of errors regarding the historical truth of the gospels and the provenance of Christ's words. By doing away with this condemnation, Schema II adopted a decidedly positive orientation relative to the study of the gospels. It formulated the attitude of the Church toward the historical value of the gospels, not with the expression of Schema I, *credidit et credit,* but with that of *tenuit ac tenet,* and preceded this not with the two adjectives of Schema I, *firma et constantissima fide,* but with the two adverbs *firmiter et constantissime.* In the new text, the adverb that previously nuanced the handing on by the gospels of what Jesus did and thought, *sincere tradere,* was also replaced by *vere tradere.* An explanation of these changes would be given later by the Doctrinal Commission in Schema IV in response to comments of a few Fathers. Among the additions made to the new text, what was said about the gospels must be particularly noticed, namely, that although "they sometimes have the form of a proclamation . . . , they communicate to us a history which is true and faithful."

Schema II was not discussed in the Council assembly. During the second half of 1963 and the first of 1964, the Fathers transmitted their comments on this schema.

c. *Schema III* developed out of the 2,481 amendments to the previous schema proposed by the Fathers. With regard to the specific problem of the historicity of the gospels, the instruction on the *Historical Truth of the Gospels,* issued by the Pontifical Biblical Commission, was to have a definite influence. The writing of this document was entrusted to the Pontifical Biblical Commission by His Holiness Pope John XXIII toward the end of 1962, immediately after appointment of the joint commission that was to prepare Schema II on Divine Revelation. Pope John

XXIII wanted the Pontifical Biblical Commission to study "form criticism" and its application to the problem of the historicity of the gospels. This study was undertaken during the year 1963, completed in 1964, in the pontificate of Paul VI, and dated 21 April although not made public until 14 May of that same year. Thus, the document of the Commission, entitled *Instructio de historica Evangeliorum veritate*, which begins with the words *Sancta Mater Ecclesia*,[23] played a major role, beginning with Schema III, in the redaction of the Dogmatic Constitution *Dei Verbum* as far as its treatment of the historicity of the gospels is concerned. The differences found in Schema III as compared with the preceding schema come therefore from suggestions made by the Fathers and the insertion into the schema of the Instruction of the Pontifical Biblical Commission on the historical truth of the gospels.

The Fathers' remarks particularly influenced the new structure of Schema III. What was in Schema II but a foreword to the whole document became in Schema III a chapter, the first, entitled *De ipsa revelatione*.[24] This made renumbering of the other chapters necessary. Thus, Chapter 4 of Schema II, which dealt with the problem of the historicity of the gospels, under the title *De Novo Testamento*, becomes Chapter 5 in Schema III, while keeping its original title. To avoid the incongruity of the general title *De Novo Testamento* being followed by a text referring almost exclusively to the gospels, the chapter was made to begin with a new number, 17, called *Novi Testamenti excellentia*.[25] The following number, 18, leaves out what had been said in number 17 of the previous schema regarding the doubts that are now expressed about the historical fidelity of the gospels and their divine authority.[26] Many fathers found the allusion to these doubts useless, particularly because it followed upon a statement of what is in effect Catholic faith in this matter. In number 19 of Schema III, dealing with the problem of the historicity of the gospels, some changes proposed by the Fathers were also made. Thus, at the end of the number, there are quoted as sources of the written gospels not only, as was the case in the preceding schema, the testimony of those who "from the beginning were eyewitnesses to and ministers of the word,"[27] but also "the memory and recollection" of the authors themselves.[28] They wanted "us to know the truth of the words in which we have been instructed (cf. Lk. 1:2–4)." Thus reads the conclusion of number

18 of Schema II.[29] These same words were kept in Schema III, but the word "truth" was put in quotation marks to emphasize the importance of the Greek word in the quotation from St. Luke.[30]

All these changes in the general composition of Schema III, together with the variations mentioned in the number concerned with the historicity of the gospels, are important because they were retained and eventually became part of the final and definitive text of the Constitution *Dei Verbum*.

The Instruction *Sancta Mater Ecclesia* of the Pontifical Biblical Commission had a still greater impact on Schema III and was later equally influential on some fundamental points on up to the definitive text. The Instruction began with a kind of prologue filled with the encouragingly positive and charitable spirit of the Encyclical *Divino Afflante Spiritu* of Pius XII. In the first number, allusion was made to the new methods of exegesis at the disposal of scholars of the Old and New Testaments. Among other things, mention was made of the positive aspects relative to study of the gospels of the "form criticism" method, always with the necessary caution concerning inadmissible philosophical and theological principles that may at time vitiate the method and its conclusions. Among the censured principles of the method was that maintained by some who "exaggerate the creative power of the community."[31] The disapproval of this creative power of the community had an influence on number 19 of Schema III of *Dei Verbum*, which asserts that the authors of the gospels have passed on to us "not fictions coming from the creative power of the early community, but the simple truth about Jesus."[32] However, the inclusion of this principle in the conciliar text was to be the subject of a further revision in the working out of the definitive text of *Dei Verbum*.

A second point developed in the Instruction of the Pontifical Biblical Commission was to have a more marked and permanent impact on Schema III. In its second number, the Instruction *Sancta Mater Ecclesia* discussed the three stages of the formation of the gospels: the first, Jesus, surrounded by the disciples who are witnesses of his works and words; the second, the apostles, taught by the glorious events of the risen Christ and the illumination of the Spirit of truth, narrate the life of Christ and repeat his words in relation to the needs of their hearers; the third, the sacred authors who put the gospels in writing through a process of selection, synthesis, and adaptation to the situations of the

Churches.[33] These three stages, described in detail in the Instruction of the Pontifical Biblical Commission, are what are contained in synthesis in number 19 of Schema III.

Number 18 of Schema II had already alluded to the first stage: "the Evangelists handed on what Jesus . . . really did and thought."[34] The Instruction's second stage was synthesized in number 19 of Schema III: "the apostles, after the death of the Lord, certainly preached to their listeners what He had said and done, with that clearer understanding which they enjoyed after they had been instructed by the events of Christ's risen life and taught by the light of the Spirit of truth."[35] The third stage, that of the writing of the authors, is thus described in Schema III: "The sacred authors wrote the four Gospels, selecting some things from the many which were already being transmitted by word of mouth or in writing, reducing some of them to a synthesis, explicating some things in view of the situation of the Churches, and preserving the form of proclamation."[36]

Schema III, developed in light of the comments of the Fathers and elements of the Instruction of the Pontifical Biblical Commission, was discussed in the Council assembly during General Congregations 91–95, from 30 September to 6 October 1964.

d. *Schema IV*, developed in light of the comments on Schema III, was transmitted to the Fathers on 20 November, during the third session of the Council. The changes made in Schema IV to the content of its predecessor on the precise point of the historicity of the gospels were relatively few, and they amount only to several omissions and a few improvements in style. Leaving aside for the moment the alterations made to improve style, the main omission consisted of suppressing the allusion to the principle of "form criticism" relative to the creative power of the community. The reason for its suppression was evident; such an allusion gave too much credit to an opinion already outmoded.[37] The expression of Schema III alluding to things handed on by the gospels and describing them as *non ficta* was likewise omitted.[38] This was, in fact, already included in the assertion that the things concerning Jesus handed on to us by the gospels are *vera et sincera*.[39] In answer to the criticisms of the Fathers who deplored the absence of the terms *historia* and *historice* applied to the gospels, it was explicitly pointed out that they were avoided on purpose because of ambiguity of these terms in modern authors.[40]

At the time of voting on number 19 of Schema IV, on 22

September, during General Congregation 155, there were 2,233 participants. Of these 2,162 voted *placet* and 61 *non placet*, while 10 were null. In the vote on the whole of chapter five, out of 2,166 participants, 1,850 voted *placet* and 313 *placet juxta modum*, while 3 were null.[41] Number 19 was the one that had the greatest number of amendments suggested by Fathers. Some of these proposed *modi* together with the responses made by the Doctrinal Commission, whether in accepting or rejecting the *modi*, shed a great deal of light on the intended meaning of number 19.

In the first place, some Fathers suggested that the Church's attitude toward the gospels, that they truly hand on what Jesus did and taught, not be expressed through the formula *tenuit ac tenet*, but rather with *credidit et credit*, because it is a question of what the Church has always believed with an act of faith. The response of the Doctrinal Commission to this proposal was a clarifying one: the Commission wrote *tenuit ac tenet* because this says better that historicity is reached not through faith alone, but through faith and reason.[42]

The most discussed point concerned the proposed addition of the term "history" or "historical" applied to the gospels. In fact, 174 Fathers asked that in the first sentence of number 19 it be said about the gospels that *juxta veritatem fidemque historicam tradere omnia facta et dicta quae in ipsis continentur*.[43] According to these Fathers, it was absolutely necessary to add the term "historical," which the magisterium had often used, to rein in exegetical audacity.[44] The Commission answered this proposition as follows:

> It is a fact that the term "historical" has often been used in previous documents of the Magisterium, for instance, in EB 560. Nevertheless, the term "history" is used today by many in a far broader sense, even, for instance, with regard to "superterrestrial" things which are perceived by faith. The term "history" can be translated by "Geschichte" or "Historie."[45]

Other Fathers, on the other hand, suggested that the terms "history" or "historical" be introduced near the end of number 19. Thus, 158 Fathers proposed that the formula of Schema IV on the authors of the gospels, *vera et sincera de Jesu nobis communicarent*, be complemented by replacing it with that of *vera et sincera de historia Jesu nobis communicarent*, or by saying that they hand on *vere historicam narrationem.*[46] To 85 Fathers, it seemed inadequate to say in Schema IV that the authors of the gospels hand on what is *vera et sincera,* because the "truth" is what the author intends to assert, according to another formula in number 12 of the schema, and it may be other than real. On the other hand, "sincerity" or absence of deceit can be found also in the narration of fantasy. That is why they consider it to be advisable, in order to save historicity, to declare that the authors of the gospels, in writing them, did it *ita tamen ut quoad factorum historicitatem, objectivam veritatem semper communicarent.*[47]

With regard to the use of the terms "history" and "historical account," the Doctrinal Commission answered as before and hence did not consider it to be appropriate to introduce these terms into the conciliar text. As for the meaning of the term *vera,* it explained it by saying that it is used for things the assertion of which agrees with reality, truth being the correspondence between the thing and understanding of it. To avoid the confusion that might result from the use of a different expression, the Council decided to suppress in number 12 the formula *veritas enim seu id quod sacer auctor scripto asserere voluit.*[48] With regard to the term *sincera,* the Commission explained that it complements the term *vera,* just as a subjective element complements an objective one.[49]

The number on the historicity of the gospels still had to surmount a last difficulty. His Holiness Paul VI was informed of the Commission's position and the reasons behind it. The Holy Father, already convinced of the appropriateness of revising the formula on the historicity of the gospels, on 17 October had a letter drafted proposing that the historical truth of the gospels be explicitly defended by substituting for the expression *vera et sincera* in number 19 that of *vera seu historica fide digna.* The letter justified this proposition by saying, "It appears that the first (expression) does not give assurance of the real historicity of the Gospels. On this point, as is evident, the Holy Father could not approve a formula which leaves room for doubt as to the historicity of these sacred books."[50]

At the meeting of the Commission on 19 October, Cardinal Bea emphasized the inappropriateness of the formula *vera et sincera* and supported the one proposed by the Pope. During the session, it was again insisted that the new formula did not remove the difficulty, because many Protestants, in particular

Bultmann and his followers, talk about the *fides historica*, identifying it with the act of the believer projecting his existential experience into a fictitious narrative from which the exegete must eliminate every mythical element. It was accordingly proposed that an unequivocal formula be placed at the beginning of number 19 that would ensure what was meant to be saved. This new suggestion also included the substance and objective of the amendment proposed by the Pope. Put to a vote, this final proposal obtained 26 affirmative and 2 negative votes from the members of the Commission. Thus, while the formula *vera et sincera* remained in the text of number 19, another one was added to express the Church's attitude toward the gospels: *quorum historicitatem incunctanter affirmat.*[51] In responding to the *modi* asking for inclusion of the term "historical," the Commission, in addition to its setting forth a double interpretation of the term "history" by *Geschichte* or *Historie,* added the following:

> And so it seemed to us preferable to assert the reality of facts and events in a concrete way by adding the term *historicity* which is not ambiguous: Holy Mother Church has held and still holds firmly and with the utmost constancy that the four Gospels, the historicity of which she asserts without hesitation, faithfully hand on. . . .[52]

On 29 October, at General Congregation 155, the Council proceeded to put to a vote the work done by the Doctrinal Commission on the *modi* proposed and the corrections inserted into the text. The voting was done chapter by chapter. In the vote on chapter five, which dealt with the historicity of the gospels, from 2,139 participants, there were 2,115 *placet* votes, 19 *non placet,* and 5 null.[53]

e. The definitive text of Schema V of *Dei Verbum* was the result of this vote. Once the text was approved by the General Congregation, it only remained to present it to the Pope and to have it solemnly approved in a public session together with promulgation of the Constitution.

In the eighth public session, the Council proceeded to the solemn vote on the Dogmatic Constitution *Dei Verbum.* There were 2,350 participants, and of them only 6 voted *non placet,* while 2,344 voted *placet.*[54] The Constitution was almost unanimously approved. Subsequently, on 18 November 1965, His Holiness Pope Paul VI, on his authority, promulgated the Constitution.[55]

Number 19 of the *Dei Verbum* on historicity of the gospels was the final step of a long journey in which a multiplicity of conciliar efforts were fused into unity as it appropriated the essential core of the Instruction of the Pontifical Biblical Commission *Sancta Mater Ecclesia.* If one wishes to characterize the contribution of this conciliar text, one must take into account a variety of aspects. It postulates, first of all, a firm and clear position of the Church toward the historicity of the gospels. Precisely to ensure that, it declined to include in the conciliar text the terms "history" and "historical" in connection with the gospels, while retaining unhesitatingly affirmation of their historicity. A clear determination was made of three stages in the formation of the gospels: the first, their original source, Jesus, who is accessible to us thanks to the writings the evangelists left us; the second, the apostles, who, during their preaching, grew in understanding of the words and deeds of Jesus, through the paschal events and the illumination of the Spirit; the third, the authors with their many-sided activity of selection, synthesis, and adaptation and proclamation of the truth that they were communicating about Jesus. The conciliar text certainly does not mention the "history of the forms method," which appeared explicitly in the Instruction *Sancta Mater Ecclesia.* The Council also declined to make even a single mention of one of the principles most censured in that document, namely, the creative power of the community. Nevertheless, one can apprehend implicitly the acceptance of what is positive in the method through the entire process of formation of the gospels that the Council established.

Thus, the conciliar text on the historicity of the gospels represents a shining beacon for every exegete wishing to penetrate, without risk of getting lost, the unfathomable depths the four evangelists have handed on to us.

The Fruits of the Conciliar Text

The conciliar text on the historicity of the gospels was not just the end of one stage; it was also the beginning of a new period that molded study of the gospels in accordance with the orientation of the Council. This article cannot review all the abundant exegetical literature that, like ripe fruit, came from the seeds planted by *Dei Verbum*. It will be enough just to sketch out the major directions that guided successive endeavors to attempt deeper penetration into the evangelical message.

1. A *new framework* governs publications that want to deal with the problem of the historicity of the gospels. The shortcomings in orientation that were prevalent in the decade preceding the Council are now clearly seen. Scholars at that time tried to reach the historical value of the gospels by beginning with the knowledge and truthfulness of those who were eyewitnesses of what they narrated, as was the case with Matthew and John, or of those who were informed by others worthy of full credibility, as was the case with Mark, who lived in Peter's company, or Luke, who was under the influence of Paul.[56] Even while the conciliar text was being developed, argumentation of this kind was under severe attack. An orientation of this kind does not take into account the environment of the community in which the gospels developed, a necessary factor for evaluating what they transmit. Some who are considered authors are not direct witnesses to what they narrate, as is the case with Mark and Luke; and their respective dependence on Peter and Paul does not suffice to guarantee their testimony in literary terms. Even the first Gospel is attributed to the apostle Matthew by tradition, and as to John the Evangelist, while he presents himself as a witness, his testimony is very late and transmitted in a work of a special character in which history, theology, and mysticism are intermingled.[57]

The new way of formulating the historicity problem takes into consideration the whole tradition that came between the Jesus of Nazareth and the Christ presented to us in the definitive redaction of the gospels, as brought into focus by the "method of form criticism" (*Formgeschichtmethode*). This whole intermediate tradition is to be retraced in different directions, either descending, beginning with Jesus and ending with the Gospels,[58] or ascending, beginning with the gospels and ending with Jesus,[59] but always trying to discover the relationship that existing Tradition presupposes between Jesus of Nazareth and the Christ of the faith. An attempt is thus being made to open the way for the orientation marked out by the Council.[60] The environment of the Christian community in which the gospels came into being has left its mark on what they have transmitted to us—the liturgical, catechistical, and missionary climate of the early Church is reflected in the evangelical narrations.[61] This positive datum of Tradition, which was brought out by the "method of form criticism" and repeated in the Instruction *Sancta Mater Ecclesia*, remained engraved on the new framework given to the study of the gospels.[62] His Holiness Pope Paul VI followed this line of the new program when, in his speech to the members of the Pontifical Biblical Commission, he emphasized that "Sacred Scripture, and in particular the New Testament, took shape within the community of the people of God, of the Church united around the Apostles."[63] From this, His Holiness implies "that it can be legitimately asserted that if God's Word has called into being and begotten the Church, the Church too has in a way begotten the Sacred Scripture, this Church that has expressed and recognized in them, for all generations to come, her faith, her hope and her rule of life in this world."[64]

2. *Access to Jesus* through this ecclesial tradition is firmly established in this new framework of the historicity of the gospels. In assimilating the positive elements of the "method of form criticism," the method itself has been surpassed by reason of the fact that the barrier separating the Jesus of history from the Christ of faith, which the whole system and its authors had erected, has been overthrown.[65] It was the Protestant exegetes,[66] and even Bultmann's disciples themselves,[67] who took it upon themselves to open a breach in the wall of separation. Just by reading the titles of recent books touching on this theme, one can see with what confidence this area of access to Jesus is now being entered into, the historicity of the gospels having thus been assured.[68]

Among other paths of access to the Jesus of history embodied in the environment of a prepaschal community, an attempt was made even during the Council itself, to widen the area of application of the "method of form criticism." A bridge was thrust out to make it possible to reach from the postpaschal tradition to the prepaschal origins of the words of Jesus. It was a matter of looking for the "Sitz im Leven" of the prepaschal community that existed around Jesus, not to determine in time and space a concrete historical happening, but to establish the typical behavior of the life of the community in which Jesus and the Twelve lived that would make it possible "to establish whether the words of the Lord are already rooted in the history of prepaschal tradition."[69] Efforts of this kind intensified in the following years.[70]

However, it is in going from the gospels to Jesus that we resort more often and with greater certainty to the criteria of historicity. Even before the Council,[71] these criteria were being studied, but it was only beginning in 1964 that the first attempts were made to systematize them.[72]

The extensive bibliography on this theme[73] was first devoted to distinguishing among indications, criteria, and proofs of historicity.[74] While indications give rise only to probability, the criteria of historicity properly speaking reach certainty as to the historical authenticity of a gospel datum. Proof or demonstration of the criteria of historicity flows from the application of the criteria of historicity to the gospel material. Studies on the criteria of historicity go on to distinguish between the various categories of criteria, namely, primary or basic, secondary or derived, and mixed. Primary criteria have intrinsic value for reaching certainty as to historicity; these are the criteria called the criterion of multiple testimony, the criterion of discontinuity with the Christian or Judaic faith of the era, the criterion of conformity with the Palestinian or Jewish milieu of the time of Jesus, and the criterion of explanation required to elucidate various elements that, if they were not authentic, would remain puzzling. The secondary or derived criterion comes from Jesus' personal style, not only from his particular way of speaking,[75] but also from his comportment or characteristic and usual way of acting.[76] This criterion helps to put us on the track of historicity. The mixed criterion comes into play when to one or more criteria there is added a literary indication that ensures the internal intelligibility of a narration, showing it to be fully adapted to its context. This mixed criterion can also be used when, relative to a gospel narration, there appear, together with other criteria of its historicity, different interpretations of each of the evangelists, who nevertheless agree at the same time on a common core.[77]

All these efforts in the end definitively break down the barrier that the system of "form criticism" had set up between the Christ of faith and the Jesus of history. Jesus himself is the original source of all Tradition and of all christology.[78]

3. *The study of the redaction of the gospels* requires once more going beyond the "method of form criticism." Just as the authors

of this method had remained imprisoned in the "forms" they had discovered, unable to reach the Jesus of history, so were they also blocked from attaining an overall view of each gospel, because they considered each one of these nothing but a juxtaposition of the literary units of the different forms. Even before the Council, the authors of the "form criticism" method had identified the redactive work accomplished by each of the evangelists in composing his work.[79] The conciliar text on the historicity of the gospels brought to the fore the work carried out by each evangelist in selecting, synthesizing, adapting, and proclaiming the material he had at his disposal. A great deal of exegetical literature has followed along this path, characterizing each of the authors of the gospels, and recognizing that, along with their faithfulness to Tradition, they exercised creative freedom in organizing the material used.[80] The study of the writing of each evangelist is henceforth commonly accepted among the exegetical methods,[81] both for presenting the whole of each gospel,[82] and for analyzing in particular the various pericopes.[83] In his speech to the members of the Pontifical Biblical Commission, Pope Paul VI himself showed that he favors biblical studies from the point of view of the history of Tradition, forms, and writing, with the necessary methodological corrections. He also showed himself to be favorable to an integration of the "diachronical" reading of the text, paying attention to its historical development, and with a "synchronical" presentation aimed at stressing the literary and existential connections in the text.[84]

4. *The fruits and the future* of the conciliar text on the historicity of the gospels represent a comforting reality and an encouraging perspective. The result obtained may well be considered as the synthesis of two previous pendular movements of "thesis" and "antithesis."[85] A first stage, of traditional conception, remained rooted in the historicity of the gospels, concerned with clarifying the data of the life and history of Jesus. This was a period of "thesis" that lasted untroubled until the eighteenth century. A second stage of radical criticism, which lasted until the appearance of the "form criticism" method, nullified the historicity of the gospels and was left with only the intermediate Tradition between Jesus and the gospels, which it considered to be a creation of the primitive community. This is the opposite position, that of "antithesis." The conciliar text on the historicity of the gospels and the exegesis that followed truly

constitute a position of "synthesis." It values the tradition that preexisted the gospels, but before this tradition there was the Jesus who was its foundation, and after it, the evangelists who organize and structure it. The orientation of the Council, and of those who accept it, give importance to the contribution of the early community to the formation of the gospels, but they are not prisoners of it but have access back to Jesus and reach back to the authors.

The conciliar text also opens up a future full of promise. To fulfill it, the exegete will have to avoid being satisfied with reaching the Jesus who is at the origin of all, but starting from him, he must find the real and living continuity that links the various stages of formation. Historicity cannot remain a mere point of arrival for reason, but must also be a point of departure for faith leading to discovery in the text of the true word of God.[86] Through study of the text, the scholar must discover the theological riches it contains. The richness of the text, which contains more than appears on the surface, has manifested itself during the long life of the Church's Tradition. The power of the evangelical word continues to be what enspirits this same Church. It is here that there comes into play the exhortation of Paul VI not to remain in just a historical-literary exegesis, but to go beyond the study of the "pure primitive text," being aware that it is the living community of the Church that "actualizes" the message for the contemporary man.[87]

Having come into being in this laborious way, the text of *Dei Verbum* on the historicity of the gospels has now brought forth abundant fruits. It also offers the hope of an ever-increasing understanding of the inexhaustible riches contained in these books that "are the principal witness to the life and teaching of the incarnate Word, our Savior" (*Die Verbum* 18).

Translated from the Spanish by Louis-Bertrand Raymond and Edward Hughes.

Notes

1. *DV* 19.
2. *DS*, 2907.
3. *DS*, 3034.
4. *EnchBib*, 189.

5. *EnchBib*, 204–209.

6. *DS*, 3479.

7. *EnchBib*, 388.

8. *EnchBib*, 398.

9. *EnchBib*, 462.

10. *EnchBib*, 538.

11. *EnchBib*, 555.

12. *EnchBib*, 557.

13. A. Bea, "Parole di chiusura del Card. Agostino Bea alla Settimana Biblica Italiana" (Rome, Pontificio Instituto Biblico, 24 September 1960), *CivCat* 111 (1960, IV), 291.

14. *Ibid.*, 295.

15. *AAS* 53 (1961), 507.

16. *AAS* 53 (1961), 507–508. The book put on the Index: J. Steinmann, *La vie de Jésus* (Paris, 1959).

17. *AS Vat. II*, vol. I, pars III, p. 22.

18. *Ibid.*, p. 22

19. *Ibid.*, pp. 22–23.

20. *CivCat* 113 (1962, IV), 597.

21. *AS Vat. II*, vol. III, pars III, p. 782.

22. *Ibid.*, pp. 788–789.

23. *AAS* 56 (1964) II, 712–718; *L'Osservatore Romano* (14 May 1964), 3.

24. *AS Vat. II*, vol. III, pars III, p. 70.

25. *Ibid.*, 97.

26. *Ibid.*, 97–98.

27. *Ibid.*, 98.

28. *Ibid.*, 98.

29. *Ibid.*, 98.

30. *Ibid.*, 98.

31. *AAS* 56 (1964), 713–714.

32. *AS Vat. II*, vol. III, pars III, p. 98.

33. *AAS* 56 (1964), 714–715.

34. *AS Vat. II*, vol. III, pars III, p. 98.

35. *Ibid.*, 98.

36. *Ibid.*, 98.

37. *AS Vat. II*, vol. IV, pars I, pp. 367, 369–370.

38. *Ibid.*, 367.

39. *Ibid.*, 370.

40. *Ibid.*, 369.

41. *AS Vat. II*, vol. IV, pars V, p. 720.

42. *Ibid.*, 722–723.

43. *Ibid.*, 722–723.

44. *Ibid.*, 722–723.

45. *Ibid.*, 723.

46. *Ibid.*, 724.

47. *Ibid.*, 724.

48. *Ibid.*, 724.

49. *Ibid.*, 724.

50. G. Caprile, "Tre emendamenti allo Schema sulla Rivelazione (Apunti per la storia del testo)," *CivCat* 117 (1966, I), 228–229.

51. *Ibid.*, 229.

52. *AS Vat II*, vol. IV, pars V, p. 723.

53. *Ibid.*, 752.

54. *AS Vat. II*, vol. IV, pars VI, p. 687.

55. *Ibid.*, 609, 687.

56. For this kind of argumentation, see L. Stefaniak, "De Novo Testamento ut chrisitanismi basi historica," *DivThom* (Plaisance) 61 (1958), 113–130, p. 115; M. Nicolau, "De revelatione christiana," in *Sacrae Theologiae Summa I*, BAC 61 (Madrid, 1958), 263–268.

57. C. Martini, "Adumbratur quomodo complenda videatur argumentatio pro historicitate Evangeliorum synopticorum," VD 41 (1963), 3–10; X. Léon-Dufour, *Les Évangiles et l'histoire de Jésus* (Paris, 1963), 32–35.

58. I. de La Potterie (ed.), *De Jésus aux Évangiles. Tradition et redaction dans les Évangiles synoptiques,* Bibliotheca Ephemeridum Theologicarum Lovaniensium 25 (Gembloux, 1967).

59. J. Caba, *De los Evangelios al Jesús histórico. Introducción a la Cristología,* BAC 316 (Madrid, 1971, 1980).

60. I. de La Potterie, "Come impostare oggi il probleme del Gesù storico?" *CivCat* 120 (1969, II), 447–463.

61. X. Léon-Dufour, *Les Évangiles et l'Histoire de Jésus,* 266–280; J. Caba, *De los Evangelios al Jesús histórico* (1980), 405–415.

62. H. Zimmermann, *Neutestamentliche Methodenlehre. Darstellung der historisch-kritischen Methode* (Stuttgart, 1966), 128–160.

63. "Allocutio membris Pontificiae Commissionis Biblicae Romae plenarium coetum habentibus (Die 14 mensis martii a. 1974)," *AAS* 66 (1974), 235.

64. *Ibid.*, 235.

65. R. Bultmann, *Jésus. Mythologie et démythologisation* (Paris, 1968), 35.

66. Thus J. Jeremias, "Der gegenwärtige Stand der Debatte um das Problem des historischen Jesus," in H. Ristow and K. Matthiae, *Der historische Jesus und der kerygmatische Christus. Beiträge zum Christusverständnis in Forschung und Verkündigung* (Berlin, 1962), 12–25.

67. Thus E. Käsemann, "Das Problem des historischen Jesus," *ZTK* 51 (1954), 125–153.

68. E. Schillebeeckx, *L'approcio a Gesù di Nazaret* (Brescia, 1972), translated from Dutch: "De toegang tot Jesus von Nazaret," *Tijdschrift voor Theologie* 1 (1972), 28–60; R. Latourelle, *L'accès à Jésus par les Évangiles. Histoire et herméneutique* (Tournai-Montreal, 1978); J.M. Casciaro, "El acceso a Jesús a través de los Evangelios," in L.F. Mateo-Seco (ed.), *Cristo, Hijo de Dios y Redentor del hombre*. III Simposio international de Teologia de la Universidad de Navarra (Pamplona, 1982), 79–110.

69. H. Schürmann, "Die vorösterlichen Anfänge der Logientradition. Versuch eines forgeschichtlichen Zungangs zum Leben Jesu," in H. Ristow and K. Matthiae, *Der historische Jesus und der kerygmatische Christus. Beiträge zum Christusverständnis in Forschung und Verkündigung* (Berlin, 1962), 342–370, cf. pp. 351–352.

70. A. Descamps, "Aux origines du ministère. La pensée de Jésus," *RTL* 2 (1971), 3–45; 3 (1972), 121–159.

71. E. Käsemann, "Das Problem des historischen Jesus," *ZTK* 51 (1954), 125–153.

72. R. Latourelle, *L'accès à Jésus par les Évangiles*, 215.

73. D.G.A. Calvert, "An Examination of the Criteria for Distinguishing the Authentic Words of Jesus," *NTS* 18 (1972), 209–218; F. Lambiasi, *L'autenticità storica dei Vangeli. Studio di criteriologia* (Bologna, 1976); F. Lentzen-Deiss, "Kriterien für die Beurteilung der Jesusüberlieferung in den Evangelien," in K. Kertelge (ed.), *Rückfrage nach Jesus* (Freiburg im Breisgau, 1974), 78–117; D. Lührmann, "Die Frage nach Kriterien für ursprüngliche Jesusworte—eine Problemskizze," in J. Dupont (ed.), *Jésus aux origines de la christologie*, Bibliotheca Ephemeridum Theologicarum Lovaniensium 40 (Gembloux, 1975), 59–72. For further bibliography, cf. R. Latourelle, *L'accès à Jésus par les Évangiles*, 238–239.

74. R. Latourelle, "Authenticité historique des miracles de Jésus Essai de critériologie," *Greg* 54 (1973), 225–262; *id.*, "Critères d'authenticité historique des Évangiles," *Greg* 55 (1974), 609–638.

75. H. Schürmann, "Die Sprache des Christus. Sprachliche Beobachtungen an den synoptischen Herrenworten," *BZ* 2 (1958), 54–84; *id.*, in *Traditions geschichtliche Untersuchungen zu den synoptischen Evangelien* (Düsseldorf, 1968), 83–108.

76. W. Trilling, *Jesús y los problemas de su historicidad* (Barcelona, 1970), 53–54; translated from German: *Fragen zur Geschichtlickeit Jesu* (Düsseldorf, 1967).

77. R. Latourelle, *L'accès à Jésus par les Évangiles*, 233–235.

78. L. Cerfaux, *Jésus aux origines de la tradition. Matériaux pour l'histoire évangélique* (Bruges, 1968); J. Dupont (ed.), *Jésus aux origines de la christologie* (Gembloux, 1975).

79. W. Marxsen, *Der Evangelist Markus* (Göttingen, 1956); G. Bornkamm, G. Barth, and H.J. Held, *Überlieferung und Auslegung im*

Matthäusevangelium (Neukirchen, 1960); W. Trilling, Das wahre Israel (Leipzig, 1959); H. Conzelmann, Die Mitte der Zeit (Tübingen, 1954).

80. A. Descamps, "Progrès et continuité dans la critique des Évangiles et des Actes," RFL 1 (1970) 41.

81. H. Zimmermann, Neutestamentlich Methodenlehre, 214–242.

82. F. Neirynck, "La rédaction matthéenne et la structure du premier Evangile," in I. de La Potterie, De Jésus aux Évangiles, 41–73; J. Delorme, "Aspects doctrinaux du second Évangile," in I. de La Potterie (ed.), De Jésus aux Évangiles, 74–99; A. George, "Tradition et rédaction chez Luc. La construction du troisième Évangile," in I. de La Potterie, De Jésus aux Évangiles, 100–129. The three articles of F. Neirynck, J. Delorme, and A. George were published in ETL 43 (1967), 41–73, 74–99, and 100–129; M. Didier (ed.), L'Évangile selon Matthieu. Rédaction et théologie, Bibliotheca Ephemeridum Theologicarum Lovaniensium 29 (Gembloux, 1971); F. Neirynck, Duality in Mark. Contributions to the Study of the Markan Redaction, Bibliotheca Ephemeridum Theologicarum Lovaniensium 31 (Louvain, 1973); M. Sabbe et al. (ed.), L'Évangile selon Marc. Tradition et rédaction, Bibliotheca Ephemeridum Theologicarum Lovaniensium 34 (Gembloux, 1974); F. Neirynck (ed.), L'Évangile de Luc. Problèmes littéraires et théologiques. Mémorial Lucien Cerfaux, Bibliotheca Ephemeridum Theologicarum Lovaniensium 32 (Gembloux, 1973).

83. F. Neirynck, "Les femmes au tombeau: Étude de la rédaction matthéenne," NTS 15 (1969), 168–190; D. Senior, The Passion Narrative According to Matthew. A Redactional Study, Bibliotheca Ephemeridum Theologicarum Lovaniensium 39 (Gembloux, 1975); J. Lambrecht, "Redaction and Theology in Mk IV," in M. Sabbe et al. (ed.), L'Évangile selon Marc, 269–307; A. Buchele, Der Tod Jesu in Lukasevangelium. Eine redaktionsgeschchichtliche Untersuchung zu Lk 23, Frankfurter Theologische Studien 26 (Frankfurt, 1978); A. Vanhoye, "La composition de Jn 5,19–30," in A. Descamps (ed.), Mélanges bibliques en hommage au R.P. Béda Rigaux (Gembloux, 1970), 259–279.

84. AAS 66 (1974), 236.

85. A. Descamps, "L'approche des synoptiques comme documents historiques," ETL 46 (1970), 5.

86. J.M. Casciaro, "El acceso a Jesús y la historicidad de los Evangelios," Scripta Theologica 12 (1980), 940.

87. AAS 66 (1974), 236.

CHAPTER 11

New Horizons and Present Needs
Exegesis Since Vatican II

Maurice Gilbert, S.J.

Summary

The recent history of the Pontifical Biblical Institute already reveals certain present-day tendencies in Catholic exegesis, especially universalism and a pastoral awareness. Note is taken of the importance of access to the texts in their original languages, and also of the main orientations of the historical-critical method and of some other recent methods. Lastly, we see how Catholic exegesis tends to be more theological, more spiritual and pastoral, more ecumenical, and how it is concerned with inculturation.

Catholic exegesis had its golden age from 1560 to 1660, in the wake of the Council of Trent, and J.B. Bossuet's 1678 victory over R. Simon (d. 1712) would prove fatal to it for two centuries. Indeed, from 1680 to 1880, there were only a few names worthy of note, such as the three Benedictines, B. de Montfaucon (d. 1741), P. Sabatier (d. 1742), and A. Calmet (d. 1757), to which we must add the names of the Oratorian C.F. Hobigant (d. 1784), and the Piedmontese priest G.B. Rossi (1742–1831). And today we hardly ever consult any nineteenth-century Catholic works, with the exception of the concordance manual for the Vulgate established by H. de Raze and two fellow Jesuits in 1852 (the twenty-second edition was published in 1950), and maybe the French translation of the Bible on the basis of the original texts by A. Crampon (who died in 1894, having seen his work published).

For the most part, people were satisfied with repeating what early authors had said, and reissuing their works–especially those of Cornelius a Lapide, which went through eight editions in the nineteenth century alone, apart from an English translation. Finally, with the papacy of Leo XIII (1878–1903), the Pope of *Rerum novarum* and the thomistic renewal, the period of the extreme poverty of Catholic exegesis, which had by then been completely eclipsed by German Protestant exegesis, came to an end. Although he was preceded by R. Cornely, a Jesuit who died in 1908, and who inaugurated the *Cursus Scripturae Sacrae* in 1885–1887 with an introduction to the Scriptures of a very high quality, M.-J. Lagrange, a Dominican, founded the Jerusalem Biblical School in 1890, under the aegis of Leo III, and undertook an extensive series of publications (the orientation of which is well explained in his little book, *La méthode historique*, published in Paris in 1903). In Lagrange, Catholic exegesis found a new master. Sad to say, with the appearance of the modernist crisis, all this work was placed in jeopardy. Leo XIII set up the Pontifical Biblical Commission in Rome in 1902, and in 1909 Pius X established the Pontifical Biblical Institute, also in Rome, thus fulfilling the wish of his predecessor. The institute was entrusted to the Jesuits, and from then onward this was where the majority of Catholic exegetes received their training in scientific methods. In the twentieth century, Catholic exegesis gradually came back to life and recovered its position. Pius XII's Encyclical *Divino Afflante Spiritu* of 1953 provided it with its credentials, and it continued its vigorous development until the eve of the Second Vatican Council, although not without its share of suffering and conflict.[1]

One of these conflicts, in fact, was to break out in earnest at the start of the Council. However, the Council came when Catholic exegesis was in a state of full expansion, and it thus took up its position on a firmly established basis, minimizing opposition, encouraging work already in course, and providing exegetes with clear guidelines—guidelines that included the pastoral orientation desired by John XXIII.[2]

The Training of Future Exegetes:
An Indication of Trends

A number of very objective reminders will be helpful in order to gain a preliminary picture of the development of biblical stud-

ies in the Church after Vatican II. The majority of future professors of exegesis in Catholic seminaries and faculties attended the
Biblical Institute, because the law stated very firmly that in order
to teach the Bible in the Catholic world, a person had to have an
ecclesiastical license in biblical sciences, and this license could
be obtained either at the Pontifical Biblical Commission or at
the Pontifical Biblical Institute. Now, it is revealing to note the
numbers of students at the Roman Biblical Institute, and where
they came from. Immediately after the Second World War, in
1946–1947, there were one hundred students. Their number had
more than doubled three laters later, so that in 1949–1950, there
were more than two hundred. This number was ten to twenty
percent lower over the next ten years, and then rose again to 215
in 1961–1962, on the eve of the Council. In 1965–1966, the
year the Council ended, there were more than three hundred
students, and as many as 380 in 1969–1970. This figure then fell
progressively, and settled down to a stable 280 to 290 between
1975 and 1985, but rose again to over three hundred in 1985.

This clear increase in the number of students coincided with
the conciliar and postconciliar periods. Some other figures can
help explain the phenomenon. In 1950–1951, out of 169 students, twenty-four came from nonwestern countries, but for the
following years the proportions were as follows:

1955–1956: 176 students, 39 of them from nonwestern
            countries
1960–1961: 195 students, 48 nonwestern
1965–1966: 305 students, 64 nonwestern
1970–1971: 343 students, 99 nonwestern
1975–1976: 288 students, 119 nonwestern
1980–1981: 285 students, 153 nonwestern
1985–1986: 304 students, 164 nonwestern

Thus, since 1980, more than half the students at the Pontifical Biblical Institute have come from nonwestern countries, so
that it is the contribution of the churches of Eastern Europe,
Africa, Asia, and Latin America that explains to a large degree
the increase observed. The most representative case is that of
India: in 1950–1951, there were only two Indian students at the
Biblical Institute; in 1960–1961, there were three; but in 1965–
1966, there were ten; in 1970–1971, fifteen; in 1975–1976,
twenty-one; in 1980–1981, there were as many as thirty; and in
1984–1985, they reached the figure of thirty-two. This growth

can, however, be explained if we remember that the numbers of seminaries and faculties in nonwestern countries have increased greatly, and that they have naturally been placed in native hands.

Lay people as well as clerics follow the courses at the Biblical Institute: in 1960–1961, there were four lay people; in 1965–1966, ten; in 1970–1971, thirteen, six of them women; in 1985–1986, eighteen, eleven of them women. There are also female religious from every part of the world: in 1970–1971, there were only two, but in 1975–1976, there were nine, and this figure has remained steady until now. Lay people and female religious usually envisage their future involvement in biblical pastoral work rather than in full-time teaching in seminaries or faculties—a pastoral choice that also applies to a certain number of clerics, diocesan priests, or male religious.

This leads us to two general observations. First, a training in scientific exegesis is no longer today confined to people from western countries, and the whole Catholic world truly does have access to such training. Second, this demanding training does not open the door only to higher teaching and research, but also to the performance of biblical pastoral work—and this applies to both western and nonwestern countries. Two major lines of development can thus be traced in postconciliar exegesis: that of universality and that of a pastoral orientation.

Another observation of a practical nature should also be made. From the beginning of the century until 1968, an ecclesiastical license in biblical sciences was needed in order to teach Bible studies in Catholic seminaries and faculties, whereas a less-rigid situation is envisaged on the basis of the Normae quaedam published by the Congregation for Catholic Education in 1968: theology faculties have been reorganized, and some have decided on a division into sections or departments, one of which would be specifically exegetical (sometimes entitled "biblical theology"); thus, there is now a curriculum leading to a license or doctorate in theology with a biblical specialization. This possibility has the advantage not only of being less heavy than the license or doctorate in biblical sciences, but also of being better integrated with theology itself. And this is another of the specific features of postconciliar exegesis.

Lastly, Catholic exegetes are no longer trained solely in Catholic academic institutions, but also in others. This observation applies particularly to certain western countries. The reason for such a choice can undoubtedly be the attraction of certain great non-Catholic academic institutions, but there are also the elements of the great ecumenical current and the openness to non-Christian religions, which have been brought about as a result of Vatican II. Even if the example is modest, it is worth noting that every year since 1975, the Pontifical Biblical Institute itself has been sending a group of its students to attend a one- or two-semester academic course at the Hebrew University of Jerusalem, where courses in Hebrew, historical biblical archeology, and an introduction to Judaism are offered to these future Catholic exegetes. Thus we can see an openness, again along the lines of Vatican II.

Access to the Original Texts

It is a point of honor for contemporary exegesis that it consults the biblical texts in the languages in which they were written, that is, Hebrew, Aramaic, and Greek. If Catholic exegesis lost ground in the nineteenth century, it has undeniably recovered it since the preconciliar period. Catholic critical editions of the New Testament by A. Merk and J. Bover are constantly being republished; the grammars of biblical Hebrew edited by P. Jouon, and of New Testament Greek by F.-M. Abel are still in constant use. The same applies to the dictionaries of Hebrew and Greek produced by F. Zorell. An in 1971, E. Vogt published an excellent dictionary of biblical Aramaic.[3]

There are very few people today who would consider this requirement of scientific rigor superfluous. The problem no longer lies in this area, but in the fact that almost everywhere in the world, the curricula of secondary education offered to young people between the ages of twelve and about eighteen do not include study of Greek and Latin—let alone Hebrew—language and culture. Even for the clergy, the study of Latin, Greek, and Hebrew is gradually being whittled down to a thin surface layer that certainly does not allow them access to texts written in these languages. A greater effort is therefore demanded of future biblicists today than was previously the case, and at an age when it is no longer so easy to learn new languages. This constitutes a new challenge for those in charge of training these future exegetes. While this situation may be inevitable for other parts of the world, we may regret its causes at least as regards European countries. Be that as it may, it would seem that the efforts so perseveringly made over the past decades have been fruitful. However, the problem will remain with us, and auxiliary solutions will probably have to be found. For instance, why should centers not be set up in different parts of the world—Africa, Latin America, and Asia—for the study of these biblical languages? Such centers could also collaborate in translating the Bible into the various local languages.

Today, the most important translations of the Bible into modern languages are normally made from the original texts. The translations that have made the greatest impact are the following: the *Jerusalem Bible,* an improved second edition of which appeared in 1974, and which has itself been translated into various languages; the *Nueva Bíblia Española,* credited mainly to L. Alonso Schökel, and much appreciated for its literary quality; the *Einheitsübersetzung der Heilige Schrift,* which appeared in 1980, and that was produced with the collaboration of the Council of the Evangelical Church for the Psalms and the New Testament; and the *New American Bible,* which appeared in 1970. Many others should obviously be recalled, for example, the new Catholic translation of the Bible into Japanese.[4]

As regards the different versions, we can say that the Latin Bible has maybe been the object of the most attention. While the Benedictine Fathers of St. Jerome in Rome were producing the great critical edition of the Vulgate of the Old Testament, Dom R. Weber, with the help of various collaborators, gave us an excellent manual critical edition of the whole of the Vulgate, which appeared in 1969 in two volumes. In 1977, Dom B. Fischer published a new five-volume concordance to the Vulgate. Apart from this, a group at the Benedictine Abbey of Beuron is slowly continuing its work on an enormous critical edition of the *Vetus Latina.* Mention should also be made of the *Nova Vulgata,* which Paul VI called for in 1965, and which appeared in 1979: the Vulgate was corrected where it was not in line with the critical editions of the Hebrew and Greek, thus highlighting the importance of the original texts and the fact that they must be correctly translated; however, the corrections were always made in the Latin of Jerome.[5]

Lastly, to say nothing of the other ancient translations of the

Bible, in 1956 A. Diez Macho (d. 1984) discovered a complete Palestinian targum of the Pentateuch in the Vatican Library. This is called *Neofiti I*, after the manuscript in which it is found. The critical edition, with translations into various languages, appeared in five volumes between 1968 and 1978.[6] This discovery revealed the amount of interest in these ancient Aramaic translations of the Bible, and has enabled us to gain a better understanding of ancient Jewish interpetations of the biblical texts—interpretations that we can sometimes detect in the Septuagint and in the New Testament, and even in patristic writings.

As far as philology is concerned, there are two very different types of work that deserve mention. On the one hand, the long study and research on the Ugaritic language carried out by M. Dahood (d. 1982),[7] with a view to solving the problems of the Massoretic text of the Hebrew, have had a major impact, even though on a certain number of points of detail, the researcher has been reproached with paying too little attention to the semantic development of languages and with not carrying out an exegetical analysis of the texts within their context. On the other hand, is there anyone today who is not familiar with the *Analysis philologica Novi Testamenti graeci* of M. Zerwick, which has also been translated into English by M. Grosvenor?[8] The pedagogical approach of this work is excellent, and it has enabled a great many beginners to gain direct access to the Greek text of the New Testament.

Lastly, any philological approach to the texts, and any study based on the actual words of the texts are today assisted by the use of computer technology—and this will apply to an even greater extent in the future. Such technology means that we can now rapidly (if not without a certain expenditure!) carry out verbal research far beyond the possibilities of any purely manual study. The Benedictine Abbey of Maredsous in Belgium has been carrying this task of computerization for some years now.[9]

The Historical-Critical Method

Exegesis today seems to be faced with problems as to method. Generally speaking, it is still true to say that the exegete seeks to understand the text he has before him, trying to hear what it

says, and understand what it means. In order to do this, he does
his best to avoid projecting himself onto the text and making it
say what he himself thinks, although he knows perfectly well
that absolute objectivity is more or less impossible. On a deeper
level, the exegete—especially if he is Catholic—seeks to listen to
what the sacred authors meant to say and do really say through
their writings. And, lastly, he tries to grasp the salvific events
and messages to which the biblical authors bear witness in their
texts. Thus, when exegetes read the gospels, their aim is basically
that of gaining a better perception of the person of Jesus. So we
can say that the ultimate object of exegesis is not the text, but
the reality to which it bears witness. And such an attitude has
certain repercussions, as we shall see in due course.

Now what means does the exegete have at his disposal for
approaching the texts (taking for granted the fact that he reads
them in the original language in which they were written)?

The basic method in exegesis is still the historical-critical one,
which aims at understanding a correctly established text by examining it in the light of everything in its historical, linguistic, and
cultural environment that can help clarify it. This means that
the exegete must have a very broad general knowledge and understanding of the ancient history of the Near East and of its various
different milieu, and in this connection he may depend on the
research of orientalists. Comparatism is therefore often vital,
even if only to show the specific originality of the biblical text.
In particular, the study of literary forms, which became firmly
established in the field of Catholic exegesis thanks to the 1943
Encyclical *Divino afflante Spiritu* of Pius XII, has enabled us to
gain a better understanding of the significance of the Psalms.
However, over ten years before the Encyclical, H. Gunkel, a
non-Catholic, had opened the way to such study. Over the past
thirty years, comparison with the Hittite treatises of the second
millenium before Christ (the so-called "treatises of vassality")
have helped us to gain a better understanding of the Old Testament texts that deal with the covenant; D.J. McCarthy (d.
1983) carried out a great deal of work in this area.[10] This study of
literary forms, together with comparison with texts from the
ancient Near East, have also meant that for a long time now
people have recognized the primordial role played by oral traditions before the texts were written down. This observation applies particularly to the traditions of the patriarchs.

Since the 1964 Instruction of the Pontifical Biblical Commission,[11] similar research has been developed with regard to the gospels. Due to the importance of the gospel witness in the eyes of faith, research in this area is extremely delicate. How are we to detect within the verses of the gospels traces of the message that was proclaimed orally before it was written down? There is no doubt that the gospel texts represent the codification—carried out in the last decades of the first century—of an apostolic preaching that began at the time of Pentecost, probably in the year 30. Do the gospel texts enable us to find out something about the preaching that preceded them for about half a century, with the gap for the Pauline writings being reduced to about twenty or twenty-five years? And if we delve even deeper, can the gospel texts and the traces of the preaching of the apostles contained therein lead us to the original events of the earthly life of Jesus? These two lines of research have already produced some appreciable results, even though it would seem that the criteria until now accepted for reaching the period of the public life of Jesus are still not totally satisfactory. It is pointed out that, with a view to determining that some specific action, phrase or behavior was that of the historical Jesus, we cannot be satisfied simply with the principle that attributes to him only those elements that cannot be traced to his Jewish surroundings or to early Christianity, for if we accept only what is truly original in Jesus, we rob him unduly of any link either with his background and origins, or with the postpaschal community that claimed to spring from him. We must, therefore, add a principle that will give us a better grasp of the consistency and connection between the actual deeds and words of Jesus, and his most natural behavior, as this is described in as many New Testament sources as possible.[12] Moreover, this type of research is not confined to Catholic exegetes; all New Testament scholars are faced with it today, particularly in reaction to the positions of R. Bultmann, with which no Catholic can agree.

If we now turn to the prophetic books of the Old Testament, we are faced with the major problem of the authenticity of these writings. Although such a statement would have been less acceptable prior to Vatican II, any exegete, even a Catholic one, can without a qualm recognize, for example, that the book of Isaiah was not totally the work of the Jerusalem prophet who lived at the end of the eighth century B.C. The same applies to all the prophetic books. Here again, research is not confined to Catholics, although they also make effective contributions in this area. The approach to the question is not simple. For example, we must decide what can be attributed, with supporting arguments, to the prophet Isaiah himself, and, on the basis of these accepted texts, decide what were the actual actions and words of the prophet in person. We must also explain the origin (often different) and the significance of what was added to his work. In this way, we can discover the extent to which a prophetic book (for this applies to all these writings) was subjected to successive rereadings in the course of the last centuries of the Old-Covenant period, in the light of the new situations in which the community read the text as it had come down to it. This means that we cannot simply reject an addition just because it is an addition to the primitive text as such, but that these additions must be taken seriously, because they too form a part of the whole book that has come down to us in the canonical Scriptures. An addition is just as canonical as a primitive text, and therefore demands equal respect. This procedure enables us to realize how closely a biblical text was linked through the centuries to the very life of the people who handed it down.

A similar problem arises with regard to a Wisdom text that Catholics, unlike the Reformation tradition, include in the canonical Bible: the work of Ben Sira, which is known as Sirach (or Ecclesiasticus in the Old Latin version). This text was written in Hebrew in about 190 B.C., and was translated into Greek after 132 B.C. It was then revised, with additions in Hebrew, and then in Greek, before being translated into Latin in the second century A.D. (with some other additions) for Christian use. There are two types of problem in this connection, because of the fact that generally speaking the commentators and translators use the first Greek translation as the basis for their work, whereas since the discovery of the Guenizah of Cairo at the end of the last century, two-thirds of the book has been recovered in Hebrew, albeit in a state calling for critical discernment. Now, is the Hebrew text of Ben Sira himself also an inspired text (insofar as it has been possible to restore it)? Moreover, since the second century A.D., the Church has been receiving and handing on the text as augmented by its own additions. This is witnessed to by the liturgy, and more recently by what is referred to as the Vatican edition of the New Vulgate, whereas most Catholic Bibles tend to place the said additions in notes. What we are trying to say is that, in our opinion, the search for the primitive text should not lead us to belittle the witnesses of the survival of the same text within the community in which it is found. The search for the UR-text (the primitive text) is helpful, or even necessary, in order to discern God's breaking through into our history, but it must not be exclusive, for this would undermine the canon of the Scriptures.

New Methods

Various methods have made their appearance in recent decades and have to some extent renewed the approach to the texts. A joke made at the end of the last century has been repeated more than once in the last twenty years: it is claimed, not without exaggeration, that historical-critical exegesis looks not at the text itself, but at its surroundings. Anyone who is familiar with such exegesis is well aware that this is indeed a joke. Even so, there is a certain tendency, manifested in various ways, that would indicate that more attention should be paid to the actual text as such.

In the present age, when the theory of unity and interconnection is seen as a scientific touchstone, exegetes are no longer concerned so much with studying small pericopes, but rather with texts taken more as a broader whole. This requirement first appeared in historical-critical exegesis with redaction criticism, which started prior to Vatican II, especially in Reform exegetes. The method in question means that one must bear in mind the fact that the evangelists, for instance, were also the real authors of the books that bear their names, and that, because of their own background and the communities to which their gospels were addressed, they had specific personal orientations in their work of putting the materials that had been handed on to them by earlier tradition into book form. In other words, they were true authors. And their specific personal characteristics must therefore be shown.

Two particular methods came into being with a view to analyzing clearly defined textual units. The first, which is in very common use today even for subunits, is analysis of the literary structure of a text. The trailblazer in this area was A. Vanhoye, with his probably definitive study on the literary structure of the Letter to the Hebrews in 1963.[13] This method requires study of the text in its original language; we then see that the sacred writer guides his reader with indications that often go unnoticed by the modern reader, who is provided by present-day printing methods with other ways of visualizing the overall structure of a text. Such indications are found principally where themes are announced. The key words will reappear in their development. The indications mark the explicit limits within which a development is contained; they are link words connecting two developments, which in their second half take up in reverse order the basic statements of the first half (A B C D C' B' A'), with the principal statement sometimes placed in the center. This method, which has the advantage of showing the order intended by the sacred author himself in his writings, enables us to gain a better understanding of the general arrangement, and also means that we can avoid projecting our own thought patterns onto an ancient work. This method therefore leads to greater objectivity, so long as it is strictly applied without any mechanical automatism.

The other method is structural analysis, which has been used in exegesis for about twenty years, especially in France.[14] It grew out of the analysis of stories and narratives proposed by the Russian masters, and tries to provide a grammar that moves beyond the words in a proposition and the arrangement of propositions in a fuller phrase, so that it comes to encompass larger units such as paragraphs, chapters, or even books. The aim is to show how the whole unit works. It is observed that this working is governed by laws, just as a simple proposition is, and that it is even possible to define this working in formal terms and draw up a grammar. However, this method has limitations. Technically speaking, it can in principle only be applied to narratives, so that it is more difficult to use it for many biblical texts that do not "tell a story." Moreover, due to its formal character, it entails a risk of paying too little attention to the message transmitted by the text, and this is why it is only one of various tools placed at the disposal of exegetes. Lastly, and contrary to what is sometimes thought, this method can sometimes lead to less important results than those offered by classical historical-critical exegesis, inasmuch as it is not concerned with the background and circumstances in which the text was produced—sometimes even to the extent of attributing little importance to the text in its original language. Nevertheless, this has not prevented this method, even in a simplified form, from drawing the attention of exegetes to certain features of literary groupings that had not been clearly perceived until then.

Also in the perspective of greater attention to the text itself, there has been a growth—but to a lesser degree—of concern to gain a better picture of the social groups or communities that the book in question reflected or to which it was addressed. This entails noting everything in the text that indicates specific political, economic, and sociological circumstances. An effort is also made to use the light of the texts to gain a better idea of the possible orientations, and indeed the conflicts, of the early Christian communities, and their history. However, in more than one case, ideological or other prejudices, or a lack of scientific rigor and objectivity, have marred such work.[15]

One last reflection on a recent method of approaching the texts: we must consider whether computer technology can help us solve certain exegetical problems, for example, the validity or otherwise of a documentary theory, or the authenticity of a text. It is interesting to note that the Pontifical Biblical Institute in Rome has recently published an important study in this area on the basis of research carried out by Israeli scholars.[16]

A Dubious Methodological Undertaking: A "Life of Jesus"

During the first half of this century, a number of "Lives of Jesus" appeared and enjoyed considerable success. It will be sufficient to recall the principal ones, which were by the following authors: M.-J. Lagrange (1928), L. de Grandmaison (1928), F. Prat (1933), J. Lebreton (1935), G. Ricciotti (1941), Daniel-Rops (1945), and A. Fernandez (1954). However, for thirty years now, no Catholic exegete of any renown has dared undertake a similar venture.

Even so, in the course of very recent years, a group of close to one hundred Italian biblical scholars has undertaken a "History of Jesus" aimed at a general audience. This enterprise, which would have appeared decidedly improbable in the present exegetical circumstances, has proved a success.[17] Today, there is, therefore, a way of rediscovering a "history of Jesus" on the basis of recent research and with the use of different methods. Even if complete chronological details of the life of Jesus are impossible, certain fundamental elements have been fixed, and if we reread the gospels in accordance with the guidelines given in the 1964 Instruction of the Pontifical Biblical Commission, it is possible to move back to Jesus during his earthly life—that is, the historical Jesus.

One particular aspect of this research that has enjoyed considerable development over the past decades is that of the extent to which Jesus himself and all the early Christian communities were rooted within Judaism. The progress in Jewish studies has helped in this research, and today it is almost impossible to imagine any study on the gospels or on the earthly life of Jesus that does not devote long pages to this Jewish background. The Jewishness of Jesus is also emphasized in present-day Jewish circles by some important works, and we would give the names of some of their authors: J. Klausner (1907), J. Isaac (1948), S. Ben Horin (1967), D. Flusser (1969), G. Vermes (1973), and P. Lapide (1974). The subject is gradually beginning to interest Catholic exegetes too.[18]

An Exegesis That Encompasses
a Movement Beyond Itself

It is wonderful to see how the Church accepts and fosters the strictest scientific research on the holy Scriptures. However, the Church also reminds Catholic exegetes—as the Constitution *Dei Verbum* of the Second Vatican Council does with solemnity— that the Bible is not simply an object of knowledge. It is an inspired work, the word of God, and if we are truly to comprehend it, we must read it in the same spirit and with the same Spirit through which it was written. Its aim is the salvation of humanity, and it therefore constantly carries out a fundamental function in our humanity. It is not simply the possession of exegetes, who are merely the servants of the people of God, to whom it speaks from generation to generation. As the gift of God entrusted to his Church for herself, and through her for every human being, it requires total faith if it is to be understood inwardly. It requires ecclesial communion today, communion with those who have lived from it for 2,000 years and with those who do so today. It builds up the Church, and it cannot become an exclusive area with entry reserved only to certain people, and where the most deep-rooted beliefs of the people of God could be overturned in the name of science. This people of God—the Church—contains its own regulating organ, the magisterium, which is assisted by the same Spirit who spoke through the prophets and the apostles and who since Pentecost has been the principle of the whole life of the Church, in order to lead us all to the wellsprings of salvation. Since Vatican II, these truths have had a strong influence on exegesis. And we shall now proceed to show the effects.

Return to Ancient Exegesis

For nearly a century, the opening out and growth of scientific exegesis in the Catholic world was marked by an increasingly clear break with the ancient exegesis of the Fathers of the Church, the medieval Doctors and the commentators of the century following the Council of Trent. Even today, many Catholic exegetes are totally uninterested in the interpretations of their early predecessors, although the present century has seen an increasing number of excellent critical editions of writings from the patristic era and the Middle Ages, not to mention the revival of study of their authors. This can be seen clearly from the fact that until 1934, the Pontifical Biblical Institute in Rome offered an optional course on the history of exegesis (which was taught by A. Vaccari), but that this course was then replaced by introductions to rabbinical literature—although this was a courageous and necessary move at that time—and it was not until 1964 that the course on the history of exegesis was revived, and not until 1982 that it become compulsory.

There are, of course, considerable difficulties to be overcome if we want to delve into ancient exegesis. Present-day archaeological discoveries have provided us with a knowledge of the milieu that is incomparably greater than that possible for our far-off predecessors. Today's critical editions of biblical texts and our knowledge of the languages of the ancient Near East are radically superior to those at the disposal of our forerunners, who (with the exception of Jerome, the Greek Fathers for the New Testament, and the humanist exegetes) could only approach the Bible in translation. Our methods of analyzing the texts are very different, so that the modern exegete is baffled by the earlier type of exegesis. Added to this is a recent and growing ignorance of the ancient languages and cultures of the Church—a situation that is particularly serious in the West.

However, such a break with this great exegetical tradition can be seen all the more clearly as an error that must be corrected if Catholic exegesis intends—as it certainly should, if it is to be true to its nature and ecclesial function—to remain an exegesis that is truly carried out within and by the Church. The Fathers, the medieval Doctors, and the humanist exegetes approached and commented on the Scriptures within the faith of the Church. Their exegesis was often to a greater extent than ours ecclesial, theological, spiritual, and pastoral, and many people today feel strongly that it is vital for modern exegesis to recover these values and orientations.

The four volumes of H. de Lubac on medieval exegesis and the four senses of Scripture (1959–1964)[19] have exercised a profound influence in favor of such a recovery, although the fruits of this influence are still hardly perceptible. And people today are less familiar with sixteenth- and seventeenth-century exegesis than with that of any other period.

A More Theological Exegesis

Although historical and literary analysis of biblical texts has become necessary and indeed indispensable, such work is seen less and less as the last word of exegesis for today. If the exegete is not able to show how his technical analyses throw real light on the actual message of the Scriptures—which, when all is said and done, belongs to the theological and even theologal order—he disappoints his readers and listeners, who expect much more from him. We do not read Isaiah or Paul in the same way that we read Homer or Virgil. The Bible has a completely different significance for the believer, inasmuch as it is the word of God, and this is why the theological significance of the texts, which are the "rule of faith," is being increasingly emphasized.

This emphasis is seen mainly in two specific orientations. The first aims at showing the unity of all the Scriptures, inasmuch as they are the work of the same Spirit who inspired both the prophets and the apostles. This unity is what, half a century ago now, Monsignor J. Coppens referred to as "the harmony of the two Testaments." It cannot of course be denied that we are increasingly coming to recognize the differences in theology within the Scriptures (although such differences must never be absolutized), and that these differences have made it more difficult to offer any integrated presentation of biblical theology. However, the diversity exists within a unity that has its origins from On High, and is the diversity of sacred authors as they work together in the one work of the Spirit for our salvation. This is noted by the authors of the *Dictionary of Biblical Theology*, which was edited in French by X. Léon-Dufour in 1962 and revised in 1970, and which has been translated into a remarkable number of languages (a sign of the times!): on this level alone, ". . . there exists a profound unity in the language of the Bible. Throughout the diversity of historical periods, environments, and events, there is a true community of spirit and of expression among all the sacred authors."[20] It is important to show this unity, because otherwise there is a risk that differences will be heightened, thus tending to undermine the unity of the Scriptures themselves, which is an essential item of faith.

The other orientation entails interdisciplinary work. Today, as yesterday, the Church is constantly faced with new problems and new challenges, and it cannot hope to solve them without the collaboration of all those whose specialized fields of study are capable of throwing some light on the questions. Because Scripture is the *norma normans* of the faith, the exegete undeniably has a contribution to make, and this is in fact part of his mission in the Church. When Paul VI renewed the Pontifical Biblical Commission in 1971, he also had in mind such a contribution from exegetes.[21] This need for interdisciplinary cooperation is felt more strongly today than ever before. And it is important that it should be developed, despite the difficulties in any such dialogue between, for example, biblicists, moralists and dogmaticians— difficulties caused by the continued overcompartmentalization of the theological disciplines in the Catholic Church. This is vital for the "analogy of faith" (Rom. 12:6)—the harmony that exists, through the same Spirit, between Scripture and the deposit of faith as a whole. The exegete may sometimes be tempted to project a particular contemporary problem onto Scripture, thus compromising the faith, but Scripture interpretation must always be fair and objective, and also be careful not to relativize elements that may seem "hard sayings" for some of our contemporaries.

A More Spiritual Exegesis

Exegesis is not only a science. Inasmuch as the Bible is the word of God for us today, if the exegete wants to attain his objective, there must be a certain "complicity" or lived connaturalness between him and this word of God. And this in turn means that on his part there must be a fidelity to the word that he is trying to hear and understand. In 1970, Paul VI emphasized the need for exegetes to have this attitude. [22]

The exegete is called more than other people to rediscover what in the Middle Ages was referred to as *lectio divina*. This is because, as a master of exegesis, he is in a better position to discern, first for himself and then for others, the orientation of the call or the Good News of God that is addressed to us today by the sacred authors. There are many exegetes today who are able to transmit this *lectio divina* as recommended by the Second Vatican Council.

A More Pastoral Exegesis

The pastoral orientation that John XXIII wanted to impart to the Second Vatican Council is also reflected in the work carried out by exegetes in these past decades. The World Catholic Federation for the Biblical Apostolate was set up in 1969. [23] We have seen the extent to which the biblical dimension of pastoral work has developed in different parts of the world, sometimes even on the episcopal level, and this is not the place to discuss this subject. However, it is worth noting once again that since the Council an ever-increasing number of people, both men and women, laity and clergy, and male and female religious, have been seeking proper exegetical training as preparation for this type of apostolate. This means that the ability of those in charge of biblical pastoral work has greatly increased. And this does not apply only in the West—indeed, quite the contrary.

A considerable effort is also being made to provide all the

people of God with suitable work tools. We have already mentioned the *Dictionary of Biblical Theology* and the main recent translations of the Bible into modern languages, but many other works of this type could also be listed.

A More Ecumenical Exegesis

Exegetical activity has also developed on the ecumenical level, especially along the lines indicated by the Council with regard to increased mutual respect and more sincere mutual understanding. This is seen both in scientific research and in joint works aimed at a wider public. Apart from this cooperation between Christians, there is now an ever-increasing cooperation with Jews.[24]

Non-Catholic exegetes are also welcomed at the congresses organized regularly by Catholic biblical scholars—for example, those of the Catholic Biblical Association of America or the French Catholic Association for Bible Study (set up in 1967), or the "Bible Study Days" organized at Louvain or the "Bible Study Weeks" in Italy. Catholics are also present in the New Testament Society and the International Organization for Old Testament Study, and at their meetings. The great Catholic exegetical journals—*Biblica, Biblische Zeitschrift, Catholic Biblical Quarterly, Estudios Biblicos, Revue Biblique, Rivista Biblica*—publish studies submitted by non-Catholic exegetes, including Jews, and Catholics submit work to non-Catholic biblical publications—for example, the *Journal of Biblical Literature, Novum Testamentum, New Testament Studies, Zeitschrift für die Alttestamentliche Wissenschaft, Zeitschrift für die Neutestamentliche Wissenschaft.* The general criterion used by everybody is that of scientific objectivity in mutual respect. Among recent initiatives, we would mention the work of two interconfessional committees made up of great experts in text criticism, including Catholics: the first, for the New Testament, published its report, edited by B. Metzger, in 1971; and the other, for the Old Testament, published the first volume of its report, edited by D. Barthélemy, in 1982.[25]

This type of cooperation extends also to works intended for a broader public, especially translations of the Bible. In 1968, an agreement was drawn up in this connection between the Executive Committee of the Universal Biblical Alliance and the

Secretariat for Christian Unity on "Directives regarding Interconfessional Cooperation in the Translation of the Bible."[26]
The ecumenical translation of the Bible into French was certainly a success,[27] and a similar project is at present being carried out in Japan.

The Bible and Different Cultures

The Church today is becoming increasingly aware of its active
presence throughout the world and in every present-day culture
and civilization. Moreover, exegetes, who know how the word of
God has made itself heard throughout biblical history in and
through very different cultures, realize that they can help in
decisions as to how the message of the Bible should be transmitted in the various different cultures. This question of inculturation and acculturation came to light a little over ten years ago in
the exegetical field.

In 1979, the Pontifical Biblical Commission investigated the
question of "Faith and Culture in the Light of the Bible," and its
reports were published in 1981. The commission showed how
concerned the biblical authors themselves were over inculturation, and pointed out that the message had to be expressed in a
manner that takes contemporary cultural circumstances into account. A short time later, but still in 1979, in the course of the
African Bible Study Meeting held in Kinshasa, African and European exegetes jointly reflected on the subject of "Christianity
and African Identity" from the exegetical viewpoint, and the
reports appeared in 1980. Interest has been wakened in different
parts of the Catholic world.[28]

The encounter of the Bible with cultures into which it has not
penetrated for centuries—unlike the situation in Europe or the
Near East—naturally leads to another type of reading. The questions asked differ according to the different culture of the person
asking them. We are sufficiently aware in the West that our
present exegetical methods are also the product of our culture.
We should, therefore, not be surprised that even within the
shared faith, Catholic exegetes of another culture tend not to
import questions that relate strictly to western culture, but try to
establish a biblical hermeneutic and methodology that are comprehensible and accessible to their own culture; this can be seen,

for instance, in India. This is bound to lead to a real enrichment of the whole Church, just as the different cultures that succeeded one another in Europe in the course of the past 2,000 years have enriched its reading of the Scriptures and its very life. If this is truly to bear fruit, it calls for at least a minimum of agreement with the exegetical world as a whole; such agreement must be found not only in the same overall faith in the mystery of salvation to which the Bible, including the Old Testament, bears witness, but also in fidelity to the biblical text as it stands, and in concern to share our own lines of questioning and discoveries with other cultures.

Despite its shortcomings and omissions, this all-too-brief overview will perhaps have been sufficient to show the great effort that has been carried out by Catholic exegetes under the impetus of their immediate predecessors and under the inspiration of the Second Vatican Council. Work is continuing in the various areas, and by now nobody can challenge the position that Scripture has recovered throughout the Church.

Translated from the French by Leslie Wearne.

Notes

1. The following are some other important names in Catholic exegesis prior to the Second Vatican Council: F.M. Abel, J.M. Bover, D. Buzy, A. Condamin, A. Fernandez, J.-B. Frey, A. Gelin, P. Heinisch, A. van Hoonacker, J. Huby, P. Joüon, E.J. Kissane, J. Levie, A. Merk, E. Podechard, F. Prat, H. Quentin, G. Ricciotti, A. Robert, A. Vaccari, L. Vaganay, and F. Zorrell. We would also recall two important congresses that demonstrate the quality of the work being carried out: that held in Louvain in 1958, J. Coppens, A.L. Descamps and E. Massaux (eds.), *Sacra Pagina*, BETL 12–13 (Gembloux, 1959), 579 and 486; and that held in Rome, *Studiorum Paulinorum Congressus Internationalis Catholicus 1961*, AnBib 17–18 (Rome, 1963), 538 and 627.

2. At the time of the conflict that broke out at the beginning of the Council, A. Bea published *pro manuscripto* and distributed his 52-page study, *L'historicité des Évangiles*, to the Council Fathers; this work would have considerable repercussions. Among the exegetes who stand out in the postconciliar period, we would note the following representative Catholic names: P. Benoit, F.-M. Braun, G.J. Botterweck, L. Cerfaux, J. Coppens, M. Dahood, A.L. Descamps, A. Diez Macho, J.

Duplacy, P. Gächter, A. Georges, A. Jaubert, C. Larcher, S. Lyonnet, G. MacRay, D.J. McCarthy, D. Mollat, A. Penna, K. Prümm, B. Rigaux, H. Schlier, J. Schmitt, P.W. Skehan, R. de Vaux, E. Vogt, R. Weber, and M. Zerwick.

3. A. Merk, *Novum Testamentum graece et latine* (Rome, 1964⁹); J.M. Bover and J. O'Callaghan, *Nuevo Testamento trilingüe*, BAC 400 (Madrid, 1977); F.-M. Abel, *Grammaire du grec biblique*, ÉB (Paris, 1927); P. Joüon, *Grammaire de l'hébreu biblique* (Paris, 1965²); F. Zorell, *Lexicon graecum Novi Testamenti* (Paris, 1961³); F. Zorell, *Lexicon hebraicum Veteris Testamenti* (Rome, 1940–1984); E. Vogt, *Lexicon linguae aramaicae Veteris Testamenti* (Rome, 1971).

4. *Bible de Jérusalem* (Paris, 1973²); *Nueva Bíbla Española*, L. Alonso Schökel and J. Mateos (eds.) (Madrid, 1977²); *Edición latinoamericana* (Madrid, 1976); *Einheitsübersetzung der Heilige Schrift* (Stuttgart, 1980); in Japanese, *The Holy Bible. Colloquial Critical Translation from the Original Languages*, Studium Biblicum Franciscanum (Tokyo, 1958ff.), 25 sections to date.

5. *Nova Vulgata Bibliorum Sacrorum editio* (Rome, 1979); A.L. Descamps, "La nouvelle Vulgate," *Esprit et Vie*, 89 (1979), 598–603; T. Stramare, "Storia e caratteristiche della Neo-Volgata," *RivB*, 27 (1979), 331–338.

6. *Neophyti I. Targum Palestinense. Ms. de la Biblioteca Vaticana* (Madrid/Barcelona, 1968–1979), 5 vols. and 1 vol. of Appendices.

7. Particularly *Psalms*, AB (Garden City, NY, 1966–1970), 3 vols.

8. M. Zerwick, *Analysis philologica Novi Testamenti graece* (Rome, 1966³); M. Zerwick and M. Grosvenor, *Grammatical Analysis of the Greek New Testament* (Rome, 1981²).

9. Cf. the quarterly bulletin published in recent times by "Promotion Biblique et Informatique."

10. Cf. his works, *Treaty and Covenant*, AnBib 21A (Rome, 1981²), and *Institution and Narrative. Collected Essays*, AnBib 108 (Rome, 1985).

11. *Sancta Mater Ecclesiae* (21 April 1964), AAS 56 (1964), 712–718.

12. Cf., for example, H. Schürmann, *Jesu ureigener Tod* (Leipzig, 1975).

13. *La structure de l'Épître aux Hébreux*, StudNeot 1 (Paris, 1963, 1976²).

14. Cf. the two collections of articles produced as the fruits of a congress: *Exégèse et herméneutique* (Paris, 1971); and *Analyse structurale et exégèse biblique* (Neuchâtel, 1971). Cf. also P. Tihon, "Exégèse et analyse structurale. Quelques réflexions d'un théologien," *NRT*, 97 (1975), 318–344.

15. Cf., for example, the following reviews elicited by F. Belo, *Lecture matérialiste de l'Évangile de Marc* (Paris, 1974): J. Delorme, "Analyse d'une lecture matérialiste de l'évangile de Marc," *Lumière et Vie*, 119 (1974), 114–118; Y. Congar, in *Études*, 342 (1975), 927–933; G. Nossent, "Sur les approches matérialistes de l'Écriture," *NRT* 98 (1976), 337–341.

16. Y.T. Radday et al., *Genesis. An Authorship Study in Computer-Assisted Statistical Linguistics*, AnBib 103 (Rome, 1985).

17. *La storia di Gesù* (Milan, 1983–1984), 6 vols.

18. C. Thoma, *Christliche Theologie von Judentums* (Achaffenburg, 1978), 163–209; F. Mussner, *Traktat über die Juden* (Munich, 1979), 176–211, English translation *Tractate on the Jews* (New York, 1980), 105–136, French translation *Traité sur les Juifs* (Paris, 1981), 187–225; L. Volken, *Jesus der Jude und das Jüdische im Christentum* (Dusseldorf, 1983); P. Sacchi, "Gesù l'Ebreo" (regarding the book of G. Vermes), *Henoch*, 6 (1984), 347–368.

19. *Exégèse médiévale. Les quatre sens de l'Écriture*, Théologie 41–42, 59 (Paris, 1959–1964), 4 vols.

20. English translation: X. Léon-Dufour (ed.), *Dictionary of Biblical Theology* (London, 1982), xvii.

21. Cf. *AAS*, 63 (1971), 666.

22. Cf. *RivB*, 18 (1970), 339–340.

23. Cf. *Documentation Catholique*, 66 (1969), 556–557; L. Feldkämper, "A Season for Everything. Today's Bible Consciousness Demands Intensified Cooperation," *World Events*, 58 (15 January 1985), 28–31.

24. Particular note should be taken of the much more respectful and positive way in which increasing numbers of Catholic exegetes view the Jewish tradition.

25. B.M. Metzger, *A Textual Commentary on the Greek New Testament* (Stuttgart, 1971); the Catholic contributor was C.M. Martini. D. Barthélemy, *Critique textuelle de l'Ancien Testament*, OBO 50/1–2 (Fribourg/Gottingen, 1982–1986).

26. Cf. *Documentation Catholique*, 65 (1968), 981–992.

27. *Nouveau Testament* (Paris, 1972); *Ancient Testament* (Paris, 1975).

28. *Fede e cultura alla luce della Bibbia. Foi et Culture à la lumière de la Bible* (Leumann/Turin, 1981); D. Atal sa Angang et al. (eds.), *Christianisme et identité africaine* (Kinshasa, 1980); L. Monsengwo Pasinya, "Exégèse biblique et questions africaines," *Revue Africaine de Théologie*, 6 (1982), 165–175; P. Beauchamp et al., *Bible and Inculturation*, Inculturation 3 (Rome, 1983). On Japanese culture, cf. K. Usami, *Somatic Comprehension of Unity; the Church of Ephesus*, AnBib 101 (Rome, 1983).

CHAPTER 12

Exegesis and Actualization in the Light of *Dei Verbum*

Ugo Vanni, S.J.

Summary

The relationship between exegesis and actualization as described in *Dei Verbum* entails an unbroken and mutual relationship between the two. This means that we can evaluate the question of exegetical method as it has developed in the past twenty years (the historical-critical method and its crisis; the birth and relative decline of the structural method; and secondary branches, such as the reading of the Bible from materialist, sociological, and psychological perspectives, and so on) and makes it possible to discern a less narrow type of exegetical methodology that is able to produce a new synthesis, making better use of the contributions of historical-literary research, the pneumatic dimension, and also the elements of testimony found in the ecclesial experience of actualization.

The Problem

Even a general overview of the development between exegesis and actualization that has taken place between the promulgation of *Dei Verbum* and the present time is of immediate interest, although it also gives rise to a certain amount of perplexity.[1]

By "actualization," we mean all those ways in which the written word of God is made meaningful and effective in the present, with particular reference to the liturgical experience. This latter aspect in fact constitutes the title of the last chapter of the Constitution ("Sacred Scripture in the Life of the Church"), and was immediately accepted and assigned its proper weight. As F. Refoulé rightly observes,[2] Vatican II and *Dei Verbum* marked a real turning point with regard to actualization. Its various aspects have been discussed, new methods of pratical application have been studied and developed, and there has been a growing move-ment that many people have seen as a rebirth. However, the aforementioned perplexity arises if we take a look at research as expressed in bibliographical listings, and note, with some sur-prise, that there is a certain stagnation. When people discuss actualization today, they very seldom refer to *Dei Verbum*. The movement that began with *Dei Verbum* is still continuing and in fact seems to be growing, but it appears to be doing so through inertial force. This leads us to wonder whether the innovating impulse that the Constitution provided in this area has already been exhausted. Is there now a praxis that fulfills the orienta-tions of *Dei Verbum* so that no reference to the document is any longer necessary, since it has already been implemented in actual life? Or, on the other hand (and the history of the great Councils teaches us that this can happen), does this dearth of references indicate a saturation of understanding, although this understand-ing is only partial with respect to the breadth of the prospects opened up by the Constitution? Is there some form of actualiza-tion proposed by *Dei Verbum* that we have yet to discover?

This problem is aggravated by the further observation that when people discuss actualization today they rarely refer to exegesis.

The increase in growth to be observed in actualization is in fact one of the factors that have put exegesis into crisis— especially in the course of the seventies. This crisis can be seen as either latent or explicit in a whole series of writings,[3] but is most fully expressed and almost explodes in two particularly significant articles, one by F. Refoulé and the other by F. Dreyfus.[4] Al-though these two authors hold different views, and also differ in mind-set and approach, they both highlight a glaring dispropor-tion between exegesis and actualization, and go so far as to talk of a "chasm" and an "abyss" between the two. Scientific exegesis— or what Dreyfus picturesquely refers to as *exégèse en Sorbonne*—is inadequate, or even meaningless and misleading, in the face of the present-day experience of the Church. Dreyfus says that what is needed is *exégèse en Eglise*. The heterogeneity, or at least the tension existing between exegesis and actualization does not seem to affect actualization itself, but it is turned against exegesis by offering a radical challenge. And this precise lack of relevance of exegesis to life has led to talk of antiexegesis.[5]

At this point, we are faced with another problem: Does *Dei Verbum* have nothing to suggest in this connection? Is it really true, as F. Refoulé states, that *Dei Verbum* consecrated scientific exegesis, understanding this as historical-critical exegesis?[6] Further, in the face of the remarkably rich and broad documentation of F. Dreyfus, we may wonder whether the relationship that *Dei Verbum* confirms as existing between exegesis and actualization makes it possible to distinguish the two levels of scientific exegesis and ecclesial exegesis from one another so clearly that they are almost isolated. Is there some type of scientific exegesis suggested by *Dei Verbum* that is still to be discovered or at least fully appreciated and implemented?

The crisis in exegesis and the accompanying debate resulted in questions being raised as to its methodology. What is known as the historical-critical method, which was the most widely used and accepted one at the time of the drafting and promulgation of the Constitution, has been and is still the subject both of radical challenge and of sometimes impassioned defense. One party has observed its limitations and even said that it is now irremediably outmoded, whereas other people try to demonstrate its value—a value considered particularly relevant today by many scholars.[7]

After *Dei Verbum*, but not directly related to the document, new methods were proposed, especially the so-called method of structural reading. It is difficult to summarize this method, partly because it has a number of different forms and also because of the number of neologisms with which it has been presented. However, the various forms do have one common denominator in their attention to the text as a whole, as a resultant literary factor, viewed synchronically in all its constitutive elements.[8]

These are the two main forms in which exegesis is carried out today, although there are others.[9] Which of the two is most capable of helping to overcome the crisis in which exegsis is presently floundering? In other words, in view of the fact that the crisis in exegesis appears to be caused by a lack of proportion between its content and contemporary life, which of the two methods is more capable of bringing us into more direct touch with lived reality? F. Dreyfus does not hide his preference for the structural method,[10] but *Dei Verbum* specifically refers to characteristic elements of the historical-critical method. We clearly cannot expect the Constitution to settle a debate as to method, but maybe a closer comparison of the two methodological approaches in the light of the Constitution, and with an eye to the relationship between exegesis and actualization, could provide some elements helpful for an evaluation. In the perspective of *Dei Verbum*, what is the authentic relationship between exegesis and actualization?

Whatever our opinion on the complex and still unsettled question of actualization and exegesis as it has developed in these past twenty years, we cannot help but recognize the varied but convergent calls for further in-depth study, and this would seem to indicate that a direct reexamination of the text of the Constitution should be carried out with a view to collecting elements helpful for an evaluation and to pinpointing possible lines of development. This is the task we plan to undertake in the present study.

The Exegetical Proposal of *Dei Verbum*

If we are to define the relationship between exegesis and actualization in the framework of *Dei Verbum*, we must first recall the picture the Constitution provides us both with regard to exegesis and to actualization, always in the perspective of the problem as we have described it above. The texts in question are well-known, but it may be extremely helpful to take another look at them.

The Constitution does not intend providing a definition of exegesis. Even so, in number 12 (which is part of Chapter III, "Sacred Scripture: Its Divine Inspiration and Its Interpretation"), it does present a picture of what is in practice the task of the exegete, whom the Constitution usually refers to as *interpres*.[11]

The starting point is a reaffirmation of what we can call the human, historical dimension of revelation. God speaks to men in a human manner, entering into the web of events and making use of men. The word of God is also the word of man. Once this basic principle is accepted, there is an immediate important consequence that concerns the overall activity of the exegete: ". . . attente investigare debet quid hagiographi reapse significare intenderint et eorum verbis manifestare Deo placuerit."

The exegete is called to carry out authentic research (*investigare*) with complete commitment (*attente*), and this investigation is seen as oriented in two parallel but clearly differentiated directions: what the sacred writers wanted in fact (*reapse*) to express (*significare*) and (*et*[12]) what God wanted to reveal through their words (*verbis*).

The Constitution refers first and most specifically to the first line, which concerns discernment of the intention of the sacred writers. It makes two specific observations. First, it speaks of literary forms: ". . . inter alia etiam genera litteraria respicienda sunt." In order that this discussion should not be left vague, the Constitution specifies what it is referring to: ". . . ad suetos illos nativos sentiendi, dicendi, narrandive modos qui temporibus hagiographi vigebant. . . ." The sacred writer expresses himself in accordance with his own culture and the thought forms of his own period.

A second observation concerns the overall picture of communications at that time, and this deserves special attention: ". . . tum ad illos qui illo aevo in mutuo hominum commercio passim adhiberi solebant." These methods of communication also concern literary forms, including or at least presuming them. However, the picture is broader than this. When we speak of a mutual exchange between men, we are in a way moving out of the sphere of the author as such. This is a clear reference to all the parallel secular literary documentation. Moreover, the reciprocal exchange between men (*mutuo hominum commercio*) encompasses not only the writer but also the reaction of his contemporaries to his message.

These details make it possible for us to produce a sufficiently precise and almost technical picture of what is required of the exegete. General attention to history, the need for careful discernment of literary forms, comparison with other texts, including nonreligious ones—all this means that the exegete is unmistakably faced with a historical-literary type of research.

In order to simplify what we are saying, we can describe these elements as a group as the "historical-literary" dimension of exegesis.

However, the exegete's task does not stop here. As the Constitution clearly states earlier on, God's intention to reveal operates through the words of the human author. Explicit attention must therefore be paid to this aspect too:

Sed, cum Sacra Scriptura eodem Spiritu quo scripta est etiam legenda et interpretanda sit, ad recte sacrorum textuum sensum eruendum, non minus diligenter respiciendum est ad contentum et unitatem totius Scripturae, ratione habita vivae totius Ecclesiae Traditionis et analogiae fidei.[13]

It is not enough to consider everything that concerns the author as author: the Spirit who guided the author must animate both the reading and the interpretation of the text, and this must be done not as some sort of superimposition or idealization, but specifically in order to extract the true meaning (*ad recte . . . sensum eruendum*). Interpretation would be empty without this attention to the Spirit when interpreting. The Constitution gives specific indication of what is to be reevaluated in reference to the Spirit: the content of the whole of Scripture, a content that tends, precisely through the action of the Spirit, to be organic and unitary.

Inasmuch as the Constitution does not intend settling the question of the *sensus plenior*,[14] the organic content of Scripture is to be understood in a global sense. Analysis of an individual text is insufficient, and the whole Bible must be considered in order to understand the meaning of the individual part. Two elements connected with the action of the Spirit are then explicitly recalled: the living Tradition of the whole Church, and the analogy of faith, which are seen as lights that are to be turned on within the text in order to illuminate its meaning.

Thus, we have a second dimension of exegesis, and one that deserves special emphasis. For the sake of clarity, we shall call it the "pneumatic" element. The attention to the Spirit that is called for goes beyond the level of any method of investigation that can be applied to nonreligious texts and applies solely to exegesis. This has the important consequence that any exegesis that intends to be truly such, and that is thus oriented toward understanding and explaining everything that the text says and nothing else, cannot do without the part that is purely literary investigation, nor without attention to the added dimension that comes from the Spirit. If either of these elements were ignored, we would have a reductive exegesis, which would lose its wholeness and specificity, and would therefore be inadequate and hence unscientific.

It is at this point that the Constitution refers explicitly to exegetes. It refers to the two dimensions we have seen—the historical-literary and pneumatic dimensions—and states: "Exegetarum autem est . . . adlaborare ad Sacrae Scripturae sensum penitius intelligendum et exponendum, ut quasi praeparato studio, iudicium Ecclesiae maturetur."

This statement has a general significance in that it refers not only to the more difficult points, but to all of Scripture as a whole. A path is thus indicated. And the expression used (*sensum penitius intelligendum et exponendum*) would seem to indicate a continuous, almost infinite, development, in which there is always some element to be discovered with regard both to the understanding of the meaning of the text and to its explanation.

Actualization

In the picture of exegesis found in number 12 of the Constitution, no explicit reference is made to actualization. It is discussed separately and at length in Chapter V, which has the definitive title of "Sacred Scripture in the Life of the Church." The whole chapter is in fact dedicated to Scripture in the life of the Church in the perspective of the various aspects it takes on there. The literary tone of the chapter has more movement and warmth than that of the foregoing chapters. The application made to the life of the Church reflects the multiplicity of this life; in other words, we might say that it follows the lines of lived experience.[15]

If we consider this chapter in the perspective of our present research, we must reflect on the picture of actualization that emerges from the text, and also on the relation of this picture to exegesis.

It is stated as a guiding fundamental principle that the life of the Church depends directly and in equal measure on the word of God and the Eucharist. The liturgy is immediately seen as the privileged place in which this twofold life-giving contact takes place.

We are in the context of actualization here, and one of its basic features can immediately be seen. In the previous chapters, Scripture is seen as a communication made by God to men, but the verbs used are usually in the past tense: Scripture, as it was produced historically, contains that which God has wished to communicate to men. This chapter also refers to Scripture as an already completed literary element, but the verbs referring to communication between God and man are in the present tense. It is worth taking another look at the text: ". . . cum a Deo inspiratae et semel pro semper litteris consignatae, verbum ipsius Dei immutabiliter *impertiant*, atque in verbis Prophetarum Apostolorumque vocem Spiritus Sancti personare *faciant.*" And a little further on: "In sacris enim libris Pater qui in caelis est filiis suis peramanter *occurrit* et cum eis sermonem *confert*. . . . "

How is the movement carried out from Scripture as a literary factor belonging to the past to the present of actualization? The Constitution indicates one elementary condition in particular: a language belonging to the past must be brought into the present through adequate translations (No. 22).

However, actualization does not stop here: "Verbi incarnati Sponsa, Ecclesia nempe, a Sancto Spiritu edocta, ad profundiorem in dies Scripturarum Sacrarum intelligentiam assequendam accedere satagit, ut filios suos divinis eloquiis indesinenter pascat . . ." (No. 23).

The task explicitly assigned to exegesis is placed within this framework of an ever-deeper knowledge of Scripture as a whole (note the plural *sacrarum Scripturarum*), the aim of which is pastoral actualization that is relevant in the different situations of different times:

Exegetae autem catholici, aliique Sacrae Theologiae cultores, collatis sedulo viribus, operam dent oportet, ut sub vigilantia Sacri Magisterii, aptis subsidiis divinas Litteras ita investigent et proponant, ut quam plurimi divini verbi administri possint plebi Dei Scripturarum pabulum fructuose suppeditare, quod mentem illuminet, firmet voluntates, hominum corda ad Dei amorem accendat.

The text carefully distinguishes between the two levels of exegetical research and actualization, and notes the respective leading actors on these two levels: on the one hand, exegetes (*exegetae*), and on the other, those who are the direct servants of the word (*divini verbi administri*) whose task is bringing this work into contact with the people of God.[16] Having made this distinction, the text then emphasizes a continuity between the work of exegesis and that of the direct ministry. Exegesis must retain its own specific character and perform its task with the tools proper to it (*aptis subsidiis . . . investigent*). However, both the research and the explanation (*ita investigent et poponant*) entailed in the task of exegesis must be carried out in such a way as to enable (*ut possint*) the immediate servants to carry out their task in an adequate manner. Any exegesis that did not have such applica-tion in view would not be accepted as such by the Constitution.

It is clear that exegesis and actualization do not merely exist side by side like two parallel lines, but are in fact in a relation-ship of dependency, inasmuch as exegesis is seen in function of actualization.

In the following paragraphs, the Constitution deals with spe-cific aspects, and particularly the relationship between study of sacred Scripture and theology.[17] Everything involved in the min-istry of the word, in other words, in pastoral activity, must be nourished *eodem Scripturae verbo* (No. 24), with particular refer-ence to the liturgy. The importance of study—and therefore implicitly that of exegetical research—is emphasized, including the recommendation in number 25 that priests and all those working in the pastoral field should familiarize themselves with the Scriptures through *lectione sacra atque exquisito studio* as well as its personal assimilation.

The relationship between reading and study is confirmed in the concluding number of the chapter: "Ita ergo lectione et stu-dio Sacrorum Librorum sermo Dei currat et clarificetur . . ." (No. 26).

The chapter then ends by confirming the parallel influence of Scripture and Eucharist in the growth of the life of the Church.

We can sum up by saying that Scripture works to nourish the whole life of the Church, penetrating its various aspects from within, and that it does so with the help and mediation of study. And the specific contribution of the exegete is to such study with a view to this actualization.

The Relationship Between Exegesis
and Actualization as Seen in Operation

The existence of an indissoluble relationship between exegesis and actualization is now clear. Can we now examine it more closely, as it is actually manifested in operation, so as to be able to reach the conclusion of our present research, providing a more precise answer to the questions we took as our starting point?

In this connection, a number of details emerge from what we have already seen. In the first place, the relationship is such that both exegesis and actualization must be completely what they are. Exegesis in function of actualization must be a full exegesis, in accordance with the two dimensions described above. An exegesis that was solely "historical-literary" would not be able to give rise to actualization, while a solely "pneumatic" exegesis would decline into the realm of imagination, and would end up by moving away from the text and providing actualization with ambiguous material. The voice of the Spirit that should resound in actualization would be weak, if not indeed falsified. On the other hand, although actualization depends on exegesis, it is not a result of it, but has its own autonomy. In other words, there is a life that is lived, guided, and organized by the Spirit, and that absorbs into itself the content proposed by exegesis. The framework of this lived experience is broad and multifaceted, inasmuch as it encompasses the situation of the Church in all its expressions. Although the liturgy is the most frequently mentioned of these and certainly the most important, it cannot be said to be the only one.

As we have seen, any partial exegesis would be inadequate for the purposes of actualization. When it came in contact with the life of the Church, it would spring back on itself and be thrown into crisis. Equally, any partial actualization would not be able to absorb exegesis. If the material provided by exegesis were brought into contact with an ecclesial life that was chronically debilitated, it would be unassimilable and would indeed remain unassimilated.

These reflections lead to a second observation. If the movement we have noted between exegesis and actualization really exists—a movement that not only respects but requires the fullness and proper functioning of both—a bond of continuity must also exist between them, because otherwise the movement could not take place. Can this relationship be defined in the light of the Constitution? The movement is not like those we can find in other somewhat similar fields—for example, the movement from a theoretical conception of human nature in a specific philosophical system to the consequences derived from this conception as they apply to behavior. The content presented by exegesis cannot be reduced to a collection of religious theorems, just as actualization is not some casuistic list of practical applications. Both exegesis and actualization have the transcendent dynamism and the vitality of the Spirit, and it is here in the life-giving presence of the one Spirit that we find the point of contact that makes the movement from one to the other possible. Thus, the bond that unites the word of God, as interpreted and focalized by exegesis, and actualization is, in the last analysis, found in the oneness of the divine life that is communicated through both. Were it not for this intentionality of life as brought by the Spirit, there would be a break between exegesis and actualization, or at best they would be merely parallel to one another. It is therefore not surprising that when the Constitution speaks of revelation, from the very beginning it places a special emphasis on life, although it does not minimize the intellectual aspect entailed in revelation.

A third observation is as follows. The continuity we have noted and reflected on between exegesis and actualization suggests a specific movement of the word of God, which is thus interpreted by exegesis and enters into the everyday practice and life of the Church. We may then wonder, again in the light of the Constitution, what the exegetical content becomes once it is inserted into the living context of actualization. The Constitution uses a variety of images in this connection, speaking of vigor, strength, illumination of the mind, strengthening of the will, renewed ardor, nourishment, renewal, etc. It is never said that the exegetical content becomes something different. The need we have seen for a correspondence between content and actualization is situated and operates within the exegetical process. Actualization does not call for some filtered type of content. On the contrary, the expressions and images used suggest that the word of God as focalized by exegesis finds its proper sphere in the presence of actualization, which enables it to release all its dynamic force. It is there, especially in the liturgy, that the word becomes fully alive and effective.

One last observation. The movement or path that, as we have just seen, is suggested by the written word of God, starts from exegesis and ends in actualization. It is in the framework of actualization that this movement is able to develop its multiple, dynamic potentialities, while retaining so to speak the form it has acquired in exegesis. And it is then, in the framework of actualization in the life of the Church, that both Tradition and that nucleus of lived truths, which make it possible to speak of the "analogy of faith,"[18] emerge and take on form. This sets up a reverse movement: the two elements of Tradition and analogy of faith, which are brought about by the impact of the word of God on the life of the Church, tend to move from actualization to exegesis, and far from acting as a restraint, they throw light on it, and in particular foster what we have described as its pneumatic dimension. There is thus a movement of reciprocity between exegesis and actualization.

These observations make it possible for us to summarize as follows: the relationship between exegesis and actualization assumes that they should both be whole, and it takes place in a continuity of life between the two as guaranteed and fostered by the Spirit, to the extent of bringing about a type of influence of reciprocal causality. At this point, and in the twofold form of an evaluation and of the new perspectives that are opened up, we are in a position to reply to the questions we set ourselves at the beginning. We shall do this by offering a number of reflections.

Concluding Reflections

We started by noting that the actualization of the word of God within the sphere of the life of the Church has spread outwards enormously since *Dei Verbum*, undoubtedly under the inspiration of this document. Any objective evaluation is made difficult by the many and varied forms that this actualization has assumed and is assuming. It is impossible to give an unequivocal answer to the question of whether this actualization, which only rarely refers explicitly to *Dei Verbum*, in fact corresponds to the document. We can, however, try to provide a rough assessment, which will at least be useful as an encouragement for further study.

It must be observed that there is a broad current in actualization that does in fact follow the orientation of *Dei Verbum* as to the uniting of actualization and exegesis. This is demonstrated by, among other things, the many publications, including some of an exegetical character, that illustrate the liturgy of the word as this is laid down in the various cycles of readings. A number of journals deal specifically with this subject.[19]

However, within the sphere of a phenomenology of actualization, there also exists a tendency to ignore exegesis. People want to listen to the word directly and hear its immediate sound, without what they see as the screen constituted by exegesis. And some people also speak of "listening to the reading" directly on opening the book.

This tendency raises some questions as to the true nature and function of exegesis. We have already seen this a number of times in the course of our study, and we now return to the subject in a synthesized way. However, taken in itself, it seems to be a movement toward superficiality and away from the type of actualization that is always linked to study and exegesis—which is what *Dei Verbum* calls for. An impoverished reading of the Bible[20] inevitably leads to a partial actualization.

According to *Dei Verbum*, the oscillating bipolarity between actualization and exegesis that we have seen is indispensable for both. The way is being opened up to improved understanding and greater appreciation of the subject, and this could lead actualization to a growth in quality, apart from the growth in quantity that has already taken place.

A second group of questions was concerned with the crisis in exegesis, which was considered especially in the form of historical-critical exegesis. On the basis of what we have seen, we can now make some observations.

We cannot agree with F. Refoulé that *Dei Verbum* consecrated historical-critical exegesis as the only scientific type. The type of exegesis proposed by *Dei Verbum* contains not only the historical-critical dimension, but also the pneumatic dimension in a unified whole. It is not surprising that a partial exegesis basically oriented toward the past should have proved irrelevant to the present. Adequate appreciation of the pneumatic dimension would have changed exegesis and certainly made it less distant from lived reality.

There is a scientific aspect that is characteristic of exegesis and that needs to be reformulated more strictly. Precisely because of its partial character, rational exegesis (*l'exégèse en Sorbonne*) cannot yet be said to be scientific, but becomes so when it moves out from the Sorbonne, through the pneumatic dimension, to enter into the life of the Church.

The reciprocal oscillating relationship between exegesis and actualization makes it possible to discern another perspective. When we speak of science and scientific strictness, we often refer to the possibility of producing proof. This possibility can be seen to be extremely limited, and indeed almost nonexistent, with regard to literary research or even to historical research alone, except maybe when it can be oriented toward the past. To put it more clearly, a given historical interpretation can be confirmed or disproved by comparison with other documents, or maybe with new discoveries. The publication of the Oxyrhynchus papyruses, and the discoveries of Qumrān and Nag Hammadi have given a new slant to various interpretations with regard to the origins of Christianity. All this can be applied in full to the historical-literary part of exegesis. However, with regard to exegesis as understood in its full sense, as it is presented in *Dei Verbum*, is there a possibility of verification in the present of actualization? This field is still to be explored, but in principle the answer would seem to be in the affirmative.

If a given exegetical proposition were seen to be completely irrelevant for the life of the Church, because of its heterogeneity or its lack of openness to actualization, it would, therefore, be suspected of being inadequate or partial. And if a formulation of exegetical content were seen to be capable of setting authentic actualization in motion, this would constitute positive confirmation, and be a certain proof of its scientific correctness.

Our examination of the crisis in exegesis raised the problem of its methodology. Faced with the two prevalent methodological lines of the historical-critical and structural approaches, we automatically wondered which of the two is in a position to fulfill the requirements of *Dei Verbum*.

The indispensable continuity called for between exegesis and actualization, as described in *Dei Verbum*, becomes a distinguishing criterion of evaluation. We considered which of the two methods offers an exegesis that is able to enter into the present life of the Church and act as a life-giving element. The observations we have made at several points have already provided an answer, and we can now summarize and explain this.

The historical-critical method is necessary, but it is not sufficient alone. Whenever it is seen as an absolute that is complete and closed in on itself, its orientation toward the past cuts it off from the present of actualization. And, as F. Refoulé's article recalls on every page, this unbridgeable separation from the present is among the various factors[21] that have brought about the crisis in exegesis.

The structural method is undoubtedly closer to actualization, and F. Dreyfus is correct here.

The text accepted as a whole is the one that is used in actualization. Its improved evaluation and appreciation reflect positively onto actualization and help foster it. However, the structural method entails a risk of turning in on itself if it does not bring the text as a whole into contact with the person to whom it is addressed, bringing out and highlighting his reaction to it, or if it follows the philosophical view that reduces man to a range of relationships—a view incompatible with that of the Bible.[22]

What can we say in this connection? On the one hand, the explicit welcome given by *Dei Verbum* to certain elements of the historical-critical method, and on the other, the pneumatic dimension of exegesis (which, as we have seen, refers most especially to the whole), and above all the continuity with actualization suggest that the exegetical method indicated by *Dei Verbum*, which encompasses valid elements from both the historical-critical and the structural methods, tends to move beyond both. A broader and more developed methodological conception is envisaged, which would be able to appreciate and make full use of the contribution of experience, of actualization, even on the methodological level. Interesting developments along this line would appear to be in view if we consider various recent contributions that increasingly emphasize the experience of the Church in order to ensure an adequate exegesis.[23]

In any case, as a necessary general conclusion, we can say that the nuanced relationship of reciprocal continuity between exegesis and actualization as this can be deduced from *Dei Verbum* would still appear to need considerable refinement, although it has basically and irreversibly been established. It requires further study and development in the areas of both exegesis and actualization, but it cannot be ignored or set aside. And *Dei Verbum* has a future in this perspective. As is the case with other conciliar documents, the experience of the past twenty years has given us a good vantage point, so that we can now understand its significance better than was possible at the time of its promulgation.

Translated from the Italian by Leslie Wearne.

Notes

1. The relationship between exegesis and actualization (the latter is also referred to as "the life of the Church") has been grasped and highlighted from the time of the first comments on *Dei Verbum*, which are the classical works in this area. We would simply refer to those of J. Ratzinger, A. Grillmeier, and B. Rigaux, in H. Vorgrimler (ed.), *Commentary on the Documents of Vatican II*, 3 (London/New York, 1969), 155–272; C. Hampe (ed.), *Die Autorität der Freiheit* (Munich, 1967); R. Latourelle, *Theology of Revelation* (New York, 1968), 453–488; O. Semmelroth and M. Zerwick, *Vaticanum II über das Wort Gottes* (Stuttgart, 1966); R. Schutz and M. Thurian, *Revelation. A Protestant View* (Westminster, 1966); L. Alonso-Schökel (ed.), *Concilio Vaticano II. Comentarios a la constitución Dei Verbum sobre la divina revelación* (Madrid, 1969). The relationship between exegesis and actualization has been noted, but to the best of our knowledge it has not been the subject of any exhaustive study.

2. Cf. F. Refoulé, "L'exégèse en question," *Supplément*, 111 (1974), 398: "Surtout la fonction de l'Ecriture depuis Vatican II a changé. La place qu'on lui a faite dans la liturgie, dans la catéchèse, la prédication, a mis en évidence la distance culturelle entre ce texte et l'expérience de l'homme d'aujourd'hui."

3. We would merely note the following contributions: G.M. Landes, "Biblical Exegesis in Crisis: What is the Exegetical Task in Theological Context?" *Union Seminary Quarterly Review*, 26 (1971), 273–298; A. Feuillet, "Réflexions d'actualité sur les recherches exégètiques," *Revue Thomiste*, 71 (1971), 246–279; D. Attinger, "Come leggere la Bibbia. Per una lettura povera della Bibbia,"*Servitium*, 6 (1972), 449–455; L. Alonso-Schökel, "L'esegesi è necessaria?" *Concilium*, 7 (1971), 1871–1880; P. Grelot, "L'exégèse biblique au carrefour," *Nouvelle Revue Théologique*, 98 (1976), 416–434; W.J. Hollenweger, "The Other Exegesis," *Horizons in Biblical Theology*, 3 (1981), 155–179. This list makes no claim to be exhaustive, but even so it does demonstrate the complexity and breadth of the phenomenon.

4. Refoulé, "L'exégèse en question"; F. Dreyfus, "Exégèse en Sorbonne, exégèse en Église," *Revue Biblique*, 82 (1976), 161–202; "L'actualisation de l'Écriture. I—Du texte à la vie," *Revue Biblique*, 86 (1979), 5–58; "L'actualisation de l'Écriture. II—L'action de l'Esprit," *Revue Biblique*, 86 (1979), 161–193.

5. The expression is that of A. Paul, "Pour la Bible, une anti-exégèse," *Cahiers universitaires catholiques* (1973/74), 7–10. The need for an alternative and counterexegesis springs from the fact that normal exegesis is addressed to the past, whereas the requirement of life refers

to the present: "Vivre c'est affirmer au présent et à l'actif, c'est travailler et produire."

6. Cf. Refoulé, "L'exégèse en question," 391: "L'exégèse historico-critique eut à mener un long combat avant que fût reconnue sa légitimité. C'est en 1943, avec l'encyclique *Divino afflante Spiritu*, qu'elle reçut ses lettres de noblesse. Sa situation demeurait pourtant encore précaire, comme l'ont montré de graves incidents au cours du Concile. La Constitution *Dei Verbum* de 1965 devait la consacrer définitivement. L'exégèse scientifique a donc triumphé. Bien plus, elle jouit maintenant du prestige de la science. 'Le donjon de la scientificité dans les sciences religieuses,' a-t-on dit, 'c'est l'exégèse.' "

7. The crisis in exegesis is basically the crisis in historical-critical exegesis. For an up-to-date bibliography on the development of the debate, cf. A.L. Nations, "Historical Criticism and the Current Methodological Crisis," *Scottish Journal of Theology*, 36 (1983), 59–71 (see note 6, p. 60). We would also add R. Brown, "Historical-Critical Exegesis and Attempts at Revisionism," *Bible Today*, 23 (1985), 157–165; P. Welles, "La méthode historico-critique et les problèmes qu'elle pose," *La Revue Reformée*, 33 (1982), 1–15.

8. The bibliography on the structural method is vast, and any detailed listing is outside the scope of the present work. We would refer to the broad review of D. and A. Patte, *Pour une exégèse structurale* (Paris, 1978), 241–243. Examples of the possible applications of the structural method to exegesis are found in the review *Sémiotique et Bible* that has been published in Lyons since 1975.

9. Other methods of exegesis have been suggested, for example, a materialist, psychoanalytical, or sociological interpretation. These drew attention to certain aspects that were ignored or neglected in other methodological approaches, but without coming to be viewed as methods in themselves. Cf. J. Kremer, "Alte, neuere und neuste Methoden der Exegese," *Bibel und Liturgie*, 53 (1980), 3–11.

10. Cf. Dreyfus, "Exégèse en Sorbonne, Exégèse en Eglise," 354–359 ("Exégèse en Eglise et structuralisme").

11. Taken in themselves, *interpres* and *exegeta* are parallel, almost synonymous terms. The only clear difference is in the derivation of the two words, with one coming from the Latin and the other from the Greek. In common use, "exegete" and "exegesis" suggest an emphasis on the technical aspect, whereas "interpreter" and "interpretation" have a broader meaning, which also includes what is called "hermeneutics" today. In its use of these two terms, the Constitution considers them interchangeable, and it is interesting to note that the same number 12 uses *interpres* when referring to the more technical part of exegesis, and *exegeta* when highlighting the more spiritual aspect.

12. This twofold dimension was explicitly noticed, as can be seen from a proposed amendment. Cf. Luciano Pacomio (ed.), *Dei Verbum. Genesi della costituzione sulla divine rivelazione. Schemi annotati in sinossi* (Turin, 1971), 97: "Tredecim Patres petunt ut, loco *et*, scribatur *quidque*, ut appareat quaestionem *de sensu pleniore* non dirimi. R. Omnes concordant de non dirimenda hac quaestione. Si scribitur *quidque*, quaestio in sensum positivum dirimeretur. Expressio *et* est neutralis."

13. The Council Fathers were particularly concerned over this aspect of the exegetical task. The principle of homogeneity in the Spirit between the composition of the texts and their interpretation was added in the fourth draft, which became the definitive text. As regards the appreciation of this dimension on the part of exegetes, the third draft only had an *etiam*, which seemed insufficient. One hundred fifty Fathers asked that this *etiam* should be replaced by *praesertim* or *ante omnia*. The expression chosen was *non minus diligenter*, which was taken from the Encyclical *Spiritus Paraclitus*. Cf. Pacomio (ed.), *Dei Verbum. Genesi della costituzione*, 100.

14. Cf. note 12. From the time it was first proposed, the *sensus plenior* has constituted a problem that is still to be resolved: Is it to be attributed only to the Old Testament (Benoit), or does it extend also to the New, where it would indicate the deepest sense that the biblical texts take on in the life of the Church (Grelot)? For the whole question, see the still relevant and stimulating observation of R.E. Brown, "The Problems of the *Sensus Plenior*," *Ephemerides Theologicae Lovanienses*, 43 (1967), 460–469.

15. Among the various difficulties that the title and approach of the chapter had raised, there was also the need for a more logical structure. However, the choice of a pastoral approach prevailed. Cf. Pacomio (ed.), *Dei Verbum. Genesi della costituzione*, 124.

16. The category of exegetes as such was deliberately broadened, so that the text reads: "Exegetae autem cathilici, aliique Sacrae Theologiae cultores. . . ." The addition is significant: exegetes are placed among *cultores Sacrae Theologiae*. Thus, their task cannot be limited to purely philological aspects, but must enter into theology. On the other hand, the task of theology must also involve Scripture, and it too is seen in function of pastoral actualization.

17. This is number 24, which states that "Sacrae Paginae studium sit veluti anima Sacrae Theologiae." We should note the implicit but clear emphasis on exegetical research. Within the present context *studium*, the term that in classical Latin means "passion," seems to have the meaning that became normal in late Roman times and in the Middle Ages: that of "study, research"; we can understand it as "impassioned research."

18. When the Constitution speaks of *analogia fidei* without further

qualification, it assumes that the concept is familiar. Its first formulation is found in the Encyclical *Providentissimus Deus*, following which it was applied in many contexts, but always with the integral unity of revelation as its basis. The context of *Dei Verbum* suggests such a unity not only in terms of intellectual content or conceptual relationships, but also that fullness of meaning that the word of God takes on when its content is absorbed and made operational. The faith to which the content of the word of God is referred is found alive and pulsating precisely within the context of actualization.

19. We should recall those journals and reviews of a more popular character that have begun to form a bridge between exegesis and actualization. For Italy, special mention should be made of *Servizio della Parola*, which was started in 1968.

20. In this connection, we refer to the article of Attinger, "Come leggere la Bibbia," already referred to in note 3 above.

21. Every method of literary research has its origin in some philosophical conception, although it may subsequently free itself of this and gain its own autonomy as a method. The historical-critical method was born at the end of the last century and comes from historical positivism. The philosophical trends that developed later—especially existentialism—created another type of requirement and a different cultural mentality. This factor also contributed to a considerable degree to a reappraisal of the historical-critical method. On the other hand, the established importance of sociology today tends to orient exegetical methodology precisely in that direction. Cf. R. Aguirre, "El método sociólogico en los estudios bíblicos," *Estudios Eclesiásticos*, 60 (1985), 305–331; T.F. Best, "The Sociological Study of the New Testament: Promise and Peril of a New Discipline," *Scottish Journal of Theology*, 36 (1983), 181–194.

22. After the explosion that took place in the seventies at the same time as the crisis in the historical-critical method, the structural method today seems to be in a recessive phase at least as regards exegesis. There can be many reasons for this, including the following: a claim to self-sufficiency, with the refusal of elements taken from the historical-critical method; the fact that the method is limited especially to narrative, and was not able to find adequate forms for other literary forms; and—maybe most important—the failure of the method to emerge from the structuralist view of man as a philosophical conception. Cf. A. McNicholl, "Strutturalismo filosofico ed analisi strutturale," *Rivista Biblica*, 28 (1980), 351–374; J. Barr, "Biblical Language and Exegesis—How far does Structuralism help us?" *King Theological Review*, 7 (1984), 48–52.

23. Cf., for example, F.F. Ramos, "Interpretación existencial de la Escritura," *Burgense*, 11 (1970), 9–61; D.H. Kelsey, "The Theological Use of Scripture in Process Hermeneutics," *Process Studies*, 13 (1983), 181–188; D.J. Lull, "What is Process Hermeneutics?" *Process Studies*,

13 (1983), 189–201; L. Legrand, "New Horizons in Biblical Exegesis," *The Bible Today*, 22 (1984), 205–222; R. Protherough, "Reading Books and Reading 'the Book,'" *Epworth Review*, 12 (1985), 68–75; A. Outler, "Toward a Postliberal Hermeneutics," *Theology Today*, 42 (1985), 281–291; J.J. Canavessi, "De la hermenéutica de la Biblia a la Biblia como hermenéutica," *Revista Bíblica*, 47 (1985), 143–157; J.B. Rogers, "The Book That Reads Us," *Interpretation*, 39 (1985), 388–401; J.P. Floss, "Sprachwissenschaftliche Textanalyse als Konkretion der hermeneutischen Regeln in der dogmatischen Konstitution 'Dei Verbum' am Beispiel Gen 2, 4a–9," *Biblische Notizen*, 19 (1982), 59–120.

CHAPTER 13

The Word of God
and Pastoral Theology
in the Contemporary Church[1]

James Swetnam, S.J.

Summary

A survey of the Bible and pastoral theology in Columbia, the Philippines, Kenya, Poland, the United States, Germany (Federal Republic), Nigeria, India, Brazil, Canada, and France suggests that a special synod of bishops dedicated to this theme would be useful for the discussion of present problems and the clarification of future goals.

Catholic school children in northern Luzon compete in writing popular songs with biblical themes.

Young Nigerian Catholics are studying Scripture in such numbers that there are not enough trained leaders to give them guidance.

Brazilian Catholics are organized into thousands of biblical circles from the futuristic national capital of Brasilia to the primitive jungles of the Mato Grosso.

Some Italian Catholics are so enthusiastic about studying the Bible that they spend several hours two nights a week in detailed and patient discussion.

Interest in the Bible is so widespread among French-speaking Canadian Catholics that in the area of Montreal alone there are three bookstores exclusively engaged in the sale of biblical material.

These are but a few of the many manifestations of a renewed interest in the Bible that is increasingly characterizing the life of many Catholics in the postconciliar Church. The phenomenon is uneven: in some countries (e.g., Brazil), the Bible is much more important in the life of Catholics than in others. Nor should the phenomenon be exaggerated: in the Church as a whole, only a relatively small number of Catholics are vitally involved. But when these qualifications have been made, it is still unmistakably clear that at the present time, the Bible is assuming an increasingly important role as an explicit element in the pastoral theology of the Catholic Church throughout the world.

Catholic Christianity is centered on the Eucharist, and it is in the perspective of the Eucharist that the Bible should be considered.[2] All use of Scripture in the Church should be regarded as being explicitly or implicitly related to the Mass. All reading or hearing of God's word is an act of sacred memory, bringing to life God's marvelous deeds in the past that have culminated in Christ.[3] It is through Christ that the past becomes meaningful for the present and for the future.[4]

The following are some indications of the way in which the word of God is being employed in the pastoral work of the Catholic Church in the world of today. No attempt has been made to be complete or systematic. But from the random examples given, there emerges a picture of the pronounced biblical trend in the ways in that the Church helps her children to recall the saving deeds and teachings of her Founder so that he lives for them again.

Colombia

In July 1966, only seven months after the promulgation of *DV*, the Colombian bishops, making explicit references to the Council document, called for encouragement of reverence for and study of Holy Scripture.[5] Specific practices were suggested (e.g., Bible days, Bible weeks, courses in Scripture) at the various cultural levels of the faithful.[6] The bishops regretted the immaturity of faith of many of the Catholics of Colombia and called for faith based on a fully conscious and personal act that accepts Christ.[7] In 1967, the bishops stressed the importance of Scripture for the formation of seminarians, pointing out that to read the divine words is to hear God's reply to the prayer that should always accompany the reading of Scripture.[8]

The response to these and other statements of the Colombian bishops has been checkered. Medellín has developed the most active center for the use of the Bible in all of Colombia. Other dioceses such as Buga, Facatativá, and Villavicencio have also seen notable developments, particularly with regard to the formation of Bible study groups. Catechesis is often linked more explicitly with the Bible. Other initiatives could be cited.

But in the eyes of one knowledgeable observer, the biblical movement in Colombia has not lived up to the promise of the conciliar texts and their initial reception by the Colombian bishops. According to this view, selected texts of the Bible (from Exodus and the prophets) have been used as a trampoline to give an impulse to ideas extraneous to the Bible. Such ideas, so goes the charge, have cornered the market with regard to the attention and efforts of Colombians that should have gone into the study, preaching, teaching, and promotion of the word of God.[9]

In July 1985, the first Latin-American Meeting of the Biblical Apostolate took place in Bogotá, sponsored jointly by the Council of Latin-American Bishops (CELAM) and the World Catholic Federation for the Biblical Apostolate. Thus begins a new chapter in the quest of Colombian Catholics for a more profound realization of the implications of God's word.

Philippines

In 1968, the Bishops' Bible Committee was formed and formally joined the Philippine Bible Society in an ecumenical project to bring translations of the Bible to all parts of the country. In 1971, a Catholic Bible Center was established (later to develop into the National Catholic Center), and in 1978, the Episcopal Commission for the Biblical Apostolate was appointed. Various practical helps were launched in the mass media (e.g., radio programs, magazines, bulletins) to make Philippine Catholics more Bible-conscious and Bible-oriented. A ten-year project known as "A Bible for Every Family" has been launched to ensure the distribution and enthronement of the Bible in every home and office, to organize Bible communities, and to form lay Bible ministers.

In February 1985, the bishops issued "The Biblical Apostolate: A Joint Pastoral Letter of the Philippine Hierarchy."[10] In it, the bishops promise "to personally nourish ourselves with the word of God, and to faithfully promote the love for it among the people. We commit ourselves to give priority to the Scriptures as basis of our pastoral programs, to nourish our ecclesial communities with the word of God, and to encourage our faithful to a greater interest in reading and reflecting on the Scriptures."[11] One specific point the bishops make in their pastoral is the insistence on the use of biblical texts in the liturgical readings and not "the words of man (writings of contemporary, even secular authors)."[12]

Kenya

For over fifteen years, the Kenya Episcopal Conference has cooperated with the Kenya Bible Society and the translations of the Society into the various languages of the country are frequently used by Catholics. This has been the most prominent effort of the Biblical Apostolate by the Catholics of Kenya up to the present time. Scripture is also more widely taught to seminarians and lay students. Other needs have been identified: for correspondence courses, for help to priests in preparing homilies, for answers from Scripture to topical questions, for commentaries to explain the meaning of different passages, for work with youth who have a great interest in the Bible, for greater use of the mass media in spreading knowledge of the Bible.

A national coordinator for the Biblical Apostolate in Kenya was appointed in 1981. Under his supervision, courses are being offered to representatives from all parts of the country, so that they can supervise the Biblical Apostolate on the diocesan level.

Nairobi is also the site of the Catholic Biblical Center for Africa and Madagascar. The center promotes pastoral use of the Bible throughout the African continent south of the Sahara.[13]

Poland

The most important single factor in the promotion of the Biblical Apostolate in Poland was the "Great Novena" of 1957–1966 to commemorate the millenium of the arrival of Christianity. About 75 percent of all the instructions of the Polish hierarchy regarding the Bible date from this period. The next most important factor was the "Conciliar Year" of 1967. For the first time, a National Bible Week was proposed (for 24–30 September, culminating in the feast of St. Jerome). Parishes were urged to mount expositions about the Bible. Specific themes were suggested, the prayer before the biblical reading was indicated, conferences were mapped out, the solemn enthronement of the Sacred Scripture was prescribed as the climax of the week. This Bible Week has since been repeated in various dioceses. In 1972, the Polish bishops published directives for the use of the Bible in paraliturgical celebrations. For the Holy Year of 1975, the bishops chose to stress the theme of reconciliation and, as one of the practical points to carry this out, they recommended enthronement of the gospels in each home, use of the gospels for gifts, and the common reading of Scripture in the family.

Implementation of specific programs for the Biblical Apostolate has varied from diocese to diocese. For example, in the diocese of Przemyśl, it is suggested that in each parish, a "Bible Hour" be held once a month in place of vespers. A special Bible Week for priests was held in 1967. In the diocese of Sandomierz, an annual Bible Week is held beginning on the first Sunday of Advent. In the diocese of Łódź, special emphasis has been given to lectures on the religious view of the world as seen in Scripture.

The cultural conditioning of Catholic life in Poland makes Bible circles impractical, hence, the concentration on functions in the churches. But even the cultural aversion to small groups is yielding to the methods of "Oasis," which was begun in the 1960s. Groups of young people meet and confront the concrete reality of their lives in the light of the gospel according to the classic steps of "see, judge, act." Such youth groups also take part in "Biblical conversations." "Oasis" is a major force in the development of the Biblical Apostolate in Poland today.[14]

United States

The pastoral use of the Bible among United States Catholics is largely unorganized on a national level. There are exceptions, to be sure. The "Renew" program originating in Newark, New Jersey, has had a notable effect in helping Catholics in parishes in many dioceses come to a better appreciation of Scripture. And the Charismatic Movement in the United States as elsewhere makes generous use of Scripture. But there is no overall concerted organizational effort to mount a national Biblical Apostolate. This is in contrast to the well-organized group of Catholic biblical scholars who for decades have taken part in the Catholic Biblical Society with impressive results: Catholic biblical scholars in the United States are probably on a par with Catholic biblical scholars in Germany both in numbers and in quality of research. But unlike Germany, Catholic scholarship in the United States is not organizationally synchronized with Catholic pastoral endeavor, such as it is.

Isolated initiatives have produced striking results, however. The "St. Louis Jesuits," a group of members of the Society of Jesus originally working in St. Louis, have produced a number of striking hymns on biblical themes that are used in the liturgy throughout the English-speaking world. Many dioceses offer courses on the Bible. In 1982, the Catholic Biblical School was founded in Denver and it already enrolls over 300 students for part-time work.[15] Study groups flourish in parishes throughout the country. Scripture is much more in evidence as the subject matter for homilies than before Vatican II. The Bible is used much more in the spiritual formation of religious and seminarians.

The Biblical Apostolate among Catholics in the United States cannot be understood apart from the pervasive and dynamic influence of Protestant Fundamentalism. Such Fundamentalists insist on the absolute primacy and infallibility of Scripture in all details according to a literal interpretation, and their self-assurance acts as a powerful magnet drawing many Catholics. The average United States Catholic is lamentably weak in knowledge of the Bible, and this compounds the problem. One bishop, Roger Mahony of Stockton, California, has attempted to remedy this situation by issuing a pastoral letter entitled "The Bible in the Life of the Catholic Church" (25 March 1983).[16]

Much organizational work needs to be done before the considerable forces latent in the United States Church can be constructively harnessed for an effective Biblical Pastoral Apostolate.[17]

Germany (Federal Republic)

In 1933, the Catholic Bible Movement was founded in Germany. Five years later, the name was changed into the Catholic Bible Work by command of the government because the term "movement" was reserved for organizations having goals consonant with National Socialism. But the influence of the Bible in German life was felt nonetheless, especially in the training of seminarians. In 1944, all publishing endeavors were suppressed and it was only with the end of World War II that unhindered activity was possible. The name Catholic Bible Work has been retained, but it covers a variety of activities, from publishing biblical books to visits to biblical lands to conferences on biblical themes.[18]

Thus, the emphasis placed on the pastoral use of the Bible by *DV* found the German Church well prepared. A unified translation for all German-speaking peoples of central Europe, both Lutheran and Catholic, was undertaken even before the end of the Council, in 1962, and finished in 1980 ("Einheitsübersetzung"). In 1972, a synod of all the bishops of West Germany gave impetus to the insertion of the Bible into all aspects of Catholic life, but the bulk of official pronouncements by the hierarchy has come from individual bishops. Today, the pastoral use of the Bible among German Catholics is highly organized. Each of the twenty-two West German dioceses is represented in the governing body of the Catholic Bible Work, which has its headquarters in Stuttgart. Seven full-time specialists conduct Bible days, Bible weeks, and Bible courses throughout the republic. Two journals, *Bibel und Kirche* and *Bibel heute,* are dedicated to the role of the Bible in the Church and in German life.[19]

Germany has long been recognized as the leading center of biblical scholarship. Today it has perhaps been equalled in this respect by the United States, but in the official coordination of scholarship with pastoral activity Germany can be compared only to France where a similar official coordination exists: recognized German scholars work closely with the German bishops in the supervision of the Catholic Bible Work just as recognized French scholars work closely with the French bishops.[20]

Nigeria

The pastoral use of the Bible in Nigeria must be set against the variegated religious background offered by this huge country (one out of every four black Africans is Nigerian). Muslims number over 40 percent of the population and dominate the northern part of the country (the Hausa-Fulani cultures). Christians probably are even more numerous and may make up almost half of the population. Protestant Christians predominate in the southwest (the Yoruba cultures). There are Anglicans, Presbyterians, Baptists, and two interdenominational evangelical groups funded largely from Europe and North America. There are also indigenous Protestant churches. Catholics are less numerous than the Protestants and are found all over the country but especially in the southeast (the Igbo cultures). There are, in addition, millions of Traditionalist or "animist" Nigerians.

A major challenge to the Biblical Apostolate is the translation of the Bible into each of the more than 250 languages in the country. Most of them are still waiting for a full and effective translation. Only the presence of English makes possible basic communication of the Good News for many people. The indigenous culture of Nigeria, with its use of sacrifice and emphasis on strong family structures, gives a certain connaturality with the biblical message. The Protestants have a nationwide organization for the study of the Bible: "SU" (Scripture Union). Some Catholics are members, but most Catholics have joined the more recently founded "Bible Society," which is organized into chapters on the parish level. There are not enough trained leaders to give guidance to all who are interested. The Charismatic Movement is strong in Nigeria, and Scripture plays an increasingly prominent part in the spiritual formation of religious and seminarians.

The Bible seems destined to play a special ecumenical role in Nigeria. Each of the major religious groupings in the country—Muslims, Protestants, Traditionalists, Catholics—is related to it in one way or another. This fact gives to the Catholic Biblical Apostolate in Nigeria a particular challenge and opportunity.[21]

India

Another country with distinctive challenges to the Catholic Biblical Apostolate is India. Catholics make up less than 2 percent of the enormous population. There are over one hundred dioceses, but so vast is the country, that there are huge areas where Catholicism or even the Bible is scarcely more than a word. There are many languages, even in areas where Catholics abound, that have not been given a translation of Scripture. In addition, and perhaps most important of all, India is heir to religious traditions such as Buddhism, Hinduism, and Islam going back hundreds or thousands of years. The Bible must vie with other sacred scriptures much more prestigious in local terms. So prestigious, in fact, that some Indian scholars have begun speaking of the inspiration of these non-Christian scriptures in terms traditionally reserved for the Bible, a practice which seems ecumenically well-intentioned but theologically ill advised.[22]

At the national level, the Catholic Bishops' Conference of India has set up a commission for the Biblical Apostolate. Each diocese has a team or an individual appointed to foster interest. Every five years, the commission organizes a national seminar on the Biblical Apostolate. The site is the National Biblical, Catechetical and Liturgical Centre at Bangalore. The Tamil Nadu Bishops' Conference (South India) has its own center at Tindivanam.

At the grass-roots level, interest in the Bible is stimulated by an annual Bible Sunday, which includes exhibitions, cultural programs on biblical themes, and sale of Bibles. Bible study groups are functioning in some parishes. Seminars and holiday programs are scheduled for some areas. Training programs for catechists teach them to train the laity in the use of the Bible for personal prayer, family prayer, and paraliturgical celebrations without official ministers. Enthronement of the Bible has taken place in a number of Indian families; it commits the family to use of the Bible in daily family prayer. In the South, cultural programs involving loudspeakers and the use of large-scale lighting have been devised to promote knowledge of the Bible among Christians and to evangelize non-Christians.

Even more fundamentally, some Indian scholars cherish hopes that the two fundamental facts of Indian life, poverty and a profoundly religious outlook, may serve as the context needed to

free the Bible from what they consider a western-oriented problem in much of its traditional interpretation.[23] In this way, they
hope that the dominant Hindu cultures in India can be pervaded
by the spirit of Christ and Christ's views about human existence
without being eliminated, and that the resulting union would be
a truly Indian Catholicism.[24]

Brazil

The Biblical Apostolate involves more Catholics in Brazil
than it does in any other country. This is fitting, for Brazilian
Catholics constitute the largest single Catholic community in
the world. The strength of the movement lies in thousands of
"biblical circles," each of which is composed of families and their
friends who come together to discuss their life in the light of
Scripture. They are schooled in the famous formula "see, judge,
act." Inevitably, poverty enters in, for 80 percent of the population in Brazil is poor, and 60 percent is very poor. There is a keen
sense of community, and stress on faith as the basis for community is prominent in the Bible circles. Liberation theology has
had a strong influence.

Leaders of the Brazilian Biblical movement face a number of
special challenges. Twenty-six percent of Brazilians are illiterate.
The concentration of such persons is especially high in the rural
areas. Many Brazilian Catholics are ignorant of their faith and
receive the sacraments without having been sufficiently "evange-
lized" as the Brazilians say. Sixty million Brazilians are practitio-
ners in varying degrees of syncretist cults that are amalgams of
religious practices found in Africa (from where many Brazilians'
ancestors came as slaves), in Catholicism, and, at times, in non-
Catholic Brazilian indigenous cultures. Attempts by scholars are
being made to see what elements of such syncretism can be
adapted into Catholicism.[25] Scriptural categories may be a help
here because of the natural affinity between many African usages
and the culture portrayed in the Bible.

The National Conference of Brazilian Bishops selects annually
a theme for the whole country in connection with the Bible. In
one recent year, the theme was "Non-Violence" and the Biblical
book selected to accompany it was Revelation. The theme is
emphasized during Lent as part of a national "Campaign for

Brotherhood." Then, in September (Bible Month because of the Feast of St. Jerome), the theme is reworked in some dioceses and culminates in Bible Sunday.

Many Brazilian leaders of the biblical movement claim that in restoring the Bible to the poor, they are restoring the perspective in which the Bible was written and thus they make possible its proper understanding today. The point is well taken provided it is not pressed too far. For just as surely as the biblical message is distorted by attachment to wealth, so it is distorted by presumption. It is presumptuous to think that the entire Bible can be explained by the untrained. There are simply too many difficult passages that require patience and expertise to unravel, given the normal workings of Divine Providence. This said, Brazil may eventually make a major contribution to the way in which the Bible is understood all over the world.[26]

Canada

One way to judge the present role of Scripture in Canada is to examine the work of SOCABI (Société catholique de la Bible) among the French-speaking, especially in Quebec. The most impressive phenomenon has been the rise of many Bible groups composed of persons desirous to better understand the Bible in order to meditate on it. SOCABI has established contact with many such groups since the early 1970s and has offered thousands of persons the opportunity to follow courses in the ambience of school or parish. And SOCABI is far from being the only organization sponsoring such courses. SOCABI also publishes a wide assortment of printed helps, such as notebooks useful for a general introduction to the Bible, correspondence courses, and a bimonthly journal, *Parabole*. According to one official of the organization, *DV* is unknown to the vast majority of those interested in the Bible in Quebec and is almost never invoked to explain why such interest exists. But he agrees that the council was nonetheless the catalyst that produced the interest.[27]

While an official of SOCABI sees *DV* as having played the role of catalyst in the biblical movement in French-speaking Canada, an official of the National Office of Religious Education (NORE) of the Canadian Conference of Catholic Bishops does not see *DV* as having had such a role in the development of

Scripture's role in the Canadian Catechism.[28] In this catechism, Scripture has been described as a "strong and continuous thrust by one authority."[29] The basic influence was not the council but kerygmatic catechesis. So much stress is given in the elementary series to the omnipresence of God's word that if biblical quotations were to be removed, little would remain except connecting material and some illustrations. On the secondary level, biblical material abounds in the second half of the series. Thus, by the time the student is fifteen years of age, he or she has been exposed not only to the New Testament but to the Old as well.

The National Liturgy Office of the Canadian Conference of Catholic Bishops published a summary of *DV* in its National *Bulletin on Liturgy*, No. 56 (November–December 1976). Other articles in the bulletin strive to help people, clergy, and readers to understand their roles in the proclamation of the word.

France

French Catholics have a long and distinguished tradition of biblical scholarship. They also have an enviable system for making scholarship, their own and others', available to nonscholars. The series "Lectio Divina" and "Parole de Dieu" are typical of this type of *haute vulgarisation*. French Catholics have a national center for applied research in the use of the Bible: "Service biblique Évangile et Vie." Both the French bishops' conference and the French Catholic exegetes' organization (Association Catholique Française pour l'Étude de la Bible) have official links with this center. Thus, a coordinated policy consonant with biblical scholarship can be officially promulgated throughout the country. This policy is quickly known in thousands of biblical discussion groups, most of which are directed by lay persons because of the lack of priests.

Among the publications of the gospel and Life Center are the monthly *Bulletin d'information biblique* and *Cahier Évangile*. The latter is a presentation of biblical themes or books. It is widely used by Bible study groups. For eighteen years, the journal *La Bible et son Message* ran a continuing commentary that eventually covered the entire Bible. As of January 1984, its successor, *Les dossiers de la Bible*, began publishing a journal on biblical themes in which scholarship and pastoral application are combined in an

attractive format. A useful publication that does not come from
the gospel and Life Center is the series "Ecouter la Bible," which
is designed to help lay persons understand the liturgical readings
used at Mass and at Scripture services.

Scripture is everywhere in the French Church: in well-
attended Bible discussion groups, in pastoral works, and particularly in catechetics. In 1981, the French bishops authorized the
publication of the book *Pierres vivantes,* a catechetical source-
book composed of "privileged documents of the faith." The book
is heavily scriptural. In January 1983, Cardinal Joseph Ratzinger,
prefect of the Sacred Congregation for the Doctrine of the Faith,
gave conferences in Lyons and Paris in response to invitations
given him by the archbishops of those two cities to discuss how
the faith should be handed on to the younger generation. The
cardinal discussed contemporary catechesis in the light of this
general theme and, among other things, expressed certain reservations about the use of Scripture in catechesis independently of
the living Tradition of the Church.[30] His remarks set off a lively
discussion in France. A new edition of *Pierres vivantes* was published in 1985.[31]

World Catholic Federation for the Biblical Apostolate

Shortly after the closing of the Second Vatican Council, Pope
Paul VI entrusted to Cardinal Augustin Bea and the Secretariat
for Promoting Christian Unity, which he headed, the study of
ways for implementing Chapter VI of *DV.* The study eventually
led to the establishment of the World Catholic Federation for
the Biblical Apostolate in 1969. Initially, the federation was
envisioned largely as a means for seeing to the production and
distribution of the biblical text for Catholics. But it soon became
clear that such limitation of the federation's aims would entail
unnecessary duplication of work already performed by the Protestant United Bible Societies.[32] And although distribution of Bibles is still part of the federation's function, that work has been
left largely to the UBS, in which Catholics now participate in
growing numbers. The federation now concentrates on the promotion of the Bible as the animating force in Catholic life,
including liturgy, catechetics, and evangelization. The head-

quarters of the federation is in Stuttgart, West Germany. The elected head is always a member of the hierarchy. A number of full-time staff members publish material useful for the Biblical Apostolate and help organize regional and international meetings. The international meetings that have been held to date are Vienna (1972), Valetta (1978), and Bangalore (1985). An executive committee composed of delegates from all parts of the world meets once a year.[33]

The achievements of the federation in promoting knowledge and interest in the Bible are already considerable, but the possibilities are more considerable still. The federation is really only beginning to find its way in the immense task of promoting the Bible as the animating force in Catholic life throughout the world.

The classic view of hermeneutics is that a text should be viewed in two intrinsically connected perspectives: meaning and significance. The meaning of a text is what the author or authors intended to say; the significance of the text is the relevance that the meaning has for the reader. The meaning is basically one and unchanging; the relevance is multiple and shifting.[34] *DV* ends with the sentence: "Just as the life of the Church grows through persistent participation in the Eucharistic mystery, so we may hope for a new surge of spiritual vitality from intensified veneration for God's word, which 'lasts forever' (Is. 40:8; cf. 1 Pet. 1:23–25)." The *meaning* of this sentence in the mind of the Council Fathers is clear: the parallelism between the word of God in the Eucharist and the word of God in Scripture is a twin basis for growth in the Church. Perseverance in taking part in the eucharistic word is a means of growth; so too should be a more intense reverence for the Bible. The implications of that more intense reverence for the Bible are being explored by the postconciliar Church. This search for the *significance* of what the Council said is not limited to a simple production and distribution of Bibles or the application of Scriptures to missionary enterprise. This search for significance touches each and every aspect of Catholic life as surely as does the Eucharist. Theology, liturgy, catechesis, spirituality, the hierarchy, the clergy, religious, laity—all things and all persons come within the purview.[35] Few emphases of Vatican II will prove so challenging—or so rewarding—if heeded.

Notes

1. An earlier title for the present study was "The Word of God and Pastoral Theology in the Third World." But study and reflection made it clear that such a limitation would skew the presentation intolerably. "Third World" is a designation based on presumed norms of economic attainment and implies inferiority. But when the norm is the pastoral use of the word of God, some economic Third World countries become First World (e.g., Brazil), and some First World countries become Third World (e.g., the United States). A general title and treatment seemed advisable to avoid prejudicing the reader into thinking that the pastoral use of the word of God was somehow more important or more necessary or more interesting in economically Third World countries: Chapter VI of *DV* is for all persons in the Church, whoever they are, wherever they may be.

2. It is noteworthy how the word of God is presented in the pastoral part of *DV* (Chapter VI). The chapter begins with a comparison between the word of God and the eucharistic body of Christ (§21), uses the image of "feeding" when speaking of the Church's desire to reach a deeper understanding of the Scriptures so as to impart it to her members (§23), speaks of "nourishment" when treating the ministry of the word (§24), and emphasizes the sacred liturgy as the privileged place of communication of the word (§25). The chapter ends as it begins, with an explicit comparison between the word of God and the eucharistic mystery (§26). But more is needed. There should be a synod devoted entirely to the pastoral use of the Bible so that key points such as the eucharistic perspective of the word of God can be explained more fully and emphasized: it is in the context of God's word sacramentally present that God's word is pastorally most meaningful.

3. "Memory revives faith. In turn, in the cultic ceremonies themselves, Israel remembers her ancient story, the works of God, his marvelous deeds in times past. Thus, cult is sacred memory becoming sacred reality and life for the participants. The bearing of all this on the role of remembrance in the words for the institution of the Lord's Supper (Lk. 22:19; 1 Cor. 11:24–25) is clear. Through the elements Christians are to remember Jesus Christ, but it follows from this meal that the presence of Christ is not merely remembered, but becomes a real presence through the remembrance" (G. Hinton Davies, "Memorial, Memory," *IDB*, III [K–Q], 345). It is improbable that the author of these words subscribed to the Catholic view of the reality of Christ's presence in the Eucharist. But the point is that the use of memory with regard to Christ and the other works of God prepares the way as a cultic act intrinsically ordered to the sacramental presence of Christ.

4. Cf. O. Fuchs, "Der Stellenwert der Bibel in der heutigen Pasto-

ral," *50 Jahre Katholisches Bibelwerk in Deutschland* (Stuttgart, n.d. [Katholisches Bibelwerk]), 104–106.

5. *Conferencias episcopales de Colombia, III, 1962–1984* (Bogotá, 1984), 160–161.

6. *Ibid.*

7. *Ibid.*, 142.

8. *Ibid.*, 375.

9. ". . . el movimiento bíblico nacional no ha sido apenas favorecido desde el principio del postconcilio. Otra preocupación ha saltado a la arena de las luchas de Colombia y de América Latina: los problemas y las angustias económico-sociales. Con la entromisión de las ideologías en la Teología han nacido algunas teologías de la liberación. En estos ambientes se ha utilizado la Biblia, sobre todo el Exodo y los Profetas como trampolín para impulsar ideas extrañas al mensaje bíblico. La Teología católica de la liberación ha acudido preferentemente al Magisterio de la Iglesia y a la reflexión teológica que al campo de la exégesis. Estas luchas y actividades han acaparado la atención y el esfuerzo que promisoriamente se hubiera dedicado al estudio, predicación, enseñanza y promoción de la palabra de Dios" (communication of Monsignor Hugo Fernández Mora, professor of Sacred Scriptures and rector of the Major Seminary of Tunja, 25 April 1985). Such a serious charge obviously merits the attention of a synod of bishops of the Church universal, for interest in liberation theology transcends the local church of Colombia.

10. The information given in the preceding paragraph was taken from the text of the pastoral letter, pp. 2–3.

11. *Ibid.*, 7.

12. *Ibid.*, 4.

13. This information about the pastoral use of the Bible in Kenya was received in a private communication from His Grace Colin Davies, M.H.M., Bishop of Ngong, 13 April 1985.

14. This information about the pastoral use of the Bible in Poland was received in a private communication from His Excellency Kazimierz Romaniuk, Auxiliary Bishop of Warsaw, 24 May 1985.

15. Cf. *St. Anthony Messenger*, 25 March 1985.

16. Available in published form in English and in Spanish from The Liturgical Press, Collegeville, MN.

17. The information and judgments in the section on the United States are based on the personal experience of the author, who is a native of that country.

18. Cf. P.-G. Müller, "Zur Geschichte des Katholischen Bibelwerks," *50 Jahre Katholisches Bibelwerk in Deutschland*, 46–60.

19. The information in this paragraph comes from a private communication sent to the author by the Rev. Dr. P.-G. Müller, Director of the Catholic Bible Work in Stuttgart.

20. Cf. "Satzung des Katholischen Bibelwerks e.V.," *50 Jahre Katholisches Bibelwerk in Deutschland,* 65–68.

21. For the information contained in this section on Nigeria, the author is particularly indebted to Sr. Bibiana Muoneke, S.I.C.M., Rev. Effiong Joseph Ekuwem of the diocese of Calabar, Rev. Christopher J. Owan Nyiam of the diocese of Ogoja, and Rev. Chudi Peter Akaenyi of the diocese of Awka.

22. Cf. the discourse of the Rev. M. Amaladoss, S.J., "Other Scriptures and the Christian," delivered at the Third Plenary Assembly of the World Catholic Federation for the Biblical Apostolate at Bangalore on 15 August 1984. The respondent for the paper, Rev. César Herrera, C.Ss.R., Coordinator for the Biblical Apostolate in Latin America, while acknowledging useful aspects of the paper, disagreed with Amaladoss including non-Christian scriptures under God's special action called "Inspiration." Herrera maintained that God's revelation in creation and in history is a sufficient basis for the salvific dimension of nonbiblical scriptures. This would seem to be the appropriate judgment based on Catholic doctrine, but the verdict of a synod of the bishops of the universal Church would be helpful in the matter.

23. Cf. G. Soares Prabhu, S.J., "Towards an Indian Interpretation of the Bible," *Bible Bhashyam* 6 (1980), 151–170.

24. This information about the pastoral use of the Bible in India comes from a number of past and present Indian students who have lived or who are living in Rome, and especially from Rev. V. Clement Joseph, C.Ss.R.

25. Cf. R. Azzi, "Religiosidade Popular," *Revista Eclesiastica Brasileira* 38 (1978), 642–654, with bibliographical indications on p. 643.

26. This information about the pastoral use of the Bible in Brazil comes from a number of past and present Brazilian students who have lived or who are living in Rome.

27. "Bien sûr, une infime partie des gens connaît la Constitution dogmatique *Dei Verbum,* mais elle n'est à peu près jamais invoquée pour expliquer l'engouement de nos contemporains et contemporaines pour la découverte de la Bible. Elle fut et reste cependant le catalyseur qui a permis et permet encore l'accès presque illimité au domaine des sciences bibliques" (private communication of Mr. R. David, production manager of SOCABI, 21 March 1985).

28. "Although the use of Scripture has been a strong and continuous thrust in the Canadian Catechism, we do not see it as an explicit response to *Dei Verbum.* In a general way it certainly has been conditioned by the renewed emphasis on Scripture encouraged by Vatican II" (private communication of Rev. L. DeMong of the National Office of Religious Education, 1 March 1985).

29. *Ibid.*

30. Cf. *Documentation Catholique* 80 (1983), 260–267.

31. This information about the pastoral use of the Bible in France came from Rev. J.-N. Aletti, S.J.; Miss Bernadette Escaffre, Institutum Apostolicum Verbum Dei; Rev. M. Fromont of the diocese of Angers; Rev. L. Gicquel de Touches of the diocese of Sées; and Rev. J. Miler, S.J.

32. On the United Bible Societies, cf. P.-G. Müller, "Zur Geschichte des Katholischen Bibelwerks," *50 Jahre Katholisches Bibelwerk in Deutschland*, 58–59.

33. On the World Catholic Federation for the Biblical Apostolate, cf. P.-G. Müller, "Zur Geschichte der Katholischen Weltbibelföderation (WCFBA)," in *Katholische Bibelarbeit in Deutschland* (Stuttgart, 1979 [Katholisches Bibelwerk]), 44–47.

34. It would be imprudent to make too rigid a distinction between meaning and significance, or to refuse to recognize that the search for significance can help in the recovery of meaning. For example, recent attempts in Brazil to come to grips with the significance of the New Testament teaching on poverty may well result in exegetes coming to a more profound understanding of the meaning of that teaching.

35. This is clear from a simple study of the text of Vatican II, where greater attention to God's word in Scripture is recommended not only in *DV*, but in other documents as well: *SC* §§24, 35, 1. 2. 4, 51, 90, 121; *PO* §§4, 13; *OT* §§8, 16; *AG* §§20, 21; *PC* §6; *AA* §§2, 6, 10, 31a, 32. The pastoral exhortations and instructions of Vatican II with regard to sacred Scripture are the result of centuries of tradition brought to a certain maturity by the immense scholarly activity of the last hundred years in the realm of biblical research. But more still needs to be done: what is needed in the not-too-distant future is a synod of bishops dedicated to the theme of the Bible in the life of the Church. Such a synod could discuss and clarify problems that have arisen in the recent attempts of the local Churches to come to grips with the significance of the Council's teaching on the pastoral use of the Bible. More importantly even, it could give a deeper insight into the vision of the Bible as the indispensable element in the understanding of the central feature of Catholic Christianity—the Eucharist.

PART III

THE CHURCH, SACRAMENT OF SALVATION

CHAPTER 14

Christ: Revealer,
Founder of the Church,
and Source of Ecclesial Life

Jean Galot, S.J.

Summary

Vatican II views Christ as "the light of the nations" and "the fullness of all revelation." Historically speaking, "the Lord Jesus gave birth to his Church," founding it and instituting the ministries it needed. He is above all the source of the life of the Church, and particularly the source of priestly activity, the consecrated life, liturgical life, apostolic activity, and unity; he reveals man to himself and establishes a new humanity.

While we find an ecclesiology that is systematically articulated under a number of aspects in the documents of Vatican II, this is not the case with christology, because the latter was not the special object of study and discussion in the work of the Council. Even so, the texts of the Council do provide us with a good number of indications of a christological nature. Our aim here is not to note all these references, but rather to pinpoint basic doctrinal orientations.

Christ, Light and Word

Christ is in the first place presented as the light, with the Church bearing the reflection of this light in order to illuminate humanity. The first words of the Dogmatic Constitution on the Church are significant:

> Christ is the light of humanity; and it is, accordingly, the heart-felt desire of this sacred Council, being gathered together in the Holy Spirit, that, by proclaiming his Gospel to every creature (cf. Mk. 16:15), it may bring to all men that light of Christ which shines out visibly from the Church.

Pope John XXIII spoke of the Church as "light of the nations,"[1] but when the Council uses this expression, it applies it firstly to Christ.[2] In fact, it is simply repeating the title given to the Savior in the prophecy of Simeon (Lk. 2:32).

This highlighting of the principle that Christ is the light reminds us of the prologue of John's Gospel: "In the beginning was the Word . . . and the Word was the true light that enlightens every man [and] was coming into the world" (Jn. 1:1, 9). The beginning of ecclesiology is found in Christ the light.

Christ's activity of revelation was dealt with specifically in the conciliar document on revelation. The first words of the Constitution *Dei Verbum* seem to refer to the "word of God" in general, but the citation that follows refers to Christ, so that this word is concretized in the person of the Revealer: ". . . we proclaim to you the eternal life which was with the Father and was made manifest to us" (1 Jn. 1:2).[3]

Later on, we are told in more precise tones that Christ "is himself both the mediator and the fullness of revelation" (*DV* 2). He is the mediator: not one of the mediators, but the sole mediator, who, by becoming man, communicates the whole of God's truth to mankind. He is the sole mediator who is both God and man, and who can therefore perform the perfection of mediation. This mediation means that in the work of revelation, he is both author and object of revelation.[4]

The unique character of this mediation is confirmed in contrast to the multiplicity of the words of the prophets. The Council cites the prologue to the Letter to the Hebrews, and comments that God "sent his Son, the eternal Word who enlightens all men, to dwell among men and to tell them about the inner life of God (cf. Jn. 1:1–18)" (*DV* 4). The citation of this epistle is all the more significant inasmuch as it replaced a paraphase of the preparatory schema, in which the unicity of Christ—and also the identity between revealer and revelation—appeared to be diminished.[5]

As the sole mediator, Christ is the "fullness" of all revelation. He is this fullness subjectively speaking, in the sense that he performs this revelation "by the total fact of his presence and self-manifestation" (DV 4). The previous draft said "through his whole person,"[6] but it seemed preferable to avoid such an expression in view of the precise meaning the concept of person, as distinct from that of nature, has taken on in christological dogma. And the intention of the text is to show that Jesus was the revealer through his whole human nature and life: ". . . by words and works, signs and miracles, but above all by his death and glorious resurrection from the dead, and finally by sending the Spirit of truth" (DV 4). All this is summed up in the phrase "presence and self-manifestation." "Self-manifestation" alone would not have been able to express the value of this work of revelation, for it could have suggested the simple exterior deployment of a reality that remained at a distance. "Presence" indicates the involvement of the person in the manifestation; the revelation does not result merely from an action but from a gift of self. It could be said that in revelation Christ has involved his own fullness, putting it at the disposal of humanity.

However, he is called the fullness of revelation in a more objective sense, inasmuch as it is the whole object of revelation that is given to us in him. This fullness obviously could not be understood in the sense of belittling the value of the revelation that took place prior to the coming of Jesus. Thus, having stated the principle that Christ is "the fullness of all revelation," the Council explains that the Word made flesh "completed and perfected revelation" (DV 4). Historically speaking, it is a fulfillment, because Jesus was preceded by a long period of revelation addressed to the Jewish people. Because he fulfills everything that has been announced beforehand, his revelation really is fullness. He takes up into himself everything that has already been revealed, in order to give it its significance and meaning. The whole light of the Old Covenant is taken up into his own light. More especially, everything that has been said of God, and of his face and actions, now receives a higher illumination in his person as the incarnate Son, in his human face, and in his activity.

Because Christ is the fullness of revelation, his work of revealing takes on a definitive character. The new covenant is definitive, says the Council: "The Christian economy . . . will never pass away; and no new public revelation is to be expected before the glorious manifestation of our Lord, Jesus Christ" (*DV* 4).

The Council did not repeat the traditional statement that revelation ended at the death of the apostles. Indeed, the end of public revelation is not represented by the death of the apostles, but concerns "the presence and self-manifestation" of Christ in the midst of humanity. Revelation is accomplished in Christ, and thus lasted until the moment of the ascension. The apostles and other witnesses simply gathered this revelation in order to pass it on and spread it.

This means that human history can add nothing in the way of public revelation to what which took place in Christ. The "glorious manifestation" will mark the end of history. Thus, men must find all the truth of their life and destiny in Christ. "Private" revelations are of course possible in God's relationship with certain individuals, but the whole of the message of salvation addressed to humanity is found in Christ, and it can be neither added to nor modified. The Church can only draw on this fullness.

It may be asked whether attributing this fullness to Christ can entail a risk of "christomonism"—a word used to describe doctrines that want to recognize only Christ in revelation or in the work of salvation. The Council offers a christocentric conception of revelation. However, christocentrism does not mean christomonism.[7] Even in the Prologue to *Dei Verbum*, the Council speaks, with St. John, of "fellowship with the Father and with his Son Jesus Christ" (1 Jn. 1:3), and then shows how God has been pleased "to make known the mystery of his will . . . that men should have access to the Father, through Christ, the Word made flesh, in the Holy Spirit" (*DV* 2). Other references to the Father and the Holy Spirit are not lacking in the rest of the document. Christ "revealed his Father and himself by deeds and words" (*DV* 17), and sent to his apostles "the Spirit, the Counsellor, who would guide them into all the truth" (*DV* 20). "Fullness of revelation" in Jesus means a fullness coming from the Father and communicated to men by the Holy Spirit.

Christ, the Founder of the Church

The Historical Action of Foundation, and Its Trans-Historical End

The origin of the Church is found in the Father's plan, which was laid down before the creation of the world. *Lumen gentium* begins by setting forth this divine plan, and then shows how it was fulfilled by the sending of the Son. The specific characteristic of the Son's action is his presence and activity in human history for the foundation of the Church. The Council emphasizes the Trinitarian origin of the Church, "a people brought into unity from the unity of the Father, the Son and the Holy Spirit" (*LG* 4). However, this Trinitarian origin, which indicates a joint action on the part of the divine persons in the constitution of the Church, does not deny each of these persons his own specific mode of action. Only the Son was incarnated, and it is he who "inaugurated the kingdom of heaven on earth" (*LG* 3).

We are given various details concerning this inauguration. Although it is carried out through a human action, the latter is different from the action of other human founders, because it is the action of the Son, the Lord. First there is the preaching: ". . . the Lord Jesus inaugurated his Church by preaching the Good News, that is, the coming of the kingdom of God, promised over the ages in the scriptures" (*LG* 5). The miracles confirm this coming, but we must recognize that the kingdom is manifested principally "in the person of Christ himself, Son of God and Son of Man" (*LG* 5). Special emphasis is placed on the decisive role of the Passion, inasmuch as the Son of Man came "to serve, and to give his life as a ransom for many" (Mk. 10:45). When it quotes these words, the Council is emphasizing the fact that the activity of Jesus as founder did not consist simply of gathering people together on the basis of his preaching and the revelation of his person, but of the fact that it brings about the liberation of humanity through his sacrifice. "The origin and growth of the Church are symbolized by the blood and water which flowed from the open side of the crucified Jesus" (*LG* 3), as was foretold by the Lord's words: "And I, when I am lifted up from the earth, will draw all men to myself" (Jn. 12:32).

His death on the cross was followed by the resurrection, in which he "was seen to be constituted as Lord, the Christ, and

Priest for ever, and he poured out on his disciples the Spirit promised by the Father" (*LG* 5). Thus, the start of the Church is brought about through an action of Christ within human history. And it is confirmed by an action that is beyond history, for it is the risen One who, as Lord, sends the Spirit of Pentecost.

To put it more fully, we should say that according to the teaching of the Council, the origin of the Church is prior to history because it is part of the primordial plan of the Father, which was hidden in the divine eternity from the beginning. Through his incarnation, the Son brings about the movement from eternity to time, thus giving a beginning to the Church within time. However, it is through his return to eternity that he becomes the source of the life and development of the Church, inasmuch as the resurrection enables him to pour out the Holy Spirit.

These views are not the result of some systematic doctrinal elaboration, but more that of a brief commentary on the statements of the Scriptures. Whereas unduly lopsided interpretations have often been attempted in this area, fidelity to Scripture means that the Church can provide an overall view of the foundation of the Church in which the various essential aspects are reunited and integrated.

The Institution of Ministries

The foundation of the Church by Christ entails the institution of ministries. When the Council speaks of the hierarchical constitution of the Church, it begins by stating that with a view to the shepherding and increase of the people of God, "Christ the Lord set up in his Church a variety of offices" (*LG* 18). It recalls the teaching of Vatican I, according to which "Jesus Christ, the eternal pastor, set up the Holy Church by entrusting the apostles with their mission, as he himself had been sent by the Father (cf. Jn. 20:21)." In presenting this doctrine in this way, it means to emphasize the fact that the sending forth of the apostles is part of the actual building up of the Church. Further, it more clearly expresses Christ's will with regard to succession: "He willed that their successors, the bishops namely, should be the shepherds in his Church until the end of the world" (*LG* 18).[8] It then justifies this declaration by reference to the perpetual character of the mission: "That divine mission, which was committed by Christ to the apostles, is destined to last until the end of the world" (*LG* 20), because the gospel must be the principle of the whole life of the Church for all time.

In this way, the Council rejects any conception of a Church that has developed by moving beyond, or even correcting, the intentions of Christ, and that has given itself its own hierarchical structure, independently of any will of the Savior. It is Christ who willed the essential structure of his Church, and who specifically wanted it to be an "episcopal" one.

The primacy of Peter and his successors must be linked to this episcopal structure. This doctrine was defined by Vatican I and is taken up briefly here: "In order that the episcopate itself, however, might be one and undivided he put Peter at the head of the other apostles, and in him he set up a lasting and visible source and foundation of the unity both of faith and of communion" (*LG* 18).

Even so, the Council does not confine itself to an outline statement on the origin of the episcopal structure, but backs it up with scriptural evidence. The institution of the Twelve is indeed one of the most outstanding events in the public life of Jesus, and its importance is shown in the long prayer that precedes it and in the sovereign will that dictates the choice. "These apostles he constituted in the form of a college or permanent assembly, at the head of which he placed Peter, chosen from among them" (*LG* 19). Thus, episcopal collegiality, the doctrine of which was developed by the Council, is a consequence of this primordial institution that was the work of Christ, and it finds solid support in the Gospels, the Acts of the Apostles, and the Letters of Paul.[9] Jesus entrusts the apostles with the mission of "gathering together the universal Church" and of spreading it, by making them share in his power of teaching, sanctifying, and governing. They must act as pastors under the guidance of the Master and in the same spirit of service as him (*LG* 19).

Christ is therefore seen as the founder of the hierarchical structure that encompasses the college of bishops and the primacy of the Pope. The Council is not so forthcoming with regard to the origin of the priestly ministry, and confines itself to stating that the bishops "have legitimately entrusted in varying degrees various members of the Church with the office of their ministry" (*LG* 28). But is this simply an initiative of the bishops, or does it not rather manifest the will of Christ? If the Council went no further than this in its statements, this was because the theology of ministry had not received sufficient reflection in this regard. The gospel account of the sending out of the seventy-two disciples—a mission similar to that entrusted to the twelve, according to Luke's description (Lk. 10:1–20)—should draw more attention to Jesus' intention of providing assistants for those who receive the supreme task of the pastoral ministry.[10] In the light of this intention, Christ is seen more clearly as the founder of the whole structure of the priestly ministry in his Church.

Christ, the Source of the Life of the Church

Christ is not only the historical founder of the Church, but retains an unbroken relationship with it by remaining, as the glorified Lord, the source of its development and life.

A Variety of Metaphors

Lumen gentium uses various metaphors to express this relationship. The Church is the sheepfold or the flock of Christ the Shepherd, and Christ therefore fulfills the prophecy that God will be the Shepherd of his people. The Church is the cultivated field of God, where the vine has been planted, the true vine that is Christ himself, who gives life and fruitfulness to the branches. The Church is the building of God, with Christ as its cornerstone; it is also called the house of God or holy temple, and we might have hoped to find this image linked to a reference to the words of Christ on the rebuilding of the temple in three days (Jn. 2:19). The Church is later seen as the bride of the Lamb, or as the bride of the Bridegroom who unites her to himself by an unbreakable alliance.

This variety of metaphors is helpful in showing that the Church exists solely in function of Christ: led by the shepherd, vivified by the vinestock, founded on the cornerstone, united to the bridegroom. Christ's role is so rich that it can be indicated only through a whole range of descriptions and metaphors.

The image of the Church as the body of Christ is more fully developed, although the Council chose not to base its doctrinal elaboration on this image, preferring the concept of the Church as the people of God.

This preference could seem surprising in view of the fact that in the preconciliar period, the doctrine of the mystical body had become very widespread. This doctrine tended to avoid legalism, pointing up the vital bond that exists between Christ and the Church, as well as the power of the social bond between its members. This doctrine had received official approval in the Encyclical promulgated by Pius XII in 1943. However, contrary to what might be imagined, it was not so recent, because even at the time of the First Vatican Council, it had already provided the inspiration behind one ecclesiological treatment.[11]

However, in the twenty years prior to the Council, the definition of the Church as the people of God had been proposed by various exegetes or theologians.[12] The concept has strong roots in the Old Testament writings, and shows how in its own manner, the Church fulfills the pilgrimage of the people with whom God made his covenant. It does not as such entail a reference to Christ. The Council states that "that messianic people has as its head Christ" (*LG* 9),[13] but the christological perspective needs some expansion.

Why was this concept given such pride of place? It would seem that the main intention was to avoid any representation of the Church that was too exclusively hierarchical, and to present the Church more specifically as the gathering of all Christians. However, it is not an exclusive preference, and the conciliar documents contain many elements of the doctrine of the mystical body. When there is a need to explain some aspect of the Church, such elucidation is often taken from this doctrine.

According to *Lumen gentium* 7, "by communicating his Spirit, Christ mystically constitutes as his body those brothers of his who are called together from every nation." He pours his life into this body, especially through the sacraments of baptism and the Eucharist. He is the source of unity, the universal head, the model to which each person must be conformed. He makes his body grow by constantly bestowing gifts of ministry. The doctrine of the mystical body explains the action of Christ as the source of the vital growth of the Church in all areas.

Source of Priestly Activity

Christ the priest is the source of all activities of the episcopal and presbyteral ministry, and it is he who is the first and principal agent of such activity: "In the person of the bishops, then, to whom the priests render assistance, the Lord Jesus Christ, supreme high priest, is present in the midst of the faithful" (*LG* 21).[14] Through them, he preaches the word of God, administers the sacraments of the faith, incorporates new members into his body, and directs and leads the people of the New Testament; in these statements, the Council gives its full power to the expression "acting in the person of Christ." It is the person of Christ who works through the bishop or priest.[15]

The effect of episcopal consecration is that of conferring the grace of the Holy Spirit and impressing a sacred character "in such wise that bishops, in a resplendent and visible manner, take the place of Christ himself, teacher, shepherd and priest, and act as his representatives" (*LG* 21). Similarly, through the sacrament of orders, priests "are signed with a special character and so are configured to Christ the priest in such a way that they are able to act in the person of Christ the head" (*PO* 2).

In this latter text, the Council fills out the words "to act in the person of Christ," specifying that this means "Christ the head." It is here that the activity of the ministerial priesthood is distinguished from that of the common priesthood, which entails a consecration that makes people capable of sharing, through the offering of spiritual sacrifice, in the sacrifice of Christ (*LG* 10). Christ operates in the activity of bishops and priests by communicating his quality as head or shepherd. Thus, "by the sacrament of Orders priests are configured to Christ the priest as servants of the Head, so that as co-workers with the episcopal order they may build up the Body of Christ, the Church" (*PO* 12). The doctrine of the mystical body makes it possible to define this role well.

The position of Christ implies two particular descriptions. He is the perfect model of the priesthood, a model that is imprinted within ministers, for the sacrament of orders "configures" them to Christ the priest; he is the model of priestly consecration of service, of the teaching mission, and of sacrifice (*PO* 3, 6, 12). And he is the source of priestly life, so that the model he constitutes is manifested in practice in the existence and activity of those he chooses as pastors. It is his priesthood as the incarnate Son that lives in the Church, both in the common priesthood of all the baptized, and more especially in the ministerial priesthood.

The conciliar texts taken as a whole provide an answer for

those who fear that this doctrine may contain an excessive exaltation of Christ, or a sort of christomonism. Christ's action certainly does not overshadow or hamper the blossoming of each
human personality; on the contrary, it fosters such blossoming in
the most radical manner. The common priesthood tends to highlight all the potential of self-offering and of Christian life; and
the ministerial priesthood extends the activity that takes place
"in the person of Christ the head." As regards mediation, the
Council states: ". . . the unique mediation of the Redeemer does
not exclude but rather gives rise to a manifold cooperation which
is but a sharing in this one source" (LG 62). In this way, Christ
the priest acts through his ministers, fostering their personal
mediation in the work of salvation. Far from suppressing the
mediations of other people around him, Christ develops such
mediation as a sharing in his own mediation. He is "the sole
source," but a true source that communicates his own life.

Source of the Consecrated Life

As the source of the priestly life, Christ is also the source of
the religious life. These two statements cannot be separated,
because the origin of the religious life is the same as that of the
priestly life. When he called men and women to follow him,
Jesus instituted a state of total consecration, which later developed along the two lines of priestly ministry and the various types
of consecrated life.

The Council is referring to this call when it states that "the
final norm of the religious life is the following of Christ as it is
put before us in the Gospel" (PC 2). Following Christ means
uniting oneself with him "by the gift of one's whole life" (PC 1),
a union that reflects that of the Church with Christ her bridegroom (LG 44; PC 12); it also means "imitating him more
closely," and taking him as model. The religious state "constitutes a closer imitation and an abiding reenactment in the
Church of the form of life which the Son of God made his own
when he came into the world to do the will of the Father" (LG
44). It means "following Christ, . . . virginal and poor," and
"obeying unto death on the cross" (PC 1).

Commitment to the service of the Church should aim at more
and more clearly manifesting Christ "in contemplation on the
mountain" or as preaching to the crowds, healing the sick, con-

verting sinners, blessing children, pouring out his goodness to all men—and always in obedience to the will of the Father (*LG* 46).

The Council makes no explicit declaration on the role of Christ in consecration. Even so, we cannot ignore the significance of an expression that tends to indicate that consecration is a divine work. Instead of saying, as is usually done, that through the vows the person dedicates or consecrates himself to God, the conciliar text states that he "is dedicated to God" and "consecrated in a more thoroughgoing way to the service of God" (*LG* 44). The turn of phrase is intentional, for in response to the objection that God alone is the author of consecration, "dedicates himself" and "consecrates himself" were corrected to "is dedicated" and "is consecrated."[16] This could be the starting point for a doctrinal reflection. If God is the author of consecration, surely here the role of Christ should be emphasized, a role complementary to the one he plays in the actual call? When Christ calls someone to follow him, he wants to accomplish within that person the consecration through which the person who is called belongs totally to him.

Source of Liturgical Life

Christ's role in the liturgy is all the more important inasmuch as this liturgy is not seen by the Council as a simple representation or remembrance: ". . . it is the liturgy through which, especially in the divine sacrifice of the Eucharist, 'the work of our redemption is accomplished' " (*SC* 2).[17] And if this work is accomplished in the liturgy, we can see in it the action performed by Christ himself. In order to understand this activity, we must remember that the earthly liturgy shares in the heavenly liturgy, "where Christ is sitting at the right hand of God, Minister of the holies and of the true tabernacle" (*SC* 8). The Council draws its inspiration here from the view of the heavenly priesthood developed in the Letter to the Hebrews, and gives to understand that the glorified Christ exercises a ministry that is manifested in the liturgy of the Church, and that brings about the accomplishment of his redemptive work therein.

It can be seen that the ministry of Christ, "sitting at the right hand of God," particularly highlights the mystery of the ascension. The liturgy has often recognized the importance of this mystery better than doctrine has. The Council also mentions the ascension when describing the work of salvation, which "Christ the Lord . . . achieved . . . principally by the paschal mystery of his blessed passion, resurrection from the dead, and glorious ascension" (SC 5). Here there is a call for greater appreciation of the consummation of the glorified state as brought about in the ascension, and also for reflection on its significance in the work of salvation. Jesus placed this mystery in relation to the Eucharist (Jn. 6:62).

The listing of the different ways in that Christ is present in the liturgy is based on a remarkable passage from the Encyclical *Mediator Dei*, which it completes by noting his presence in the word.[18] It begins by a general declaration of his presence, stating that in order to accomplish the work of redemption, "Christ is always present in his Church, especially in her liturgical celebrations" (SC 7). This means that the liturgy is the privileged locus of the presence of the Redeemer. What follows is in the nature of a justification of this statement.

Each time the Council wants to express these different forms of presence, it uses two linked words: *praesens adest. Adest* means an existence oriented toward someone. This intentionality of the presence shows that it is not simply an action of the Lord in the liturgy. Christ wants to be present to those who take part in the liturgical action, and such a presence highlights the relationship of one person to another. Thus, Christ is more clearly seen as the center of interpersonal relations between human beings. "He is present in the Sacrifice of the Mass not only in the person of his minister, 'the same now offering, through the ministry of priests, who formerly offered himself on the cross,' but especially in the eucharistic species" (SC 7). The two forms of presence are closely united, for Christ becomes present on the altar through the fact that the minister offers the sacrifice in his name and pronounces the words of consecration in his name. However, they are very different: on the one hand, there is a presence that works subjectively through the ministry of the priest; and on the other hand, the presence of Christ in one place as an objective reality under a visible sign. The latter presence is "maximal," as the liturgical reproduction of the presence of the incarnate word.

Christ's presence in the sacraments is indicated by St. Augustine in the reflection that "when a person baptizes, it is Christ himself who baptizes."[19] This is a presence of Christ "through his virtue," through his power, for it acts sacramentally. However, this presence cannot be reduced to a simple activity.

When the Council added presence in the word to the text of *Mediator Dei,* it wanted to recognize the importance of this word in the liturgy. A first version of the conciliar document read: "It is he [Christ] who speaks when the words of sacred Scripture are read or explained in the Church."[20] However, some people objected that Christ does not speak in the same way in the reading as in the explanation of Scripture.[21] The Council, therefore, confined itself to a declaration of his presence in the reading of Scripture, while elsewhere it referred to his action in preaching. The presence of Christ in the reading of the sacred texts is all the clearer in that he personally is the word. In him there is identity between the person and the word of God, to which the Scriptures bear witness.

"Lastly, he is present when the Church prays and sings, for he has promised 'where two or three are gathered together in my name there am I in the midst of them' (Mt. 18:20)" (SC 7). We must remember that through his prayer, Christ inaugurated Christian prayer, and it is through him that his Church continues to pray.

"The liturgy, then, is rightly seen as an exercise of the priestly office of Jesus Christ" (SC 7). This invisible aspect of the liturgy is thrown into strong relief.

We would again note that this primordial action of Christ does not mean some type of christomonism. On the one hand, the Council considers that the final object of worship is the Father: when the Church calls on Christ its Lord, "through him [it] offers worship to the eternal Father." On the other hand, the activity of the Church in the liturgy is always united to that of Christ: ". . . full public worship is performed by the Mystical Body of Jesus Christ, that is, by the Head and his members," and every liturgical celebration is "an action of Christ the Priest and of his Body which is the Church." Christ's action confers the highest value on the action of the Church: "No other action of the Church can equal its efficacy by the same title and to the same degree" (SC 7).

Source of Apostolic Activity

As the source of the life of the Church, Christ is more specifically the source of all apostolic activity, and the Council emphasizes this when referring to the apostolate of the laity: "Since he wishes to continue his witness and his service through the laity also, the supreme and eternal priest, Christ Jesus, vivifies them with his spirit and ceaselessly impels them to accomplish every good and perfect work" (*LG* 34). It is he who grants lay people a share in his priestly responsibility for the performance of spiritual worship; it is he who, through their witness, carries out his prophetic function; and it is he who, through them, spreads his kingdom (*LG* 34–36).

This gives rise to the norm that governs this apostolate: "Christ, sent by the Father, is the source of the Church's whole apostolate. Clearly then, the fruitfulness of the apostolate of lay people depends on their living union with Christ" (*AA* 4). This text contains a clear echo of the words of the Master: "He who abides in me, and I in him, he it is that bears much fruit, for apart from me you can do nothing" (Jn. 15:5).

In order to express the doctrinal foundation of missionary activity, the Decree *Ad gentes* explains the scope of the mission of the Son and the mission of the Holy Spirit, according to the plan of the Father. It shows how "Jesus Christ was sent into the world as the true Mediator between God and men" (*AG* 3). As God and man in virtue of a true incarnation, he came to enable men to share in the divine nature. He came to give his life as a ransom for all—wresting men from Satan's sway, bringing about the reconciliation of the world with God, and saving those who were lost—and he was made head of a regenerated humanity. "Now, what was once preached by the Lord, or fulfilled in him for the salvation of mankind, must be proclaimed and spread to the ends of the earth (Acts 1:8)" (*AG* 3). In order to accomplish this plan, Christ sent the Holy Spirit from the Father.

The duty of the Church to spread the faith and salvation of Christ flows from the express mission given to the apostles and their successors, and is carried out in virtue of the impulse of life that Christ communicates to its members: ". . . this mission continues and, in the course of history, unfolds the mission of Christ, who was sent to evangelize the poor" (*AG* 5). The whole missionary activity of the Church is therefore carried out through the will of Christ and through the communication of his life.

Source of Unity

The ecumenical perspective also opens out through reflection on the will of Christ the Lord, who instituted one single Church. The separation of Christians is in open opposition to this will, and it is "as if Christ himself were divided." This opposition to Christ is seen as intolerable by the ecumenical movement, which is made up of "those who invoke the Triune God and confess Jesus as Lord and Savior" (*UR* 1).

When the Decree gives the Catholic principles of ecumenism, it reminds us of the work of unification carried out by Christ. The unique Son was sent by the Father in order to regenerate, redeem, and reassemble the whole human race in unity. Before his sacrifice, he prayed that "they may all be one" (Jn. 17:21). He instituted "the sacrament of the Eucharist, which expresses and brings about the unity of the Church." He gave his disciples a new commandment of mutual love. When he had entered into glory, he poured out the Spirit, "through whom he has called and gathered together the people of the New Covenant, which is the Church, into a unity of faith, hope and charity" (*UR* 2).

With regard to the earthly work of Jesus, special mention is made of the mission entrusted to the college of the Twelve, from among whom he chose Peter, determining "that on him he would build his Church." He promised him the keys of the kingdom, and "entrusted all his sheep to him to be confirmed in faith and shepherded in perfect unity." In this expressly instituted unity, Jesus Christ "forever remains the chief cornerstone and shepherd of our souls" (*UR* 2).

The sacred mystery of the unity of the Church is thus "in Christ and through Christ." Here again there is no christomonism, because "the highest exemplar and source of this mystery" is the unity of the divine persons in the Trinity (*UR* 2).

Christ and the Mystery of Man

The Mystery of the Individual Person

How does the Constitution *Gaudium et spes* define the position of Christ with regard to the mystery of man?

In the first place, Christ performs an action of revelation:

. . . it is only in the mystery of the Word made flesh that the mystery of man truly becomes clear. . . . Christ the Lord, Christ the new Adam, in the very revelation of the mystery of the Father and of his love, fully reveals man to himself and brings to light his most high calling (*GS* 22a).

The revelation of God is therefore simultaneously a revelation of man.

Christ also performs a work of restoration. "He who is the 'image of the invisible God' is himself the perfect man who has restored in the children of Adam that likeness to God which had been disfigured ever since the first sin" (GS 22a). In order to throw this restoration into relief, the Council takes the incarnation itself as the basis before commenting on the redemptive sacrifice.

In the first place, there is the incarnation: when the Son of God became man, he raised human nature up to a sublime dignity. On the one hand, he became a man, similar to us in all things excepting sin, while on the other hand through the incarnation, he "in a certain way united himself with each man" (GS 22b). How is this union to be defined? It means that in taking on the nature of an individual man, the Son of God transformed the condition of all men.[22] The scope of the incarnation is universal, and this universality flows from the infinite breadth of the divine person of the Son.

Then there is the redemption, in which the spotless Lamb won life through his blood: "In him God reconciled us to himself and to one another, freeing us from the bondage of the devil and of sin" (GS 22c).

The paschal mystery opened up a way for all humanity. Christians are given a share in this mystery through the struggle against evil at the price of many trials and tribulations. The same applies to all men of good will: ". . . since all men are . . . called to one and the same destiny, which is divine, we must hold that the Holy Spirit offers to all the possibility of being made partners, in a way known to God, in the paschal mystery" (GS 22c–e). "It is therefore through Christ, and in Christ, that light is thrown on the riddle of suffering and death which, apart from his Gospel, overwhelms us" (GS 22f). The problem of suffering, which so often tortures man's mind and heart, finds its only answer in Christ the Redeemer.

In the description of the quality and grandeur of the mystery of man, the mystery of the resurrection attracts particular attention. "Christ has risen again, destroying death by his death, and has given life abundantly to us so that, becoming sons in the Son, we may cry out in the Spirit: Abba, Father!" (GS 22f). The risen Lord is thus the source of divine life and divine filiation. He has a transforming effect on all men, acting "in the hearts of men by the power of his Spirit" (GS 38a). He purifies and strengthens the generous aspirations that are oriented toward an improvement of human society.

The Mystery of Man as Community

Together with the transformation of the individual destiny of the person, the Council emphasizes Christ's significance for man's destiny as community. The incarnate word himself wanted to enter into the human community, thus expressing his solidarity with men: he shared meals; he used metaphors taken from the most everyday life in order to reveal to men the Father's love and the beauty of their calling; and he sanctified human bonds, especially those of the family. He was obedient to the laws of his country and led the life of a craftsman of his time and place (GS 32b).

Further, he wanted to establish a new unity among men. Through his preaching, he declared the obligation of the sons of God to behave as brothers to one another. He prayed for unity. He sacrificed himself for all. He ordered his apostles to proclaim the gospel message to all peoples, "in order that the human race would become the family of God, in which love would be the fullness of the law" (GS 32c).

> As the firstborn of many brethren, and by the gift of his Spirit, he established, after his death and resurrection, a new brotherly communion among all who received him in faith and love; this is the communion of his own body, the Church (GS 32d).

In this communion, mutual service must be the rule, and solidarity must constantly increase.

The "foundational" role of Christ is referred to when the document describes the assistance the Church wants to offer to human society: "The union of the family of man is greatly consolidated and perfected by the unity which Christ established among the sons of God" (GS 42a). This reference to Christ is all the more significant inasmuch as it was expressly inserted into the text in order to highlight the supernatural destiny of society. [23]

The new bonds of union established by Christ do not involve only human beings, but everything in the universe. ". . . as perfect man he could save all men and sum up all things in himself" (GS 45b). The summing up proclaimed by St. Paul (Eph. 1:10) and later developed by St. Irenaeus, places the accent on the cosmic value of the transforming action of Christ.

The whole of history thus converges toward Christ: "The Lord is the goal of human history, the focal point of the desires of history and civilization, the center of mankind, the joy of all hearts, and the fulfillment of all aspirations" (GS 45b). The first part of the conciliar document is also brought to a close with the words of the Lord in the book of Revelation (22:13): "I am the alpha and the omega, the first and the last, the beginning and the end."

Conclusion: Christ as Omnipresent in the Church

The conclusion of this brief study is that the essential foundation of all the ecclesiology expressed in the documents of the Council is christology—and not only implicit christology. Although it is true that the christological starting point sometimes remains a simple assumption, there are a certain number of texts in which the christological statements are explicit, even within the limits imposed by the need for brevity. The mystery of the redemptive incarnation is described in some detail at several points.

In virtue of this mystery, Christ founded the Church within history, and he continues to exercise a determining influence on its present development. When he came to earth, the incarnate Son established his Church, providing it with a ministerial structure. Having come to the glory of his resurrection and ascension, he remains the source of light and life for the "people of God" who are his body. It is he who acts in all aspects of ecclesial activity.

There is no christomonism here, for the Council is careful to place Christ within the divine plan of salvation. The Son is sent by the Father and acts through the Holy Spirit. Moreover, his predominant action in the life of the Church does not curb the activity of the members of his body, but tends rather to develop it as much as possible.

Christ draws his Church into the paschal mystery, and also brings the whole of humanity onto this path. He reveals man to himself, transforms the condition of all people, and establishes a society of brotherhood. He governs and directs history, which has as its objective the summing up of all things in him.

Translated from the French by Leslie Wearne.

Notes

1. Pope John XXIII, " 'Ecclesia Christi, lumen gentium,' Nuntius radiophonicus universis catholici orbis christifidelibus, mense ante quem Oecumenicum Concilium sumeret initium" (11 September 1962), *AAS*, 54 (1962), 678–685. In this message, the Pope referred to the "Lumen Christi" pronounced with regard to the paschal candle: "Yes, it is the light of Christ, the light of the Church, the light of the nations" (p. 680).

2. As Y.M.-J. Congar notes, in *Le Concile de Vatican II. Son Église peuple de Dieu et Corps du Christ* (Paris, 1984), 167, ". . . au prix d'une construction latine heurtée" ("Lumen gentium cum sit Christus").

3. H. de Lubac, "Commentaire du Préambule et du Chapitre I," in B.-D. Dupuy (ed.), *La Révélation divine, Constitution dogmatique "Dei Verbum,"* 1 (Paris, 1968), 159, emphasizes that *Verbum* is capitalized, so that it is impossible to say whether it means the abstract word or Christ.

4. R. Latourelle, "La Révélation et sa transmission selon la Constitution 'Dei Verbum,' " *GR*, 47 (1966), 19: "Le Christ étant ainsi le Fils du Père, la Parole éternelle faite chair, il s'ensuit qu'il est à la fois le Révélateur suprême et la suprême Objet révélé."

5. De Lubac, "Commentaire du Préambule et du Chapitre I," 219, mentions this change of perspective from the time of the schema *De Fontibus revelationis.*

6. "Tota sua persona revelationem complendo perficit." The objections are given in de Lubac, "Commentaire du Préambule et du Chapitre I," 222.

7. Congar, *Le Concile de Vatican II*, 164–165, also rejects this accusation with regard to *Lumen gentium:* "Relecture attentive faite, j'affirme qu'on ne peut taxer *Lumen Gentium* de 'christomonisme.' "

8. Vatican I simply said: ". . . so he wished shepherds and teachers to be in his Church until the consummation of the world (see Mt. 28:20)" (Sessio IV, Prol., DS 3050; English translation, Jesuit Fathers of St. Mary's College, *The Church Teaches* [St. Mary's, KN, 1955], 94).

9. This is shown in greater detail in S. Lyonnet, "La collégialité épiscopale et ses fondaments scripturaires," in G. Baraúna and Y.M.-J.

Congar (eds.), *L'Eglise de Vatican II, Etude autour de la Constitution conciliaire sur l'Eglise* (Paris, 1966), 829–846.

10. The silence of Vatican II on this point should no more be interpreted as a negation than the previous reserve of the Council of Trent on the subject of the divine institution of bishops; cf. J. Galot, *Prêtre au nom du Christ* (Chambray, 1985), 82, 185.

11. This is noted by O. Semmelroth, "L'Eglise, nouveau peuple de Dieu," in Baraúna and Congar (eds.), *L'Eglise de Vatican II*, 2, 400, with regard to the rough draft produced by Kleutgen.

12. The movement started with the work of M.D. Koster, *Ekklesiologie im Werden* (Paderborn, 1940), in which he reacted against the idea of the Church as the mystical body.

13. Father Congar is personally responsible for the use of the expression "messianic people," which was previously used by Father M.-D. Chenu; cf. *Le Concile de Vatican II*, 135.

14. This text is inspired by a sermon of St. Leo on the anniversary of his elevation to the position of Bishop of Rome: *Serm.*, 5, 3, in *PL*, 54, 154.

15. This presence of Christ in the episcopal ministry shows that we are "au-delà de l'aspect sociologique," to which some people give exaggerated consideration, as J. Lécuyer notes, "L'episcopat comme sacrement," in Baraúna and Congar (eds.), *L'Eglise de Vatican II*, 3, 761.

16. *Mancipatur, consecratur*. An objection had been made to *consecrantes*, because the consecration is performed by God and by his grace (*AS*, II/III, 609). The doctrinal commission commented on the new text with *consecratur*: ". . . sub forma passiva, subintelligendo 'a Deo' " (*AS*, III/VIII, 131). Cf. P. Molinari and P. Gumpel, "La dottrina della Costituzione dogmatica 'Lumen gentium' sulla vita consacrata," *Vita Consacrata*, 21 (1985), 10.

17. The Constitution on the Sacred Liturgy is based on a vigorous christological doctrine. Cf. J. Galot, "La Cristologia nella 'Sacrosanctum Concilium,' " *Notitiae* (*Sacra Congregatio pro sacramentis et cultu divino, sectio pro cultu divino*), 20 (1983), 305–319.

18. *Mediator Dei* 20c, in DS 3840.

19. *In Jo. Evang. Tract.*, VI, 1, 7, in *PL*, 35, 1428.

20. AS, I/I, 265.

21. AS, I/III, 705.

22. Cf. J. Mouroux, "Situation et signification du chapitre I: Sur la dignité de la personne humaine," in Y.M.-J. Congar and M. Peuchmaurd, *L'Eglise dans le monde de ce temps. Constitution pastorale "Gaudium et Spes,"* 2 (Paris, 1967), 250. Mouroux notes that the Council does not confine itself to the essentialist perspective of a transfiguration of the whole of human nature, but affirms union with each human person.

23. Cf. P. Delhaye, "Histoire des textes de la Constitution pastorale," in Congar and Peuchmaurd (eds.), *L'Eglise dans le monde de ce temps*, 1, 270; Monsignor Delhaye cites this text in its definitive version as compared with the Ariccia text to give an example of the change in perspective. The Ariccia text reads: "In the first place, inasmuch as the order of redemption includes the order of creation, the ministry of the Church necessarily extends, under a certain perspective, to all human situations and problems taken as a whole."

CHAPTER 15

Postconciliar Ecclesiology

Expectations, Results, and Prospects for the Future

Angel Antón, S.J.

Summary

This ecclesiological assessment intends to compare the hopes aroused by Vatican II in the field of ecclesiology with the results achieved. The most urgent tasks that postconciliar ecclesiology must deal with follow from this comparison in regard to:

1. the reasons for a number of disagreements relative to both method and content in current ecclesiology (the confusion present in every postconciliar period, profound changes in society and the Church, the doctrinal ambiguities and pastoral character of the conciliar decrees);
2. the methodological options open to postconciliar ecclesiology (a return to the sources, centrality of the mystery of the Church, a historical-salvific focus, priority of the *congregatio fidelium*, the real *universality* of the Church and the problems it presents for the Church and for ecclesiology);
3. the question of the model of the Church as mystery of communion (the key notion of "communion" in postconciliar ecclesiology; the relationship between ecclesiology and christology, the Church in the service of communion among men, ecclesial communion and base communities);
4. the renewal of institutional structures (the immutable and the mutable in the Church, the reasons for conflicting interpretations of conciliar ecclesiology, compromises between wording and content, theological language and canonical language);

5. one Church–many Churches (the universal Church or the local Church as center of gravity in ecclesiology, the model of the Church as *communio ecclesiarum;*
6. the primacy and episcopal collegiality (the declaration of the principle of collegiality and problems of its application at all levels of the postconciliar Church, compromises in the wording but not in the content in Vatican II);
7. the relationship between hierarchy and laity (the hierarchical ministry at the service of all the faithful, doctrinal ambiguity in Vatican II as to the concept of "lay persons" and their place in the Church, the new *Codex iuris canonici* and its theory on the *potestas,* which returns in part to preconciliar positions);
8. the "Church–world" relationship (the *Gaudium et spes* presentation at the center of ecclesiological discussion since Vatican II, affirmation of both terms as the starting point of *Gaudium et spes,* plurivalent meaning of the term "world," the *Gaudium et spes* option for dialogue, its message of sound ecclesiological optimism).

Introduction

The twenty-five years that have elapsed since the opening of Vatican II are obviously not enough to enable one to make a definitive judgment on this Council of the Church and on the Church. Nevertheless, one can describe in broad outline the impact which Vatican II, the Church parliament with the greatest number of participants in the whole history of the Councils, has had on ecclesiology and on the very life of the Church.

Twenty-five years of conciliar and postconciliar Church history invite us to ask what *results* have been obtained in ecclesiology and what *new problems* have been raised for it for the future. An assessment of postconciliar ecclesiology, even provisional, requires examination both of the reception of Vatican II, the level of the Church, of Christianity, and of all humanity, and of the study of the *Lumen gentium* and of the *Gaudium et spes,* the two pillars on which the entire ecclesiological concept of the Council is based. Neither aspect can be separated from the other, because the Church, in search of a new awareness of herself and of new contacts with the other churches, with non-Christian religions, and with the modern world, is at the very center of the ecclesiological doctrine of Vatican II.

While recognizing that ecclesiology is enriched by the elements it steadily receives from a Church that has been renewed in its historical aspect and its mission of salvation, and that at the same time it definitely affects that same renewal—the mutual exchange of elements between the *real* and the *doctrinal* aspects in the historical evolution of the Church and of ecclesiology has been extremely fruitful—as a methodological matter, we must opt here for an assessment of ecclesiological doctrine during the period of twenty-five years that have elapsed since the opening of Vatican II. In view of the proliferation of ecclesiological publications in the past twenty-five years, a whole book would not suffice for that, so we shall have to confine ourselves to comparing, in an overall view, the *expectations* that Vatican II aroused in the field of ecclesiology with the *results* achieved. The most urgent tasks that postconciliar ecclesiology must deal with in the future follow from this comparison.

The Reasons for Some Disagreements in Present Ecclesiology

1. Solid knowledge of the history of the Church led J.H. Newman to say, a month after the closing of Vatican I, that "it is uncommon that a Council not be followed by great confusion."[1] This realistic comment of the English cardinal is equally applicable to Vatican II, both as regards the practical reform of the Church and relative to the strictly doctrinal heritage of the Council centered in the theology of the Church. Nevertheless, the *confusion,* and in some circles the *crisis,* that have conditioned the development of postconciliar ecclesiology, whether in *method* or in *content,* should not be imputed simply to the Council and to the ecclesiological doctrine in its decrees, although the latter certainly contains significant deficiencies and anomalies that have given rise to conflicting positions in interpretation.

2. To delve deeper into the origin of the most outstanding divergences in the development of postconciliar ecclesiology, a series of exterior and interior *elements* in the ecclesiological doctrine of Vatican II must be mentioned.

During the past twenty-five years, so many changes have taken place in the society and the Churches of the Christian West that very serious problems have arisen for western Christianity as regards spreading the Christian message. Economic and scientific development have grown at a dizzying pace. The classical model of society went into crisis. The superiority of the West was challenged by the revolt of the Third World against all forms of neocolonialism. The Churches there cannot turn a deaf ear to the emancipation of women, the spread of a new cultural model among the young, and the tremendous problems of an economic, demographic, and ecologic nature. There are strong tendencies within them toward a greater participation by all their members in the dual function of preparing and making decisions (*decision making–taking*) and toward a real dialogue with the other Churches and religions. Its commitment to man presents the Church with the task of defending his rights wherever they are violated.

– On the South American continent, the episcopate, theologians, and Church leaders have made the preferential option for the "poor," the latter being understood in a wider sense than that of economic poverty. The "poor" have actually begun to take part in recent years in the political and ecclesial life of the Latin American nations. From being subjects of evangelization, they have converted themselves into evangelizers. This awakening of ecclesial consciousness in the great masses of the baptized who now feel themselves to be active participants in the life of the Church is a symptomatic feature that has, in certain ecclesiological circles, made some speak of a Church "which is born of the people." Provided it is not understood in an exclusive sense, we have here a postulate common to the Churches of the Third World to which postconciliar ecclesiology must give a satisfactory response.

3. The ecclesiological *confusion* that became widespread after Vatican II—thus confirming Newman's observation regarding the preceding Councils—has its roots in the very nature of the conciliar doctrine. Referring to the decrees of Vatican II, J. Grootaers speaks of *doctrinal atrophy.*[2] This characteristic is, in a way, common in the doctrinal heritage of every Council. The confrontation among the various theological trends within a Council ends with the imposition of one on all the others. Conciliar dynamics tend, however, to produce decrees relative to

which there are neither winners nor losers. All have had to make concessions so that the Council's decrees might be approved as unanimously as possible. Regarding the most debated themes, the conciliar text is a mosaic of interpolated clauses seeking to satisfy the various theological trends of the assembly. Besides, Vatican II fully endorsed the hermeneutic principle of previous Councils of not deciding questions still being debated among theologians. And to this, we must add the prevalently *pastoral* orientation—without belittling in any way the value of the dogmatic documents of Vatican II—which both Popes imprinted on the Council from the time it was convened. The assembly having decided against issuing dogmatic definitions, the body of doctrine it has bequeathed to us is aimed at giving a doctrinal foundation to the options elected by Vatican II for reaching four proposed objectives: (1) to determine with greater precision the *idea,* or if it be preferred, consciousness of the Church; (2) to bring about a genuine *renewal* of the Church; (3) to restore *unity* among all Christians; and (4) to intensify the *dialogue* between the Church and men of our time, and to build a bridge to the contemporary world.[3] Finally, the postconciliar Church has concentrated all its energy on reform of its institutions at both the universal and the local levels, while with regard to the "doctrinal atrophy" mentioned above, it did not make enough progress to change the situation and to avoid the tendency to return to the positions of the past.

4. In all fairness, it must be said that, as regards putting the principle of collegiality into practice at the level of the individual Churches, the assessment is clearly positive. The already existing national episcopal conferences have been reorganized in a more collegial way and their influence is steadily growing in the life of their respective Churches. Other episcopal conferences have been organized at the continental level, and their meetings have become a decisive element in the life of the Church in their respective continents. The synodical organizations at the diocesan and parochial levels, together with presbyteral and pastoral councils, have opened up new paths in pastoral practice and been given an initial regime in the *Codex iuris canonici.* As regards the central government of the Church, mention must be made of the periodical celebration of the Synod of Bishops, reform of the Curia, and regulation of the work done by some of its important departments, the creation of new secretariats and com-

missions, which have been opened up to a greater number of members—clergy and laity—residing in Churches scattered throughout the world, and, in recent years, the repeated convening of the entire College of Cardinals to deliberate with the successor of Peter serious questions concerning the government of the Church. However, the creation and application of some forms of collegial activity have raised new problems in the field of ecclesiology, regarding which ecclesiology does not find a direct response in the decrees of the Council. With regard to the problems that the postconciliar renewal of these ecclesiastical institutions and the creation of new ones have raised, bishops and theologians have not found solutions that go much beyond what is contained in the decrees of the Council. Postconciliar ecclesiology has proved to be not only unable to prevent certain conflicts, but unable even to follow the breathtaking pace with which they have arisen in the various facets of ecclesial life.

In these past twenty-five years, ecclesiology has been challenged by new problems for which it had to furnish solutions that are at once new and faithful to the ecclesiological options regarding *method* and *content* adopted by Vatican II.

The Methodological Options
of Postconciliar Ecclesiology

Postconciliar ecclesiology, whether in the magisterium of the Pope and of the various episcopates of a nation or of a whole continent or in the field of research, has faithfully accepted the methodological options introduced by Vatican II.

1. This faithfulness is shown above all in a return to the very *sources* of theology, that is, to the word of God, alive in the Church and transmitted alive, under the guidance of the Spirit, in the teachings of the Fathers, of the Councils, and of the magisterium of the Church, and in the testimony of the liturgy and the Christian life of the People of God.

2. Postconciliar ecclesiology, in full conformity with the most important methodological option of Vatican II, is rooted in the very *mystery* of the Church, has cut its ties with the sociojuridical concepts that monopolized apologetic preconciliar ecclesiology, and is developing a genuine theological perspective that de-

scribes the Church as an object of faith, the study of which must be infused with faith.

3. Postconciliar ecclesiological publications have been faithful to the *historical-salvific* perspective adopted by Vatican II, and they describe an ecclesiology more open to the historical dimension of the Church and fully aware of the place it has in the history of salvation. The Church thus appears as *fructus salutis,* or creation of God and Father through the redeeming work of the Son and in the Spirit, and, at the same time, as *medium salutis,* through which God gives his grace to man. This Trinitarian origin of the Church is the point of departure of the three conciliar constitutions and various of its decrees and declarations that have a more doctrinal character. Vatican II, by deciding to change the axis of ecclesiology to make it revolve around the ecclesial mystery, preserved a permanent value through the development of ecclesiology during the past twenty-five years.

4. On many occasions, we have insisted on another profound change—called Copernican by Yves Congar—that was introduced by the Council with the insertion in *Lumen gentium* of Chapter II on the People of God before Chapter III on the ecclesiastical ministry.[4] The reach of this decision, taken when the writing of the *Lumen gentium* was almost finished, did not find adequate expression in the Constitution itself. There, the priority of the People of God, in consideration of its finality and its prophetic and sacerdotal character as a whole with respect to the various categories of persons who constitute it, is recognized. In Chapter II, the *Lumen gentium* outlines a whole theology of community in which the fundamental equality of all its members and the communion that unites them all in one identical Christian vocation and one identical hope of eternal salvation. The ecclesiastical ministry, at all levels, appears here in intimate communion with all those who have been regenerated in Christ and ordained, by virtue of their election and respective sacramental consecration, to transmit the blessings of redemption to the entire body of the faithful.

5. According to K. Rahner, the truly transcendental change introduced by Vatican II into the Church and into postconciliar ecclesiology consists of this having been the first Council in which consciously and officially the Church actualized itself as the universal Church.[5] A judgment as categorical as this has to be explained if Rahner's thought is to be understood in its precise

meaning. The real universality of the Church, which was reached centuries ago in relation to the extra-European world, is characterized very accurately by Rahner as a worldwide exportation activity by a European religion that made no attempt to adapt its merchandise.[6] Vatican II, on the other hand, was the first council in which the Church became a universal Church in the fullest sense. This likeness of the universal Church revealed itself in a very clear and efficacious way in the periodic celebration of the Synod of Bishops. The indigenous episcopates of the Churches of the Third World are ever more aware of the need for their contribution if the Church is to go beyond western particularism. To make this universality an effective reality presents the Church and postconciliar ecclesiology with *serious problems.* Is a valid canon law codification possible for the Church of Christ that is called to actualize itself in such different ways on each of the five continents? Are the organs of the central government of the Church in Rome aware of the legitimate aspirations, the results achieved, and the serious problems requiring rapid solutions of the Churches dispersed throughout the world? Is the Church keeping abreast of the profound changes taking place in the various cultures worldwide as to which she must be culturally informed so that her message may be truly universal?

Both the Church, in its magisterial and disciplinary activities, and ecclesiology, in its theological study, must look for a response beginning with the fact that Vatican II was truly the "first gathering of the universal episcopate in its entirety,"[7] and that "the Church, in this Council, at least inchoately began to act magisterially as the universal Church, qua universal."[8] In his evaluation of some of the most significant data of the doctrinal legacy of Vatican II relative to this opening to its universality, K. Rahner speaks of the dawn of a new era of its history characterized by the changeover from western Church to universal Church, in a sense analogous to what occurred through the evangelizing work of Paul, when the Church passed from being a Church of Jews to being a Church of pagans. In his comparison of the two situations, Rahner maintains that the "dejudaization" of Christianity inaugurated by Paul did not represent a greater change than the one required by "the differences between Western culture and the present cultures of the whole of Asia and Africa, relative to which the Christianity of today must become inculturated, so as to be finally a universal Church, as it has already begun to be."[9] This opening to a necessary religious and cultural pluralism, while facing with Pauline audacity all the consequences it entails in the various fields of the Church's life without betraying the unity of faith or the truly immutable elements of its nature, has been, during the past twenty-five years, a source of strong tensions in the Church and in postconciliar ecclesiology.

6. These changes of a *methodological nature* that were introduced by Vatican II have proved to be *inadequate* in postconciliar ecclesiology, although very promising in themselves. The dynamics of the opposition between the sociojuridical, abstract, and apologetic ecclesiology that was prevalent since the time of the counter-Reformation and the new ecclesiology, rooted in Scripture and the Fathers, historical and concerned with communion, which eventually prevailed in the Council, did not make the synthesis hoped for possible. We must acknowledge the ecclesiology of Vatican II, as to which it would admittedly be premature to make any judgment, presents a certain *juxtaposition* of both ecclesiological trends, as can be easily seen by comparing the first two chapters of *Lumen gentium* (I and II) with the second two (III and IV). *Lumen gentium* furthermore outlined a vision of the Church in its relationship to the modern world from a theological viewpoint, the main themes of which were drawn up in *Gaudium et spes* after the promulgation of *Lumen gentium*. This fact is a clue to a certain inconsistency regarding the "church–world" relationship between *Lumen gentium* and *Gaudium et spes*. The Churches of the Third World have also adversely criticized Vatican II for reflecting the situation of the Church as it exists in the social, cultural, economic, and political environment of the developed world. This criticism is not unfounded. The world with which the Church is carrying on a dialogue in *Gaudium et spes* seems to be identified with the scientifically and technically developed world, at a high western economic and cultural level, whereas the Churches of the Third World could, from this point of view, consider themselves part of the Churches of silence.

There is a reason for this. Despite the great awareness of the Church of Vatican II that it was fundamentally a *universal* Church, the great theological protagonists of the Council, bishops and theologians, belong to the developed world. The vision that *Gaudium et spes* presents of the "Church–world" relationship cannot but look somewhat optimistic and ingenuous to the Churches of the Third World, and certainly contrary to the daily experience

of the great masses of Christians in those countries who are struggling to rise above the state of economic, political, and cultural
abandon they live in. The reaction of the spokesmen of these
Churches of the Third World was not long in coming. They made
their voices heard with ever-greater insistence in the synods of
bishops convened periodically in Rome. In the general assemblies
of the bishops of entire continents (e.g., Africa: Kampala, 1969;
Far East: Manila, 1970; Latin America: Mandellín, 1968; Puebla,
1979), they outlined evangelization plans for their Churches that
contained innovative elements. At the same time, theological
ideas of local inspiration were being developed that, while avow-
ing faithfulness to Vatican II as their source of inspiration and
constant point of reference, proposed to outline a new model of
ecclesiology, more in conformity with the legitimate aspirations of
the faithful in their respective Churches. The limitations of the
ecclesiological model outlined by Vatican II and of changes in
theological methodology were more and more obvious. New paths
had to be opened up to make up for the deficiencies in conciliar
ecclesiology through local elements. These elements were the
fruit of faith experience in their respective ecclesial communities
and of strictly theological thought produced within these same
Churches and having their origins in their concrete situation.
With this inversion of method, one may hope that a certain historical inertia and the abstract neutrality that the ecclesiology of
Vatican II offers to theologians, pastors, and the faithful of the
Churches of the Third World may be overcome.

The Model of the Church as Mystery of Communion

1. The concept of *communion* is without a doubt the key concept for interpreting the ecclesiology of Vatican II and the one
that best summarizes its results in ecclesiological doctrine and in
the renewal of the Church.[10] The fact of having focused the theology of the mystery of the Church on this concept of *koinonia*
represents perhaps the most transcendent innovation of Vatican II
for postconciliar ecclesiology and the life of the Church. The
ecclesiological content of this concept is not new; rather, it was
latent in ideas and models of ecclesiology prior to Vatican II.
Moreover, the notion of a "dynamic communion" in the "service
of communion" is "the heart of traditional ecclesiology."[11] Yves

Congar had anticipated before the Council that among the notions describing the Church that of "communion" would hold a central place in the ecclesiology of the future.[12]

2. This prophecy has been fulfilled. "In fact, beginning with Vatican II, the idea of communion is at the very center of the ecclesiological debate. It is intimately linked to the other key idea of the People of God which, through the conciliar constitutions and decrees, has obtained an important place in Catholic ecclesiology, even though it has also given rise to tensions which remain to be resolved."[13] The present relationship between the *dynamic* reality and the *social* reality of this *koinonia* is a continual source of *tensions* in the ecclesiological doctrine and in ecclesial life itself. In ecclesiological terminology, we make a distinction between these two aspects and refer to the former favoring the term *communion*, and to the latter the term *community*. In the theology of the Church, however, monistic solutions are unacceptable. The ecclesiology of Vatican II began with this key concept of Church-*communion* of all mankind in Christ and went on to see it actualized in the People of God of the New Covenant, which has Christ as its head in accordance with the universal plan of salvation of the *Father*, who has revealed himself in a fully open and irrevocable way in the mission of the Son, and, through the mission of the Spirit, preserves its integrity in time and space until the eschatological consummation, when God will be all in all (cf. 1 Cor. 15:28).

3. While the ecclesiology of Vatican II presents the Church of Christ as the fruit of the divine plan of salvation (*fructus salutis*) that begins with the Father and finds its culmination in the Christ event and the mission of the Spirit and it therefore insists on unity and universality, the new elements of each stage of the *historia salutis* being conserved, attempts have been made in some theological circles since Vatican II to locate the *birth of the Church* solely in the response of faith to the apostolic preaching of the resurrection.

In postconciliar ecclesiology, there is no option but that of presenting the birth of the Church-communion in the unbroken line of the Israel of the Old Covenant—its prefiguration and historical preparation—giving full value to new elements added to the global mystery of Christ through the mission of his Spirit.[14] Therefore, the birth of the Church is not circumscribed by the *intention* of the historical Jesus and his messianic activity, but rather extends to the *global Christ* event, that is to say, God's action in the *mysterium Christi* from his incarnation and birth and his public life up to his death and resurrection and the communication of his Spirit to the group of believers and witnesses to his resurrection.

Here is the connection between the Church-communion model and Christ in the double perspective of *being* and *acting.* *Ecclesiology* is linked to *christology* in this historical bond of the Church with the very person of the word incarnate and the mission he has entrusted to her. In the Catholic ecclesiology, the relationship of the Church with the person of Jesus cannot be disavowed. Vatican II presents the birth of the Church as inseparable from Christ, because he himself founded her,[15] through an act of his will on Peter and the Twelve, constituting her as universal sacrament of salvation. Hence, the Church is not a mere "result," nor a simple consequence set in motion by the evangelizing activity of Jesus. In opposition to certain ecclesiological tendencies in the context of Latin American theologies of liberation, the Puebla document declares that "it certainly springs from the evangelizing activity of Jesus . . . but in a direct way, since the Lord himself called together his disciples and gave them the power of the Spirit, endowing the nascent community with all its essential properties and elements, which the Catholic people recognized as of divine institution."[16] Here the reductionist currents that relativize the historical foundation of the Church by the historical Jesus and the risen Lord, including the mission of the Spirit, are decidedly rejected.

4. The bond of the Church of Christ in its birth and existence may also be compromised by its being presented as only "the event which finds its completion when the message of Christ is proclaimed."[17] To emphasize the dynamic aspects of the *Church-communion*, S. Dianich sums up his notion of the Church in the formula "announcement for communion" and its equivalent "communion born of announcement." Basing himself on the concept of *event* and emphasizing the interpersonal relationships among its members, he asserts that the Church "is not an idea, but rather the result of the relationship between these two facts of experience, namely, that of announcement and that of communion. Both the elements of these two facts and connotations flowing from the relationships between them constitute a conjunction of such complete and precise elements as to be a suffi-

cient basis for the entire reality of the Church."[18] From these premises, Dianich goes on to locate the birth of the event-Church in Peter's preaching on the day of Pentecost.[19] This offers ecclesiology a link between the nascent Church and the historical Jesus, not only as regards the community—in this sense, we would have to speak of an *autogenesis*—but also because Jesus laid its foundations before the paschal mystery by announcing the coming of the kingdom; calling and teaching the disciples, especially the Twelve; institution of the Eucharist; association of his disciples in the messianic activity; assigning certain leadership functions related to his future Church, etc. Jesus let it be seen in his prepaschal preaching, as a community at the service of the proclamation of the kingdom. In spite of Dianich's efforts to link the Church-communion to Christ, the *christic* dimension remained very much a secondary aspect.

5. In the postconciliar period, the Churches of the Third World reflected upon this ecclesiological model of the Church-communion in a truly autonomous and original fashion from their state of oppression and dependence. The ecclesiological model emanating from this spontaneous reflection of faith on the part of every category of persons comprising the respective ecclesial communities is centered in an ecclesiology of communion revolving around the *poor* and the *oppressed* of our world. This is a matter of a *preferential option* that interprets the basic concepts of the ecclesiology of Vatican II in the light of the masses of those who are the poor in spirit of the Sermon on the Mount.

The Church, like every *sacrament,* signifies and realizes the mystery of the communion of men with God and among themselves. But it realizes it because it signifies it. To be a *sign* and to be an *instrument* are two complementary and inseparable dimensions of its sacramental structure. It is not yet the complete and definitive kingdom, but it already constitutes on earth the germ and principle of this kingdom. The Church lives at the service of the *communion* of men with God and mankind, even though this mystery finds its realization beyond its visible limits. It is the *universal People of God,* but it does not come into conflict with any other people, and can be incorporated in all and serve in planting the kingdom of God in them. This People of God lives the mystery of communion in the Church of the Third World as the *great family of God.* The Church is not just a place where men are seated, but where they make themselves really and ontologically the *family of God.*

Faithfulness to the most fundamental ecclesiological principles of Vatican II does not allow comparison of this model of the Church-communion with that of an anarchic *populism*—"the Church which is born of the people"—or with an exclusive and sectarian *elitism*—an ideal followed by certain kinds of base communities—because these are ecclesiological tendencies that exclude, both in theory and practice, constituent elements of the local Church. The very terms "popular Church" and "born of the people" are not very felicitous for sound ecclesiology, because the call to the Church through faith is always a grace "from above." Besides, "the people's Church" is often presented as opposed to the Church that certain circles of the theology of liberation characterize as the "official" and "institutional" Church, which they consider "alienating." The assembly of Puebla rejected this attitude as a deviation from the ecclesiology of Vatican II inspired by well-known ideological influences.

On the other hand, at the level of the universal Church, although with greater strength in the Third World, there has arisen spontaneously—and we must see in this the fruit of intervention by the Spirit—a series of models for living the mystery of ecclesial communion within intraparochial groups or communities that, while stripping themselves gradually of certain forms of sectarianism, offer the Church today some very efficacious help in its evangelizing task. These ecclesial base communities constitute the first and fundamental ecclesial nucleus, the initial cell of communion, a center of evangelization and a primordial element of human advance and development.

The Renewal of Institutional Structures

1. The postconciliar Church, under the energetic direction of the successors of Peter, has put into effect with great commitment the mandate of Vatican II that it renew itself in its organizational structures. The process of renewal of ecclesial structures involves the introduction of experiments, changes, and transformations together with the risk of adopting extreme positions. In this task of renovation, the postconciliar Church is faced with the problem of distinguishing what is *immutable* in it from what is

mutable, and of maintaining substantial faithfulness to its origins while at the same time remaining open to the circumstances of the historical moment. For the postconciliar Church, the question has been to determine whether certain changes in matters touching on doctrine and the Church's constitution can be considered as being within the framework of an historical evolution, which may honestly be characterized as a *new beginning,* without it being of necessity a deviation or substantial alteration with regard to the *Ekklesia* that the risen Lord left when he ascended into heaven as the definitive presence of his grace and eschatological event of his mercy for the salvation of all mankind. This new beginning has bristled with difficulties. Its realization has involved successive stages of euphoria, crisis, and resignation, and it has aroused conflicting reactions within the Church.

2. Ecclesiology is not so much interested in characterizing the progressive and traditionalist tendencies that have come onto the scene during the postconciliar period—there are publications enough on the subject on both sides—as to furnish an impartial explanation of the reason for this truly antinomic situation regarding people who want to give greater service to the Church. We must start here from the ecclesiological principle that the Church is by its very nature a *complexio oppositorum* and that tensions are naturally innate in it. In focusing our attention on analysis of postconciliar ecclesiology, we are concerned here with pointing out a few of the more specific reasons that are related to the very character of the ecclesiological legacy of Vatican II.

a. The first reason for the present status of postconciliar ecclesiology—which is, according to some, stagnant or even in the process of going backwards, and according to others, compromised by an undiscriminating progressivism—lies in certain fundamental ambiguities in the conciliar texts.[20] Obviously, this criticism does not lessen the value of the positive results obtained by ecclesiology in Vatican II, and it could be made regarding any other Council. This ambiguity is certainly a characteristic of the crucial texts regarding conciliar ecclesiological doctrine as to which it was more difficult to reach a compromise acceptable to the great majority of the assembly. This furthermore deals with essential points of ecclesiology that now condition its development and even the renewal of ministries and institutions in the Church. It will suffice here to mention two central themes of the ecclesiology of Vatican II on which it has focused in the two last decades: first, that of the relationships between the papacy and the episcopate for the purpose of identifying an exercise of the papal primacy that would take into account all the implications of the principle of episcopal collegiality; and second, that of the role of the laity in the Church, so as to draw out all the consequences of the declaration of *vera aequalitas*, although *in varietate*, between pastors and lay persons.

b. Some authors, going more deeply into the ambiguity of the conciliar texts, have put forward hypotheses of a more general significance to explain the indecisions and antinomies of one trend or other in postconciliar ecclesiology. From an analysis comparing the preceding schemas with the definitive text of the *Lumen gentium*, A. Acerbi has come to the conclusion that it contains a *juxtaposition of two ecclesiologies*—one prevalently juridical and the other focused on the notion of the Church-communion.[21] H.J. Pottmeyer sees the origin of the profound divergences and of opinions that are even contradictory in the postconciliar ecclesiology and Church in *two tendencies* that already existed within the conciliar assembly and that represented two very different notions of the Church.[22] One tendency sees the universal Church as above all the communion of local Churches (*communio ecclesiarum*) and each of these as the congregation of the faithful united by vital bonds of communion (*communio fidelium*). In this ecclesiological perspective, one may speak, with the necessary reservations that the principle of analogy requires, of federative and democratic structures. However, it would be theologically more accurate to use the categories of *sacramental* and *collegial* to express a reality that the Church of the early centuries lived intensely. The other tendency has been prevalent in Catholic ecclesiology since the counter-Reformation, and it has always emphasized the hierarchical structure and the juridico-institutional authority of the Church's ministries, and in particular of the papal primacy. Perhaps the euphoria at seeing the ecclesiology of communion strengthened in the Council made it difficult to see realistically that the documents contained both ecclesiologies juxtaposed. This juxtaposition was felt even more distinctly in particular conflicts in dealing with the renewal of ecclesiastical institutions.

Let us abandon any attempt simply to identify the ecclesiological tendency called hierarchical with Vatican I and that of communion with Vatican II. In fact, the two tendencies were present and active in both assemblies. What is certain is that the ecclesiology of the minority of Vatican I was transformed into the majority of Vatican II, whereas the ecclesiology of the latær minority was that of the majority of the former. This fact explains why in order to resolve the most acute conflicts, both in theory and in practice, in postconciliar ecclesiology, some seek support in the ecclesiology of Vatican I, which was reaffirmed in Vatican II, while in others disenchantment increases with a Church of communion, which has not succeeded in finding its place in the structures of the Church.[23] The tensions between these two tendencies have brought them to totally unilateral, and consequently unacceptable, positions. One consists in considering Vatican I obsolete, challenging its decisions from the historical and theological point of view.[24] The other tries to impose the hegemony of an interpretation of the texts of Vatican II in the ecclesiological key of Vatican I, and thus slowing down application of the ecclesiology of communion in the reform of ecclesiastical institutions. A third proposal, by an international group of theologians, begins from the idea, for them unquestionable, that Vatican II was a Council of transition, and they have launched a campaign to demand as necessary the convening of Vatican III for the purpose of effecting a synthesis of the two preceding Councils and of drawing from it its ultimate consequences relative to reform of the Church, and dialogue with the other Churches and with the world.[25]

c. Yves Congar, referring specifically to the problems that postconciliar ecclesiology faces (i.e., ecclesiological christocentrism and pneumatocentrism; primacy-episcopate; ministry-laity), declared recently that *Vatican II stopped halfway*, setting forth compromise solutions not only as to the formulas used, but also as to the ecclesiological content behind these statements. Hence, it is that in their concrete application with regard to renovation of ecclesiastical institutions, very divergent interpretations of them are given. It is necessary here to make a hermeneutical comment applicable both to Vatican II and to any other Council. This regards the distinction between compromise regarding *content* and that which refers only to wording. When an agreement on content is reached in a conciliar assembly, one can review this decision of the assembly in the documents covering the discussions of the conciliar texts in order to resolve problems concerning their interpretation. On the other hand, it becomes impossible to apply this hermeneutical norm when the compromise reached concerns only the formulas used, which remain subject to very divergent, and even contradictory, interpretations. This distinction between compromise in content and compromise in wording is a matter of the greatest current interest in the interpretation of the decrees of Vatican II. On fundamental points, this Council reached a compromise, not on content, but solely on the formal wording. This explains why such divergent positions have been adopted in interpreting the conciliar texts, which, in themselves, for lack of a compromise on content, remained necessarily ambiguous. The most important texts deal precisely with the relationships between the universal Church and the other Churches, the primacy and the episcopacy, the hierarchy and the laity. They have also been the points most hotly debated in ecclesiological discussions and a source of serious conflicts in the postconciliar Church.

d. Another cause of confusion has been the difficulty of harmonizing *theological language* with *canonical language*. The discussion set off in theological circles by the draft "fundamental law of the Church" and controversies about other central themes on the theology of the Church, which the new codification of canon law raised, have made this difficulty evident. While a fruitful dialogue between theologians and canonists was initiated in the course of preparation of the new *Codex iuris canonici*, we must not forget that ecclesiology cannot do without canon law if the conciliar decrees are to be given full application in the life of the Church. Promotion of this collaboration between theologians and canonists will help the ecclesiology of communion to find suitable expression in the reform of ecclesiastical institutions at the various levels of the Church's life. For the model of the *Church-communion* being fundamental in the ecclesiology of Vatican II, it must be translated into institutions fully in harmony with it. In carrying out this task common to both theologians and canonists, it must be recognized that the problems presented to postconciliar institutions are more dogmatic than canonical.

One Church–Many Churches

In the "one Church–many Churches" relationship, one fact is very clear: Vatican II chose as *point of departure* the reality and the idea of universal Church or congregation of all the faithful in communion with the center, the supreme Pastor and the whole body of bishops.[26] As soon as Lumen gentium was promulgated, a certain amount of resignation, not free of disillusionment, could not help but be evident in light of this fact.[27] When Lumen gentium decided not to adopt the theology of the local Church as point of departure, it certainly did not do so to emphasize the socioinstitutional aspect of the Church, but rather to focus its ecclesiology on the very mystery of the social organism, vivified by the Spirit, and made up of members united in the closest communion of spiritual life.

This fundamental notion of the Church, which is prevalent in all the decrees of Vatican II and is based on the reality and the idea of universal Church, is legitimate, and there is nothing to do but accept it, although it has hidden in it a *risk* from which it is not easy to liberate itself. It would be easy to pass from legitimate emphasis on this unity to the imposition of uniformity and centralization as necessary accompaniments of unity, when in reality it is only an avoidable consequence of this prerogative of ecclesiology. Hence, the task of postconciliar ecclesiology has consisted in warding off more and more every day this risk of centralism and uniformity in the Church, and in progressively shifting the center of gravity toward the local Churches. Progress in this task during the last twenty-five years has been very slow because it has been necessary to overcome the inertia that has dominated the western Church for centuries.

The living experience of the Fathers of the Council of the *real universality* of the Church of Christ, spread over the five continents, proved to be decisive in the effort to reach integration of the theology of the universal Church and the theology of the local Church. K. Rahner saw in this living experience a "permanent significance" of the last Council. This experience of the universality of the Church has been even stronger in the synods of bishops periodically convened during the past two postconciliar decades. The voice of the episcopates of the Churches of the Third World has been widely diffused, and it seems that its most fundamental theses have had considerable acceptance. This is a fruit that ripened since the end of Vatican II. Some essential elements of the theology of the local Church had already found acceptance in the decrees of the Council, although at the last minute and because of that without reaching a synthesis with the theory of the Church universal. Within the context of the sanctifying office of the bishop, a brief theology of the Church as concrete local community and as eucharistic assembly around the altar of the Lord with its legitimate pastor was outlined.[28] Moreover, the theology of the local Church was more fully developed in other conciliar decrees drafted after *Lumen gentium,* such as those dealing with the pastoral duties of bishops, the eastern Churches, and the missionary activity in the Church. Thus, Vatican II tried in its ecclesiology to find equilibrium between the centripetal and the centrifugal forces, or, in other words, between unity and diversity in the Church.

The Council laid the theological foundations of the model of the Church-*communio ecclesiarum.* The particular Churches are not simply parts and even less administrative districts of a confederation of Churches called the universal Church, but rather the same supreme reality of the one Church of Christ, present and really actualized in a specific place. In light of this ecclesiological principle, one understands the tensions aroused during the postconciliar period between the center and the periphery, between the base and the vertex of the Church, to use terms now in current use while avoiding consideration of them as forces of themselves antagonistic. These tensions and conflicts helped to open the way to the ecclesiological model of the Church-*communio ecclesiarum.* In other words, a *first* concept prevailed for many centuries that, having had its origin in the center of unity in the Church, led necessarily to an exaggerated centralism and uniformity. The way is now being opened up for a *second* concept that, starting from the periphery and local diversity, could easily degenerate into sectarian particularism or nationalism. We must, therefore, opt for a *third* concept of a correct theological and practical equilibrium that can be phrased this way: it is a matter of making Rome more present in Paris, New York, Manila, etc., and that these and all the local Churches be more present in Rome. This motion will always be pendular because the complex reality of the Church is between these two poles of strength. Since the closing of Vatican II, important steps have been taken to permit the voice of the Churches to be heard in Rome (Synod of Bishops, more or less periodical meetings of the College of Cardinals, periodical intervention of local bishops in the departments of the Roman Curia, etc.), and to make Rome present in the numerous Churches. The apostolic journeys of the successors of Peter effectively contribute to keeping this

exchange of charisms and ecclesial experiences between the center and the periphery alive, as the ecclesiological model of the
Church-communion of sister Churches demands.

Primacy and Episcopal Collegiality

The search for full and consistent truth on the primacy and
the episcopacy has been a task bristling with serious difficulties
both theoretically and practically, not only in the debates within
the assembly, but also in postconciliar ecclesiology. While there
is good reason to rejoice over the dawning of collegiality, its
theoretical and especially its practical difficulties cannot on that
account be glossed over. In the practical application of collegiality, we are all learners. There is so much to learn about this task
of all the Christian faithful that twenty-five postconciliar years
have not sufficed to reach the goal.

It is not surprising that the application of collegiality at all
levels of the postconciliar Church has been a source of tensions,
whether in the relationships between the episcopate and the
Pope or among the various categories of persons making up the
local Church. The reason for this—and here it is necessary once
again to have recourse to the hermeneutical norm mentioned
above in the interpretaion of conciliar decrees—is to be found in
the lack of a compromise in the *content* during the debates on this
theme in Vatican II. The Council took no substantial decision
on the most controversial points but rather limited itself to emphasizing the intimate unity between primacy and the collegiality of the bishops, as truths both of which emanate from the same
divine revelation. The attitude of Vatican II is clearly not to
oppose the two terms "primacy–episcopate" to one another. Just
as the concept of bishops as simple vicars and delegates of the
Pope is unacceptable, so also is the concept of the Pope as vicar
and delegate of the college of bishops.

The extreme positions in the interpretation of the binomial
expression "primacy–episcopate" certainly cannot appeal to the
ecclesiological doctrine of Vatican II. However, for the purpose
of zealous pursuit of the integral truth and of complementing the
doctrine on the primacy with one on collegiality, positions exist
between the two bridgeheads—to use a clarifying figure—
positions in the center, positions nearer to the primacy point of

view, and positions nearer to the episcopate point of view. The image cannot, however, be carried too far. It involves two poles within the area of one single *communion* that is a mystery of faith, charity, and unity. It is within this very wide area that ecclesiological research can and must go deeper into the fundamental structure of the binomial term *primacy–episcopal collegiality*, and draw out from it the pastoral implications it contains for the central and peripheral government of the Church.

Once more, we must take note that Vatican II succeeded in reaching only a compromise on the *formulas*, [29] while as to *content*, a propensity for ambiguity prevailed in the conciliar assembly between the majority and the minority. This gave rise in the postconciliar period to two kinds of ecclesiology relative to the doctrine of collegiality in its concrete application, one of which starts from the universal Church and the other, on the contrary, from the individual Churches. Depending on its point of departure, each of these ecclesiological models emphasizes its respective element in the binomial term "primacy–episcopate" and founds it on an appeal to the compromise formulas that abound in the conciliar decrees.

Relationships Between Hierarchy and Laity

1. The insertion of Chapter II on the People of God in the *Lumen gentium* gives us the key to *interpretation* of the place and mission of the lay persons in the Church, by reason of their being included in the mystery of this pilgrim people who, in the divine plan, belong to the category of *end*, whereas the hierarchial ministry is a *means* toward this end.

This definitive structuration of the *Lumen gentium*—in conformity with the data of the New Testament on the Church—to the elements common to all categories of persons, namely, *unity, solidarity, essential equality* in the compass of Christian existence, the *mystery of communion* through which we are all brothers in Christ.

The Council did not, however, expressly take on the issue of reconciling this principle of fundamental equality—although *in varietate*, that is to say, with full recognition of the specific office of the hierarchy—between pastors and ordinary believers, to make any inferences about the participation of the latter with full rights, that is to say, with a *deliberative* and not merely a *consultative* vote, in decision making of various directive organs instituted since the Council at the local and universal levels of the Church. Vatican II awakened in lay persons a keen consciousness of the place they occupy in the Church and of their mission and responsibility in the world. In one or another of its decrees, it speaks of the presence of the Church in the world through lay persons. Hence, it will come as a surprise to no one to see that lay persons, aware of their mission, rely on the Council when they ask to be heard on issues concerning marriage, family, and the attitude of the Christian toward the world. Moreover, they are not satisfied with merely carrying out decisions in which they participated neither in the preparation (*decision making*) nor in the decisions (*decision taking*). These legitimate aspirations of the laity do not reject nor do they challenge hierarchical authority, but rather they are an obvious application of the ecclesiological model of the Church-*communion* that demands active participation of all the faithful in the mission of the Church.

2. If the postconciliar Church does not show great progress in this participation of the laity in the various decision-making organs of the Church, the causes of this situation must be looked for as well in the *doctrinal ambiguity* of the conciliar decrees on significant points of the theology of laity.

a. We find this ambiguity in the purely descriptive idea of the lay person that *Lumen gentium* has bequeathed to us after choosing not to develop an *ontological definition* that would take a stand on points still under discussion in ecclesiology and canon law.[30] In a *negative* way, the lay person is declared to be neither a cleric nor a religious. This does not mean that the Council thus ratified the theory of the "three statuses" of persons in the Church; to the contrary, it refutes it expressly as regards the religious.[31] In a *positive* way, the generic element of the idea of lay person, as to how he realizes his Christian being, the expressions used ("in their own way" and "in the role they play") do not say much. What is peculiar to the *laity* is cautiously insinuated in the following terms: "their secular character is proper and peculiar to the laity." The question arises here whether to give this sentence a strictly theological meaning, or whether it is rather a sociological statement. In the first hypothesis, it becomes very difficult to label as "lay," for example, the Christian education that children receive within the family. On the other hand, it must be admitted with *Lumen gentium* that "secular affairs" are not totally pro-hibited for *clerics* because they may "sometimes be concerned with them," and even "carry on a secular profession," although "by their particular vocation they are principally and expressly intended for the sacred ministry." The ambiguity of the expres-sion "lay" in the Church is obvious, and this has influenced the position adopted by the postconciliar Church regarding the par-ticipation of the laity in the pastoral mission of the Church.

b. Vatican II was no clearer on the question of whether it is necessary to situate lay persons alongside the hierarchy when they participate in certain ecclesiastical offices (*munera*),[32] or supple-ment ministers in certain sacred functions (*officia sacra*),[33] or are called by the bishop to dedicate themselves entirely to apostolic tasks.[34] The Council was extremely cautious on the subject of a further *diversification* of the ecclesiastical ministry, and it is under-standable why, after establishment of the competence of lay per-sons to assume certain ministerial offices in the Church by virtue of their participation in the sacerdotal, prophetic, and kingly character of Christ,[35] this subject of diversification and creation of new ministries should have been warmly debated during the postconciliar period and, in a special way, in the Churches of the Third World, where the urgent need for bolder solutions than those adopted in the Churches of Europe does not permit further delays. The individual episcopal conferences have made decisions on creation of certain ministries to be conferred on lay persons called to dedicate themselves wholly to apostolic tasks in close collaboration with regularly ordained ministers.

3. Theological studies on the problems presented are being called upon to continue the search for clearer solutions on into the future. We are disappointed to see that the new *Codex iuris canonici* did not go deeper into the ecclesiological and canonical significance of the distinction introduced by Vatican II between *munus* and *potestas* regarding the subjects of ecclesiastical minis-try, but decided rather to use again the term *potestas jurisdictionis*, from which the Council had moved away, being fully aware of the negative effects of the net distinction (in some authors end-ing up in *separation*) between the *potestas jurisdictionis* and the *potestas ordinis* had had on the evolution of the ecclesiological ideas. Even more lamentable than the use of the term *potestas jurisdictionis* was the decision to separate in the new *Codex iuris canonici* codification concerning the power of jurisdiction (*munus*

regendi) from that concerning *munus docendi* and *sanctificandi.*
This decision was equivalent to going back to preconciliar positions. This structuration of the *Codex iuris canonici* conceals something that cannot be explained by having recourse to the *ratio
methodi,* that is to say, that one cannot deal with everything at
the same time. Having in mind this basic adverse criticism of the
new *Codex iuris canonici,* there is certainly no reason to be surprised that it approved participation of the laity in the synodal
structures of the Church in a merely consultative role.

The "Church–World" Relationship

With three long years of gestation, *Gaudium et spes* is the
document of Vatican II that most faithfully reflects the progressive alteration of the theological concepts of the "Church" and
"world" among the participants in the assembly. However great
the enthusiasm of the experts and Council fathers may have been
when they approached the subject, they found themselves somewhat at a loss and divided not only as to what solutions to offer,
but also as to work methods and the structure to be given to the
document. Its drafting required them to take a position on this
complex issue regarding the relationships between the sacred and
the profane, the natural and the supernatural, and the Church
and the world. Vatican II could not, however, elude its responsibility. It was better to risk making an incomplete statement, but
one capable of establishing the immutable, although dynamic
principles, contained in revelation, and to furnish certain orien-
tative indications, than to give up when faced with the problem
of not being able to write a conciliar document that would be on
a par in style and precision with those of other Councils. To
overcome the impasse, it was decided to give *Gaudium et spes* the
character of *pastoral* constitution.

No other document of Vatican II had an impact on the development of postconciliar ecclesiology as decisive as *Gaudium et
spes.* Moreover, the situation of the Church itself in this postconciliar period has been inevitably affected, even more in the
Churches of the Third World than in those of the developed
world, by a solid commitment to put into practice the principles
set forth in *Gaudium et spes* and to try new solutions to questions
that are also new. It is a fact beyond discussion that in the two

decades following Vatican II, ecclesiological thinking in the Churches of the Third World gave priority, both in theory and practice, to the subject of its mission of salvation among men in the sense of *integral application of the evangelical message* in the life of these peoples. These ideas had provided information for renovating the structures of these Churches and even for creating new ones that can ensure more effective accomplishment of their mission among men.

2. The conciliar assembly, in accepting the third draft of *Gaudium et spes* as the basis of discussion, made a decision to start from the immanence (*unity*) of the Church in the world and to deal subsequently with transcendence (*difference*) in the "Church–world" relationship. The choice of a point of departure in this as in so many other ecclesiological problems, where it is similarly necessary to acknowledge the two poles of energy in this relationship, has an impact beyond the *methodological order* and influences the very content of the particular ecclesiological concept. In the debate on this theme, two ecclesiological currents have confronted one another, one of which, to correct a too *optimistic* vision of the world, insists on differences and their implications, as, for instance, the presence of sin in the world and the reality of the cross, of death and of redemption; the other, on the other hand, aims at avoiding a pessimistic perspective of the world at any cost, and to this end, begins with unity as an implication of the dogmas on creation, the incarnation, and the dominion of Christ over the world and history. From this direct confrontation between the concepts—which are opposed only in the point of departure chosen and the consequent emphasis on the aspects implied respectively in difference and in unity—a harmonious synthesis of the two ecclesiological currents was not reached and could not be reached.

By approving *Gaudium et spes*, Vatican II proclaimed its intention to advance without breaking with tradition in its approach to man. This commitment presented a challenge to postconciliar ecclesiology, especially in the Churches of the Third World. The approach bristles with difficulties, and it is not surprising that, in the face of these, radical positions have been taken. In the present ecclesiological panorama, there are unmistakable signs that tensions and disagreements are weakening. It is to be hoped that the phase characterized by demonstrations of euphoria and utopia will be followed by another distinguished by rethinking of one's own theoretical and practical positions in the search for as large a consensus as possible among theologians and Church leaders. It will only be on the basis of such a consensus and of collaboration by everyone in the common task of bringing man the Christian message in all its integritys that the Church may make progress in the directions outlined by Vatican II in *Gaudium et spes*.

3. As regards the content of *Gaudium et spes*, its concept of "world," already used in the preamble of the constitution and fully described in other passages, must be pointed out as a key element. Although the Council clearly endeavored to bring out the positive aspects of the world as the work of the Creator, *Gaudium et spes* left us a concept of the world theologically little developed. Ratzinger has written that this concept is still in a pretheological stage,[36] and that it therefore needs to be further clarified by postconciliar ecclesiology. Nevertheless *Gaudium et spes* did contain a few positive aspects regarding the plurivalent concept of the world.

a. While this concept presents in biblical language—from which it passed into Christian literature—a negative impression because of sin and the powers of the evil one that operate in the world, its positive aspects, such as the totality of the work created by God and renewed in Christ, are by far more prevalent, and this *Gaudium et spes* reflects.

b. By "world," *Gaudium et spes* means also the men who inhabit the earth. Among these there are good and bad in the moral and spiritual sense mentioned above, and there are also Christians, believers, and atheists. This fact does not simply mean that the former must be separated from the latter. The Church, while not of this world, lives *in* and *for* the world.

c. Finally, *Gaudium et spes* includes in the concept of world *earthly realities* and the *temporal tasks* that man is called upon to perform during his existence on earth. The realities of this world created by God have a certain autonomy that man must respect. By establishing the principle of the distinction between the Church and human society, *Gaudium et spes* affirmed this relative autonomy of the temporal. This distinction should not be understood in the sense of two realities that exclude every mutual exchange or influence. Nor does *Gaudium et spes* support the thesis that for the Christian, the profession of his faith and his existence in the world are carried on in two separate and impermeable fields.

It would have been utopian to hope that Vatican II would be more specific about such a theologically complex concept as that of the world and would establish the definite implications it has in the various aspects of the life of the Church and of a Christian. The Council entrusted theologians with the task of delving more deeply into this problem, which is so basic in ecclesiology. During the twenty-five years following the Council, considerable progress has been made on this subject. In fairness, we must point out that the results obtained by the theologians of the Third World represent an original and innovative contribution to the ecclesiology prevailing in the developed world.

4. *Dialogue* is another of the fundamental categories that *Gaudium et spes* adopted, and it had a definite impact on postconciliar ecclesiology during the past two decades. Vatican II proclaimed its choice of dialogue in the very preamble of *Gaudium et spes:* "The Council, witness herald of the faith of all the people of God gathered by Christ, can give no better proof of its solidarity, respect and love for the whole human family than that of carrying on dialogue with it about all its problems . . . clarifying them in the light of the Gospel. . . ."[37] The assembly here made a decision in favor of this path of dialogue with the world, which includes a search together for solutions to the serious problems that trouble man today and discussion as to the most effective ways of solving them. The fundamental function of the *dialogue* that *Gaudium et spes* enjoins on the postconciliar Church requires that the Church identify and defend *authentically human values* and collaborate with all men of good will in building a more human world. The assertion of the fundamental unity between the order of creation and that of redemption implies that the Church must fully recognize the dignity of human nature and all the natural rights of man. In so doing, the Church reinforces and ennobles them. The decision to engage in dialogue includes acceptance by the Church of a *coexistence* with civil society, which is the beginning of mutual cooperation. On the other hand, this is a question of a cooperation that is not intended to have as its goal socializing or, still less, ecclesiasticizing, because it recognizes the autonomy that, by will of the Creator, the temporal order possesses. With its cooperation, the Church brings the priceless gift of the light of the gospel. With this, it is able to announce words of eternal validity beyond the wisdom of this world.

5. A last characteristic of *Gaudium et spes* is the message of *optimism* that it has spread throughout the postconciliar Church and to which postconciliar ecclesiology has not turned a deaf ear. The Church clearly opted for solidarity with man and his successes, presenting to him the ultimate meaning these things have in the divine plan of the Creator. To spread this *message of optimism* has been the essential task of the postconciliar Church and ecclesiology, both at the universal level and in a special way in the Churches of the Third World. Of one accord, pastors, theologians, and the faithful have participated in this task—tensions have never put this fundamental cooperation in doubt; to the contrary, they have been a source of new energies. As regards the fruit of this, one may speak of the awakening of a new ecclesiastical consciousness among the great mass of Christians who now consider themselves participants, and in some ways protagonists, in the ecclesial life of their communities. Moreover, Christians are learning to make themselves men among men without renouncing their divine vocation. This demands that they harmonize their earthly task with their supraterrestrial goal. Their Christian faith prompts them to put themselves at the service of men and to see in the most helpless of them a brother they must help to free himself from all oppression and to live like a Son of God.

The need to draw all the consequences out of this message of optimism of *Gaudium et spes* has induced pastors and theologians to take innovative decisions, conscious of all the risks they entail. Vatican II has not become a dead letter. Twenty-five years ago the seed was sown. The period of germination has been long and laborious. Moreover, it cannot be considered to have been completed in these twenty-five years since the opening of the Council. But one can speak of very considerable fruits both in theory and in practice. The renewal of postconciliar ecclesiology has made it clear to Christians today that in abandoning their temporal commitment they would be led to disfigure the order of creation established by God and restored in Christ.

Conclusion

In this summary treatment of postconciliar ecclesiology, of necessity brief, there are lights and shadows, positive results and problems awaiting solution. As sons and daughters of the Church, our Mother, and as theologians, we must accept this situation of the postconciliar Church and ecclesiology, with all its challenges and promises, in the light of faith. We did not choose the *Kairos* in which we live. God put us there. To seek refuge in the past or lose ourselves in a utopian future would not be responses we could characterize as Christian. The Church lives its mystery in every period of history by striving to respond to the requirements of the moment in the light of the past and with its aim on the future. Without taking anything away from the value of the transformations we have observed, both in *doctrine* and in the *existential reality* of the Church in the most crucial moments of its history, it remains true that these changes did not alter this *permanent substratum* of the Church, which defies the centuries. There is nothing new in saying that ecclesiology is presently in a period of transition. In every other time of its history, the theology of the Church has tried to find new solutions to the theoretical and practical problems it had to face. Faith tells us that each era is a gift of God for the Church and for the Christian, because time belongs to God. It is up to the Church to accept it and use it in a responsible way. The history of ecclesiology has gone through situations quite similar to the present one and is for the theologian the *magistra* who guides him in his difficult task of giving new solutions to new problems without betraying the past.

Translated from the Spanish by Louis-Bertrand Raymond and
Edward Hughes.

Notes

1. J.H. Newman, Letter to O'Neill Daunt (7 August 1970) quoted in Y.M.-J. Congar, *Regard sur le concile Vatican II à l'occasion du 20e anniversaire de son annonce;* in H. Stirnimann, J. Brantschen, and P. Selvatico (eds.), *Unterwegs zur Einheit* (Freiburg im Breisgau, 1980), 786.

2. J. Grootaers, "Dynamisme et prospective de l'ecclésiologie de Vatican II." Colloque international de Bologne: 8–12 April 1980, *Iren* 53 (1980), 200.

3. Cf. John XXIII, Disc. (8 December 1962), *Vat. II-BAC,* 759–760; Paul VI, Disc. (29 September 1963), *AAS* 55 (1963), 850; John XXIII, Enc. *Ad Petri cathedram, AAS* 51 (1959), 511; Paul VI, Disc. (29 September 1963), *Vat. II-BAC,* 966–968.

4. A. Antón, "El capítulo del Pueblo de Dios en la eclesiología de la comunidad," *EstEcl* 42 (1967), 155–181; *id.*, *Primado y Colegialidad* (BAC-Minor 15), 32–79; *id.*, "La Iglesia comunidad," in *Comunidad eclesial y Misiones* (XXIII Sem.esp.mis.) (Burgos, 1971), 43–63; *id.*, *La Iglesia de Cristo. El Israel de la Vieja y de la Nueva Alianza* (BAC-Maior 15), 27–36, 58–70.

5. K. Rahner, "Die bleibende Bedentung des II Vatikanischen Konzils," *StimZ* 197 (1979), 796.

6. *Ibid.*, 796.

7. K. Rahner, "Una interpretación teológica a fondo del conc. Vaticano II," *RaFe* 208 (1979), 186.

8. *Ibid.*, 188.

9. *Ibid.*, 191.

10. A. Antón, *Primado y Colegialidad* (BAC-Minor 15) (Madrid, 1970), 32–78.

11. P. Cesare Bori, *Koinônia. La ideal della comunione nell'ecclesiologia recente en nel Nuovo Testamento* (Brescia, 1972), 55.

12. Y.M.-J. Congar, *Sainte Eglise. Etudes et Approches ecclésiologiques* (Paris, 1963), 21–24.

13. P. Cesare Bori, *Koinônia*, 55–56.

14. A. Antón, *La Iglesia*, 21–54; 115–134, 316–420.

15. Cf. *LG* I, 5; *GS*; 40; *UR*, 1.

16. Puebla. *Il messaggio della Speranza* (Rome, 1979), n. 129, 137–138.

17. S. Dianich, *La Chiesa mistero di comunione* (Turin, 1975), 12.

18. *Ibid.*, 12.

19. *Ibid.*, 16–17.

20. This is one of the conclusions of the International Symposium of forty theologians (Bologna, 1980) on the ecclesiology of Vatican II: *Christ Stor* 2 (1981), 1–327.

21. A. Acerbi, *Due Ecclesiologie: ecclesiologia giuridica ed ecclesiologia di communione nella "Lumen Gentium"* (Bologna, 1975).

22. H.J. Pottmeyer, "Kirche auf dem Weg: 20 Jahre nach dem II Vat Konzil," *Universitas* 37 (1982), 1251–1264; *id.*, "Continuità e innovazione nell'ecclesiologia del Vaticano II," *Crist Stor* 2 (1981), 71–94.

23. Pottmeyer, "Kirche auf dem Weg," 1256.

24. H. Küng, *Unfehlbar. Eine Anfrage* (Einsiedeln, 1975); A.B. Hasler, *Pius IX; (1846–1878), päpstliche Unfehlbarkeit und I. Vatikanisches Konzil. Dogmatisierung und Durchsetzung einer Ideologie* (Stuttgart, 1977).

25. D. Tracy, H. Küng, and B. Metz (eds.), *Toward Vatican III. The Work That Needs To Be Done* (Dublin, 1978); G. Alberigo (ed.), *Verso la Chiesa del terzo millenio* (Brescia, 1969).

26. We have emphasized this fact in many publications as the cause of serious attitudes relative to a series of hotly contested issues to which Vatican II gave a unilateral response, cf. A. Antón, *Primado y Colegialidad*, 79–101.

27. K. Rahner, "Das neue Bild der Kirche," *GeistL* 39 (1966), 3.

28. *LG*, III, 26.

29. *LG*, III, 22–23 with the prior explanatory note.

30. *LG*, IV, 31.

31. *LG*, VI, 43.

32. *LG*, IV, 33.

33. *LG*, IV, 35.

34. *LG*, IV, 41.

35. *LG*, IV, 31.

36. J. Ratzinger, *Der Weltdienst der Kirche: Zehn Jahre nach Vaticanum II*, A. Bauch, A. Glasser, and M. Seybold (eds.) (Regensburg, 1976), 37.

37. GS, 3.

CHAPTER 16

The Biblical Question
of "Charisms" After Vatican II

Albert Vanhoye, S.J.

Summary

The Council saw some lively discussions on charisms. In its wake, certain authors revived the theory that the Pauline churches had a purely charismatic structure. An examination of the New Testament texts does not in any way bear out this systematic theory. No precise notion of charisms yet existed, and such a concept was only just being sketched out. The New Testament offers some dynamic perspectives on this subject, but also encourages us to use discernment.

Pope John XXIII had expressed the hope that the Council would be the occasion for a "new Pentecost," and the remarkable development of the "charismatic movement" in the years following the Council has often been seen as a fulfillment of this wish. Like the apostles on the day of Pentecost, many Christians have felt themselves to be filled by the Holy Spirit and have started "speaking in tongues."[1] At the same time, attention has been directed to the "charisms," which were discussed by the Council. Many works have been published on this subject. Without making any claim to provide an exhaustive account—for this would take too much time—this modest article seeks at least to clarify certain aspects of the question from an exegetical viewpoint.

The word *charism* in fact has to do with exegesis, for it is a biblical term: the simple transcription of the Greek word *cha-risma* that is used in the New Testament.[2] The concept of charisms has its starting point in certain New Testament texts that speak of *charisma*. However, this raises a considerable number of questions, inasmuch as not all the uses of the word in the New Testament present the same perspective, so that they do not provide a univocal basis for the theological notion of charism. Moreover, this notion was then seen to be open to evolution in relation to the life of the Church and not only to Scripture.

Linguistic Situation

In order to reach a clear idea of the questions to be answered, we must first note a linguistic factor that indicates a necessary difference in status between the English word "charism" and the Greek word *charisma*. It might appear at first glance that there is a perfect correspondence between the two terms, inasmuch as one is simply the transcription of the other. How could we hope to find any more faithful translation? However, this is a misapprehension. It is in fact impossible for a transcription to be a faithful translation. When a word moves from one language to another, it inevitably undergoes a change in linguistic status: in its original language it is at home, whereas in another language it is a foreigner, cut off from its family. It therefore changes in sense, or at least in connotations. In Greek, *charisma* has many relatives that contribute to its meaning. It is derived from the verb *charizesthai*, which means "to show oneself generous, to present." It is related to *charis* (grace), *eucharistein* (to give thanks), and many other terms. Like *pragma* or *ktisma*, it is formed with the aid of the suffix *-ma*, and expresses the result of the action indicated by the verb. It therefore has a general meaning of "gracious gift" or "gratuity." Like any other word that becomes specialized through usage, it can also acquire a technical sense, while never losing its general sense. "Charism," on the other hand, is an isolated word in English (and the same goes for French or other modern languages). It has no perceptible relationship with "grace" or with "gift," and there is nothing that enables us to guess its meaning. It is inevitably a technical term. Its precise meaning is the subject of debate among theologians. The latter, of course, take into account the New Testament texts. However, it is a good idea to examine the precise significance of these texts.

In the theology of the Latin Church, the generalized use of the technical term "charism" is of relatively recent date.[3] This is because this word is found only once in the Vulgate, in 1 Corinthians 12:31: "Aemulamini autem *charismata* meliora." This is the only passage in which the Vulgate is satisfied with a transcription, and in every other case it offers a translation. It most often translates the Greek *charisma* as *gratia* (Rom. 1:11; 5:16; 6:23; 1 Cor. 1:7; 12:4, 9, 28, 30; 1 Tim. 4:14; 2 Tim. 1:6; 1 Pet. 4:10), a translation that is based on the relationship between *charisma* and *charis*, but that eliminates the difference between these two terms. In some texts, the Vulgate uses *donum* (Rom. 5:15a; 11:29; 1 Cor. 7:7), which makes *charisma* equivalent to *dōrea* (Jn. 4:10; Acts 2:28; Rom. 5:15c). In still other cases, we find *donatio* (Rom. 12:6; 2 Cor. 1:11), which has the same drawback, inasmuch as *donatio* is used to translate *dōrea* in Romans 5:17 and Ephesians 4:7. These translations are, therefore, not precise. Nevertheless, from a linguistic point of view, they amount to more than a simple transliteration, for the reasons already given.

The fact that Latin theologians hardly ever used the word "charism" does not mean that they had no corresponding concept. On the contrary, they were attentive to the statement of 1 Corinthians 12:4, "Divisiones vero gratiarum [*charismatōn*] sunt" and other similar texts,[4] and thus elaborated the concept of *gratia gratis data* as distinct from that of *gratia gratum faciens*. According to St. Thomas Aquinas,

> Accordingly, grace is of two kinds. Firstly, there is the grace by which man himself is united to God, and this is called sanctifying grace [*gratia gratum faciens*]. Secondly, there is the grace by which one man cooperates with another so that he might be brought back to God. Now this kind of grace is called freely bestowed grace [*gratia gratis data*].

Theologians are in agreement over the identification of *gratia gratis data* with "charism."[5] In the section on *gratiae gratis datae*, St. Thomas does in fact discuss the different gifts listed in 1 Corinthians 12:8–10: prophecy, the gift of tongues, the gift of words, miracles (II/II, qq. 171–178), to which he adds ecstasy, referring to 2 Corinthians 12:2–4.

The word "charism" does now belong to the theological vocabulary of the Latin Church. Vatican II marks a definite stage in this connection, for the official texts of the Council, written in Latin, use the Latin transliteration of the Greek word *charisma* fourteen times. These occurrences are not in direct quotations from the New Testament, because for these the Council uses the Vulgate, and the Vulgate, as we have just said, prefers to translate rather than transliterate. *Charisma* is used in the explanations given by the Council.

Charisms at the Council

During the Council, there was a lively debate between the supporters of two different ways of understanding charisms and their function in the life of the Church. On the one hand were those who saw the charisms as extraordinary, miraculous gifts granted by God in exceptional cases; on the other were those who viewed them in a much broader way, as gifts of grace of all types oriented to fostering the growth of the Christian people.

The first view had a claim to be seen as "traditional" in theological teaching. It was warmly defended by Cardinal Rufini, who rejected the idea that all Christians could have a charism of one sort or another, and claimed on the contrary that charisms are extremely rare and are exceptional manifestations of the power of God, aimed at confirming the presence and action of God in a holy person or in some particular situation.

The other point of view was supported by Cardinal Suenens,[6] who declared that charisms "are not some secondary phenomenon in the life of the Church," but that each Christian, whatever his cultural level, can have charismatic gifts in his everyday life. Rather than resorting to scriptural or theological arguments. Suenens appealed to the pastoral experience of the Council Fathers and asked:

Does not each one of us know lay people, both men and women, in his own diocese who are truly called by God? These people have received various different charisms from the Spirit, for catechesis, evangelization, apostolic action of various types, social work, and charitable activity. . . . Without these charisms, the ministry of the Church would be impoverished and sterile. . . .

The second position eventually prevailed, and a text on charisms was adopted by the Council. This constitutes the second part of number 12 of the Dogmatic Constitution on the Church, *Lumen gentium*. The first part of this same number describes the prophetic aspect of the people of God, after the previous numbers had described its priestly aspect: "The holy People of God share also in Christ's prophetic office: it spreads abroad a living witness to him, especially by a life of faith and love . . ." because "the supernatural appreciation of the faith [*sensus fidei*]" is that of "the whole people," this is not some special grace granted to some Christians and not to others. We can, therefore, see a clear difference between this first part of number 12 and the following part, which presents charisms as "special graces" that are distributed in a broad variety of ways. In the Latin text, the word *charismata* is expressly applied to these "special graces."[7]

In order to define the charisms, the Council distinguishes them from the graces that the Holy Spirit grants to the people of God "through the sacraments and the ministries of the Church"—graces of sanctification, leadership, or government, and of growth in virtue. The charisms are "special graces" (*gratiae speciales*) that the Spirit distributes "as he wills" (1 Cor. 12:11) "among the faithful of every rank." These graces "make them fit and ready to undertake various tasks and offices for the renewal and building up of the Church, as it is written, 'the manifestation of the Spirit is given to everyone for profit' (1 Cor. 12:7)." The following sentence adds that "these charisms" (*quae charismata*) are very varied, ranging from "the very remarkable" to "the more simple and widely diffused." They are above all "fitting and useful for the needs of the Church."

The Council invites people to adopt a positive attitude toward charisms: ". . . they are to be received with thanksgiving and consolation." Even so, it does issue a warning against possible excesses in connection with "extraordinary gifts," which "are not to be rashly desired, nor is it from them that the fruits of apostolic labors are to be presumptuously expected."

The number concludes by describing the role of those who have charge over the Church, whose task it is to "judge the genuineness and proper use of these gifts." The instructions given to the Thessalonians by the apostle Paul are applied especially to these leaders: they are "not to extinguish the Spirit, but to test all things and hold fast to what is good (cf. 1 Thess. 5:12, 19–21)."

The concept of charism that emerges from this text provides us with a number of specific elements.

In the first place, we note a clear distinction between institution and charism. On the one hand, there are the "sacraments and ministries," and on the other, the "special graces," which are "charisms." The latter do not depend on institution, and no programming can be made in their regard, because they depend on the free initiative of the Spirit, who distributes them "as he wills." The distinction between institution and charism also appears in other passages of *Lumen gentium.* In the first chapter, it is stated that the Spirit provides the Church with "varied hierarchic and charismatic gifts" (*LG* 4), and a little further on, the Council observes that among the various gifts of the Spirit "the primacy belongs to the grace of the apostles to whose authority the Spirit himself subjects even those who are endowed with charisms [*charismaticos*]" (*LG* 7).

The distinction does not, however, go so far as opposition. The ministries and the charisms are attributed with a common origin, both of them coming from the Holy Spirit. It is the same Holy Spirit who, on the one hand, "through the sacraments and the ministries of the Church . . . makes holy the People," and who, on the other, distributes "special graces" to certain members of the faithful without any necessary link with the sacraments (*LG* 12). Both "hierarchic" gifts and "charismatic" gifts are granted by the same Spirit (*LG* 4).

Moreover, the charisms have a special relationship with the ministries, and the Council describes them as useful gifts: "By these gifts he makes them fit and ready to undertake various tasks and offices [*opera et officia*] for the renewal and building up of the Church" (*LG* 12). The formula *opera et officia* is obviously very broad, and is applied to the various services in the Church undertaken by lay people. However, there is no justification for claiming that it applies only to lay people and excludes ordained ministers. Formal pastoral responsibilities are certainly *officia* helpful for the development of the Church. And how can we deny that certain priests and bishops receive "special graces" from the Spirit for one or another aspect of their ministry? The Council expresses a distinction between these special graces and sacramental grace strictly speaking, which is bestowed on all those who receive the sacrament with the necessary dispositions. However, it would be ridiculous to see sacramental grace as an obstacle to the reception of charisms!

There is another type of relationship between charisms and institution, in that the pastors of the Church have a right and duty to exercise discernment with regard to charisms. In its number 7, on the Church as the Body of Christ, the Council bases itself on the text of 1 Corinthians 14 to state that the Spirit himself subjects those with charisms to apostolic authority, and returns to discuss this point at greater length at the end of number 12.

As regards the nature of charisms, the Council visibly draws its inspiration from the theological distinction between *gratia gratum faciens* and *gratia gratis data,* thus refraining from indicating any relationship between charisms and sanctification or virtues. It is through the sacraments, not through the charisms, that the Spirit sanctifies the members of the Church and enables them to advance in virtue. The charisms are situated solely within a perspective of usefulness to the Church, and are described as conferring readiness and willingness to undertake activities helpful to the Church.

In order to justify this point of view, the Council cites the phrase of 1 Corinthians 12:7: "The manifestation of the Spirit is given to everyone for profit." St. Thomas states that the profit intended was that of others, but there are grounds for considering whether this statement in fact corresponds to the thought of St. Paul.

In order to define the function of charisms better, the Council highlights the "renewal" (*renovatio*) of the Church, thus suggesting a distinction between the ordinary administration of grace and new initiatives. The Holy Spirit uses the sacraments and institutional ministries for ordinary administration, but when he wants to bring about something new, he inspires people with charisms.

Nevertheless, the following phrase invites us not to take this distinction as hard and fast, admitting the existence of "more simple and widely diffused" charisms alongside the "very remarkable" (*clarissima*) ones. We can see here that the Council adopted the position of Cardinal Suenens. It follows from this position that many charisms play their role in the ordinary life of the Church. They do not represent sensational innovations, but are applied to activities necessary for the constant building up of the Church. Cardinal Suenens could thus speak of a charism for teaching catechism, as well as one for caring for the poor and the sick. Many members of the faithful have special gifts for these ordinary Christian activities, and they use them with remarkable spiritual fruitfulness, although this does not mean that they are innovators.

The statements of the Council give rise to more than one question. Here we must consider the extent to which they can be seen as based on New Testament texts. In this connection, it is helpful to distinguish between the question of vocabulary and that of content. As regards vocabulary, the exegete must consider whether the word *charisma* already possesses a technical meaning in the New Testament, and, if it does, whether this technical meaning corresponds to the conciliar concept of charism; even if it does not possess such a technical meaning in the New Testament, the exegete must still consider whether the facts narrated in the New Testament justify the conciliar position with regard to the relationship between charisms and institutions, and with regard to the diversity and function of charisms.

Charism and Ministry According to E. Käsemann

Although it appeared prior to the Council, E. Käsemann's study on "Ministry and Community" deserves our attention, for it exercised its influence in the period following the Council.[8] The complexity of Käsemann's positions means that it is difficult to summarize them. In his study, the author expresses a great many thought-provoking ideas that we cannot recall here. The point that interests us particularly is that in his introduction, Käsemann gives his answer to a number of the questions we have just been considering: he states clearly that the word *charisma* possesses a technical meaning in Pauline theology and that the concept of *charisma* "describes in a theologically exact and comprehensive way the essence and scope of every ecclesiastical ministry and function."[9]

Käsemann emphasizes the importance of this concept not only for Pauline ecclesiology but for the whole theology of the apostle—an importance that, in his opinion, flows from the fact that Paul gave a technical sense to the word *charisma*. [10]

After such clear statements, we might expect to find some convincing evidence. However, we seek in vain in the following paragraphs. Käsemann begins by citing Romans 6:23, which he translates: "The charisma of God is eternal life in Christ." This indicates definite linguistic confusion, for it is clear that in this text *charisma* is not used in a technical sense and does not refer to the variety of functions in the Church. In Romans 6:23, *charisma* has its general meaning of "generous gift." Translating the text as "The *charisma* of God is eternal life" is simply an error in translation. What should be said is, "The generous gift of God is eternal life," giving up any idea of using the text as a demonstration of a technical sense of *charisma*. The same must be said of Romans 5:15–17 ("But the gift [*charisma*] is not like the trespass"), although Käsemann tries to use this text as well. No translator has ever thought that charisms were being spoken of here.

Käsemann then notes the alternation of *charismata* and *diakoniai* in 1 Corinthians 12:4–5 and the connection with the call of God in Romans 11:28 and 1 Corinthians 7:7, 17–22. He concludes that a charism is "the specific part which the individual has in the lordship and glory of Christ; and this specific part which the individual has in the Lord shows itself in a specific service and a specific vocation."[11] Here we are offered a precise idea. If it were witnessed to in a sufficient number of texts, it would allow us to consider *charisma* a technical term. However, Käsemann does not take the trouble to carry out any methodical demonstration. None of the texts he cites corresponds to the definition given. Neither Romans 11:29, nor 1 Corinthians 7:7, 17–22, nor 12:4–5, speaks of "a part in the lordship and glory of Christ"; nor does any of these texts define a charism as a service or a vocation.

The text that corresponds least ill to the definition would be that of Ephesians 4:7–13, which attributes the power to distribute gifts to the glorified Christ. However, this text cannot be taken to prove a technical sense of *charisma*, for the simple reason that the word *charisma* is not used there. This does not, however, prevent Käsemann from taking Ephesians 4:7–13 several times to prove his theory.[12] Such a lack of scientific precision is astonishing.

Käsemann is no more careful when drawing up lists of charisms.

Without in any way bothering about the presence or absence of the term charisma, he lists all the names of functions to be found in the Pauline *corpus* and calls them charisms (p. 69): among the charisms of service, he includes "the widows" of 1 Timothy 5:9–13, although this text does not mention charisms; with regard to charisms of government, he refers to five texts, not one of which uses the word *charisma.* He then adds "charismatic suffering," stating that two texts speak of this clearly; however, we seek in vain in these texts (2 Cor. 4:7–9 and Col. 1:24) for the slightest allusion to *charisma.* With such a method, we could find charisms everywhere, but it would be purely arbitrary.[13]

Käsemann goes on to say that the meaning of *charisma* must be broadened still further, and he states: "This becomes quite clear in 1 Corinthians 7:17. It is true that the term charisma is not employed here. But the formula 'as the Lord has distributed to each man, as the Lord has called each man' must bear the same meaning." If we examine the context, we can see that this claim is extremely debatable, because Paul is not speaking here of gifts of grace but of social and cultural circumstances—circumcision or uncircumcision, slavery or the condition of a free man—and he does not say that God has called the person to this or that condition, but that God's call to the Christian faith has come to the person in this or that condition. Ignoring all this, Käsemann claims that in Paul's view, everything has the value of a charism: circumcision and uncircumcision, slavery and freedom. Again, his exegesis is arbitrary. It is quite clear that Paul has no intention of giving the value of a charism (in other words, a religious value) to circumcision or uncircumcision. On the contrary, he denies them any religious value: "For neither circumcision counts for anything nor uncircumcision" (1 Cor. 7:19; Gal. 5:6; 6:15). And the same applies to the person's social position: "Were you a slave when called? Never mind." If Paul had had the intention of giving slavery a value by attributing it with the dignity of a charism, he would certainly not have said: "Never mind." Käsemann supports his interpretation by referring to the passage in Romans 12:3 where the expression "each according as God has assigned him" appears shortly before a passage on the charisms (Rom. 12:6–8). However, this argument is fallacious. A partial parallelism between Romans 12:3 and 1 Corinthians 7:17 cannot lead to a conclusion of a total parallelism (God has distributed various charisms; God has distributed various social conditions;

therefore, social conditions are charisms—God has given me eyes; God has given me ears; therefore ears are eyes!).

Moreover, this position of Käsemann is very far removed from his initial definition of charism. If we must consider circumcision and uncircumcision as charisms, it is difficult to see how the notion of charism can be "a concept . . . which describes in a theologically exact and comprehensive way the essence and scope of every ecclesiastical ministry and function." Must we accept that according to Paul circumcision is an ecclesial service? And that the same applies to uncircumcision? Simply asking this question is enough to show how illogical it is.

Käsemann does not hesitate to make some resounding declarations as to the importance of charisms in the theology of Paul: "Paul bases the prescriptions of the so-called 'household code' [*Haustafeln*] firmly on the idea of charisma" (p. 71); "Paul has based not only the household code, but all his catechetical matter on the concept of charisma" (p. 71); "Rom. 12–15 is speaking, as we have already seen of ch. 14, exclusively of charismata and those conditions that are the raw material of charismata" (p. 73)—it will be recalled that the word *charisma* does not appear even once in Romans 14 and that the only time it is used in Romans 12–15 is in the phrase in 12:6. Käsemann goes so far as to refer to "the strong and indeed decisive penetration of every area of Pauline theology by the doctrine of charisma and . . . the clarity with which the Apostle's basic theological conception emerges from it" (p. 75). "The whole question of order within the Christian community is also treated from this standpoint" (p. 76). "We have now reached the point at which we must speak explicitly of the relation between community [*Gemeinde*] and ministry [*Amt*]. This relationship also is treated by Paul exclusively on the basis of the charisma concept" (p. 78). We can see that in this last phrase, Käsemann is giving his answer to the question studied in his article: "Ministry and Community."

We must sadly observe that not one of these ringing declarations is effectively proved by their author. Indeed, it would be impossible to prove them, because the necessary texts do not exist. It is very clear that in Paul's theology, the notion of charism does not have the importance that Käsemann attributes to it. We would note in passing that he ignores the pastoral letters, where he considers that the notion of charism is not only different from that of the other letters, but in fact the opposite

(p. 85). As a consequence, *charisma* is found in only three letters (Romans, 1 Corinthians, and 2 Corinthians). The texts that can be used as the basis for a technical meaning are only two (Rom. 12:6–8; 1 Cor. 12), whereas three other passages provide overly rapid references (Rom. 1:11; 1 Cor. 1:7; 7:7). The other Pauline occurrences are not relevant because they take the word in a general sense (Rom. 5:15, 16; 6:23; 11:29) or apply it to some specific factor (2 Cor. 1:11). How is it then possible to claim that Paul's ecclesiology, and indeed his whole theology, is based on the concept of charism? We are clearly dealing with a case of gross exaggeration.

With regard to the relations between community and ministry, Käsemann states that Paul "set his doctrine of charisma in opposition to the theory of an institutionally guaranteed ecclesiastical office [*institutionell ausgewiesenen Amtes*]" (p. 84). He does not cite any text in this connection, and one would indeed seek such a text in vain, because Paul never expressed such an opposition. Starting from a correct idea (i.e., that each baptized person has a certain responsibility in the Church), Käsemann takes up a very confused position when he claims that "all the baptized are office-bearers [*Amtsträger*]" (p. 80), in other words, that they have a pastoral responsibility of the same order as that of priests and bishops. In order to prove his point, Käsemann refers to the text of 1 Peter 2:5–10, which in fact mentions neither charisms nor pastoral responsibilities.

The last pages of his article consider the pastoral letters (1 Timothy, 2 Timothy, and Titus), stating that these texts present a notion of charisms that "cannot be reconciled with the Pauline doctrine of the charismata" (p. 87), because charisms are here linked to ordination. On this point as on others, Käsemann attributes the texts a significance that they do not have. Paul never claimed that no charism could be conferred through ordination. When he made a strong declaration as to the spiritual efficacity of baptism (Rom. 6:3–4; 1 Cor. 12:13; Gal. 3:27), the apostle showed that he fully accepted the links between graces and sacraments—links that are in harmony with the mystery of Christ's incarnation and with the existence of the Church as the body of Christ. It is therefore difficult to see why his notion of charism would exclude any possible relationship with an ordination.

Käsemann concludes his article with a significant question:

"Why has Protestantism itself . . . never made a serious attempt to create a Church order which reflected the Pauline doctrine of charismata," an order in which "all responsibility and every kind of ministry in the community would be grounded on baptism," by proclaiming and exercising "the common priesthood of all believers" (p. 93)? This question clearly shows Käsemann's underlying intention, which is that of setting charism and institution—with the exception of baptism—in opposition as two incompatible factors, in the dream of a purely "charismatic" Church. [14]

The Charismatic Structure of the Church
According to H. Küng

A short while after the close of the Council, an article by H. Küng, entitled "The Charismatic Structure of the Church," appeared in the review *Concilium*. [15] Its author was in the process of producing a major work on the Church, in which he would express the same positions in the same terms. [16] Küng cites Käsemann's article a number of times. [17] In doing so, he expresses reservations, stating that he cannot "agree with his conclusions," [18] although he does in fact adopt many of Käsemann's positions and often reproduces sentences from "Ministry and Community" word for word without bothering to place them in quotes; the unwary reader will think that these sentences come from the pen of H. Küng, whereas they in fact belong to E. Käsemann.

Küng disagrees with Käsemann on some points, stating, for example:

The Catholic theologian . . . will not . . . draw the same conclusions as many Protestant scholars did, that the pastoral letters are at best a kind of programme in contrast with the true Evangelium. . . . The Catholic interpretation demands that the New Testament must be taken seriously *kath' holou*, as a *whole*, including *all* the writings. [19]

Küng must, therefore, be credited with avoiding Käsemann's exclusivism on an important point. However, he follows him faithfully in everything else.

Thus, on his own account, and without giving any reference

or inserting quotation marks, he takes up Käsemann's statement that the concept of charism "exactly describes the essence of all ecclesial services and functions."[20] Further on, he draws on Käsemann to define charism thanks to a mixture of charism, vocation, and ministry.[21] In order to justify this mixture, Küng is satisfied with the arguments provided by Käsemann—and we have already noted the inadequacy of these.

Following in the steps of Käsemann, Küng uses very different notions of charisms in succession. When he wants to show that "charismata are therefore in no way limited to the extraordinary, [but] are rather altogether ordinary phenomena in the life of the Church," he broadens the notion of charism as much as possible, to the point of robbing it of any identifying characteristic. On the basis of 1 Corinthians 12:31—13:3, he states that "the highest charism" is "precisely the least exceptional and the most ordinary, love." It is true that the text of 1 Corinthians 12:31—13:3 allows for various different interpretations, and we can wonder whether Paul is here implicitly applying the term *charisma* to charity. However, if we are to be consistent, a choice must be made between two possibilities: either *charisma* must be taken in its general sense of "generous gift," in which case there is nothing to stop it from being applied to love, which is a gift of God; or *charisma* must be given the technical sense of a special grace granted to one Christian and not to another, in which case it cannot be applied to love, which is indispensable for any Christian life. In other words, we can and must say that love is a gift, but we cannot say that it is a charism. When Küng says that it is, he is falling prey to inconsistency and illogicality.

When he then insists on the existence of a very broad range of charisms, Küng meekly follows Käsemann, and sees charisms everywhere: circumcision and uncircumcision, slavery and freedom, marriage and celibacy, "even drinking and eating."[22] In this "infinite diversity," the concept of charism is watered down to such an extent that it loses any substance and it becomes difficult to see how the charisms could then provide the Church with a "structure."

In his struggle against three misunderstandings and his efforts to demonstrate that "the charismata are not primarily extraordinary, but common; . . . not of one kind, but manifold; . . . not limited to a special group of persons, but truly universal in the Church,"[23] Küng shows that he is especially anxious to limit the sphere of responsibility of the pastors of the Church as much as possible. And this is the use he makes of his two ways of understanding charisms.

In the first place, he uses the very broad concept and emphasizes that the charisms are not reserved to the hierarchy of the Church. It is difficult to recall who has ever held "that there is only one kind or class of charismata, for instance, those that are linked with ordination of one kind or another,"[24] but Küng is very anxious to counter this possible error, and, in order to quash it more definitively, he describes everything as a charism, from theological charity to the action of eating and drinking. In this way, the authorities of the Church are, so to speak, drowned in an ocean of charisms possessed by all the members of the faithful. Küng also feels the need to point out that "the infinite variety of charismata is not concentrated on a few people, such as community leaders."[25]

Toward the end of his article, another maneuver is executed, this time with the support of the carefully defined notion that the charism is "*God's call to the individual person in view of a specific ministry within the community, including the ability to perform this service.*"[26] According to this definition, a charism is a very specific personal gift, and is in close relationship with a specific ministry. Clearly we cannot say that love—or indeed drinking and eating—corresponds to this notion of charism! However, this is the concept that provides the foundation for Küng's thesis of a "charismatic structure" of the Church. He does not clearly explain what he means by this, but because each individual charism "gives one the ability" to perform a "specific ministry," we can understand that each Christian receives directly from God some ministry to be carried out within the Church, and that he has the right to perform this ministry without interference from the hierarchy.

This interpretation is confirmed by the fact that in his article, Küng refrains from citing the conciliar phrase indicating the role of pastors in the discernment of charisms and their properly ordered use. Küng asks the question: "How can unity be preserved in all the variety, and order in all this freedom, in this many-sided cosmos of charismata which fills the Church?" His answer is unilateral: "The answer (and there is no other) lies in the fact that it is the same Spirit who creates this unity and this order."[27] This amounts to ignoring the fact that the Spirit makes use of mediation, and that in the apostle Paul's long discussion on the spiritual gifts and the charisms (1 Cor. 12–14), he is certainly not satisfied with the fundamental answer given by Küng. Paul adds another, which is not in contradiction with the first, but that he considers is also necessary: that of apostolic authority. Paul makes a show of authority and has no hesitation over entering into details. He lays down clear and strict rules for the members of the Corinthian congregation who have charisms: no more than two or three of the members will speak "in tongues" in one gathering, and they will only do so on condition that there is someone present to interpret what they say; no more than two or three are to prophesy, and any prophecy must be followed by a discernment (1 Cor. 14:27–29). Paul is no dreamer. He certainly shows a deep respect for the gifts of the Spirit, but he is no less convinced that the body of Christ has a structure and that this structure must be respected. Otherwise, we cannot truly live in love, the gifts of the Spirit are distorted, and everything becomes delusion and confusion (1 Cor. 14:37).[28]

Can *Charisma* Be a Technical Term?

Anyone wishing to study the question of charisms from the exegetical viewpoint must first of all consider whether, apart from its general meaning of "generous gift," the Greek word *charisma* sometimes takes on a technical meaning in the New Testament texts. Opinions on this point differ, and this is only to be expected, inasmuch as there are too few texts available and none of these throws any conclusive light on the question. It is useless to look for a technical definition of *charisma* in the New Testament.

As we have already seen, in a number of texts, *charisma* clearly has its general meaning, and translating it as "charism" would distort the phrase. This is the case with Romans 5:15–16, where Paul points out the opposition between original sin and justification in Christ, and where he describes this justification as grace (*charis*), gift (*dōrea*), donation (*dōrēma*), and free gift (*charisma*): "But the *free gift* [*charisma*] is not like the trespass . . . ; for the judgment following one trespass brought condemnation, but the *free gift* following many trespasses brings justification." In this passage, Paul uses many terms formed with the suffix -ma (*paraptōma, dōrēma, krima, katakrima, dikaiōma*) in order to em-phasize the concrete aspect of the elements referred to. *Charisma* is therefore useful to him from this point of view, and it is impossible to see any restricted technical meaning here.

The same must be said with regard to Romans 6:23: "For the wages of sin is death, but the free gift of God is eternal life in Jesus Christ our Lord." Here *charisma* is contrasted with *opsonia*, the "wages" earned by sin. *Charisma* indicates the "free gift" of God in all its fullness, which is eternal life. The notion of a "special grace" for some specific activity is certainly in no way present here.

However, in some texts, *charisma* is applied to specific gifts, but these gifts are so special that our notion of charism cannot be applied to these either. In 2 Corinthians 1:10–11, Paul expresses the hope that God will deliver him from a danger of death, and he refers to this liberation as a *charisma*, to which the prayers of the Corinthians will have contributed. No translator is tempted to use the word "charism" here, for it is simply referring to a specific event that takes place due to the goodness of God. The text of Romans 1:11 also refers to a specific event—the hoped-for meet-ing between Paul and the Christians of Rome—but here *charisma* means a grace that can be passed on. "For I long to see you," writes the apostle, "that I may impart to you some *spiritual gift* [*cha-risma . . . pneumatikon*] to strengthen you. . . ." The expression is vague and does not enable us to define *charisma* with any preci-sion. Paul then goes on to expand on it (*touto de estin*) as a spiritual consolation: ". . . that we may be mutually encouraged by each other's faith, both yours and mine." In our way of speaking, a spiritual consolation does not correspond to the notion of a charism.

Other texts are so short or so lacking in precision that they do not permit any sure conclusion (Rom. 11:29; 1 Cor. 1:7). There are, in fact, very few texts that are really helpful for the discus-sion. These are 1 Corinthians 7:7; 12:4, 31; Romans 12:6; and 1 Peter 4:10–11 to which we can then compare 1 Timothy 4:14 and 2 Timothy 1:6. The concept of special grace is seen in these texts, that is, the notion of a gift that is granted to one Christian and not to another, because it is not necessary for everyone. This first characteristic is essential to our notion of charism and is clearly expressed in 1 Corinthians 7:7: "But each has his own special *charisma* that comes from God, one of one kind, and one of another." In 1 Corinthians 12:4–10, Paul returns to the same idea, illustrating it with a list:

> Now there are various *charismata,* but the same Spirit. . . . To each is given the manifestation of the Spirit for some useful purpose. To one is given through the Spirit the utterance of wisdom, and to another the utterance of knowledge, . . . to another . . . , to another. . . .

The metaphor of the body and members is then used in order to highlight the necessary diversity between the members that make up the one body. The same elements are found again in Romans 12. Romans 12:3 uses the same "each" of 1 Corinthians 7:7 and 12:7, 11, 18; in Romans 12:4–5, we find the same metaphor of the body and members as in 1 Corinthians 12:12–27; and Romans 12:6–8 describes the diversity of *charismata,* followed by a list of examples as in 1 Corinthians 12:8–10. The text of 1 Peter 4:10–11 is much shorter and gives only two examples—that of speaking and that of service—but it does contain the characteristic *hekastos* and the reference to the diversity of the gifts: "As each has received a *charisma,* employ it in the service of one another, as good stewards of God's varied grace. . . ."

In these texts, it seems possible to translate *charisma* as "charism," because the concept of charism has in fact been developed on their basis. However, such a translation is not obligatory and has the regular drawback of restricting the openness of the text. In any semantic study, we have to distinguish carefully between the strict meaning of a word and the qualities that have been added on by the context in which it is used. The word "building," for example, could be used throughout a study of religious architecture to indicate a church, but it does not follow that it actually means "church." N. Baumert has recently published a careful analysis of all the uses of the word *charisma* in the New Testament, and he comes to the conclusion that this word never has a technical meaning by itself.[29] In every case, it could be given its general sense of "free gift" (*Geschenk, Gabe*). This general meaning is then qualified by other words in the various contexts, but in a way that varies from one text to another, and these variations prove that no fixed concept of charism yet existed.

The only unvarying feature of the use of *charisma* in the New

Testament is that it always refers to divine gifts, and is never used for a gift given by one human person to another.[30] From this viewpoint, it is more specialized than the word *charis* itself, which is sometimes used in the New Testament to indicate a favor granted by a human being (Acts 24:27; 25:9). However, the rarity of the occurrences of *charisma* means that we cannot conclude whether this constant characteristic is significant or not; it could be simple coincidence, and the New Testament may not have offered any opportunity for a profane use of the word. Be that as it may, *charisma* is several times placed in explicit relationship with the relationship sense of *charis*, not only in Romans 5:15–17, where it is used to indicate the justification brought about by grace, but also when it indicates special gifts: according to Romans 12:6 Christians have "gifts [*charismata*] that differ according to the *grace* given to us," and 1 Peter 4:10–11 places the same diversity of *charismata* in relationship with the multiform aspects of God's grace.

Having said this, the divine origin of the special graces is not always indicated in the same way. When we speak of charisms today, we tend to emphasize their connection with the Holy Spirit. However, this relationship is expressed in neither Romans 12:3–8 nor 1 Peter 4:10–11, which confine themselves to speaking to God, as is also the case with 1 Corinthians 12:28. With regard to the relationship of charisms and the Spirit, we therefore cannot say that there is any constant New Testament teaching, although it must be admitted that a relationship between *charismata* and the Spirit is thrown into strong relief in 1 Corinthians 12:4, 7–11. The same observation applies to the gifts of prophecy and glossolalia in Acts (2:4; 10:44–47; 19:1–7).[31] The perspective of Mark 16:17, 20 is different, and this text makes no mention of the Holy Spirit; it attributes the accomplishment of "signs" to the risen Lord, and among these we find glossolalia and healings. The Letter to the Ephesians likewise attributes the distribution of "gifts" to the glorified Lord, although it does not refer to them as *charismata* (Eph. 4:7–11). It is clear that these different presentations are in no way contradictory. The author of Acts makes a sort of Trinitarian summary when he explains the "charismatic" phenomena of the day of Pentecost in the following terms: "Being therefore exalted at the right hand of God, and having received from the *Father* the promised *Holy Spirit*, he [*Jesus*] has poured out this which you see and hear" (Acts 2:33). The exegete must, however, respect the perspective of each text, and he must not hastily assume that they are equivalent.

The list of gifts given in 1 Corinthians 12:8–10 has sometimes been seen as a complete list of charisms. This was the position of St. Thomas, who raises the question in his *Summa Theologiae:* "Is the Apostle's division of freely bestowed grace [*gratia gratis data*] satisfactory?" He replies in the affirmative.[32] In his great commentary on 1 Corinthians, E.-B. Allo follows this opinion: "Here we have a complete list of 'charisms' (in the sense of *gratiae gratis datae*), in an intentional order."[33] Other exegetes express the opposite opinion,[34] and examination of the text shows that they are right, as does comparison with other texts. In 1 Corinthians 12:8–10, Paul is in no way concerned to provide a complete and correctly graded list of charisms; he is simply trying to emphasize the variety of the gifts of the Spirit, in order to counter the tendency of the Corinthians to attribute excessive importance to the gifts of prophecy and glossolalia. The apostle's intention is seen clearly in 1 Corinthians 14, but, prior to this, it is also seen in 1 Corinthians 12:8–10, where prophecy and glossolalia are relegated to the end of the list. The fact that Paul has no precise concept of "charism" in mind can be seen from various details, but particularly from the expression *charismata iamatōn* used in 12:9 and twice repeated (12:28, 30). Those exegetes who want to see charisms here, translate this expression as "the gift of healing."[35] However, this entails a twofold infidelity to the text, because Paul did not use the singular with the article ("the gift"), but used an indefinite plural ("gifts, blessings"), and he did not add the verb "to heal," but another noun ("of healings"). *Charismata iamatōn,* therefore, does not mean a capacity to bring about healing, but a certain number of healings generously granted by the Holy Spirit. Similarly, when he speaks of wisdom or knowledge in 12:8, Paul is not thinking of some habitual capacity, but simply of occasional inspirations: "To one, through the Spirit, is given an utterance of wisdom, and to another an utterance of knowledge. . . ."

The improvised and incomplete nature of the list given in 1 Corinthians 1:8–10 can also be seen from a comparison with other lists (1 Cor. 12:28; Rom. 12:6–8). A certain number of omissions and additions are immediately clear, as well as a difference in the order. Prophecy, for example moves from sixth place (1 Cor. 12:20) to second place (12:28), and then to first place

(Rom. 12:6). Extraordinary gifts (miracles, healings, glossolalia) mentioned in 1 Corinthians 12:8–10 and 12:28 are not found in the list given in Romans 12:6–8, whereas some gifts not found in 1 Corinthians 12:8–10 appear in 12:28 ("helpers, administrators") and others in Romans 12:6–8 ("he who comforts," "he who contributes," "he who presides," "he who performs acts of mercy"). The forms vary, sometimes appearing as an abstract noun ("prophecy"), sometimes as a title ("prophets"), and sometimes as a participle (literally "the comforting one," "the contributing one"). The perspective is never the same: as we have seen, in 1 Corinthians 12:8–10, Paul seems to be presenting the "gifts" as occasional blessings; in 12:28, he no longer speaks of gifts of the Spirit, but of positions established by God in the Church, and he defines a hierarchy ("God has appointed in the Church first apostles, second prophets, third . . ."); in Romans 12:6–8, he describes the way in which the "gifts" are to be exercised ("prophecy, in proportion to our faith; . . . he who contributes, in liberality," and so forth). The very diversity of viewpoints demonstrates that for Paul, *charisma* does not have a precise technical meaning, and that no fixed concept of charism is to be found in these texts. We can simply note that the extraordinary gifts are mentioned only in 1 Corinthians 12—14, and that here they are the subject of serious warnings (13:1–3). The later texts (Rom. 12:6–8; 1 Tim. 4:14; 1 Tim. 1:6; 1 Pet. 4:10–11 to which we can add Eph. 4:11) only speak of ordinary gifts, which are of constant usefulness for the life of the Christian community. This observation provides a good grounding for the position of the Council, which, while not denying the existence of "ordinary" charisms, draws attention to the usefulness of the "more simple and widely diffused" charisms (*LG* 12).

Is a Charism a Grace for the Good of Others?

In order to define *gratiae gratis datae*, St. Thomas says that they are oriented to the good of others. As we have seen, the Council followed this orientation. St. Thomas cites 1 Corinthians 12:7 in support of his definition: "Unicuique autem datur manifestatio Spiritus ad utilitatem," and completes this sentence by adding, "scilicet aliorum."[36] The Council uses the same text to define the "special graces" that are charisms (LG 12). But how should we view this interpretation?

Translators most often give 1 Corinthians 12:7 the same sense as St. Thomas. The *pros to sympheron* of Paul is translated as "for the *common* good" (RSV). The expression used by Paul does not in fact say this much: it simply speaks of usefulness, without any indication of whether this usefulness is to the individual or the community. In Matthew 5:29–30, *sympherei* is qualified in the sense of personal usefulness: ". . . it is advantageous *for you.*" In Hebrews 12:20, an expression similar to that of 1 Corinthians 12:7, *epi to sympheron,* is applied according to the context to personal sanctification. It is true that most of the gifts mentioned in 1 Corinthians 12:8–10 are of use to others: healings bring health to the sick, miracies kindle or strengthen faith. However, in the case of glossolalia, this orientation cannot be maintained, and the explanations given by Paul are clearly opposed to such a view. The apostle dictates that "one who speaks in a tongue speaks not to men but to God" (1 Cor. 14:2), and compares the usefulness of glossolalia, which is only individual, with that of prophecy, which is for the community: "He who speaks in a tongue edifies himself, but he who prophesies edifies the church" (14:4). For this reason, Paul does not hesitate to forbid the use of glossolalia in the church gatherings when there is nobody present who is able to provide an interpretation: "But if there is no one to interpret, let each of them keep silence in the church and speak to himself and to God" (14:28). This does not mean that Paul is in any way denying that glossolalia is a gift (*charisma*) of the Spirit—a gift that he himself has received, and that he exercises abundantly (14:18). Even so, he attributes its usefulness only for personal prayer.[37] This very clear position means that we cannot give the phrase in 1 Corinthians 12:7 the meaning attributed to it in many translations and commentaries, adding to the expression *pros to sympheron* a qualification (*scilicet aliorum*) that is not found in the text. The usefulness aimed at by the "gifts" of the Spirit may very well be that of the person who receives them.[38] This means that in Paul's mind, there is no necessary link between *charisma* and *diakonia*. A *diakonia* (service or ministry) is always directly oriented to the good of others, whereas this is not always the case with a *charisma*.[39]

Having said this, it is still possible to distinguish among the many gifts of grace a series of gifts that are characterized by their usefulness to the Church, and to reserve the title "charism" for these. This is what the Council does, following a theological tradition. This specialized use is not found in St. Paul, but does correspond to an orientation that he recommends. In 1 Corinthians 14, he shows how concerned he is to regulate the use of the gifts within Christian gatherings on the basis of their usefulness to the community. And the same orientation is expressed in 1 Peter 4:10, which exhorts Christians to place the gift (*charisma*) they have received at the service of one another.

However, in this connection, it is wise to avoid a unilateral view that would see charisms as gifts oriented exclusively to the good of others, in other words, as being without any advantage for the person who possesses them. This would mean accepting the view that God reduces the person in question to the simple role of an instrument, whereas God also has the good of the person himself in view. For example, the grace of the apostolate is obviously given for the good of those to whom the apostle is sent; however, it is also a grace for the apostle himself, for whom it is an opportunity for personal union with Christ in love. Communicating a gift of God to others is always an opportunity for advancing in love. We are therefore justified in criticizing any definition of charisms in which they are seen as gifts oriented exclusively to the good of others.

Nevertheless, certain New Testament texts do show that a separation between community and personal benefit is possible, although such a separation does not correspond to the will of God. A very harsh text of Matthew describes a case in which charisms have been exercised and been helpful to others, although the person possessing the charism was not himself placed in true personal relationship with Christ: "On that day many will say to me, 'Lord, Lord, did we not prophesy in your name, and cast out demons in your name, and do many mighty works in your name?' And then will I declare to them, 'I never knew you; depart from me, you evildoers.' " (Mt. 7:22–23). Paul himself shows that he is aware of this danger, when he writes: ". . . I pommel my body and subdue it, lest after preaching to others I myself should be disqualified" (1 Cor. 9:27). In his eulogy of charity, he describes the situation of a person who has the most sensational gifts but to whom they are of no use because he lacks love (1 Cor. 13:1–3). Such a situation is obviously not normal, but it is presented as possible. Further, the remark in 1 Corinthians 12:21 about the eye that cannot tell the hand, "I have no need of you," indicates that the charisms of knowledge entail a temptation to pride and to a lack of charity. This is also confirmed in the famous saying: "Knowledge puffs up, but love builds up" (1 Cor. 8:1).

We should, therefore, distinguish between graces that sanctify the person directly and gifts that do not necessarily sanctify. A good number of these gifts can be helpful for the spiritual progress of other people without contributing to the progress of the person concerned, through his own fault. And in this sense, we can speak of charisms as special gifts granted "for the good of others." Even so, this definition is not really satisfactory, because it opens the door to certain false ideas.

Charisms and Institution

What can be concluded from all the foregoing with regard to the question of the relationship between charisms and institution in the Church? Is it correct, as Käsemann states, that in the letters of Paul, *charisma* is used to express "a critical posture over against other . . . views about the relation between the ministerial office and the community"?[40] The answer must be that it is not, in the first place because it is impossible to demonstrate that *charisma* has a technical meaning for Paul, and in the second place because Paul never uses *charisma* in opposition to institution. Far from putting charisms on one side and positions of authority on the other, Paul declares in the same breath that within the Church God has set up a hierarchy of offices and multiple gifts (1 Cor. 12:28). Instead of expressing some opposition between inspiration and institution, whenever the occasion arises, he describes the action of the one God, "who inspires everything in everyone" (12:6) the presence of the one Lord (12:5), and the activity of the one Spirit (12:4, 11).

In 1 Corinthians 12:12–30 and Romans 12:3–8, Paul emphasizes the need for the various gifts—let us say "charisms"—to be properly placed within the body of the Church. His way of speaking with authority to those who possess charisms shows very clearly that he does not view charisms as gifts of the Spirit that grant the right to some autonomous ministry in the Church. There is no serious basis for crediting the apostle Paul with the idea of a purely charismatic community, and a great many exegetes have recognized this. In concluding his article "Charisma," in the *Theologisches Wörterbuch zum Neuen Testament*, without beating about the bush, H. Conzelmann states that "the famous distinction between charismatics and authorities in the Church is untenable,"[41] and E. Cothenet observes that "placing charism in opposition to hierarchy means abandoning the very Pauline categories that they are in fact claiming to support."[42]

The New Testament writings as a whole tend rather to confirm that the Church possesses an institutional structure that is also charismatic, although it does not hold a monopoly on charisms. The foundation and model of this structure is found in the institution of the Twelve, whom Jesus chose "through the Holy Spirit" (Acts 1:2; Lk. 6:12–13), and who were "filled with the Holy Spirit" (Acts 2:4) with a view to the performance of their mission. The Church is, therefore, not some great administrative machine, but is "the body of Christ" (1 Cor. 12:27; Rom. 12:5; Eph. 4:12), which has its life from the Holy Spirit (1 Cor. 12:13; Rom. 5:5). The concept of an ordained ministry that is transmitted as a gift of God (*charisma*) under the inspiration of the Spirit (*dia prophēteias*) with a human liturgical action (*meta epitheseōs tōn cheirōn tou presbytēriou*) (1 Tim. 4:14) is perfectly consistent with this doctrine. The context of this passage from 1 Timothy shows that simple human capacities are not enough for the proper fulfillment of the demands of a position of responsibility in the Church. Personal obedience to the Spirit is needed, and a normal consequence of such obedience is a positive attitude toward the varied gifts of God and charisms, which appear "among the faithful of every rank," as the Council states (*LG* 12). St. Paul acts as an example of this positive attitude, even for those gifts that cause difficulties in the community at Corinth.

However, the apostle also shows that a positive attitude does not mean a paralysis of authority in the presence of charismatic manifestations. The pastors of the Church have the task of watching over the good of the whole community, and this task includes the right and duty to set clear limits so as to avoid disorder and confusion (1 Cor. 14:26–30). Paul expresses the certainty that, far from being incompatible with the gifts of the faithful, these limitations imposed by apostolic authority have the same divine origin and must be accepted in the same way: "If any one thinks

that he is a prophet, or inspired by the Spirit, he should acknowledge that what I am writing to you is a command of the Lord" (1
Cor. 14:37). This revealing statement clearly shows the close
union in the Church between inspiration and institution. Tensions can always, of course, arise, but the idea of resolving these
by suppressing either of the two aspects would mean giving in to
a destructive delusion.

Conclusion

Careful exegesis of the New Testament writings leads us to two
observations, one negative, the other positive.

The negative observation is that these texts do not offer any
clear teaching on what are today referred to as "charisms." They
do not say what people sometimes want them to say. It is not
possible to demonstrate that the word *charisma* has a technical
sense in the New Testament, and it is in particular impossible to
give a clear definition of the relationship between *charismata* and
ministries, and between *charismata* and hierarchy on the basis of
the New Testament texts. We must neither confuse these different aspects of the reality of the Church, nor separate them, still
less place them in opposition to one another. Nor is the relationship between the *charismata* and their usefulness for others a
decisive element. Christians should place their *charismata* at the
service of others, but this orientation does not as such help
define the *charismata* themselves.

The positive observation is that the New Testament testifies
to the great variety of God's gifts, and the word *charisma* is used
in some significant texts (1 Cor. 7:7; 12:4–10; Rom. 12:3–8; 1
Pet. 4:10–11) to indicate this variety, and particularly to emphasize the fact that the gifts vary with the people concerned. Apart
from the gifts that are essential for any Christian life, such as
justification by faith, shared hope, and living in charity, there
are gifts that are distributed differently. Some believers are called
to be apostles and pastors, and others are not; some have the gift
of "prophecy," in other words, inspiration, and others do not;
some "speak in tongues," and others do not; some have special
gifts for organization, teaching, or caring for the sick or the poor,
and so on. St. Paul uses the metaphor of the body and its members in order to show that this variety is certainly not contrary to

unity, but is in fact necessary to it: "For the body does not consist of one member but of many" (1 Cor. 12:14).

Taking this as a starting point, we can work out a concept of "charism." Such a theological development is possible and legitimate. However, we must bear clearly in mind the fact that this specialized notion is a later development, and that its relationship to the New Testament data will not necessarily be consistently close. The New Testament gives direct support to the distinction between "very remarkable" charisms (glossolalia, miracles of various types) and "more simple and widely diffused" charisms (gifts of teaching, and various types of dedication or service). It quite understandably does not speak of the charisms of founders of religious orders or of the charisms of different religious institutions. It is the history of the Church that leads the Council to apply the words of Romans 12:5–8 and 1 Corinthians 12:4 to the latter (PC 8).[43] Reference to the New Testament remains the norm, not in the sense of an obstacle to development, but in that of dynamic inspiration accompanied by discernment.

Translated from the French by Leslie Wearne.

Notes

1. In the Catholic Church, the birth of the "charismatic movement" was a postconciliar event. It took place in 1967 at the Catholic University of Pittsburgh, Pennsylvania. However, it took place in dependence on the pentecostal movement, which had its origins in 1901 in a Methodist community in Kansas, and which had developed in the face of strong opposition. For further details, cf. Francis A. Sullivan, *Charisms and Charismatic Renewal. A Biblical and Theological Study* (Ann Arbor, MI, 1982), 52.

2. There is no known occurrence of *charisma* in classical Greek, and it is only found at a later period. The word is very rare outside the New Testament and Christian writings. In the New Testament, it occurs 17 times: 16 times in the Pauline letters (6 times in Romans, 7 times in 1 Corinthians, and once each in 2 Corinthians, 1 Timothy, and 2 Timothy), and once in 1 Peter 4:10.

3. In the theology of the Greek Church, the word *charisma* is not restricted to a precise technical sense, but can be applied to the Holy Spirit, baptism, the remission of sins, the Eucharist, chastity, alms giving, etc. Cf. the word *charisma* in the *Patristic Greek Lexicon* of Lampe.

4. Romans 12:6: "Habentes autem donationes [*charismata*] secundum gratiam quae data est nobis differentes. . . ." Ephesians 4:7: "Unicuique autem nostrum data est gratia secundum mensuram donationis [*dōreas*] Christi. . . ." 1 Peter 4:10: "Unusquisque sicut accepit gratiam [*charisma*]. . . ."

5. Thus, in the Italian translation of the *Summa Theologiae*, the section dealing with *gratiae gratis datae* (II/II, qq. 171–178) is entitled "Carismi" and the expression *gratia gratis data* is translated therein as *grazia carismatica* or *carisma*. The expression *charismata spiritualia* is used by St. Thomas in *Op. 57 in festo Corporis Christi*. Cf. V. Garcia Manzanedo, *Carisma-ministerio en el Concilio Vaticano Segundo* (Madrid, 1982), 129.

6. The debate took place in October 1963; cf. *AS*, II/3, 175–178.

7. The French translation (Paris, 1965) does not translate *charismata* here as *charismes* but as *grâces*.

8. E. Käsemann, "Amt und Gemeinde in Neuen Testament," a paper given in 1949, but not published until 1960 in the collection *Exegetische Versuche und Besinnungen*, I (Gottingen, 1960), 109–134. The English translation, "Ministry and Community in the New Testament," was published during the Council in *Essays on New Testament Themes*, Studies in Biblical Theology 41 (London, 1964), 63–94. (Translator's note: This English translation has been slightly modified on a few minor points of terminology.)

9. "Ministry and Community in the New Testament," 63–64: "While there is no real equivalent in the New Testament for our present-day conception of 'office,' there is a concept in Pauline and sub-Pauline theology which describes in a theologically exact and comprehensive way the essence and scope of every ecclesiastical ministry and function—namely, the concept charisma." The phrase cited indicates an opposition between the present notion of institutional ministry ("office")—a notion that in Käsemann's opinion does not exist in the New Testament—and the presumably noninstitutionalized ministries (or services) and functions, the essence and scope of which are expressed in the New Testament by the term *charisma*.

10. *Ibid.*, 64: ". . . it was Paul who first used it in a technical sense and who indeed introduced it to the vocabulary of theology."

11. *Ibid.*, 65.

12. *Ibid.*, 68–69, 73–74.

13. One detail reveals the lack of attention Käsemann sometimes pays to the texts. In his article, he places the charisms in relationship with Christ Cosmocrator (twice on p. 68, and once each on pp. 71, 72, and 73). Now this title is never applied to Christ in the New Testament. Its only occurrence (Eph. 6:12) is to indicate demons, and it corresponds to the expression "the prince of this world" (Jn 12:31;

14:30; 16:11) and other similar expressions (1 Cor. 2:6; 2 Cor. 4:4; Eph. 2:2). The Bible uses a different title for God: Pantocrator (2 Cor. 6:18; Rev. 1:8; etc.).

14. It must even so be observed that Käsemann does not envisage this Church as an assembly given over to the extravagances of every type of inspiration. On the contrary, he constantly warns against "enthusiasm."

15. H. Küng, "The Charismatic Structure of the Church," *Concilium: Ecumenism 1* (1965), 23–33. (Translator's note: This English translation has been slightly altered at a few points.)

16. H. Küng, *Die Kirche* (Freiburg im Breisgau, 1967); *The Church* (London, 1967), 179–191, 401–403.

17. Küng, "The Charismatic Structure of the Church," 33, note 7, presents Käsemann's article as "the most penetrating study of the biblical data" of the Pauline theology of charisms. He then refers to Käsemann, in note 8, to indicate that he has borrowed his list of charisms, and again in note 12 with regard to the "basic importance of this concept of charisma in St. Paul's ecclesiology."

18. *Ibid.*, 33, note 7.

19. *Ibid.*, 26.

20. *Ibid.*, 30; Käsemann, "Ministry and Community in the New Testament," 63–64 (cited above, note 9).

21. Küng, "The Charismatic Structure of the Church," 31; Käsemann, "Ministry and Community in the New Testament," 65 (cited above, note 11).

22. Küng, "The Charismatic Structure of the Church," 29.

23. *Ibid.*, 30; this sentence summarizes the three misunderstandings and the answers Küng gives to these in the preceding pages.

24. *Ibid.*, 28.

25. *Ibid.*, 29.

26. *Ibid.*, 31 (italics in the original).

27. *Ibid.*, 31.

28. Cf. P. Grelot, "La structure ministérielle de l'Eglise d'après saint Paul. À propos de 'l'Église' de H. Küng," *Istina*, 15–16 (1970–71), 389–424.

29. N. Baumert, "Charisma und Amt bei Paulus," in A. Vanhoye (ed.), *L'Apôtre Paul. Personalité, style et conception du ministère*, BETL 73 (Leuven, 1986), 203–228.

30. Outside the New Testament, the meaning of "gift" is witnessed to, for example, in this expression from a papyrus: "dothenta hyper charismaton nauton" ("objects given as gifts to sailors"); cited by F. Preisigke and E. Kiessling, *Wörterbuch des griechischen Papyrusurkunden* (Berlin, 1925–1944), *sub verbo*.

31. Prophecy and glossolalia are referred to more than once in 1

Corinthians 12 in the discussion of the *charismata*. However, it should be remembered that in the Acts of the Apostles, they are not described with this term. The word *charisma* never appears either in Acts or in the gospels.

32. *Summa Theologiae*, I/II, q. 111, a. 4.

33. E.-B. Allo, *Saint Paul. Première épître aux Corinthiens*, EB (Paris, 1934), 319.

34. C.K. Barrett, *A Commentary on the First Epistle to the Corinthians* (London, 1986), 286; H. Conzelmann, *2 Corinthians* (Philadelphia, 1975), 109: "The enumeration in vv. 8–10 is unsystematic."

35. This is the translation of the Jerusalem Bible.

36. I/II, q. 111, a. 1.

37. The perspective of Acts is different: glossolalia is of use to the Church. However, Acts cannot be used to provide a definition of Paul's position as contrary to what he himself expressly states.

38. This is recognized by Sullivan, *Charisms and Charismatic Renewal*, 30; as also by Baumert, "Charisma und Amt bei Paulus," 220.

39. As we have seen above, Käsemann confused *charisma* and *diakonia*, stating that *charisma* "describes . . . the essence and scope of every ecclesiastical ministry and function" (see above, note 9). Such confusion cannot be justified.

40. Käsemann, "Ministry and Community in the New Testament," 64.

41. *TWNT*, IX, 396.

42. "Prophétisme," *DBSup*, VIII, 1302. Other exegetes who hold the same position are mentioned by A. Lemaire, "The ministries in the New Testament. Recent Research," *BTB*, 3 (1973), 138.

43. Cf. M. Augé et al., *Carisma e Istituzione. Lo Spirito interroga i religiosi* (Rome, 1983).

CHAPTER 17

Mary in Postconciliar Theology

Stefano De Fiores, S.M.M.

Summary

After an appreciation of Chapter VIII of *Lumen gentium* as a successful summary of Church doctrine with regard to Mary, the elements and causes of the mariological crisis in the immediate postconciliar period are considered. The stage of the eclipse of mariology is progressively overcome in a threefold manner: the conciliar path of *renewal* leads to a return of mariology to the theological fold and to a reopening of the subject of Mary in ecumenical terms; the complementary path of *recovery* fills the pneumatological vacuum of mariology and reassesses popular marian piety; and the hitherto unknown path of *cultural encounter* not only reflects on Mary in a perspective of theological esthetics and theodrama, but offers examples of mariology that are acculturated, or based on the feminine, and starts on the delicate process of revision of the marian dogmas. The future of mariology is bound up with the deeper study and appreciation of the function of Mary in the mystery of Christ, but also with opening up discussion on Mary to the contemporary world and to its various cultures, in such a way as to highlight the salvific and anthropological significance of the mother of Jesus.

For mariology, as for other sectors, the Second Vatican Council represents both a *point of arrival* and above all a *starting point,* inasmuch as it marks the convergence and fusion of manualistic mariology as centered on Mary in the mystery of Christ, and the

469

innovative currents (biblical, liturgical, patristic, kerygmatic, anthropological, and ecumenical) that rediscover Mary in the mystery of the Church.[1] The history of the laborious drafting process
of Chapter VIII of *Lumen gentium* can thus be seen as

> . . . the microhistory of mariology of the first half of the
> twentieth century: the four years of drafting of the marian text
> reproduce the development of mariological thought in the
> forty years between 1920 and 1960, in which the systematic
> christological perspective alternated with the ecclesiological
> perspective as proposed by the innovative movements.[2]

At the same time the Council transformed contemporary theology into "a vast workshop in the center of which an imposing
building fully under restoration rises up,"[3] involving mariology
too, and setting it in motion as regards methodological approach
and content.

In view of the importance of Chapter VIII of *Lumen gentium*
from the viewpoint of the magisterium, theological quality, and
actual influence, it represents a watershed, and we must take it as
our starting point for an understanding of the direction of mariological trends in the postconciliar period.

The Perspective of Salvation History
as Chosen by the Second Vatican Council:
Mary in the Mystery of Christ and of the Church (1964)

The history of Chapter VIII of *Lumen gentium* has been described in great detail by a number of authors,[4] but here we are
concerned to note the slow but sure maturation of the Council
Fathers toward a new way of approaching the subject of the
mother of Jesus. The movement from the first text, which was
entitled *De Beata Virgine matre Dei et matre hominum* and was
distributed on 23 November 1962, to the definitive one, which
was entitled *De Beata Maria Virgine Deipara in mysterio Christi et
Ecclesiae* and was approved almost unanimously on 21 November
1964, was basically due to the historic vote that took place on 29
October 1963. Voting on this chapter was preceded by addresses
by Cardinals Rufino Santos and Franz König, who respectively

presented the arguments for and against the insertion of the marian schema into the treatise on the Church, and by a small majority, it approved the insertion (*placet*, 1,114; *non placet*, 1,074). This conciliar choice, which would be consolidated in the course of the debate on the chapter dedicated to Mary, represents "a notable event for marian theology,"[5] inasmuch as it is a formal expression of the tendency to view ecclesiology as an appropriate context in which to treat the mother of our Lord, thus marking an end to the isolated mariology[6] that had become established in the posttridentine period.

Although the new text, which was inserted into the Constitution on the Church as its eighth and last chapter, bears the marks of the alternating influence of the approaches represented by its chief drafters, G. Philips and C. Balic, it testifies to the clear evolution toward a marian approach that is essentially biblical, christocentric, ecclesiological, ecumenical, and pastoral.[7] Underlying the whole approach, and unifying it, is the perspective of salvation history:

> The person, the mission and the privileges of Mary, and also the devotion offered to her, are not considered in themselves or in relation to her dignity as mother of God. Rather, the whole treatment is developed and expanded in the broader framework of the history of salvation. The perspective of salvation is the true new theological perspective. . . .[8]

The Council's adoption of the perspective of salvation history represents a movement away from a deductive type of mariology that was centered on Mary and her privileges, had a tendency to foster marian titles and dogmas, and was closed to dialogue with our brothers of the Reform tradition. Vatican II did not really intend carrying out any speculative advance, because it did not wish "to decide those questions which the work of theologians has not yet fully clarified" (*LG* 54), and it did not proclaim any marian dogma, despite the fact that in the preparatory stages, 300 bishops had postulated the dogmatic definition of the universal mediation of Mary. The conciliar approach to mariological reflection penetrates more deeply when it presents the Virgin not in isolation, but in her functionality within the overall context of the divine plan of salvation; the very title of *Theotókos* is viewed primarily as a "function" and only secondarily as a "dignity" ("high office and dignity"—*LG* 53). Another distinguishing feature of Chapter VIII of *Lumen gentium* is its ecumenical concern, which leads it to adopt the biblical perspective as the basis for discussion on Mary (*LG* 55–59), to ignore or relativize the term "mediatrix," which is considered ambiguous or false by Protestants, preferring to translate its more authentic content with "salutary influence" or "function as mother" (*LG* 60), and to take care not to use maximalistic terms or other expressions that could lead to misunderstandings of Catholic doctrine concerning Mary.

Overall evaluation of the work of the Second Vatican Council in the sphere of mariology varies according to the different viewpoints of those examining it.

From the viewpoint of its doctrinal value, Chapter VIII of *Lumen gentium* is seen as "a document of the Church," a text that the Church "has made her own and proposes to all—bishops, theologians, and simple members of the faithful—as an official expression of her faith."[9] The importance of this conciliar chapter cannot be underrated if we observe, with Paul VI, that "this is the first time . . . that an ecumenical Council has presented such a broad-ranging synthesis of Catholic doctrine on the place that the Blessed Virgin Mary holds in the mystery of Christ and of the Church."[10] The authority of Chapter VIII is derived from the fact that it is part of a Dogmatic Constitution, which is given this title because it sets forth truths of the faith that are already unquestionably held in the Catholic Church, and thus "it is to be seen as an act of the extraordinary magisterium, and as such takes on universal value that is doctrinally binding for the whole Church."[11] John Paul II can quite legitimately state that "Chapter VIII of *Lumen gentium* is in a certain sense a *magna charta* of the mariology of our era."[12] In this text, we find

> . . . a theological synthesis of the surest doctrine concerning the Virgin Mary, as studied in the light of revelation, oriented by a cultural and religious awareness relevant to modern days, and reexamined in the perspective of the history of salvation, so that the whole Church might have a perfect picture of the whole mystery of Mary.[13]

From the viewpoint of the historical evolution of mariology, the marian chapter of the Council can be seen as "a point of arrival that provides a criticism and corrective to a certain way of

doing mariology that can be conventionally called "the posttridentine manner.' "[14] The voting on 29 October 1963 "took on
the significance of a spiritual watershed,"[15] marking the moving
away from an isolated mariology and the breaking down of speculative structures that were either extraneous or were out of proportion to the overall information revealed:

> When the Council placed its declarations on Mary in a con-
> text of the Church and of salvation history, *it eliminated the
> perspective of an autonomous marian discourse* and any mariologi-
> cal isolation. From the time of the Council onwards,
> mariology could no longer be a catalogue of marian truths or
> privileges, because Mary belongs to the history of salvation
> and has a functional character with regard to the mystery of
> Christ and of the Church. This clear orientation means a
> radical change in direction and methodology; from now on it
> will no longer be possible to discuss mariology in isolation, as
> in the posttridentine approach, which, with Suarez (1585)
> and Nigido (1602), produced a separated "mariology" that
> came down to our days.[16]

From the hermeneutical viewpoint, it must be recognized that
Chapter VIII of *Lumen gentium* bears the marks of the historical
and cultural moment at which the text was produced, and therefore also of its conditioning. It tried to "combine opposing mariological orientations,"[17] and can thus be seen as

> . . . an attempt at conciliation between the traditional cur-
> rent that wanted a return to its origins, with a view to the
> cause of ecumenism. . . . Although it has normative value as
> the expression of such a broad and authoritative consensus, it
> is not written in a normative style. It does not intend crystalliz-
> ing the faith and piety of the faithful, but simply ensuring that
> what is essential is safeguarded while research and ecumenical
> dialogue continue.[18]

Because of its thorny history—and, going back further, because of its theological and cultural grounding—Chapter VIII
has limitations that have been observed by the various commentators. H. Mühlen criticized the effects of the pneumatological
vacuum of conciliar theology in attributing to Mary, without the

necessary clarification, "identical functions to those that according to Scripture are attributed above all and univocally to the Holy Spirit."[19] It is equally easy to notice the absence of a patrological theology that brings out all the consequences of the relationship of Mary to the Father. The most glaring omission in the main marian text of the Second Vatican Council is of an anthropological and cultural nature, inasmuch as it does not refer to the problems of daily life and the legitimate aspirations of men and women of our days, the relationship between mariology and anthropology, and its encounter with the various cultures so as to make the figure of Mary meaningful. This omission has an effect both on the conciliar instruction based on the negative criterion of "not leading the separated brethren or any others whatsoever into error" (*LG* 67) when speaking of Mary, and also on the conservative-sounding recommendations (that ignore any renewal or creative impulse) with regard to devotional practices and cult images (cf. *LG* 67).

The Apophatic and Parenthetic Period: The Crisis in Mariology (1964–1974)

Despite the spur provided by the positive conciliar presentation of Mary and devotion to her, the immediate postconciliar period saw what had been referred to as "the decade without Mary":

> . . . it is surprising that the conciliar innovation found no answering echo in the Church. Mariology and marian devotion are disturbingly close to nil. The choral praise of the mother of God in the days of Pius XII has been succeeded by a deep silence.[20]

Apart from the verbal exaggerations of this description of the postconciliar period, which ignores both the various marian publications and also the continuation of devotion to the Virgin in the majority of the faithful, the atrophying and stagnating effect of Vatican II on mariological development cannot be denied. Indeed, in 1970, a good number of mariologists from various cultural areas jointly recognized the crisis situation of mariology and marian devotion.[21] While Pastor Richard Molard could note that the Council "acted as a great damper on mariology,"[22] the

Catholic R. Laurentin had already declared that "the marian movement is finished"[23] and that in 1972, we were observing a "slow and above all relative recession, but one that goes hand in hand with a rise in the quality level" in the field of publications on the Virgin.[24] When we consider the absence of any reference to Mary either in ecumenical dialogue or in the large treatises on christology and ecclesiology,[25] we cannot deny that there has been a tendency to place her in parenthesis and marginalize her.

The various authors consider different factors to have been decisive in bringing about this apophatic and parenthetic phase in mariology; however, they do agree on the influence of Vatican II with its choices and omissions.

The Council in fact rightly gave priority to the most vital problems in the contemporary crisis of the faith, proclaiming a "hierarchy of truths." In this listing, pride of place is given to God, Christ, the Church, and man; interest in Mary, therefore, tends to be pushed into the background, because her mystery does not appear to occupy a primary position.[26] In particular, "the establishment of the new ecclesiocentric mariology led to the temporary collapse of mariology as such" and to an "absorbing of mariology into ecclesiology."[27]

A. Müller sees the causes of a weakening in marian interest in the "second illuminism" or the assimilation of critical thought that led Vatican II to oppose "the expression of a Christianity that was above all ritual, sentimental, introverted, impregnated with popular piety, and supported by a theology that was conceptually very rigid but that even so was ingenuously realistic." With the Council,

> . . . the ritualistic tone, with its religious manifestations of veneration, gave place to an ethics characterized by "the Sermon on the Mount and the preaching of the kingdom of God." In ritual in the strict sense, the liturgical aspect is highlighted, with popular devotions receiving less emphasis.[28]

Apart from this falloff in affective religiosity, W. Beinert notes a deeper cause: the new theological way of thinking, which explores the sources according to the historical-critical method, and moves from a mariology of privileges to a more functional and ecclesial view of Mary.[29] While from the viewpoint of content a certain type of exegesis and theology throws doubt on the

traditional fact of the virginity of Mary, doubt is also thrown—
also for hermeneutical reasons—on the legitimacy of the mariological construction itself:

> From the methodological viewpoint, mariology has suffered a
> great many consequences: the tendency to submit magisterial
> pronouncements to a hermeneutical reading that relativizes
> their significance seems to rock one of the most basic elements
> of the entire mariological structure; the fashion for "demytholo-
> gization" entails a risk of reducing a good part of the "Mary-
> event" to the status of symbol; the acclaimed need to place man
> at the basis and conclusion of the theological task gives rise to a
> shift of interest toward subjects and sectors in which the figure
> of Mary of Nazareth seems to have no meaning. [30]

H. Mühlen remains within the sphere of ecclesiology *ad intra*
when he states that "the deep crisis in mariology . . . is a pneumatological crisis," which proposes a reorientation of people's
attention from Mary to the Holy Spirit. [31] With greater intuition,
Paul VI seeks the root of the crisis in the cultural sphere, in the
"discrepancy existing between some aspects of this devotion [to
the Mother of the Lord] and modern anthropological discoveries
and the profound changes which have occurred in the psycho-
sociological field in which modern man lives and works." [32] The
Council is certainly not responsible for this discrepancy, because
the latter existed prior to the Council; indeed, "the split between
the gospel and culture is without a doubt the drama of our
time." [33] Vatican II resolved the "marian problem" very well by
offering a synthesis with regard to Mary that was capable of
reestablishing the consensus of the various movements within
the Church. It must still be regretted that the spirit of *Gaudium et
spes,* which was oriented toward dialogue with the contemporary
world, did not enter into Chapter VIII of *Lumen gentium.* The
time had not yet come for this dialogue with a view to inculturation—something that would later be seen as one of the primary tasks of postconciliar theology.

Because the marian crisis has cultural roots, it is clearly not
enough to seek a balanced solution of the requirements of the
various movements within the churches. Undoubtedly, "the ultimate reason for the overcoming of the crisis in marian piety is to
be found in the respect that the Church owes to the free and wise

plan of God."[34] The *sensus fidei* that accepts the biblical revelation, and the mission and person of the Virgin within it, and lives this on a deep level in its daily experience, is indispensable and cannot be replaced by any acculturation. Even so, if mariology is to overcome the "rejection phenomenon" and the "lack of meaning" of Mary for our times,[35] it must open itself to the just perspectives, requirements, and acquisitions of culture, and express itself in a way that is suited to it. Thus, a new mariology is needed—one that is faithful to God and to man, vivified by a creative impulse, and integrated not only into the present ecclesial universe, but also into the symbolic and cultural one.

The Conciliar Path of Renewal

Postconciliar mariology does not move along some independent path, but takes its place within the framework of the great theological trends, thus overcoming its period of eclipse. As for theology, three paths are opened up for mariology, corresponding to three successive stages. These paths sometimes cross one another and sometimes move forward side by side. They are those of *renewal, recovery,* and *cultural encounter.*[36]

The path of renewal was inaugurated by the Second Vatican Council, which, with its spirit of renewal, led the way to an overall review of the life of the Church, especially as regards the liturgy, canon law, ecumenism, and theology, under the prudent leadership of Paul VI, who "immediately demonstrated an intuitive and precise grasp of the fact that one cannot turn back."[37] Theology in particular has been renewed in its methods and content, returning to its biblical foundations, reinterpreting texts of the Fathers and of the magisterium, and reworking the various treatises on the basis of a new ecclesial awareness.[38]

The mariological renewal was neither immediate nor universal, but has moved forward laboriously and in a relatively disjointed manner.

A "Reentry" of Mariology into Theology?[39]

The hoped-for "reentry" of mariology into theology, from which it broke away in 1602 with P. Nigido,[40] has only taken place to a small degree. In the postconciliar period, there have been at least thirteen completely separate treatises on mariology,[41] and out of eight courses on theology, five devote a separate volume to Mary, which is divided from the other treatises and has no organic link with them,[42] whereas only three include the subject of Mary within the context of christology, ecclesiology, and anthropology.[43] Two great shortcomings are very clear to see in all this treatise production: not one of the postconciliar mariological manuals adopts the methodology indicated by the Council in *Optatum totius* 16; and even when they are part of a series on theology or one of its branches, not one of them is structurally and logically linked to the whole theological *corpus*.[44]

The sole exception is represented by K. Rahner's *Foundations of Christian Faith*, where two pages are devoted to the "new" marian dogmas in the section entitled "Christianity as Church."

In this context, Rahner is concerned to show that the developments in marian dogma (the Immaculate Conception and the Assumption) are not some "addition to the real and ultimate substance of Christianity," nor something that "would basically contradict the real substance of the faith."[45]

In a positive perspective, the author applies to recent marian definitions the postulate (that is established elsewhere) of presenting every individual statement "in its coherence both with the one totality of faith and with the original and unifying center of the reality of faith"[46]:

> . . . the "new" Marian dogmas . . . have to be seen within the context of the total understanding of Christian faith. They can be understood correctly only if a person really believes in what we call the Incarnation of the eternal Logos himself in our flesh, and counts this as part of Christianity's very existence.[47]

Rahner relates understanding of Mary and of mariological developments to the initial—but decisive and definitive—moment in the history of salvation, in other words, the incarnation, where "God communicates himself and man accepts the divine self-communication, and they thus become irrevocably one single individual (that is, Jesus Christ)."[48] And Mary, the believing mother of Christ, is linked in a unique way precisely to this fundamental event:

From this perspective it has to be said immediately and according to the witness of scripture that Mary is not simply and only an individual episode in a biography of Jesus which has no theological interest, but rather that she is someone who has an explicit historical role in this history.[49]

For Rahner, Mary cannot be considered either solely from a biological viewpoint, or in an individual and privatistic perspective. The open and responsible attitude she assumed at the annunciation with her assent of faith gives her a formal place in the history of salvation. It must, therefore, be stated

> . . . that Mary was not only the mother of Jesus in a biological sense. Rather Mary is seen as someone who assumes a quite definite and indeed unique function in this official and public history of salvation.[50]

While this maternal function of Mary plays a decisive role in the salvation of mankind, it constitutes her own salvation in a supreme manner inasmuch as it represents full acceptance of Christ in body and spirit. In other words, "Mary is someone who has been redeemed radically. . . . Mary is . . . the highest and the most radical instance of the realization of salvation. . . ."[51]

Rahner relates the dogma of the Immaculate Conception to this principle, as explanation of the special redemption of Mary. Further, by uniting the perspective of original sin to that of a contemporaneous and more intense redemption of mankind on the part of Christ, Rahner thinks that he is smoothing the way to ecumenical acceptance of the marian dogma:

> Take the case of an Evangelical Christian today who says that he sees a great problem with original sin itself if today more than ever, and quite biblically at that, we understand Adam's sin to have been transcended and encompassed by God's salvific will and by the redemption of Christ. Consequently we have to say that we are always sanctified and redeemed insofar as we have our origins in Christ, just as we are sinners without the Spirit insofar as we regard ourselves as having our origins in Adam. From this perspective there really is no special difficulty with the statement that the mother of the Son was conceived and willed from the beginning by God's absolute salvific will as someone who was to receive salvation in faith and love.[52]

The application of the principle of the perfect redemption of Mary in the context of the assumption is equally detailed but clear. Rahner does not go into the question of the source of this belief within the Church; nor is his intention that of defending the timeliness of the definition of the dogma of the assumption. Rather, he is concerned with the aspect of theological coherence and consistency that he sees as fulfilled in it:

> The Assumption of the Blessed Virgin, body and soul, into heaven says nothing else about Mary but what we also profess about ourselves in an article of faith in the Apostles' Creed: the resurrection of the body and eternal life. . . . But in any case it is at least a possible opinion in Evangelical theology that the fulfillment of the single and whole person does not necessarily take place on a temporal axis which is our own, but rather that it takes place for a person with his death and in his own eschatology. If, then, as Catholics we assert that Mary has reached fulfillment because of her quite special place in the history of salvation and because we profess that she is the most radically successful instance of redemption, then at least from a theological point of view it is impossible to see why this dogma has to contradict the basic substance of Christianity.[53]

Despite its brevity, *Foundations of Christian Faith* provides a valid attempt to integrate Mary within theology, as involved at the same time in anthropology, christology, protology, ecclesiology, and eschatology.

With a View to an Ecclesiological Understanding of Mary

The first axis of postconciliar theological reflection is "the subject of the renewal of the Church as proposed by the Second Vatican Council."[54] Strange to say, the patristic teaching on Mary as "the type of the Church," which was used in Chapter VIII of *Lumen gentium,* is completely absent from the various treatises on ecclesiology and in the articles on "The Church" in various dictionaries.[55] This means an impoverishment of the Church, which is deprived of one of its specific and highly evocative images; it also leads to a mutilation of mariology, which is deprived of its ecclesial dimension and therefore runs the risk of being reduced to a marginal and unconnected chapter.

The timeliness of an in-depth comparison between the Church and Mary was pointed out by O. Semmelroth at the International Theological Congress that took place in Rome in 1966. Semmelroth had previously worked out a system of mariology that took as its starting point Mary as the type of the Church.[56] For this theologian, the union between ecclesiology and mariology eliminates in both the twofold danger of *mysticism* (or monophysitism) and *naturalism*:

> Whoever venerates Mary as the personal type of the Church cannot identify the Church with Christ himself. Indeed Mary, and thus the Church, is intimately united to Christ, although they can never be identified with him. . . . Whoever venerates Mary also avoids ecclesiological naturalism, since in all her mysteries the Blessed Virgin prefigures the grace of Christ, through which the Church becomes the Bride of Christ, within whose maternal womb individuals are children of grace.[57]

Similarly, the fact that Mary points toward the Church enables us to avoid both the *mariological mysticism* that tends not to see Mary as a member of the redeemed Church, and also the *mariological naturalism* that forgets that she has been raised up to the position of a daughter of God through grace.[58]

The relations between ecclesiology and mariology are explained by C. Journet in *L'Eglise du Verbe incarné* (three volumes: 1940, 1962, and 1969), which was judged by Y.M.-J. Congar to be "the most profound dogmatic work to have been written on the Church in our century."[59] Journet takes as his starting point the grace of Christ, which is communicated to the Virgin and to the Church, and thus discovers a "deep relationship, a necessary involvement, and a mutual inclusion"[60] between the two. It follows, in an approximative manner, that "mariology and ecclesiology can be seen as two parallel treatises," although, more strictly speaking, it must be said that "mariology is a part of ecclesiology—the part that studies the Church in its highest and never equalled point."[61]

Mary is thus within the Church not as a shared fulfillment, but as its privileged part: the Church "finds in the Virgin its highest success. . . . Mary is the purest and most intense fulfillment of the Church."[62] To put it simply, "Mary is the prototype of the Church," a title that signifies

> . . . that, within the Church, Mary is more mother than the Church, more bride than the Church, and, through her exemption from original sin, more virgin than the Church. . . . Mary is mother, bride and virgin *before* the Church and *for* the Church; *in* her above all and *through* her, the Church is mother, bride and virgin.[63]

There is a corollary of immense ecclesiological significance: "The whole Church is marian," in the sense that "Mary is interiorized in the Church, to whom she communicates her spirit." She is indeed "the intrinsic modalizing form, . . . the model, the type of the Church," so that imitation of Mary is necessary, because "the more the Church resembles the Virgin, the more it becomes bride."[64]

Journet continues along this line of argument, and draws on the Orthodox theologian V. Lossky, calling Mary "the mystical personification of the Church," and explaining this description in relation to the Spirit.[65]

The typological relationship that unites Mary and the Church is accepted and studied in greater depth by authors such as H.U. von Balthasar and L. Bouyer.[66] It will find its fruitful soil in the history of salvation, which places the Church and its archetype Mary not only within the ancient people of God but also within the Trinitarian mystery,[67] where the exaltation of Mary-and-Church is kept within the limits of the created and does not usurp the divine glory.

As regards the reciprocity between Mary and Church, it is clear that any unilateral or constricting analogy must be avoided. Nor can the image of Mary be fixed for all time, because it is actualized in every age, drawing on the inexhaustible sources of the biblical and ecclesial tradition, on the experience of faith, and on history and culture. Nor again can Mary be seen as the only icon of the Church, because it has other archetypes (starting with the supreme one of Chirst) and other hermeneutical spectrums (including the historical one) in which to discover its reality and vocation.[68]

The following are among the postconciliar tasks of ecclesiology: "reflection on the understanding of Mary in an ecclesiological key, and of the Church in a mariological key"[69]; clarifying marian typology, with particular attention to the use of metaphor[70]; and carrying out an in-depth study of the title "Mater Ecclesiae," which was discussed at the Council and proclaimed by Paul VI.[71]

Mary in the Postconciliar Christological Approach

From such intense investigation of the Church that there was even fear of ecclesiocentrism, postconciliar theology soon moved to christology, which is still the fulcrum of reflection on the Church.[72]

Here another undeniable observation must be made: an overwhelming majority of the vast number of books on Jesus seems to ignore the fact that he is the son of Mary, or at least does not attribute any importance to this element, despite the fact that, as M. Bordoni observes, mariology and christology are so closely interconnected that one draws benefit from the other.[73] Indeed, as can be seen from an examination of contemporary christology, "where there is the greatest christological richness, there we find the greatest mariological richness, and vice versa."[74]

1. *The "metadogmatic" christology* of E. Schillebeeckx and H. Küng, who set out to study Christ "by moving beyond the dogma of the Church" or "without dogmatic bias,"[75] interprets the virginal conception of Jesus as "a functional christological statement," which indicates the messianic dignity of the Son of God, but does not transmit anything in the way of biology or physical fact.

While the theologian from Nijmegen eliminates Mary as virgin from his formula of faith, the theologian from Tubingen also takes his distance from the other marian dogmas. Küng criticizes the title "Mother of God," saying that it has no biblical basis, that it was historically approved at Ephesus because of "Cyril of Alexandria's successful manipulation of the Council" under the influence of the people and of the mediterranean religion of the Great Mother, and that it is theologically ambiguous inasmuch as it "might imply a Monophysite conception of divine sonship and incarnation, hypostasizing God."[76]

As regards the most recent dogmas (those of the Immaculate Conception and the Assumption), Küng is convinced that they should be subjected to an honest evaluation, on the basis of which we can discern the basic intentions that we may possibly share and the concrete formulations that are to be rejected.[77]

Küng's critique of mariology eventually accepts only a small nucleus formed of two statements that have their basis in the Bible:

> Mary is the mother of Jesus. She is a human being and not a heavenly being. As a human being and as a mother, she is witness of his true humanity, but also of his origin from God. . . . Mary is the example and model of Christian faith. Her faith, which feels the sword of scandal, dissension and contradiction, and is required in face of the cross, according to Luke, . . . provides a pattern for Christian faith as a whole.[78]

A. Amato reaches the following conclusion as regards this archaizing reductionism:

> The metadogmatic perspective is revealed to be in fact a metaecclesial perspective, if not indeed an antiecclesial one, impoverishing both theological consideration of Mary and also her exemplary aspects as authentically human and Christian. And is it really true that in order to enrich the image of women we must impoverish the biblical and ecclesial image of Mary?[79]

2. *The "transcendental" christology* of K. Rahner, on the other hand, is anchored in the "creative acceptance of tradition" (J.-B. Metz) and thus in the marian dogmas, which the theologian relates to the Theotókos and thus to christological dogma:

> Mary is only intelligible in terms of Christ. If someone does not hold with the Catholic faith that the Word of God became man in Adam's flesh so that the world might be taken up redemptively into the life of God, he can have no understanding of Catholic dogma about Mary either. It may indeed be said that a sense of Marian dogmas is an indication of whether Christological dogma is being taken really seriously; or whether it is being regarded (consciously or unconsciously) merely as a rather outmoded, problematic, mythological expression of the fact that in Jesus (who is basically just a religious man) we undoubtedly feel God (here again a cipher for an unexpressed mystery) particu-

larly close to us. No, this Jesus Christ, born of Mary in Bethlehem, is at once, as One and Indissoluble, true man and true
Word, consubstantial with the Father. And so Mary is in truth
the Mother of God. It is only to someone who truly and unre-
servedly confesses this that the Catholic Church can continue
to speak meaningfully about her other Marian dogmas.[80]

When Rahner brings discussion of Mary back to transcendental christology, which sees Christ as the definitive fulfillment of
man's movement of transcendence toward God, he highlights
the theological function of Mary in the incarnation. Her acceptance of the will of God, which makes her mother in a personal
and not only a biological sense, not only constitutes "an event in
the public and official history of salvation," but also represents—
and supremely so—the role of man in accepting redemption:
"Since Mary stands at that point in salvation history at which
through her freedom the world's salvation takes place definitively
and irrevocably as God's act, she is most perfectly redeemed."[81]

In its turn, Rahner's mariology, with its details and explanations that range from the title of Theotókos to the dogma of
the Assumption, can act as a criterion for discerning authentic
christology.

3. *Latin-American christology* attributes new value to the figure
of the Virgin. At its meeting at Puebla in 1979, the Conference
of Latin-American Bishops carried out an evaluation of the
christologies of liberation elaborated by J. Sobrino and L. Boff,
and referred to the Christ of popular religion, who is the Christ
of the Tradition of the Church, true God and true man, who
must not be

. . . distorted, factionalized, or ideologized . . . either by
turning him into a politician, a leader, a revolutionary, or a
simple prophet on the one hand; or, on the other, by restricting him, the Lord of history, to the merely private realm.[82]

Christ is a "living presence" within the Church, leading people "to their liberation." Nor is this a reductive liberation, inasmuch as it

. . . is gradually being realized in history, in our personal
history and that of our peoples. It takes in all the different

dimensions of life: the social, the political, the economic, the cultural, and all their interrelationships.[83]

Although she is not inserted directly into the context of the truths concerning Christ, but into that of the Church and man, Mary is always linked to the Son as the foundation of her motherhood and her status as example:

She becomes the Mother of God, of the historical Christ, with her *fiat* at the Annunciation, when the Holy Spirit overshadowed her. She is the Mother of the Church because she is the Mother of Christ, the Head of the mystical body. She is also our Mother. . . . Mary shows quite clearly that Christ does not annul the creativity of those who follow him. She is Christ's partner, who develops all her human capabilities and responsibilities to the point where she becomes the new Eve alongside the new Adam. By virtue of her freely proffered cooperation in Christ's new covenant, Mary is the protagonist of history alongside him. . . . Her whole life is one of complete communion with her Son. . . . Her divine maternity led her to total self-surrender. It was a clear-eyed, generous gift that was consistently maintained.[84]

Mary belongs "to the intimate identity" of the peoples of Latin America, and, with Christ the Liberator, she stands at the side of those who want to cooperate with the liberating energies of mankind and society. With the spirituality of the *Magnificat*, which is "the culmination of the spirituality of Yahweh's poor," the Virgin

. . . presents herself as the model for all those . . . who do not passively accept the adverse circumstances of personal and social life and who are not victims of "alienation" . . . , but who instead join with her in proclaiming that God is the "avenger of the lowly" and will, if need be, depose "the mighty from their thrones."[85]

4. *Orthodox christologies* reserve a privileged place for the Theotókos, and this is of very deep significance. In the sophiological current of Soloviov, Bulgakov, and Florensky, the mother of the Lord is the first ontological point of contact of the Logos and

the Holy Spirit, and thus possesses a "cosmic power" and a "radiant sophianity" to purify the world.[86]

In the ecclesial and neopatristic christologies of Evdokimov and Lossky too, the Virgin is seen as consanguinous with Christ and as the "mystical center" of the Church.[87] Orthodoxy sees mariology as a chapter of christology, or, rather, states with N. Nissiotis that "there is no Christian theology without continuous reference to the person and role of the Virgin Mary in the history of salvation."[88]

Two ancient titles attributed to Mary—*Theotókos* and *Panaghía*—ensure her proper position in the divine economy in relation to Christ and the Holy Spirit:

> The two terms point to the fundamental truth that one can think, speak and write, or one can meditate, worship and pray with Mary at the centre of the Church community only when one thinks of her always as in inseparable unity with the Christ-event in the Spirit and the ecclesial gathering as communion of saints and the sanctified people of God.[89]

The Theotókos does not allow any detachment of the discussion of Mary from the incarnation, inasmuch as she not only gives a body to the word, but is "fully involved because a distinctive and elect person sharing . . . in the hypostasis of the Logos." This cooperation is articulated through reference to the early christological controversies and through the title of Theotókos, without which we fall into the old errors:

> The insistence of early Christian theology on using only the term *Theotókos* is important and is a result of the appropriate understanding of Christology, i.e., in terms of the union in one person of the two natures, divine and human. Either one affirms by faith that this mystery occurred fully right from the beginning or one risks all kinds of deviation: dyophysitism (separating the two natures), monophysitism (accepting only one in the birth of Christ), or docetism (endorsing the idea of an "appearance-like," but not the happening of the event itself). Behind this insistence there is the firm and self-evident conviction of faith in regard to the incarnation of the Logos that one cannot speak of nature (*physis*) outside a concrete person (*hypostasis*) without falling into an abstraction or nega-

tion of one of the two (in *Christotókos*, the divine nature) and
thereby destroying the full understanding of the incarnation.[90]

Fidelity to the Council of Ephesus is the guarantee of Orthodox christology, so that acceptance of the Theotókos is not optional but necessary:

> The third Ecumenical Council of Ephesus (431) used a Chris-
> tological term that preexisted in the Eastern patristic tradi-
> tion, and so placed Mariology within Christology for ever. In
> the right Christology we affirm what happens in the incarna-
> tion of the Logos, i.e., that "He who was from the beginning
> as the eternal Logos, the Son of God took flesh from the
> Virgin *Theotókos* Maria and become fully man also" (Athan-
> asius, *PG*, 26, 383) and therefore "if one does not accept and
> recognize the Holy Maria as the *Theotókos* one is without a
> sense of divinity (in the incarnation)" (Gregory of Nazianzus,
> *PG*, 37, 177).[91]

This leads to a corollary of great importance: that "the *Theotókos* stands within the right Christology as the proof and the
guardian of the reality and fullness of the divine-human hypostatic union."[92]

Having noted "an organic link between Mary and the eucharistic event," and also the anthropological typology of the Theotókos, Nissiotis concludes with the following positive statement:

> It is clear what great importance the word about Mary has for
> Church life, theology and especially for Christian anthropol-
> ogy today. It becomes imperative to speak today of a Mario-
> logical anthropology if we are to deal Christologically with the
> place of the virgin Mary in the economy of salvation and of
> her motherhood in the Church.[93]

Our overview of christology has shown that there has been a
certain degree of recovery of Mary with regard to the Christ
event. Future mariological reflection will not be able to avoid
taking account of certain vital points of contemporary christology, and drawing new orientations from these. While "a return
to the earthly Jesus is fruitful and necessary today,"[94] equally to
be hoped for is a rising mariology that takes place from below and

that restores to Mary her historical, human, and creaturely dimension. If present-day judgment on Chalcedon has had to accept the "inalienable significance" of its christological formula, this does not mean that the latter is necessarily exhaustive and cannot be developed along narrative, soteriological, and eschatological lines, involving also the Theotókos. The real character of the incarnation and its kenotic aspect make it possible to overcome certain reservations of traditional mariology, seeing in Mary the pilgrim of faith, who is subject at least as much as Christ to temptations and above all to cultural conditioning. Similarly, mariological conclusions must be drawn both from the fresh presentation of christocentrism, and also from the various soteriological interpretations of our times.[95]

Mary in Ecumenical Dialogue

The question of Mary has not yet been officially faced by the mixed commissions, although such discussion has been strongly recommended from various quarters, and at Nairobi in 1975, the World Council of Churches envisaged a future study "on the significance of the Virgin Mary in the Church."[96] Far from being relegated to a marginal position in ecumenical dialogue or postponed until the future, the subject of Mary has in the meantime been seriously considered by individual theologians belonging to different churches at a number of the ecumenical meetings at which joint declarations are worked out, and in publications of considerable interest that help discussions move forward. The most important contributions in this field concern the new approach to dialogue on Mary and some elements of dogma and worship.

1. *The Relaxation of Rigidity and the Ecumenical Reopening of Discussion on Mary.* The preconciliar atmosphere of closure and defense of one's own confessional positions with regard to the mother of Jesus is slowly giving way to an atmosphere of authentic dialogue in a shared search.

On the Catholic side, an increasing need is felt for "a critical study of marian theology and its history"[97]—indeed, for a "catharsis" of mariology,[98] which must free itself of maximalistic rigidity, give up its structural independence, reduce the "degenerative hypertrophy" of devotionalism, submit marian dogmas to honest criticism, and steer clear of any parallelism between Mary and

Christ.[99] As regards the procedure for dialogue, the steps to be taken together can be listed as follows: to start with the points on which there is agreement, to become aware of the changed ecumenical climate, to establish the relationship between devotion and doctrine, to return to the sources, and to respect the hierarchy of values.[100]

Among the Evangelicals, alongside certain expressions of resistance to dialogue,[101] there have been some contributions based on a new approach to Mary that is both more critical and deeper.

At a meeting of the Protestant Faculties of Theology, which took place in Rome in 1981, Jean-Paul Gabus would draw attention to "the eclipse of the marian theme in Protestant theology" since the seventeenth century. He suggests two explanatory causes: the development of the *historical-critical method*, which, when applied to the biblical texts, strips the virginal conception of its basis; and *puritanism*, which suppresses any reference to sexuality and to the female archetype. He states that present-day Protestant theology should shake off its twofold scientific-liberal and puritanical heritage in order to "reopen the marian file."[102]

Having come to the defense of a "theological poetics" that would give space to the fundamental imagery of male-female and to a concrete anthropology (as Choan-Song Song does in *Third-Eye Theology*), Gabus examines the disputed mariological questions and makes a notable effort to move in the direction of a solution.

The title *Mother of God* was not viewed with a kindly eye by Calvin because it can lead people into error. Even so, the thinking of the Reformer is opposed to Nestòrius and in line with Ephesus, and will be more acceptable in the measure in which we believe in "the corporality of revelation" (W. Stählin) and in God as truly made man. *Virginity, Immaculate Conception,* and *Assumption* can be recovered through archetypes and symbols of purity, holiness, and nuptiality, not retrospectively, but in an eschatological perspective that looks forward to the new reality that is still being accomplished. As regards *human cooperation in the work of salvation*, Gabus rejects the idea of the self-glorification of man and of the "parity" between divine initiative and human response. Even so, he wonders why the Protestant theology of salvation should not include "the free response of man, the 'Yes' of Mary and of every believer to the offer of divine grace." And as regards *Mary's intercession*, he says that

. . . to the extent that the Catholic dialogue partner agrees to confirm the unique mediation of Christ, and the Protestant partner the reality of a communion between visible Church and invisible Church, dialogue and mutual understanding have become possible.[103]

Lastly, while refusing any mariolatry and autonomous mariology, Gabus fully agrees with "the criteria for a healthy mariology" proposed by *Marialis cultus:* the essentially christological character, the pneumatological dimension, the ecclesiological significance, the importance of biblical emphasis, the integration of praise of Mary into liturgical renewal, ecumenical concern, attention to the contemporary social conditions of life, the elimination of risks (credulity, sterile sentimentalism, narrowness of mind, exaggerations as to content, the appeal to legendary elements).[104]

In the interesting document *Maria,* produced by the Evangelical-Lutheran German Churches, we would recall the statement that "Mary is not only Catholic but also Evangelical" and that "for the Christian faith Mary performs an illuminating role and not a normative one. Mary can illustrate Christian existence but is not its foundation."[105]

A great effort at understanding has been carried out by Pastor W. Borowsky, who discerns three areas for ecumenical dialogue on Mary: *common ground* in which all parties agree is that of the biblical figure of Mary, the believing, suffering, serving mother of the Lord; the *area of pluralism*—in other words, that of unity in diversity—also includes the last two marian dogmas, which do not necessarily have any biblical standing but are something more that Catholics claim to know, and do not threaten unity; and, lastly, the *area of disagreement* covers the titles given to Mary in parallel with Christ, and devotion offered to her. In order to work together, the disagreement must be gradually brought into the area of pluralism, and pluralism into the area of unity.[106]

While G. Maron holds that Protestant theology performs an important role in the search for "the true image of the mother of our Lord, hidden behind the luxuriant overflowing mass of a mythical 'mariology,' "[107] J. Moltmann points out three types of prejudice that would compromise mariology and prevent Mary "from being a figure in the liberating history of the gospel of Christ": (1) the link with *celibacy* when this is not lived out evangelically in the mixed community of believers; (2) the connection between mariology and *politics*, which transforms the apocalyptic Mary into a symbol of struggle against reform or attack against the established order; and (3) the link between mariology and *popular religion*, which has made of marian devotion "a storehouse of the most varied needs and religious aspirations," and of the *sensus fidelium*, the criterion of new mariological dogmas. [108]

Moltmann's observations challenge Catholics to reconsider their own assumptions (and not only those of the Evangelicals) and to work out a mariological approach that is *biblical* (expressing the "true Mary"), *ecclesial* (in the context of other believing women), *pneumatological* (oriented toward the presence of the Spirit), and above all *christological:* "Without Christ, no Mary; and without christology, no mariology!"

M. Thurian sets himself outside any rigid patterns with his further movement in the direction of an encounter with the person of Jesus and with that of his mother, who "lives today in the communion of saints"—an encounter that is to take place through contemplation and liturgy, and not only through exegesis and theology. Having highlighted the links between Scripture and Tradition ("Scripture alone" is not the same as "Scripture isolated"), and between grace and freedom, Thurian distinguishes five forms of marian prayer (memory, recollection, acclamation, request for intercession, direct request), placing the last two within the sphere of Christian freedom. [109]

Some important ecumenical progress with regard to mariology can be seen on the part of the Anglicans. Anglican theologians play an active role in the Ecumenical Society of the Blessed Virgin Mary, which was founded in 1967 by the Catholic layman Martin Gillet. Articles and addresses submitted to this association have been published in a thick volume. [110] J. de Satgé's book, *Mary and the Christian Gospel,* is noteworthy for its serious approach and ecumenical openness; the author writes that it was "written in an attempt to find an attitude towards the Lord's mother which will include the essentials of Catholic teaching about her, and at the same time do justice to the central impulses of evangelical Christianity." [111]

The Final Report of the Anglican-Roman Catholic Commission (1982) contains a page on Mary. This notes the Anglican difficulties with regard to the last two Marian dogmas, but also expresses considerable agreement in other areas:

We agree that there can be but one mediator between God and man, Jesus Christ, and reject any interpretation of the role of Mary which obscures this affirmation. We agree in recognizing that Christian understanding of Mary is insepara- bly linked with the doctrines of Christ and of the Church. We agree in recognizing the grace and unique vocation of Mary, Mother of God Incarnate (*Theotókos*), in observing her festi- vals, and in according her honour in the communion of saints. We agree that she was prepared by divine grace to be the mother of the Redeemer, by whom she herself was redeemed and received into glory. We further agree in recognizing in Mary a model of holiness, obedience and faith for all Chris- tians. We accept that it is possible to regard her as a prophetic figure of the Church of God before as well as after the Incarna- tion. Nevertheless the dogmas of the Immaculate Conception and the Assumption raise a special problem for those Angli- cans who do not consider that the precise definitions given by these dogmas are sufficiently supported by Scripture.[112]

2. *Ecumenical Meeting Points with Regard to Mary.* Together with various subjects that are considered every now and then, the thorny questions of the *mediation* of Mary and of *devotion* to her are the object of debate and understanding between the representatives of different confessions.

The subject of *mediation* reappeared in 1974 in a basic text that the Calvinist H. Chavannes proposed for ecumenical discus- sion.[113] In the analysis of this theologian, the different interpreta- tions given by Catholics and Protestants to the *unus mediator* springs from "different metaphysical attitudes." For Catholics, these are constituted by the doctrine of participation, according to which there is both radical difference and also similarity be- tween God and the world; Mary can share in the one unique mediation of Christ in an analogous sense, that is, with a shared, dependent mediation that is oriented to that of the sole Media- tor. On the other hand, the metaphysical presupposition of Prot- estants is nominalism, which reduces the analogy to a distinction of reason, placing God and man on the same plane of action, and thus in competition, because "if cooperation between man and God belongs to the same order it is clear that God's action within man diminishes the latter's part." In practice, Chavannes con- cludes, we should return to the thomistic concept of participation in order to overcome the disagreement on conceptions of the relationship between man and God.

Chavannes' text received the formal agreement of the Catholic S.C. Napiórkowski in the name of the creeds of early Protestantism (*Confessio augustana, Liber concordiae,* etc.), which accept a salvific mediation in things and in persons, but "in Christo."[114] R. Laurentin also accepts Chavannes' proposal, recognizing that the key to the present disagreements and confusion is to be found in the different philosophical presuppositions and in the questioning of "the philosophy of participation." However, he does not align himself with the notion of "mediation," which "has many meanings, and is ambiguous and full of traps, so that it must be used with the utmost circumspection."[115]

While the Anglican E.L. Mascall states that he is "in virtually full agreement" with the views of Chavannes,[116] certain reservations or radical criticisms are voiced on the Protestant side.[117]

The subject of mediation remains open to further study.[118]

As regards the place of Mary in Christian worship, the most valuable contribution is offered by the International Mariological Congresses of Zaragosa (1979) and Malta (1983). The first deals with the problem of terminology, bearing in mind "the psychological difficulties . . . which many Christians experience . . . in particular over the use of the word 'cult' (worship or devotion) in relation to created persons."[119] Thus, the twenty-two signatories of the ecumenical declaration of Zaragosa prefer to speak of "the facts in which our worshipping attitude reveals itself" (No. 5). As regards the fundamental attitudes of praise, imitation, veneration, and invocation of Mary, the text is nuanced but generally positive:

1. We recognize together that all Christian *praise* is praise of God and of Jesus Christ. If we praise the saints, and, in particular, if we praise Mary as the Mother of God, our praise is essentially to the glory of God, who "in glorifying the saints, crowns his own gifts" (Latin Preface of the Saints). This praise is expressed in the liturgy, in hymns, and in the life of the faithful. In relation to Mary, it corresponds to the words of the Magnificat: "Henceforth all generations will call me blessed." The practice of the praise of the Mother of God has become an urgent question for all Christians.

2. We recognize the importance of *imitation* as an element which is common to the traditions of our different churches concerning Mary. As we find particularly in the Magnificat, Mary is seen as the humble and most holy servant of the will of God. This imitation involves, in a special way, the Gospel understanding of poverty before God. The spiritual attitude of Mary was her total response to the Word of God, and, thus, she became the temple of the Holy Spirit who accomplished in her the Incarnation of the Son of God (Lk. 1:35–38).

3. This *veneration* of the Mother of God, which is lived in our churches in different ways already mentioned, is never the adoration which is due to God alone. The distinction made by the Second Council of Nicaea, that is, between the adoration (or worship) of God and the veneration of the saints (*proskunesis-latreutiké/proskunesis-timetiké*) remains vital for all of us.

4. The problem of the *invocation* and *intercession* of Mary was examined afresh in this congress. We have considered it against the background of the communion of saints. As a Christian can and should pray for others, we believe that the saints, who have already entered into the fullness which is in Christ (amongst whom Mary holds the first place), can and do pray for us sinners who are still suffering and struggling on earth. The one and unique mediation of Jesus Christ is in nothing affected by this. The meaning of the direct invocation of the saints who are alive in God, an invocation which is not practiced in all the churches, remains to be elucidated.[120]

At Malta, a further step was taken toward a marian piety inserted into communion with the heavenly liturgy as centered on the Lamb. Within the communion of the saints in heaven, Mary continues the prayer she prayed in the upper room while waiting for Pentecost (Acts 1:14). If "praying to Mary" clashes with the "Apologia" of the *Confessio augustana,* it is possible to "pray with Mary," as the ecumenical declaration of Malta states in its central passage:

Mary the Mother of God has a place within the Communion of Saints. It is precisely the relationship to Christ which gives her a singular role in the Communion of Saints, a role that is of christological origin. Further, the prayer of Mary for us should be seen in the context of that worship of the entire heavenly Church described in the Apocalypse, to which the Church on earth wishes to unite itself in its own corporate prayer. Mary prays with the Church, as once she prayed in expectation of Pentecost (Acts 1:14). There is no reason preventing us, even with our confessional differences, from uniting our prayer to God in the Spirit with the prayer of the heavenly liturgy, and especially with the prayer of the Mother of God.[121]

It is to be hoped that these ecumenical agreements on Mary will move toward official approval and popular acceptance.

The Complementary Path of Recovery

During the postcontestational period of a return to the private sector or the reconstruction of its group identity, in the Church too there is a tendency to turn to the past in order to recover some vital elements that were not sufficiently developed by the Second Vatican Council. And the pneumatological dimension of mariology, and popular piety, must be included among these elements.

The Pneumatological Dimension of Mariology

The Second Vatican Council undoubtedly contains "a precious, if incomplete, series of orientations" on the relationship between Mary and the Holy Spirit, although it "did not give details of this relationship in any special paragraph."[122]

Two particular cases of pneumatological shortcomings with regard to the pneumatological dimension can be seen in Chapter VIII of *Lumen gentium.* Number 62 attributes to Mary the titles of "Advocate, Helper, Benefactress, and Mediatrix," without adding, as it did for Christ, that these are to be understood "in such a way that it neither takes away from nor adds anything to the dignity and efficacy" of the Holy Spirit.[123] Then, in number 68, which presents Mary in an eschatological perspective, there is not "even the briefest of references to the Holy Spirit."[124]

In the postconciliar period, various theologians filled the pneumatological vacuum that also involved mariology, considering the relationship between Mary and the Paraclete in greater depth.

Among the first to work along these lines was H. Mühlen. In the second edition (1967) of his *Una mystica persona,* he adds a broad study on Mary and the mediation of the Spirit, in which he sets out "to prove that the Trinitarian-pneumatological horizon of ecclesiology must apply also to mariology."[125]

Although Mühlen accepts that Mary is to be considered "the normative subjectivity of the Church in her response as bride to Christ," he takes his distance from the position of von Balthasar with regard to the subject of the Church:

> We would thus not say that the Church, which proceeds from Christ, has its "personal center" in Mary; Mary is, rather, the historical *beginning* of the Church as bride of Christ—and this beginning also has an "exemplary" power, since it is the highest and matchless point. We should instead indicate that the personal center, in which the whole Church (including Mary as "act-of-us") has its unceasing source, is in fact the Holy Spirit.[126]

Mühlen goes on to discuss the legitimacy of the "mediation" of the Spirit, which, although derived from Christ, has a biblical basis in the formulae *en* and *diá* as referred to the Spirit (Eph. 2:18; 4:30; 1 Cor. 12:4–11). The mediation of Mary cannot, however, be compared with that of the Spirit, which has a character of immediacy. Further, all exaggeration will be avoided if we realize that mariology "must move through the crucible of pneumatology in such a way as to be freed of those 'theologoumenons' that could give the impression that Mary is *de facto* placed in the position and function of the Holy Spirit."[127]

Among these "theologoumenons," we must include the "treasury of grace" conceived of by Clement VI as a mass of graces entrusted to Peter or distributed by Mary. This is a "quantitative" concept of declining scholasticism, which tended to forget that "the Holy Spirit himself is that storehouse of graces that Christ has won for us." Mühlen says that we must reject the idea that Mary can "authoritatively" attribute grace to us, because this would mean conferring on her a power over the Spirit—although she can, with her intercession, obtain the descent of the Spirit for us, as she did on the first Pentecost.[128]

On the contrary, it is the Spirit who has power over Mary, because she "is under the dominion of the Spirit like no other man," both through the biological processes necessary for the growth of Jesus within her womb (the "personological" function willed by God), and also through her free and conscious act of faith, and her cooperation in the redemptive work of the Son (the "personal" function). Such cooperation must also be interpreted as "first and foremost a collaboration in the collaboration that the Holy Spirit gives to the redemptive work of the Son."[129]

In *Marialis cultus* (1974) and in his letter to Cardinal Suenens on the occasion of the Mariological Marian Congress held in Rome (1975), Paul VI demonstrated great sensitivity to the requirements expressed by Mühlen with regard to the theoretical and vital recognition of the role of the Spirit, and also the possibility of a wrongful substitution of the Virgin for the Paraclete. However, unlike Mühlen, Paul VI denies that Catholic piety should be diverted from Mary to the Spirit:

> We must consider, therefore, that the action of the Mother of the Church, for the benefit of the redeemed, does not replace or compete with, the almighty and universal action of the Holy Spirit, but implores and prepares it, not only with *prayer* of intercession . . . , but also with the direct influence of *example*, including, what is extremely important, maximum docility to the inspirations of the divine Spirit.[130]

Theologians of the postconciliar period have considered how best to express the intimate bonds uniting Mary and the Holy Spirit from the moment of the Annunciation—or, rather, from the Immaculate Conception—up to the Assumption. R. Laurentin faithfully follows the conciliar choice, and refuses to accept the title "bride of the Holy Spirit" because it ignores the Bible, in which Christ is presented as bridegroom (Eph. 5:25–33; 2 Cor. 11:2) and the Spirit as bond of love.[131] Other theologians hold, with *Marialis cultus*, that "a nuptial aspect" can be discerned in the hidden relationship between the Holy Spirit and Mary—as was seen by the poet Prudentius (d. ca. 405) and St. Francis of

Assisi (d. 1226), the first western author to attribute the title "bride of the Holy Spirit" to Mary.[132]

Alongside this path of nuptiality, a number of authors follow that of a certain identification of the Holy Spirit with Mary on the level of activity or synergy (Bertetto), visible mission (Manteau-Bonamy), transparency (Pikaza), and even personal unity (Boff's hypothesis).

D. Bertetto reflects on the fact that Scripture speaks of the prayer of Christians as an effect of the joint action (synergy) of themselves and the Spirit (cf. Rom 8:15). He sees the incarnation as the most outstanding case of such synergy, and says that in this mystery "on the level of *action* (not that of being) it can be said that the principle is one: Mary and the Holy Spirit in *synergy*, so that the same action is attributed to Mary and to the Holy Spirit."[133]

H.-M. Manteau-Bonamy holds that in the incarnation the Holy Spirit descended in person on Mary, and it follows that the Virgin Mother becomes "the physical manifestation of the personal presence of the Holy Spirit" and that her motherhood is divine not only because its end is the person of the word, but also because its source is the person of the Holy Spirit.[134]

In 1981, X. Pikaza published a long study on "Mary and the Holy Spirit," in which he gives a careful interpretation of Acts 1:14, a text that mariologists have tended to leave on one side. Biblical analysis of this verse leads us to a distinction between the person of Mary as expressly named, and the group of apostles, women, and brethren of Jesus (here the *and* is always disjunctive). Although Mary stands out because of her importance, as witnessed to by the gospels, she is integrated into the community of disciples and friends of Jesus. She is part of "all those" who receive the Spirit at Pentecost and who speak in tongues (Acts 2:1, 13).

In order to understand the importance of Mary's presence at Pentecost, we must remember the angel's promise to the Virgin and reread it with deep attention: "The Holy Spirit will come upon you . . ." (Lk. 1:35). This text can be interpreted in three different ways: the approach of *eschatological creation* (Barret), which sees Mary as the chaotic and infertile earth of the beginning of time, but as made fruitful by the Spirit; the approach of *sacred indwelling* (Laurentin and Feuillet), which sees Mary as the sacred place in which the Spirit dwells in order to pour himself

out over all people; and the approach of *personal transparency*
(Pikaza), which sees in Mary the encounter with God in freedom
and love, "the expression of the Spirit," "a manifestation of the
power and reality of God among men."

This biblical interpretation is to be distinguished both from
that preferred by the Protestant tradition, which recognizes primarily the *believer* in the mother of Jesus, and from that of the
Catholic tradition, which emphasizes the Virgin as Christ's *collaborator*. It is in line with the Orthodox interpretation, which
admires the Theotókos as the *icon of the Spirit*. For the Orthodox
Bulgakov and Evdokimov, Mary is "the instrument and the place
of the manifestation of the Spirit," the "pneumatophore *par excellence,*" "the hypostatic revelation" of the Spirit. [135]

It can be seen from this postconciliar overview that western
theology is overcoming the pneumatological vacuum and the
tendency to christomonism. And this has immediate applications to mariology.

The movement to a mariology that is open to consideration of
the Spirit does not mean giving up christocentrism, because the
Paraclete (and with him the Virgin) has the primordial function
of uniting us to Christ, who remains the sole mediator of salvation. However, it means that Christ and Mary should no longer
be seen in a closed relationship but within the Trinitarian context. Hence, the need not to neglect the Spirit (and, analo-
gously, the Father) when dealing with the function of Mary and
of devotion to her. Clear symptoms of pneumatological underde-
velopment can be seen in the fact that discussion of Mary is
concentrated on Mary without reference to the Holy Spirit, on
which she in fact depends in her mission and holiness, and in the
simplification of the biblical *taxis* or "order" (cf. Eph. 2:18) to
such an extent that no trace of the Father and the Spirit is left, as
is seen in the motto "Ad Iesum per Mariam," which should at
least be completed and expanded to: "Ad Patrem per Christum in
Spiritu Sancto cum Maria." [136]

Theological research has established an area of agreement in
which Mary is recognized as the *place of encounter, witness* or *sign,*
and *sanctuary of the Spirit:* through her special acceptance of the
Paraclete at the Annunciation and at Pentecost, the Virgin became *par excellence* "she who bears and is conformed to the
Spirit." [137]

Theology is trying to use this consensus as a base camp for

moving toward new frontiers, but it has met with some hesitation as to terminology and some rash hypotheses. While theology rejects the identification between Mary and the Spirit on the personal level,[138] it does tend to emphasize the unity existing between them on the operative level. As the exemplary expression of a creature molded by the Spirit, the Virgin becomes a pattern for the Church and for man, and her very "presence" within history is seen as the effect of her pneumatic sharing in the condition of the risen Christ.[139]

Mary in Popular Piety

After the fierce criticisms of Protestant theology and prophecies of the end of popular religion issued by sociologists and theologians of secularization, various sociological and pastoral factors brought the subject to the forefront in the seventies.

It is of interest as a mass phenomenon that encompasses values such as community openness, the sense of celebration, and a deeply felt relationship with Mary, and which is rich in inspiration for theology, symbology, and culture. Indeed, popular religion is identified with Mary, the symbol of the age-old tragedy of poverty and suffering that is at present acting as a spur to liberation:

This fundamental paschal dimension comes to us through devotion to the Virgin Mary, especially by means of meditation and the recitation of the mysteries of the rosary. The people of Latin America feel they are interpreted and absorbed into Mary.[140]

The first Protestant theologian to take an interest in the marian aspect of Latin-American Catholicism was H. Cox, who was impressed by two elements, which he describes in his diary: the Mass of the Assumption as celebrated by Bishop Mendes Arceo in Cuernavaca Cathedral in Mexico in 1971, and a fresco in Santa Fé representing Christ and our Lady of Guadalupe together with national heroes.

Bishop Mendes Arceo's sermon was vigorous and simple:

Mary is poor like the oppressed people of the Third World. The "Assumption" does not mean that she "goes up" . . . but that she is now united with Christ, who is "the liberator in our midst." Together at this very moment they are "tearing the imperial powers from their thrones," . . . sending the rich away empty, lifting up the downtrodden, supporting "us" in our fight against dependency and imperialism. Therefore, on with the battle![141]

According to Cox, in almost all cases "through prescribed marian piety, the anger and aspiration of women is sapped and deflected."

Mariology often functions, among poor men and poor women, in ways that are cruelly alienating and repressive: Mary as royal benefactress, a cosmic lady bountiful; Mary as virginal mother; Mary as sentimental pleader to Those Higher Up. . . . Official Mariology is a form of seduction, a calculated misuse of the spirit.[142]

The sermon preached in Mexico has its place in another perspective, and performs a process of consciousness raising and political radicalization, showing that the religions of the downtrodden have moved from expression to protest, and from protest to action. There is thus a hidden value in marian piety, which must not be abandoned because of its official abuse: "Those who support justice for the poor cannot spit on their devotions. They must realize that the faith of the poor is not *just* opiate but also cry." And, continuing this line of reasoning, Cox recognizes that "especially for millions of very poor women, Mary is the central religious reality in their lives, the spiritual energy center that gets them through many tiring days and trying years." It is no coincidence that God "in Hispanic popular piety is almost always pictured as dead: as Christ in a casket, being lowered from the cross, being placed in the tomb. Mary on the other hand is the radiant incarnation of life and flesh." "As Queen of Heaven, Mary is depicted without any child in view. . . . Mary is not just a woman but a powerful, maybe even liberated women." "If God is dead, Mary is alive and well, and she deserves our attention."[143]

The Santa Fé fresco, which shows our Lady of Guadalupe under the guise of Tonantin, the Toltec goddess of fertility, suggests "another religious epistemology" to Cox: "Mary allows us to plumb again, in ourselves and in our cultural unconscious, that psychic sector which lies dormant but not dead beneath our overdeveloped cognitive intelligence." "Mary is so obviously an aggregate of human fantasy, myth making, projection and all the rest" that she "takes us completely away from our obsession with true-or-false games. She puts us literally 'beyond belief,' " carrying us into a perspective of symbology and meaning.[144]

The official Catholic position is expressed in the Apostolic Exhortation *Evangelii nuntiandi* of Paul VI (8 December 1975), which describes popular religiosity, with its limits and values, as a "reality which is at the same time so rich and so vulnerable," but one that must not be ignored because "when it is well oriented" it constitutes "a true encounter with God in Jesus Christ" (No. 48). Paul VI observed elsewhere that the presence of Mary within the people is a vital reflection of the plan of salvation:

> It is in fact true that Mary occupies a privileged position in the mystery of Christ and of the Church, and she is therefore always present within the souls of our faithful, permeating them in their every religious expression and manifestation within their depths and also outside.[145]

A large number of studies have moved in the direction of an analysis of the more notable forms of marian devotion, examining shrines and places of pilgrimage, and collecting marian material (songs, poems, customs, and traditions) for some specific geographical area.[146] This has provided a fresh and varied picture of popular ways of honoring Mary, and this material is now awaiting a serious study in the field of theological hermeneutics.

L. Lombardi Satriani has penetrated into the sphere of popular legend, tradition, and poetry, and has collected details of "the Madonna of folklore." within an anthropological perspective. The picture that emerges is that of a woman who is part of a family, a young woman who still has things to learn, a model to help in overcoming negativity and death, a mediatrix with the wrathful Son, chosen worker for the poor.[147]

On the theological side other features of the Madonna of the people are being noted, and G. Agostino summarizes these as follows:

a. Mary is welcomed as a living presence;
b. as a maternal presence, who is relevant as individual and universal mediatrix;

c. she shares human suffering;

d. because she is mother, she is the vehicle of communion;

e. she is the model of Christian existence, the pattern of what we should be, and the fulfillment of what we should like to be.[148]

Theology is still faced with the task of working out a "popular mariology" that integrates the authentic figure of the Virgin into the roots of the ecclesial tradition and the cultures of the various peoples. This work must have a biblical and patristic foundation, deal with inculturation, and act as a life-giving translation of the message of salvation.

If the people are taken seriously and viewed as a "theological locus," this will also lead to an appreciation of their intuitions with regard to Mary. This is an effect of the *sensus fidelium,* whose role in fostering closer adherence to the truths of the faith was seen in the definition of the marian dogmas of the Immaculate Conception and the Assumption.

The central aspect of popular understanding of Mary today is undoubtedly the perspective in which she is seen in faith as a living, glorified, holy person, endowed with power and maternal goodness, and thus as able to intervene in human affairs.

There is one result of this that is of great practical value and that has been formulated as follows by the Church of Latin America:

A purely typological marian piety has no value for formation, and is simply a pastoral illusion. It is not enough to say that the Virgin is an example of fidelity to the word and of strength in suffering . . . and that we must therefore imitate her. If we do not foster the bond of love and healthy affection for the person of Mary, the call to imitation of a prototype is simply a categorical imperative. In order to make the charisma of Mary fruitful, the marian bond (which has pedagogical priority) must lead to a marian attitude (which has concrete priority).[149]

Further, the working out of a "popular mariology" should move from the eschatological condition of Mary in her influence in bringing about the "marian factor" in the Church, in order to descend into the bibical events of her life and her divine motherhood; it will thus be a new type of mariology, which reverses the method of the manuals.

The Path of Cultural Encounter

The period from 1966 to the present day [1980] has not been marked by some fearful turning back of theology into itself. On the contrary, alongside in-depth study of the conciliar texts, we have also seen a great deal of research activity which consists of exploring new paths, and in which hastiness sometimes goes hand-in-hand with generosity of intention.[150]

The new paths of theology in general act as a counterbalance for mariology, which is thus forced to measure itself against the cultural trends of our days. The western consciousness has been shattered, so that we have realized that other cultures exist within which new theologies have been growing up, such as the liberation theology of Latin America or "black theology," which have hitherto unimagined ways of approaching the subject of Mary.

At the same time, mariology is also involved in the feminist movement and in that of feminine theology, which emphasize the otherwise generally ignored fact that Mary is a woman, and also the need for an "alternative" type of mariology.

Lastly, there are the tendencies to secularization, demythologization, and structuralism, as well as development in the human sciences of language, and all these elements confront theology (and mariology) with the problem of the interpretation of the information that has been handed down. Mariologists are therefore encouraged to carry out a revision of the various dogmas and to discern the significance of Mary for our present age.

Mary in Theological Esthetics and in the Theodrama of H.U. von Balthasar

The work of H.U. von Balthasar can be situated within the broad range of a theology anxious to carry out an in-depth study of transmission of revelation in a way accessible to the contemporary mentality, but without falling victim to cultural fashions. He devotes a broad space to the mother of the Lord, and in his work mariology becomes fertile ground for the application and testing of new paths, such as theological esthetics and theodrama.

1. *Mary as the Masterpiece of the* ars Dei. In his fundamental work *Herrlichkeit. Eine theologische Aesthetik,*[151] von Balthasar sets about a systematic interpretation of revelation, making use of a category neglected by contemporary theology: "beauty," which is the object of esthetics.

> Theological esthetics means contemplating God, not as he communicates truth, or as he is good to man and helps him, but as he draws near to man in order to manifest himself in the eternal splendor of his trinitarian love. This is the reason why this theological esthetics is called *Herrlichkeit* (that is, Glory).[152]

In the development of his system, the author does not omit explicit reference to Mary and to her function as prototype of the Church, thus showing "the great significance that mariology has within a theological esthetic."[153] Discussion of Mary has its place in the twofold task of theological esthetics: the esthetic perception of revelation as the uncovering of God who reveals himself (subjective evidence), and the manifestation of the glory of God in the figure (objective evidence).

Unlike rationalistic theology, theological esthetics wants to view the figure in concrete terms without giving in to the reduction of logical procedures. In "conversion to the image," the idea shines forth in a visible and plausible manner, and its significance is felt intuitively as in a work of art.

Now in the Virgin Mary, we have an image or figure of very strong esthetic value. As God's "work of art," Mary's essence is like a malleable substance at the disposition of the divine action: "Mary's life must be regarded as the prototype of what the *ars Dei* can fashion from a human material which puts up no resistance to him."[154]

Following the line of Fichte and Hegel, von Balthasar emphasizes the esthetic quality of the image of Mary on the natural level too:

> The image of Mary is incontestable, and even to nonbelievers it represents a treasure of inviolable beauty, even when it is understood not as an image of faith but only as a sublime symbol interpreted according to universal human categories.[155]

In the Christian sphere, the meaning of the figure of Mary lies in the revelation of the Church as christiform. The Church is undeniably very complex and cannot be revealed totally by Mary: it has other archetypes in Peter, as regards its hierarchical function, and in Rahab, as symbol of its position as *casta meretrix.* Even so, Mary's special position "can at least set us on the path toward integral response, in view of the fact that it is the infinite openness of her attitude of faith . . . that makes Mary the ideal (moral) and real (physical) sense of the Church."[156]

If we want to eliminate the weakened image of the Church, which overshadows it to the extent of making it unrecognizable, then we must turn to Mary, who reveals "its supreme beauty— that of the Bride-Church of the New Testament": "The Lord does not want his Church to stand before him as a unique out- standing failure, but as a glorious bride who is worthy of him. At this point the marian principle necessarily plays its role in the Church."[157] Christians must therefore keep their eyes fixed on the interior image of Mary if they want to be the holy and christiform Church that is capable of making the work of God shine forth in the world: "To the extent that the Church is Marian, she is a pure form which is immediately legible and comprehensible; and to the extent that a person becomes Mar- ian . . . , the Christian reality becomes just as simply legible and comprehensible in him."[158]

It will be remembered that in 1975 Paul VI indicated not only the *via veritatis,* but also the *via pulchritudinis* as approaches to the mystery of Mary.[159] His words cannot be said to be an echo of those of von Balthasar, but rather an intuitive view that had developed maybe in the light of scholastic philosophy. They put forward a threefold problem:

> The *methodological* problem, concerning research in the field of mariology; the problem of *content,* which has the task of discerning the meaning of Mary's beauty; and the *cibernetic* problem, with a view to an artistic communication of the marian message.[160]

Studies on the *via pulchritudinis* are still few in number.[161] The document *Fate quello che vi dirà* describes its significance as "the path of ascetic commitment, the path adhering to the Word, the filial path."[162]

2. *Mary as a Theological Character in the Theodrama.* Von Balthasar takes the category of theatrical drama as an interpretative presupposition and starting point, and then within this perspective sees God's activity as "fulfilled salvation, reconciliation of the world in Christ with God (2 Cor. 5:19) through an initiative of love that gives itself only." Thus men can become actors in the theodrama only if they are integrated into Christ and in response to a call.

These two conditions are fulfilled in Mary, who is transferred, because of a vocation beyond her expectations, into the "dramatic sphere" of Christ:

> Sterile women are unsuited to conceiving and giving birth to promised sons or to prophets—Sara, Anna, Elizabeth; and the Virgin Mary is even more unsuited to bringing the Son of the Most High into the world. . . . The *bat qol* (voice from heaven) that introduces Mary into her vocation and mission tells her something absolutely new. [163]

While this mission of Mary represents a "space open to further figures, both contemporary and future," it is strongly theodramatic because the Virgin is part of the "constellation" of Christ.

Because human beings are made up of the man-woman polarity, it is clear that "if the Word of God truly became man, this fundamental aspect cannot be excluded from the sphere of the theodrama or remain neutral towards it." [164]

As a woman, Mary has her part in the incarnation, we might say of necessity, through her motherhood with regard to God:

> The Word of God cannot truly enter into the generational series of humanity except through conception, pregnancy and birth from a woman. In this way, the "adamitic" relationship is reversed, as Paul notes: ". . . as the first woman was made from man, so man is now born of woman" (1 Cor. 11:12). . . . If the mother in question is the mother of a human child who is personally God, then she will rightfully be called Theotókos, the Birth-giver of God. [165]

This prior position of Mary in regard to the human birth of Christ is reflected in connection with the Church and with her motherhood of believers, which "always has as its presupposition the fact that Mary conceived and gave birth to the Messiah for the world." Thus, although mariology is bound up with ecclesiology, "it must claim a priority inasmuch as it deals with the mother of the Savior, without whom there would be neither a structured church nor as a rule a divine grace."[166]

Von Balthasar does not ignore the difficulty that exists for anyone who wants to study the *intimate closeness* and *infinite distance* between Mary and Christ. The history of mariology is the history of a pendulum movement between the praise and oblivion of Mary:

> This makes it possible to understand the historical ups and downs in mariological seasons: a wave of attributes, titles and exalting honors is almost necessarily followed by a counter-wave, which can, however, also run aground in a theologically unworthy oblivion.[167]

Such a pendulum movement is articulated in a further threefold swing that the theologian discerns and describes as a stimulus to a new and deeper approach to mariology:

> It is first of all the swing of feminism as such: since woman is molded along the pattern of man, but with identity of rank in the same human nature, this irreducible twofold character is not known to man in the same way; it works against any reduction.
>
> In the second place, there is the especially marian swing between the "lowliness of the maidservant" and the "all generations shall call me blessed"; the beatification (as "queen") threatens to obscure the lowliness . . . , and entails the risk of forgetting it especially in the sense that in Mary lowliness is not the depths of sinfulness, even original sin, but that of the nothingness of the creature before God.
>
> There is lastly the swing that is so difficult to define and that operates between the ages: simultaneous membership of the spura- and infra-lapsaric sphere, and moreover, within the latter, simultaneous membership of the Old Testament sphere ("of flesh and blood") and the eschatological New Testament sphere ("overshadowed by the Spirit"). It is especially here that discussion of the essence, meaning and dimension of Mary's virginity is developed.[168]

Inculturated Mariologies

In the postconciliar atmosphere of theological pluralism and relationships between gospel and culture (GS 58), there has been a growing awareness of the legitimacy and need of local theologies, as well as acculturated evangelization of different peoples. Alongside European theology, we have "African theology" (a term first used by F. Tshibangu in Kinshasa in 1960), and that of Latin America, while similar efforts are being made in the different cultures of Asia.

The rise of these theologies that are bound to a specific sociocultural context has consequences for the way of seeing and presenting the figure of the mother of Jesus on the part of Christian communities outside Europe.

1. *Mariology in the Latin-American Context.* Latin America is rediscovering some of the relatively unknown aspects of the figure of Mary on the basis of its sociopolitical situation, the history of its evangelization, and attention to its own culture. Reference to the Virgin appears in various waves, not in an academic or commonplace perspective, but in a dimension of life-giving authenticity, although certain aspects may need closer examination.

Liberation theology, which has arisen as a *witness* to historical-political commitment and as a *criticism* of the practice of the Church in the light of the word of God, recovers aspects of the biblical message that had long been ignored. Among these aspects, we must include the hymn of the Virgin with all its spiritual and liberating power:

> The Magnificat expresses well this spirituality of liberation. A song of thanksgiving for the gifts of the Lord, it expresses humbly the joy of being loved by him. . . . But at the same time it is one of the New Testament texts which contains great implications both as regards liberation and the political sphere. This thanksgiving and joy are closely linked to the action of God who liberates the oppressed and humbles the powerful. . . . The future of history belongs to the poor and exploited. True liberation will be the work of the oppressed themselves; in them, the Lord saves history. The spirituality of liberation will have as its basis the spirituality of the *anawim.* [169]

In a pastoral perspective, and in the face of the felt presence of Mary in the popular Catholicism of Latin America, there have been three stages in orientation. First, there was an effort to strengthen the link between the people and Mary, teaching the significance of her motherhood and intercession, and placing greater emphasis on affection for the mother than on the content of her relationship to the Trinity. Then, with secularization, there was a purifying and iconoclastic crisis, which gave birth to a typological kind of pastoral approach that lacked affective bonds and resembled a categorical imperative. Lastly came Puebla in 1979, which fused the motherhood and the ecclesial exemplarity of Mary. Using universally valid expressions ("Mary, mother and model of the Church"), Puebla avoids a-historical generalization, and gives these titles a context in relation to the sociocultural circumstances of the Latin-American region.

The Puebla document sees the Guadalupe event as a "sign" that God offers to the people in Mary in order that they should understand his closeness and become a community. It is a maternal sign, because a mother is suited to showing God's tenderness and carrying out a mission of unification:

From the very beginning—with her appearance in Guadalupe and the dedication of a shrine to her there—Mary has constituted the great sign of the nearness of the Father and Christ, inviting us to enter into communion with them; and she has served as a sign endowed with a maternal, compassionate aspect. Mary has also been the voice urging us on to union as human beings and as peoples (No. 282).

Through her link to Christ, Mary becomes the historical basis of fidelity to the Lord, "teacher of the Gospel in Latin America" (No. 290), so that when the "Latin American Church wishes to take a new step forward in its fidelity to its Lord," it must focus its "gaze on the living figure of Mary" (No. 294). All this is founded on the primordial task of Mary, which consists of connecting God to man and of incarnating the word in the concrete circumstances of history:

Through Mary, God became flesh, entered a people, and became the center of human history. She is the bond of interconnection between heaven and earth. Without Mary the Gospel is stripped of flesh and blood and is distorted into an ideology, into a spiritualistic rationalism (No. 301).

The people of Latin America, who are not able to accept a Church that is not a family (No. 41), "recognize the Church as the family whose mother is the Mother of God" (No. 285). The presence of Mary in the Church is in no way anonymous:

> Here we deal with a feminine presence that creates the family atmosphere, receptivity, love and respect for life; a sacramental presence of the maternal features of God; and a reality so deeply human and holy that it evokes from believers supplications rooted in tenderness, suffering and hope (No. 291).

2. *Mary in African Theology.* This chapter is only just beginning, but it is rich in promise and is being carried out through studies restricted to specific local churches. This can be seen in various doctoral dissertations presented to the Roman universities between 1974 and 1986, which examine Mary in Dahomey (what is now Benin), Uganda, Malawi, and Swaziland, with particular attention to the historical and cultural elements underlying typically African expressions of marian devotion.[170] On a more general level, there is the study of R. Laurentin, "Mary and the African Theology,"[171] which studies the four forms of "blackness" (suffering, aggressive, serene, triumphant) and the values of African culture in the context of a precomprehension of Mary. Such anthropological presuppositions should pave the way to acceptance of certain aspects of the gospel that are difficult for European culture to assimilate.

Mariology and Feminism

Mary and women are linked by a bond of a historical and cultural nature that lies in the fact that Mary is not only a woman but is the most outstanding figure in the Christian West. Whether negative or positive, her influence on the conception of women is undeniable, as Marina Warner observes in no uncertain terms:

> Whether we regard the Virgin Mary as the most sublime and beautiful image of man's struggle towards the good and the pure, or the most pitiable production of ignorance and superstition, she represents a central theme in the history of western attitudes to women. She is one of the few female figures to have attained the status of myth—a myth that for nearly two

thousand years has coursed through our culture, as spirited and often as imperceptible as an underground stream.[172]

For its part, feminism provides a spur to mariology, encouraging it to review both the conception of women and the traditional image of Mary. If the "scandal" of feminist theology is the "maleness" of Jesus, Mary constitutes just as great a stumbling block and is viewed as an ambiguous and dangerous model: a symbol of passivity, sexual repression, and the exaltation of motherhood.

Faced with this ambiguity, the feminists swing between rejection of the figure of Mary or her recovery within a liberating perspective. Thus, so long as Mary's holiness is "measured by the number of clothes washed" or is projected into a sphere of total perfection and inimitability, women today tend to become "anti-Mary,"[173] and to take their distance from an overly domestic and idealized view of Mary.

Instead of entrenching themselves in closed attitudes toward the mother of Jesus, other feminists prefer to look to the discovery of the "true" Mary of the bible, free from cultural accretions, disguises, or ideological instrumentation.[174]

Within the context of interconfessional history, Rosemary R. Reuther has discovered that it is at least possible to produce an "alternative" mariology to the dominant one. This new mariology is potentially capable of "breaking the mold of the female patriarchy,"[175] In the view of C. Halkes, from Holland, a twofold liberation is needed:

a. Mary asks to be *freed* from the image that has been made of her and *from the projections that a male ecclesiastical hierarchy has attributed to her*. Under the promptings of a deep feeling of solidarity or historicity, I do not wish to diminish her in this way.

b. It is also necessary to *free women from those images of Mary* that still dominate and hold them in subjection. Such images must be analyzed and unmasked.[176]

The most pressing tasks with a view to a liberated and liberating mariology can be summarized as follows: restoring Mary to humanity, overcoming the image of her as almost not a woman but a semigoddess[177]; relativizing Mary's biological motherhood, as Jesus does in his preaching, in order to highlight her faith in the word of God[178]; seeing Mary not as the image of femininity or the model of femaleness, but above all as the model of every believer—the "autonomous" person who responds freely to God, the "radical symbol of a new humanity, . . . the original and eschatological representative of humanity"[179]; avoiding the approaches of the "new Eve," the "bride," and the "relational being," which perpetuate a subordination not properly entailed by service and *diakonia,* and transpose the androcentric schema from the order of creation to that of redemption[180]; opening the ministerial priesthood to women, because restrictions in this area are based on an irrelevant past, and more precisely on prohibitions against blood that make a woman "impure" because of her biological functions.[181]

Apart from radical feminist challenges, theology continues in its elimination of certain commonly held attitudes to the femininity, maternity, and virginity of Mary, freeing her image of historical and cultural presuppositions, and highlighting the revelatory capacity of the Virgin with regard to God and women.[182] The theologian who carried out "the first attempt of an integrated and major type, in which the encounter between mariology and the female takes place,"[183] is L. Boff, with his already cited work *O rosto materno de Deus* (of which we are using the Italian translation, *Il volto materno di Dio*).

With a clear striving for a systematic method, Boff examines the organizing nucleus of mariology "on the basis of which all the marian events can be explained and understood," or, in other words, "the master-plan of the divine wisdom with regard to Mary."

The seven answers offered by contemporary mariologists, who base their treatment of Mary on the foundation of her relationship with Christ or the Church, or who reject any organic and integrated discussion, are held to be defective. They do not encompass the whole salvific significance of Mary in the plan of God, because they neglect the feminine aspect, or fall into "historical positivism," because they confine themselves to describing the events concerning Mary without seeking their theological framework.

Boff's intention is to resolve this situation, observing that "the fact that Mary was a woman is not without significance." Indeed, this very fact can become "a fundamental anthropological category" that would be capable of "systematizing all the facts that the faith bears witness to about Mary."[184] The theologian supports this choice with a philosophical and theological analysis of the female, revealing its sacramental structure ("it speaks of God, evokes God, and points towards God").

If the male is divinized in Christ in a full and direct manner, Boff wonders "why we cannot hope that, in the order of being, the female should not be divinized in a similar way." The theologian offers an affirmative response in the form of a "theological hypothesis (theologoumenon)," holding that it is up to the Holy Spirit to divinize the female at the end of history, but giving an eschatological foretaste of this in the mystery of the Virgin Mary:

> We support the hypothesis that the Virgin Mary, the Mother of God and of men, fulfills the feminine in an absolute and eschatological form, because the Holy Spirit has made her his temple, his sanctuary and his tabernacle in such a real and true way that she must be considered to be hypostatically united to the third Person of the Most Holy Trinity. [185]

This hypothesis has been much criticized by theologians, who consider it unfounded, exaggerated, and antiecumenical. [186]

There is still a good deal of heavy ground to be covered in the area of the relationship of mariology to the feminine and to the pneumatological dimension if we are to harmonize historical and cultural requirements (without giving in to the temptation of hubris) and the facts of biblical revelation (without sticking obstinately to old clichés that deprive the figure of Mary and the person of the Spirit of logical and life-giving significance for contemporary men and women). Despite his "theological hypothesis," Boff must be credited with having thrown into relief the limitations of "unisex" theology, indicated mariology as the "catalizing and conditioning nucleus" of the whole question of women, and taken Mary as the "privileged subject of anthropological reflection." [187]

Revision of Marian Dogmas

The urgent need for a reflection on dogmas, not with a view to diminishing their content, but rather with a view to increasing their understanding and expressing them in a way more accessible to contemporary culture, has also been felt in the field of mariology. [188] The process of revision also brings the four marian dogmas into the dynamic movement of the crisis, and in these circumstances, some of them are not only subject to challenge and attack, but also see new horizons of understanding opening up, beginning with the virginity of Mary.

1. *The Virginity of Mary.* The publication of the *Dutch Catechism* in 1966 marked the start of discussion on the virgin conception. This document states that Jesus is "God's gift to humanity" and "the son of the promise, like none other," but avoids clarifying the content of this in any traditional sense. Following the Gazzada and Nemi meetings in 1967 between theologians of the Holy See and of the Dutch conference of bishops, in its declaration of 15 October 1968, the Commission of Cardinals stated:

It must be openly professed in the Catechism that the holy mother of the incarnate Word remained always adorned with the honour of virginity. It must teach equally clearly the doctrine of the virginal birth of Jesus, which is so supremely in accord with the mystery of the Incarnation. No further occasion shall be given of denying this truth—contrary to the tradition of the Church in reliance upon Sacred Scripture—retaining only a symbolic meaning, merely indicating for instance the gift inspired by pure grace, which God bestowed on us in his Son. [189]

The matter seemed on the way to a definitive solution with the publication of the "Supplement" to the *Dutch Catechism.* However, it then arose again in Germany with H. Halbfas, who was forbidden to take up his professorship in religious education in Bonn by order of the Vicar General of Cologne, because of the position he had taken up especially with regard to the virgin birth in his work *Theory of Catechetics,* in which we read: "Jesus' birth 'of the *Virgin* Mary' is not presented for belief as a biological fact (Jesus had no human father) and is not available to a preacher as information about any psychological, let alone gynecological process. . . ."[190]

H. Küng caused rather more of a stir with his best seller *On Being a Christian,* in which he unequivocally asserted that "the virgin birth cannot be understood as a historical-biological event," but should be interpreted as a "meaningful *symbol*" of the new beginning brought about by God in Christ. [191]

The debate moved to Spain with X. Pikaza, who follows R.E. Brown in placing himself midway between the historical, biological fact and the theologoumenon, and with an article by R. Scheifler, who casts doubt on the virgin conception and birth.[192]

A number of points have become steadily clearer in the theological discussion of Mary's virginity between champions of the "theologoumenon"[193] and supporters of the traditional interpretation.[194] These points are as follows: the uniqueness and independence of the virginal conception of Mary from theogamic models, the need to understand it within the perspective of a developed christology, the movement beyond contingent patristic lines of reasoning, the recovery of the significance of Mary's virginity for salvation history and of its biblical and theological foundations.[195]

2. *The Immaculate Conception.* E. O'Connor was the first mariologist to see the repercussions of contemporary theories about original sin on the dogma of the Immaculate Conception, and in 1969 he produced an article examining this subject.[196] Reference to the Immaculate Conception is generally ignored or relatively undeveloped in such theories, although their evolutionary, sociological, or existentialistic perspectives do in fact throw light on certain aspects of marian dogma.[197]

Other theologians throw more light on the question when they specifically consider the intelligibility of the content of the dogmatic definition of 1854 in a christological context and using a cultural hermeneutics. Beginning from the principles that the "starting point cannot be Adam and sin, but Christ," and that the redemption must be seen above all in its "positive aspect," D. Fernández asserts that "we must see the mystery of Mary in its true theological dimension: that is, as a mystery of divine election, of holiness, of fullness of grace, and of fidelity to the plan of God."[198]

The negative formulation of the Bull *Ineffabilis Deus* should thus give way to a positive formulation. The negative is, in fact, always an imperfect expression: for example, what sort of holiness would it be that was free of sin but was not accompanied by grace and divine election, as well as by a life of faithful commitment to God and men?

In a 1985 article, Fernández repeats his twofold thesis with increased conviction: we must bid "a definitive farewell" to the doctrine of original sin and at the same time reject the existence of any "intrinsic and essential relationship" between it and the dogma of the Immaculate Conception, inasmuch as it is possible to envisage a redemption that is not a "liberation from sin" but is principally a "capacity to possess God."[199]

Alejandro de Villalmonte examines the relationship between
original sin and the Immaculate Conception, and comes to the
same conclusion as D. Fernández with regard to the need to
move beyond the negative formulation of the dogma of the Immaculate Conception. He says that historically speaking, this
dogma "was the result of the progressive, centuries-long deepening of the Christian religious understanding of the content of the
New Testament affirmation concerning Mary: Mother of Christ,
full of grace."[200]

Theological investigation regarding the Immaculate Conception will investigate, with K. Rahner,[201] the place of "the individual statement in its coherence . . . with the one totality of faith,"
and especially in relation to Christ and the Church. However,
attention is also given to the anthropological significance of marian dogma with regard to "the new humanity"[202] or "the holy
remnant" of the people of Israel.[203] While ecumenical difficulties
concerning the Immaculate Conception are dying down,[204] this
dogma is interpreted by St. Maximilian Kolbe with mystical and
metaphysical intuition in reference to the Holy Spirit.[205]

3. *The Theotókos.* Although the title "Theotókos" has been
defined, it still causes some problems from the viewpoint of content and terminology: "The question of the divine maternity always has, and still does, presented difficulties both as concerns
content (it concerns the mystery of the hypostatic union) and also
as concerns terminology, as was the case in the fifth century,"[206]

Despite the thought-provoking nature of this marian title,
postconciliar theology has produced no work on the Theotókos
that is both wide ranging and has an actualizing cultural impact.
Even the new christological trends, such as metadogmatic ones
and those concerned with liberating action, do not offer valid
elements for a new understanding of the mother of Jesus.[207] The
most interesting contributions come from those mariologists who
are concerned to clarify and justify the marian title that received
official approval at the Council of Ephesus.

While the term "Theotókos" literally means "she who gives
birth to God," J. Galot does not stop at this biological meaning,
but feels that the title of "mother" should be taken on in all its
anthropological depth and significance:

Maternity does not consist only of an act of generation with
which the woman conceives and gives birth to the child. It

sets up a permanent relationship between one person and another, on the basis of this generation. A mother is the mother of the person of her child.[208]

When this first observation about motherhood is applied to Mary, it takes on an extraordinary dimension, because, unlike the motherhood of other human women, that of the Virgin does not result in any ordinary human person, but in the person of Jesus:

> According to the expression repeated a number of times by the Council of Chalcedon, Jesus Christ, true God and true man, is "one and the same." First, therefore, there is not some relationship of Mary to the man Jesus, to which a relationship to Jesus the Son of God is later added. There is only "one and the same" relationship of the person of Mary to the divine person of the Son. This is a direct relationship with God, since the Son is God.[209]

The filial relationship (which is real and not just in the sphere of reason) of the Son of God with Mary corresponds to this maternal link between Mary and the person of the incarnate word. It brings Christ into other interpersonal relationships, and also sets up a relationship that is not one of identity, but of participation and sign, with the divine filiation:

> The temporal filiation is distinct, but has its place as the extension of the eternal filiation, as its manifestation in the world. The Father generates his Son within time through the operation of the Holy Spirit, and does so with the cooperation of Mary. Mary's greatness lies in the fact that she is the partner of the Father in this process of generation.[210]

According to Galot, the second element of a true motherhood is also found beyond the biological level. This element is the "educational task," which makes Mary "she who brought God up." There is no need to follow those theologians who are puzzled "in the face of this view of some moral influence of Mary on the one who was God," because this aspect falls within the terms of the incarnation.[211]

In his book *Theotókos*, M.J. Nicolas also reflects on Mary's motherhood as a psychophysical process and a spiritual reality. He comes to this view by taking as his joint starting point the biblical information according to which the Virgin "became the mother of God not in a purely physical and material way" but "in faith and assent," and also the concept of truly human generation, which entails a complete love coming from the Spirit. The Fathers saw this clearly when they stated that Mary "conceived first in her mind and then in her womb," and St. Augustine also added that she "conceived not in the ardor of the concupiscence of the flesh, but in the fervor of love and faith."[212]

Apart from any dichotomy between natural and supernatural, Mary's motherhood is itself a grace, because it establishes a total bond between mother and Son, and is made up of "a relationship of an ontological order, pointing to and encompassing a relationship of knowledge and love." And even though adulthood entails separation of the son from the mother, "motherhood is a relationship that should be deepened rather than eliminated with time," inasmuch as conscious human parenthood provides the basis for a lasting relationship with those who have been generated.[213]

A. Müller tries a new approach to the divine motherhood of Mary, laying aside the mariologists' attribution of priority to metaphysical concepts in order to attribute it instead to biblical revelation. It follows that we must be careful to avoid seeing the divine motherhood as "completely isolated from other theological categories"; it must, rather, be seen "in relationship with the whole doctrine of the incarnation." In the divine plan, "the Son of God becomes man in order to give man a share in his divinity, through his humanity." This is the biblical category that makes it possible to understand Mary's motherhood in a context of salvation: "The divine motherhood reveals itself as the highest and truest sharing in the humanity of Christ and as the highest cooperation as member in his work of redemption."[214] Müller goes on to interpret the messianic motherhood of Mary with the category of "the revelation of transcendence" that belongs to the Bible and is critically guaranteed by theology. Mary's motherhood becomes a "discourse on the mediation of transcendence." It follows that the Ephesian title of "Theotókos" is seen to "provide a very lively description of the active participation of man in this event of transcendence."[215] If we reject the erroneous meaning of "the maternal production of God himself," the title of

"Birth-giver of God" is clearer for tradition; however, the term "Mother," which is of a personal and relational type, "is more expressive for the present-day mentality."[216]

The Theotókos is certainly anything but a revealed mystery. After recent theological reflection, this title requires further explanation through in-depth biblical research and cultural insights as to the meaning of motherhood.[217]

4. *The Assumption.* Contemporary eschatological perspectives have repercussions for the dogma defined by Pius XII in 1950, and particularly as concerns the abolition of the intermediate state that would deprive Mary's Assumption of its character of privilege and anticipation. This line of reasoning is taken by O. Karrer, and after him by D. Flanagan, who observes that the formula used in defining the Assumption—unlike that used for the Immaculate Conception—does not present the new dogma as "a singular grace and privilege," and concludes that the Bull of definition leaves the question open of whether other people apart from Mary have reached the final state of glory.[218]

While S. Meo and C. Pozo defend the traditional position,[219] which would be confirmed in the letter *Recentiores episcoporum synodi* ("On the Reality of Life after Death") of the Sacred Congregation for the Doctrine of the Faith in May 1979, other theologians feel that it is urgent to reinterpret the Assumption in the light of biblical revelation and theological anthropology.[220]

The journal *Ephemerides mariologicae* ranges itself with this revisionist position in a 1985 issue devoted to "L'Asunción de María desde las antropologías y la escatología actuales." E. Barón emphasizes the need to avoid a *dualistic* anthropology that places body and soul in opposition, and a *materialistic* anthropology that confuses body and inanimate substance. It must be stated with Merleau-Ponty that the body is animated and the soul embodied. The corruption of Mary's body is itself seen as a biological fact, while the *aphtharsía* of the Fathers implies fullness of life. As regards the Assumption, this is not a matter of honoring Mary's body in memory of her holy past, nor of adding an accidental (bodily) glorification to the substantial one (of the soul). In a unified anthropological perspective, the Assumption means "calling the whole person to himself" in a fulfilled vocational maturity; establishing an intersubjective relationship through the body; resolving, in the interpersonal bond with God, a process of Assumption that continued through the whole of Mary's earthly life; actuating the dynamic potential of obedience; and taking up the gift of her body and binding it to the body of Christ.[221]

D. Fernández sees the hope of new possibilities in the biblical basis of the Assumption, and this could have positive repercussions in the ecumenical sphere.[222]

J.M. Hernández is equally favorable to the hypothesis of immediate resurrection, and considers the biblical model of the Assumption particularly suited to expressing the transferral of the righteous to the sphere of divine life: in biblical terms, this is not the privilege of a few, but the destiny of all (1 Thess. 4:17; Rev. 11:12).[223]

As we can see, mariology has sufficient resources to be able to assimilate new theories, even if these are not yet securely founded or universally accepted. The discussion on intermediate eschatology must not totally absorb mariological study, because apart from this aspect, there are still the marian, christological, and ecclesial meanings indicated by *Marialis cultus* (No. 6) and celebrated in the liturgy. The subject of the Assumption is still open to further study, proof, and development.

The Future of Mariology

A backward glance gives us an idea of the ground that has been covered by mariology since the Council. This progress has been marked by two events of undeniable historical value that open discussion of Mary to ever-broader horizons.

The first turning point was brought about by the Second Vatican Council in 1964, when it diverted mariology from its posttridentine unidirectional development and placed it within the framework of theology as a whole, and ecclesiology in particular. The integration, or reentry, of mariology into ecclesiology marked the end of an isolated marian discourse, and also the decline of a conception of Mary in a perspective of privileges and titles. The latter has given way to functionality, service, communion, and typology in a context of participation. In other words, the Second Vatican Council called on mariology, which had been following a path of its own, to correct its orientation, reintegrating itself into the common movement, and becoming more biblical, ecclesial, and ecumenical.

The second turning point was represented by *Marialis cultus* in 1974, which opened mariology to the anthropological perspective, understanding that the mariological crisis that has broken out since the Council will not be resolved by some well-balanced personal and structural reasoning that might attract acceptance within the Church, but by taking account of the full extent of the cultural changes taking place in our age.

At this point, mariological approaches are branching out in three directions: the conciliar impulse inspires theological renewal, which attempts a different mariological approach, bringing mariology back into theology and into unified worship, and encompassing ecumenical dialogue; in the meantime, an operation has been launched for the recovery of the charismatic experience and of popular piety, which some people may consider a regression, but which develops the pneumatic dimension of mariology and absorbs the values of popular marian religiosity; and, lastly, mariology feels called to enter on the path of cultural encounter so that the figure of the Virgin can once again become meaningful for our age.

To sum up, postconciliar mariology is moving along its threefold path in the conviction that it can make up for past shortcomings by basing itself on the points securely stated in the documents of Vatican II and in *Marialis cultus*: strengthening its own integration with the theological movement of the Church, always considering Mary in relation to the *center* and *mainspring* of the faith, in other words, "within the mystery of Christ and of the Church," and also opening itself to serious encounter and dialogue with the contemporary world (that is, with the historical movement of the different cultural areas) in such a way that the subject of Mary, with its typological power and its ability to foster values, can enter into the dynamic movement of society. Postconciliar mariology must introduce the spirit of *Gaudium et spes* into Chapter VIII of *Lumen gentium* in order to develop inter-Church communion on the basis of the word of God regarding Mary, and the mission of proclaiming the whole plan of salvation to all cultural areas.

In view of these serious tasks, "unemployment certainly poses no threat to mariologists,"[224] because "mariology has not reached its conclusion. Today it still has a history oriented to the future which is as yet totally undiscovered. In this history the Church seeks the essence of woman, of Mary, and also of itself."[225]

A repetitive mariology that is incapable of accepting challenges and facing new paths has no future, because it makes the
crisis chronic instead of resolving it. Mariologists must act as
antennas sensitive to contemporary challenges and appeals: they
will evaluate the successive cultural trends as they arise, discerning and accepting the values in these trends that are capable of
purifying, developing, and rediscovering many doctrinal and
cultal elements regarding the Virgin; they will make use of different thought forms and lines of investigation that have been
developed in recent years (the *linguistic-analytical, sociocritical,*
and *hermeneutical* models)[226]; and they will follow paths that are
parallel or complementary to the path of reason, such as those of
symbolism, typology, and *theological esthetics.*

Only by remaining within the mainstream of history will
mariology be able to present a view of Mary that is truly meaningful and that acts as a "living reference point," not acting as a
brake, but as a spur to a better future, and indeed offering insights for a solution of contemporary problems on a deeper level.
In the past, iconography has reflected a mirror image of Mary as
seen by the Church in its encounter with history and the different cultures, so that it showed her as the mother with the Child
in her arms, or at the foot of the cross, or bathed in glory in a
heaven populated by angels. It would seem that the marian icon
of the future will show the Virgin of the *Magnificat:* as the Daughter of Sion who is transmuted into the Church and who, bearing
Christ within her, moves along the paths of history, assimilating
in the Spirit the sad and joyful events of history and seeing them
as reasons for offering praise to God, who leads his children
through the varying fortunes of the world and onto the path of
authentic salvation and liberation and of the definitive covenant. Mariology is entrusted with the mystogogical task of unseal-
ing for future generations the salvific secrets found in the one
who is "blessed among women" and whose name is Mary.

Translated from the Italian by Leslie Wearne.

Notes

1. For an analysis of the history of mariology from the beginning of
this century until the Second Vatican Council, cf. S. De Fiores, *Maria
nella teologia contemporanea* (Rome, 1986[2]).

2. *Ibid.*

3. R. Winling, *La théologie contemporaine* (*1945–1980*) (Paris, 1983), 462.

4. Cf. R. Laurentin, *La Vierge au Concile* (Paris, 1965); *Doctrina mariana del Vaticano II,* Estudios marianos 27–28 (Madrid, 1966); *La Vierge Marie dans la constitution sur l'Eglise,* Etudes mariales 22 (Paris, 1966); G. Besutti, *Lo schema mariano al Concilio Vaticano II. Documentazione e note di cronaca* (Rome, 1966); G. Philips, *L'Eglise et son mystère au IIe Concile du Vatican. Histoire et texte de la constitution Lumen gentium,* 2 vols. (Paris, 1968); F. De Fiores, *Maria nel mistero di Cristo e della Chiesa. Commento al capitolo mariano del Concilio Vaticano II* (Rome, 1984³).

5. G. Baraúna, "La ss. Vergine al servizio dell'economia della salvezza," in G. Baraúna (ed.), *La Chiesa del Vaticano II* (Florence, 1965), 1198.

6. Y.M.-J. Congar, "Sur la conjoncture présente de la publication de l'exhortation 'Marilis cultus,' " *La Maison-Dieu,* 121 (1975), 118, situates the isolationist tendency of mariology within that of western theology in its medieval roots: "On peut situer cette tendance dans un courant plus général assez caractéristique du Moyen Âge occidental. . . . On a volontiers isolé une personne ou une réalité de l'ensemble commun, on l'a élevée au-dessus de lui, on s'est attaché à définir ses prérogatives propres; ainsi le Pape par rapport au Corps des évêques, les prêtres par rapport aux fidèles, les religieux, le moine par rapport à la consécration baptismale, les sacrements par rapport à la sacramentalité générale de l'Eglise, enfin la Vierge Marie par rapport à l'ensemble des saints et à l'Eglise."

7. These features of the marian text of the Council are illustrated, for example, by S.C. Napiórkowski, "La situazione attuale della mariologia," *Concilium,* 3/9 (1967), 123–143; G. Gozzelino, "Maria negli orientamenti della teologia attuale dal Concilio Vaticano II alla *Marialis cultus* e al su seguito," in A. Pedretti (ed.), *La Madonna dei tempi difficili. Simposio mariano salesiano d'Europa 1979* (Rome, 1980), 40–52.

8. S. Meo, "Concilio Vaticano II," in S. De Fiores and S. Meo (eds.), *Nuovo dizionario di mariologia* (Cinisello Balsamo, 1985), 386–387.

9. G. Philips, "El espíritu que alienta en el cap. VIII de la 'Lumen gentium,' " in *Doctrina mariana del Vaticano II,* Estudios marianos 27 (Madrid, 1966), I, 187.

10. Paul VI, Discourse at the Close of the Third Session of the Second Vatican Council (21 November 1969).

11. Meo, "Concilio Vaticano II," 393.

12. John Paul II, Discourse at General Audience (2 May 1979).

13. Meo, "Concilio Vaticano II," 393.

14. Gozzelino, "Maria negli orientamenti della teologia attuale," 38.

15. J. Ratzinger, "Considerazioni sulla posizione della mariologia e della devozione mariana nel complesso della fede e della teologia," in J. Ratzinger and H.U. von Balthasar, *Maria Chiesa nascente* (Rome, 1981), 19.

16. S. De Fiores, "Maria nelle prospettive post-conciliari," in S.A.E. (ed.), *Maria nella comunità ecumenica* (Rome, 1982), 70.

17. "Maria la Madre di Gesù," *Enciclopedia Europea*, 7 (1978), 222.

18. R. Laurentin, "Attuali indirizzi di 'teologia mariana,'" *Settimana del clero* (20 December 1970), 4.

19. H. Mühlen, *Una mystica persona* (Rome, 1968), 572.

20. W. Beinert, "Devozione mariana: una *chance* pastorale," *Communio*, 7/37 (1978), 88.

21. Cf. the issue of *Ephemerides mariologicae*, 20 (1970), which was dedicated to the "crisis en mariología."

22. R. Molard, "Editorial," *Réforme* (13 October 1979), 2.

23. R. Laurentin, "Crise et avenir de la mariologie," *Ephemerides mariologicae*, 20 (1970), 54.

24. R. Laurentin, "Bulletin sur la Vierge Marie," *Revue de sciences philosophiques et théologiques*, 56 (1972), 433.

25. There are no substantial references to Mary in the following treatises on ecclesiology: J. Hamer, *La Chiesa è una comunione* (Brescia, 1964; first French ed., 1962); H. Küng, *Die Kirche* (Frieburg im Breisgau, 1967); B. Gherardini, *La Chiesa arca dell'Alleanza* (Rome, 1972); S. Dianich, *La Chiesa mistero di comunione* (Turin, 1975); A. Anton, *La Iglesia de Cristo. El Israel de la Vieja y de la Nueva Alianza* (Madrid, 1977). And little or no attention is paid in the following treatises on christology: W. Kasper, *Gesù il Cristo* (Brescia, 1975); P. Schoonenberg, *Un Dio di uomini. Questioni di cristologia* (Brescia, 1971); C. Duquoc, *Cristologia* (Brescia, 1973); W. Pannenberg, *Cristologia. Lineamenti fondamentali* (Brescia, 1974); B. Forte, *Gesù di Nazaret, storia di Dio, Dio della storia* (Rome, 1981); M. Serenthà, *Gesù Cristo ieri, oggi e sempre. Saggio di cristologia* (Leumann, 1982).

26. This is the line of thought followed by L. Scheffczik, "Maria Exponent des katolischen Glaubens," in *Schwerpunkte des Glaubens. Gesammelte Schriften zur Theologie* (Einsiedeln, 1977), 306–308.

27. Ratzinger, "Considerazioni sulla posizione della mariologia e della devozione mariana," 22–23.

28. A. Müller, "Il culto mariano nella teologia cattolica e nel dialogo ecumenico," *Il Regno/documenti*, 28 (1983), 241.

29. Beinert, "Devozione mariana: una *chance* pastorale," 90.

30. J. Calabuig, "In memoriam Pauli VI eiusque erga Deiparam pietatis. La riflessione mariologica al tempo di Paolo VI. Travaglio e grazia," *Marianum*, 40 (1978), 6.

31. Mühlen, *Una mystica persona,* 575; "Neuorientierung und Krise der Mariologie in den Aussagen des Vaticanum II," *Catholica,* 20 (1960), 19–53.

32. Paul VI, Apostolic Exhortation *Marialis cultus* (2 February 1974), No. 34.

33. Paul VI, Apostolic Exhortation *Evangelii nuntiandi* (8 December 1975), No. 20.

34. 208th General Chapter of the Servants of Mary, *Fate quello che vi dirà. Riflessioni e proposte per la promozione della pietà mariana* (Rome, 1983), No. 11.

35. S. De Fiores, "Incontro vivo con Maria oggi," in *Maria presenza viva nel popolo di Dio* (Rome, 1980), 236–241.

36. Cf. B. Forte, "La teologia europea di fronte alla sfida del pensiero moderno e dei mutamenti ecclesiali," *Melta teologica,* 33 (1982), 34–42; Winling, *La théologie contemporaine* (1945–1980); F. Ardusso et al., *La teologia contemporanea. Introduzione e brani antologici* (Turin, 1980). For the threefold path of renewal, recovery, and cultural encounter, cf. De Fiores, *Maria nella teologia contemporanea.*

37. G. Martina, *La Chiesa in Italia negli ultimi trent'anni* (Rome, 1977), 100.

38. Cf. K. Rahner, "Un compito della teologia dopo il Concilio," in *La teologia dopo il Vaticano II* (Brescia, 1967), 737–749; C. Geffré, *Una nuova epoca della teologia* (Assisi, 1973); U. Benedetti, "Un nuovo concetto e un nuovo metodo di teologia," *Rivista di teologia morale,* 6 (1974), 242–243.

39. S. De Fiores, "Mariologia," *Nuovo Dizionario di teologia* (Alba, 1977), 880: "La mariologia dovrebbe perciò effettuare un rientro nella teologia, da cui si era staccata per esigenze di organicità particolare. Ciò significa la fine di un discorso mariano separato, con i suoi svantaggi di isolamento, perdita del senso della globalità, polarizzazione su Maria e sviluppo unidirezionale. Integrando Maria nell'insieme del piano della salvezza risulterà una kenosi della mariologia, da non considerarsi come perdita o soppressione della propria realtà, ma come ricupero della funzione di servizio. . . ."

40. On P. Nigido, who published the *Summae sacrae Mariologiae pars prima* (Panhormi, 1602), coining the term "mariology," cf. A. Segovia, "Nota sobre el autor y el contenido de la primera 'mariologia,' " *Estudios eclesiasticos,* 35 (1960), 287–311; De Fiores, *Maria nella teologia contemporanea.*

41. C. Fuerst, *Mariologia. Adnotationes ad usum privatum auditorum* (Rome, 1964); Z. Kraszewski, *Mariologia* (Paris, 1964); M.J. Nicolas, *Theotókos. Le mystère de Marie* (Tournai, 1964); id., *Marie Mère du Sauveur* (Paris, 1967); A. Royo Marín, *La Virgen Maria. Teología y espiritualidad mariana* (Madrid, 1968); G.M. Roschini, *Maria santissima* *nella storia della salvezza. Trattato completo di mariologia alla luce del Concilio Vaticano II* (Isola del Liri, 1969); G. Girones Guillem, *La humanidad salvada y salvadora. Tratado dogmático de la Madre de Cristo* (Valencia, 1969); C. Amantini, *Il mistero di Maria* (Naples, 1971); C. Curty, *Le mystère de la Vierge Marie. Théologie mariale* (Paris, 1971); D. Bertetto, *La Madonna oggi. Sintesi mariana attuale* (Rome, 1975); L. Melotti, *Maria e la sua missione materna* (Turin, 1977); B. Albrecht, *Kleine Mariankunde* (Meitingen, 1979); *Handbuch der Mariankunde* (Regensburg, 1984).

42. The separate treatises on mariology, but forming part of a theology series, are the following: M.J. Nicolas, *Marie Mère du Sauveur*, Le mystère chrétien, Théologie dogmatique (Paris, 1967); C. Pozo, *María en la história de la salvación*, Historia salutis, Serie monográfica de teología dogmática (Madrid, 1974); G. Söll, *Mariologie*, Handbuch der Dogmengeschichte (Freiburg/Basel/Vienna, 1978); R. Laurentin, *Maria nella storia della salvezza*, Teologia attualizzata (Turin, 1972); D. Bertetto, *Maria Madre universale*, Nuova collana di teologia cattolica (Florence, 1965).

43. The following collections include Mary within one or another treatise of theology: *Mysterium salutis. Grundriss heilsgeschichtlicher Dogmatik*, 12 vols. (Einsiedeln, 1967–), discusses Mary within christology and ecclesiology; J. Auer and J. Ratzinger, *Kleine katholische Dogmatik*, 9 vols. (Regensburg, 1971–1983), dedicates a few pages to Mary within ecclesiology; M. Schmaus, *Der Glaube der Kirche. Handbuch katholischer Dogmatik*, 2 vols. (Munich, 1970), discusses Mary in Chapter V of Part IV, "The Justification of the Individual" (Chapter V, "Mary as Fully Redeemed," 657–697), although the author proceeds in an autonomous manner in structuring this mariological treatment.

44. As an example, we would refer to the study of A. Müller, which represents a broad and deep chapter of the christology of *Mysterium salutis*. Despite the intention of offering a treatment "not as mariology either outwardly or inwardly complete unto itself, but as part and parcel of the whole history of salvation" (p. 510), in practice the inclusion within christology turns out to be only formal, because the text does not benefit from the perspectives opened up in the other chapters on the mysteries of Christ, on kenosis, on the logic of the cross, etc. Müller himself would admit later that his contribution "substantially covered the same ground as the 'old' theology, although making an effort to take up a relatively critical position". A. Müller, *Discorso di fede sulla madre di Gesù. Un tentativo di mariologia in prospettiva contemporanea* (Brescia, 1983), 6.

45. K. Rahner, *Foundations of Christian Faith. An Introduction to the Idea of Christianity* (London, 1978), 387–388.

46. K. Rahner, "Mary's Virginity," *Theological Investigations*, 19 (London, 1984), 220.

47. Rahner, *Foundations of Christian Faith*, 387.

48. *Ibid.*, 172.

49. *Ibid.*, 387.

50. *Ibid.*, 387.

51. *Ibid.*, 387.

52. *Ibid.*, 387–388.

53. *Ibid.*, 388.

54. Kasper, *Gesù il Cristo*, 9.

55. There is no reference to Mary in L. Sartori, "Chiesa," *Nuovo Dizionario di teologia*, 122–148, or in S. Dianich, "Ecclesiologia," *Dizionario teologico interdisciplinare*, 2 (Turin, 1977), 13–31.

56. O. Semmelroth, *Urbild der Kirche. Organischer Aufbau des Mariengeheimnisses* (Wurzburg, 1950).

57. O. Semmelroth, "Quomodo mariologiae cum ecclesiologia conniunctio adiuvet utriusque mysterii interpretationem," in *Acta congressus internationalis de theologia concilii vaticani II, Romae diebus 26 septembris–1 octobris 1966 celebrati* (Vatican City, 1968), 268.

58. *Ibid.*, 269.

59. Y.M.-J. Congar, *L'Eglise de saint Augustin à l'époque moderne* (Paris, 1970), 465.

60. C. Journet, *L'Eglise du Verbe incarné*, 2 (n.c., 1962), 428.

61. *Ibid.*, 393.

62. *Ibid.*, 392–393.

63. *Ibid.*, 427.

64. *Ibid.*, 428, 432–433.

65. *Ibid.*, 3, 637.

66. The perspective of Mary as the "type of the Church" in her assent to Christ in faith is the *leitmotiv* of the mariological thought of H.U. von Balthasar; cf., for example, *Sponsa Verbi* (Brescia, 1969), 161–162; L. Bouyer, *L'Eglise de Dieu, corps du Christ et temple de l'Esprit* (Paris, 1970).

67. Cf. G. Vodopivec, "Le dimensioni di Maria all'interno della Chiesa sacramento di salvezza," in *Sviluppi teologici postconciliari e mariologia* (Rome, 1977), 54, 58, 69.

68. J. Galot, "Maria tipo e modella della Chiesa," in Baraúna (ed.), *La Chiesa del Vaticano II*, 1156, observes that we must not, even in a parallel sense, seek in Mary the example of all the graces and all the charisms granted to the Church. K. Rahner, "Mary and the Christian Image of Women," *Theological Investigations*, 19 (London, 1984), 212–213: "The Church will always see in Mary the one who had a unique function in salvation history. . . . Nor [will the Church] give way to a pseudo-democratic resentment, unwilling to accept a situation in which everyone does not have the same task in history. . . . Mariological statements refer to a particular individual, an historical and finite human being, who has a definite (albeit unique) place in mankind as a whole and in its history. This person's unique function in history does not permit us to see her in the light of what is ultimately a mistaken Platonism and to ascribe to her alone the whole fullness of human reality which can be realized only in mankind as a whole and in its whole history."

69. L. Sartori, "Orientamenti attuali della teologia e il problema della mariologia," in *Sviluppi teologici postconciliari e mariologia*, 21.

70. Cf. C. Molari, "Maria nella Chiesa. Reflessioni sul valore di alcune formule teologiche," in *Maria e la Chiesa oggi* (Rome/Bologna, 1985); H. Petri "Überlungen zu Sprachproblem der Mariologie," in *ibid.*, 452–463.

71. The title "Mater Ecclesiae" has been the subject of some valid reflections; cf. A. Rivera, "Bibliografía sobre María, Madre de la Iglesia," *Ephemerides mariologicae*, 32 (1982), 265–271.

72. Cf. Serenthà, *Gesù Cristo ieri, oggi e sempre*, 12.

73. M. Bordoni, "L'evento Cristo ed il ruolo di Maria nel farsi dell'evento," in *Sviluppi teologici postconciliari e mariologia*, 31–33: "La prospettiva cristologica pone la mariologia nella sua giusta luce che le compete in rapporto essenziale a Cristo, liberandola dal pericolo di fare di Maria, nel piano divino della salvezza, come un principio a parte ed isolato, che sarebbe continuamente tentato dal pericolo di cadere in forme di mitologizzazione più vicine alle concezioni di divinità pagane che non alla vera immagine evangelica dell'umile serva del Signore. . . . L'approfondimento del ruolo di Maria nell'ambito dell'evento Cristo, non è solo un vantaggio per il discorso mariologico; esso dà un rapporto importante per lo studio del significato e dell'ampiezza storica dello stesso evento Cristo. . . . Uno dei pericoli in cui può incorrere il cristocentrismo teologico è infatti quello di giungere a forme di 'pancristismo' o 'riduzione cristologica' che nell'intento di sottolineare l'unicità e la totalità dell'evento Cristo e della salvezza da esso apportata, finiscono per misconoscere il ruolo della partecipazione umana all'evento, del principio teologico della cooperazione dell'uomo alla propria salvezza. Ora, tale principio, proprio nel tempo in cui le teorie emancipatorie richiamano all'esigenza di sottolineare il ruolo attivo della creatura nella storia salvifica trova una salvaguardia precisamente nel dogma mariano. . . ."

74. A. Amato, "Gesù Cristo," in De Fiores and Meo (eds.), *Nuovo dizionario di mariologia*, 615.

75. E. Schillebeeckx, *Jesus: an experiment in Christology* (New York, 1979), 27; H. Küng, *On Being a Christian* (London, 1977), 116.

76. Küng, *On Being a Christian*, 459–460.

77. *Ibid.*, 462.

78. *Ibid.*, 459.

79. A. Amato, "Rassegna delle principali cristologie contemporanee nelle loro implicazioni mariologiche. Il mondo cattolico," in *Il Salvatore e la Vergine Madre* (Rome/Bologna, 1981), 49.

80. K. Rahner, "The Immaculate Conception," *Theological Investigations*, 1 (London, 1974), 202–203.

81. *Ibid.*, 206.

82. *Puebla. Evangelization at Present and in the Future of Latin America* (London, 1980), No. 178.

83. *Ibid.*, No. 483.

84. *Ibid.*, Nos. 287, 292, 293.

85. *Ibid.*, No. 297.

86. P. Florenskij, *La colonna e il fondamento della verità* (Milan, 1974), 418: "Se il Signore è il capo della Chiesa, la mite Maria è 'la trasmettitrice del divino favore,' il vero cuore per mezzo del quale la Chiesa distribuisce ai suoi membri la vita, l'eternità e i doni dello Spirito, la vera 'datrice di vita,' la vera 'fonte vivificante.' Perché Maria è 'la Signora tutta immacolata, la sola pura e benedetta . . . , la piena di grazie . . . , la sola colomba incorrotta e buona.' Essa è il simbolo vivò e il principio del mondo che si purifica, la purificatrice; è il roveto ardente circondato dalle fiamme dello Spirito Santo, l'approvazione viva e anticipatrice dello Spirito sulla terra, *il tipo della pneumatofania.*"

87. V. Lossky, *The Mystical Theology of the Eastern Church* (London, 1968), 193–194: ". . . the very heart of the Church, one of her most secret mysteries, her mystical centre, her perfection already realized in a human person fully united to God, finding herself beyond the resurrection and the judgement. This person is Mary, the Mother of God. She who gave human nature to the Word and brought forth God become man, gave herself freely to become the instrument of the incarnation which was brought to pass in her nature purified by the Holy Spirit. But the Holy Spirit descended once more upon the Virgin, on the day of Pentecost; not this time to avail Himself of her nature as an instrument, but to give Himself to her, to become the means of her deification. So the most pure nature which itself contained the Word, entered into perfect union with the deity in the person of the Mother of God."

88. N. Nissiotis, "Mary in Orthodox Theology," *Concilium*, 8 (1983), 25.

89. *Ibid.*, 26.

90. *Ibid.*, 27.

91. *Ibid.*, 27.

92. *Ibid.*, 27.

93. *Ibid.*, 35.

94. Commissione Teologica Internationale, "Alcune questioni riguardanti la cristologia," *La Civiltà Cattolica* (1980/4), 259–270.

95. For a development of these perspectives, cf. De Fiores, *Maria nella teologia contemporanea.*

96. Cf. *Briser les barrières. Nairobi 1975* (Idoc-France/L'Harmatton, 1975), 171.

97. M.J. Guillou, "Mouvement marial et mouvement oecuménique: convergences et divergences," *Études mariales*, 21 (1964), 13.

98. S.C. Napiórkowski, "Le mariologue peut-il être oecuméniste?" *Ephemerides mariologicae*, 22 (1972), 72. The author studies the roots of the mariological-ecumenical problem in "Ecumenismo," in De Fiores and Meo (eds.), *Nuovo dizionario di mariologia*, 518–522.

99. Cf. B. Gherardini, "Maria e l'ecumenismo," in *Maria mistero di grazia* (Rome, 1974), 266; Küng, *On Being a Christian*, 461; A. Müller, "Il culto mariano nella teologia cattolica," *Il Regno/documenti*, 28 (1983), 242–243.

100. W.J. Cole, "Mary in Ecumenical Dialogue," *Ephemerides mariologicae*, 33 (1983), 447–454.

101. Cf. the rigid positions of K. Barth, *Domande a Roma* (Turin, 1967), 76; V. Subilia, "Ecumenismo e mariologia," *Protestantesimo*, 39 (1984), 99–102; A. Sonelli, "Aggiornamento," in G. Miegge (ed.), *La Vergine Maria. Saggio di storia del dogma* (Turin, 1982–1983), 311–320.

102. J.P. Gabus, "Point de vue protestant sur les études mariologiques et la piété mariale," *Marianum*, 44 (1982), 482.

103. *Ibid.*, 489.

104. *Ibid.*, 491–493.

105. "Maria. Evangelische Frage und Gesichtspunkte. Eine Einladung zum Gespräch," *Marianum*, 44 (1982), 584–607.

106. W. Borowskj, "Incontro delle confessioni in Maria," in *Maria ancora un ostacolo insormontabile all'unione dei cristiani?* (Turin, 1970), 35–43.

107. G. Maron, "Maria nella teologia protestante," *Concilium*, 19 (1983), 104–105.

108. J. Moltmann, "Editoriale," *Concilium*, 19 (1983), 23–26.

109. M. Thurian, "Figura, dottrina e lode di Maria nel dialogo ecumenico," *Il Regno/documenti*, 28/7 (1983), 245–250.

110. *Mary's Place in Christian Dialogue. Occasional Papers of the Ecumenical Society of the Blessed Virgin Mary 1970–1980* (Middlegreen, 1982).

111. J. de Satgé, *Mary and the Christian Gospel* (London, 1979[2]), 130.

112. Anglican-Roman Catholic International Commission, *Final Report* (London, 1982), 95–96.

113. H. Chavannes, "La médiation de Marie et la doctrine de la participation," *Ephemerides mariologicae*, 24 (1974), 29–38.

114. S.C. Napiórkowski, "Mediatio ad—mediatio in. Quelques remarques sur la symbolique protestante," *Ephemerides mariologicae*, 24 (1974), 119–125.

115. R. Laurentin, "Observation . . . sur le papier d'Henry Chavannes . . . ," *Ephemerides mariologicae*, 24 (1974), 143–145.

116. E.L. Mascall, "Some Comments on Dr. Henry Chavannes's Paper . . . ," *Ephemerides mariologicae*, 24 (1974), 369.

117. Cf. especially H. Düfel, "Die Mittlerschaft Marias und die Lehre von der Anteilnahme," *Ephemerides mariologicae*, 24 (1974), 137.

118. Cf. the Acts of the Mariological Symposium *Il ruolo di Maria nell'oggi della Chiesa e del mondo* (Rome/Bologna, 1979).

119. *Ecumenical Trends*, 9 (1980), 26.

120. *Ibid.*, 25.

121. *L'Osservatore Romano* (English edition) (26 September 1983), 11–12.

122. D.M. Montagna, "Maria e lo Spirito Santo," *Servitium*, 2/1 (1968), 6.

123. Mühlen, *Una mystica persona*, 572–573.

124. E. Vigani, *Spirito Santo e Maria nel concilio ecumenico vaticano II*, cyclostyled thesis (Rome, 1974), 365–366.

125. Mühlen, *Una mystica persona*, 565.

126. *Ibid.*, 560.

127. *Ibid.*, 574–575.

128. *Ibid.*, 579–581.

129. *Ibid.*, 584.

130. Paul VI, Letter to Léon Josef Cardinal Suenens (13 May 1975), *Osservatore Romano* (English edition) (5 June 1975), 9.

131. R. Laurentin, "Esprit Saint et théologie mariale," *NRT*, 99 (1967), 38–40; *Dio mia tenerezza. Esperienza spirituale e mariana, attualità teologica di san Luigi Maria da Montfort* (Rome, 1985), 180–190, 197–199. The path of nuptiality is also rejected as an expression of the relationship between Mary and the Holy Spirit by G. Philips, "Le Saint-Esprit et Marie dans l'Église. Vatican II et perspectives du problème," *Études mariales*, 25 (1968), 29.

132. Cf. O van Assendonk, "Maria, sposa dello Spirito santo in s. Francesco d'Assisi," in *Credo in Spiritum Sanctum. Atti del congresso internazionale di pneumatologia, Roma 1982* (Vatican City, 1983), 1123–1132.

133. D. Bertetto, "L'azione propria dello Spirito santo in Maria," *Marianum*, 41 (1979), 436.

134. H.M. Manteau-Bonamy, *La Vierge Marie et le Saint-Esprit. Commentaire doctrinal et spirituel du chapitre huitième de la constitution dogmatique "Lumen gentium"* (Paris, 1972²), 209.

135. X. Pikaza, "María y el Espíritu santo (Hech 1, 14. Apuntes para una mariología pneumatológica)," *Estudios trinitarios*, 15 (1981), 3–82.

136. Cf. A. Amato, "Lo Spirito santo e Maria nella ricerca teologica odierna nelle varie confessioni in Occidente," in *Maria e lo Spirito santo. Atti del 4° simposio mariologico internazionale, Roma 1982* (Rome/ Bologna, 1984), 94–95.

137. Cf. D. Fernández and A. Rivera, "Boletín bibliográfico sobre el Espíritu santo y María," *Ephemerides mariologicae,* 28 (1978), 265–273.

138. The theological hypothesis of a "hypostatic union" between the Holy Spirit and Mary will also be discussed in the subsection on "Mariology and Feminism."

139. Cf. this "pneumatic" interpretation in A. Pizzarelli, *La presenza di Maria nella vita spirituale* (Rome, 1983).

140. E. Pironio, "Relazione sull'America latina, presentata al Sinodo 1974," *Il Regno/documenti,* 19 (1974), 510.

141. H. Cox, *The Seduction of the Spirit: The Use and Misuse of People's Religion* (New York, 1973), 175.

142. *Ibid.,* 76, 199.

143. *Ibid.,* 177, 181, 182.

144. *Ibid.,* 183, 182–183.

145. Paul VI, "Ai rettori dei santuari d'Italia" (23 November 1976).

146. Cf. G. Besutti, *Bibliografia mariana* (Rome, 1980), 268–351; "Santuari e pellegrinaggi nella pietà mariana," *Lateranum,* 48 (1982), 450–504; A. Rossi, *Le feste dei poveri* (Bari, 1971–1972); R.M. Baratta, *Montevergine. Tradizioni e canti popolari religiosi* (Montevergine, 1973); P. Toschi and R. Penna, *Le tavolette votive della Madonna dell'Arco* (Cava dei Tirreni/Naples, 1971); E. Foti, *Preghiere popolari alla Madonna nel santuario di Dinnammare,* cyclostyled edition (Rome, 1980); P. Borzo-Mati, "Per una storia della devozione mariana in Calabria nell'età contemporanea," in *Studi storici sulla Calabria contemporanea* (Chiaravalle, 1972), 171–194.

147. L. Lombardi Satriani, "Il canto religioso specialmente mariano nel contesto della cultura popolare," *La Madonna,* 26/1–2 (1978), 21–31.

148. G. Agostino, "Chi è Maria per il popolo," *La Madonna,* 35/5–6 (1984), 66–70; id., "Pietà popolare," in De Fiores and Meo (eds.), *Nuovo dizionario di mariologia,* 1111–1122; S. De Fiores, "La Madonna anima della pietà popolare per un autentico incontro con Cristo," in *Maria presenza viva nel popolo di Dio* (Rome, 1980), 166–184; F. Tortora, *Per una devozione popolare autentica verso la Madre di Dio* (Turin, 1982); R. Pannet, *Marie au buisson ardent* (Paris, 1982).

149. J. Alliende Luco, "Diez tesis sobre pastoral popolar," in Equipo Seladoc, *Religiosidad popular* (Salamanca, 1976), 122.

150. Winling, *La théologie contemporaine (1945–1980),* 213–214.

151. H.U. von Balthasar, *Herrlichkeit. Eine theologische Aesthetik:* I, "Schau der Gestalt"; II, "Fächer der Stile"; III, "Im Raum der Metaphysik"; III, 2/1, "Theologie. Alter Bund"; III, 2/2, "Theologie. Neuer Bund" (Einsiedeln, 1961, 1962, 1965, 1967, 1969). English translation: *The Glory of the Lord*, 3 vols. (of 7) already published (Edinburgh, 1981–   ): I, "Seeing the Form"; II, "Studies in Theological Style: Clerical Styles"; III, "Studies in Theological Style: Lay Styles"; IV, "The Realm of Metaphysics in Antiquity"; V, "The Realm of Metaphysics in the Modern Age"; VI, "Theology: The Old Covenant"; VII, "Theology: The New Covenant."

152. H. Vorgrimler, "Hans Urs von Balthasar," in *Bilancio della teologia del XX secolo*, 4 (Rome, 1972), 142.

153. Von Balthasar, *The Glory of the Lord*, 1, 563.

154. *Ibid.*, 564.

155. *Ibid.*, 565.

156. H.U. von Balthasar, *Sponsa Verbi. Skizzen zur Theologie*, 2 (Einsiedeln, 1961), 189–283.

157. *Ibid.*

158. Von Balthasar, *The Glory of the Lord*, 1, 562.

159. Paul VI, Discourse to the Participants in the International Mariological-Marian Congress, Rome (16 May 1975): "In this regard two paths can be followed. In the first place there is the *path of truth*, that is, the way of biblical, historical and theological speculation, which is concerned with the precise position of Mary in the mystery of Christ and of the Church: it is the path of scholars, the path that you follow and that is certainly necessary, and which assists mariological doctrine. However, there is another path that is accessible to all, even the simplest of souls. This is the *path of beauty*, to which we are led by the mysterious, wonderful and marvellous doctrine that is the subject of the marian congress: Mary and the Holy Spirit. Indeed, Mary is the creature who is *tota pulchra*; the *speculum sine macula*; the highest ideal of perfection, which artists have sought in every age to reproduce in their works; the 'woman clothed with the sun' (Rev. 12:1), in whom the purest rays of human beauty meet with the sovereign, but accessible, rays of the supernatural beauty."

160. Cf. S. De Fiores, "Bellezza," in De Fiores and Meo (eds.), *Nuovo dizionario di mariologia*, 224.

161. Cf. P. Evdokimov, *Teologia della bellezza. L'arte dell'icona* (Rome, 1981–1982); D.M. Turoldo, *Laudario alla Vergine. Via pulchritudinis* (Bologna, 1980); A. Gouhier, "L'approche de Marie selon la Via pulchritudinis et la Via veritatis," *Études mariales*, 32–33 (1975–1976), 70–80.

162. 208th General Chapter of the Servants of Mary, *Fate quello che vi dirà*, Nos. 63–71.

163. H.U. von Balthasar, *Theodramatik*, vol. II, "Die Personen des Spiels," 2, "Die Personen in Christus" (Einsiedeln, 1978),

164. *Ibid.*

165. *Ibid.*

166. *Ibid.*

167. *Ibid.*

168. *Ibid.*

169. G. Gutierrez, *A Theology of Liberation* (New York, 1973), 207–208. Cf. also A. Paoli, *La radice dell'uomo. Meditazioni sul vangelo di Luca* (Brescia, 1972), 196–209; J. Moltmann, *Il linguaggio della liberazione, Prediche e meditazioni* (Brescia, 1973), 122–131; L. Boff, *Il volto materno di Dio. Saggio interdisciplinare sul femminile e le sue forme religiose* (Brescia, 1981), 180–190. The Congregation for the Doctrine of the Faith has warned against taking the "prophetic reading of the *Magnificat*" as the "principal and exclusive" dimension (*Instruction on the Theology of Liberation*, 6 August 1984), and against yielding "to the ideologies of the world and to the alleged need for violence" in contrast to "that hymn to the God of mercy that the Virgin teaches us" (*Instruction on Christian Freedom and Liberation*, 22 March 1986, No. 99)

170. J. Amoussou, *Le culte de Marie dans la spiritualité africaine au Dahomey en Afrique noire*, extract from a thesis defended at the Pontifical Theological Faculty "Marianum" (Oudiah, 1974); J.M. Bukenya Biribonwa, *The devotion to Mary in Uganda in the light of the doctrine of chapter VIII of Lumen gentium*, extract from a thesis defended at the Pontifical Urbanian University (Rome, 1980); P. Gamba, *Mary in the Evangelization of Malawi. History and culture for a spiritual Project*, thesis cyclostyled at the Pontifical Gregorian University (Rome, 1983); M.M. Tsabedze, *The mission of the Servants of Mary in Swaziland from its origins (1913) until 1933: Historical development and marian devotion*, thesis cyclostyled at the Pontifical Theological Faculty "Marianum" (Rome, 1986).

171. R. Laurentin, "Mary and the African Theology," in *Mary in Faith and Life in the New Age of the Church* (Dayton, 1983), 3–44.

172. M. Warner, *Alone of All Her Sex: The Myth and the Cult of the Virgin Mary* (London, 1976), xxv.

173. C.A. Douglas, *Mary Anti-Mary* (Christmas, 1973).

174. C. Zanon Gilmozzi, *Per un'autentica liberazione della donna* (Rome, 1979).

175. R.R. Reuther, "Cristologie e femminismo," in *La sfida del femminismo alla teologia* (Brescia, 1980), 134–137.

176. C. Halkes, "Maria e le donne," *Concilium*, 19/8 (1983), 135.

177. J. O'Connor, "The Liberation of the Virgin Mary," *Ladies' Home Journal* (December 1972), 75, 126–127.

178. Halkes, "Maria e le donne," 142–143.

179. R.R. Reuther, *New Woman, New Earth* (New York, 1975), 12.

180. R. Børresen, "Maria nella teologia cattolica," *Concilium*, 19/8 (1983), 111.

181. L.M. Russel, *Teologia femminista* (Brescia, 1977), 89.

182. Cf. A. Manaranche, *L'Ésprit et la femme* (Paris, 1974), 140–150; Rahner, "Mary and the Christian Image of Women," 210–219; J. Galot, *Maria la donna nell'opera della salvezza* (Rome, 1984); M.X. Bertola, "Maria e le istanze del mondo femminile," in *Il ruolo di Maria nell'oggi della Chiesa e del mondo*, 153–187; P. Schmidt, *Maria, Modell der neuen Frau. Perspektiven einer zeitgemässen Mariologie* (Kevelaer, 1974).

183. A. Bonazzi, *Implicazioni morali della mariologia de Leonardo Boff*, cyclostyled thesis (Rome, 1983), 5.

184. Boff, *Il volto materno di Dio*, 17–24.

185. *Ibid.*, 93.

186. Cf. J. Galot, "Marie et le vrai visage de Dieu," *Marianum*, 44 (1982), 427–438; X. Pikaza, "¿Unión hipostática de María con el Espíritu Santo? Aproximación crítica," *Marianum*, 44 (1983), 439–474; D. Fernández, "El Espíritu santo y María en la obra de L. Boff," *Ephemerides mariologicae,*, 32 (1982), 405–419; A. Amato, "Lo Spirito santo e Maria nella ricerca teologica odierna delle varie confessioni cristiane in Occidente," in *Maria e lo Spirito santo*, 67–75.

187. Bonazzi, *Implicazioni morali della mariologia de Leonardo Boff*, 5, 32.

188. Two well-known mariological societies are anxious to face the revision of the marian dogmas in different perspectives: Sociedad mariológica española, "¿Mariología en crisis?" *Estudios marianos*, 42 (1978); Société française d'études mariales, "Faut-il réviser les dogmes concernant Marie: Mère de Dieu, Vierge, immaculée?" *Études mariales*, 38 (1981).

189. *AAS*, 60 (1968), 688. English translation in *A New Catechism, with Supplement* (London, 1974), 24.

190. H. Halbfas, *Theory of Catechetics: Language and Experience in Religious Education* (New York, 1971), 137.

191. H. Küng, *On Being a Christian* (London, 1977), 451.

192. Cf. respectively: X. Pikaza, *Los orígines de Jesús. Ensayo de cristología bíblico* (Salamanca, 1976); R.E. Brown, *La concezione verginale e la risurrezione corporea di Gesù* (Brescia, 1977); R. Scheifler, "La vieja natividad perdida. Estudio bíblico sobre la infancia de Jesús," *Sal terrae*, 65 (1977), 835–851. The following react to these positions, appealing to the faith of the Church: C. Pozo, "La concepción virginal del Señor," *Scripta de Maria*, 1 (1978), 131–156; D. Fernández, "Maria virgen y madre. Una presentación inaceptable de la maternidad virginal," *Ephemerides mariologicae*, 30 (1980), 333–357.

193. J.B. Bauer, "Parto verginale," in Auer and Molari (eds.), *Dizionario teologico*, 494–500; O. da Spinetoli, *Itinerario spirituale di Cristo*, vol. I, "Introduzione generale" (Assisi, 1971), 72–88, 101–107; E. Schillebeeckx, *Gesù. La storia di un vivente* (Brescia, 1977), 586–

589; L. Évely, *Il Vangelo senza miti* (Assisi, 1971), 69–71; A. Malet, *Les Évangiles de Noël: Mythe ou réalité* (Lausanne, 1970).

194. H. Urs von Balthasar, *Cordula ovverossia il caso serio* (Brescia, 1968), 94. The following are among those who defend the traditional position: C. Balic, "La verginità di Maria e la problematica teologica," in *La collegialità episcopale per il futuro della Chiesa* (Florence, 1969), 301–316; J.A. De Aldama, "El problema teológico de la virginidad en el parta," in *Studia Mediaevalia et mariologica, P. Carolo Balic . . . dicata* (Rome, 1971), 497–514; R. Laurentin, "Sens et historicité de la conception virginale," in *ibid.*, 515–542.

195. Cf. S. De Fiores and A. Serra, "Vergine," in De Fiores and Meo (eds.), *Nuovo dizionario di mariologia*, 1418–1476.

196. E. O'Connor, "Modern Theories of Original Sin and the Dogma of the Immaculate Conception," *Marian Studies*, 20 (1969), 112–136. Cf. also J.M. Alonso, "Demitologisación del dogma de la Inmaculada Concepción de María," *Ephemerides mariologicae*, 23 (1973), 95–120; J.M. Cascante Davila, "El dogma de la Inmaculada en las nuevas interpretaciones sobra el pecado original," *Estudios marianos*, 42 (1978), 113–146.

197. Cf. S. De Fiores, "Immacolata," in *Nuovo dizionario di mariologia*, 699–703.

198. D. Fernández, *El pecado original ¿Mito o realidad?* (Valencia, 1973), 183.

199. D. Fernández, "La crisis de la teología del pecado original ¿afecta al dogma de la Inmaculada Concepción?" *Ephemerides mariologicae*, 35 (1985), 291–293.

200. A. De Villalmonte, "La teología del pecado original y el dogma de la Inmaculada," *Salmanticenses*, 22 (1975), 39.

201. Rahner, "The Immaculate Conception," 202; cf. also G. Rovira (ed.), *Im Gewande des Heils. Die Urbild der menschlichen Heiligkeit* (Essen, 1980).

202. Boff, *Il volto materno di Dio*, 126–130, 226–227.

203. J. Ratzinger, *La figlia di Sion. La devozione a Maria nella Chiesa* (Milan, 1979), 59–68.

204. Apart from Borowsky and Thurian, on the Protestant side, cf. A. Stawrowsky, "La sainte Vierge Marie. La doctrine de l'Immaculée Conception des Églises catholique et orthodoxe. Étude comparée," *Marianum*, 35 (1973), 36–112.

205. Cf. F.S. Pancheri, "L'Immacolata Concezione al centro della mariologia Kolbiana," in *La mariologia di s. Massimiliano M. Kolbe. Atti del congresso internazionale 1984* (Rome, 1985), 417–476.

206. D. Fernández, "El concilio de Efeso y la maternidad divina de María," *Ephemerides mariologicae*, 31 (1981), 363.

207. Cf. the reviews of J.T. O'Connor, "Mary Mother of God and

Contemporary Challenges," *Marian Studies*, 29 (1978), 26–43; L.M. Alonso, "Maternidad divina y cristologías recientes," *Ephemerides mariologicae*, 30 (1980), 7–68; E. Sauras, "La maternidad divina de Maria en las nuevas cristologías," *Estudios marianos*, 52 (1978), 73–92; A. Amato, "Rassegna delle principali cristologie contemporanee nelle loro implicazioni mariologiche. Il mondo cattolico," in *Il Salvatore e la Vergine Madre* (Rome/Bologna, 1981), 9–112; D. Fernández, "Maria en las recientes cristologías holandesas," *Ephemerides mariologicae*, 32 (1982), 9–32.

208. Galot, *Maria la donna nella storia della salvezza*, 99.

209. *Ibid.*, 99–100.

210. *Ibid.*, 102.

211. *Ibid.*, 106–107.

212. Nicolas, *Theotókos. Le mystère de Marie*, 73, 78.

213. *Ibid.*, 99–101.

214. Müller, "La posizione e la cooperazione di Maria nell'evento Cristo," 512.

215. Müller, *Discorso di fide sulla Madre di Gesù*, 92.

216. *Ibid.*, 91.

217. John Paul II calls motherhood "a keystone of human culture" (General Audience, 10 January 1979). For other dimensions, cf. T. Koehler, "Qui est Marie-Theotókos, dans la doctrine christologique et ses difficultées actuelles," *Études mariales*, 38 (1981), 11–35.

218. O. Karrer, "Das neue Dogma und die Bibel," *Neue Züricher Zeitung* (26 November 1950); A. Flanagan, "L'escatologia e l'assunzione," *Concilium*, 5/1 (1969), 153–165.

219. S.M. Meo, "Riflessi del rinnovamento della escatologia sul mistero e la missione di Maria," in *Sviluppi teologici postconciliari e mariologia*, 107–127; C. Pozo, "El dogma de la Asunción en la nueva escatología," *Estudios marianos*, 42 (1978), 173–188.

220. Cf. S. Folgado Florez, "La Asunción de María a la luz de la nueva antropología teológica," *Estudios marianos*, 42 (1978), 166–167.

221. E. Barón, "La Asunción corporal de María desde la antropología, *Ephemerides mariologicae*, 35 (1985), 9–35.

222. D. Fernández, "Asunción y Magisterio," *Ephemerides mariologicae*, 35 (1985), 106.

223. J.M. Hernández Martínez, "La Asunción de María en el debate actual sobre la escatología intermedia," *Ephemerides mariologicae*, 35 (1985), 78.

224. Rahner, "Mary and the Christian Image of Women," 216.

225. C.S. Napiórkowski, "La mariologie et ses problèmes dans notre siècle," in *La mariologia di S. Massimiliano M. Kolbe*, 575.

226. Müller, *Discorso di fede sulla Madre di Gesù*, 22–28.

CHAPTER 18

The *Christifidelis* Restored to His Role as Human Protagonist in the Church

Piero Antonio Bonnet

Summary

After considering certain conciliar premises concerning ecclesiology, this article proceeds to examine the teaching of the Second Vatican Council as regards the *christifidelis* (or "member of the Christian faithful"): first of all, the author discusses the break with the old hierarchical models, which makes it possible to situate the *christifidelis* himself in a varied ministerial and vocational context, and then to construct the *communis christifidelium status* (or "common status of the members of the Christian faithful") in order to permit the diversity created by liberty to express the equality brought about by unity, around which the identity of the people of God is established. The author then proceeds to attempt discernment of this plan of the Council, through light and shadows, in the new Code, which is considered the Code of the Second Vatican Council.

Some Ecclesiological Premises

In order to gain a correct understanding of the place of the *christifidelis* in the people of God, we must take our lead from the ecclesiological teaching that Vatican II so admirably constructs and summarizes in number 8 of the Constitution on the Church.[1] The Council declares:

> The one mediator, Christ, established, and ever sustains here on earth his holy Church, the community of faith, hope and charity, as a visible organization through which he communicates truth and grace to all men (*LG* 8a).

These first words, referring back as they do to previous papal teaching, and throwing light upon it in depth, affirm the capital *sustaining* presence of Christ in the Church, which is brought about by means of the "vital" mission of the Spirit. For if we consider "this vital force and power, through which the whole community of Christians is upheld by its Founder," "we shall easily understand that it is none other than the Paraclete, the Spirit who proceeds from the Father and the Son, and who in a special manner is called the 'Spirit of Christ' or the 'Spirit of the Son.' "[2] Thus, the mystery of the Church is involved in the first and greatest of all mysteries, that of the Trinity: "Hence the universal Church is seen to be 'a people brought into unity from the unity of the Father, the Son and the Holy Spirit' " (*LG* 46, quoting St. Cyprian).

In this way, the human sphere is unceasingly sustained and nourished by the divine sphere that mysteriously pervades it in depth, and both these dimensions, *together,* constitute the totally incomparable community that is the Church:

> But, the society structured with hierarchical organs and the mystical body of Christ, the visible society and the spiritual community, the earthly Church and the Church endowed with heavenly riches, are not to be thought of as two realities. On the contrary, they form one complex reality which comes together from a human and a divine element (*LG* 8a).

A detail of the greatest importance is therefore added to our understanding of the essential and effective structure of the people of God. This is naturally composed of two principles that are absolutely inseparable from each other, although they must in no way be confused with each other. In the admirable unity of its essential being, *the Church incarnates the perfect primacy of the divine over the human.* All this is better explained if it is considered that the human dimension has been taken up as a "sign" of its "sharing" in the divine dimension. In this way, we shall grasp the full significance of the words of the Council itself—and these words have the ring *almost* of a definition about them—according to which "the Church, in Christ, is in the nature of sacrament— a sign and instrument, that is, of communion with God and of unity among all men" (*LG* 1). The divine life as manifested and incarnate in the mystical body can in this way reach men, continually transforming many of them from amongst the most varied peoples of the world into *a people* (horizontal dimension), which, experiencing his grace in this way, belongs to, and is of God (vertical dimension). And thus the Church, structured by Christ "as the instrument for the salvation of all" (*LG* 9b), also takes on a sacramental character as the fundamental framework of its very efficacy, with its visible activities connected—indeed, bound—to invisible grace.[3]

> In Christ and through Christ in the Church, grace has taken on a human dimension; it transforms Christ's humanity, and, by means of Christ's humanity, the whole of mankind (and, through mankind, the universe), so that it is made manifest and communicates with what is human—by divinizing what is human, it "becomes human." In Christ and through Christ in the Church, grace is "sacramentalized": as it transforms man, it is expressed and transmitted in him. . . . Every effect of God's grace in man is a *sacramentalization.* Grace takes up what is human in order to divinize it; simply by taking it up, it divinizes it. This is why every effect of grace has an ecclesial character, inasmuch as it tends towards the sacramental.[4]

At this point, in order to give a more profound understanding of the mystery of the Church, the magisterium of the Council points out the *nexus mysteriorum:*

> For this reason the Church is compared, not without significance, to the mystery of the incarnate Word. As the assumed nature, inseparably united to him, serves the divine Word as a living organ of salvation, so, in a somewhat similar way, does the social structure of the Church serve the Spirit of Christ who vivifies it, in the building up of the body (*LG* 8a).

Thus, according to this teaching of the Council, just as the divine word employed human nature for his salvific work in showing forth the Father among men, so also the human component of the Church has been structured solely so that the Spirit might render Christ historically present in the world. In this way is shown forth how the connection and at the same time the distinction between the mystery of the incarnation and that of the Church are linked to the very relationship between the "mission" of the Son and that of the Spirit.

In the mystery of the immanent Trinity, in which the essential unity of nature is the basis for distinguishing the persons, the Spirit is in contrast to the Father and the Son inasmuch as he proceeds from each of them at the same time and is thus the only immediate relationship that unites them as a single person in the Father and the Son. Because it is this same Trinity whom we know in the economy of salvation, we can say[5]

. . . that the distinction within the Trinity between the Father and the Son on the one hand and the Holy Spirit on the other, is shown forth *as such* in the mystery of the Church, and that in the economy of salvation not only do the Father and the Son contemplate the Holy Spirit as a further mode of existence on the one divine nature, but they contemplate this mode of existence as the principle unifying the multiplicity of persons. Thus in this sense, the Spirit of Christ is, in the economy of salvation, the "we-relationship" of ourselves among the many—i.e., among the persons united in the "bride"—and the bridegroom, Christ. The salvific "love-of-self" which is characteristic of the Son ("whoever loves his own wife loves himself"—Eph. 5:28) reaches the fullness of "we," reigning in the economy of salvation, only when the Church "emanates" from him.[6]

In the Church, the Spirit is the person who, with extraordinary immediacy (for the divine word is in him himself), unites the many to Christ, and thus also to each other. In this way, we come to a deep understanding of the *original* significance of the ecclesial relationship as being a relationship of love.[7] The Church is defined—and this then clarifies its significance and importance—as *communion*: the people of God are also characterized in this manner as regards their being the body of Christ. As has been stated, the Spirit of Christ,

. . . in the social framework of the Church—i.e., in this absolutely unique, universal and personal interplay of relationships—is the relationship of the relationships, and the immediacy of every immediacy. (We are at present surveying the depths of a strict mystery of faith, which is absolutely unique of its kind, and practically incapable of any possible analogy.) Thus neither can this interplay of ecclesial relationships nor can the very Spirit of Christ be called the "subject" of the Church; this subject is made up (*coalescit*) of human and divine elements, as Vatican II teaches us.[8]

The *Christifidelis* in the Spheres of Ministry and Vocation of the Church: The Council Breaks with Old Models by Restoring a Traditional Value (Pluralism in the Spheres of Ministry and Vocation)

This is the ecclesiological context in which the Council situates its teaching on ministry and vocation. This represents a *break* with certain preconceived ideas that had also taken hold in canon law, and at the same time a *restoration* of an ecclesially traditional value.

In the preconciliar era, it was perfectly normal to give a picture of the Church that was primarily hierarchical, centering the structure of the Church above all on the "cleric," who thus also became the principal figure juridically, as we can see from the admirable treatment reserved to him in the 1917 Code of Popes Pius X and Benedict XV, which represented a faithful expression of the theologically and canonically dominant culture of the time. This also led to the contrasting of the cleric with the noncleric—the layman[9]—whose position and function were definitely marginalized by the Code in the Church itself, but were clearly, and sometimes with an abundance of norms,[10] submitted to the authority of the hierarchy. In point of fact,

. . . until the renewal of ecclesiology in the last forty years, which was, as it were, consecrated by the Council, the vision of the Church as popularized in the manuals was dominated by the idea of a *societas inaequalis hierarchica* [= an unequal hierarchical society] and not by the idea of community or that of people of God. The doctrine of the mystical body occasionally made a breach in the clerical rampart, but it was itself sometimes interpreted in the context of an unequal and hierarchical society. . . . There was a spontaneous tendency towards a clerical view of the Church.[11]

The Second Vatican Council wished to break with this situation by moving beyond this rift that, while it was widening in canonical terms, was also growing in incomprehensibility, as on the one hand, the Church was becoming established *almost* exclusively around the clergy, who were the only ones authorized to carry out the Church's mission, and on the other hand, the laity were being attributed a degree of secularization in their functions that *almost* placed them outside the Church. By contrast, the ecclesiology developed, as we have seen, by Vatican II authoritatively rendering it obligatory to bring right into the foreground— as, indeed, we find thrown into very fine relief by the systematic theology of the Dogmatic Constitution of the Church, which is itself a result of prime importance of these same discussions at the Council[12]—the common matrix of the whole Church:

> There is, therefore, one chosen People of God: "one Lord, one faith, one baptism" (Eph. 4:5); there is a common dignity of members deriving from their rebirth in Christ, a common grace as sons, a common vocation to perfection, one salvation, one hope and undivided charity (*LG* 32b).

The communion of the Church is eschatologically oriented (the communion of saints), and is already *in via peregrinationis* (or "on pilgrimage"), for it was dynamically "founded to spread the kingdom of Christ over all the earth for the glory of God the Father, to make all men partakers in redemption and salvation, and through them to establish the right relationship of the entire world to Christ" (*AA* 2a). *Furthermore,* this quality of communion in its objective means that the latter, in the people of God, is put into action according to the proper understanding thereof as the mission of *all* the *christifideles,* as is emphasized in a passage of fundamental importance by the same Second Vatican Council, where it speaks of the very laity whom the theological and canonical culture, which had up to that point held undoubted and exclusive sway, had attempted to exclude[13] from this common responsibility:

> Gathered together in the People of God and established in the one Body of Christ under one head, the laity—no matter who they are—have, as living members, the vocation of applying to the building up of the Church and to its continual sanctification all the powers which they have received . . . (LG 33a).

In order to effect this certainly very complex mission, the Church itself "by divine institution . . . is ordered and governed with a wonderful diversity" (LG 32a). And it is this very diversity that covers the one mission of the Church, with all the potential capacities in which the diverse expresses the one, that permits all the members of the faithful in Christ without exception to be partakers, according to the special gifts of each, in the building up of the Church. For

> In the organism of a living body no member plays a purely passive part; sharing in the life of the body it shares at the same time in its activity. The same is true for the Body of Christ, the Church: "the whole Body achieves full growth in dependence on the full functioning of each part" (Eph. 4:16). Between the members of this body there exists, further, such a unity and solidarity (cf. Eph. 4:16) that a member who does not work at the growth of the body to the extent of his possibilities must be considered useless both to the Church and to himself (AA 2a).[14]

And because every *christifidelis*, "through those gifts given to him, is at once the witness and the living instrument of the mission of the Church itself 'according to the measure of Christ's bestowal' (Eph. 4:7)" (LG 33b), it follows that, although the shared responsibility in effecting the one mission of the Church belongs to every member of the Christian faithful, it does not, however, belong in any way to each of them in equal measure. For if this complex sphere of ministry within the Church is to be sufficiently and suitably effective—in other words, be a diverse yet harmonious collection of activities functionally aimed at a particular goal[15]—a personal capacity is necessary, that is, a power that is subjectively articulated in different ways. More specifically, while it is true that, in order to develop certain ministries, the ministerial priesthood (hierarchical power) is indispensable, for others, the common priesthood is sufficient. However, we should not forget that both these forms of priesthood, "though they differ essentially and not only in degree, . . . are nonetheless ordered one to another; each in its own proper way shares in the one priesthood of Christ" (*LG* 10b).

Thus, it is in the multifold and multiform framework of the sphere of ministry, and only on the basis of their operative capacity for putting into effect (and thus for exercising the ministerial office), that is situated this diversification of those who, having been invested therewith by the hierarchical power, constitute the hierarchy as such, and those who, not possessing this power, form the laity as such. More specifically, in the people of God, as the Second Vatican Council teaches,

> . . . each part contributes its own gifts to other parts and to the whole Church, so that the whole and each of the parts are strengthened by the common sharing of all things and by the common effort to attain to fullness in unity. Hence it is that the People of God . . . is made up of different ranks. This diversity among its members is . . . *secundum officia,*—some exercise the sacred ministry for the good of their brethren (*LG* 13c).

In this way, Vatican II, with an ecclesiological approach of an importance, including its canonical impact, that no one can fail to appreciate, overcomes, without in any way altering its undeniable radical truth, the preconciliar dualism that placed the clergy in opposition to the laity, envisaging a harmonious complementarity of the one and the other in the organic unity of the people of God, affirming an essentially diverse capacity for the exercise of a multiplicity of ministries that, even when they require a hierarchical power, are, "in the strict sense of the term, a service, which is called very expressively in sacred scripture a *diakonia* or ministry" (*LG* 24a).

Now, if the one mission entrusted to all the *christifideles* is rendered living and vital by becoming incarnated "pluralistically"[16] in a varied diversity of ministries, some of which are of necessity linked with the hierarchical priesthood, whereas others are connected with the common priesthood, it follows that the selfsame vocation to God to which every *christifidelis* is called, is once again realized "pluralistically" in a diversity of forms and manners. For, as Vatican II again teaches, in the people of God, there is a diversity among its members, "due to their condition and manner of life—many enter the religious state[17] and, intending to sanctity by the narrower way, stimulate their brethren by their example" (*LG* 13c).

More particularly, the general vocation to holiness, which is proper to every baptized person, is expressed in numerous forms, some "common"—as personal realizations of the individual *vocatio ad Deum*—and some "special." This latter kind of vocation, which is lived out in a life consecrated to God by the practice of the evangelical counsels of chastity, poverty, and obedience,[18] in turn covers a multiplicity that is the richest series of different forms in the Church. Indeed, if we wish to contemplate the richness and "diversity" of incarnations of the consecrated life alone (which could even make it seem inappropriate to group them into the category of institutes, which would not cover, for example, eremitical styles of life), it will suffice to turn our attention to the multiplicity of forms of monastic life and of dedication to the apostolate of the vast number of male and female "religious" congregations that, in the most varied of forms, bear public witness to their profession of the evangelical counsels, that also finds external expression in the special habits they wear, and that is lived out in brotherly community with the Eucharist as its focal point.[19] Yet, the religious institutes do not exhaust the possibilities of consecrated life, which also covers at least certain of those "societies of apostolic life"[20] that are so very difficult to define because of the very diversity of their forms, both, when such is the case, in the context of their vows to the evangelical counsels (which are, nonetheless, in some way of a public nature), and also in the kinds of brotherly life, as well as in the goals of their apostolate, which are very frequently, as is natural, incorporated into the life of the various local churches, both those founded in the days of early Christianity and also those of more recent origin. We must add to this list, in order to complete the picture we are discussing, the microcosm of the Church in all its rich variety that is constituted by the "secular institutes"[21] that, in contrast to religious institutes, in numerous different ways live out their vocation in the world, seen as the context of their commitment and Christian responsibility, whereby they are nonetheless distinct (albeit in no way losing their common, lay origin) from the other laity by virtue of the "consecration" that characterizes and reinforces their secular character.[22] On the other hand, in the spirit of Vatican II, there have budded and flourished, with an evermore clearly defined character, *new* "various and vital forms of consecrated life, which have in common the features of the Council and those of the present day."[23]

Thus, the unity of communion of the people of God is never corrupted, owing to the continual support and sustenance of the Spirit,[24] and is continually expressed in diversity. This latter feature is, of course, a modality entirely characteristic of man, whose nature can be grasped only in the remarkable unrepeatability of all individual men who are socially interconnected, and in whom mankind is incarnated diachronically and synchronically. Thus, diversity is simply the modality that is entirely consonant with man's nature, so that he may be able to truly lay hold on the unity of the Church in depth, given that he cannot really say he is capable of making this his own other than by means of a personal "interpretation"[25] that must of necessity[26] be mediated by the "culture"[27] of the specific social context of which he forms part.

Hence we find, alongside certain constant elements, an endless variety of ministerial expressions of the Church's mission, and of vocational expressions of the common calling to God. For

Since the kingdom of Christ is not of this world (cf. Jn. 18:36), the Church or People of God which establishes this kingdom does not take away anything from the temporal welfare of any people. Rather she fosters and takes to herself, in so far as they are good, the abilities, the resources and the customs [or, we could say simply, the cultures] of peoples. In so taking them to herself she purifies, strengthens and elevates them (*LG* 13b).

And then, more specifically, by the term "culture," we can refer to all the means

. . . which go to the refining and developing of man's diverse mental and physical endowments. He strives to subdue the earth by his knowledge and his labor; he humanizes social life both in the family and in the whole civic community through the improvement of customs and institutions; he expresses through his works the great spiritual experiences and aspirations of men throughout the ages; he communicates and preserves them to be an inspiration for the progress of many, even of all mankind (GS 53b).

Thus, if by the term "culture," we mean all the above, we shall have no difficulty in sensing the necessary variety of forms of ministry and vocation that must be established alongside those directly established by God, so that the *christifideles* in their context within all the peoples who constitute the one people of God, may be able to realize God's vocation and the Church's mission in a manner that is really capable of deeply involving them.[28]

Indeed, it is only through their own cultural identity that a people can live as the Church, making it truly and radically their *own,* in such a way as not to feel estranged from it, as would be only natural if membership of the Church were to be considered linked to a particular culture that was different from their own, and especially so if this extraneous culture were alienating, inasmuch as it were that of a dominating or even colonial power. This synchronic diversity that is rooted in the cultural variety of so many peoples is also of necessity accompanied by a diachronic diversity, inasmuch as "culture necessarily has historical overtones" (GS 53c), for it is in itself a *continuum* that dynamically progresses in discontinuity.

Once we have grasped this ministerial and vocational diversity that unity incarnates in the communion of the Church, we shall easily understand the role not of separation but of union proper to the difference between the common and particular vocations to God as well as that between the hierarchical and common priestly power. The following text presents closer treatment of this latter difference:

The distinction which the Lord has made between the sacred ministers and the rest of the People of God involves union, for the pastors and the other faithful are joined together by a close relationship: the pastors of the Church—following the example of the Lord—should minister to each other and to the rest of the faithful; the latter should eagerly collaborate with the pastors and teachers. And so amid variety all will bear witness to the wonderful unity in the Body of Christ: this very diversity of graces, of ministries and of works gathers the sons of God into one, for "all these things are the work of one and the same Spirit" (1 Cor. 12:11) (*LG* 32c).

What is more, this admirable structure of the people of God thus comes to find, prior to all the distinctions, its center in the *christifidelis* who is therefore the true and effective *human protagonist* in the Church. In this perspective of unity, the basic condition of *christifidelis* is destined never to change in an essential manner, although it will of necessity have to adapt itself with all due flexibility to the numerous requirements of diversity, particularly when the latter takes on very specific connotations, as for the exercise of the hierarchical ministries. Nevertheless, even in this latter case, these variations that arise *solely* from the need to best favor the exercise of the ministry, and thus from "objectively" functional and not "subjectively" personal causes, must not establish themselves—by exchanging the conditions for putting the ministry into effect for personal circumstances—into "statuses" that are juridically distinct from a socially subjective point of view and that, following the inevitable process of involution of legal structures, will in time become separate strata, as recent history has shown in practice, especially as regards the opposition between clergy and laity, and will finally become a sign of division. On the contrary, these variations must avoid generalizations[29] to the greatest possible extent, and express, by contrast, solely the needs of each of the numerous incarnations of the spheres of vocation and ministry within the Church, and must develop as the diaconal gift of each ministerial and vocational "rank" to all the others, so that all may build up unity together in harmony, because, as Vatican II recognizes, "the people of God . . . is made up of different ranks" (*LG* 13c). Nevertheless, in order to gain a sufficient and proper understanding of this central position occupied by the member of the Christian faithful within the economy of the Church, we must move on, after our consideration of this general context, to examine the basic condition of this *christifidelis*, in other words, the *communis christifidelium status*.

The *Christifidelis* as the Incarnation
of Pluralism in the Church:
The Council "Constructs" Liberty (Diversity)
in the Manner of Living out Equality
(Unity in the Church)

The richly varied structure of the spheres of ministry and vocation within the Church, of which we have attempted to give an outline above, has as its human barycenter, as we have seen, the *christifidelis*, whose "state . . . is that of the dignity and freedom of the sons of God, in whose hearts the Holy Spirit dwells as in a temple" (LG 9b).[30]

It is a fact that the Church's understanding of itself as promulgated in the teachings of Vatican II is particularly centered on a detailed study of its own mystery (whereby it sought not to contradict but certainly to complement comparable studies attempted in former ages), by means of the exemplary figure of the "people of God," which was more specially understood, as we have said, in terms of the *communion* of all the members of the Christian faithful with each other and with God, as a *communio fidei, sacramentorum et disciplinae* (or "communion of faith, sacraments, and discipline"), as Paul VI had occasion to express it on one occasion.[31] In this way, we can confidently identify the communitarian dimension of the Church in the profound *equality* that unites all in the Church in a relationship that corresponds to the same law of love, bringing, in the one heritage of faith, God close to each *christifidelis* and each to him, in the unity of the sacraments themselves.[32] We can therefore emphasize that

> Fully incorporated into the Church are those who, possessing the Spirit of Christ, accept all the means of salvation given to the Church together with her entire organization, and who—by the bonds constituted by the profession of faith, the sacraments, ecclesiastical government, and communion—are joined in the visible structure of the Church of Christ, who rules her through the Supreme Pontiff and the bishops (LG 14b).

The equality of all, so strongly affirmed in the teaching of the Second Vatican Council (also in the very structure of its Dog-

matic Constitution on the Church, in which the chapter on all
the people of God precedes the assuredly more traditional one on
its hierarchical structure), is translated into the "effective" participation of all, according to their own spiritual needs, in the
supernatural benefits, especially those of word and sacrament,
that are present in a communitarian manner in the Church.
Beyond this realm of equality, there is a wide diversity of situations that are of varied juridical importance as a result of canonical legislation,[33] as "the Church knows that she is joined in many
ways" (*LG* 15) to every non-Catholic baptized person, while
"those who have not yet received the Gospel are related to the
People of God in various ways" (*LG* 16). Within this same equality, however, are active all the various subjective positions that,
by their admirable diversity, nourish the extraordinary personal
vitality within the Church. Equality, functioning essentially as a
fulcrum, builds up the communitarian dimension within the
Church, and is to be considered as a "unifying" matrix of the
diversity of all subjective positions, which are thus possible *only
consecutively*.

More specifically, equality is hence to be seen as a feature of
the *basic identity* of every member of the Christian faithful, who
shares in the *same* word and the *same* sacraments within a *sole*
community, the absolute necessity of which for the *christifidelis*
can be seen to be self-evident. Indeed, in this perspective,

> . . . the fundamental Christian experience of the New Life
> cannot exist other than conjointly as the Church and as an
> individual personality; each of these aspects is clearly defined
> in itself and yet always in relation to the other. There cannot
> exist a Church in which the members of the faithful are not at
> the same time interior worlds which repose alone within them-
> selves with their God. There cannot exist a Christian personal-
> ity that is not integrated in the community of the Church as a
> living member.[34]

The individual discontinuity of each *christifidelis* is thus able to
live out in harmony the "continuity" of the community, in order
to move toward God by means of the Church.

Hence, the nature of this equality is such that it constitutes
the matrix most suited to develop those areas of freedom that
permit each individual day after day to transform her own radi-

cally undetermined human existence into the self-realization whereby each member of the Christian faithful fashions herself and works out her own salvation. Thus, we can conclude our discussion of this point with the words of the Second Vatican Council:

> In Christ and in the Church there is, then, no inequality arising from race or nationality, social condition or sex, for "there is neither Jew nor Greek; there is neither slave nor freeman; there is neither male nor female. For you are all 'one' in Jesus Christ.". . . In the Church not everyone marches along the same path, yet all are called to sanctity and have obtained an equal privilege of faith through the justice of God (*LG* 32b–c).

Thus, it is on the basis of this equality that the freedoms of the *christifideles* are grafted—and hence, above all, the freedom that includes and summarizes all the others, the freedom to move toward union with God:

> It is therefore quite clear that all Christians in any state or walk of life are called to the fullness of Christian life and to the perfection of love. . . . In order to reach this perfection the faithful should use the strength dealt out to them by Christ's gift, so that, following in his footsteps and conformed to his image, doing the will of God in everything, they may whole-heartedly devote themselves to the glory of God and to the service of their neighbor. . . . Each one . . . , according to his own gifts and duties must steadfastly advance along the way of a living faith, which arouses hope and works through love (*LG* 40b–41a),

so that "those who believe might have access through Christ in one Spirit to the Father" (*LG* 4a).

More specifically, the *christifidelis,* who thus needs God, is able to find his own "total" fulfillment in God's personal (inasmuch as he gives himself *totally* to him) gift of himself, without any obligation, of truth and love, which takes place within the Church.[35] For when a member of the faithful responds freely to God's call, she gives life to a personal dialogue, given that she has been rendered capable of this by God's love itself. This dialogue involves knowledge of the very life of the Trinity, in God's word, and sharing in it, and this sharing takes on a very special sense in the sacrament:

> In the same love with which the Father loves the Son, we too are re-conformed to the form of love, and in it the Father himself loves us; for through this very love, which is the Holy Spirit who is given from the Father to the Son and from the Son to the Father and from both to us for our sanctification, illumination and perfection, we are drawn back to this very fount of love.[36]

Now, if we consider this freedom of sanctification as such, we shall see that it is the modality whereby the member of the faithful continually renews herself in God, because she is truly acting freely, also forming her own Christian identity with her own human existence. This becomes what it is ecclesially within *time*. More specifically, in the *christifidelis* freedom shows forth her own personal Christian existentiality as she moves toward God. This existentiality is at once perceived by the *christifidelis* as being "situated" within history. More particularly, from this specific viewpoint, the *christifidelis* perceives her existence immersed in a temporal dimension. Time also transmits to her, with its basic relativity, the sense of her continuing becoming in God, who is definitive, instant after ever-indefinite instant. Her free existence within time, which cannot be arrested in any way, is therefore *diversity*, because during her progress in God, she is never for a moment what she was the moment before. This condition whereby she is never complete in her own eyes also produces a considerable degree of anxiety; this is strictly linked to the fact that she is moving *freely* in God. For this continued growth and inexhaustible movement cannot be achieved following a tranquil plan that would permit only a development along the sure lines of a predetermined progress. However, existence, including in the *christifidelis*, comes about in God within time according to a dynamic creativity that is governed by the freedom that belongs to her individually.

The member of the Christian faithful thus discovers herself in her existential dimension as "radical indetermination," revealing herself to herself as a being truly entrusted to herself and finding fulfillment in God in successive moments of time in the "individuality of her Christian identity" through freedom. By means of an unceasing diachronic dynamism, freedom also makes the *christifideles* in the people of God different from each other and absolutely unique in themselves.

However, diversity and uniqueness in our ecclesial relationship with God, according to the reasoning we have followed up to this point, must actually mean the *creatively* personal modality of a human existence that is unmistakably characterized by the identity incarnated in the common heritage of the communion of the Church, dynamically constructed in proportion to the gifts received. Thus, diversity, originating from freedom, is shown forth in the Church by life in the same unity as expressed and formed by each *christifidelis*, who invents it afresh day by day according to her own personal individuality, forming it in such a way as to give life to the charisms received from the Spirit. Indeed, as the Second Vatican Council itself teaches in a passage that is assuredly fundamental for an understanding of this diversity of the *christifideles*,

> From the reception of these charisms, even the most ordinary ones, there arises for each of the faithful the right and duty of exercising them in the Church and in the world for the good of men and the development of the Church, of exercising them in the freedom of the Holy Spirit who "breathes where he wills" . . . , and at the same time in communion with his brothers in Christ, and with his pastors especially. It is for the pastors to pass judgment on the authenticity and good use of these gifts, not certainly with a view to quenching the Spirit but to testing everything and keeping what is good (AA 3d).

The freedom of self-fulfillment in God must therefore be considered in the people of God not solely contemplating its necessity, as a "duty" to be performed—which certainly needs to be stated—but, for the very reason that it is a creative freedom, also much more significantly as a "right," and more specifically as a *right and duty to salvation*, which in its "uprightness" cannot be limited other than in itself. This fundamental right and duty, as we have come to present it, *demands* for its suitable and sufficient realization a whole series of ecclesial actions so that the canonical legislation may be centered on the member of the Christian faithful, with an authentic overturning of the old positions that placed the hierarchy at the center, and that can no longer be maintained after Vatican II, the teaching of which clearly placed the *christifidelis* at the center of a Church that in the divine plan was intended for *her* service and *her* salvation.

This basic right and duty is also incarnated and expressed by means of a series of other rights and duties, all of which, as is obvious, already form part of this primary, fundamental right and duty to salvation, and are thus closely and inseparably *incorporated* in each other, in such a way that an offense proffered to the one must of necessity in some way inflict a wound on the others. Leaving aside the more-or-less complete lists and the various classifications that can be made of these rights and duties, the Second Vatican Council—although here we cannot give a full account of a subject that is certainly very complex[37]—did not fail to indicate at least the lines along which the basic areas must develop in which, both in the universal Church and in the local, individual churches, the diversity of the individual's own self-realization in God must grow, specifying in this way the rights and duties that must form a suitable expression of this diversity,[38] whether these be—even if it may prove not to be easy or even feasible to impose such a distinction in the light of the conciliar texts—of an *individual* nature, whether "personal," or "communitarian" (among the latter, an assuredly very important place would be occupied by the rights and duties that we could call those "of dialogue"[39]), or of a *collective* nature.

The *christifidelis*, who is the true incarnation of "pluralism"[40] in the people of God, expresses in diversity, in other words with freedom (in line with her own individual personality), the common heritage of faith and sacrament that is rooted in the communion of the Church, and thus becomes capable in the Church of realizing in God her own existentiality within time, directing and forming the being that she is able to release from her own radical indetermination. Thus, *from within* (from a free self-determination made possible by grace, which has interiorly put aright all deficiencies by giving added strength in every way), every *christifidelis* gives life to a self that is unique and unrepeatable, and of which she is consciously the maker inasmuch as she lives out an existentiality that is favored by the Church and protected by canon law. This existentiality is rooted in her own Christian identity. She is able to give life to this self after having formed and molded it in its historical context by means of her own freedom, which is thus for her "the power of self-definition within a horizon of indefinite possibilities," the power whereby she achieves "stability in the unforeseeable flux" of her own "existence," and provides a basis for her own "eternity."[41] Hence, canon law must work effectively in the service of the human protagonist, whom the magisterium of Vatican II has fully restored to the "awareness" of the people of God, in order to permit her, "pluralistically," in a diversity that must be a genuine manifestation of unity, to attain the Father in the Spirit through the Son.

The *Christifidelis* in the Code of the Council: A "Consequence" of the Council in the *Communis Christifidelium Status* (or "Common Status of the Members of the Christian Faithful")

The magisterium of the Second Vatican Council found its juridical dimension in the Code of Canon Law promulgated on 25 January 1983 by John Paul II. In the very Constitution *Sacrae disciplinae leges* by which it was promulgated, authoritative emphasis is also given to the "note of complementarity which the Code presents in relation to the teaching of the Second Vatican Council."[42] Furthermore, this same Constitution states that "what constitutes the substantial *newness* of the Second Vatican Council, in line with the legislative tradition of the Church, especially in regard to ecclesiology, constitutes likewise the *newness* of the new Code," so that

> . . . if . . . the Second Vatican Council has drawn both new and old from the treasury of tradition, . . . then it is clear that the Code should also reflect the same note of fidelity in newness and of newness in fidelity, and conform itself to this in its own subject matter and in its own particular manner of expression.[43]

However, it is more the spirit of the teachings of the Council than the letter that reappears, because the Code itself as such— although this was not always successful or really satisfactory— had to give a juridical form to these teachings, creating them anew in the form of norms. What is more, the Code, which followed almost twenty years after the Council, cannot simply have put the latter into effect, because in the meantime, the Church had certainly not stood still but had continued along the same path, questioning and understanding itself better and better, including in the light of the teaching of the Council, which represented the point of reference for a reflection that, too, has certainly not ended and that, on the contrary, has, owing also to the needs that the new times have gradually produced within the people of God, ceaselessly become enriched by new developments. The 1983 Code of Canon Law, albeit of course, as the promulgator himself authoritatively emphasized, the Code of Vatican II, of which it has become the authorized interpreter from a juridical point of view, nevertheless constructs this "continuity," which is, more profoundly, continuity with the two millenia of the Church's canonical tradition, by means of an equally unavoidable and traditional "discontinuity," which is, as we have just stated, the unmistakable sign of the times, which are also changing for the people of God. [44]

On the other hand,

> . . . the Code will become what the life of the Church makes of it. It is not a point of departure, nor a point of arrival; it is not a monolithic block set up once and for all. It would not be a real Code if it did not permit the life of the Spirit to express itself in the institutions which he has brought into being and which will become more and more open to his action. It is this very openness to life, this adaptability and this respect for what the Spirit will bring into being, that constitute one of the new and promising features of this new legislation. [45]

With this necessary openness to the divine law—which is, after all, an inalienable feature of Church law—the 1983 Code truly and effectively represents an interpretation of God's word, under the impact of the Second Vatican Council. Not only is this hermeneutically of outstanding importance, but it also avoids in the juridical experience of the people of God every form of immobilization of the life of the Church, which would be in open contradiction with the living action of the Spirit in the Church.

If we search the 1983 Code for the lines of the conciliar teaching we have tried to sketch in this study, we shall observe the great effort that has been made to translate it into terms of juridical norms, even though it must be confessed that the results obtained are obscured by the frequent superimposition of the old juridical forms of the 1917 Code of Popes Piux X and Benedict XV. More specifically, as regards more closely the subject we are discussing, we are obliged to affirm this above all for the general ministerial and vocational context that is the necessary basis in the Church for the position and the role that the Second Vatican Council wished to proclaim for the *christifidelis* in the Church.

More specifically, even though we cannot examine all this in detail here, as concerns the sphere of ministry, we can perceive in the 1983 Code the basic outlines of the conciliar magisterium. In the first place, the opposition between the hierarchy and the laity has disappeared, and the two states have been situated in a more varied and structured ecclesial context in which are integrated, as has been observed, "all Christians, each according to his rank or role. The new Code has opened up this path by speaking first of the Christian faithful, then of the laity, then of the clergy, and lastly of the institutes of consecrated life."[46] Nevertheless, not only will we search in vain for all the richness of forms and options the Council had been able to perceive—albeit, as is indeed the case with life itself, in a confused and disordered manner—but, in our opinion, the Code failed to give their full value, in depth at least, to the personal *ordines* as such. That is to say, it did not consider them as adaptations to the ministerial individuality of the common condition of *christifidelis,* which would have avoided certain unnecessary generalizations, focusing better, by contrast, on the individual features derived from the specificity of each ministry and, above all, pointing up diversity as the pluralistic expression of a fundamental unity, and in its norms, it was not capable of entirely avoiding setting persons in opposition.

This is all particularly evident as concerns the laity.[47] Thus, although in the 1983 Code we find the major features of the conciliar teaching on ministry, these are not translated into a truly unifying principle; rather, they are confused with principles of a different origin. In point of fact, in the 1983 Code,

. . . different traditions are found in contrast; if certain of them are followed, it will prove possible . . . to demonstrate the richness as well as the complexity of the nature of the Church and of the doctrinal research it necessarily involves.[48]

On the other hand, although the common vocation receives inadequate treatment, a more felicitous juridical account is undoubtedly reserved (because of the clearer conciliar impact of at least the special vocation represented by the various forms of consecrated life) for the diversity of vocations in the 1983 Code, for here the Code has successfully formulated better norms, under the impact of the Council, for the living reality of the people of God, which can thus draw benefit from a juridical system that is, as it should be, at its service. The sphere of vocation receives very varied and well-structured treatment in the 1983 Code, just as it appears in the lived experience of the people of God, where

> . . . the diversity of charisms has produced, on a common basis, different groups of monastic and apostolic institutes. The same can be said of societies of common life, which are so different one from another. The secular institutes have the same experience. Each institute forms a compact group of persons. This group cannot be a "rank of persons" in the Church; however, awareness has now grown to the effect that "ranks of persons" could find new life not only in law, but also in the real life of the Church, whereby excessively general classifications could be overcome, such as those of clerics and laity. The term "clerics" is gradually giving way to the terminology that suits them better, namely "sacred ministers." They are divided into three holy orders. The laity will engage in similar research as soon as freedom of association permits them to give themselves a better organized structure within the Church.[49]

As we have stated, this view of the Church is not always presented as it should be in the Code, and it is our opinion that this is above all owing to the rather confused impression given by the passage in Canons 208–223 outlining the *communis christifidelium status*, although the very fact that this figure in the 1983 Code is to be considered a new element of capital importance for a correct understanding of the laws of the Code as well as of the theological and canonical culture—that of the Second Vatican Council—that is the basis on which the new Code is founded.

The first thing we are obliged to point out is that the norms referring to the series of fundamental rights and duties of the *christifidelis* are not always consciously centered on the most fundamental right and duty, that to salvation, and are mostly limited simply to enumerating these subjective positions, on the whole without the specific value that juridical statements should always possess. Above all, however, a clear treatment is lacking of the group of elements of negative protection—safeguards against unwarranted interference on the part of others, including the hierarchical authorities themselves—and in particular of positive protection, as expressed in the premises necessary for an effective and real exercise of all the rights and duties in the daily life of the people of God.[50] What is more, not all these rights and duties (not even the fundamental ones) have been mentioned in the norms. Above all, we must also regret the lack of specification, with any subjective juridical position of a collective nature, of those rights and duties that give an active voice to those who socially and individually are in situations of grave difficulty and emargination.[51] Although it is true that those that are "forgotten" by the Code are contained in the fundamental right and duty to salvation, had they been specifically noted in the legislation, this would have permitted especially the definition of their positive and negative elements, their more adequate protection, and their more proper influence on the lives of the *christifideles*.

The *communis christifidelium status*[52] does, however, figure in the Code as concerns one of its primary fundamental features: that of equality. In the first place, the element of unity that is the common heritage of all *christifideles* in the people of God is emphasized by the 1983 Code in Canon 205, which rules that "Those baptized are fully in communion with the Catholic Church on this earth who are joined with Christ in its visible structure by the bonds of profession of faith, of the sacraments and of ecclesiastical governance." On the basis of this fundamental communion, it is then possible to state, as is established by Canon 208 of the same Code, that

> In virtue of their rebirth in Christ there exists among all the Christian faithful a true equality with regard to dignity and the activity whereby all cooperate in the building up of the Body of Christ in accord with each one's own condition and function.

Without this principle of equality, which is for good reason given such prominence by the magisterium of the Council, it would certainly be impossible to give a juridical outline of the

ecclesial condition of the Christian faithful, because equality is
the element of identity that, while it binds together the individual members of the people of God, at the same time forms the
common matrix from which the freedom of each individual
christifidelis will form her own personal physiognomy as she moves
toward God. However, it can also not be disputed that the continuous repetition[53] of this principle under the most varied of
forms in the norms of the Code can lead, by encouraging incorrect legal interpretations, to an obfuscation of its value, which is
that of a solely intrinsic limit (because it is of necessity a consequence of its function that is indicative of the element of unity in
the *communis christifidelium status*) whereby it takes on the character—which is alienating by this principle—of an external limit
imposed by force in order to put a brake on the free expansion of
the same *christifidelis* toward God.

Even in the Code, the *communis christifidelium status* has its
own complement, and hence its other basic feature, in the norms
concerning the areas of freedom that are established around the
fundamental rights and duties that permit each member of the
Christian faithful to build up, in diversity, according to her own
role and her own charisms, her own Christian identity, and thus
her own progress toward God. Although these numerous rights
and duties are not always individually specified in the norms of
the Code, they are all, nonetheless, centered on the most fundamental and all-embracing right and duty of each *christifidelis* to
salvation, as is solemnly stated in Canon 210 of the Code: "All
the Christian faithful must make an effort, in accord with their
own condition, to live a holy life and to promote the growth of
the Church and its continual sanctification."

Despite the considerable legislative uncertainty—the sign of
an incipient progress in the norms of Church law—the *communis
christifidelium status* confirmed by the 1983 Code constitutes an
element of capital importance, not only as a fundamental "consequence" of the Council in juridical terms, but also and above all
because it situates the *christifidelis* in the center of the juridical
economy of the people of God, making her the human protagonist of the Code promulgated on 25 January 1983, inasmuch as
all the other norms to a certain extent depend on and must be
interpreted on the basis of those that regulate this *communis
christifidelium status*. In order to render this juridical progress,
achieved under the impact of the Council, ever more real and

effective even in the daily life of the people of God, hermeneutical practice is of fundamental importance. In order not to lose the major values contained in these norms, this practice must always consider them in the light and spirit of the same Second Vatican Council, and thus of a Church that is perceived as a communion in which pluralistically each *christifidelis* can *freely* build up the "diversity" of her own progress in God, thus expressing, in the manner uniquely and personally her own, *equality*, which is the unity around which the identity of the people of God is established.

Translated from the Italian by Ronald Sway, Andrew Wade, and Leslie Wearne.

Notes

1. For a much more detailed although partially different approach to this conciliar text, cf. P.A. Bonnet, "Diritto e potere nel momento originario della 'potestas hierarchica' nella Chiesa. Stato della dottrina in una questione canonisticamente disputata," *Jus canonicum*, 15/29 (1975), 77–91.

2. Pius XII, Encyclical Letter *Mystici Corporis Christi* (29 June 1943), in *AAS*, 35 (1943), 220 and 219; English translation published by the Catholic Truth Society (London, 1944), 35 and 34.

3. It is clear that in this broad sense of the term, every activity of the Church must be described as sacramental, even though a grace could exist that is not bound to any sign, or a sign could exist that is sometimes performed without fruits of grace.

4. J. Alfaro, *Cristologia e antropologia. Temi teologici attuali* (Assisi, 1973), 129–130.

5. H. Mühlen, whose line we follow in his vast and perceptive research on the analogy between the mystery of the Church and that of the incarnation.

6. H. Mühlen, *Una mystica Persona. La Chiesa come il mistero dello Spirito Santo in Cristo e nei cristiani: una persona in molte persone* (Rome, 1968), 559.

7. Cf. P.A. Bonnet, "Carità e diritto: la dimensione comunitaria quale momento della struttura interna del diritto della Chiesa," *Investigatione theologico-canonicae* (Rome, 1978), 75–98.

8. Mühlen, *Una mystica Persona*, 555; but cf. 470–561.

9. Cf. P.A. Bonnet, "De laicorum notione adumbratio," *Periodica de re morali canonica liturgica*, 74 (1985), 227–271.

10. Cf., for example, inasmuch as it refers to the very central phenomenon of associations of *christifideles*, P.A. Bonnet, "De christi-fidelium consociationum lineamentarum, juxta Schema 'De Populo Dei' codicis recogniti anni 1979, adumbratione," *Periodica de re morali canonica liturgica*, 71 (1982), 576–579.

11. Y.M.-J. Congar, *Misteri e comunione ecclesiale* (Bologna, 1973), 34.

12. Cf. C. Moeller, "Il fermento delle idee nella elaborazione della costituzione," in G. Baraúna (ed.), *La Chiesa del Vaticano II. Studi e commenti intorno alla costituzione dommatica "Lumen Gentium"* (Florence, 1967³), 175–176.

13. Cf. J. Beyer, "De statuto iuridico christifidelium iuxta vota Synodi Episcoporum in novo codice iuris condendo," *Periodica de re morali canonica liturgica*, 57 (1968), 559.

14. Cf. P.A. Bonnet, "Est in Ecclesia diversitas ministerii sed unitas missionis," in E. Corecco, N. Herzog, and A. Scola (eds.), *Les droits fondamentaux du Chrétien dans l'Eglise et dans la Société* (Freiburg im Breisgau/Milan, 1981), 291–308.

15. Cf. P.A. Bonnet, "Una questione ancora aperta: l'origine del potere gerarchico nella Chiesa," *Ephemerides iuris canonici*, 38 (1982), 62–121.

16. On this concept as the fundamental key to understanding the whole of canon law, cf. P.A. Bonnet, "Pluralismo (in genere), a) diritto canonico," *Enciclopedia del diritto*, 36, 956–983.

17. This matter should be further discussed with reference not only to the religious life, but to the whole of consecrated life. Cf. J. Beyer, *Verso un nuovo diritto degli Istituti di vita consacrata* (Rome/Milan, 1976). It should be mentioned that the elaboration of the final redaction of the chapter on religious in the Dogmatic Constitution on the Church was not without its difficulties. Cf. M.J. Schoenmackers, *Genèse du chapitre VI "De religiosis" de la constitution dogmatique sur l'Eglise "Lumen gentium"* (Rome, 1983).

18. Cf. J. Beyer, *De vita per consilia evangelica consecrata* (Rome, 1969).

19. Cf. Beyer, *Verso un nuovo diritto degli Istituti di vita consacrata*, 173–189.

20. Cf. J. Beyer, "Le società di vita comune," *Gregorianum*, 48 (1967), 747–765.

21. Cf. J. Beyer, *Les instituts séculiers* (Paris, 1954).

22. Cf. S. Holland, *The Concept of Consecration in Secular Institutes* (Rome, 1981).

23. J. Beyer, "Novità dello Spirito," *Vita consacrata*, 14 (1978), 576.

24. Cf. P.A. Bonnet, " 'Continuità e 'discontinuità' nel diritto ec-clesiale e nell'esperienza giuridica totale dell'uomo," in G. Barberini (ed.), *Raccolta di Scritti in onore di Pio Fedele*, 1 (Perugia, 1984), 44–45.

25. The Second Vatican Council itself gave authoritative expression to the same idea (cf. GS 53a).

26. Cf. Bonnet, " 'Continuità' e 'discontinuità' nel diritto ecclesiale," 37–47.

27. As regards the central importance of the element of culture in the economy of the Church, cf. from a mostly specific viewpoint that could, however, be broadened to general considerations, P.A. Bonnet, "Il diritto-dovere fondamentale del fedele migrante," *On the Move*, 13/39 (1983), 66–115.

28. This would not be possible if the life of the people of God were lived in forms and manners that were extraneous to the local culture. This extraneous nature would in fact entail a Church identity that was mostly incomprehensible and above all alienating, and for this very reason rather superficial. Cf. concerning the relationship between faith and culture, B. Lonergan, *Doctrinal Pluralism* (Milwaukee, 1972²).

29. Cf. Bonnet, "Est in Ecclesia diversitas ministerii sed unitas missionis," 301.

30. Cf. P.A. Bonnet, "Habet pro conditione dignitatem libertatemque filiorum Dei," *Il diritto ecclesiastico*, 91/1 (1981), 556–620.

31. Allocution "Ad Praelatos Auditores et Officiales Tribunalis Sacrae Romanae Rotae, a Beatissimo Patre novo litibus iudicandis ineunte anno coram admissos" (19 January 1970), *AAS*, 62 (1970), 116.

32. Cf. P.A. Bonnet, "Eucharistia et ius," *Periodica de re morali canonica liturgica*, 66 (1977), 583–616.

33. Cf. W. Bertrams, "De gradibus 'Communionis' in Doctrina Concilii Vaticani II," *Gregorianum*, 47 (1966), 286–305.

34. R. Guardini, *La realtà della Chiesa* (Brescia, 1967), 50.

35. Cf. Bonnet, "Eucharistia et ius," 583–598.

36. Albert the Great, "In sacrosancta Evangelia luculenta expositio, In Caput IX Marci," in S.A. Borgnet (ed.), *Alberti Magni . . . opera omnia*, 21 (Paris, 1894), 546.

37. Cf. P.A. Bonnet, "De christifidelium communi statu (iuxta Schema anni 1979 L.E.F.) animadversiones," *Periodica de re morali canonica liturgica*, 71 (1982), 463–529.

38. Cf. J. Beyer, "La 'communio' comme critère des droits fondamentaux," in Corecco, Herzog, and Scola (eds.), *Les droits fondamentaux du Chrétien*, 79–96.

39. Cf. J. Beyer, "La 'communio' criterio dei diritti fondamentali," *Vita consacrata*, 19 (1983), 200–210.

40. Cf. note 16 above.

41. J.B. Metz, "Libertà," in H. Fries (ed.), *Dizionario di teologia*, 2 (Brescia, 1967), 199.

42. *AAS*, 75/2 (1983), XII. The English translation of this Constitution, and that of the canons is taken from that published by the Canon Law Society of America (Washington, DC, 1983); here, xiv.

43. *AAS,* 75/2 (1983), XXI; English translation, xv.

44. Cf. P.A. Bonnet, "La codificazione canonica nel sistema delle fonti tra continuità e discontinuità," in *Perché un codice nella Chiesa (Il codice del Vaticano II)*, 1 (Bologna, 1984), 57–125.

45. J. Beyer, "Dal Concilio al codice," in *Il nuovo codice e le istanze del Concilio Vaticano II (Il codice del Vaticano II)*, 2 (Bologna, 1984), 32.

46. *Ibid.*, 71.

47. Cf. Bonnet, "De laicorum notione adumbratio," 167–201.

48. Beyer, "Dal Concilio al codice," 72.

49. *Ibid.*, 91–92.

50. Cf. Bonnet, "De christifidelium communi statu," 492–504.

51. For a particularly detailed systematic account, cf. Bonnet, "Il diritto-dovere fondamentale del fidele migrante," 66–115.

52. Cf. P.A. Bonnet, "De omnium christifidelium obligationibus et iuribus (cann. 208–223)," in P.A. Bonnet and G. Ghirlanda, *De christifidelibus. De eorum iuribus, de laicis, de consociationibus. Adnotationes in codicem* (Rome, 1983), 19–52.

53. Cf. Bonnet, "De christifidelium communi statu," 516–529.

CHAPTER 19

Does the So-Called
Theology of the Laity
Possess a Theological Status?

Giovanni Magnani, S.J.

Summary

The present study does not intend to deal with all the problems of the so-called "theology of the laity," but only, focusing on Vatican II, to investigate certain questions that are fundamental for determining its theological status. After an historical section, the study concentrates (a) on the conciliar texts on the theological status of the laity, and, briefly, on the process of their redaction, (b) bearing in mind the background of the postconciliar debate on this topic, along with an indication of the solution given by the new Code of Canon Law, (c) throwing into relief certain central problems that have not yet been solved or have not yet received sufficient clarification.

Methodological Premises

The conciliar texts in their final redaction must be examined in the first place for their intrinsic value, with the intentions and content that are explicitly present in them. However, if we are to gain a fuller understanding of them, they must be situated in their time as a response to problems and debates of that moment as they were perceived by the relevant conciliar commissions and subcommissions. Lastly, we must indicate at what point, and why, questions and problems have arisen in the postconciliar debate. Nevertheless, we shall have to limit ourselves to a few basic indications lest we exceed the limits of the present article.

Our study, which is dedicated to the determination of a possible theological status for the "theology of the laity," is centered on only two interconnected problems that, in our opinion, exert a determining influence on this field of research. We shall express these in the form of two questions:

1. Is it possible to determine a theological status for the (Christian) "laity" on the basis of the texts of Vatican II? Is it possible to define the layperson in justifiable and unobjectionable theological terms?

2. Is it strictly possible to indicate a "specificity" of the layperson? If so, on what plane of reflection is this to be situated? If not, is it still strictly possible to speak of a "theology of the laity"? What relationship exists between lay status and the layperson?

It is obvious that the two questions are interconnected.

However, these questions reveal all their importance if we bear in mind that if a solution can be found to them, this will modify the understanding the pilgrim Church is gaining of itself, and of its—or, in its—relationship with the world. The first question, which implies that there is a basis for a status of the laity in the "one sacred deposit of the word of God" of Scripture and Tradition—in the sense established by the Dogmatic Constitution on Divine Revelation (*DV* 10, with the observation made in No. 9 concerning sacred Tradition: ". . . thus it comes about that the Church does not draw her certainty about all revealed truths from the holy Scriptures alone")—already reveals the difficulties implicit in the very posing of the question, to which our research intends replying in the following paragraphs.

Brief Account of the History
and Present Situation of the Problem:
The Term "Layperson" in Tradition
and in Postconciliar Thought

It is not our intention to carry out a full study, but to offer some reflections on the difficulties behind our two questions.

1. The *first difficulty* for a theological basis of the term "layperson" comes from the well-known fact that λαϊκός does not figure in the Greek Bible (the Septuagint and the New Testament). This is, of course, also true for the words derived from it: laity, lay status, etc.

Hence, pioneer theologians in the "theology of the laity," such as Congar, have tried to transfuse into the term λαϊκός, which is undoubtedly derived philologically from the noun λαός, all the semantic and theological content that this term had acquired in the Jewish and Christian contexts, that is, the most frequently used expression of "people of God" in contrast to the pagan nations.

"Layperson" is thus taken to mean the simple member of the faithful, inasmuch as he or she is a "member of the people of God." This idea was commonly accepted until 1958, including by the present author, who used it in a series of conferences. It was based on two basic lines of reasoning: (a) it was considered that the expression did not exist in pre-Christian pagan usage, and (b) it was thought that it was a "new usage" in the Church, rich in theological content. It was said to have been first used in a passage of the First Letter of St. Clement of Rome, written probably in 95 A.D. No importance was given to the fact that here the term is introduced in a cultal contexts in which "laypersons" were seen in contrast to "priests and levites" who had specific functions in the cult, in which they were clearly distinct from laypersons and also from each other.[1]

This theory was expressed succinctly by Congar in *Jalons pour une théologie du laicat:*

> Our word "layperson" thus comes from a word that in Jewish, and later in Christian, usage was applied specifically to the consecrated people in contrast to the profane peoples. Those who spoke Greek, at least, over the period of the first four centuries or even longer, were aware of this nuance.[2]

Hence, we can define this theory as the affirmation that the theological value of the notion of the "layperson" is "directly derived" from that of the "people of God," and this gave the theological basis for the "theology of the laity."

2. However, in 1958, Father I. de la Potterie published an

article in which he brought valid arguments to bear against this theory.[3] As concerns the *first argument*, he observed that from the very beginnings of Greek literature, λαός had not only the meaning of people "in general," but also that of the "mass of the people in contrast to the leaders." This twofold meaning is also to be found in the Greek Bible. The adjective λαϊκός already existed, albeit only in hellenistic papyri, but hence also in popular parlance, in the third century B.C., and, like all adjectives ending in -ικός, expressed membership of a group or of a category in a specific manner: in other words, it had a categorizing force. And because in the papyri, λαός had this restricted meaning, the derived adjective λαϊκός preserved the significance of something belonging to the "mass of the inhabitants, the population, as distinct from those who govern it."

Later, in Jewish and Christian tradition, although the term λαϊκός is not found in the Septuagint, but only in the late Greek translations of Aquila (c. 120–140), Symmachus and Theodotion (end of the second century), it is always employed in the context of the *cult* with the contrast of the profane and the sacred, which in Symmachus became the contrast of the "sacred" and the "lay," against the background of the typically priestly teaching of those passages of the Old Testament in question, which refer to sacred things, not persons. It is therefore not justified to attribute to the adjective "lay" the full theological meaning of the biblical usage of the term λαός as "people of God."

As concerns the *second argument* of the theory proposed by Congar and others, based on the *use* of the term λαϊκός *in the Fathers*, its very infrequency prior to the third century—a single passage in St. Clement of Rome, three instances in Clement of Alexandria, and one in Origen—prevents us from considering it "so central a theological notion," as though it were derived from the biblical usage of λαός as "people of God." St. Clement of Rome is the first to apply it to persons, but the term λαϊκός continues to be employed in the context of the cult in contrast to the ministers. Thus, we find three categories: priests, levites, and laypersons, who, in Clement of Alexandria, become priests, deacons, and laypersons. This gives even greater emphasis to the separation of the latter from the former, in a context of contrast between the sacred and the profane (the laity). In this way, the laity acquires a "frankly pejorative nuance." Hence, the context remains one of *categorization,* of *contrast,* sacral, and not able to be attached semantically to the prime meaning, full of theological implications, of the biblical term λαός.

Father de la Potterie also reaches these same conclusions from an examination of the earliest Latin texts, both as regards the transliteration of the term *laicus,* and also in connection with the terms *plebs* and *plebeius,* contrary to the opinion of Congar. With Tertullian, this use of "lay" to express the contrast with the sacred can be considered to be established.

He therefore concludes: "As we can see, we find the same distinction everywhere: 'layperson' means a Christian who is neither a bishop, nor a priest, nor a deacon; one who, in a word, does not belong to the clergy." Thus the term "lay" was not created in Christian circles, but had already been in existence for a long time, denoting a contrast. More specifically, in Jewish and Christian texts, it refers to a category within the people of God, qualifying the laity as those "who are not consecrated for the service of God." Lastly, from a semantic viewpoint, there is no historical evidence for an evolution of the term.

Nonetheless, the author considers it to be an error to understand the role of the laity as solely negative, because they always retain an ecclesial meaning, and "theologically speaking, it remains entirely true that the laity are members of the people of God." The early Church was aware of this, given that the general use of λαός as the "people of God," that is, the first sense with a theological content, was also more frequent than the restricted sense denoting contrast, although it is to this latter sense that the use of λαϊκός is exclusively connected.

In an article published the following year (1959), J.B. Bauer[4] confirmed de la Potterie's theory, completing it in certain aspects. After examining various papyri and translations of the Old Testament other than the Septuagint, referring also to Hebrew and Talmudic texts, he concludes:

> λαϊκός is already found as an adjective referring to persons in a heathen context in the third century B.C., probably also in places such as Isaiah 24:2 and Hosea 4:9 in Greek translations apart from that of the Septuagint. These could justifiably be considered as the place of birth of λαϊκός in the sense in which it is employed by Clement of Rome.

Thus, as concerns de la Potterie's theory, Bauer also finds an adjectival use of the term λαϊκόυ that is personal and not limited to objects, both in papyri and also in the post-Christian Greek translations. This does not, however, weaken de la Potterie's theory, but supports its substance. Nor did other later studies, such as that by Jourjon in 1963,[5] nor the whole series of references that have appeared in connection with the history of the term "lay" (cf., in the volume *Laicità, problem e prospettive,*[6] the summaries by Pizzolato and Picasso[7] in 1977), change the substance of the above-mentioned conclusions. Congar himself in a sort of recantation[8] accepted de la Potterie's theory, as did Schillebeeckx more recently, along with others who have examined the question afresh in consequence. Unless we can be satisfied with a theological context for the expression "laity" that is only indirect, we shall have to find some other path than that described here, which has been shown to be mistaken, if we wish to provide a respectable theological basis for the so-called "theology of the laity."

3. Despite the foregoing, the line of *indirect* reference retains its considerable importance. It remains unaffected, despite the greater weight of the direct line (that of contrast), which is still rather confused as regards its logical connotations. The secondary, indirect line already mentioned by de la Potterie acquires particular stature in a text that has received a great deal of attention from scholars: that of the *Didascalia* (c. 225):

> Audite ergo etiam vos laici, electa Dei ecclesia. Nam et prior populus ecclesia vocabatur; vos autem estis catholica sacrosancta ecclesia, regale sacerdotium, multitudo sancta, plebs adoptata, ecclesia magna, sponsa exornata Domino Deo.
> [Therefore also hear this, you lay people, the chosen church of God. For even in former times the people was called "church"; but you are the most holy catholic church, the royal priesthood, the holy gathering, the adopted people, the great church, and the bride bedecked for the Lord God.]

This is certainly not the only text of its kind, even though others are not so solemn and complete, with the obvious reference to 1 Peter. Other people have employed this text in an attempt to reconstruct in particular the history of the notion of the common royal priesthood.

However, a more detailed examination of the *Didascalia* itself shows that it has some suprises in store. Scholars tend to forget to cite the rest of the passage given above. The anonymous bishop who is writing concludes in a manner that leaves us definitely puzzled:

> Quae primum dicta sunt, tu nunc audi: delibationes et decimae [et] primitiae sunt principi sacerdotum Christo et ministris eius, decimae salutaris, initium [n]om[i]nis eius.
> [Now you listen to the things said in the first place: Libations, tithes and firstfruits belong to Christ the prince of priests and to his ministers, of the salutary tithe, the beginning of his name (or: all is his beginning).]

What is more, if we examine the thirty or so other passages in this work in which the term *laicus* occurs, we shall have great difficulty in interpreting any of them in a positive sense rather than as a contrast with the bishops or the presbyters and deacons.[9]

If we were to conduct a full study of the historical development, we would need, despite the positive tradition, especially that concerning the common baptismal priesthood, to specify the ratio, as in the case of the *Didascalia,* of positive texts to texts expressing contrast. The latter are not infrequently emphasized in the periods following the fall of the Roman Empire in a sense that is very negative for the lay people, who are called *idiotes,* or illiterate, as Congar and others have observed. What is certain is that no uniform historical judgment can be given. Nevertheless, even the best cases are not devoid of doubts and uncertainties, as can be seen in the study by Pizzolato on the first Christian centuries.

4. Indeed, Pizzolato defends the methodological principle according to which an historical study cannot be considered complete unless it not only considers the historical development of the term "lay," but also investigates the "attitude of respect and use of the word for soteriological ends which is proper to Christian doctrine and which derives from the concept of the goodness of nature,"[10] which he calls "layness." Nevertheless, he recognizes the negatively categorizing meaning that the term "lay" acquired as early as the subapostolic era within a community that was closed in on itself and that "tended to develop the theme of the laity while ignoring the values of the lay state." The absence of a lay spirituality is further evidence of this.

However, despite the fact that in the era of the martyrs and of the apologists, the lay state received rather more positive treatment—especially in the anonymous *Letter* (or, rather, *Apology*) *to Diognetus*—while the eschatological theme continued, vis-à-vis history, which was in turmoil, along with the awareness that "the lay choice of the world is a creative option," this does not seem to have freed the term "lay" from its connotations of contrast with the hierarchy. On the contrary, after the lay state had lost its eschatological role during the Constantinian era, the separation of the clergy from the laity became more extreme, to the point of an "ontological difference of categories" with a slow process of "expropriation" "of the eschatological dimension to the disadvantage of the lay state," leading to a reduction of the importance of the functions of the laity within the Church, increased hierarchization, and the shifting of emphasis to the monastic ideal and the concept of being "not of this world." This led to the monastic eschatological desire attracting the clergy itself into its orbit (as Bodin[11] observed in 1969).

Of course, in the period following the third century, during which the category of monks appeared alongside those of the clergy and the laity, several great fourth-century bishops frequently recognized certain risks inherent in monasticism. However, according to Pizzolato, in order to preserve a link between monastic and lay values, both in the West (for example, St. Benedict) and in the East, the Fathers and the great canonists of the Church, to whom he devotes a documented historical section, eventually came to emphasize in the lay state "more its ontological affinity with the monastic state than its lay specificity," and thus "there is an absence of a sure conviction of the link between clerical acts and the laity in a soteriological perspective."

Neither did Chrysostom's repeated witness in favor of a reintegration of lay values free the laity from a heavy ascetic burden that, with the sole variant of marriage, tended to assimilate the laity to the monastic state. In the West, we find similar tendencies in Gregory the Great, with his tripartite division of Christians into *pastores, continentes, conjugati* ("the pastors, the chaste, and the married"), although there are differences in detail. And although in his *Ordines*, Augustine spoke of the laity in a way that seemed to restore them to the profane state, his diffidence toward the things of the world and his radical approach concerning the relinking of lay values to eternity

. . . did not substantially favor the lay dimension of Christianity, even though the laity, in Augustine's pastoral teaching, occupies a major position inasmuch as lay people are members of the people of God and have roles to fulfill within the Church.

However, we should add that with the theories Augustine begins to expound in the *Ordines,* he too fails to overcome the contrasting characterization of the laity with respect to the hierarchy.

The theory of the lay character of the State as formulated by Augustine on the basis of ideas advanced by St. Ambrose (despite the text of Pope Pelagius—maybe the last to affirm the distinction between State and Church; cf. Diez Alegria, 1967[12]) led gradually to an affirmation of the superiority of the Church over the State, which had become Christian, with a progressive "substitution" of the clergy, who ended up by expropriating the laity—although the transcendent value of their lay identity was not actually denied—of their autonomy in the political sphere, responding to oriental caesaro-papism with clericalism; already in Gregory the Great, we see the clergy functioning in the guise of civil authorities. "While in the East the lay State was despised," through asssimilation to the monastic ideal, "in the West the laity was emptied of its roles and functions."

Whatever judgment may be reached on the individual historical affirmations in this study, it has the merit of pointing up the complexity of the thorny problem of the interplay, against the background of the relationship of the Church and the world, between the laity and lay identity.

In the Middle Ages, the meaning of the term *laicus* denoting a contrast came to be used as a synonym for *popularis,* from its Greek root meaning *populus* ("people"), as Isidore of Seville observed, passing on the usage, in his *Etymologiae.* From that point onwards, the meaning of "people of God" is never given again as its root.

However, it is through Gregory the Great that the tripartition of the Church into *three ranks* is finally established, thus completing a long process of reflection from Tertullian through Augustine to Jonas of Orleans.[13] However, even in texts that give greater attention to the laity, as in the *De institutione laicali* by the above-mentioned Jonas of Orleans, lay spirituality is seen more as an imitation of the clerics than as having an independent existence, even though, as Picasso pointed out in 1977, certain texts, referring to the father of a family, seem to foreshadow the passages of Vatican II on the "domestic church" (*LG* 11; *AA* 11).

5. The fact of the matter is that the laity *always* occupied *the lowest place* and was defined *in function of contrast* in all the kinds of classification that took hold in the Church, up to and including the 1917 Code of Canon Law.

Although the classifications that gradually came to be used did not acquire the value of a "category" in the Church, nevertheless, following the assimilation of clerics to monks (and vice versa) and particularly from the twelfth century onwards, which granted greater autonomy to the laity, these classifications remained within the *contrasted dualism of the two ranks*, two "lives," or else two "peoples," or two "sides of the body," while together they form "the whole body of Christ, which is the Church."

Although some progress may be observed in the renewed attention of the theology to baptismal dignity and in the recognition of marriage as a sacrament, it remains true that the royal priesthood was not permitted to be exercised with all its possibilities and eventually became almost forgotten, for complex historical reasons, even in theological thought. The War of Investitures and the struggle for the freedom of the Church in the face of the abuse of the lay state on the part of princes, entailing ecclesiastical reactions from Popes up to Gregory VII, the theological reaction to the first heresies that refused the ordained priesthood, and even the difficult conditions of life in those centuries (as Picasso observes, commenting on the study of Le Goff,[14] published in 1969), all combined to produce a context in which "there really could be little room for the lay condition." What is more, the pessimism of the *De contemptu mundi*[15] of Innocent IV provides a background for the subsequent affirmation of the theocratic principle, which reached its apex under Boniface VIII.

A truly independent State, neutral in religious questions—in other words, a truly lay State—was inconceivable in Church circles then, and continued to be so, even once the theocratic teaching had been dropped, up to the threshold of Vatican II. Faced with such a weight of history, it is easy to understand how the first affirmations of the "lay spirit," from Marsilius of Padua onwards, took on, with ups and downs and various complications, strong laicizing connotations.

To conclude, even the late Middle Ages were unable to de-

velop a theological basis for the laity that would point up its full
dignity and that would be a foundation for the lay functions of
taking up created reality and transforming it into Christ. The
theology of creation and of Christ as being all in all were largely
stifled by a theology and a spirituality that were guided by clerics
and monks who in turn were biased in favor of a theology of
redemption that therefore appears rather unbalanced, concentrating as it does more on the "not yet" of the kingdom and a certain
flight from the world rather than on a proper appreciation of the
lay state. The emphasis on an eschatology and a concept of
salvation that paid little attention to the kingdom as "already
here" also subjugated the laity, although this was not necessarily
due to the continuing influence of monasticism or the new religious foundations. In such a context, even though the expression
imperfecti ("imperfect") given to the state of life of lay people by
ecclesiastical writers was dropped, a real theology of earthly matters and their autonomy was not even imaginable, and the definition of the "lay state" or "rank" and its tasks remained within a
conception expressing a contrast that was more tolerated than
encouraged. The seeds of a lay approach to be found in St.
Francis or in the ideology, which was more practical than theoretical, of the medieval corporations,[16] or in certain passages
from St. Thomas Aquinas, received no followup.

The theology of the laity and the search for its basis were even
more completely stifled during the tridentine period and later,
and the character of the laity as contrasted with the hierarchy
was accentuated. There was a brief parenthesis occasioned by the
first Christian humanism, which has not been sufficiently explored with regard to our subject and which might hold some
surprises in store. However, the continuing influence of medieval spirituality was later compounded by the reaction of the
counter-Reformation which, in the face of Luther's rejection of
the hierarchy and of the ordained priesthood with a one-sided
exaltation of the common priesthood and the suppression of the
distinction between clergy and laity, could not be expected to
favor a balanced reflection on the layman and the lay state
within Catholic theology. No full blossoming was possible for
certain seeds of a lay spirit that might be identified in lay movements over the tridentine period, in a positive approach to the
active life of regular clerics and of the series of religious congregations with the lay movements accompanying them, in St. Igna-

tius' *Spiritual Exercises* with its spirituality that was attentive to the creation and that was particularly intended for lay persons (cf. also the final "Contemplation to obtain love"), and the attitudes of Jesuit neoscholasticism. Reflection on the nature and tasks of the laity remained detached from any theological basis and was entrusted to a spirituality that, despite certain new features, nonetheless continued to consider it against the yardstick of a clerical spirituality that was sometimes also to a certain extent "religious." The prime feature of this approach was the search for the "salvation of the soul" or of souls, rather than that of the "world," despite the increase in charitable activism (cf. St. Vincent de Paul, etc.), and despite the importance given by the Jesuits to the influence to be exerted—so as to obtain a better Christian order of society—on princes and on the ruling classes. Hence, this approach never reached the consideration of the autonomy of temporal things and of a task of lay people within this autonomy. The laity remained subordinate to the clergy, and politics subordinate to the ideal of the "perfect society." The path toward holiness of lay people in the world remained inferior to the "more perfect" path of the clergy and religious.

At most, considering the different situation of Catholics in States adhering to the Reformation or mission countries as opposed to that of those in States of the counter-Reformation, a "tolerance" was invoked that remained intolerant in the Christian states.[17] The ideal of State–Church relations remained that of St. Robert Bellarmine of the "perfect society," which, in the course of time, was codified as the "indirect power of the Roman Pontiff," and of the Christian State. This finally ended up as the system codified as "ecclesiastical public law."[18]

6. If, in order to complete our historical study, we now take a look at the attitudes to the laity in local Councils and in the development of the codification of canon law concerning laypersons, we shall find the same increasing emphasis given to a concept that developed over centuries and confirms the character of contrast—and mainly negative contrast—of the prevailing traditional view.

a. For the Councils, a glance at the documents found in the well-known *Enchiridion Symbolorum* of Denzinger-Schönmetzer (1967 edition) will suffice. While it shows the great antiquity of their use of the term "lay," it also bears witness to the meaning expressing an essentially negative contrast, for the systematic index of this *Enchiridion* gives a series of references regarding the laity that turn out to be nothing other than a list of prohibitions even in the texts given under the title "The Function of the Laity in the Church," and its two more specific references are entitled "Laymen Require Canonical Authorization in Order to Preach," and "Sins Are Not to Be Confessed to Laymen."[19] Nevertheless, it would be a mistake to jump to conclusions on the basis simply of the usage of the term "laymen" here as elsewhere, without distinguishing the more complex ecclesiological thought lying behind it. However, the texts aim more at indicating limits rather than at taking a positive stance in favor of laypersons: this did not seem to be to their advantage.

Yet it is a fact that the concept of the Church as a pyramid had been gradually taking hold ever since the Middle Ages—in line with the hierarchical concept of civilian society—eventually reaching the exaggerated positions that prompted Congar to coin the adjective "hierarchological." In the specific theological treatises entitled *De Ecclesia* following Vatican I, various scholars have noted that the Church is described entirely as a pyramid and as a society that is both perfect and unequal. There is no room for the element of communion or for the charisms and gifts of the Spirit, nor yet for its fundamental nature as a communion. With this view, it is impossible even to ask our question as to the definition and specificity of the laity.

b. From a *juridical point of view*, as has been shown in recent studies,[20] it is not possible to compare the situation of the laity in the early Church with that brought about by later and increasingly restrictive developments. Caron can give indications for the first centuries showing a participation of lay people in the power of order, the power of teaching, and the power of jurisdiction, apart from what is an essential and specific part of the ordained priesthood. As a sign of the beginning of progressive decadence in the functions of the laity in the Church, and because of the influence this had in canonical codification, authors often cite the text of Gratianus on "two kinds of Christians," where he contrasts the first kind (the clerics and monks, who have already been assimilated to each other) with that of the "lay people," whose condition appears as a concession:

These are allowed to possess temporal goods, at least in order to use them. . . . It is granted to these to take a wife, to till the soil, to judge between one man and another, to plead causes, to place offerings upon altars, and to pay the tithe, and thus they will be able to be saved, if, however, they do good and avoid vices.[21]

The consequence of this is that the layperson is permitted no active part in the Church. Bruno may be right when he connects the view of disqualifying the layperson with the general concept of perfection in which flight from the world is of major importance, so that "life in the world, in Christian terms, cannot but lead to a compromise," and thus "at the base of the whole question is the idea that, in Christianity, the concept of 'world' has gradually acquired."

It is a fact that, following the theology of the treatise *De Ecclesia* that took shape after Vatican I, the codification of the 1917 Code of Canon Law followed the lines of this devaluation, although it would be an exaggeration to accuse it of a purely negative view of the laity, as Congar has already observed in his *Jalons.*

The canonical definition remained fundamentally one of contrast to the clerical hierarchical office, although it retains evidence of a number of unresolved tensions: tension because of the reference to baptism in contrast to the predominantly pyramidal picture of the Church, and tension because of the reductionist choice in contrast to the history of the most active tasks being attributed to the laity in different eras. One might also ask to what extent the picture of the Church as a perfect society and an unequal society may have acted as a background. This would have entailed reducing the complex nature of the Church to a single dimension, and failing to provide a sufficient guarantee of the distinctions in the structure of the Church, which was considered to be bipolar. These two poles, the hierarchy and the laity, were recognized by canonists as being of divine institution. We may also ask ourselves how much influence may have been exerted by the continuing idea of the Catholic state and the theory of the indirect power of the Roman Pontiff (all of which was mitigated by the idea of tolerance).

Congar has observed that the law of the Church should not be expected to give an answer to the question of the laity because "by its origin, its history, and its very nature, the law of the Church is principally a system organizing sacramental worship, and thus it is normal that it should be above all a law concerning clerics and sacred things."[22] This view must not only be answered by saying, with Bruno, that "although this canonical point of view was legitimate, it eventually also determined the Church's point of view concerning the laity, and this is the real evil,"[23] but we must also indicate the limits of this view of the Code, namely, its dependence on an ecclesiology that is theologically reductionist and one-sided. An answer to this was given by the new Code of 1983 and the Constitution *Sacrae disciplinae leges* with which it was promulgated.

7. Various theologians have attempted to produce a synthesis from the historical development we have outlined here. In his account of the expression "lay people," Congar distinguishes three periods. More recently, Forte highlights the term "communion" and speaks of four divisions, according to the structure of two poles in mutual tension: the pole of communion or community, and the ministerial or hierarchical poie. He concludes that "the history of the Christian laity, in practice and as the object of reflection, can be seen wholly in terms of the varied relationship of these two poles."[24]

We felt the situation to be more complex, and thus these classifications and periods puzzle us somewhat. Nevertheless, bearing in mind the background provided by history to the two questions we asked at the outset, we feel the following conclusions are tenable:

a. The point of reference and of departure is provided by the New Testament, where we find a Church or a community that is structured in various different ways. Recent historical-critical studies have moved beyond the rigid positions of early form criticism, and have tended increasingly to recognize the existence of an incipient tradition in the prepaschal community that bears witness to the beginnings of a fundamental structure originating from Christ. By his conscious intention,[25] a circle of "disciples" was formed around him as "Master," and from among them, he chose a group with particular teaching functions. Tradition refers to this group by the technical term "the Twelve," among whom Peter occupies a position of preeminence. Around the structure of this prechurch, there is the circle of the crowd to whom the kingdom is proclaimed and who are invited to become "disciples." The continuity between the prepaschal and postpaschal Traditions can be shown by critical analysis.[26] The radicalization between the Aramaic and the Greek communities, which was seen as the innovatory basis for fundamental structures, is no longer accepted by critics. The prevailing mentality in the whole of the New Testament remains that of "Tradition," with analogies—without being identical—to that found in rabbinism or the other expressions of Judaism.[27]

The common terms used to indicate all the followers of Jesus both in the prepaschal and postpaschal Traditions of the New Testment is that of "disciples," without any distinction of "categories." This is the earliest term with which the community referred to themselves, and it is preserved only in the four Gospels and the book of Acts. Acts 12:26 shows its ancient usage when speaking of the antiochene origin of the new term "Christians," which was maybe an extrinsic denomination given by the pagans. Here, "disciples" refers to all the followers of Jesus without distinction. The same applies to the global terms used within the community, which are found in the New Testament from the earliest Pauline writings: elect (κλητοί), brothers (ἀδελφοί), saints (ἅγιοι), believers (πιστοί), with or without the article, but all having a strongly theological content. This was not the case for the terms taken from outside, although those absorbed into the Tradition, such as "Christians," did receive some of the rich theological content of the term "disciples" and other similar terms.

The same cannot be said of the nontestamental adoption of the term "laypersons," which was also received into Tradition. The theological content remains *indirect,* as we said above, and is dominated by the prevalent semantic usage expressing contrast. Obviously nothing of the kind occurred for the external denominations that were pejorative in content and were rejected by the community, such as those used by the Jews: first of all the term "Nazarenes," and then that used to refer to the Judeo-Christians of Palestine, Minīm. The terms taken in from outside, especially those expressing a contrast, such as "laypersons," have a content that contains more contingent historical aspects that, as time goes on, can crystallize and become harmful for a fuller self-understanding on the part of the Church.

The institution of "the Twelve" and the development of a presbyterate established the hierarchical study on the Church in the New Testament, and introduced *on the practical level* a basic complexity that is respected by the whole of subsequent New

Testament and Church Tradition. This includes the canonical
Tradition preceding the 1917 Code, which considers it of divine
institution, and the Code retains traces of this in its reference
(which is not developed theologically) to baptism for all the
faithful, including laypersons.[28] However, *on the theoretical level,*
the New Testament distinction does not permit categories to be
established: it is not "the disciple" who is contrasted with the
hierarchy, but "one who is not endowed with hierarchical offices." This means we cannot really speak of two distinct circles
around Christ, or two poles, or of derivation from the essential
institution of the hierarchy in the phenomenon of the "disciples," or else, as would be said, of the *christifidelis,* whose essential
nature is logically to be sought on another level, and is not
derived from the existence of the hierarchy. The lack of attention in mixing on the practical level the different theoretical
natures of institution has led over the centuries to arbitrary conclusions, thereby leaving room, especially after the introduction
of the nonbiblical term "laypersons," to cultic, sociocultural, and
juridical influences that have proved decisive.

Even so, it does not seem to me that this took place in the
New-Testament communities as concerns the later structures
that appeared alongside the fundamental one *of* the Church and
directly due to Christ, and which we shall call structures *in* the
Church.[29] Through the *traditio apostolica,* some of these can be
referred back indirectly to Christ—for example, the hierarchical
order—whereas others can be attributed to the inspiration of the
Spirit or else were instituted by the community under the guidance of the apostles, which was also subject to the action of the
Spirit. In any case, there is no important evidence in the New
Testament, neither for the fundamental institution nor for the
concomitant structures, of the *categorical character expressing contrast* that we have observed following the introduction of the
term "lay" as a constant element in subsequent Tradition, until
the 1917 Code.

b. The consequences of this confusion of logical levels is also
reflected in theological reflection under various guises, from the
period of the barbarian invasions through the Middle Ages to
modern times. The loss of traditional riches such as the common
priesthood, and the impoverishment of the biblical notions of
the people of God and the body of Christ in the two Pauline
versions, the more organic of which in Ephesians and Colossians

does not permit an interpretation that is predominantly hierarchical, progressively gave way to the predominance of the hierarchical conception and the devaluation of the laity and their active roles in the Church. The dimension of negative contrast dominates the few relics of the positive dimension, despite the ups and downs we have indicated. What is more, the modern period, despite its diversification, appears to have widened the gap.

c. Against this background, the twofold question of the theological definition and the specific nature of the laity *does not even arise:* we are obliged to conclude that the fate of the lay identity has been historically connected with that of the importance and value attributed to the laity; and also with the problem of reflection of the "foundation" and "justification and connection" of anthropologies and cosmologies, and not solely of philosophical and religious theologies that underlie it and that sometimes remain implicit or undeveloped.[30]

8. To finish at our point of departure, we can appreciate the great merits of the scholars who have developed a "theology of the laity" outside the framework of the classical treatises *De Ecclesia,* which excluded the laity. Even though we have criticized the attempt to derive the theological value of the "layperson" directly from the notion of the "people of God," and have demonstrated that such an attempt is unfounded, it is nevertheless true that biblical, patristic, and historical research on the one hand, and greater attentiveness to the life of the people of God on the other hand (the facts precede the theory), led, after the first studies in the 1930s and 40s to the committed treatises of the period 1945–1959 immediately prior to Vatican II, which they influenced (J. Leclerq, Y. Congar—cf. *Jalons*—K. Rahner, E. Schillebeeckx, G. Philips, de Montcheuil, etc.).[31]

a. Pride of place must go to the complex study of Congar, which we have mentioned above, and which appeared in 1953. This work is a veritable *Summa,* which, with the *Addenda* supplementing the third edition in 1964, remains irreplaceable. Congar deals with all the major subjects that lead up to the theology of the laity as such: the relationship of the Church and the kingdom (already here, and not yet), the relationship between the Church and the world, the reference to its christological basis and to a "global ecclesiology." His development of these subjects reveals a rich and original line of thought, as centered on a basic area of research on the relationship between structure and life in the

Church, the unity of which flows from the fact that it is a communion. "The Church lives by a living relationship between two poles which can be called the hierarchical pole and the pole of community" (*Jalons*, p. 356). We cannot follow the unfolding of this thought, various aspects of which have been criticized by other theologians, including Daniélou and Rahner; Congar tried to answer these criticisms in the *Addenda*—not entirely convincingly, in my opinion.[32]

The theology of the laity claims its origins in that of the people of God, although this does not make it a separate chapter of ecclesiology; rather, it refers to a "total ecclesiology," with an approach that is not static, but dynamic, attentive to the "life" of the Church, belonging to it no less than the structure, which refers back to life so as to *se plénifier* (or "find fullness") in it. Life is the Church's constant adaptation of itself to events, under the influence of the Holy Spirit. Congar does not approve of positions such as that of Bouyer and others who hold that work in the world is extraneous to the preparation and maturing of the kingdom. It is this very world which, remaining ontologically the same, will become the kingdom. In it a whole power of transformation is already active. This is the royal, priestly, and prophetic power of Christ and of the Holy Spirit he has given. Congar rejects both a medieval type of Christianity that does not always attribute their true causality to secondary causes, that is, the opposite of a separation of the two cities. The Christian is between the two: he is in relation to the fullness of the Pasch, and thus receives everything from Christ (this is the basis of the hierarchical function, in relation to the Parousia), and he must lead all the riches of creation back to God, engage himself in the temporal sphere in respect for the truth (the autonomy) of created things, and make them his own in the paschal mystery. The relationship of Christ with his "body" is seen under the twofold aspect of power and animation. For Congar, the Church as an institution and the Church as the community of the faithful correspond to these two aspects. In the institution, kingship, priesthood, and magisterium are powers, and means to obtain life for the members; in the community, the triple function exists as a form of life that qualifies the members as such. However, the energies Christ has placed within his Church are passed on to the lay people, not only for the building up of the body, but also as dimensions for the world and for history "so as to bring back to

God all the riches of his creation, of which Christ is the first-born and the king" (*Jalons*, p. 125).

The *two initial descriptions* given by Congar in *Jalons* are well known. Critics have objected that it is difficult to reconcile them. Most have opted in favor of the second:

> A layman is a man for whom things exist; for him, their truth is not, as it were, engulfed and abolished by a higher sphere of reference, since for him, in Christian terms, it is the very reality of the elements of this world, the appearance of what is transitory, that is to be referred to the Absolute (p. 45).

The author himself later took pains to correct the one-sided interpretation given by certain critics, who seemed to think he intended resuming "the ridiculously simplistic formula: spiritual things for the priest, and temporal matters for the layman." On the contrary, "the whole of our book is a protest against the reduction of the specific quality of being 'lay' to a reference to the world or the temporal sphere" (*Addenda*, p. 648). Nevertheless, he ends up by drawing close to Rahner's formula,[33] whereby the layperson is someone whose Christian existence and responsibility are determined by his integration into the life of the world. However, certain difficulties remain, despite Congar"s subsequent and decisive linking of the lay condition to sacramentality (both baptismal and eucharistic) and his description with a wealth of research of the participation of the lay condition in the threefold priestly, royal, and prophetic task of Christ, and in the evangelizing and apostolic mission of the Church, thereby revaluing the active role of the lay people. He examines this threefold *munus* from the point of view of "lay people in the life of the Church," which turns out in the end to be reductionist as regards the concept of kingship with respect to the "taking up" of the world in order to "bring it to fulfillment," and gives undue emphasis to a spirituality of sanctification in the activity of the layperson—as we see in the last chapter—thus neglecting the spirituality of creation.

We must still ask whether the difficulties raised by the critics have been entirely satisfactorily answered by this thinker, who was always willing to polish and revise the whole of his thought in response to that of others and to the life of the Church. Certain critics spoke of an excessive division between structure and life, between the institutional Church and the Church as the "congregation of the faithful," between the Church and the world, and between hierarchy and laity, with texts that appeared to give the laity a role that belonged not to the *esse* of the Church, but only to its *plus esse*, even though both of these are constituent elements of the Church. We may ask if he really replied to the difficulties raised by Daniélou in his review of the book:

> I am disturbed by this idea which suggests that there is always a danger that reference to God is an alienation for human values, and that they have to be considered in their own right. This appears to constitute a concession to the lay spirit in the worst sense of the expression. Quite to the contrary, it would seem that human realities can only acquire a meaning when referred to God, if their essential character is that of being created, and that, according to the fundamental meditation on the *Exercises* of St. Ignatius, "everything that is on the surface of the earth is nothing but a means to permit man to achieve his sole purpose," which is to glorify God.[34]

It seems to me—as can be seen clearly in the pages where Congar compares lay people, clerics, and monks—that he does not entirely escape the categorizing mentality of contrast that spills over into the sphere of reality and mixes diversified logical matters with others that cannot be directly compared with them and that govern the identification of each of them in its own sphere, as we shall see more clearly in due course. It is necessary to remain within the limits of each sphere: in the sphere of clerics, the contrasting element is "the rest of the people of God" (as is correctly stated, for example, in *Lumen gentium* 32), and not "the lay people"; a direct comparison ends up by falling into illogicality by introducing negative consideration in the sphere of reality, hardening into contrasting categories what is characterized in different spheres that have their validity only in terms of contraposition for their logical opposite: lay/nonlay (or remaining people of God), and the same can be said for cleric/noncleric, religious/nonreligious.

b. We cannot accord even the summary attention we have given to Congar to all the various theologies of the laity we have mentioned above. The opinion of J. Grootaers may be helpful here, inasmuch as he summarizes the common and fundamental position as regards the question, "Who is the layperson?":

(i) negatively: the layperson is the Christian who is distinguished within the Church both from the priest and from the religious;

(ii) positively: the sphere proper to the layperson is the temporal sphere;

(iii) positively: within the Church, the layperson is called to make an active contribution.

Two features pinpoint the spirituality of this layperson: a married and family life; and involvement in a professional life and social relationships. The author observes that this picture of the layperson corresponds to the retreat of the priest from a leadership that had invaded the sphere of the profane (in countries dominated by a clerical form of Catholicism), and that was based on the definition of the layperson principally as the person of temporal matters in contrast to the priest as a man of Church matters, or even of "spiritual" matters. There is a dualism between *ad intra* and *ad extra*.[35] Grootaers' position invites debate, especially point (ii): it has the merit of defining situations we have experienced, but it neglects the strictly theological approach of the authors he considers.

However, if Grootaers' point (i) is true, we may ask, despite the declared will to promote the laity and to restore and give a positive development to all the potentialities of the gospel and patristic tradition, whether in all this theological reflection, there is not still the radical ambiguity of an identification of the "layperson" that takes as its starting point a predominantly *ad intra* description in contrast to the hierarchical functions, and of a mode of sharing in the life of the Church that may still be too conditioned by gracious concessions? In this position, lay people are defined by their *nonclerical state* and *not by their "lay state*," and this indicates that the contrast mentioned above is still there, hardened into categories or *ordines*, with the confusion of logical spheres we have already pointed out. Lastly, this position also retains a contrast that has not been entirely overcome between the "Christian identity" of the layperson and his "lay identity" in relation both to the Church and to the world. All these have yet to be overcome in theological reflection.

9. *Postconciliar research* does not really seem to have paid suffi-

cient attention to this distinction of spheres. One group of scholars[36] has taken as its starting point the observation that it is
impossible to give a true definition or a really distinctive specificity for the layperson. They thus concluded that "layperson" and
"Christian" were identical. Finally, even if they did not actually
state that the term "layperson" was useless, they concentrated
their theological reflection on the abstract idea of "lay identity,"
detached from the term and the existential situation of the layperson. At best, they said it remains useful to retain reference to the
layperson as a means to avoid a possible future reclericalization of
the Church, or else the secularization of the clergy—which
seems to me to be the greater danger at present. In any case, the
conciliar use of the term "lay" is credited with having brought the
Church to the discovery or rediscovery of its own "lay identity"
or "secularity."

On the other hand, there are also certain commentators of
Lumen gentium who interpret the texts, especially number 31, in
the sense of a definition of the laity and of the determination of a
truly "specific" character. This would consecrate the survival of a
certain character of "contrast" in a single sphere of consideration, and thus of categories within the people of God, with the
inevitable mutual negative projections. Certain authors, such as
Klostermann,[37] speak of a definition, and even discern in number 31 a *genus proximum* (the link to the *christifidelis*) and a
specific difference (31a: in general in the expression *pro parte sua;*
31b: with the precise indication in *indoles saecularis*). However,
this interpretation is contradicted by the conciliar text, as we
shall see. Nor does it seem to be consistent with the observations
Klostermann makes later on, still with reference to *Lumen gentium* 31. We shall discuss Schillebeeckx' opinion on a definition
in the next section. Other authors who comment on the texts
avoid the issue (and it certainly cannot be said, for example, in
the case of Philips,[38] that they were unaware of its existence).
Others wearily repeat, without raising great difficulties, the idea
that the Council indicates a "specific character" for the laity in
the *indoles saecularis;* still others observe that there are questions,
and speak more openly of a quasidefinition or a quasispecificity,
yet do not pursue the matter in any depth or draw the consequences, so that they remain, like almost all the authors of this
second group—despite their desire to give a positively expressed
doctrine or maybe even a theology of the laity—on counter-

positions that mask a contrast and that are implicitly negative and limiting with regard to the layperson and his or her role in the Church and the world, and they end up limiting the very concept of lay identity. Others shift the whole problem onto the distinctions between "vocation," "functions," "ministries," and "states of life," with various emphases without asking the basic question of the *direct* theological origin of the dignity of the laity, on which the quality and value of the interpretations they give depend, and also the quality and value of the various "spiritualities of the laity," which are modeled on "theologies of the laity" that are in crisis due to aggressivity and the arguments in favor of the opposite position, and that are incapable of renewing themselves, as has been observed in the decrease of writings on the laity in latter years.

However, the first group, which I refer to as those of the *abstract lay state,* who tend to eliminate the terms "layperson" and "laity" from theological considerations and abandon reflection on them to a spirituality or pastoral theology with a weak theological basis, also has major problems. Leaving aside considerations that will be better dealt with later, I shall simply observe that this tends to empty the rich theological aspects acquired concerning the layperson, such as the relationship of this term— even though it has proved to be indirect—to the "people of God," in the earliest theologies of the laity, which, revised and reinforced, enabled them to be received into the Council. Remaining in the background of the concerns of the Pastors, they had decisive influence on a line of magisterium and reflection that is still to be found in the most recent Synods and in documents and concerns expressed for the forthcoming Synod on "The Vocation and Mission of the Laity in the Church and in the World, Twenty Years after the Second Vatican Council" (at the beginning of the *Lineamenta*). The *Lineamenta* recall the "very rich doctrinal heritage" and not only the "spiritual and pastoral" heritage that we have received from Vatican II on the subject of the laity (No. 4). An excessively abstract theology of the lay condition of the whole Church, despite the truths contained in it and pointed up by it, runs the risk of losing it by losing contact with a large area of life and with the more suitable, permanent *locus theologicus* that is the laity, and that can also fully explain the *ratio* of the *christifidelis* in relation to his or her task toward the world.

It is not difficult to see how the objections and negative declarations in response to this abstract vision of the lay condition on the part of the whole Church, of outstanding laypersons, and of the thinkers of the "lay movements," as we shall see, can be considered to be a protest from the *sensus fidelium*. They feel that they have been expropriated or threatened through the awareness they have acquired of a task that is irreplaceably theirs, in the Church and in the world, and thus they rush to the defense of the *indoles saecularis* in the face of the attacks of this new abstract theology, which no longer corresponds to the method of reflection that takes life as its starting point, informed by faith, which—above all—the Church movements most actively engaged in the temporal sphere try to cultivate together. With this they become aware of their active presence as Christian witnesses, as people who, in a Christian manner, in all seriousness "take up" the whole reality of creation and of history in order to bring it to fulfillment—without bypassing the whole of the paschal mystery—in Christ who is all in all.[39]

A new position must be found that, without neglecting the critical reasoning of the theologians (most of whom are still, unfortunately, clerics), will strike the right balance with the line of reasoning of the laity. The present work hopes to provide a first contribution to this end. The problem posed by history must be joined with that studied by research following Vatican II, and our reflection on the difficulties outlined briefly above have convinced me (and I hope the reader is also beginning to think this way) that we must make a fresh start from a new and more thorough consideration of the dogmatic conciliar texts on the laity, respecting the distinction on the complex level of reality in order to overcome any remaining opposition. This is the intention we find in the Council itself—in its texts taken as they stand, in conformity to the demands of modern hermeneutics. It also seems clear to me at this point after our historical study of the pre- and postconciliar periods, that an effort must be made to clarify the twofold question of the "definition" and the "specific character" of laypersons, that this has revealed itself to be a starting point of essential importance. It may be that the present modest attempt will indicate a path for further reflection. The hermeneutical principle we have cited, which finds the actual intention within the texts, cannot, however, dispense us—in order to gain a better understanding of the historical context—

from also taking into consideration those texts (to be found particularly in the introductory *Relationes* by the subcommissions that drafted the text itself) that present terminologies, intentions, and propositions that might be absent from the text itself. This might be at the origin of a certain degree of subsequent confusion, and now gives greater clarity to the outlines of the state of our question.

10. The next section is devoted to an account of "the novelty" of the Council as regards the laity, shown against the general background of novelty, which we shall outline briefly but only partially. This consists of the consistent manner in which the Council as a whole spoke of the laity in entirely positive terms, with clear admonitions in the text to eliminate all categorizing positions of contrast.

The section after next will attempt an examination of the novelty of the Council's response to the problem of the supposed definition and the claimed determination of the "specific character" of the layperson, giving an answer that seems to be definitive: the layperson is the *christifidelis* (or "member of Christ's faithful") who fully recognizes the *ratio* itself of the *christifidelis* in relation to the world (*distinctio nominalis*).

The Novelty of Vatican II as Regards the Laity

Vatican II was of course not the first Church Council to deal with the laity, as we have pointed out, but it was certainly the first Ecumenical Council to do so, and, moreover, it was the first to consider the question of the Church's understanding of itself in such a way as to give prominence or restore prominence in a positive sense to all the potential dignity of the laity to be found in revelation. We shall first give a general background of novelty and then describe the specific novelty with regard to the laity.

A Background We Experienced

My generation of young theologians, who had already received their formation and were involved in pastoral work and in the effort to promote the theology of the laity, experienced the Council as a great Pentecost of the Spirit. Many, if not all, of the problems that worried us received an answer.

In our work, which consisted of research and apostolate in the State universities, we were constantly tormented by the question as to the value of the pyramidal ecclesiology of the treatises we had studied, in the face of the cultural outlook of today's world, and we felt frustrated at the failure to use so many cultural resources in the believing laity and at the persistence of the official Church culture on embattled and defensive positions. We were also worried by the phenomena of incipient cultural disintegration within the Church, with the ill-considered and irresponsible irenic reactions they prompted. Clericalism, which was under attack from the outside, remained oppressive from within.

In relations between Church and State, the old doctrine of the ecclesiastical public law was dominant, connected with the idea of the perfect society, with the positions of St. Robert Bellarmine and the theory of thesis and hypothesis. This was becoming daily more untenable in a sincere dialogue with contemporary culture.

Pioneers of the theology of the laity did not pay sufficient attention to the changes taking place in the educated lay world as regards the very concept of the "layperson" and the "lay condition." Congar saw it as meaning primarily laicism and atheism; in the new international context, this could appear a judgment too closely dependent on European history. New, more neutral conceptions of the lay condition were becoming accepted.

Furthermore, developments in biblical sciences were posing new problems concerning the foundation for many of the important traditional theses, especially following the prudent openings of *Divino afflante Spiritu* in 1943 and the flourishing of biblical research that both preceded and followed, up to the threshold of the Council. The growing demand for lay participation in the liturgy could not be contented with the means of compromise thought out on the pastoral level by enlightened pastors, which ended up by satisfying only part of the cultivated and educated laity.

The novelty of Vatican II must also be seen in the context of these expectations, of which other authors have spoken in this work with specialized knowledge for individual areas. It is especially the four Dogmatic Constitutions that answered the legitimate expectations of renewal: *Lumen gentium* and *Gaudium et spes* for the more general ones, the admirable *Dei Verbum* for the specific expectations in the field of biblical studies, and, to a lesser degree, *Sacrosanctum concilium* for the renewal of the liturgy. New vistas seemed to open up for those seeking a new conception of the relations between Church and State, with the statements on religious freedom and freedom of conscience in the Declaration *Dignitatis humanae,* in which we saw an implicit affirmation of the lay character of the State, and the clear statement in *Gaudium et spes* to the effect that "the political community and the Church are autonomous and independent of each other in their own fields" (No. 76c).

The General Response to the Expectations Regarding the Promotion of the Laity

Vatican II provided an ample response to the expectations regarding the *promotion of the laity,* to use the expression then currently in use. It was the first Ecumenical Council to deal with the position and function of lay people as a dogmatic and pastoral chapter of fundamental significance in the reflection the Church was conducting on itself and on its mission. The importance the Fathers attached to this theme can be appreciated from the fact that the term "layman" occurs 206 times in the documents of the Council. To these we must add three instances of "laity" and seven of the adjective "lay."[40] There is, however, no occurrence of the abstract expression "lay condition," nor is there a direct reflection on this subject.

However, the very importance given to the subject of lay people permits a reflection that may seem in contradiction to the large number of times the term is used. In the history of the Councils, an important question introduced for the first time in one of them has rarely found an exhaustive answer; other Councils and further reflection were necessary in order to obtain a more complete and satisfactory doctrinal treatment of the subject—especially when terms and concepts were introduced that were not found in the biblical text. Thus, we should not be surprised that this occurred regarding the introduction of the term "layman" in Vatican II.

The Council Fathers' desire to give a *positive description* of the layperson in a perspective of communion is beyond doubt. However, this question is mixed with the problems of the Church's understanding of itself, including its institutional organization, as well as the changes and history of the various drafts required by the Constitution *Lumen gentium* before the definitive text.

There has not been an exhaustive scientific study on the discussions *concerning the laity* that can be compared, for example,
with that of Acerbi on the two ecclesiologies or that of Father
Ghirlanda on the *Hierarchica Communio.*[41] For this reason, it is
still difficult to reflect on the part played by the discussions on
the laity in the overturning of the "pyramidal" schema proposed
to the Fathers by the commission responsible for preparing the
schema on the Church—although even this commission introduced the subject of laypersons in Chapter VII in terms that
expressed a positive approach. A glance at the Acts of the Council cannot replace a systematic, analytically documented, and
developed study, which so far does not exist and which would
require years of critical research. The systematic accounts of
Lumen gentium, and the comments on the position of lay people
in the general discussion, printed prior to the publication of the
Acts of the Council, do not seem to give much weight to the
discussions of the texts concerning the laity in the development
of the ecclesiological teaching of the Council. The overturning
of the first pyramidal schema seems to have been influenced
more by other concerns that were widely shared by the Fathers,
such as the subject of collegiality.

In any case, reflection on the *position of the "laity" in the Church*
benefited from the *novelty* of the Church's understanding of itself
as expressed in *Lumen gentium,* although we can only give a
partial description of this here: the Council gave preference to
the more general and broader aspects as opposed to those that
appeared more particular, juridical, and historical in the previous
pyramidal schema. It highlighted the aspect of the Church as
"mystery," the object of the threefold action of the three divine
Persons, and as the "sacrament" of Christ and thus the "sign and
instrument . . . of communion with God and of unity among all
men" (No. 1); it gave an account of the doctrine of the body of
Christ, placing greater emphasis on the relationship of Christ to
believers than on the hierarchical relationship. The predominant category became that of *communion,* and the predominant
perspective that of unity. All this was the consequence of the
rejection in the Council Hall of the schema presented by the
preparatory commission and the ecclesiological view that predominated in it, as well as—after the famous intervention of
Cardinal Suenens—of the ecclesiological discussions that threatened to produce a rift between Fathers supporting opposing ten-

dencies and that led to the compromise in the final text of *Lumen gentium*.

The insertion of Chapter III (cf. especially No. 21) between the two sections of the schema concerning the laity (so that the general aspects became Chapter II on the people of God, and the more specific treatment of the laity became Chapter IV) broke down a certain linear system that seemed to lead logically as a passage from more general and common matters to ones more particular and specific, so that in Chapter IV on the laity, it was necessary in number 31 to give not so much a definition or a theology of the laity as an indication, but one that is *relational* and that sounds apparently negative: "The term 'laity' is here understood to mean all the faithful [*omnes christifideles*] except [*praeter*] those in Holy Orders and those who belong to a religious state. . . ."

Although the negative interpretations given by certain theologians such as Weinzierl[42] cannot be accepted, it cannot be denied that the preservation of a *relational expression that seems to be negative* in this context poses the question of the extent to which the Council overcame the meaning of categorizing or at least cultic and sociocultural contrast that clings to the term "layperson" from the past, of which we have given an account above (cf. below, especially paragraph 2 of the second subsection in the next section).

A Positive Vision, Not One of Contrast, To Define the Laity

The answer to this problem can be given by observing that the conciliar texts on the laity—both those that are more concerned with the so-called ontological status of their "being" as Christians, and also those seeking to define the specific character of the laity—are *all* clearly *positive*.

The above-cited passage from number 31 of *Lumen gentium* goes on to refer back to what was said in general terms concerning the Christian in Chapter II:

That is, the faithful who by Baptism are incorporated into Christ, are placed in the People of God, and in their own way share the priestly, prophetic and kingly office of Christ, and to the best of their ability carry on the mission of the whole Christian people in the Church and in the World.

However, if we leave aside the few passages in the conciliar texts that, like this one, prepare the way for the attempt to determine the "identity" [*indoles saecularis*] of the laity, there can be no doubt that the theological basis and the details of the tasks of the laity given in the conciliar texts *add nothing specific to the status and the tasks that are common to all Christians,* even when they attempt to give more precise indications of the application of the schema on the threefold *munus,* or of the evangelizing and apostolic or missionary task of lay people. This will be seen more clearly when we speak of their "definition" and the "specific character" in due course.

1. I must therefore conclude that all the general indications given by the conciliar text as it stands when it makes statements concerning the laity, seem more or less to prepare the way for a status of identity between the "Christian" and the "layperson" rather than affirming any substantial differentiation. We shall discuss the intentions of the subcommission in due course.

Recognition of the *ministries and charisms* proper to lay people (*LG* 30, for example) and of their multiple *functions* is subordinate to the basic teaching of the unity of the people of God, of the common dignity of the members of the one body of Christ, and of the common calling to holiness. All Christians share in the one mission of the Church: they are called to be prophets and witnesses, they exercise the common priesthood and royal service, and they share in the common task of evangelization and mission.

When the Council speaks of lay people, it avoids the expressions denoting contrast that are to be found in Tradition. In the approved texts, it never uses the term "category," it speaks very rarely of the term "status," and avoids emphasizing the original cultic contrast. It avoids speaking of the "specific character" of the layperson, and tries to eliminate all sociocultural references denoting contrast.

2. Although the conciliar documents such as *Apostolicam actuositatem* that depend more on *Lumen gentium* do not introduce any substantial variations, they do provide certain details that need to be borne in mind in our context: *Apostolicam actuositatem* closely links the "distinctive task" of lay people with

that of Christ who is all in all, especially as regards the autonomy
of the temporal order and its laws (AA 7e).

What is more, it says that, as bearers of the mission of the
people of God "to establish the right relationship of the entire
world to Christ" (AA 2a), it is their task to "extend God's kingdom, [and] make the Christian spirit a vital energizing force in
the temporal sphere" (AA 4d; cf. 5a), for "it is the work of the
entire Church to fashion men who are able to establish the
proper scale of values on the temporal order and direct it towards
God through Christ" (AA 7d). It also states that

> Laymen ought to take on themselves as their distinctive task
> this renewal of the temporal order. Guided by the light of the
> Gospel and the mind of the Church, prompted by Christian
> love, they should act in this domain in a direct way and in
> their own specific manner (AA 7e).

The document also makes *a certain effort to specify this distinctive task of the laity:* they are empowered to act because every
member of the mystical body of Christ receives from the Spirit a
special energy in order to carry out the tasks he or she assigns to
each according to the gifts, charisms, and ministries he or she has
already distributed and the situation of life in which God has
placed each individual. In addition to evangelization, witness,
and Christian presence, it is the particular task of the laity to
take up all temporal things in Christ. Hence, exercising their
apostolate in the Church and in the world "in the temporal order
as well as in the spiritual," lay people must bear clearly in mind
with the whole Church that "although these orders are distinct,
they are so closely linked that God's plan is, in Christ, to *take* the
whole world *up again* and make of it a new creation, in an initial
way here on earth, in full realization at the end of time."

Nevertheless, the text seems to end up by adding a concern
that breaks the tension: "The layman, at one and the same time a
believer and a citizen of the world, has only a single conscience,
a Christian conscience; it is by this that he must be guided
continually in both domains" (AA 5). It is as if, after the peak of
the grandiose conception of Christ who takes history up again in
himself has been reached, the conciliar declaration suddenly
drops the tone, instead of stating all the great potential contained within this idea.

3. It seems that neither *Lumen gentium,* nor *Apostolicam actu-osit atem* which depends on it, manages to express the connection—despite intuitions that draw close to it—of the ordering toward God of temporal realities with the whole fullness of Christ's great role in taking up the whole of history again into himself. The royal function seems to stay restricted in a forced manner to "service," which is not extended to the fullness of "bringing to fulfillment" the whole of creation.

It is not a simple matter to find out why the reflection suddenly cuts out at this point. I can only express the opinion that, on the one hand, the late introduction of more precise christological references did not permit a rethinking of the whole of a schema that had already been drafted without these references, and, on the other hand, the dominance of an *ad intra* approach to the understanding of the royal *munus* seems to have impeded the recovery of a more broadly based theology of creation. However, these are no more than plausible explanations. We should also not ignore the weight of an earlier theology of the laity that imposed the same limitations, as well as the intrinsic conditioning of history affecting the very usage of the term "layperson." Despite this, the dynamism of the Council's thought moved *toward the identification* of "Christian" and "layperson" and thus toward assuming as the task of the entire Church that which was held to be distinctive of the laity.

4. The same dynamism of thought seems to be behind *Gaudium et spes,* in which the introduction of the christological texts appears to be, at least partially, the fruit of later revision.

Nevertheless, there is a point that has not yet received attention and that may throw a little more light on our problem: the drastic reduction to *only six instances* of the term "layman" in the text, which —what is more—does not figure at all until number 43. This goes against the current of thought found in *Lumen gentium* and *Apostolicam actuositatem,* which would have emphasized the reference to the laity precisely in the Constitution that spoke of the relationship between the Church and the world, and thus dealt more closely with the area that had formerly been designated as the "distinctive" sphere of the laity.

Instead of this, however, *Gaudium et spes* drastically cuts down on its use. It is as if the Fathers had realized that the task of ordering temporal things toward God, of taking them up to transform them in Christ, and of the recapitulation that involves the whole of the created order is now seen to be *distinctive of the whole Church and not only of lay people,* or not to be attributed to them exclusively or to an excessive degree. This may be why the Constitution prefers to use the more general terminology of "Christian," "member of the Christian faithful," or, indeed, the term "Church."

The use of "layman" returns, however, in the body of number 43, which deals with the help the Church intends giving to human activities. Here the main subject is "[all] Christians," "citizens of both cities," an expression that recalls the two "ranks" of *Apostolicam actuositatem* 5, where mention was made only of the laity. In *Gaudium et spes,* the perspective is broader and the introduction of the term "layman" in a context of "animating the world with the spirit of Christianity," which refers back to *Lumen gentium* without actually citing it, is accompanied not only by a call to skill, cooperation, and the assumption of personal responsibility, in the light of Christian wisdom, but also by the observation that secular occupations and activities belong to them "distinctively albeit not exclusively." This text already sets before us the theme of the specific character of the layperson, which we must now discuss. It is legitimate to ask at least why there is no reference here in the notes of *Gaudium et spes* to *Lumen gentium* 31.

A Remaining Tension

Despite the incomplete nature of the summary observations we have made up to this point concerning the theological status of the laity and their tasks, they have pointed out not only that categorization and contrasts within the tasks of the Church have been overcome, showing an "inadequate" distinction between the Christian and the clergy, which is not tenable on the same plane of thought, but they also tend to cast doubt upon the possibility of speaking logically of an inadequate distinction between the Christian and the layperson, and rather, they show these tend to be identical. This means that the distinctive task attributed to the layperson tends to become the distinctive task of the Christian—in other words, of the whole Church.

Even so, *a tension remains.* The term "layperson" is still weighed down not only with an historical and cultural linguistic usage expressing contrast, but also one expressing a relative identity that seems to be negative and that *Lumen gentium* 31 was not able to avoid, although it reduced it to a minimum. Thus, the documents derived from it, especially *Apostolicam actuositatem,* show signs of this, and maybe compound its effect in certain passages, even though they remain faithful to purging their references of the negative features of the historical and cultural and the cultic usage.

Toward a Postconciliar Development

Leaving aside extremist eccentrics, and resuming the positive aspects of what we have stated above, we can understand that the most recent postconciliar theology concerning the "laity" seems to have taken up the following positions: (a) it tends to take for granted the identification between layperson and Christian; (b) as a result, it asks why the term "layperson" should be maintained in the theological field; the problem of pastoral use, however, remains a separate problem; (c) it transfers the area of research to the more general subject—which requires a different kind of identification that is more problematic—of the "lay" or "secular condition" of the whole Church; (d) it tends toward the construction of a total ecclesiology as the context in which all the problems still extant can be resolved.

However, there are several others who seek a solution of these extant problems and tensions in ecclesiology, including what is referred to as "total ecclesiology," by having it depend more precisely on a more general theological view that takes as its starting point the conciliar text, which is so rich in intuitions that have often remained partially unexplored, or at least not theologically coordinated. These theologians—at least in Italy among those who have contributed to the debate on the lay condition, which is more of a burning issue in Italy than elsewhere at present—try to highlight more thoroughly the aspect of communion (Dianich) or ministry (Sartori) of a systematic theological account of the Trinitarian mystery (Forte), or of pneumatology, or else, in a similar approach to that of the present writer, they think that we should explore the great opportunities offered by developing a *total christology.*

This total christology does not exclude but includes—or can include, more systematically—not only what the Council highlighted regarding the laity, but can also make considerable contributions to the task of overcoming the two ecclesiologies that

Acerbi's study discerns are not wholly integrated in the Council, and clarify the problematic solutions produced in the striving for a total ecclesiology.

The Crucial Point

Analyses of the positive conciliar elements as regards the laity and later references to the questions of development made in this section seem to indicate even more unequivocably than appeared above that the crucial and prime issue of the debate is constituted by the two problems set at the outset: in other words, whether or not the Council gives a theological definition of the "layperson" and the "laity," and therefore whether or not it provides a solid basis for the ambiguous expression "theology of the laity" and lastly whether or not (quite apart from the question of a formal definition) the Council gives any truly typological indication—in other words, any "characteristic and distinctive" indication—of the presumed "specific character of the laity" (*indoles saecularis*, etc.). If this is the case, we may ask what status and specific theological area should be assigned to a "theology of the laity" that does not come down to a mere collection of pastoral questions.

The lack of any examination of these questions, or the fact of simply taking them for granted without proper consideration, is one of the reasons for the confusion still reigning in the contemporary debate.

Vatican II and the Problem of the
Definition and the Specific Character of the Layperson

Although the two questions of the definition and the specific character of the layperson in the texts of Vatican II are closely linked, I prefer to discuss them separately. I am taking for granted that a study of all the passages given above in which the terms "layman" and "laity" appear will lead to the clear conclusion that there are really only two texts in the Dogmatic Constitutions that are fundamental and foundational for our twofold question: *Lumen gentium* 31, and *Gaudium et spes* 43. These are the texts that provide the keys respectively to the whole Chapter IV of *Lumen gentium* (and the related passages in *Apostolicam actuositatem* and *Optatam totius* that depend on it) and to the remaining citations (all of them later) of the term "layman" in *Gaudium et spes.*

A Definition of the Layperson?

1. The assumption that the Council intended giving a genuine "definition" of the "layperson" seems to have interested eminent laypersons in the cultural and apostolic spheres more than theologians, whether lay or not.[43] It would seem that the reasons for this defense can be found in the need, which is more pastoral than basically theological, to defend the space for freedom and initiative that the Council recognized as belonging to laypersons, and which, after having been accepted in theory, can be seen and felt to be threatened by the viscosity of a persistent and centralizing clerical pastoral practice, even where this practice does not actually resist acceptance of the Council.

However, most frequently, this defense has neglected or completely ignored the question of the definition, and has concentrated on the interpretation of the *indoles saecularis* and similar statements of the Council as the specific and *exclusive sphere of the laity.*

Even so, those who think otherwise should not forget the positive aspect of these opinions: the danger of putting the clock back, of stagnation, or of reversing the theological process begun by the Council, dreams of restoration, and abuses of clerical power, with a conspiracy of silence and weakness on the part of those who should step in, are examples from our history. Thus, Lazzati[44] is right when he issues a warning to theological colleagues exploring the new frontiers of the "secularity" or "lay character" of the Church—of the whole Church—against the dangers of worldliness and of a return to clericalism. Even so, this position is rightly refuted by theologians from the secular and regular clergy who support their arguments both with the conciliar texts and with a warning against the danger of a disincarnated spiritualism. And, to tell the truth, we think both warnings should be extended to the lay movements, especially those referred to as "of the third order" (i.e., those without explicit ecclesial recognition).

However, it is maybe necessary to emphasize the fact that, even without attributing an exclusive character to the specific task of the laity as indicated by the Council (which involves the *recovery for the whole of Christianity of a theology of creation and of earthly things* that is clearer than that expressed by the current that prevailed—without excluding this recovery—in the elaboration of the conciliar text on the laity), it is still necessary to state very strongly, as Lazzati does,[45] that the primary vocational task of the layperson is that of "engaging in temporal affairs and directing them according to God's will" (*LG* 31), and that this constitutes the layperson's distinctive path to holiness. It is also important that in his or her effort to demonstrate the theological basis of this, he or she should take as the starting point the theology of creation, and should reflect on the christological foundations of the "specific character" of the laity. This is the path toward a total christology.

2. If we now turn our attention to professional theologians, we shall find very few who use the term "definition" to indicate the theological status of the laity. Two questions should be carefully distinguished in this connection: (a) the attribution to the Council of a desire to provide a definition, and of what type; (b) the personal attempt of the theologian to achieve a definition, and of what type.

In contemporary thought, there are many ways of understanding the concept of "definition." And it is also easy to understand that those—for instance, Schillebeeckx[46]—who sought to provide a positive answer to the second question, should have concentrated on the importance of the use of the word as found in various of the interventions of the Council Fathers with regard to the text of the chapter on lay people that was presented by the conciliar subcommission in the second session (the later variants did not affect the substance as far as our subject is concerned). Schillebeeckx interprets it as he prefers, in terms of a "descriptive definition," which is different from the classic one of Tradition. Now it is a fact that the preparatory commission had already ruled out (we may interpret this as that they were unable to give) an "ontological" definition, which seems to indicate nothing other than a "classical, practical definition according to type and specific difference."

Now the nonspecific use of the term "definition" by the Fathers (as Schillebeeckx seems to observe) can certainly not be interpreted as a defense of the classical sense; but neither does it support other restrictive definitions. This is important for the essential element of our problem, which is that of seeing whether or not the intention of the Fathers, and above all that of the "received text," should be interpreted as the indication of a "specific character in a strict sense," in other words, through exclusive and excluding elements or distinguishing and distinctive features.

However, in support of the retention of the term "definition," Schillebeeckx also seems to cite the presentation to the Council made by Cardinal Wright in the name of the subcommission. Yet the tone of this speech did not indicate this: it did not speak of a definition but only of "a broad description of the layperson," with the precise indication that "here" was being added to the beginning of number 31

> . . . so that it may be understood that the Council does not wish to give a definition, which would be harmful for the discussions of scholars, e.g., whether Religious, and—with even greater reason—the members of a secular Institute, are to be counted amongst laymen, and in what sense. Further, the Council does not propose an "ontological" definition of the layman, but rather a "typological" description.[47]

The general tone of the speech seems on the whole to reject any connection between the terms "definition" (and not only an ontological definition) and "description" in interpreting *Lumen gentium* 31a, which is being discussed here, while with regard to the second part of the number on the "secular character," it speaks only of "the typology of the layperson in the world."

There is, therefore, no basis for stating, following the subcommission itself, that the Council wanted to give a definition of the laity. As regards the personal interpretation of Schillebeeckx of a "descriptive definition" or a "typological definition" with which "against the common background the specific character of the layman is defined more precisely, seen in contrast to that of the clergy," we must wonder precisely what a "descriptive definition" is in good logical terms and if it can be properly suited to the conciliar text of number 31.

Among the various types of definition, A. Menne includes that of "connotation or description," which "highlights an object, indicating its characteristic identity, which must so far as possible be *unique* and *typical* of this object, in such a way as to distinguish it from others."[48] The typological—or as some people call it, "phenomenological," using the term correctly in this field—description is used as an indication of "distinguishing and distinctive" features,[49] in other words, ones that here too are exclusive. Hence, while concluding this consideration of the first question with the view that the Council seems, on the whole, not to have wanted to give a true definition of the laity or the layperson, we must still consider whether it did not end up by permitting one *de facto*, by indicating in the "secular character" or equivalent expressions a distinguishing and distinctive, and thus exclusive, feature that we can take as a new basis for a definition.

The *Indoles Saecularis* ("Secular Character") as the *Proprium* ("Specific Character") of the Laity

Is this a distinguishing and distinctive feature of the laity, or does it allow another, nonexclusive interpretation?

In order to answer this question, we must reexamine the precise tone of the final text of Chapter IV of *Lumen gentium*, in which number 31 gives the meaning, and the text of *Gaudium et spes* 43, which offers the final conciliar interpretation.

We shall first consider the text as it stands in the intentions it demonstrates, without reference to the suggestions of the subcommission that drafted it: these can sometimes give rise to misunderstandings or point us in the wrong direction. For these reasons, we shall leave our examination of the tone of its *Relatio generalis* (or "General Report") until later, but shall begin instead with the conciliar text of number 30.

1. After recalling that what it has stated in general concerning the people of God also holds good for lay people, in number 30, the Council adds: "Because of their situation and mission [*condicionis et missionis*], however, certain things pertain particularly to the laity, both men and women, the foundations of which must be more fully examined owing to the special circumstances of our time." In view of the fact that the text began by speaking of *status* with regard to lay people, who are being addressed here, from the beginning we are faced with the crucial question of whether *status* is to be understood in a specific sense, already in some way expressing a contrast. For if we compare it with the immediately preceding text, which was revised by the subcommission, we shall see that *status* has been used to replace *condicio et missio* in order to avoid repetition, because the latter

phrase is found a few lines later in the new text; this expression did not express a contrast, nor does it now.[50] If the text had wished to speak more specifically in this sense, it would have used a term such as *categoria.* However, *categoria* is not found in the Council at all (except in UR 13, in quite a different context), and we have moreover observed its general tendency to avoid this approach.

In this case, the opinion of the subcommission can be of help: it explains that *status* was introduced, as stated above, in order to avoid repetition, and also as "an honor" they wished to attribute to lay people. However, the term is understood by the subcommission "only in the broad sense"; "only" may indeed seem puzzling, but all that seems to be meant is the honorific intention, and not some forced categorization, which is excluded by the expression "in the broad sense." Moreover, for the first time, the text expressly mentions with regard to lay people "their contribution and charisms," which are to be recognized by the pastors.

2. Number 31 should be studied as follows: first the beginning (already cited), then the rest of the first paragraph, and then the second paragraph. *The introduction to the first paragraph* is a sort of reminder that calls for some further consideration than that already carried out:

> The term "laity" is here understood to mean all the faithful [*christifideles*] except those in Holy Orders and those who belong to a religious state approved by the Church. That is, the faithful [*christifideles*]. . . .

What then follows indicates that the second *christifideles* merely indicates the *ratio* of the *christifidelis*—the *ratio communis,* which, on its own, the Council considers suited to indicating in positive terms who the layperson is. If the first *christifideles* were also to be viewed solely on the level of the *ratio* and were not instead to be taken on the complex *practical level* of the people of God, there could be no distinctions between clerics and religious, because no such distinctions can be deduced from the term. Thus, what we have here is a listing and comparison, which the text keeps on the *practical level;* and indeed clerics and religious are correctly referred to in the only way logically possible in the circumstances, that is, by introducing the different level on which their positive character (*ordo* and *status sancitus*) is seen.

Consequently, in order to preserve logic, it must be stated that the *positive character of the layperson* in the practical order coincides with the pure and simple content of the *ratio* of *christifidelis* that becomes fully "real" and present in the "layperson," whereas the positive character that distinguishes the cleric and the religious is drawn from other levels of logic[51] that cannot be derived from the *ratio* of the *christifidelis*, although they too are *christifideles*. Thus, the only thing that can be stated with regard to the layperson is a pure and simple identity with the *christifidelis*—and this at once eliminates the possibility of interpreting "layperson" as a category. On the other hand, the "inadequate distinction" of the other two with respect to the simple *christifidelis* does not allow one to make them into categories, but only, in strict logic, to distinguish their specific positive character, which is definable not on the level of the *ratio* of the *christifidelis*, but in what they receive "from outside": through the institution of Christ or the raising up of the Spirit, as recognized by the Church. On the practical level, it is not possible logically to speak of negative conclusions on the basis of the different *rationes* we are discussing; and therefore the "except" at the beginning of the text can likewise not be held to be such.

However, had the Council wanted to say nothing but this, it is impossible to see why it should have retained the term "layperson." But before moving on to examine this aspect in the second part of number 31, we need to describe the *content* of the first part: the laity,

> That is, the faithful who by Baptism are incorporated into Christ, are placed in the People of God, and in their own way [*sua modo*] share the priestly, prophetic and kingly office of Christ, and carry out their own part [*pro parte sua*] in the mission of the whole Christian people [*missionem totius populi christiani*] in the Church and in the world.

The logic of this text retains a certain tension between the pure and simple participation of the entire common content of the *christifidelis* and *suo modo*, which seem to restrict it, and between *missionem totius populi christiani* and *pro parte sua*, which again seem to restrict it. If we presume the idea of categories, or at least presume that here a genuine specific character is introduced— this would be indicated in the second part of number 31—then these two expressions could not be seen as limitations. However, in this case, they would be in contradiction with what has been stated so far. We can see how Klostermann, who starts with the idea of a specific character, finds it foreshadowed here.

However, in the light of the Council's desire to produce a purely positively oriented description, and also of the tendency toward the identification we have mentioned above, it is strictly speaking possible to give a different interpretation to the text. *Pro parte sua* and *suo modo* could have not a limiting sense, but an *intensive* one, because (as was said above with regard to clerics or religious) a comparison made on a complex practical level cannot avoid highlighting the positive character; however, the positive character is not yet fully outlined here, although it is to be found in the very *ratio* of the *christifidelis* and cannot be separated from it. It will be sought in the next section of our study in the relationship of the Church *to the world:* thus *pro parte sua* indicates that only the layperson fully carries out the mission of the Church toward the world, inasmuch as he or she alone is totally immersed in it according to the divine plan. On the other hand, *suo modo* could refer to the kingly task in the sense of "taking up the whole of creation in order to bring it to fulfillment," which only the layperson can do because of his or her full, unlimited role in God's plan. However, it would be better to speak of the laity as a whole.

The *Relatio*, or report, of the subcommission on this first part of number 31 expresses the intention of giving in it "the general and positive *ratio* of the *christifideles.*" It does not seem to me that "general" (*generica*) here is meant to indicate a *genus proximum*, as Klostermann interprets it to mean; rather, it simply means *communis*, and, as we have seen, in this context, this does not entail a limiting or categorizing sense.

Thus, if our interpretation is correct, *laicus*, as shorn of any intention to denote a contrast, neither adds nor subtracts anything from the *ratio* of the *christifidelis* from the theological viewpoint, so that between these two terms there can only be a nominal distinction. However, this does not mean that the term *laicus* does not have any theological value: on the contrary, it gives it the *fullness* of the theological value of *christifidelis* in relationship to the world, with the further connotation of the *area* where this fullness comes to fulfillment and is situated *in practice.*

The conciliar text wishes to retain both the practical level of comparison and the indication of the different logical *rationes* whereby lay people, clerics, and religious are distinguished from one another, and it therefore finds itself in a context that was difficult to reconcile in logical terms, which, if read with presuppositions different from ours (for example, owing to a certain way of understanding the *Relatio generalis* on the "specific character," which we shall discuss at the end of this section), has given rise to interpretations that in our opinion destroy the logical structure by introducing categorizing approaches. However, the subcommission that drafted Chapter III must bear even more responsibility for this than the subcommission that produced Chapter IV: the former subcommission—and not the conciliar text—ventured to speak at one point of "categories," and in an imprecise sense, what is more. To the best of my knowledge, in their oral and written interventions in the Council Hall, the Fathers themselves refrained from using the term "category," and I have found only one occurrence of this nonconciliar term in the *Acta Synodalia*, volume III, part X—and this too is used with imprecision.

3. It is the *second part of number 31* that has given rise to discussion on the "specific character" of the layperson. Here again we shall first of all read the text as it stands. Not only does it not contain the expression "specific character," not even in a broad sense, but, in the light of what is said in the first paragraph, it completes the first paragraph with logical consistency, providing greater clarification as to the intensifying (and not contrasting) indication of the practical positive character that it wishes to indicate by using the term *laicus*, while remaining within the *ratio* of the *christifidelis*. The essential part of the text follows:

> Their secular character is proper and peculiar to the laity. . . . By reason of their special vocation it belongs to the laity to seek the kingdom of God by engaging in temporal affairs and directing them according to God's will. They live in the world, that is, they are engaged in each and every work and business of the earth and in the ordinary circumstances of social and family life which, as it were, constitute their very existence. . . .

The terms that could be interpreted as indicating a *specificus* in the text are those of *proprius* and *peculiaris*, used either separately or together here in order to strengthen the *indoles saecularis*. Now the term *proprius* harks back to that of *specificus* (which does not belong to classical Latin, but only to medieval scholastic Latin) in a context of definition, or, we might say, of typological description in the strict sense—which has already been discussed above and eliminated. When used outside this context alone, the term *proprius* has a broader meaning: "stable," "firm," "secure," "unchangeable," for example, as found later in the text in the expression *proprium munus*. *Peculiaris* also is broader and less specific than *specificus*. *Proprius et peculiaris*, which refer here to *indoles saecularis* in such a way as to indicate the maximum intensity desired by the Council, never attain—even when taken together—the pregnant significance of *specificus*, which refers to a species precisely as distinct from others. *Proprius*, which is also attributed to the vocation or *munus* of lay people, does not therefore seem to indicate any more than something stable, firm, secure, such as their actual area of existence, which is undoubtedly permanent. It is therefore not possible to draw anything more than this from the text—and certainly not the definition of a distinguishing and distinctive *unicum*. [52]

This is confirmed by the phrase that we omitted and that shows the intention of the text, even here, to remain (consistently with the first paragraph) on the practical level, in order to permit the only possible comparison—in other words, a positive one—retaining the individualizing logical distinctions without mixing levels:

> Although those in Holy Orders may sometimes be engaged in secular activities, or *even practice a secular profession*, yet by reason of their particular vocation, they are principally and expressly ordained to the sacred ministry. At the same time, religious . . .

It is not our task to extend our reflections to clerics and religious, but we shall simply note that as regards the content of the *indoles saecularis*, or "secular character," *Lumen gentium* in this passage eliminates any possibility of seeing this as a "specific character" in a strict sense. The Council correctly remains within the indication of the positive character of the respective distinguishing levels; nor does it introduce, but implicitly refers elsewhere (and the subcommission explicitly refers to Chapters III and VI) for any other observations that are possible only on these levels and not for comparison on the practical level; if on this level the specific vocations set limits in relation to the world, nothing of this should be echoed on the level of the *christifidelis* in his or her specific *ratio*. However, the comparison, which has remained on the razor's edge of logic, has the effect of highlighting to an even greater extent this *intensification* that affects the laity as the only area in which (without either adding or removing anything essential) the *ratio* of the *christifidelis* in relation to the mission of the Church toward the world, and in particular to the task of "taking up the whole of created reality, the world and history in order to bring them to fulfillment" in Christ, finds entire fulfillment which is permanent, stable, and full: in a few words, "its own."

It is important to note that the *theological foundation* for all the above lies in the identification of *laicus* with *christifidelis*, which gives a "new" and fuller theological meaning to the word *laicus*—a meaning that it never had before and that is the fruit of the wish of the Council only to give positively oriented indications and to eliminate any meaning expressing contrast. In this way, as our analysis has shown, it has also restored full theological dignity to the laity.

Thus, despite the nominal distinction, the term *laicus* is fully justified, and comes indispensable for the intensification, permanence, and indication of the full and specific area without which the lay character of the whole Church would remain abstract, ineffective, and handicapped.

4. The exclusion of the "secular character" as *the true and specific distinctive character* of the laity is definitively supported by the forceful text of *Gaudium et spes* 43, the first in which this Constitution takes up the subject of the laity: "It is to the laity, though not exclusively to them, that secular duties and activity properly belong."[53] It is remarkable that this fresh affirmation of a "specific" task of the laity should be found in the Constitution in which the Council became aware that the task of assumption, human promotion, and salvific transformation in Christ of all created things belongs to the whole Church. Number 43 itself applies to "Christians," who are indicated generically, what it wishes to say concerning "help that the Church wants to give to human activity": its observations on the harmony between religious life and commitment on the one hand and commitments in daily life and professional and social activities on the other,

recalling "the example of Christ, who worked as a craftsman," lead to the following statement: "The Christian who shirks his temporal duties shirks his duties towards his neighbor, neglects God himself, and endangers his eternal salvation." Now it is in this context that the *proprium* of lay people is reaffirmed, "albeit not exclusively," linked to statements about skill, cooperation, initiative, and the possibility of pluralism in solutions that raise problems of new relations, including those with the authority of the Church.

It therefore seems to me that what we have said concerning the "laity" as the only specific theological area in which the lay character of the Church is truly brought to fulfillment, and as the root from which the "specific" characteristics derive, in the sense indicated, of vocation, *munus,* and whatever else the Council indicates, finds its confirmation. It will be necessary to study all the consequences of this, even though this is beyond the limits of the present study, which must, nevertheless, conclude with a few remarks to this effect.

5. As the last observation in this analysis, one of the *reasons for the deviation of the discussion* onto the "specific character" can now be given as certain unfortunate and ambiguous statements of the conciliar subcommission that drafted Chapter IV of *Lumen gentium.*

We have already discussed the use of "typological description" and "the typology of the layperson" in the *Relatio* to number 31, together with the misunderstandings it caused. However, it was above all the *Relatio generalis* that used this ambiguous and unfortunate expression that set off certain commentators, who did not pay enough attention to what the text said as it stands, on a false trail: ". . . in the same chapter on the laity it was necessary to discuss more clearly and also at greater length *those things which specifically appertain to the lay people. . . .*" However, the subcommission itself indicated the difficulty, adding: ". . . which was easier said than done."

The truth is that the subcommission labored under a number of influencing circumstances: it had to work on previous drafts without very much freedom to rework them, and it had to take differing opinions into account; and lastly, it was also conditioned by the limitations of the "theology of the laity" of that time. Its concerns are expressed in the following text, which we shall examine in two parts: "In the new order and revision of the text, several dangers had to be avoided, as is obvious. For the lay people do not simply coincide with the faithful, who include both the hierarchs and the faithful." Unless it is simply a printing error, the last *fideles* ("the faithful") for "members of the religious state" (*LG* 31a) is a real slipup. In any case, the phrasing indicates a difficulty of expression and a lack of clarity. It may possibly be capable of a right interpretation, but it can give rise to the idea of a contrasting bipolar view. The subcommission continues as follows: "It was also necessary clearly to distinguish between the natural and the supernatural order, and between temporal and spiritual matters, so that on the one hand a dangerous confusion, and on the other hand a no less dangerous separation, might be avoided." And lastly, we should note its terminological considerations: "Finally, as regards the use of terminology: the words cleric, layman, religious, clericalism, laicism, the world and its consecration or condemnation are used quite differently in sacred, juridical, and everyday vernacular language." The warning that follows concerning the distinction between hierarchy and laity provides a good example of the fundamental concern, which was above all to highlight cooperation in communion.

Lastly, it reaffirms that *Lumen gentium* IV lays the "dogmatic basis" for the questions that were then being dealt with in the schema *De apostolatu laicorum* (which later became *Apostolicam actuositatem*).[54]

6. Our research has been particularly concerned with identifying this "dogmatic basis," which, as concerns lay people, does not appear to lie in the identification of some "specific character" that analysis of the texts simply does not reveal, and consequently it can lead only to relatively imprecise and incomplete functional distinctions. On the other hand, it seemed to us that the conciliar text indicates the *theological root* of the identification of the laity in the basic identity between *christifidelis* and *laicus*, seeing in the latter not a category or a division within the people of God, but rather the normal situation of the *christifidelis* who, in accordance with the divine will, fully lives out the lay task of the whole Church: that of bringing all created things, the world, and history to fulfillment in Christ who takes all things up again in himself. This leads us to the specific indication of a "distinctive character" that is not specific because it is not exclusive.

Even so, the revaluation of the specific theological area that we have made of the "laity" seems more significant than a reflection solely in terms of closely defined, classified, and hierarchicized functions and ministries. A difficulty in the way of this revaluation (although it is not in direct contradiction to it) of the term "layperson" could come from the extension of the term *ordines* that the Council uses to the "laity" as a whole. Now the Council uses the term *ordo* in many very different ways. Those that can be involved here are not concerned with the strict usage reserved for those who have received the sacrament of orders, but the broader yet still determining usage of a traditional flavor which the Council certainly uses in *Lumen gentium* 13c:

> Hence it is that the People of God is not only an assembly of various peoples, but in itself is made up of different ranks [*variis ordinibus*]. This diversity among its members is either by reason of their duties—some exercise the sacred ministry for the good of their brethren—or it is due to their condition and manner of life—many enter the religious state and, intending to sanctity by the narrower way, stimulate their brethern by their example.

However, neither here nor elsewhere do the Council texts attribute the term *ordo* to the laity—and even less so in this second, more restricted sense. And the *Relatio* to number 13 follows this same line.[55]

Are we to see a possibility for expansion in the preceding number of *Lumen gentium* (12c; cf. also SC 26), which states: "The Holy Spirit . . . distributes special graces among the faithful of every rank [*omnis ordinis fideles*]"? It does not seem at all certain that here the word *ordo* has the same meaning as in the previously examined text, and the *Relatio* to this number says nothing. If this restricted meaning were intended, why does number 13, which follows it and which should therefore define it more clearly, not include the laity among the *ordines*? Further, the context speaks of "charisms" and therefore seems to belong to another type of consideration on various kinds of sacramental and ministerial orders, as is expressly stated at the beginning of the text. Moreover, it does not use terminology that could refer back to a "category," "state of life," or similar contexts expressing contrast. It therefore seems to me that a use of *ordo* to distinguish the laity in a strict sense cannot be justified by supposed intention of the conciliar text.

It is easy to understand that certain categorizing mentalities, or scholars blocked by the nonconciliar term "specific"—or by the context of the past expressing a contrast that has not been wholly overcome, or by concentrating more on functions and ministries than on the theological root we considered above—can find it easy to extend the term *ordo* to the laity. However, they would have to specify in what sense they were using it both in order to preserve the distinction of logical levels without inappropriate slips that would reproduce the mentality of contrast, and to respect the theological root and the fullness that are proper to the laity in the *ratio* of the *christifidelis*, without introducing coercion into it from other levels. We must still consider it if this is what we find in the new Code.

7. Taking into account my limited experience and specialized knowledge with regard to the new Code of Canon Law, I shall confine myself to a few observations taken from the first commentaries to appear. Furthermore, we are not concerned here with what it has to say in detail about lay people, which certainly represents a decisive break with the previous canonical tradition and especially that codified in the 1917 Code. It clearly draws its inspiration from—and wishes to adhere firmly to—the spirit and texts of the ecclesiology of Vatican II. This adherence to the conciliar text is clear in Book II, "The People of God," which deals with "The Obligations and Rights of All the Christian Faithful" (Title I) and in particular "The Obligations and Rights of the Lay Christian Faithful" (Title II). And the conciliar text is sometimes cited word for word (cf. also the Introductions to the individual books that are found in some editions).

We are concerned with two specific questions here: that of the determination of the fundamental structure of the Church in relation to the distinction between sacred ministers and lay people; and the way in which the Code classifies lay people.

The first question seems to be dealt with above all in Canon 207, the last of the introductory canons to Book II. Here I will make use of a recent commentary that calls for some discussion. (All italicization is mine.)

The last of the four introductory canons, No. 207, gives us the *fundamental structure* of the Church. Its first paragraph distinguishes between sacred ministers and lay people according to divine institution. In this way the hierarchical structure of the

Church is given. However, in the second paragraph it is presumed that this is not the fundamental structure of the Church, considering consecration, through the profession of the evangelical counsels by means of vows or other sacred bonds recognized and approved by the Church, to be proper to the life and holiness of the Church, even though they do not concern its hierarchical structure (cf. *LG* 43b; 44d). It is thus implicitly recognized that there is a *primordial,* fundamental *structure* of the Church, which is of a charismatic and institutional type, and on which this hierarchical structure is grafted.

The author takes "institution" to mean "all the relationships between various subjects that are ruled by norms of conduct that are binding on the subjects involved in the relationship," and he links the charism to its need for "a practical form of expression," which requires these norms of conduct even if they are not approved by a positive law. He can therefore conclude that "even prior to its positive determination, an institution arises as the direct work of the Spirit, and hence as the immediate expression of the charism." It is the task of hierarchical authority to recognize the charism and provide suitable and consistent laws for it. However, is this truly "the primordial structure," or does it lie in the unity of communion, known by the two names "community" and "ministries"?

On this basis the author—who is primarily interested in the *communio hierarchica* and the juridical structure that derives from it—feels he can deduce from his view and interpretation of the charisms that the above-mentioned canon

> . . . gives us a vision of a Church organized into a number of *ranks* or *categories* of persons, which have their source in the action of the Spirit, and are recognized and approved by the Hierarchy, which is itself a fruit of the action of the same Spirit.

But we may ask whether the Spirit truly wished to make lay people a category or rank.

The author reveals in a note what is the foundation of this extension of the term *ordo,* and even that of "category" to the laity:

We can say that in the Church there are three general ranks that correspond to three different charisms: the lay charism which entails profession of the faith in direct dealings with temporal matters, thus according to a specific secular character. . . .[56]

We see here how a canonical mentality can manage to resume the categorizing distinctions that inevitably express a contrast that analysis of the conciliar text as it stands had exluded. This may of course be inevitable in the translation of conciliar texts into terms of rights and duties in a Code written in a different spirit. However, if this were so, similar conclusions should be found in all commentaries on the Code.[57] At this point, we come to our second question.

We may ask ourselves whether we should apply to the words of the Code the same hermeneutical principle we employed for the conciliar texts—that of reading them as they stand, and distinguishing the intentions found in the text from those of the commentators. Now, if we are not mistaken, in the canons that deal with the faithful, and in particular with the lay faithful, we do not find any consecration of the terms "rank," "category," or similar words—just as we saw was the case for the conciliar texts. It seems to me even less possible to infer from an interpretation of a "specific" lay character that, after what has been said, it can only have a precise sense in the term *proprius* understood without categorizing inferences or even of a "rank." In any case, the *Relatio generalis* to *Lumen gentium* IV rejected the attribution of a juridical meaning to the terms. Of course, in view of its needs, and in its references back to the conciliar texts, the Code can introduce details and clarifications—as we find, for example, in the case of the above-mentioned Canon 207, §1—which do correspond entirely to the conciliar terminology; in fact, in our example, a clear distinction is drawn between sacred ministers "who are also called clerics in law" and "other Christian faithful, who are also called laity." *Laici* has a broader meaning here than *Lumen gentium* 31a had given it, even though it introduced it with "here." We must leave it to the competent canonists to show how such variations and solutions can be reconciled with respect for the logical levels on which the conciliar distinctions are made, and the more complex practical level on which the Council moves. However, the specific note of the conciliar text and of the legitimate interpretations to which it gives rise must in any case be respected. We are, therefore, greatly disturbed by interpretations that apparently tend to go too far in reducing the basic and fundamental *communio* to a *communio hierarchica* that seems to emphasize the *hierarchica* aspect unduly. We are also disturbed by those interpretations of the laity that do not retain the rediscovery of the lay character of the whole Church, hardening the term *laici* into a category or rank on the basis of a "specific character" that is not strictly specific.

However, the difficulties remain for others as well as canonists. There are several postconciliar studies on "the people of God" or the Church in which reflection on lay people is minimal or almost completely lacking, while, on the other hand, there are others that maybe harden the term "state of life" and thus seem to move toward a renewed quasiassimilation of the spirituality of the layperson to that of the cleric or religious. There is still a great deal of ground to be covered before lay people are recognized as having that fullness that is their right on the basis of the theological root of the *christifidelis*: the layperson is the *christifidelis* who alone carries out in its fullness the task of taking the world up and transforming it. And, if I may be permitted to end with an impression that the new Code of Canon Law leaves me with, despite everything, it seems to me that in its fundamental spirit and apart from the details of individual canons and commentaries, it too moves toward that identification between *christifidelis* and *laicus* that we found in the Council. In any case, I hope that the conciliar interpretation upheld in this article may provide a subject of discussion that will result in clearer comprehension for the good of the whole Church and an ever-improved understanding of the position and tasks of the laity.

Conclusion

In the perspective of the postconciliar theological debate on the "laity," a view has been proposed that is based on a fresh consideration of the conciliar texts and that seems to set about the difficult task of reconciling two opposing tendencies. The first seems to us to be concentrated on the rediscovery and increasing value given to a "lay character" that it thinks is a quality of the Church, and that therefore tends to diminish the value of the term "lay" as introduced by the Council. The second, on the other hand, wants to retain it and give it its full value, and therefore concentrates on the defense of a "specific character" in the full sense of the term, claiming that this was asserted by the Council. We have observed the dangers that can be entailed in both positions.

We have conducted a review of the most significant conciliar texts in the light of the hermeneutical principle of reading the texts as they stand, without allowing ourselves to be influenced by any opinions, however authoritative, that might dominate our impression, and of the logical principle of respect of the different logical *rationes* that regulate distinctions, avoiding undue mixing of issues on the practical level on which the Council moves. This has enabled us to give a structured reply.

1. As regards the first tendency, we concluded that it was impossible either to speak of a conciliar definition of the layperson, or to indicate a specific character of the layperson that would define the laity as a particular sector, a category, or an *ordo* in the strict sense, retaining the character of contrast as found in the long preceding Tradition. This enabled us to recognize a highly positive value in the rediscovery of the "lay character" of the whole Church.

2. As regards the second tendency, we recognized that the specific value of the "lay character"—its practical implications and its creativity—is not ensured if we take refuge in an abstract lay character divorced from the practical theological area wherein alone it can find complete fulfillment, in other words, from the "layness" of lay people.

3. Our interpretation consists in the fact that we do not consider that the nominal distinction—affirmed on the basis of the negation of the specific character of the new conciliar use of the term "lay" purged of any residual connotation of contrast, of the affirmation that the theological root of the lay character of the whole Church lies in the very *ratio* of the *christifidelis* who shares in Christ's task of taking all things up again into himself—leads to a reduction in the theological value of the term *laicus*. On the contrary, if we distinguish the theological root in this *christifidelis*, we feel the "layperson" absorbs the whole theological significance of the *christifidelis*, seeing the term "layperson" not as something more or something less than the *ratio* of the *christifidelis* but as the only practical area (distinguished by its own

specific charisms and ministries) where his relationship to the world and to the lay condition indicated in it can come to complete fulfillment. It is a permanent, practical, and stable way that we see indicated in the conciliar affirmation of a *proprium* (or "distinctive character"), ("although not an exclusive one") of the laity, which finds its full justification here.

This interpretation, which we propose as a working hypothesis for further discussion needs to be verified and backed up by further study. I would indicate some lines of inquiry that seem to me to be important:

1. We should explore all the potential of the "seeds" of the lay character that are contained in the New Testament, especially where the text speaks of the "faithful," and other terms that, prior to any distinction, indicate or can indicate the same area.

2. Research in "biblical theology" should be pursued, with reference to "the foundation of the lay character," with a fuller appreciation of a theology of creation. B. Maggioni has produced a good systematic study in this field, with reference to the wisdom tradition.[58] However, as a comparative phenomenologist of the history of religion, I wish he had given more serious attention to modern criticisms of the ambiguity of the term "sacred," which he sometimes even confuses with the object of religious experience—in other words with the Ultimate or Divine Reality in his salvific relationship with man.[59]

3. Lastly, it is to be hoped that there will be more detailed study of "total christology," of the "total Christ" who pervades the whole of history in order to draw everything and everybody back to the Father; this study should be based on a theology of the creative word, according it its full importance and harmonizing it with the role of Redeemer, in a fuller reflection on Christ who takes all things up again into himself. In this approach, the layperson would receive greater consideration as the most appropriate area in which the Church can with special competence and experience discover and evaluate "the seeds of the word," the movements that are "the signs of the times" sown in history by the Spirit—those seeds of eternity (cf. GS 18) and of creative reminder, which, while fully respecting the autonomy of temporal realities, the eye of faith discovers as "intrinsic," "ordering toward God."

Within the perspective of the search for an increasingly perfect balance between the theology of creation and the theology of redemption as envisaged by the Council (GS 41 and 43; cf. 22 and 45; LG 31c, etc.) and as seems to be favored by a total christology, and for a harmonious conception of the eschatology of the already here and the not yet, the position and revelation accorded to the "laity" could avoid the abstraction of a theory of the lay character without lay people. Our historical survey has convinced us that wherever the laity is undervalued, the lay character is also undervalued, and vice versa, and, on the other hand, the christic dimension of all created things and the cosmic dimension of Christ taking up the whole of creation again into himself, according to which everything must be taken up in order that everything may be saved—and this is the task of the whole Church—would not reach its practical and creative fullness without this specific theological area that is the "laity" with all the fullness of the gifts, charisms, and ministries with which the Spirit enriches it and without stripping it of all its other tasks considered by the Council that we have mentioned above (see p. 598).

Only a position of this sort can be a sufficient basis for those further studies and reflections on the degree of participation in the tasks of the hierarchy itself (apart from those that are essential to the latter), which postconciliar research has been developing, following what the Council opened up in view of a full restoration, also *ad intra*, of the tasks and dignity of the laity. Elsewhere, as an example of this approach, and on the basis of *Apostolicam actuositatem* 6d, which attributes to lay people according to their ability and "according to the mind of the Church" their own role "in expressing Christian principles," I have been able to describe the right and duty of a "sharing of lay people in the doctrinal definitions of the (ordinary) magisterium."[60] For example, in the face of constantly changing economic problems and the many types of specialized knowledge that are needed in this and other spheres, everybody must recognize that reference to a skilled and professionally competent laity is necessary if the Church is to be an effective presence and avoid the risk of proposing a doctrine and solutions to human problems that are incomprehensible because they are obsolete.

As regards the initial question of the possibility of a theology of the laity, it is clear that this cannot be envisaged as a classical treatise or as an independent part of another treatise, despite the fact that the theological revaluation of the layperson as seen in direct relation to the richness of the *christifidelis* has witnessed to specific identification for him or her, with the charisms of his or her "distinctive character." However, here again it becomes clear that there is no way in which reflection on the relationship between the Church, the lay character, and the laity[61] could be passed over in a study concerning ecclesiology based on a total christology.

In conclusion:

> A "theology of the laity" which was always based on the exclusive institutional superiority of the hierarchy, is followed by a "theology of the people of God," which is based on the condition of "member of the faithful," within which vocations and ministries are structured.[62]

Further, in the interpretation of the conciliar text, certain remaining traces of contrast must be overcome, and we must move forward in a balanced fashion on the path that it has opened up for postconciliar reflection by its rejection of the view that clerics, religious, and laypeople are "categories."

*Translated from the Italian by Andrew Wade, Ronald Sway, and
Leslie Wearne.*

Notes

1. St. Clement of Rome, 40, 5, in Funk and Bihlmeyer, 57.

2. Y. Congar, *Jalons pour une théologie du laïcat* (Paris, 1954²), 19; *idem*, *Sacerdoce et laïcat devant leurs taches d'évangélisation* (Paris, 1962), 318.

3. I. de la Potterie, "L'origine et le sens primitif du mot 'laïc,' " *NRT*, 80 (1958), 840–853.

4. J.B. Bauer, "Die Worgeschichte von 'Laicus,' " *ZKT*, 81 (1959), 224–228 (here 228).

5. M. Jourjion, "Les premiers emplois du mot laïc dans la littérature patristique," *LumVit* (1963), 37–42.

6. *Laicità, problemi e prospettive. Atti del XLVII Corso di aggiornamento culturale dell'Università Cattolica, Verona, 25–30 settembre 1977.*

7. L. Pizzolato, "Laicità e laici nel cristianesimo primitivo," in *ibid.*, 57–83; G.G. Picasso, "La laicità nel medioevo," in *ibid.*, 84–112.

8. In the "Addenda" to the 1964 edition of *Jalons*, Congar accepts

the view of de la Potterie, 647–648; cf. also *Ministeri e comunione ecclesiale* (Bologna, 1973), 11–28.

9. *Didascalia*, II, 26, 1, in F.X. Funk, *Didascalia et Constitutiones Apostolorum* (photographic reprint, Turin, 1962).

10. Pizzolato, "Laicità e laici nel cristianesimo primitivo," 57; S. Vanni Rovighi, "Fondazione critica del concetto di laicità," in *Laicità, problemi e prospettive*, 235–248; the foundation of the lay character is given in the statement to the effect that "everything has a value in itself, and not only as a symbol, as a shadow of a higher reality" (237).

11. Y. Bodin, "Saint Jérôme et les laïcs," *RevEtAug*, 15 (1969), 134–135.

12. J.M. Diez Alegria, *Teoria generale del diritto e dello stato* (Rome, 1967); cf. *idem*, *La liberdad religiosa. Estudio teologico-filosofico-juridico y historico* (Barcelona, 1965).

13. Y.M.-J. Congar, *Ecclésiologie du haut moyen âge. De Saint Grégoire le Grand à la désunion entre Byzance et Rome* (Paris, 1968); G.G. Meersseman, *Ordo fraternitatis. Confraternite e pietà dei laici nel Medioevo*, 3 vols. (Rome, 1977).

14. J. Le Goff, *La civiltà dell'Occidente medioevale* (Turin, 1981).

15. Pope Innocent III, *De contemptu mundi*. This is the better known title of the work composed in 1194–1195, but only the following can be attributed to the author: *De miserie condicionis humanae*, ed. by R.E. Lewis (Athens, 1978), 51–53. As a rejoinder to the work of Innocent, the humanist Giannozzo Manetti wrote his *De dignitate et excellentia hominis* in 1452.

16. *I laici nella "Societas Christiana" dei sec. XI e XII. Atti della terza settimana di studio, Mendola, 21–27 agosto 1965* (Milan, 1968).

17. J. Lecler, *Histoire de la tolérance*, 2 vols. (Paris, 1955); *Studi sul Medioevo Cristiano, offerti a R. Morghen* (Rome, 1974).

18. F.M. Cappello, *Summa juris publici ecclesiastici* (Rome, 1954[6]).

19. H. Denzinger and A. Schönmetzer, *Enchiridion Symbolorum* (Rome, 1967[34]), 889.

20. A. Doglio, *De capacitate laicorum ad potestatem ecclesiasticam, praesertim iudicialem* (Rome, 1962); P.G. Caron, *I poteri giuridici del laicato nella Chiesa primitiva* (Milan, 1975[2]).

21. *Decretum Magistri Gratiani*, II pars, Causa XII, Quaest. I, Cap. VII, in *Corpus juris canonici*, pars prior, ed. by A. Friedberg (Leipzig, 1879), 678; cf. Congar, *Jalons* (1954), on Hugh of St. Victor, 32; other texts in the same line as Gratianus: the Bulls of Urban II (1029) and Honorius II (1124).

22. Congar, *Jalons* (1954), 11.

23. P.G. Bruno, *Anche i cristiani sono laici. La dimensione laicale della missione della Chiesa* (Avellino, 1982), 31, note 50.

24. Y.M.-J. Congar, "Laicato," *DizTeol*, ed. Fries (Brescia, 1967),

2, 124–140: Church of martyrs, Constantinian age, modern world. B. Forte, "Laicato," *DizTeolInterd* (Turin, 1977), 2, 354: the term "polo comunitario" indicates "l'appartenenza a un popolo," and the expression "polo ministeriale e gerarchico" is used to mean "l'appartenenza ad una categoria opposta ad un'altra all'interno di questo stesso popolo."

25. R. Riesner, *Jesus als Lehrer. Eine Untersuchung zum Ursprung der Evangelien-Ueberlieferung* (Tubingen, 1981), 2–18, gives an account of the contemporary situation of criticism with regard to the synoptic question, form criticism, and the history of tradition.

26. H. Schürmann, "Die vorösterlichen Anfänge der Logientradition. Versuch eines formgeschichtlichen Zugangs zum Leben Jesu," in H. Ristow and K. Matthiä (eds.), *Der historische Jesu und der kerygmatische Christus* (Berlin, 1961²), 342–370; this work marks the beginning of the move beyond form criticism.

27. G. Magnani, *Introduzione alla cristologia fondamentale: I. Metologie e richerche storiche su Gesù di Nazareth* (Rome, 1976), 312–419.

28. J.B. Ferreres, *Institutiones canonicae* (Barcelona, 1917–1918), 1, 87; A. Wermeersch and J. Creusen, *Epitome iuris canonici* (Mechelen/Rome, 1921–1925), 1, 87, 96, 346 (referring to Acts 13:2; 20:28–29; etc.); F. Wernz and P. Vidal, *Jus canonicum* (Rome, 1928–1930), 2, 47.

29. Intervention of Mgr. A. Charue, in *AS*, II, III, 382–384; C. Moeller, "Storia della Struttura e delle idee della LG," in J.M. Miller (ed.), *La teologia dopo il Vaticano II* (Brescia, 1967), 185.

30. The observation of a certain contemporary line of reflection is even more applicable to the historical and theological sciences than it is to the philosophy of science. For example, at the International Congress of Philosophy held at Varna in 1973, McMullin observed that 75 percent of philosophers of science held that every account even of physics and chemistry implied a "metaphysics"; cf. G. Magnani, *La crisi della metapsicologia freudiana* (Rome, 1981), 78, note 76. And T. Kuhn, *The Structure of Scientific Revolution* (Chicago/London, 1966), "Preface," X, etc., says that in any given age of the sciences, there are predominant "paradigms" that are always linked to a *Weltanschauung*. Any reflection of faith, and, *a fortiori*, any theological view implies a basic metaphysics or ontology, an anthropology and cosmology with various possibilities for successive systematic explanation. This means that it is impossible in our case to speak of a purely "functional" theology, or only of "functions" in the Church; it is thus necessary to indicate the theological basis for the use of the term "layperson," and this does not necessarily entail reference, among the possible ontologies, to a "static" ontology of the past.

31. J. Leclerq, *Vivre chrétiennement notre temps* (Brussels, 1957), 61–62; E. Schillebeeckx, "De leek in de Kerk," *Tijdschrift voor Geestelijk*

Leven, 15 (1959), 684; K. Rahner, "Über das Laienapostolat," in *Schriften zur Theologie*, 2 (Einsiedeln, 1955), 339–373; Congar, *Jalons* (1954), 45; G. Philips, *La mission de l'Eglise* (*Document de base pour le IIe Congrès de l'apostolat des laïcs* (Rome, 1957), *passim;* Y. de Montcheuil, *L'Eglise et le monde actuel* (Paris, 1945); *id.*, *Aspects de l'Eglise* (Paris, 1948).

32. P. Guilmot, *Fin d'une église cléricale?* (Paris, 1969), 151–250, on Congar; Guilmot's theory on the ordained priesthood seems excessively reductionist to me.

33. Rahner, "Über das Laienapostolat," adopted by Y. Congar, "I laici," in Miller (ed.), *La teologia dopo il Vaticano II*, 301: ". . . il laico è colui il cui essere cristiano e le responsabilità cristiane sono determinate dalla sua inserzione naturale nella vita e nella trama del mondo." However, even Rahner's view is debatable because it is incomplete and restrictive.

34. J. Daniélou, "Compte rendu des *Jalons*," *Dieu Vivant*, 25 (1953), 151.

35. J. Grootaers, "Quatre ans asprès. Une texte qui est loin déjà," in Y.M.-J. Congar (ed.), *L'apostolat des laïcs. Décret "Apostolicam Actuositatem"* (Paris, 1970), 215–237, esp. 232–234. As regards the widespread criticism that *Apostolicam actuositatem* is less advanced than the two Dogmatic Constitutions *Lumen gentium* and *Gaudium et spes*, see also Guilmot, *Fin d'une église cléricale?*, 313–314; L. Sartori, "La laicità nella dottrina del Vaticano II," in *Laicità nella Chiesa* (Milan, 1977), 32–66; P. Colombo, "Il compito dei laici nell'azione pastorale della Chiesa," in *Atti del Convegno su "I laici nella pastorale del lavoro"* (Rome, 1980), 9–10. Colombo and Sartori extend the discussion to the requirements of the postconciliar debate—with the need to overcome the abstract way of viewing the relationship between Church, world, and society according to the western model, and concern over the so-called "theology of liberation" and the relationship between evangelization and human promotion, as discussed by the 1974 Synod of Bishops, in *Evangelii nuntiandi* (cf. Nos. 70 and 73), and the Puebla Conference— and place the discussion on lay people and laity against this background (cf. Colombo, 11–16).

36. Reflection on the "lay character" has been discussed not only by Sartori and Colombo, but has developed to a great extent in Italy with: S. Dianich, "Chiesa e laicità oggi," *Quaderni di azione sociale*, 28 (1980), 95–106; *id.*, *Chiesa in missione. Per una ecclesiologia dinamica* (Alba, 1985), 267–271: ". . . l'ecclesiologia più recente tende a lasciare al margine il problema dei 'laici' come categoria specifica di cristiani, per concentrare la sua attenzione sulla laicità come carattere dell'intera chiesa" (269, note 9); and B. Forte, *La chiesa icona della Trinità* (Brescia, 1984), especially Chapter II, p. 35, where he states that "the category of the laity" must be overcome—which is not the same thing as our thesis of overcoming the laity "as a category."

37. F. Klostermann, "The Laity," in H. Vorgrimler (ed.), *Commentary on the Documents of Vatican II* (London/New York, 1966), 231–260, with commentary on *Lumen gentium* 31 (236–238). As regards the theory of Schillebeeckx, 1965, see the text of the following number. V. Porter, *Anthropologie et Apostolat des laïcs* (Paris, 1965, but written prior to the Council) stresses the distinction and separation in terms of power.

38. G. Philips, *La Chiesa e il suo mistero nel Concilio Vaticano II* (Milan, 1966), 2, 16–26, commenting on *Lumen gentium* 30 and 31. The position of J.-G. Page, *Qui est l'Eglise? III. Le peuple de Dieu* (Montreal, 1979), 119–207, is nuanced, using "definition" for *Lumen gentium* 31, but also stating: "Il ne faut donc pas définir le laïc d'abord par sa 'condition séculière,' par le fait qu'il est plus mêlé à la vie propre du monde que le ministre ou le religieux . . . ; il faut le définir avant tout par son insertion dans l'Eglise, par sa qualité de baptisé. . . ." However, he also says that living this life of a baptized person "en plein coeur du monde" constitutes "ce qui caractérise plus spécifiquement le laïc." Further on, he also speaks of lay people as a "category," alongside priests and religious.

39. Indicatations are found in the theology of earthly things, of work, etc. (cf. C.L. Scalicky, "La teologia dell'impegno cristiano nel temporale," *Lateranum* [1977], 198–243) and in authors of the trend referred to as "liberation theology," who need rethinking in a more balanced manner. The study of their restoration in *Gaudium et spes* and the intense and complex postconciliar debate on the relationship between Church and world and between evangelization and human promotion, the search for a theological basis for the autonomy of human affairs while retaining their intrinsic ordering to God, and the meaning of "salvation" in relation to them, are all involved here, but do not yet appear to have found a proper equilibrium, especially with regard to the theological basis for the rediscovery of the "lay character" of the Church and of the position of the laity within it. The concepts of "Christ who takes up again into himself the whole of created reality" and of the "total Christ," who pervades history in order to bring all things and all people to the Father—bringing the whole created world to fulfillment in redemption, but without viewing this as detracting from the integral development of creation—and the truth that "only what has been taken up is redeemed" have not yet been developed satisfactorily. Indications are found especially in Irenaenus' theology of this taking up; cf. E. Scharl, *Recapitulatio mundi. Der Rekapituationsbegriff des heiligen Irenäus und seine Anwendung in die Körperwelt* (Freiburg im Breisgau, 1941); J. Daniélou, *Message évangélique et culture hellénistique* (Tournai, 1961), 156–169; A. Orbe, *Antropologia de San Ireneo* (Madrid, 1969). Bibli-

cists and biblical or dogmatic theologians—almost all clerics and monks—do not seem particularly interested in producing a theology of creation and of "bringing the world to fulfillment" in the plan of taking all things up into Christ; at the most, they highlight the role of Christ who takes up all created things again into himself, but they pay little attention to his participation in the "body" and the position of the laity in it; cf. G. Siegwalt, "Introduction à une théologie de la récapitulation. Remarques sur le contenu dogmatique du prologue de Jean," *RTP*, 113 (1981), 259–278. Indications in J.L. Witte, "La chiesa *sacramentum unitatis* del cosmo e del genere umano," in G. Baraúna (ed.), *La Chiesa del Vaticano II* (Florence, 1965), 491–521; R. Russo, *Cristo nel mondo. La cristologia nella Costituzione Pastorale "Gaudium et Spes" del Concilio Vaticano II* (Naples, 1983), 119–152, with the bibliography on *Gaudium et spes* concerning the relationship of the Church with the world and the "focusing" of the incarnation. Cf. also J.M.R. Tillard, "Il sottosuolo teologico della Costituzione: la chiesa e i valori terrestri," in E. Giammancheri (ed.), *La Chiesa nel mondo contemporaneo. Commento alla Costituzione "Gaudium et spes"* (Brescia, 1967²), 213–250; B. Lambert, "La problematique générale de la Constitution Pastorale," in Y.M.-J. Congar and M. Peuchmaurd (eds.), *L'Eglise dans le monde de ce temps. Constitution pastorale "Gaudium et Spes"* (Paris, 1967), 2, 131–170; S. Lyonnet, "I fondamenti biblici della Costituzione," in G. Baraúna (ed.), *La Chiesa nel mondo d'oggi. Studi e commenti intorno alla Costituzione pastorale "Gaudium et Spes"* (Florence, 1966), 192–212; J. Gremillion, "La chiesa nel mondo contemporaneo: un appello alla teologia," in Miller (ed.), *La teologia dopo il Vaticano II*, 653–686; F. Houtart, "Proposte per un futuro sviluppo dottrinale," in *ibid.*, 687–696; Y.M.-J. Congar, "Pastorale Konstitution über die Kirche in der Welt von heute," in H.S. Brechter et al. (eds.), *LThK, Das Zweite Vatikanische Konzil, Documente und Kommentare* (Freiburg im Breisgau, 1968), 3, 400–402; cf. also No. 58.

40. P. Delhaye, M. Gueret, and P. Tombeur, *Concilium Vaticanum II. Concordance, Index, Listes de fréquence, Tables comparatives* (Louvain, 1974).

41. A. Acerbi, *Due ecclesiologie. Ecclesiologia giuridica ed ecclesiologia di comunione nella "Lumen Gentium"* (Bologna, 1975); G. Ghirlanda, *"Hierarchica Communion." Significato della formula nella "Lumen Gentium"* (Rome, 1980).

42. E. Weinzierl, "Laici nella Chiesa," in J.B. Bauer and C. Molari (eds.), *Dizionario teologico* (Assisi, 1974), 291. According to Y. Congar, "I laici," in Miller (ed.), *La Teologia dopo il Vaticano II*, 302, "Il Concilio . . . si è accontentato di dare una descrizione positiva e nello stesso tempo negativa o esclusiva (*LG* 31)"; our interpretation will be different.

43. For example, A. Oberti, *Il Concilio e i laici* (Milan, 1964), 16, where he speaks, without any discussion, of an "esatta e completa definizione del laico." Other lay commentators insist on the "specific character" of the laity; cf. H. Rollet et al., *La mission des laics. Décret conciliaire sur l'Apostolat des laïcs* (Lyons, 1966), *passim*.

44. G. Lazzati, *Laicità e impegno cristiano nelle realtà temporali* (Rome, 1985). This author too insists on the *indoles saecularis* as the specific lay character. Cf. the discussion between G. Lazzati, "Secolarità e laicità. Le caratteristiche del laico nella Chiesa e per il mondo," *Il Regno*, 12 (15 June 1985), 333–338, where he draws a distinction between the secularity of the whole Church and the *indoles saecularis* as the specific character of lay people, and S. Dianich and B. Forte, "Laicità: tesi a confronto," *Il Regno*, 16 (15 September 1985), 459–461.

45. Lazzati, *Laicità e impegno cristiano nelle realtà temporali*, 9–10. The author refers to the following: *Lumen gentium* 36; *Gaudium et spes* 34, 36, 38 (14); John Paul II, *Laborem exercens*, especially Nos. 4 and 25 (cf. Gen. 1:28); St. Peter Chrisologos on man as the "vicario di Dio nell'opera della creazione" (67); the conception of the "liturgia universale fuori del tempo" of Orthodox theology (J. Lagovsky, P. Evdokimov; 21). He emphasizes Christ as the "centro del disegno di creazione e redenzione" and the Church as the "sacramentum renovationis totius mundi." Lastly, he refers to Paul VI, *Evangeli nuntiandi* 70, 73. Thus, his thought is basically and rightly concentrated on the "continuità che esiste fra la linea della creazione e dell'incarnazione" (90).

46. E. Schillebeeckx, "Definizione del laico cristiano," in Baraúna (ed.), *La Chiesa del Vaticano II*, 960–977. Schillebeeckx speaks of a "definizione esatta" (961), a "definizione tipologica" (968, in a specific sense), and of the "carattere specifico del laico in contrapposizione con quello del chierico" (969).

47. AS, III, I, 291–292 (*Relatio generalis* to Chapter IV); 281–282 (*Relatio* to No. 30); 282–283 (Relatio to No. 31), here 282. There is an evolution between the second and third sessions of the Council: the term "definition" is used most frequently with regard to lay people in the discussion of what was then Chapter III of *Lumen gentium* in the course of the second session; cf. note 52 below.

48. A. Menne, "Definizione," in H. Krings, H. Baumgartner, and C. Wild, *Concetti fondamentali di filosofia* (Brescia, 1981), 1, 540.

49. Cf. G. Magnani, "Il metodo della fenomenologia storico-comparata della religione," in A. Molinaro (ed.), *Le metodologie della ricerca religiosa* (Rome, 1983), 28–77; the phenomenological "type" is defined through "tratti caratterizzanti e distinctivi"—in other words, unique and exclusive features (p. 74).

50. AS, III, I, 281 (B).

51. Acerbi, *Le due ecclesiologie*, is the only author to observe, with regard to clerics, religious, and lay people, that "in realtà le tre istituzioni non sono accumunabili in uno stesso piano logico" (299, note 147), but he does not carry his line of thought to its fulfillment, although his aim is to overcome categories (521). Here he notes that "la LG rifiutò di proporre una definizione del laico e del religioso" and that "l'intervento del laico nel mondo non è esclusivo, ma è solo 'peculiare.' La molteplicità dei ministeri e delle vocazioni non esclude nessuno dalla totalità delle funzioni esercitate dal corpo." For the correction to *precipuum* (in place of *principes* in the previous text) in the definitive number 36 of *Lumen gentium,* which is important for our interpretation of the specific character, cf. AS, III, I, 288 (E); here the *Relatio* seems to reduce to a role of assistance what *Lumen gentium* 31 had said, when speaking of clerics and religious, with regard to their "lay" activity (and in this, we must prefer the text; cf. also GS 43); it concludes, with regard to *activitatem "laicalem"*: ". . . universaliter tamen loquendo pro huiusmodi activitate laicis substitui nequeunt." See Acerbi's comment (444) on number 39, in which he says that here it was a question of excluding a definition "sia per i laici che per i religiosi."

52. The exclusion of a definition of exclusive characters was already present in the *textus prior* of the definitive *Lumen gentium* 31: "Laici vero tota ratione vitae peculiariter, *etsi non exclusive,* ad res temporales gerendas et secundum Deum ordinandam vocantur." The *Modi* proposed and aimed at a more positive description of the layperson and not, as such, at the "peculiariter, etsi non exclusive," that in *Gaudium et spes* 43 becomes "proprie, etsi non exclusive." Acerbi (300, note 150) shows how the tendency (proposed, for example, by I. Menager) "di non dare una definizione, ma una descrizione quanto più larga e positiva" eventually prevailed in the discussions during the second session; he also notes (301) that the Council moved beyond the traditional doctrine on *status.*

53. The brief conclusive text of *Lumen gentium* 38 returns to the two fundamental themes of the whole of Chapter IV: the christological dimension and the communitarian dimension of the involvement of lay people, followed in the approach of Chapter II on the people of God. In conclusion, in the words of Acerbi (413–414), the text of Chapter IV "escluse che la presentazione del laico in contrapposto alla gerarchia e ai religiosi costituisse una definizione (ciò avrebbe avvallato una visione in cui gli elementi giuridici entrano come costitutivi della natura del laico) . . . , esplicò maggiormente la fondamentale unità del popolo di Dio, come esse si rifletteva nei rapporti tra laici e gerarchia," and through the "natura 'esclusivamente' laicale dell'impegno nel mondo. . . . Il capitolo si limita a dire che è un imgegno 'precipuo' dei laici, e nella spiegazione che dà è manifesta l'intenzione di rispettare i rilievi avanzati dai padri contro ogni tentativo di elevare compartimenti stagni all'interno del popolo di Dio. Ma se escluse pretese di esclusiva da parte dei laici, il capitolo, affermò anche l'esistenza di una missione come tale, non solo di una missione della gerarchia. Alla missione della chiesa i laici partecipano come tali. . . . La gerarchia appare, dunque, con una funzione insostituibile, ma specifica, che non assorbe in sè tutte le funzioni della chiesa, bensì rappresenta uno dei ministeri, istituito stabilmente da Cristo. . . ."

54. *Relatio generalis* to Chapter IV, in *AS*, III, I, 291.

55. *Relatio* to No. 13 (Chapter II), in *AS*, III, I, 200–201.

56. Cf. G. Ghirlanda, "I laici nella chiesa secondo il nuovo codice di diritto canonico," *Civiltà Cattolica* (1983/2), 531–543.

57. Cf. G. Thils, *Les laïcs dans le Nouveau Code de Droit Canonique et au IIe Concile du Vatican* (Louvain-la-Neuve, 1983).

58. B. Maggioni, "La fondazione della laicità nella Bibbia," in *Laicità, problemi e prospettive*, 39–56; cf. also C. Ghidelli, "Fondazione biblica del discorso sui laici evangelizzatori," *Presenza Pastorale* (November 1978), 18–39.

59. H. Bouillard, "La categoria del sacro nella scienza delle religioni," in *Il sacro. Studi e richerche* (Padua, 1974), 33–56; A. Vergote, "Equivoques et articulations du sacré," in *ibid.*, 471–492; G. Magnani, *Introduzione storico-fenomenologica allo studio della religione*, 1 (Rome, 1977), 89–114.

60. *Atti del II Colloquio su Vocazione e Missione dei Laici nella Chiesa e nel mondo a venti anni dal Concilio Vaticano II, 3–5 gennaio 1986* (at present with the printers): this meeting was organized by the Theological Faculty of Sicily, Palermo.

61. In relation to the new conciliar sense of "layperson" described above, the expression "lay character" could usefully be compared with meanings that are new and natural (with respect to faith) and that seem to be emerging in the best of contemporary culture, beyond the mutual remains of anticlericalism and clericalism. The terms are used in varied and inconsistent ways in earlier polemics. Professor P.L. Grasselli, National Head of *Rinascita Cristiana* (the present writer is National Assistant), based himself on this neutral concept in the debate of the National Council of the Movement on 3–4 June 1978 (*Atti, ad uso interno: Un concetto positivo di laicità*, 12 pp.; cf. my own contribution, *Spunti per un inquadramento teologico della nostra laicità*, 11 pp.). As regards the history of the expressions "lay character" and "laicism," cf. F. Traniello, "Clericalismo e laicismo nell'età moderna fino al Concilio Vaticano II," in *Laicità, problemi e prospettive*, 113–140; P. Scoppola, "Laicismo borghese e laicismo operaio nell'Italia unita," in *ibid.*, 141–162; N. Morra, "Laicismo," in *Novissimo Digesto Italiano* (Turin, 1963), 438, with a positive and neutral sense of "lay character." Those Christian movements that are more involved in temporal affairs, in the face of the "abstract lay character" of the theologians, call for a dimension and space proper to the "lay character" and an inductive method of theology; cf. "La comunità cristiana e le associazioni dei laici," *Studi Sociali,* 10 (1984); *Atti del Convegno Nazionale della Pastorale Sociale e del Lavoro, Ariccia, 26–30 agosto 1984;* and as regards method, cf. "Per una riflessione teologica," which was produced by P. Doni and G. Magnani and approved by the assembly (121–128).

   62. Acerbi, *Due ecclesiologie,* 513.

CHAPTER 20

Internal Forum—External Forum
The Criterion of Distinction

Francisco Javier Urrutia, S.J.

Summary

Recent canonists have tended to concentrate on the question of the juridical character or otherwise of the internal forum, but have neglected the definition of the concept of the internal forum. On the basis of the Code, the criterion of distinction between the two forums is seen to be the hidden or public manner of acting. The effects of the one power of governance are of the external forum if they can be recognized in the community; otherwise they are of the internal forum. However, when the law so decides, the latter move into the external forum, with the provision of proofs, without any new exercise of power. The forums are not separate spheres without any mutual relationship, and therefore a solution given for the internal forum can be based on the norms for the external forum.

Introduction

1. The principal orientation of the modern canonist is toward consideration of the juridical or nonjuridical character of the internal forum. Even when the distinction was no longer considered acceptable between the two powers of jurisdiction, so that only that for the external forum could properly be called juridical,[1] canonists decidedly tended toward recognition of the juridi-

cal character of the internal forum. The proofs cited are as varied as the concept of canon law proposed by the different authors, because those who deny the juridical character of the internal forum do so on the basis of their conception of canon law.[2]

About ten years ago, De Paolis collected the various elements of the debate, considering mainly the thought of Ciprotti on the one hand, and that of Bertrams on the other, in order to examine, by way of examples, the mutual relations between the forums in penal canon law. De Paolis does not consider it a good method to take civil juridical experience as the starting point in order to understand canon law, which is what happens when the internal forum is relegated to the exclusive sphere of morals.[3] Inasmuch as the Code accepts the validity of (juridical) power for the internal forum, it does not appear to view the latter as the exclusive sphere of morals. Nor does it seem possible to deny that dispensations and absolutions in the internal forum represent the exercise of juridical power, and that the effects produced are juridical. Under the form of questions "which do not make any claims," it is clear that De Paolis is claiming to demonstrate his convictions regarding the juridical character of the internal forum as regulated by the power of jurisdiction of the external forum; the internal forum is, together with the external forum, an integral part of the canon law system, and in this internal forum, the power of jurisdiction is operative with effects that have consequences for the community. Indeed, he says that in the act of absolving from sins, the priest acts not only with the power of orders, but also with that of jurisdiction, readmitting the Christian into the Church; nor can it be said that the person who absolves from censures in the internal forum, or the person who dispenses from ecclesiastical laws in the internal forum, remains in the extrajuridical sphere. De Paolis very precisely notes that when there is a conflict between internal forum and external forum, "it is not simply a conflict between conscience (internal forum) and law (external forum)," but rather a conflict between "two juridical norms within the same legal system."[4]

2. Although the debate on the juridical character or otherwise of the internal forum has undoubtedly helped provide deeper understanding of the concept of canon law, it seems to me that, paradoxically, it has not contributed similarly to a clarification of the actual concept of the internal forum. To put it another way, what do we mean when we speak of the internal

forum and the external forum? What is the criterion for distinguishing one forum from the other, and for distinguishing when an act (whether of authority or not) is performed within the internal forum or the external forum? This will be the object of the present study, which will take Canon 130 as its starting point.

Exercise of the Power of Governance

Of itself the power of governance is exercised for the external forum; sometimes however it is exercised for the internal forum only, but in such a way that the effects that its exercise can cause for the external forum are not acknowledged in this forum unless such acknowledgement be established by law for specific cases.[5]

3. In the first place, we must note that this canon develops the concept of power of governance in the Church (which is introduced in the preceding Canon 129) inasmuch as it first lays down the twofold manner in which it is exercised, and then the sphere or extent of its effectiveness in these two types of exercise.

This means that in this canon, we do not find a division of the power of governance.[6] The divisions of this power are described in the following Canon 131, §§1–2, and also in Canon 135, §1. It will be remembered that commentators on the 1917 Code divided jurisdiction into jurisdiction in the external forum (which was properly such for some of these commentators) and jurisdiction in the internal forum.[7] They were also led to this division by the text of Canon 196, which corresponded to the present 130: "The power of jurisdiction or governance . . . is divided into that of the external forum and that of the internal forum. . . ." It was precisely in changing these words and speaking of the exercise of one power of governance for both forums that Canon 130 introduced a first important correction to the previous canon. The power of jurisdiction or governance referred to in Canon 129—the sole power of governance, which was given by Christ to his Church—can be exercised in either forum.

The Internal Forum Is No Longer Called
"The Forum of Conscience"

4. Canon law has never defined the two expressions "external forum" and "internal forum," which are, as we know, peculiar to canon law.

It should be noted that Canon 130 also omitted another expression found in the previous Canon 196, which described the internal forum as the forum of conscience, making this latter expression synonymous with the former: ". . . internal forum, or the forum of conscience." However, if the forum of conscience is "man's most secret core, and his sanctuary, [where] he is alone with God whose voice echoes in his depths" (GS 16), the canonical internal forum certainly cannot simply be identified with the forum of conscience, because it is subject not only to the human intellect, as making judgments in close and exclusive relationship with God, but is also subject to the power of governance of the Church.[8]

5. Canon 196 of the previous Code was undoubtedly based on the work of the many canonists throughout history who, in their efforts to describe the internal forum, had referred to it as the "forum of conscience." The first to speak of the forum of conscience—but as opposed to the forum that was not yet described as "external," because the terminology of "external/internal forum" did not yet exist, but as "judiciary"—were the scholastic theologians, describing as the forum of conscience the forum that was referred to as "penitential" and that was the sacramental forum. After Trent, canonists returned to the term "forum of conscience," but no longer identified it with the penitential-sacramental forum. The term "forum of conscience" can be said to have been consecrated by Suarez,[9] and its identification with the internal forum would become almost axiomatic, especially for those who saw the internal forum as the sphere of obligations and moral decisions.

Shortly before the 1917 Code, for example, Ojetti wrote:

The internal forum, or that of conscience, is in turn either sacramental . . . or simply of conscience. . . . The penitential forum sometimes means the sacramental forum, and sometimes the extrasacramental forum, in other words simply that of the conscience.[10]

Later, in his 1931 commentary on the Code, he would write:

> . . . these two forums differ in this, that the penitent is judged
> in the external forum, and is thus absolved or condemned
> according to allegations and proofs; on the other hand, in the
> internal forum, [this takes place] according to his conscience,
> which comes to be known by the manifestations of the peni-
> tent himself. . . . They are also distinguished from one an-
> other by the means used in pursuing the ends; in the internal
> forum these means are reduced to the judgment of conscience
> and its confession. . . .[11]

6. I feel that it is important to realize that when the 1917
Code made the internal forum synonymous with the forum of
conscience, it was practically eliminating the concept of the
internal forum that had been introduced by Berardi (1719–1768)
against the teaching of the previous posttridentine canonists, if
not always in contrast with some of their expressions. This concept had a considerable influence on later canonists, including,
curiously enough, the commentators on the Code. Berardi
thought that the two forums should be distinguished according to
the purpose for which the jurisdiction was exercised; thus the
jurisdiction was different, one type being that of the external
forum, and the other, in a fairly broad sense, that of the internal
forum, according to the purpose intended. Jurisdiction would
belong to the external forum when it concerns directly and principally the public utility of the ecclesial community, whereas it
would be exercised in the internal forum when what is being
directly and principally sought is the private spiritual utility of
the individual Christian.[12] It is obvious that with this criterion,
the internal forum could no longer be considered as synonymous
with the forum of conscience—and Berardi did not in fact consider it so.

Today, we may be surprised to note that for Berardi the administration of the sacraments—all the sacraments—is an activity
viewed as belonging to the internal forum, and that the same also
applies to the celebration of *public* prayer, and to canonical moni-
tions imposed by a superior, because all these cases concern an
activity ordered to the spiritual good of individuals.[13]

7. As I said, even among commentators on the Code, and

despite the fact that the Code identified the internal forum with
the forum of conscience, the distinction between public utility
and the private utility of individuals was often seen as one of the
criteria for distinguishing between internal forum and external
forum. Apparently, they did not realize the contradictions inherent in this view. As an example of all these commentators, we
would cite Vidal-Aguirre:

> Jurisdiction *of the external forum* is that which refers primarily
> and directly to the public good, whether the *common* good of
> the faithful or that of the Church. It regulates the social rela-
> tionships of the members of the Church. . . . Jurisdiction *of
> the internal forum* (forum of conscience) is that which concerns
> *primarily* and *directly* the private good of the faithful. It regu-
> lates their moral relations with God (it is the *forum poli*; cf. c.
> 43, C. XVII, q. 4), not the social relations with the Church as
> a visible society (*forum fori*). . . .[14]

A Return to the Public/Private Criterion?

8. The suppression of the identification of the internal forum
with the forum of conscience in the 1983 Code cannot be interpreted as an indication of a return to the criterion proposed by
Berardi. And the Code makes not the slightest reference to the
public/private criterion (in the sense of the public utility of the
community as such or the spiritual good of the member of the
faithful as an individual) for distinguishing the two forums.

The criterion that is seen is more that of the *public/hidden*
exercise of power, so that the examples of jurisdiction for the
internal forum that were provided by Berardi cannot in any way
be accepted as valid.

9. A first reading of the canons that mention the forums
confirms this view. An administrative act concerning the external forum *is to be set forth in writing*[15] (Canon 37). In order to use
a favor that has been granted orally in the external forum, this
concession *must be proven* if authority requests it (Canon 74). If a
matrimonial impediment *can be proven in the external forum*, it is
to be considered public, and if it cannot be proven, it is to be
considered occult (Canon 1074).[16] If the impediment *is occult*, a
confessor can dispense from it for the internal forum, in danger of

death (Canon 1079, §3). However, if the dispensation is granted for the external forum, the local Ordinary *must be informed of it*, and it *is to be recorded* in the relevant register (Canon 1081). The Penitentiary can dispense from occult impediments for the internal forum, and (if the internal nonsacramental forum is involved) this dispensation *must be recorded* in a register that is to be kept *in the secret archive* (Canon 1082). Thus, whenever a marriage is convalidated in the external forum, or is declared null, or is legitimately dissolved, the pastor of the place *must be informed*, so that it can be *recorded* in the marriage and baptismal registers (Canon 1123). Declarations and promises made in preparation for mixed marriages must be *established* in the external forum (Canon 1126). The fact that the interrogation has taken place and its outcome must also *be lawfully established* in the external forum (Canon 1145, §3). The remission of penalties in the external forum is to be given *in writing* (Canon 1145, §2). In urgent cases, the confessor can remit in the internal sacramental forum censures of excommunication or interdicts *latae sententiae* that *have not* been declared (Canon 1357, §1).

10. The immediate criterion used by the Code therefore seems clear: the exercise of jurisdiction of which the community has legitimate knowledge, because there are legitimate proofs of it, is the exercise of jurisdiction for the external forum or in the external forum. And the effects of this exercise, publicly known, belong to the external forum. On the other hand, if the exercise of jurisdiction remains hidden from the community as such, and the effects produced remain similarly hidden, because there are no legitimate proofs, then this is the exercise of jurisdiction for the internal forum or in the internal forum.[17]

Proofs can be written or by testimonial. Indeed, if the facts are made known, any other proof will be perfectly superfluous.

The Meaning of Canon 130

11. In the foregoing brief examination of the canons, I deliberately omitted consideration of Canon 130 itself, because it is here that we have the clearest confirmation of the criterion given.

I said at the outset that the canon not only lays down the twofold manner of exercising the power of governance, but also defines the sphere or extent of the effectiveness of this exercise.[18] As regards the exercise of power of governance for the internal forum, the canon tells us that when this power is exercised *for the internal forum only*, it can even so have effects for the external forum; however, these effects are not recognized in this forum, except insofar as is established by law. This in fact means that the same power is exercised for the internal forum, if the effects it has there remain hidden and cannot be observed or recognized by the community for lack of legitimate proofs, as has already been said after examination of the other canons that deal with the forum. Canon 130 adds that there are certain cases established by law in which these same effects for the internal forum become effects in the external forum without the need of any fresh exercise of power; they simply become public, and thus observable, recognizable, and recognized by the community.[19]

12. The hypotheses of Canons 74 and 1082 seem to be the clearest commentary on what is laid down in Canon 130, because they deal with applications of the latter to specific cases. Canon 74 discusses favors granted orally, in other words, an exercise of power that can remain occult. The granting of a favor made in this way will remain in the internal forum while the means remain occult. We suppose that the favor has been truly granted, is valid, and can hence be used by the beneficiary; however, if such utilization takes place publicly in the life of the community, it cannot be "imposed" on the community, which does not know that it has been granted, and, as Canon 130 says, the community cannot acknowledge it in the external forum unless the beneficiary provides proof, to anyone who may lawfully demand it, that the favor has in fact been granted. The proof can be provided either by the testimony of persons who were present at the moment the favor was granted, or through some document if it was put into writing after it was granted.

13. In the same way, the exercise of the power of the Penitentiary, when it dispenses from an occult impediment to marriage, is for the internal forum. If the forum was nonsacramental, the dispensation must be recorded in a document that is to be kept in the secret archive of the curia (Canon 1082). Now the impediment has been removed, and consequently the persons involved are free to contract marriage—which is naturally an act in the external forum. However, the impediment (which no longer exists) might later become public; in other words, the facts that

gave rise to the impediment could become public knowledge. Were this to happen, the impediment (which has in fact been removed) still apparently exists for the community, having moved into the external forum, while, on the other hand, the dispensation granted for the internal forum, with the occult exercise of power, remains occult, and its effect in removing the impediment therefore also remains occult. In this case, the effect of the power exercised for the internal forum alone cannot be recognized by the community in the external forum, unless the document that has been kept in the secret archive is produced; "no other dispensation is necessary for the external forum" (Canon 1082).[20]

The Matter or Object Is Not an Adequate Criterion

14. Canonists have not infrequently followed a path that we must consider mistaken in distinguishing the forums, basing the distinction between the two on the matters or objects proper to each, as if matters and objects of their very nature belonged to one or other forum. Capobianco, for example, wrote that "the internal forum concerns only occult matter and has the same extent as that of the occult,"[21] as if occult or public matters were to be considered immutably such, and thus as belonging exclusively to one or other *area* of the internal forum or the external forum. In this case, full validity could be ascribed to the objection raised by Mostaza, who pointed out that public censures can be remitted in the internal forum.[22]

15. It is in a certain sense true that the object of the internal forum is always occult, just as it is true that the exercise of power is for the internal forum when it is occult. Thus, when public censures are remitted with an occult exercise of power, this remission is also occult, and inasmuch as the censure is public, it is not the object of the remission; and this is precisely why a further remission will be needed with the public exercise of power. Public censure, of course, also entails an occult dimension, inasmuch as its effects in restricting the rights of the person who has fallen under the penalty are equally binding on his conscience for the internal forum—in other words, for occult actions that are performed without the knowledge of the community—as for the external forum—in other words, for acts openly performed in the

view of the community. Thus, remission from the public penalty for the internal forum considers the penalty primarily as it concerns the occult behavior of the believer, and in this sense, it can to some extent be claimed that the object of the remission is the *occult* dimension.

16. Naturally, even if the primary intention is that of allowing the penitent to act freely for the internal forum, if the censure has been truly remitted, he or she can also behave within the community in a manner consistent with this, and ignore a penalty that no longer exists, so long as this does not cause scandal, given that the community is unaware of the fact of the remission, or so long as the superior does not call for conformity with a penalty that still *apparently* exists.

As we recalled above, under the 1917 Code, the occult exercise of the remission of a public penalty became public, and hence moved into the external forum, with the production of proof—or even only with the legitimate presumption—that this power had truly been exercised. Similarly, under the present Code, it is sufficient to produce the document kept in the secret archive, in order for the dispensation from the matrimonial impediment that was previously occult and given for the internal forum, to be recognized in the external forum once the impediment has become public.[23]

Ambiguous Expressions

17. Expressions such as that used by Capobianco are, to say the least, ambiguous, inasmuch as they seem to suggest that the two forums are separate areas or spheres, and not different modes of action, whether of the individual believer or of the authority in the exercise of its power. Unfortunately, ambiguous expressions of this type are frequent, and they have given rise to a feeling of obscurity and uncertainty with regard to the concept of the internal forum and the external forum.

This is what happened when canonists, apparently developing the criterion proposed by Berardi, took the social or private dimension of acts as the criterion for distinguishing between forums. "The internal forum encompasses primarily and as such the private actions of the faithful, and within it the private good—or that of the conscience of the individual—is considered foremost."[24] "Inasmuch as it is exercised in the internal forum, jurisdiction concerns directly and primarily the spiritual good of the individual believer and his individual relations with God."[25]

18. However, if it can be said that the internal forum is the sphere of personal relations with God, and of the individual's spiritual good, is this not equally true of the exercise of power for the external forum? Surely a law or a precept imposed by a legitimate superior in the presence of witnesses, or a sentence handed down by a tribunal, also regulates the personal relations of the individual? Surely it also concerns the individual's relations with God? Surely its primary and direct objective is also the personal spiritual good of the individual? And, vice versa, surely certain acts that are considered strictly personal also have a communitarian dimension? Surely relations between spouses in the whole interpersonal sphere, or the personal observance of one or another precept of the Church (for example, the Sunday obligation, or days of penance) are also acts that equally involve the social dimension of the activity of the individual within the community of the Church?[26] If some acts belong to the internal forum and others to the external forum, this is not because they belong to different areas or spheres, one of which concerns acts of a social nature and the other acts of an individual nature. Rather, it depends on how the acts in question are produced: whether in a secret manner or in a manner that can be recognized by the community.

An act with social dimensions is not an act of the external forum because it is social, but because it is made publicly and in such a way that the community can see it. Similarly, a so-called personal act is not an act of the internal forum *because it is not social,* but because and to the extent that it remains occult and cannot be recognized by the community. If it is inconceivable that a certain act, such as the promulgation of a law, belongs to the internal forum, this is because the promulgation of the law is by definition a public act. On the other hand, an instruction imposed by the legitimate superior is necessarily for the external forum only if it is imposed in the presence of witnesses or with a lawful document that is publicly known, while the same instruction could have been imposed in an occult manner, and hence for the internal forum, if it had been imposed without witnesses, or with a lawful document that is, however, kept secret. Thus, the difference between the exercise of power for the internal forum and for the external forum lies neither in the matter ruled on, nor in the nature of the act itself, but in *the way* in which the power is exercised.

Effects of the Exercise of Power for the
Internal Forum and for the External Forum

19. When the exercise of power takes place for the external forum, the effects it produces are valid in this forum inasmuch as they can be observed and required by the community, and they are equally valid in the internal forum when the person acts in a way that cannot be observed by the community because it is hidden. The effects brought about by the exercise of power for the external forum, for example, certain obligations, do not belong solely to the public (or exclusively and formalistically social) domain, but are personal obligations that are to be respected at every moment and on every level, even when the believer acts alone, without supervision, witnesses or publicity.[27]

Conversely—and Canon 130 states this explicitly—the exercise of power for the internal forum alone can also produce effects that concern the external forum, but because the power is exercised in an occult manner and for the internal forum, these effects are not recognized by the community in the external forum. Because it is a matter of the occult exercise of power, which cannot be observed and of which there is no lawful proof, it is easy to see that the effects also remain occult and unrecognizable, and have no possibility of lawful proof. The community is unaware of these effects, which remain unknown to it.

20. The Apostolic Penitentiary can grant a *sanatio in radice* of an invalid marriage for the internal forum. This occult exercise of power has an effect that must of necessity also involve the external forum, in view of the fact that it concerns the validity of a marriage that was invalid until this moment, even though it may have appeared and been considered valid in the external forum if the impediment invalidating it remained occult. Now, although the marriage is validated from the moment of the *sanatio*, the validation is not recognizable in the external forum, because the *sanatio* has been given for the internal forum, in other words, in an occult manner, so that the community has no proof in order to be able to recognize it.

The Criterion Proposed by Bender in 1954

21. This criterion of distinction on the basis of *the manner in which power is exercised,* which is now suggested in Canon 130, was proposed in the 1950s by the Dominican Bender: "It is said that juridical acts that are performed in such a way that they are known, or can be known, with that knowledge proper to the public life of society, belong to the external forum and take place in the external forum,"[28] and this applies also to acts performed with some authentic document or before two trustworthy witnesses.

"All those things that are known with private knowledge belong to the internal forum. . . . Indeed, all things, whether public or secret, can be known with private knowledge," while there is a limit to the number of things that can be known with public knowledge, which is the knowledge according to which public life is governed.

Almost as if commenting in advance on Canon 130, Bender wrote that while acts performed for the internal forum alone may be valid, their validity "is not recognized in the external forum" because of the lack of public knowledge of them, although this does not mean that their validity is in any way denied. Thus, despite the apparent distinction made in Canon 196 of the Code then in force (". . . that of the external forum and that of the internal forum . . ."), Bender denied that there were two types of power of jurisdiction, stating decidedly that the expression of the canon "concerns its exercise both as regards the way it is performed and also as regards its effects." He also gave the example of a parish priest who refuses to celebrate the marriage of two people related through consanguinity in a degree that allows dispensation, even though one of them swears that he or she has been dispensed by the confessor in circumstances of danger of death. He said that the priest is denying neither the fact of the dispensation, nor its validity, so that the impediment no longer really exists, but it is simply that he cannot recognize these facts and take them into account for the external forum because of the lack of public knowledge of them.[29]

22. As I said earlier, Bender also claimed that it is not only the *matter* that determines the forum, because, although occult facts are normally to be dealt with in the internal forum, they can also *change* forums, due to the simple fact that the subject

acts in a public form. For example, according to the Code then in force, a superior could grant a dispensation both occultly and publicly from a private and occult vow, and occult censure due to the occult offense of heresy, absolution from which was reserved to the Apostolic See, could be absolved from for the *external* forum if the penitent voluntarily confessed it and thus moved it into the external forum.[30]

23. Not everybody greeted Bender's point of view with the same decisiveness as Deutsch: "If the juridic act is so performed that it can be established by juridic proof, it is done in the external forum. If not, it is done in the internal forum."[31]

Ineffective Criticisms

24. Consideration of certain criticisms that were at the time expressed against Bender's explanation can help us to understand more clearly that it is precisely in the distinction of the way of exercising power (as also in that of the personal actuation of the members of the faithful) that we can find the right criterion for distinguishing between the internal and external forums.

Despite the fact that Mostaza approves of the distinction between whether the act of power can be demonstrated or not, he does not believe that it can be accepted as a criterion for distinguishing between the forums. However, the reasons he advances for this view do not seem to have been sufficiently considered. In the first place, he states that occult acts can be subject to juridical proof, as is clear in the case of marriage impediments or of irregularities.[32]

25. I find the objection somewhat puzzling, because it in fact seems to imply confirmation of the criterion given, that is, that we cannot consider any matter as belonging exclusively to one or the other forum, but that the same matter will be dealt with in one or the other according to the way of actuation. A fact that can be established with juridical proofs will always remain in the internal forum until it is in fact demonstrated, because the possible proofs remain occult. At the very moment when the juridical proofs are made public, the facts will no longer be occult acts, nor will they remain in the internal forum; they will have become public, and will now belong to the external forum. Surely, this is the precise hypothesis envisaged in Canon 1082, which

concerns the dispensation granted by the Penitentiary from an *occult* matrimonial impediment, and lays down that this dispensation must be recorded in the secret archive, in case the impediment becomes *public* at some later date? In what sense does Mostaza therefore claim that it is obvious that the distinction between the forums on the basis of whether the power is exercised in a public or occult manner does not correspond to the Code?

26. The objection that the distinction between the forums on the basis of the way in which power is exercised, or the manner in which a given juridical act is performed, does not correspond to the conception historically held in canon law, would truly be serious (although not necessarily decisive, if we accept that there can also be progress in the field of canon doctrine) if Mostaza could define precisely *what* the conception in the history of canon law is with which the proposed criterion must be reconciled. However, he confines himself simply to making this statement. Now, if there is a clear lesson to be drawn from the excellent historical study carried out by Mostaza himself, I think it is the very fact that no precise and constant conception can be found in the history of canon law as regards the distinction between the internal and external forums.[33]

27. Another objection raised by Mostaza seems to me to be equally lacking in foundation. He bases himself on a statement of Bender that all acts, both occult and public, belong to the internal forum insofar as they are the object of private knowledge. Mostaza perceives a contradiction: the statement means that it is not true that everything that is occult belongs to the internal forum!

The meaning of Bender's assertion seems only too clear, and is in fact nothing else but what Suarez had stated (as Mostaza himself reminds us): that internal forum and external forum are not two separate extremes, but "are to be understood as including and included."[34] "These two forums are in a mutual relationship as part and whole."[35]

28. Salazar Abrisqueta's criticism of Bender seems no more valid to me. Indeed, it seems even less so because it proceeds—as the author clearly recognizes—from the a priori philosophical assumption that no juridical character can be recognized for the internal forum.[36] For him, the only acts that concern the internal forum are those exclusively directed toward personal sanctifi-

cation; the question of whether they can be juridically proven or not has no relevance because they are merely moral acts. Similarly, it is of little importance that social, and thus juridical, acts can take place although we have no juridical proof of them. For him, therefore, the distinguishing criterion is the matter, or the acts as objectively considered, according to whether its objective is moral and individual and it is subject exclusively to the judgment of conscience, or whether its objective is social and of a communitarian order and it is subject to the authority that governs the social order for the common good. Obviously, just as acts of the external forum have consequences for personal sanctification, in the same way, we can say that some acts of the internal forum can have social consequences. However, this does not change their nature, but simply concerns a juridical dimension of the moral act; *under this aspect* of their relationship to the just social order, they can be said to be acts of the external forum, while remaining acts of the internal forum *in their dimension* of being ordered to personal sanctification.[37]

29. An act will be of the external forum, only if it is juridical, if it is suited to the creation of a just social order, which is the aim of the law with its characteristics of intersubjectivity, imperativity, and compulsoriness. The sphere of the jurist is the external forum—a sphere that is limited to just social relations.[38]

It can also be said that occult acts will be seen as oriented primarily toward the sanctification of the individual, and public acts toward the creation of a just social order. However, we are still left with the fact that for Salazar Abrisqueta, it is not the occult or public character of the act, but whether its primary and immediate objective contributes or otherwise to the just social order, that determines whether an act belongs to one forum or to the other. "The internal forum operates in the moral field and its specific direct objective and its characteristics are thus moral and not juridical."[39]

30. The clear separation of the two forums on the basis of differing matters or objects that are ordered to differing objectives is not convincing. In my view, in canon law, we should not consider that there can be acts of the faithful (principally external, although not necessarily public, acts) that aim at attaining eternal salvation but that do not at the same time also promote the social ends of the Church. We can separate these two aspects only if we hold a narrow concept of what is social in the Church

and see this as being concerned only with human justice. In the Church, what is social cannot be dissociated from the specific ends of the Church. Conversely, it cannot truly be said that an external and public act that is oriented primarily toward the social organization of the Church is not equally oriented to the salvation of the individual member of the faithful. This is why I spoke of an *a priori* philosophical assumption.[40]

31. Lastly, Salazar himself must agree that the distinction between forums on the basis of the aims that can be found in the same act is only formal and conceptual. Recognizing that all human acts can be considered from the viewpoint of salvation, so that *all* human acts are the object of ecclesiastical *jurisdiction* for the internal forum, he holds that only certain of these acts will be considered juridical if considered from the viewpoint of their social orientation. "It follows, therefore, that there is no perfect separation between these two orders."[41]

Practical Applications

32. When two people, with the permission of the local Ordinary and for a serious and urgent reason, contract marriage secretly (Canon 1130), the marriage is no less valid than if it had been celebrated with the normal publicity. Given that the canonical form has been observed, there is lawful juridical proof (Canon 1131, 2°), but despite this, the proof must be kept secret, and the marriage is to be recorded in the register that is kept in the secret archive (Canon 1133). While the marriage remains secret in this way, it is a valid factor for the internal forum (the 1917 Code spoke of "marriage of conscience"), and it is equally valid for the external forum, even if it cannot be recognized in this external forum because the proofs are not publicly known, and it is a marriage "which remains hidden in the shadows and is unknown to all."[42] As regards circumstances that permit secret celebration, the example given by Benedict and drawn from the practice of the Penitentiary is the case of persons whom everybody believes to be honorable and to be legitimately married, whereas in actual fact they are living in an irregular union. This is an irregular situation of the internal forum, because it is unknown to the community, and it is corrected with a measure that is equally of the internal forum.[43] The former irregularity of the

union may later become known to the community, and thus move into the external forum; it will then be necessary for the Ordinary to produce proof of the celebration in order to avoid any possible scandal (Canon 1132).

It is clear that the provision regarding secret celebration is an attempt to foster the salvation of the souls of the spouses. However, it also seeks to correct their canonical position; indeed, we could follow the logic of someone like Salazar and say that it is in fact through this correction of their canonical position, through which they are brought into the just social order, that the salvation of these souls is fostered.

33. Consideration of another practical case, which is at present causing concern in the pastoral ministry, can also be helpful in providing a better understanding of the criterion proposed. When some people seek a solution in the internal forum for irregular matrimonial situations, whether those known as "hardship situations" or those known as "conflict situations,"[44] the difficulty in accepting the solution does not lie in the fact that it proposes a norm of action different for the internal forum from the public one for the external forum. The problem arises because a norm of action is proposed for the internal forum as if we were dealing with a sphere totally unconnected with the external forum and its norms.

As I said above, citing De Paolis,[45] the conflict between internal forum and external forum is a conflict of juridical norms, which are different because they are related to different facts—occult in the first case, and public in the second. However, given the close bonds between the two forums, a valid norm given for the internal forum in order to deal with occult facts also has value for the action of the believer in the community life of the Church, in other words, in the external forum. Only when the occult facts become public must the solution that was given occultly also become public through the production of proofs, so that the apparent contradiction between the public facts and a manner of behaving that is founded on unknown facts will be eliminated.

34. The impossibility of accepting the so-called solution of the internal forum in the case of "hardship situations" springs from the fact that it does not deal with the real problem even in the internal forum. The prior marriage is known to be valid and does not allow a new union (Canon 1085, §1), and the new

union remains invalid, and therefore inadmissible, not only in the external forum but also in the internal forum. The solution suggested in no way provides a solution to the defectiveness of the new union for any forum. It is merely a palliative for the conscience of the persons involved, but an unlawful palliative because it clashes with principles that are valid both for the external forum and for the internal forum.

35. On the other hand, for "conflict situations," in which it is objectively speaking certain that the prior marriage was invalid but there is no possibility of producing proof of this in the external forum before the tribunal,[46] there is the theoretical possibility of an internal forum solution that meets the requirements of the external forum, even if in practice this possibility remains decidedly hypothetical. It amounts to the consideration that neither the need for proof before the tribunal, nor the need for the canonical form for the new union, are binding in the specific case.[47] This is a valid position entailing a reasonable application of canonical fairness, as this is formulated in the classical principle that ecclesiastical legislation does not oblige in the case of disproportionately severe penalties.

In this case the new marriage, without the canonical form, is valid. However, because the fact of the celebration of a prior marriage is known in the external forum and there is no proof of its nullity, the validity of the new union remains a fact of the internal forum, because it is occult and cannot be proven. Hence, it cannot be recognized in the external forum, just as is laid down by Canon 130. And this is precisely why even if the internal forum solution truly deals with the problem, in such cases it can be applied only where the fact of the prior union and the fact that its nullity has not been declared are not known by the ecclesial community.

36. If we were to try to apply it in cases where the community has learned of the existence of the previously celebrated union that has never legitimately been declared null, conflict would arise between the two juridical norms: the norm for the internal forum upholds the validity of the new marriage and the legitimacy of behaving as spouses, while the norm for the external forum, although not denying the validity of the marriage, cannot recognize it. And because it cannot be recognized, scandal would arise from the sight of members of the Church behaving in a

manner in contradiction with its public norms and claiming that this behavior is based on reasons that remain completely hidden. The internal forum solution cannot become an external forum solution unless there is certainty in the community as regards the nullity of the first union and the valid celebration of the second—a certainty that we cannot reasonably expect to be based on the subjective conviction of the persons involved, who are not in a position to communicate this conviction to the community through the competent instances.

Conclusion

37. I should like to conclude these reflections on the criterion for distinguishing between internal forum and external forum according to the way in which the power of governance is exercised, and more generally to the manner of acting within the ecclesial community, by indicating that this criterion can in fact be linked to the criterion that was used in the first historical distinctions between the forums. Thus, as Mostaza shows, the first distinction (which was apparently made by Bernardo Papiense) was between manifest judgment and occult judgment. This distinction then came to be seen as between the contentious forum of tribunals, in which everything is public and is admitted in proportion to the proofs accepted, and the forum that would be called either "spiritual" or "penitential." The same distinction was held by St. Thomas, who referred to the penitential forum (as opposed to the judicial forum) as the forum of conscience, of confession, of God, of penitence, even though no clear distinction was yet made in this forum, as opposed to the judicial forum, between the secret forum and the public forum, and Navarro had not yet made his distinction of an external forum different from the judicial one.[48]

We are therefore not moving away from the first criterion of distinction when we hold that the internal forum and the external forum are not separate areas or spheres, but that they merely indicate different ways in which the power of governance is exercised or in which the faithful act—ways that can be public and socially demonstrable, or occult and socially unrecognizable. When the forms of the exercise of power are distinguished in this way, it is not a matter of determining its effectiveness for the production of valid effects, but only of the possibility or otherwise of recognition by the community of the effects produced.

Translated from the Italian by Leslie Wearne.

Notes

1. A. Van Hove, *De legibus ecclesiasticis* (Malines/Rome: H. Dessain, 1930), 181 (No. 175), wrote: "Potestas iurisdictionis fori interni sese extendit ad interna, at potestas legislativa in foro interno non est. Iurisdictio *aequivoce* sumitur, prout agitur de iurisdictione fori externi et interni. Iurisdictio proprie est potestas publica ordinata ad bonum commune et absolvitur potestate legislativa cum annexa potestate praeceptiva ac dispensativa, potestate iudiciaria et coercitiva. Iurisdictio autem fori interni est ab bonum privatum; vocatur tamen iurisdictio, quia conceditur et ordinatur per potestatem iurisdictionis fori externi." Again, in 1945, in *Prolegomena* (Malines/Rome: H. Dessain, 1945), 31 (No. 32), he wrote: "Ecclesia duplici potestate pollet in ordine ad finem suum assequendum, iurisdictione *fori interni et fori externi* (can. 196). Prior efficaciam suam habet ex se coram Deo et in conscientia, altera insuper coram societate ecclesiastica eiusque auctoritatibus." However, in the same paragraph (pp. 31–32), he spoke in contradictory terms of the one power that "concedi et exerceri potest vel in foro externo et ideo de se in foro interno [?], vel limitari potest ad solum forum internum, prouti iure positivo Ecclesiae determinatur. Est exercitium unius eiusdemque potestatis vel vicariae vel propriae."

2. In 1968, A. Mostaza recalled a good number of authors who considered the internal forum as belonging to the domain of morals, and hence to the metajuridical sphere, and certain others who considered only the nonsacramental internal forum to be juridical. He himself, with others, accepted the juridical character of the whole internal forum as "una conclusión obligada" (p. 358) of his study, as presented in three long articles; cf. "Forum internum—Forum externum. II. Naturaleza de la Jurisdicción del fuero interno," *Revista Española de Derecho Canónico*, 24 (1968), 339–364. In his opinion, "Apud canonistas postredentinos luce meridiana apparent cum aspectus moralis fori interni tum eius indoles plene iuridica" ("De foro interno iuxta canonistas postridentinos," *Acta conventus internationalis canonistarum, Romae, 21–25 maii 1968* [Vatican City, 1970], 269–294; here 293 [VII]).

At the same meeting, P. Ciprotti confirmed the ideas he had previously expressed; Mostaza, "Forum internum—Forum externum, II," 342, note 16, had cited: *Lezioni di diritto canónico* (Padua, 1943), 12, 59 (Nos. 10–13, 45); and "Sulla potestà della Chiesa," *Archivio di Diritto Canonico*

(1941), 49–61, 189–197. See P. Ciprotti, "Potestas iurisdictionis fori interni et productio iuris in Ecclesia," *Acta conventus internationalis canonistarum, Romae, 21–25 maii 1968,* 262, 268 (here 265): "Interdum autem apud auctores legimus potestatem iurisdictionis fori interni esse iuridicam, vel etiam aeque esse iuridicam ac potestatem iurisdictionis fori externi: hae propositiones sunt omnino aequivocae, eas vitare oportet, et, si qua mentio iuris vel iuridicitatis fiat quoad attinet ad iurisdictionem fori interni, oportet, ne confusio fiat, perspicue declarare quid quisque velit et intellegat."

Another contribution at the same meeting—F. McManus, "The Internal Forum," *Acta conventus internationalis canonistarum, Romae, 21–25 maii 1968,* 251–261—used different terminology and involved considerations of a pragmatic order, but shared the same general view, on the basis of the codal definition of the internal forum as the forum of conscience, and of the confusion "of juridic and moral order . . . created by moralists blindly relying upon the sacred canons . . . as well as by canonists posing as moralists" (p. 251). "It is really undesirable that the law . . . wear a badge or moral admonition . . ." (p. 252). "The law has entered legalistically into areas where the order of the Church society was hardly at stake" (*ibid.*). "The canon law of the future would do well to make this a clear pattern; determining, or, better, describing a juridic order in the Christian community without threat of moral sanction" (*ibid.*). "The law should be explicitly intended as an external norm of conduct imposed when necessary for the Church society but without direct reference to obligation except in the juridic way" (p. 253). "This area of the canon law, namely, the public and social norms governing the exercise of the power to forgive and to retain . . ." (p. 256).

However, we should also note a phrase that seems difficult to reconcile with the foregoing ones: "Canonically, a greater emphasis upon the social aspects of the sacrament [of reconciliation] could only help to relate the external norms of the Church society to this internal forum of conscience, both to justify the norms and to emphasize the essential unity of the two ecclesiastical forums" (p. 257).

3. "Natura e Funzione del Foro Interno," *Investigationes Theologico-Canonicae* (Rome, 1978), 115–142 (here 136–137): "Nello studio del foro interno ci si può domandare se sia giusta la strada intrapresa di volerne spiegare la natura attraverso categorie giuridiche desunte dall'esperienza giuridica profana. . . . La via più facile potrebbe essere quella di eliminare addirittura il problema, relegando il foro interno al puro campo della morale."

With particular reference to the view of Ciprotti, he justly criticizes not only this unilateral "civilistic" view, but also the fact that he confines himself to the aspect of the production of the norm, without considering other acts of the power of jurisdiction, such as dispensation and absolution (pp. 137–140).

4. *Ibid.*, 140.

5. The translation is the author's. The English translation is based on that of the Canon Law Society of Great Britain and Ireland, with the main difference being the use of the phrase "that the effects that its exercise can cause for the external forum" in place of "that the effects which its exercise is designated to have in the external forum." The legislator chose "*pro* foro," rather than "*in* foro," but it does not seem to me that the choice of one or the other formula can lead to any clear conclusions as to doctrine, such as the conclusion that "in foro" refers to the way in which the power is exercised, whereas "pro foro" refers to its effect; for this view, cf. C. De Smet, *De Sponsalibus et Matrimonio* (Bruges, 1927[4]), No. 737, note 3. We find both formulas in the same Canon 130, and both refer to the effects of the exercise of power. Indeed, if it can be said that one particular formula refers more to the exercise of power, this would be "*pro* foro." It seems to me in fact that both "pro" and "in" can refer either to the way of exercising power or to its effects. However, I would say that with certain nuances "pro" tends to refer more to the dynamic moment of the exercise of power and of the effects as produced, while "in" suggests a static moment of exercise that has been performed and effects that have been produced.

6. At the beginning of his comments on Canon 130, Monsignor P.V. Pinto, *Commento al Codice di Diritto Canonico* (Rome, 1985), 78, states, on the contrary: "La prima divisione di potestà di giurisdizione . . . ," while further on he says: ". . . il canone vuole precisare l'*ambito* . . . in riferimento ai due fori."

7. See Van Hove, *De Legibus ecclesiasticis*. See also, among others, E.F. Regatillo, *Institutiones Iuris Canonici* (Santander, 1961[8]), I, 273 (No. 365), where he collects the true criteria of distinction frequently found in the different authors: "*DIVISIO* (*potestatis*): 1. *Fori externi*, quae: (a) subditos regit in ordine ad societatem; (b) quasi in publico exercetur; (c) effectum in facie Ecclesiae sortitur; (d) immediate se refert ad bonum commune. *Et fori interni*, quae: (a) subditos regit in ordine ad Deum; (b) in secreto exercetur; (c) effectum habet in conscientia; (d) immediate et directe bonum privatum respicit. . . ." F. Maroto, *Institutiones Iuris Canonici* (Rome, 1921[3]), I, 857–859, speaks of "other types of jurisdiction," in the first place the jurisdiction of internal forum and external forum, although he immediately tells us that "*iurisdictio*, prout in hoc foro *interno exercetur* . . . *respicit*" (italics mine). Further on, though, he writes: "Iurisdictio fori externi . . . eam potestatem designat, qua . . . ," and again: "In iure canonico viget omnino distinctio et separatio utriusque fori . . . (d) *ex potestate* qua in ipsis agitur, nam potestas seu iurisdictio in uno foro necessario et semper non importat iurisdictionem pro alio."

8. The Commission for the Revision of the Code, in its 1977 "Praenotanda allo Schema De Normis Generalibus," *Communicationes*, 9 (1977), 235, said decisively: "Ceterum non potest haec potestas quae pro solo foro interno exercetur dici fori conscientiae."

9. According to A. Mostaza, "Forum internum—Forum externum. I. En torno a la naturaleza jurídica del fuero interno," *Revista Española de Derecho Canónico*, 23 (1967), 253–331 (here 262), St. Thomas may have been the first to describe the penitential (sacramental) forum as *forum conscientiae* as opposed to the contentious forum or the forum of judgment *exterius*. Again according to Mostaza, *ibid.*, 275, it seems that among canonists we must wait until after the Council of Trent in order to find the description, but now without identification of the *forum conscientiae* with the sacramental forum. Mostaza also says, *ibid.*, 277, that, as in so many other fields, it was Suarez who consecrated the identification *internum/poenitentiale/conscientiae*, while always remembering that according to him the penitential forum "no se limita al juicio del sacramento de la penitencia, sino que se extiende a todo juicio que puede tener efecto en el fuero de la consciencia. . . ."

10. *Synopsis Rerum Moralium et Iuris Pontificii* (Rome, 1911³), II, No. 2236: "Internum seu conscientiae iterum vel sacramentale est . . . vel *conscientiae* simpliciter. . . . Sic potestas quam exercet superior ecclesiasticus extra confessionem a censura absolvens, vel dispensatio super voto, est potestas fori interni extra-sacramentalis, seu conscientiae simpliciter. Forum poenitentiae modo significat forum sacramentale, modo forum extrasacramentale seu conscientiae simpliciter." It can be noted that, unlike Canon 196, Ojetti instead identifies the forum of conscience with the internal extrasacramental forum.

11. *Commentarium in C.I.C. Liber II, De Personis (cann. 145–214)* (Rome, 1931), 157.

12. C.S. Berardi, *Commentaria in Ius Ecclesiasticum Universum* (Turin, 1766), I, 12–13 (dissertatio 1, cap. 2): "Imprimis ecclesiastica iurisdictio dicitur alia interni, alia externi fori. Quae fori interni iurisdictio appellatur, praecipue et directo refertur ad singularem uniuscuiusque fidelis spiritualem utilitatem, nec nisi secundario in utilitatem publicam, utpote quae ex privatorum utilitate coalescit. . . . Hinc magnis proprie iurisdictio appellatur, quae in foro externo consistit, utpote quae valde similis est, salvo potestatis utriusque discrimine, iurisdictioni illi, quae publicis magistratibus competit et publicam utilitatem directo curat, quamquam secundario etiam foveat privatorum utilitatem singularem. . . . Quartum corollarium est, tantum distingui invicem iurisdictionem fori interni et iurisdictionem fori externi, quantum distinguuntur invicem, et utilitas publica et

privata. . . . Postremum corollarium est, maxima opus esse prodentia in definiendo, quaenam ad fori interni, quaenam ad fori externi iurisdictionem pertineant: siquidem non adeo facile est secernere, quae publicam, aut quae privatam directo curent utilitatem, propterea quod utilitas publica vix sine privatorum commodo, aut commodum privatum vix sine utilitate publica intelligitur."

13. *Ibid.*, I, 12 (nt. praec.): "Exercetur autem [the jurisdiction of the internal forum] in sacramentis administrandis . . . , in sacramentalibus similiter faciendis, in orationibus publicis fundendis, documentis, admonitionibus atque his similibus, quae cum leniora officia sint, nonnisi latiore significatione iurisdictionis esse dicuntur." In the fifth and last corollary, *ibid.*, I, 13, he gives as examples of jurisdiction of the internal forum the faculties to preach the gospel and to absolve sins, and also the censures as regards the bond of spiritual union with Christ, whereas he considers the jurisdiction that grants such faculties as belonging to the external forum.

14. *Ius Canonicum*, vol. II: *De Personis* (Rome, 1943³), 423. Another criterion is also noted in the same text—a criterion that is in fact far from being in perfect accord with that previously proposed, following Berardi: ". . . atque [the power in the external forum] exercetur publice in facie Ecclesiae et cum effectibus iuridicis et socialibus," while the power of the internal forum "per se et ordinarie exercetur in occulto et cum effectu coram Deo, non publice in facie Ecclesiae cum effectibus iuridicis et moralibus."

We can also note that the citation of Graziano to identify *forum poli* with the internal forum, and *forum fori* with the external forum (an identification very often made by canonists) does not take into account the fact that Graziano writes *"ius* poli" and *"ius* fori," and identifies them with *canon law* and *civil law*; cf. Mostaza, "Forum internum—Forum externum. I," 257.

15. ". . . to be set forth in writing" is the translation of the Canon Law Society of America. Compare with the translation of the Canon Law Society of Great Britain and Ireland: ". . . to be effected in writing," which could suggest that the written form is the intrinsic form of the administrative act, and is therefore necessary for its validity, rather than being a mere instrument for proof of the act. The Latin "scripto est consignandus" does not suggest that the written form is necessary for validity.

16. The formulation of Canon 1074 is particularly expressive, even if it creates a certain difficulty inasmuch as it seems to be tautological. If the impediment can be proven *in the external forum* it is public. And how can something be proven in the external forum except by public proof? Maybe the formulation could have been: "publicum . . . quod legitime probare potest" (cf. Canon 1145, §2: interrogations and their outcome "in foro externo legitime costare debet"), and maybe adding for greater precision: ". . . potest coram communitate."

It might be thought that the concept of public/occult impediment given in Canon 1074 conflicts with the proposed criterion, inasmuch as it can be of such a nature that it can be proven, despite the fact that it remains secret. We can say that so long as the impediment remains unproven, it is secret and belongs to the internal forum. In other words, it is in fact occult, even though through its nature it may be public. This distinction was accepted as early as 1927 by the Commission for the Interpretation of the Code; cf. AAS, 20 (1928), 61: ". . . verba 'pro casibus occultis' can. 1045, §3 intelligenda . . . etiam [de impedimentis] natura sua publicis et facto occultis." Present-day commentators recognize that the "occult" of Canon 1074 takes on the sense of "actually secret" in Canons 1079, §3, and 1080; e.g., J. Hervada, Código de Derecho Canónico. Edición anotada, P. Lombardía and J.I. Arrieta (eds.) (Pamplona, 1983), 633, 641, 642; and F. Aznar, Código de Derecho Canónico. Edición bilingue comentada (Madrid, 1983³), 516, 519.

17. We should also note the change in formulation from that of the old Canon 207, §2, ". . . sed potestate pro foro interno concessa . . . ," to the present Canon 142, §2: "Actus . . . ex potestate delegata, quae exercetur pro solo foro interno . . . ," which also seems to suggest that the canons on power consider the latter from the viewpoint of its exercise specifically when dealing with the distinction between forums.

On the other hand, the formulation of Canon 596, §2, may seem less clear in this regard: "In institutis autem religiosis clericalibus iuris pontificii pollent [superiors and chapters] insuper potestate ecclesiastica regiminis pro foro tam externo quam interno," inasmuch as, at least explicitly, it is power itself, rather than its exercise, that is being spoken of. I tend to feel that the formulation was an attempt to preserve so far as possible the wording of the previous Canon 501, §1: ". . . in religione autem clericali exempta, habent iurisdictionem ecclesiasticam tam pro foro interno quam pro externo," without any particular intentions as regards our problem.

I do not think there is any need to emphasize that *public* is not the same as *external*, because *external* activity or exercise of jurisdiction can remain *occult*. Public exercise is always external, but the reverse is not true, because *external* exercise is not always *public*.

18. See note 3 above. The *sphere* of power is understood differently by Jimenez Urresti, who discerns in Canon 130 a division of the power of governance "según el ámbito donde se ejerce," into the "ambito social y público," and the "ambito privado y secreto." The view that the sphere is the *extent* of the effectiveness of the power according to the *way* in which it is exercised, rather than as the area of exercise, may be viewed as irrelevant pedantry; however, the search for greater precision in a question that is somewhat confused in the works of the various authors could in fact help to clarify things.

19. I do not think it necessary to linger over the clarification made by Canon 130 as compared with the norm of the previous Canon 202, §1: "Actus potestatis iurisdictionis . . . pro foro externo, valet quoque pro foro interno *non autem e converso.*" The authors admitted that if the act *was* valid, it *was* so for both forums, whereas the act that was not valid could *be considered* valid in one of the forums, and vice versa. Having explained various cases, Bender, *"Potestas Ordinaria et Delegata." Commentarius in canones 196–209* (Rome, 1957), 68 (No. 85), concluded: "Norma can. 202, §2 [sic] proprie habet sensum; actus potestatis iurisdictionis positus in foro interno [tantum] in foro externo non agnoscitur validus, cum eius validitas probari nequeat ideoque ignoratur illa scientia, quae est norma agendi in foro externo."

Regatillo, *Institutiones Iuris Canonici,* I, 278 (No. 270), states very briefly: "Actus iurisdictionis . . . ; sed non e converso, *nisi probetur;* nam in foro externo non esse et non apparere pro eodem sumuntur."

20. In the case of an undeclared censure (even a public one) being remitted (only for the internal sacramental forum) in the circumstances of urgency described in Canon 1357, §1, by a confessor who does not have this faculty, the confessor must impose on the penitent the obligation to have recourse to the competent authority or to another priest endowed with faculties. In §2, this canon imposes such recourse for the purpose of "standi huius mandatis." However, bearing in mind the corresponding Canon 2254 of the previous Code, it seems clear that this means above all the reception of a new remission that is operative for the external forum. (§2 stated that after carrying out such recourse, the penitent could present himself to a priest endowed with faculties in order to obtain from him both remission and "mandata," and that he was then not bound to obey the norms imposed by the superior to whom he had made recourse.)

Canon 1357 thus applies the norm of Canon 130: that the effect of the remission of the penalty for the internal forum (in the sacramental case) is not recognized in the external forum.

Even when a person who had the faculty to remit censures did so only for the internal forum (whether sacramental or not), a new remission was then needed for the external forum, when this was requested in order to avoid scandal or when the superior demanded its observance, even if the penalty had in fact already been removed (Canon 2251 of the 1917 Code). This canon was not retained, undoubtedly because it was judged superfluous, given the general norm of Canon 130: except as otherwise established by law, the effect of power exercised for the internal forum is not acknowledged in the external forum.

However, Canon 2251 added: ". . . nisi concessio absolutionis probetur aut saltem legitime praesumatur," a norm that was not taken up by the present Code. For this case, therefore, Canon 130 applies fully in its normative part, because the exception that could have been established by law does not exist.

Mostaza, "De foro interno iuxta canonistas postridentinos," 294, had proposed that the new Code should include the same norm that allowed proof or presumption for the external forum of the remission of censure given for the internal sacramental forum, also with regard to matrimonial impediments dispensed from by a confessor.

However, while there is still the possibility of proof (Canon 1082) for impediments dispensed from in the internal nonsacramental forum, this is not so for those removed in the internal sacramental forum (this can apparently be inferred from the same canon, as also from Canon 1081), nor for censures remitted in the internal sacramental forum. Indeed, except for this case of urgency, the rule is that remission is to be granted in the external forum; cf. Principius 9 ex directivis, *Communicationes*, 1 (1969), 85. In the words of V. De Paolis, *De Sanctionibus in Ecclesia. Adnotationes in Codicem: Liber VI* (Rome, 1986), 103, this means that "remissio poenae in foro interno sacramentali . . . sit quid anomalum, cum poena per se remittenda sit in foro externo."

21. P. Capobianco, "De ambitu fori interni ante Codicem," *Apollinaris*, 8 (1935), 591–605 (here 590–591): ". . . generale principium statui potest: forum internum respicit tantum materiam occultam et eiusque se extendit qua ipsum occultum. Quare quaestio de ambitu fori interni coincidit cum quaestione de notione occulti in iure canonico." *Id.*, "De notione fori interni in iure canonico," *Apollinaris*, 9 (1936), 364–374 (here 366): "Vocatur etiam 'forum conscientiae' quia actiones internas, seu relationes conscientiae ad Deum pro obiecto habet."

22. Mostaza, "Forum internum—Forum externum. I," 294.

23. See note 20 above, and Canon 1082 of the present Code.

24. A. Vermeersch, I. Creusen, A. Berche, and I. Greco, *Epitome Iuris Canonici* (Malines/Paris/Bruges, 1963⁸), I, 294 (No. 313, 1): "Ad forum internum pertinent primario et per se actiones privatae fidelium, in eoque bonum privatum seu conscientia singulorum primario attenditur." *Ibid.*, I, 22 (No. 22, 4): "Foro interno respondet iurisdictio quae immediate in bonum singulorum exercetur; dum iurisdictio fori externi bonum commune immediate curat." It should be noted that, while the intention of the expression appears to be that of following Berardi (see note 12 above), the "public utility" to which Berardi refers is replaced with the "common good." And while Berardi attributes the care of the spiritual good of individuals to the power for the internal forum, in no way does he identify this internal forum with the conscience.

25. Maroto, *Institutiones Iuris Canonici*, I, 857 (No. 718): "Iurisdic-

tio prout in hoc foro interno exercetur, directe et primario uniuscuiusque fidelis spiritualem utilitatem respicit et eius ad Deum indi-
viduale relationes."

26. Berardi and those who follow him are careful to state that when
they speak of the objective as being the good of the individual or of the
community, they mean this *primarily* and *directly,* or *per se.* In the case
of the occult exercise of power, it is easy to accept that it aims primarily
and directly at the good of the individual for whom it is exercised;
however, it is not so clear that the exercise for the external forum aims
primarily and directly at the communitarian and social good—except
on the strength of some specific conception of *canon* law. There is
considerable significance in the reason for which Berardi considers
jurisdiction for the external forum as more properly such "utpote quae
valde similis est . . . iurisdictioni illi, quae publicis magistratibus
competit" (cf. note 12 above).

27. Canon 130 is not explicit on this question. However, canon
doctrine has never doubted that the law is not only binding on the level
of conscience, but that all the other juridical effects also have full value
on that level. Thus, the penalty is binding on the penitent even when he
acts without publicity. Even if in certain circumstances, the law provides
for the *suspension* of certain prohibitions *for the external forum* (Canon
1335), the penalty subsists and is still binding on the conscience.

28. *"Potestas Ordinaria et Delegata"*, 14 (No. 19). Three years earlier, he had already expressed his thinking in "Forum externum et forum
internum," *Ephemerides Iuris Canonici,* 10 (1954), 9–27.

29. *"Potestas Ordinaria et Delegata"*, 14–15, and note 6.

30. Thus in Canon 2314 of the 1917 Code. Today, however, according to Canon 1330, is there no occult offense of heresy? It does not
seem to me that this canon forces an interpretation according to which
every offense of heresy is necessarily public: the manifestation as perceived by only one person is sufficient to constitute the offense, but not
to render it public. F. Voto, lawyer of the relevant group of the Commission for the Revision of the Code, had already noted, *Communicationes,*
8 (1976), 168: "Nonnulli proposuerunt ut non satis sit si manifestatio
animi vel mentis percipiatur ab aliquo, sed exigatur ut percepta sit
publice. Relator censet hoc verum non esse, nam typiphicari potest
etiam delictum ab uno tanto perceptum, ex.gr. in casu contumeliae."

31. B.F. Deutsch, *Jurisdiction of Pastors in the External Forum* (Washington, DC, 1957), 95. The author clearly follows Bender in accepting
the validity of the internal forum in the Church, given its *sui generis*
nature and also because of consistency between the two forums, so that
an act that is valid for the internal forum cannot but be so for the
external forum, even though certain conclusions in the latter forum can
be erroneous because of ignorance of what can take place for the inter-

nal forum; such conclusions are inevitable, but this does not mean that they are any less erroneous (*ibid.*, 93). He also follows Bender in explaining the statement of Canon 202, §1, that the exercise of power for the internal forum *is not valid* for the external forum: "One thing may be done so that it can be established by way of *juridic proof,* and another thing may be done so that it cannot be thus established. . . . If the juridic act is so performed that it can be established by juridic proof, it is done in the external forum. If not, it is done in the internal forum" (*ibid.*, 95). "Therefore, one may distinguish acts of the external forum and acts of the internal forum according to the manner of performance, namely, as juridically public or as juridically not public, or occult. Before one can be said to act publicly in the juridic order, one must so act that the accomplished fact can be established by way of juridic proof" (*ibid.*).

32. Mostaza, "Forum internum—Forum externum. I," 287, 295: "Para Bender, pertencen al fuero externo aquellos actos jurídicos que se realizan de manera que puedan demostrarse *probatione iuridica.* De lo contrario, pertenecen al fuero interno. En teoría, nada tenemos que objetar a esta definición del P. Bender . . . , pero es obvio que ella no se adapta a la concepción histórica ni a la que nos da el *Codex,* ya que para éste puede ser oculto un asunto—y en consecuencia, ser ventilado en el fuero interno—que es susceptible de *prueba jurídica,* como es evidente respecto a la dispensa de impedimentos matrimoniales e irregularidades."

33. In *ibid.*, 298–304, Mostaza himself lists a great variety of criteria also proposed by commentators on the 1917 Code. In the course of this same article, he demonstrates a clear evolution from a first distinction between *ius poli* and *ius fori,* understood by Graziano as canon and civil law, up to the distinction of the Code, passing by way of distinctions between forum of judgments and penitential forum, penitential forum (which would then be considered the forum of God) and external forum, while the forum of judgments would also broaden out to a noncontentious external forum. Only relatively late, in the early sixteenth century, would the sacramental penitential forum be distinguished as different from the nonsacramental one. According to Mostaza's study, Suarez was the first to identify the internal—even nonsacramental—forum with the forum of conscience. And Suarez would thus propose various criteria, which later canonists would then use in proposing very different points of view. (Mostaza himself, "De foro interno iuxta canonistas postridentinos," 289, criticizes a number of canonists for using certain expressions of Suarez and others "a sua contextu distortas.") Berardo would then propose a truly new criterion, which was taken up by many others, even when they did not give up various previously proposed criteria. Lastly, does not Mostaza himself

remind us that even today authors propose contradictory examples of matters belonging to one or the other forum, for example, marriage of conscience belongs to the internal forum according to Moersdorf, and to the external forum according to Bertrams? Further, various sentences that he recalls ("Forum internum—Forum externum. II") with regard to the nature of the internal forum only go to demonstrate how unreasonable it is to appeal to a lack of conformity with *traditional and modern canonical doctrine,* as he says in the first article in 1967 ("Forum internum—Forum externum. I," 196).

34. For Bender's assertion, cf. *"Potestas Ordinaria et Delegata",* 14 (No. 19); Mostaza cites Bender's article "Forum externum et forum internum," 26–27. For Mostaza's criticism, cf. "Forum internum—Forum externum. I," 295. In *ibid.,* 196, he cites Suarez, *De leg.* 8.6.11 (already noted previously on p. 278): ". . . haec autem duo membra (forum externum—forum internum) ita sunt intelligenda ut se habeant tanquam includens et inclusum, non tanquam mutuo se excludentia."

35. Bender, *"Potestas Ordinaria et Delegata",* 14 (No. 19).

36. J. Salazar Arbisqueta, "La jurisdicción social y el fuero interno," *La Potestad de la Iglesia. Análisis de su aspecto jurídico. Trabajos de la VII Semana de Derecho Canónico* (Barcelona, 1960), 149–203 (here 183): "Salta a la vista, teniendo en cuenta lo que arriba hemos dicho sobre el concepto del fuero interno, que no podemos admitir este criterio de distinción, porque la Iglesia puede procurar la sanctificación de las almas . . . mediante actos que son susceptibles de prueba jurídica, y puede haber actos de sus miembros susceptibles de prueba jurídica que no les haga objeto de sus normas jurídicas." *Ibid.,* 185: "Se nos objetará que esto es separarnos de lo que encontramos en el Código de Derecho Canónico y en sus comentariastas. En efecto. Ya dijimos al principio que íbamos a estudiar este problema de la jurisdicción social y el fuero interno a la luz de la Teología [?] y Filosofía del Derecho. . . . Ahora bien, teniendo en cuenta las definiciones del fuero interno que dan todos los canonistas . . . , éstes se ha de poner en el campo moral."

37. *Ibid.,* 184: ". . . y aun los actos externos, si los miramos desde el punto de vista de la sanctificación personal, ofrecen una perspectiva completamente distinta y hay que tratarlos de una manera absolutamente distinta que si los consideramos en cuanto influyen en el estado jurídco de los otros."

Ibid., 184–185: ". . . estos actos pueden pertenecer siempre al fuero interno porque siempre pueden ser considerados desde el punto de vista de si me sirven o no para mi santificación personal y podrán pertenecer al fuero externo cuando, por razón de una ley o contrato, sean exigibles jurídicamente."

38. *Ibid.,* 150: "Jurisdicción social bajo este segundo aspecto es la que tiene como meta la organización jurídica de la sociedad de los bautizados; ordena las acciones jurídicas de los mismos en orden a la salvación; trata de conseguir el orden social justo." *Ibid.*, 153–154: ". . . podrán ser materia de la jurisdicción social sólo aquellas acciones que tengan un valor jurídico, prescindiendo de la mala o buena disposición de ánimo del agente." *Ibid.*, 169, 184: ". . . el fin del fuero externo o jurídico, que es . . . organizar la actividad social del hombre . . . a veces hace el derecho *amoral,* al tener que prescindir de las disposiziones subjetivas de la persona y fijarse únicamente en el objeto de la acción humana." *Ibid.*, 171: "Tenemos el caso del médico bueno como médico; pero pésimo como hombre. Aquí será *jurídicamente* bueno, moralmente malo." *Ibid.*, 172: ". . . ejercer la justicia [not the virtue of justice] o hacer un acto de justicio sólo significa *dar a cada uno lo suyo.* Y aquí están los reales del jurista." *Ibid.*, 155: ". . . si se da al deudor [*sic*] lo que se le debe, aunque sea de mala gana y odiándolo, se ha hecho un acto de justicia."

39. *Ibid.*, 181, 185: ". . . porque el fuero interno se mueve en el campo moral y su fin específico y directo y sus características, por consiguiente, son morales y no jurídicas."

40. The author, *ibid.*, 181, is perfectly frank on this point: "Quizás alguno podría decir que el concepto de lo jurídico, que hemos desarrollado en la primera parte del trabajo, está calcado sobre el derecho civil y que se refiere a éste. De ningún modo. Hemos cogido la noción del derecho en sí, de lo jurídico, de la justicia en abstrato, lo que todos los teólogos [?] y filósofos del derecho han entendido por derecho, y no hemos hecho más que desarrollar las notas esenciales del derecho 'así entendido.' . . . Es muy fácil decir que el ordenamiento canónico tiene una índole especial, que es 'sui generis,' que al concepto del derecho canónico no se pueden aplicar todos los elementos que atribuye la filosofía del derecho a lo jurídico, que el concepto del derecho que tenemos es tomado del derecho civil. Pero es necesario demostrar en qué consiste esa índole especial, qué elementos hay que excluir y cuáles incluir y dar un concepto de derecho que sea verdadero derecho y, al mismo tiempo, excluya e incluya esos elementos, si es posible. . . . Mientras tanto seguiremos sosteniendo que, si entra el fuero interno en el ordenamiento jurídico de la Iglesia como parte integrante esencial del mismo, es imposible salvar su juridicidad, porque el fuero interno se mueve en el campo moral y su fin específico directo y sus características, por consiguiente, son morales y no jurídicas."

Whether this is, or has in fact ever been, the concept of *canon* law is quite another question. The author starts from a univocal concept of law—a concept drawn, with philosophical reasoning, from human juridical experience—which can be applied perfectly as a *generic* concept to different types of law, and hence also to canon law. The latter thus has its own peculiarities or specific attributes, but in no way is it a different category. And the author, *ibid.*, 182, does not allow us any doubts on this point either: "Los conceptos de animal y racional distintos se unen para formar al hombre. Este nuevo ser no podemos decir que es animal sólo ni racional sólo, ni puede decirse que su animalidad o su racionalidad son como la animalidad o racionalidad que se encuentran en un ser puro animal o puro racional, sino que su animalidad es de especie distinta: humana, lo mismo que su racionalidad." (He should, rather, have said not that animality is of a different species, but that it is a generic concept specified in a different way from rationality!)

We must instead say that it is the actual concept of canon *law* that is analogous, being *sui generis*, of a different genus. In itself it is similar; yet in itself it is also dissimilar from the concept of law rationally derived from human juridical experience. The specificity of *canon law* does not therefore come primarily from any specific difference that marks a differentiation in the generic character of law, but comes from the generic concept itself. Cf. my articles: "De natura *legis* ecclesiasticae," *Monitor Ecclesiasticus*, 100 (1975), 399–418; "Aequitas canonica," *Periodica*, 73 (1984), 33–88; "Notio legis ecclesiasticae," *Periodica*, 75 (1986), 303–333.

41. Salazar, "La jurisdicción social y el fuero interno," 168: "Tenemos, pues, que entre estos dos órdenes no hay separación perfecta." Then, in the conclusion of his article, *ibid.*, 203, Salazar considers as objects of the juridical power of the Church, or social power, those acts that refer to relations to others, that is to say, juridical acts (which, from what has already been said, must be said to be acts of the external forum); these, being of the external forum, are said to be public, and, being of the internal forum, are said to be occult! And with apparently equal inconsistency he speaks, *ibid.*, 203, of the specific end "de la potestad eclesiástica jurídica o jurisidicción social tanto de fuero interno como de fuero externo. . . ." Where, then, does this leave the statement, *ibid.*, 182, that "De aquí que para salvar la juridicidad del ordenamiento canónico es necesario que reduzcamos a éste al fuero externo"?

42. Benedict XIV, Encyclical Letter *Satis vobis* (17 November 1741), §2, in *Fontes*, I, 702 (No. 319): "Quod in tenebris delitescit et ab omnibus ignoratur."

43. *Ibid.*, §6, p. 703.

44. Following the Americans, authors speaks of a "hardship situation" when the partners in a second union know that the first was valid, but it has irremediably failed. A "conflict situation" refers to circumstances in which the partners in the second union are convinced that their first union was certainly invalid, although they are unable to provide proof that is acceptable for the ecclesiastical tribunal.

45. Cf. "Introduction," note 1, above.

46. It is naturally the spouses who are convinced of the invalidity of the first union, and thus this is a subjective certainty. However, it is clear that this certainty of the subjects can in reality correspond to the truth, and it is in this sense that we must speak also of objective certainty.

47. Cf., for example, U. Navarrete, "Conflictus inter Forum Internum et Externum in Matrimonio," *Investigationes Theologico-Canonicae* (Rome, 1978), 332–346 (here 339–340); M. Zalba, "Cooperatio materialis ad malum morale," *Periodica,* 71 (1982), 410–441 (here 437–440).

48. Cf. Mostaza, "Forum internum—Forum externum. I," 256–274. Of particular interest in connection with the subject under consideration here is the citation of A. di Asti, *ibid.,* 165, who not only contrasts the penitential forum, as the forum of conscience and of God, to the forum of the Church or the judicial forum, but also "nos dice que en la Iglesia existe un doble fuero—unum secretum . . . aliud est publicum—según que sea pública o secreta la manera del procedimiento."

CHAPTER 21

The Maintenance of the Clergy
From the Council to the Code

Velasio De Paolis, C.S.

Summary

Starting with the situation on the eve of the Council, the author examines the ground covered by the Council before reaching the formulation—particularly in the Decree *Presbyterorum ordinis*—of new guidelines for the maintenance of the clergy. These conciliar guidelines are then compared with the norms of the new Code of Canon Law.

Economic questions undoubtedly—and inevitably—play a very large role in the life of man, and also in the life of the Church. We find evidence of this even in the very early Church.[1] Among these problems, that of the maintenance of the clergy took on particular importance: engaged in the pastoral ministry, the priest had to find ways of supporting himself within his ministry itself.[2]

The ordination of sacred ministers who had no secure economic means of support eventually caused so many problems that even ecumenical councils had to take a hand in the matter. We can recall that the Council of Chalcedon laid down that nobody could be ordained if he had not been enrolled with a particular church.[3] Then the church that requested his ordination had to ensure the maintenance of the minister.[4] This gave rise to the institution of the title for ordination, which underwent various modifications through the centuries, but which had the basic aim of guaranteeing the maintenance of the sacred minister.[5] The title that eventually came to take on the greatest importance was that of the benefice. Although the rise of benefices was viewed with a certain amount of disapproval by Church authorities, who were unable to eliminate them but did try to purify them of certain aspects that could lead to distortions,[6] for many centuries they were the main institution for the maintenance of the clergy.[7] Indeed, not even laws for the expropriation of ecclesiastical property on the part of quite a number of states, particularly in the second half of the last century,[8] were sufficient to lead the legislator of the first Code, in 1917, to reduce the dimensions of the institution of benefices and to set the question of clergy maintenance on a different footing. Regulations regarding the benefice system, therefore, occupy a large space in the 1917 Code,[9] which places the benefice in first place as a title for ordination (cf. Canon 979, §1), although it does not ignore other possible solutions; and it goes on to lay down detailed rules with regard to benefices, devoting eighty canons in Part V of Book III to this matter.[10] The benefice system is seen as pivotal for clergy maintenance and is closely linked to the ecclesiastical office, to the extent that the benefic juridical person is described in Canon 1409 as being formed of two essential elements: "officio sacro et iure percipiendi reditus ex dote officio adnexos." This refers to the benefice properly so-called, as the codifier had inherited it from tradition. In fact, at the time of the codification, the situation had changed considerably, particularly in countries in the new world. The legislator notes the new situation and tries to adapt the institution of benefices to it too. Thus, we have a benefice improperly so-called: where there is no endowment in the form of property, beneficial endowments are considered

> . . . sive certae et debitae praestationes alicuius familiae vel personae moralis, sive certae et voluntariae fidelium oblationes, quae ad beneficii rectorem spectent, sive iura, ut dicitur, stolae intra fines taxationis dioecesanae vel legitimae consuetudinis (Canon 1410).

Thus, alongside the traditional type of benefice, another type is established that is not strictly speaking a benefice, and that is made up of the free offerings of the faithful or of so-called stole fees.[11]

Because the benefice was a juridical person made up of two closely linked and inseparable elements (office and right to the revenues of the endowment linked to the office on the part of the holder of the office), it followed that, in principle, the revenue could not be subtracted either wholly or in part from the holder of the benefice, except in exceptional cases, and in any case with many restrictions (cf. Canon 1429). In such a situation, although the office is theoretically the *pars potior,* inasmuch as the revenue is at the service of the holder of the office for his maintenance, in fact the right to the revenue takes on a greater importance.[12] In any case, the beneficial title makes provision (not always in an adequate manner) for the holders of offices alone. Above all, situations of economic inequality among members of the clergy come into being, inasmuch as the holder of the office has as his source of maintenance the right to the revenue from the endowment, whether this is abundant and more than necessary, or whether it is insufficient. If we then consider that the setting up of a beneficial endowment often depends on extremely contingent situations, rather than on the real requirements of the office itself, we can see that it is easy for situations of inequality—and sometimes, indeed, of iniquity—to come into being. The endowment is not proportionate to the office, and its size is independent of the requirements of the latter. Property does not therefore seem to be sufficiently regulated in function of ecclesial objectives—in particular according to the pastoral service performed—and, in any case, according to requirements, linked as these are to a specific office.[13]

It is true that Canon 1473 imposes the obligation "impendendi superfluos pro pauperibus aut piis causis, salvo praescripto, can. 239, §1, 19." However, this obligation, the nature of which is in any case the subject of doctrinal debate,[14] is certainly not sufficient to eliminate inequality and ensure the proper end of ecclesiastical property. Canon 1473 imposes this obligation after conferring on the incumbent the right to free enjoyment of the fruits of the benefice to the degree necessary for his maintenance, even though he may have family or some other type of property at his disposal; this places a mortgage, or at least a question, on the poverty of sacred ministers, equality of retribution, and communion of life.[15]

Further, bearing in mind that the benefice system means that the incumbent administers the property of the benefice,[16] there can also be other consequences. A good part of the time and ability of the officeholder must be taken up in administration, at the expense of pastoral work. And if he has no administrative ability, the property of the benefice is in serious danger. Because it is not always possible to find incumbents who have both pastoral and administrative qualities, there is a risk of having either excellent administrators at the expense of the care of souls, or excellent pastors at the expense of the security of Church property.[17]

If we situate this question within contemporary culture and society, particularly those of the western world (in other words, against a background of disregard for the Church and its property), we have a fairly good basis for an evaluation of the shortcomings of the benefice system of the Code.

Lastly, we must also note the effects the benefice system can have—and has in fact had in not a few cases—on the spiritual life of the clergy, with some priests having to make do as best they can due to the inadequacy of the income from their benefices, while others live in at least relative luxury. Apart from damaging the spiritual life of the clergy, such inequality and inadequacy also create scandal for the members of the faithful. The benefice system is also at least in part to blame for the move away from the living of a common life among clerics.[18]

Such was the situation on the eve of the Council, and we must now move forward from the situation as we have summarized it, in order to understand the Council and the new Code of Canon Law.

The Maintenance of the Clergy in the Second Vatican Council[19]

The Antepreparatory Stage

The need for a reform of the system laid down in the Code for the maintenance of the clergy is felt even in the antepreparatory stage of the Council. The shortcomings of the benefice system, to which we have just referred, are criticized by all those who deal with the question when sending in proposals for the forthcoming Council.[20] Unfortunately, however, not many people in fact pay attention to the problem. To make up for this, we find interventions that deal with the problem in a serious and far-reaching manner, proposing an alternative to the benefice system, or at least suggesting substantial modifications that would eliminate the major defects. We shall refer to only three of these interventions that are of special value because they come from pontifical universities or faculties, and that sum up all the basic elements of the problem and propose solutions that will then be debated at the Council.

1. *The Vote of the Pontifical Lateran University.* The vote of the Pontifical Lateran University[21] takes the shape more of a reform of the benefice system than of its abolition. It is considered that such a reform can take place through the conferral of special faculties on the bishop to mitigate the severity of Canon 1429 and decide the amount of the surplus to be devoted to the poor and to pious causes—which would give substance to the obligation laid down in Canon 1473. A third remedy could be added to these two, but it should receive careful reflection: the withdrawal of administration from the individual incumbent, and the setting up of a central administrative organization for all diocesan and benefice property. Material inequality would thus be avoided, and it would also mean that the incumbent would not have to devote a large portion of his time to administration—or, if he is incapable of such administration or would have neglected it, the threat to the security of the property itself is averted.[22]

2. *The Vote of the Pontifical Salesian Athenaeum.* The Salesian Athenaeum expresses itself decidedly in favor of the abolition of the benefice system.[23] In support of this proposal, the vote gives an historical overview. (a) For seven or eight centuries, there was one common fund and a unified administration of diocesan property, under the responsibility of the diocesan bishop. Later a division was made, not of the property and its administration, but of the income, according to the various purposes for which it was destined, and only later were these different purposes institutionalized and set up as juridical persons. It was not until this institutionalization that the property was divided among the different titulars, with the administration also being divided up accordingly. (b) In this context, the benefice system arose, and it was inserted into the Code when it was already giving clear signs of having outlived its purpose. The Council should take note of this situation and definitively abolish the benefice system in order to return to the original system of a single centralized administrative

organization for all diocesan property, which should be seen as one single estate. (c) This estate, or accumulation of property, should be made up of all the other property: benefice property, whether movable or immovable, property derived from other sources, including from the civil authorities, the offerings of the faithful, stole fees, income from pastoral activities, and all the income or property that comes to the Church in whatever form. The only exception suggested is offerings for the celebration of Mass. This single estate should provide whatever is necessary for pursuing the objectives of the Church, including the maintenance of the clergy and of those who in any way work in the service of the Church. (d) If the benefice system were abolished along these lines, the present problems would be in large part eliminated, and justice and equity among the clergy would be fostered, together with priestly holiness and perfection. In particular, "vita communis totius cleri facile in praxim deducitur et insuper in eius sustenantione magnis pecuniae summis parci potest."[24] (e) The following vote is formulated in conclusion:

> Systemate beneficiali relicto, omnia bona ecclesiastica dioecesana ab Ordinario loci administrentur et, aequa proportione servata, clero, ecclesiis, populo et operibus curae animarum, ordinariis et extraordinariis, pro rata distribuantur.[25]

3. *The Vote of the Theological Faculty of Naples.* The vote of the Theological Faculty of Naples[26] starts from a technical juridical perspective, but does so in order to resolve some very real problems, in other words, to reach the proposal of some practical solutions that eliminate the drawbacks of the benefice system. (a) The definition of benefice, as it is proposed in Canon 1490, is a juridical muddle and encompasses not a few contradictions on the practical level: the subjective perpetuity of the title, inequality in remuneration, harm "spiritui paupertatis et zelo apostolico, quia beneficiarius, vel candidatus, magis a sponsae dote trahi et occupari contingit quam ab ipsa sponsa eiusque amore et servitio," arguments and scandal among the faithful. (b) It is proposed that the benefice system should be replaced by a system of stipends to be paid to all those who fulfill an office, in proportion to the requirements of the office in question and to differences as to place and circumstances. The so-called benefice endowment, which is referred to in Canon 1410, would be freed from the

benefice and would form part of the patrimony of the juridical person or set up as a pious foundation. Stole fees should become part of the general estate, from which stipends should be drawn; offerings for the celebration of Mass should be similarly treated and used. (c) Once subjective perpetuity has fallen, parish priests should be removable.

As can be seen, these proposals represent an indictment of the benefice system. The evils are clearly seen. And there is also a certain amount of agreement—although with various nuances, sometimes quite large ones—on the measures to be taken to eliminate these problems. In particular, from the very beginning, we can see the twofold approach that would be proposed again and again both during and after the Council, sometimes with the emphasis on one side and sometimes on the other: abolition or reform of the benefice system? In actual fact, apart from the question of emphasis, we often have the impression that it is more a question of terminology and of confusion that springs from the fact that not enough of an effort has been made to gain a clear idea of the essence of the benefice system. However, once this essence has been pinpointed, it should not be difficult to see the difference between reform and abolition of the system itself. Now the cornerstone of the benefice system is the connection between the office and the right to the income from the property attached to the office on the part of the titular himself. It is indeed a juridical muddle, as the vote of the Theological Faculty of Naples said, with the technical consequences deriving from this muddle. The benefice system is abolished precisely when this connection is removed; on the other hand, it is reformed, but still remains, when this connection is merely lessened, as in the vote of the Pontifical Lateran University, which speaks simply of deciding the sum to be assigned to the titular, and of the possibility of entrusting the administration of the benefice to some centralized diocesan administrative organization. We must, therefore, move beyond terminology in order to consider first and foremost the substance of things. As we shall see, the Council will move beyond the terminological question, not lingering too much over the problem of reform versus abolition but clearly indicating the essential point when it will lay down in the Decree *Presbyterorum ordinis* 20:

Officio vero, quod sacri ministri adimplent praecipuum momentum tribuere oportet. Quare systema sic dictum beneficiale relinquatur aut saltem ita reformetur ut pars beneficialis, seu ius ad reditus ex dote officio adnexos, habeatur tamquam secundaria, et princeps in iure tribuantur locus ipsi officio ecclesiastico.

However, it should be noted here that the Council does not say whether the link is broken or merely loosened.

The Preparatory Stage

In the preparatory stage of the Council, we have two schemata. The first, proposed by the Commission for the Discipline of the Clergy and of Christian People, is entitled: *De officiis et beneficiis ecclesiasticis deque bonorum ecclesiasticorum administratione*.[27] And the second is entitled: *De officiis et beneficiis ecclesiasticis minoribus deque bonorum ecclesiasticorum administratione*.[28]

These two schemata clearly adopt the approach of the vote of the Pontifical Lateran University, with great caution and circumspection. It is a question of rectifying certain defects, for instance, guaranteeing a fair remuneration to those whose office is not endowed with a benefice, or ensuring that the surplus from the incumbents should truly go to the poor and to pious causes. It is also a question of meeting new requirements, such as those of insurance and a pension. Such objectives can be fulfilled by modifying the concept of office and limiting the right of the incumbent to the revenue from the benefice. In other respects, the schemata basically reiterate the teaching of the Church with regard to the administration of worldly goods. However, in this connection, there are certain new elements resulting from the reform they intend proposing for ecclesiastical benefices. Thus it is prescribed that the revenues of benefices that are not necessary for the fitting maintenance of the incumbent himself, as is to be defined in particular local law, or for the fulfillment of other tasks connected with the benefice, should devolve upon a common fund made up of the property of the diocese. The Ordinary can also set up a unified system for the administration of various secular benefices in such a way that the revenues are distributed in an equitable way for the maintenance of the clergy, to promote apostolic works, and to help meet other needs of the diocese. However, where such a centralized administrative system is not set up, the Ordinary could establish the sum to be paid to the parish priest of the benefice, while the rest should be paid into a common fund. In any case, a common estate should be formed in each diocese for the different requirements of the same diocese. This estate should be made up of the revenues from diocesan property, taxes, voluntary offerings, and charitable contributions from richer dioceses.[29]

The Conciliar Stage

In the conciliar stage, the question of clergy maintenance was included in the schema on the clergy—a schema that went through a good number of different drafts.[30] If we examine the different schemata, we can see the extent to which the subject of temporal goods and that of clergy maintenance concerned the Council Fathers.[31] The inclusion of the subject in the schema on the life and ministry of priests undoubtedly served to frame the problem of clergy maintenance and of the consequent reform or abolition of the benefice system in a broader context, encompassing the significance of temporal goods, priestly poverty and spirituality, and the living of a common life among clergy. As far as this subject is concerned, the long path traveled by the Council led to numbers 17, 20, and 21 of the Decree *Presbyterorum ordinis.*

Two different aspects can be clearly distinguished in the discussions of the Council Fathers: that of the values to be ensured, and that of the technical means or instruments that will guarantee such values so far as possible.

1. *Values.*

a. Discussion of the maintenance of the clergy should be seen within the broad context of the mission of the Church and of the proper ends of the temporal goods the Church has the right to possess precisely in connection with the mission it is to fulfill. Such goods are for ecclesial ends, and such ends must be attained with their effective use for those ends to which the goods are ordered.

b. Priests or clerics have the right to receive a fair and just remuneration for the service they give to the Church, and also adequate social security, health insurance, and retirement pension. Even so, they must be poor and should live as poor people, not setting their hearts on riches. And whatever happens, they must not take the ecclesiastical ministry as a pretext for enriching themselves or their families. The material goods that come to them from the Church or through the ecclesiastical ministry must in fact be used for the purposes of the Church. Any surplus must revert to such purposes and must particularly be distributed in favor of the poor.

c. Just remuneration must be ensured for all those who fulfill ecclesiastical offices, avoiding any scandalous inequality. This requirement points toward the communion and communication of material goods, on the basis of a living solidarity.

d. A clear reference point is charity toward the poor.

2. *Technical Instruments Envisaged.* From a technical viewpoint, the protection of such values is entrusted to the solution of a number of technical juridical problems.

a. From the very beginning, *the new notion of ecclesiastical office* was more or less accepted. If there is any intention at all of setting in motion a reform of the system of clergy maintenance, which would cover all clerics who carry out some function in the Church on a permanent basis as well as lay people, the concept of ecclesiastical office given by Canon 145, §1, of the 1917 Code can no longer be accepted in any strict sense, inasmuch as this concept entails participation in the power of order or of jurisdiction. Anybody who carries out a permanently instituted function for the purposes of the Church, whether through divine law or ecclesiastical law, must be recognized as the holder of an office and thus as worthy of remuneration. Ecclesiastical office would therefore have to be taken in a broad sense on the basis of Canon 145, §1, of the 1917 Code.[32]

b. A second problem concerns the *abolition or reform of the benefice institution.* The early conciliar schemata simply speak of the abandonment of the benefice institution, even though the implementation of this step is entrusted to the revision of the Code.[33] Schema D, *De ministerio et vita Presbyterorum,* however, speaks of reform,[34] while Schema E, the last text before the definitive one, speaks of both abandonment and reform.[35] The wish to give up the benefice system seems clear. However, practical difficulties led the Council Fathers to leave greater freedom to the Commission for the Revision of the Code, even though they give the commission some clear reference points: (1) office is to be understood in the broad sense; (2) the office is preeminent with regard to the right to revenues.

c. As far as the maintenance of the clergy is concerned, it is recommended that an *institution should be set up for the maintenance of the clergy,* and also that a common diocesan fund should be set up for other needs.

The Decree *Presbyterorum ordinis*[36]

The fruits of the conciliar debate are found in numbers 17, 20, and 21 of the definitive text of the Decree *Presbyterorum ordinis.* The following are the more important elements.

1. It is a question for priests above all of having a correct relationship with the goods of this world, through the spiritual discernment that is the fruit of freedom and that leads to freedom. In any case, priests ". . . quippe quorum Dominus sit pars et hereditas (Num 18, 20), bonis temporalibus uti debent tantummodo eos in fines, ad quos iuxta Christi Domini doctrinam Ecclesiaeque ordinationem eadem destinari licet" (No. 17).

2. Ecclesiastical property is a means for the achievement of the purposes of the Church. In particular, such worldly goods are "ad cultum divinum ordinandum, ad honestam cleri sustenationem procurandam, necnon ad opera sacri apostolatus vel caritatis, praesertim erga egenos exercenda" (*ibid.*). The clergy must therefore use them for their own maintenance and only for the purposes of the Church.

3. As regards moneys or other goods acquired on the occasion of the exercise of the sacred ministry, although these do not strictly speaking belong to the Church,[37] the priest must not use them to enrich himself or his family: because they are acquired through an office that comes from the Church, they must return to the purposes of the Church. In this way, priests will be free from the slavery of riches, and will thus avoid any avarice and anything that could give rise to scandal, and will be more fully prepared for their ministry in voluntary evangelical poverty (No. 17).

4. In particular, "aliqualis verum communis usus, ad instar bonorum communionis quae in historia primaevae Ecclesiae extollitur, caritati pastorali optime viam sternit et per eam vivendi formam Presbyteri laudabiliter ad praxim reducere possunt spiritum paupertatis qui a Christo commendatur" (*ibid.*).

5. Even so, priests who dedicate themselves to the ministry of the kingdom of God must be provided with a just remuneration in proportion to their office. The faithful have the obligation to see that the priest receives this, and bishops must remind the faithful of this duty.

6. There is, therefore, a need for the abolition or reform of the benefice system, in such a way that the office, to be understood "quodlibet munus stabiliter collatum in finem spiritualem exercendum," is given "princips locus" with respect to the right to revenues.

7. The Council appeals to the significance of the temporal goods of the Church. They are in a way common, like spiritual goods, and they must thus be communicated and shared. As an example, it gives the primitive Church in Jerusalem, in which "erant illis omnia communio" (Acts 4:32) and "dividebatur autem singulis prout cuique opus est." Richer dioceses are also invited to help poorer ones "ut illarum abundantia harum inopiam suppleat" (No. 21).[38]

8. However, the Council does not have a great deal to say with regard to practical, technical, and juridical solutions, and it expresses itself with great circumspection in this regard. It speaks of an "institutio quaedam diocesana" for the maintenance of the clergy, and this institution "summopere congruit" in "regionibus saltem in quibus cleri sustentatio penitus aut magna ex parte a fideliim oblationibus pendet" (No. 21). Apart from this "institutio," which should be set up as a juridical person, as a "fundatio autonoma," the document also speaks of a "massa bonorum communis," with which bishops can meet the other needs of their dioceses. This "massa communis bonorum," which need not necessarily be set up as a juridical person, is only "in votis"; it should be established "quantum fieri possit in singulis dioecesibus vel regionibus" (ibid.). Episcopal conferences in particular are entrusted with the task of making sure that provision is also made for health assistance and for the proper support of priests in old age (ibid).

If we reflect a little on the path traveled by the conciliar texts, it is easy to see how the Council in fact took note of the strong suggestions made on its eve. It was certainly not the task of the Council to make new laws with regard to ecclesiastical property. Even so, it provided some very important orientations, both directly as regards priestly spirituality (the proper attitude to temporal goods and their use, poverty, common life, solidarity, and communion of goods), and in the form of instructions of immediate juridical relevance. The Council could not, of course, go into details; even so, what it had to say as concerns the concept of ecclesiastical office, the remuneration of the clergy, the fund for clergy maintenance, health insurance and old-age pensions, and diocesan property as a whole, was all of major importance. The Council did not feel it wise for it to decide whether the benefice system should be abolished or reformed. The circumstances militating against any abolition pure and simple were enormous, particularly in the area of external civil law.[39] However, the Council did lay the foundations for its abolition, at least in the long run and once the circumstances preventing such an abolition have gradually been eliminated.

The 1983 Code[40]

Although the revision of the Code was announced by Pope John XXIII on the same day that he announced the Second Ecumenical Vatican Council, a good deal of ground still had to be covered before this revision could actually take place. In particular, it had to wait until the end of the Council, and the documents for the implementation of the Council provided its basis and helped in its elaboration.[41] Among these documents, great importance must be given to the Motu Proprio *Ecclesiae sanctae* of 1966,[42] which also concerned itself closely with the subject under discussion here.

The Motu Proprio *Ecclesiae sanctae*

The Motu Proprio *Ecclesiae sanctae* (I, 5) entrusts episcopal conferences

> . . . eas de usu bonorum ecclesiasticorum opportunas statuere ordinationes, quibus, attentis quidem imprimis ipsarum dioecesium territorii necessitatibus, dioecesibus subsidia quaedam imponuntur solvenda in favorem sive operum apostolatus vel caritatis, sive Ecclesiarum quae parvis opibus sunt praeditae aut ob peculiaria adiuncta in agestate versantur.

Similarly, episcopal conferences are entrusted with the task,

> . . . ut, sive pro singulis dioecesibus sive pro pluribus earum in communi sive pro toto terriotrio, normae statuantur, quibus apte consulatur debitae sustentationi omnium clericorum, qui in populi Dei servitium munere funguntur vel functi sunt.[43]

Further, episcopal conferences are entrusted with the task of making sure that funds for the maintenance of the clergy are set up in the individual dioceses, in accordance with the decisions of the Council.[44] Lastly, episcopal conferences must also make sure that the conciliar orientations with regard to the health and social insurance of the clergy are implemented.[45]

On the other hand, the reform (no mention is made of abolition) of the benefice system and the setting up of a common fund for the other requirements of the diocese are entrusted to the Commission for the Revision of the Code. In the meantime, however, "curent Episcopi, suis auditis consiliis Presbyterorum, ut provideatur aequae distributioni bonorum, etiam redituum ex beneficiis provenientium."[46]

These texts seem clearly to indicate a tendency to go further than the Council itself in their emphasis on the role of episcopal conferences. The responsibility the Council attributes simply to the individual bishops in their respective dioceses tends to be attributed to episcopal conferences by the Motu Proprio, so that the conferences have at least a role of supervision over individual bishops. This tendency can also be seen in the first drafts of the canons on temporal goods, although it was eventually eliminated in later drafts and in the definitive text, inasmuch as it was observed that such a role of supervision compromises the autonomy of the individual bishops in their respective dioceses.[47]

The 1983 Code

In drafting Book V of the Code of Canon Law, "De bonis Ecclesiae temporalibus," the commission bore two points of reference particularly in mind: the Council, and the principle of subsidiarity.[48] As regards the Council, the commission did not mean to codify what the Council had said about temporal goods, but only what it had required should be regulated by norms of canon law.[49] And the application of the principle of subsidiarity led the commission to leave many things up to local law, given the great variations in circumstances and also the canonization of the civil law of the country in quite a number of cases.[50]

The drafting process of the Code was lengthy, and the definitive text is the outcome of broad consultation and a good number of drafts.[51] We cannot describe this process in full, but shall refer immediately to the definitive text, although, where necessary, we shall mention specific details of the process that led to this text. It should be borne in mind that the Code does not refer so much to the *documents* of the Council as to its *acts*. Indeed, it should be remembered that the Council specifically chose not to deal with many matters of a disciplinary nature that are proper to the Code. The difference between the Council and the Code also lies in the fact that the Council did not want to deal with all the problems of the Church, whereas the Code is a text that must necessarily be complete in its own sphere. It is thus easy to see that the Code will be broader and more complete, and will deal with aspects that the Council left untouched.[52]

1. The new Code no longer speaks of the "title of ordination" inasmuch as the system for the maintenance of the clergy is based on the office performed in the service of the Church, for which the individual must receive adequate remuneration, even if he is not incardinated into the specific church in question. However, although reference to the title of ordination is now abandoned, this does not mean that independent clerics are permitted. Every cleric must be incardinated "aut alicui Ecclesiae particulari vel praelaturae personali, aut alicui instituto vitae consecratae vel societati hac facultate praeditis" (Canon 265). Canon 266, §1, lays down that every cleric receives holy orders for the service of the institution into which he is incardinated. And the institution for which he has received orders or in which he performs his service must provide him with the necessary maintenance. Canon 269 lays down that the bishop is not to incardinate a cleric except where "necessitas aut utilitas suae Ecclesiae particularis id exigat, et salvis iuris praescriptis honestam sustentationem clericorum respicientibus" (Canon 269, 1°). Canon 295, §2, lays down, for those who have been incardinated into a prelature: "Praelatus prospicere debet sive spirituali institutioni illorum quos titulo praedicto promoverit, sive eorum decorae sustentationi." For members of institutes of consecrated life, the

profession of the evangelical counsel of poverty means that those concerned must use temporal goods in dependence and according to the limitations laid down in the specific law of each institute (cf. Canon 600), and for religious in particular, there is the obligation of common life (cf. Canon 668).

2. Canon 281 lays down the fundamental norms with regard to the *remuneration of the clergy*, and we reproduce it here in full:

§1. Clerici, cum ministerio ecclesiastico se dedicant, remunerationem merentur quae suae condicioni congruat, ratione habita tum ipsius muneris naturae, tum locorum temorumque condicionum, quaque ipsi possint necessitatibus vitae suae necnon aequae retributioni eorum, quorum servitio egent, providere.

§2. Item providendum est ut gaudeant illa sociali adsistentia, qua eorum necessitatibus, si infirmitate, invaliditate vel senectute laborent, apte prospiciatur.

§3. Diaconi uxorati, qui plene ministerio ecclesiastico sese devovent, remunerationem merentur qua sui suaeque familiae sustentationi providere valeant; qui vero ratione professionis civilis, quam exercent aut exercuerunt, remunerationem obtineant, ex perceptis inde reditibus sibi suaeque familiae necessitatibus consulant.

a. It should be noted that the text bases remuneration on the fact that the cleric performs an *ecclesiastical office*, independently of whether or not he is incardinated into the diocese or institute in which he performs this office. Nor does the text speak specifically of a right, but confines itself to saying, "remuneratione merentur."[53] The source of this canon can be found in number 20 of the Decree *Presbyterorum ordinis*, and the history of its drafting process reveals that the word "merces" was purposely avoided in order to eliminate any connotation of an ordinary relation between job and wages. It should also be noted that for married deacons who give their services to the Church full time, but who have their own sources of income, Canon 281, §3, indicates that such service should be offered free.[54]

b. Such *remuneration*, which clerics deserve, must be *adequate* for their circumstances, bearing in mind both the nature of the office and also the conditions of time and place, so that they can provide for the needs of their own lives and also for the just remuneration of whoever works in their service.

c. Following the conciliar orientations, §2 of the same canon also lays down norms for *social assistance* and *old age pensions*.

3. These norms regarding the maintenance of the clergy should be read in the same gospel spirit that the Council sought to emphasize and that the Code confirms:

a. Thus Canon 282 states that clerics are to lead a *simple life* and avoid anything that has a semblance of vanity. Any goods they have received on the occasion of exercising an ecclesiastical office and that are superfluous to their needs should be used for the good of the Church and for works of charity. Although such goods do not strictly speaking belong to the Church, they are acquired because of the exercise of an ecclesiastical office and must therefore return to the Church.[55]

b. The instruction or the strong recommendation that clerics should live a *common life*, which is spoken of in Canon 280, should also be read in the perspective of poverty. Historically speaking, a common life among clerics was practiced when there was a common table and when the evangelical counsel of poverty was professed. It suffered a heavy blow with personal remuneration, and particularly with the spread of the benefice system.[56]

4. The *benefice system* comes to lose its meaning and sense with regard to the maintenance of the clergy. While the Code does not simply abolish it in Canon 1272, this is not in order to allow its survival with a view to the maintenance of the clergy, but because its abolition with a single stroke of the pen would have created problems of a different sort. The language of the Code leaves no room for doubt: the benefice system is destined for extinction. No new benefices can be established, and existing ones are to be regulated by some temporary rulings by episcopal conferences, as agreed and approved by the Apostolic See. Whatever these temporary norms may be, the link between office and right to incomes is to be abolished, inasmuch as benefice revenues, and so far as possible the benefice endowment itself, must accrue to the institute for the maintenance of the clergy that is envisaged in Canon 1274, §1.[57] However, it should be noted that the Code speaks of benefices "proprie dicta," which even at the time of the conciliar debates existed in only a few parts of the Church. Hence the qualification, "ubi . . . adhuc exsistunt." Reform or abolition can take place gradually, and the adverb

"paulatim" clearly indicates this. However, the conclusion of this process is the abolition of the benefice system as an instrument for the maintenance of the clergy.

5. After the benefice system has been set aside and the obligation has been imposed of providing a just remuneration for clerics inasmuch as they perform their ministerial office, *the funds must be found for the necessary maintenance of the clergy*. The Code indicates the solution in Canon 1274, §1:

> Habeatur in singulis dioecesibus speciale institutum, quod bona vel oblationes colligat eum in finem ut sustentationi clericorum, qui in favorem dioecesis servitium praestant, ad normam can. 281, provideatur, nisi aliter eisdem provisum sit.

A few observations may be of help in understanding the significance of this norm more clearly:

a. It may be helpful to carry out a comparison with the conciliar text, which speaks as follows with regard to the setting up of such a fund: ". . . in regionibus saltem in quibus cleri substentatio penitus aut magna ex parte a fidelium oblationibus pendet, bona in hunc findem oblata colligat institutio quaedam dioecesana."[58] The text of the Code gives the following details: this fund is to be set up in each diocese for those clerics who perform an office within the diocese, whether they are diocesan or not. Is the setting up such a fund obligatory? The verb "habeatur" leaves no room for doubt, because it is in the imperative. However, the final phrase, "nisi aliud eisdem provisum sit," gives the impression that bishops are free to make alternative arrangements for the maintenance of their clergy, although this cannot be an excuse for the prolongation of the benefice system.[59] However, bearing in mind that Canon 1272 very definitively calls for the creation of such a fund, on which the income and even the original endowments of benefices are to devolve, it may be thought that the phrase refers not so much to some other possible means of clergy maintenance as such, but more to some different way in which provisions may be made for clerics in certain cases. This final phrase may refer not so much to an alternative system to the creation of the fund for the maintenance of the clergy, but more to an alternative way of giving clerics a just remuneration in certain cases. Be that as it may, the language of the Code certainly indicates more urgency than that of the Council with regard to the establishment of the fund. Where the Council simply says "summopere . . . congruit,"[60] the Code has "habeatur," even though it adds the close "nisi aliud eisdem provisum sit"; and where the Council envisages such a fund for areas where the maintenance of the clergy depends almost totally on the free offerings of the faithful, the Code states "in singulis dioecesibus."[61]

b. As regards sources, the Council simply speaks of "bona in hunc finem oblata," whereas the Code speaks of "bona vel oblationes" for the maintenance of the clergy. And the Code specifically refers back to this fund in Canon 1272, when it speaks of the management of benefices, and in Canon 1303, §2, when it lays down instructions as to the disposal of the goods of nonautonomous pious foundations once their purposes have been fulfilled. The perspectives of the Council and the Code are certainly different. The Council is thinking of places where the maintenance of the clergy depends on the offerings of the faithful, and hence the fund that is to be established is made up of such offerings. The Code, on the other hand, is considering a general situation, and thus the fund can be made up of goods that are already earmarked for the maintenance of the clergy and of other goods that may be given for such a purpose. Benefices are to be included among those goods that already have this purpose. However, in Canon 1272, the Code unfortunately does not distinguish between benefice goods that have this purpose and other benefice goods; and Canon 1303, §2, gives a general rule, with the only exception being where the donor has expressly wished otherwise. The Council seems to have been more sensitive than the Code with regard to the wishes of donors. However, it must be said that the Code has the task of defining the constitution, nature and purposes, and also the goods that make up such funds, and it therefore had to provide solutions to problems that the Council had merely noted.

6. In response to the conciliar directives on social security, the Code lays down a norm in Canon 1274, §2, and in response to conciliar orientations on mutual assistance between dioceses, in Canon 1274, §3, it envisages the setting up of a common estate or fund, the purposes of which include that of helping poorer dioceses.

7. Having established the principle of fair and just remuneration for those who perform any ecclesiastical office, and having

ruled on the reform of the benefice system, the Code gives different instructions also as to *any income linked to the priestly ministry.*
Such income no longer goes to the priest (parish or otherwise),[62]
but to the common account of the parish, or to that of the
juridical person in the service of which the priest carries out his
ministry.

a. Thus, Canon 531 lays down:

Licet paroeciale quoddam munus alius expleverit, oblationes
quas hac occasione a christifidelibus recipit ad massam
paroecialem deferat, nisi de contraria offerentis voluntate
constet quoad oblationes voluntarias; Episcopo dioecesano,
audito consilio presbyterali, competit statuere praescripta,
quibus destinationi harum oblationum necnon remunerationi
clericorum idem munus implentium provideatur.

The following reflections can be made:

(1) It is very easy to understand the principle that the offerings should go to the common parish account. The cleric has no
right to personal possession of them, because in accordance with
Canon 281, he already receives a fair remuneration for the service he performs.

(2) Respect for the wishes of donors is in conformity with
justice and has been the constant tradition of the Church.[63]

(3) It may not seem so easy to understand why the diocesan
bishop,[64] after consulting the presbyteral council,[65] should have
to issue instructions as to the allocation of these offerings and the
remuneration due to those who perform the ministerial service.
Because these funds belong to the parish, they should be used for
the needs of the parish. However, this ruling seems to be a clear
reference to the problem of the maintenance of the clergy. If it is
true that a fair remuneration must be provided (Canon 281), and
also, unless otherwise provided for, that a fund is to be set up for
this purpose (Canon 1274, §1), then it is also necessary to find
the moneys for this fund or at least for the fair remuneration.
Thus, such offerings could be earmarked specifically for the maintenance of the clergy and go to feed the fund set up for this
purpose. The reference to the remuneration of the priest may
seem stranger when we remember that he already has his fair
remuneration under Canon 281. However, this norm indicates
something more than the simple remuneration referred to in

Canon 281. In other words, the possibility is envisaged that part of the offering should be given to the priest who performed the ministerial action on the occasion of which the donor made his offering. This is a recognition of the action performed and also an encouragement to pastoral zeal, inasmuch as less zealous priests might leave every possible task up to others if they gained nothing from ministerial actions. A similar prescription is found in Canon 951, §1, which says that offerings for a second or third Mass on the same day are to be given for the purposes laid down by the Ordinary "admissa quidem aliqua retributione ex titulo extrinseco" for the celebrating priest.[66]

b. Canon 551 states that Canon 531 applies in respect of offerings made on the occasion of the exercise of the pastoral ministry by the assistant priest. Offerings determined by the competent authority, as laid down in Canon 848, and also in Canon 1181, in accordance with the norms of Canon 1264, are also to go to the common fund. Canon 1267 should also be observed.

8. Offerings received for the *application of Mass* for specific intentions deserve separate consideration. Canon 945, §1, confirms the centuries-old practice of the Church: "Secundum probatum Ecclesiae morem, sacerdoti cuilibet Missam celebranti aut concelebranti licet stipem oblatam recipere, ut iuxta certam intentionem Missam applicet." Through long tradition, offerings for such Masses belong to the celebrant. The 1917 Code laid down very detailed regulations for the "stipendia Missarum." In particular, Canon 1509, 5, considered such stipends as matter that was not subject to prescription, and Canon 1506 ruled out any possibility of a levy on Mass offerings. The fact that the Mass stipend belonged to the celebrant also explained the norm laid down in Canon 840, which stated that if the Mass was celebrated by another priest, the *whole* offering should be passed on, "nisi aut oblator expresse permittat aliquid retinere aut certo constet excessum supra taxam dioecesanum datum fuisse intuitu personae."

The Council does not speak of Mass offerings, although it did discuss them in the antepreparatory stage, the preparatory stage, and in the actual conciliar debates. Specifically, certain proposals and votes to the Council said that Mass offerings should not be included in the "massa bonorum" of the diocese,[67] whereas others proposed that they should be included, like other stole fees, in the common fund for the maintenance of the clergy.[68] In the drafts of the preparatory phase, it is explicitly stated: "Nullum autem tributum imponi potest super eleemosynis Missarum sive manualium sive fundatarum."[69] However, the subject would not return again in the documents of the conciliar stage, and is not referred to at all in the definitive texts. Even so, it should be noted that when mention is made of the goods that must go to make up both the fund for the maintenance of the clergy and also the common fund for other requirements, the specifications of local law are deferred to.[70]

The subject is not broached in the early drafts of the new Code. In the 1980 draft, Canon 1213, which speaks of the power of bishops to impose levies, the text of Canon 1506 of the 1917 Code is repeated: ". . . nullum vero tributum imponi potest super eleemosynis missarum." But this norm would disappear in the definitive text.[71]

While the new Code repeats various norms from the previous Code, it also introduces some new ones.

a. Canon 945 reconfirms the lawfulness of offerings for the application of Mass for specific intentions, although not for more than one intention on the same day, in accordance with Canon 951 and taking into account the further regulations given therein.[72]

b. Such offerings belong to the celebrant, and must therefore be passed on in full to the priest who is entrusted with celebrating the Mass for which the offering was given (cf. Canon 955, §1).

c. The offerings for a second or third intention on the same day are to be used as decided by the Ordinary, in accordance with Canon 134—in other words, the bishop of the place in the case of priests subject to him, or the religious superior in the case of religious.[73]

All this would seem to indicate that offerings for Mass intentions cannot be taxed or made subject to any levies. However, in justification of the practice of the faithful of making offerings for the application of Masses, Canon 946 indicates a twofold reason: ". . . ad bonum conferunt Ecclesiae atque eius curam in ministris operibusque sustinendis ea oblatione participant." Thus, Mass offerings are not only for the maintenance of the clergy, but also for the works and activities of the Church. In such a perspective, the possibility of some sort of taxation cannot be wholly ruled out,[74] even if the tradition of excluding such offerings from taxation should be respected.[75]

9. Thus the Code establishes a general norm for the maintenance of the clergy, on the basis of which the institution that
incardinates the cleric through ordination must also provide for
his maintenance. Canon 281 gives another norm of a general
type, stating that a cleric who performs an office must be given a
fair remuneration. In order to meet this obligation, the Code
rules that a fund is to be set up, in accordance with Canon 1274,
for the maintenance of the clergy. However, it is envisaged that
the cleric may also receive part of the offerings of the faithful, as
described in Canon 531, or part of the offerings for a second or
third Mass intention, apart from that for the first.

10. As can be seen, the legislation of the Code has a different
emphasis from that of the conciliar approach, which was very
broad ranging as regards the significance of temporal goods in
general, and ecclesiastical goods in particular, in the life of
priests, and their effects on detachment from temporal goods, a
life of poverty and solidarity, and community life.

The discussion of the significance of ecclesiastical goods is less
explicit where the purposes of the temporal goods of the Church
are discussed in Canons 1254 and 1260. The attitude of clerics
with regard to ecclesiastical goods is discussed only in Canon
282. Communion of goods is referred to in very general terms in
Canon 280, which recommends a common life. Canons 1271
and 1274, §2, speak of the communion and sharing of goods. To
tell the truth, this does not seem sufficient, especially in view of
the fact that these elements are very broadly scattered and not
found in the context in which the Council had placed them, so
that they lose some of their strength. [76]

As far as technical aspects are concerned, the Code has codified the conciliar directives on the concept of office, the reform/
abolition of benefices, the setting up of a fund for the maintenance of the clergy, and the common fund for the other requirements of the diocese. In providing the conciliar directives with a
clearer practical expression, it has introduced a fairly large number of new elements as regards these technical aspects; and in
some cases, as we have seen, it has in fact moved beyond what
the Council said. Given the nature of a Code, this was bound to
be the case.

At the close of this study, we should like to emphasize that
this broad and sometimes very detailed legislation should be read
in the context and spirit of the conciliar documents, which the

Constitution *Sacrae disciplinae leges* states are still the interpretative criterion for the Code of Canon Law.[77] We can even go so
far as to say that, if the norms are not to lose their underlying
spiritual significance, they must be interpreted in the light of the
word of God, which, as Pope John Paul II said in his discourse on
the presentation of the new Code, is the supreme rule of the life
of the Church.[78] If this criterion of the underlying inspiration of
the Canons is borne in mind, it will be easy to avoid and overcome any legalism or degeneration of the authentic sense of the
laws in our interpretation of them.

Translated from the Italian by Leslie Wearne.

Notes

1. Acts 6:1–2; A. Humbert, *L'atteggiamento dei primi cristiani verso
i bent terreni* (Rome, 1972); L. Orabona, *Cristianesimo e proprietà*
(Rome, 1964).

2. J. Piñero Carrion, *La sustentacion del clero, sintesis historica y
studio juridico*, Doctoral dissertation (Seville, 1963).

3. *Conciliorum Oecumenicorum Decreta* (Bologna, 1973), VI, 90:
"Nullum absolute ordinari debere presbyterum aut diaconum nec quem-
libet in gradu ecclesiastico, nisi specialiter ecclesiae civitatis aut posses-
sionis aut martyrii aut monasterii qui ordinandus est pronuntietur. Qui
vero absolute ordinantur, decrevit sancta synodus, irritam esse huiusce
modi manus impositionem, et nusquem posse ministrare, ad ordinantis
iniuriam." The Council of Chalcedon intended banning absolute ordi-
nations, but in the West the prohibition was understood mainly in the
context of the title of maintenance.

4. Concilium Lateranense III, in *ibid.*, 214 (No. 5): "Episcopus si
aliquem sine certo titulo, de quo necessaria vitae percipiat, in diaconum
vel in presbyterum ordinaverit, tamdiu necessaria ei subministret, do-
nec in aliqua ei ecclesia convenientia stipendia militiae clericalis as-
signet; nisi forte talis qui ordinatur exstiterit, qui de sua vel paterna
hereditate subsidium vitae possit habere." Cf. C. Vogel, "Titre d'Ordination et lien du Presbytre à la communauté locale dans l'Eglise ancienne," *La Maison-Dieu*, 115 (1973), 70–85.

5. V. De Paolis, "Titolo di ordinazione," *Dizionario degli Istituti di
Perfezione* (Rome, 1974–   ).

6. For the benefice system, cf. V. De Reina, *El sistema beneficial*
(Pamplona, 1965).

7. Cf. "Dal beneficio feudale all'officio ecclesiastico ed ecclesiale,
Bibliotheca," *Monitor Ecclesiasticus*, 33 (Naples, 1971); "Dal beneficio

feudale all'officio ecclesiastico ed ecclesiale o comune, Bibliotheca," *Monitor Ecclesiasticus,* 34 (Naples, 1971).

8. As regards, for example, Spain and France, see Piñero Carrion, "La sustentacion del clero," 243–297; for Italy, see G. Molteni Mastai Ferretti, *L'amministrazione dei benefici ecclesiastici* (Milan, 1974), 1–71.

9. For a comment on the Code, cf. G. Stocchiero, *Il beneficio ecclesiastico* (Vicenza, 1942).

10. For other titles, cf. Canons 981–982.

11. In fact, the 1917 Code attributes the so-called stole fees to the holder of the office (Cann. 1507 and 563). The possibility of a benefice made up from the free offerings of the faithful is envisaged in Canon 1410. It should also be recalled that another possible source of income is represented by Mass intentions (Cann. 824, 1506).

12. Molteni Mastai Ferretti, *L'amministrazione dei benefici ecclesiastici,* 107–137.

13. See the works listed in note 7 above.

14. A. Vermeersch and I. Cresusen, *Epitome Iuris Canonici,* 2 (Rome, 1954[7]), No. 798.

15. This problem can already be seen in the words of St. Augustine, *Sermo* CCCLVI, XIV, in *PL,* 39, 1580: "Quia placuit illis socialis haec vita, quisquis cum hypocrisi vixerit, quisquis inventus fuerit habens proprium, non illi permitto ut faciat testamentum, sed delebo eum de tabula clericorum. Interpellet contra me mille concilia, naviget contra me quo voluerit, sit certe ubi potuerit, adjuvabit me Deus, ut ubi ego episcopus sum, illic clericus esse non possit."

16. Canon 1476 of the 1917 Code.

17. Piñero Carrion, *La sustentacion del clero,* 527–550.

18. As we shall see, this is found among the proposals made at the Council for the reform of the benefice system.

19. Cf. D. Faltin, "De recto usu bonorum ecclesiasticorum ad mentem Concilii Vaticani II," *Apollinaris* (1967), 409–441; X. Ochoa, "Ratio bonorum temporalium in Ecclesia et Institutis perfectionis post Conc. Vat. II," *Commentarium pro Religiosis* (1967), 339–348; *id.,* "Acquisitio, distributio ac destinatio bonorum temporalium Ecclesiae Institutorumque perfectionis ad mentem Concilii Vaticani II," *Commentarium pro Religiosis* (1970), 20–33; V. Rovera, "De structuris oeconomicis in Ecclesia renovandis," *Periodica* (1971), 197–250.

20. Cf. N. Girasoli, *Significato ecclesiale dei beni temporali della Chiesa,* Doctoral dissertation (Rome, 1984).

21. See *Acta et documenta Concilio Oecumenico Vaticano II apparando, Series I (Antepraeparatoria)* (Vatican City, 1960–1961), 282–284.

22. The vote also lists the shortcomings of the benefice system that we have recalled above.

23. *Acta et documenta Concilio Oecumenico Vaticano II apparando,* Series I (*Antepraeparatoria*) (Vatican City, 1961), 206–209.

24. *Ibid.*

25. *Ibid.*

26. *Ibid.,* 714–710.

27. *Acta et documenta Concilio Oecumenico Vaticano II apparando,* Series II (*Praeparatoria*), *Commissio Centralis 1* (Vatican City, 1965), 685–689.

28. *Sacrosanctum Oecumenicum Concilium vaticanum secundum. Schemata constitutionum et decretorum (ex quibus argumenta in Concilio disceptanda seligentur,* Series IV (Vatican City, 1963), 37–42.

29. *Ibid.*

30. In the course of the Council, the following schemata on clerics dealt with the problem of the maintenance of the clergy: (1) *De clericis,* Nos. 27–39, in *AS,* III, III/IV (Vatican City, 1974), 837–842; (2) *De sacerdotibus,* Nos. 24–35, *ibid.,* 872–877; (3) *De sacerdotibus,* Nos. 7–10, *ibid.,* 848–849; (4) *De ministerio et vita sacerdotali,* Nos. 9–12, *AS,* III, II/IV (Vatican City, 1974), 230–232; (5) *De ministerio et vita presbyterorum,* Nos. 17–19, *AS,* IV, IV/IV (Vatican City, 1977), 857–860; (6) *De ministerio et vita presbyterorum,* Nos. 16–18, *ibid.,* 366–369; (7) *De ministerio et vita presbyterorum,* Nos. 17, 20–21, *AS,* IV, IV/VI (Vatican City, 1978), 378–380; (8) *De presbyterorum ministerio et vita,* Nos. 17, 20–21, *AS,* IV, IV/VII (Vatican City, 1978), 725–726.

31. Girasoli, *Significato ecclesiale dei beni temporali della Chiesa.*

32. O. Robleda, "Notio officii ecclesiastici in Concilio Vaticano II," *Quaestiones disputatae iuridico-canonicae* (Rome, 1969), 132–150.

33. Thus we find, in the schema *De clericis,* No. 29, "relicto systemate beneficiale"; the same words are also found in the schema *De sacerdotibus,* No. 25, the schema *De sacerdotibus* A, No. 8, and the schema *De ministerio et vita sacerdotali* B, No. 10; while in the schema *De ministerio et vita presbyterorum* C, No. 17, we find, "suppresso systemate beneficiali."

34. On the other hand, in the schema *De ministerio et vita presbyterorum* D, No. 16, we find, "reformato systemate sic dicto beneficiali."

35. A further variation is found in the schema *De ministerio et vita presbyterorum* E, No. 20: ". . . systema sic dictum beneficiale relinquatur aut saltem ita reformetur ut pars beneficialis . . . habeatur tamquam secundaria. . . ." This expression would remain in the definitive text (*Presbyterorum ordinis* 20).

36. O. Robleda, "De systemate beneficiali supprimendo aut reformando ad normam Concilii Vaticani II," *Quaestiones disputatae iuridico-canonicae* (Rome, 1969), 151–166.

37. Only those goods that belong to a public canonical juridical

person are ecclesiastical; cf. Canon 1257, §1, as compared with Canon 1497, §1, of the 1917 Code.

38. Cf. also *LG* 13, 23.

39. In a good number of countries, benefices are the subject of concordats with the state in question. For Italy, cf. Pontificia Universitas Urbaniana, *I nuovi Accordi Concordatari tra Chiesa e Stato in Italia* (Rome, 1985); G. Feliciani, "Il trattamento economico del clero nella nuova legislazione concordataria," *Aggiornamenti sociali*, 6 (1985), 451–462; *Norme per il sostentamento del clero* (Brescia, 1985).

40. L. Colombo, "Alcune questioni sulle finalità del patrimonio ecclesiastico," *Il nuovo Codice di diritto canonico* (Bologna, 1983), 243–252; V. De Paolis, "Schema canonum Libri V. De iure patrimoniali Ecclesiae," *Periodica*, 68 (1979), 673–713; *id.*, "De Bonis Ecclesiae temporalibus in novo Codice iuris canonici," *Periodica* (1984), 113–151; *id.*, "I beni temporali e la loro amministrazione," *I Religiosi e il nuovo Codice di diritto canonico* (Rome, 1983), 134–159; *id.*, *De bonis Ecclesiae temporalibus, Adnotationes in Codicem: Liber V* (Rome, 1986); T. Mauro, "Gli aspetti patrimoniali dell'organizzazione ecclesiastica," *Il nuovo Codice di diritto canonico* (Bologna, 1983), 207–226; S. Mester, "I beni temporali della Chiesa," *Il nuovo Codice di diritto canonico* (Rome, 1983), 296–306; A. Mostaza Rodriguez, "El nuevo derecho patrimonial de la Iglesia," *Studios eclesiasticos*, 58 (1983), 183–216; V. Rovera, "I beni temporali della Chiesa," *La normativa del nuovo Codice* (Brescia, 1983), 261–283; F.R. Aznar Gil, *La administracion de los bienes temporales de la Iglesia* (Salamanca, 1984); L. Chiappetta, *Dizionario del Nuovo Codice di diritto canonico* (Naples, 1986).

41. F. D'Ostilio, *E' pronto il nuovo Codice di diritto canonico* (Vatican City, 1982).

42. *AAS*, 58 (1966), 757–787.

43. *ES*, I, 8.

44. *Ibid.*

45. *Ibid.*

46. *Ibid.*

47. With regard to Canon 5 of the 1977 schema, we read in *Communicationes* (1980), 402: "Plures animadvertunt in schemate nimiam potestatem tribui Episcoporum conferentiis circa aliqua instituta, ita ut instauretur aliquod ius vigilantiae supra Episcopos, quod quidem intolerabile videtur attentis sive principiis doctrinalibus sive consectariis practis. Consultores concordes sunt ut e schemate expungatur quidquid implicare possit vigilantiam Conferentiae supra Episcopos, vel attentare possit Episcoporum iuri regendi suas Ecclesias uti pastores ordinarii et immediati."

48. *Schema canonum Libri V. De iure patrimoniali Ecclesiae* (Vatican City, 1977), 3: "In recognitione huius schematis praeterea 'principia quae recognitionem Codicis Iuris Canonici dirigant' adamussim Commissio secuta est, illus praesertim quod subsidiarietatis vocatur, quodque maxime in hac materia de bonis temporalibus attendi debuerat, cum circumstantiae diversarum regionum speciale influxum habeant in regimine bonorum."

49. *Ibid.:* "Uti notum enim est, in documentis Concilii Vaticani II praescriptiones habentur quae materiam de bonis temporalibus tangunt, quorumque consectaria in lege ordinari debent."

50. Cf. Canons 22, 197, 1290.

51. Cf. D'Ostillo, *E' pronto il nuovo Codice di diritto canonico.*

52. In his inaugural discourse to the Commission for the Revision of the Code, Paul VI himself indicated the Council as a point of reference. See *Communicationes* (1969), 41: ". . . ius canonicum, prudentia adhibita est recognoscendum, scilicet accomodari debet novo mentis habitui, Concilii Oecumenici Vaticani Secundi proprio, ex quo curae pastorali plurimum tribuitur, et novis necessitatibus populi Dei."

53. Cf. T. Marchi, "La remunerazione dei chierici," *Lo stato guiridico dei ministri sacri nel nuovo Codex Iuris Canonici* (Vatican City, 1984), 191: "E' difficile determinare se questo nel chierico sia un diritto in senso stretto. Infatti non si dice a chi incombe il dovere di provvedere." E. Cappellini, "Vita e ministero del presbitero," *Il presbitero nel nuovo Codice* (Brescia, 1985), 96, speaks, with regard to Canon 281, of the "insieme dei diritti relativi alla remunerazione e alle previdenze sociale," but in the discussion that follows he does not seem to attribute any precise connotation to this word: "Si tratta di un canone di enorme portata, perchè contiene alcune determinazioni fondamentali: anzitutto il principio: chi esercita un ministero ne ricavi il necessario per la propria sussistenza; la gratuità è principio evangelico, che si coniuga armonicamente con l'altro: chi serve all'altare viva dell'altare." However, in ecclesiastical tradition, it is difficult to see any right to maintenance for those who had other sources—even private—of income, precisely on the basis of the gospel principle. This does not mean that positive law cannot confer this right. Further study should be given to what E. Cappellini himself says in another article, "Beni ecclesiastici e onesto sostentamento del clero," *Norme per il sostentamento del clero* (Brescia, 1985), 165: ". . . la adeguata remunerazione per il chierico che si dedichi ad un ministero ecclesiastico è un diritto personale: indipendentemente dalla situazione della sua famiglia di origine."

54. Canon 281, §3, indicates that the ministry as such is not the basis for any right to remuneration, but that remuneration is merely a necessity that arises from the fact that the person devotes himself to the ministry.

55. Cappellini, "Beni ecclesiastici e onesto sostentamento del clero," 13, note 3.

56. Piñero Carrion, *La sustentacion del clero*, 134–192.

57. However, it must be borne in mind that Canon 1274, §1, is not in complete harmony with Canon 1272, inasmuch as the latter states that there should be a reform based on the existence of the fund described in Canon 1274, §1, while the latter does not say that the setting up of such a fund is obligatory except "nisi aliter eisdem provisum sit."

58. PO 21.

59. F. Salerno, "Commento al can. 1274," *Commento al Codice di diritto canonico* (Rome, 1985), states that Canon 1274, §1, "lascia liberi gli Ordinari di provvedere in modo alternativo al mantenimento del clero, senze tuttavia consentirne con ciò di protrarre nel tempo il sistema beneficiale."

60. PO 21.

61. Canon 1274, §1.

62. Canons 531, 551, 1181.

63. Canon 1267, §3; cf. also Canons 121–123.

65. Canon 134, §3.

65. As laid down in Canon 127, such consultation is necessary for validity.

66. Traces still remain of a widespread idea that a certain financial incentive is needed in order for people to devote themselves to their work!

67. The vote of the Salesian University, 5, rejects this (see note 23 above).

68. See, for example, the vote of the Faculty of Naples (see note 26 above).

69. *De officiis et beneficiis ecclesiasticis minoribus saecularibus deque bonorum ecclesiasticorum administratione*, no. 40 (cited in note 28 above).

70. PO 20.

71. It does not appear that the reason was a wish to authorize the possibility of imposing a levy on Mass offerings, because no trace of such a possibility is found in any canon. The text should therefore be interpreted in accordance with Canon 6, §2. In any case, the legislation assumes that offerings for the application of Mass to specific intentions should go to the celebrant, and that it should be passed on in its entirety (Canon 955).

72. See also Canon 951, §2.

73. It is easy to understand why it is the Ordinary of the place who can authorize a priest to celebrate twice or three times in one day (Canon 905), because this is a pastoral matter, while it is the Ordinary who is to decide as to the intention of the second and possible third Mass (Canon 951, §1), because this is not strictly speaking a pastoral matter. In any case, this was already the practice, on the basis of faculties granted by the Holy See.

74. This takes place in certain dioceses, but we really do not feel that this practice has sufficient foundation.

75. For other reasons, Cappellini, "Beni ecclesiastici e onesto sostentamento del clero," 19, note 9, states that he is against such taxation.

76. Our observations are confined to the question of the maintenance of the clergy. We do not intend examining the whole approach of Book V to see whether or not it corresponds to the ecclesiological perspective of Vatican II. On this question, we cannot share the criticisms made by E. Corecco, "I presupposti culturali ed ecclesiologici del nuovo Codex," *Il nuovo Codice di diritto canonico* (Bologna, 1983), 52.

77. *Codex Iuris Canonici* (Vatican City, 1983), XI: "Immo, certo quodam modo, novus hic Codex concipi potest veluti magnus nisus transferendi in sermonem canonisticum hanc ipsam doctrinam, ecclesiologiam scilicet conciliarem. Quod si fieri nequit, ut imago Ecclesiae per doctrinam Concilii descripta perfecte in linguam canonisticam convertatur, nihilominus ad hanc ipsam imaginem semper Codex est referendus tamquam ad primarium exemplum, cuius lineamenta is in se, quantum fieri potest suapte natura experimere debet."

78. See *Communicationes* (1983), 16: "Accanto al Libro contente gli Atti del Concilio c'è ora il nuovo Codice canonico, e questo mi sembra un abbinamento ben valido e significativo. Ma sopra, ma prima di questi due Libri è da porre, quale vertice di trascendente eminenza, il Libro eterno della Parola di Dio, di cui centro e cuore è il Vangelo."

Bibliography

This bibliography contains the books and articles published on the Second Vatican Council by the contributors to Volume One.

Zoltán Alszeghy, S.J.

"L'immagine di Dio nella storia della salvezza," in La Chiesa e il mondo contemporaneo nel Vaticano II, Collana Magistero Conciliare 11 (Turin, 1966), 419–452.

"Quid reflexio ad historiam salutis a theologia catholica exigat," in Acta Congressus Internationalis de Theologia Concilii Vaticani II (Vatican City, 1968), 444–454.

"Salvezza, mistero, storia della," in Dizionario del Concilio Ecumenico Vaticano II (Vatican City, 1968), 1760–1772.

"La crisi della Chiesa interpella la nostra fede," in: AA.VV., Come interpretare la crisi della Chiesa oggi? (Rome, 1972), 35–46.

"A 'hivatás' fogalma a II. Vatikáni Zsinat után," Szolgálat, 48 (1980), 5–11.

Angel Antón, S.J.

"Conciencia posconciliar," Razón y Fe, 173 (1966), 597–610.

"De ratione discriminis in theologica qualificatione Constitutionis 'Lumen Gentium,' " Periodica, 55 (1966), 549–593.

"Il progresso della Chiesa nel tempo," in Laici sulle vie del Concilio (Assisi, 1966), 29–46.

"Base sacramental de la estructura jerárquica de la Iglesia," Estudios Eclesiásticos, 42 (1967), 355–386.

"El capítulo del Pueblo de Dios en la Eclesiología de la comunidad," Estudios Eclesiásticos, 42 (1967), 155–181.

"Episcopi per orbem dispersi: estne collegiale eorum magisterium ordinarium et infallibile?" Periodica, 56 (1967), 212–246.

"Estructura teándrica de la Iglesia. Historia y significado eclesiológico del numero 8° de la 'Lumen Gentium,' " *Estudios Eclesiásticos*, 42 (1967), 39–72.

"Episcoporum Synodus: partes agens totius catholici episcopatus," *Periodica* 57 (1968), 495–527.

"Iglesia, Cuerpo de Cristo," *Manresa*, 40 (1968), 283–304.

"Revelación y Tradición. 'Gesta et Verba' sus elementos constitutivos," *Estudios Eclesiásticos*, 43 (1968), 225–258.

"El tratado 'De Ecclesia' nuevo centro de perspectiva en la enseñanza de la Teología," *Gregorianum*, 50 (1969), 661–688.

"Episcopato e primato garantiscono la diversità e l'unità nella Chiesa," *La Civiltà Cattolica*, 120/4 (1969), 110–124.

"Hacia una síntesis de las nociones 'cuerpo de Cristo' y 'pueblo de Dios' en la eclesiología," *Estudios Eclesiásticos*, 44 (1969), 311–364.

"La comunidad creyente portadora de la revelación," in *Comentarios a la 'Dei Verbum,'* BAC 284 (Madrid, 1969), 311–364.

"La Iglesia 'pueblo de Dios' en la nueva alianza," *Estudios Eclesiásticos*, 44 (1969), 465–501.

"Sinodo e Collegialità estraconciliare," in V. Fagiolo and G. Concetti (eds.), *La collegialità episcopale per il futuro della Chiesa* (Florence, 1969), 62–78.

Primado y Colegialidad, BAC-Minor 15 (Madrid, 1970).

"Primado y Colegialidad en la discusión del Sínodo," *Estudios Eclesiásticos*, 45 (1970), 5–34.

"La Iglesia comunidad," in *Comunidad Eclesial y misiones*, XXIII Semana Espanola de misionología (Burgos, 1971), 41–93.

"Iglesia universal—Iglesias particulares," *Estudios Eclesiásticos*, 47 (1972), 409–435.

"Infalibilidad: problema ecuménico," *Gregorianum*, 53 (1972), 759–770.

"Lo sviluppo della dottrina sulla Chiesa nella teologia della teologia dal Vaticano I al Vaticano II," in *L'Ecclesiologia dal Vaticano I al Vaticano II* (Milan, 1973), 27–87.

"Curso de aggiornamento en Eclesiología," *Iglesia Pascual*, 7 (1981), 39–56.

"Magisterio de la Iglesia y Fe del cristiano," *Sillar*, 3 (1983), 41–54.

"Magisterio y teología: dos funciones complementarias," *Sillar*, 3 (1983), 57–72.

La Iglesia de Cristo. El Israel de la Vieja y de la Nueva Alianza, BAC-Maior 15 (Madrid, 1977), 5–54, 707–792.

"La collegialità nel Sinodo dei Vescovi," in J. Tomko (ed.), *Il Sinodo dei Vescovi. Natura. Metodo. Prospettive* (Vatican City, 1985), 59–111.

Piero Antonio Bonnet

"Est in Ecclesia diversitas ministerii sed unitas missionis," in E.

Corecco, N. Herzog, and A. Scola (eds.), *Les droits fondamentaux du Chrétien dans l'Église et dans la Société. Actes du IVe Congrès International de droit canonique, Fribourg (Suisse) 6–11.X.1980* (Fribourg/ Freiburg im Breisgau/Milan, 1981), 291–308.

"De christifidelium communi statu (iuxta Schema anni 1979 L.E.F.) animadversiones," *Periodica*, 71 (1982), 463–529.

"Una questione ancora aperta: l'origine del potere gerarchico nella Chiesa," *Ephemerides Iuris Canonici*, 38 (1982), 62–121.

"Pluralismo (in genere) a) diritto canonico," in *Enciclopedia del Diritto*, 33 (Milan, 1983), 956–983.

"Habet pro conditione dignitatem libertatemque filiorum Dei", *Il diritto ecclesiastico*, 92/1 (1981), 556–620; in *Diritto, persona e vita sociale. Scritti in memoria di Orio Giacchi II* (Milan, 1984), 157–203.

"De laicorum notione adumbratio," *Periodica*, 74 (1985), 227–271.

José Caba, S.J.

"El problema de la historicidad de los evangelios en el concilio Vaticano II: Constitución dogmática 'Dei Verbum,' " in *De los evangelios al Jesús histórico. Introducción a la Cristología* (Madrid, 1980²), 50–73.

"Il problema della storicità dei vangeli nel concilio Vaticano II: Costituzione dogmatica 'Dei Verbum,' " in *Dai vangeli al Gesù storico* (Rome, 1979²), 55–75.

"En torno a los autores de los evangelios: Constitución dogmática 'Dei Verbum,' " in *De los evangelios al Jesús histórico. Introducción a la Cristología* (Madrid, 1980²), 107–117.

"Gli autori dei vangeli: Costituzione dogmatica 'Dei Verbum,' " in *Dai vangeli al Gesù storico* (Rome, 1979²), 106–116.

Stefano De Fiores, S.M.M.

Maria presenza viva nel popolo di Dio (Rome, 1980).

Maria nel mistero di Cristo e della Chiesa. Commento al capitolo mariano del Concilio Vaticano II (Rome, 1984³).

"Mariologia," in G. Barbaglio and S. Dianich (eds.), *Nuovo dizionario di teologia* (Rome, 1985⁴), 850–884.

"Maria," in S. De Fiores and T. Goffi (eds.), *Nuovo dizionario di spiritualità* (Rome, 1985⁴), 878–902.

Maria nella teologia contemporanea (Rome, 1986²).

Nuovo dizionario di mariologia, S. De Fiores and S. Meo (eds.) (Cinisello Balsamo, 1986²).

Ignace de la Potterie, S.J.

"La verité de la Sainte Écriture et l'Histoire du salut d'après la Constitution dogmatique 'Dei Verbum,' " *Nouvelle Revue Théologique*, 88 (1966), 149–169.

"La verdad o inerrancia de la Sagrada Escritura e historia de la salvación a la luz de la constitución 'Dei Verbum,' " *Hechos y dichos*, 301 (1966), 171–183.

"Verità della S. Scrittura e storia della salvezza alla luce della Costituzione dogmatica 'Dei Verbum,' " in *La verità della Bibbia nel dibattito attuale*, Giornale di Teologia 21 (Brescia, 1968, 1972²), 281–306.

Jean Galot, S.J.

"Réflexions sur la structure du Concile," *Revue du Clergé africain*, 19 (1964), 143–148.

"Mère de l'Église," *Nouvelle Revue Théologique*, 86 (1964), 1163–1185.

"Pour le renouveau," *Vie Consacrée*, 38 (1966), 321–338.

"Marie, type et modèle de l'Église," in G. Baraúna and Y. M.-J. Congar (eds.), *L'Église de Vatican II. Études autour de la Constitution conciliaire sur l'Église* (Paris, 1966), 1243–1259.

"Le sacerdoce selon la doctrine du Concile," *Nouvelle Revue Théologique*, 88 (1966), 1044–1061.

Renouveau de la vie consacrée. Le décret du Concile. Présentation et commentaire (Gembloux-Paris, 1966).

Les religieux dans l'Église selon la Constitution 'Lumen Gentium' et le décret sur la charge pastorale des Evêques (Gembloux-Paris, 1967).

Porteurs du souffle de l'Esprit. Nouvelle optique de la vie consacrée (Gembloux-Paris, 1967).

Consécration au coeur du monde. Gaudium et Spes et la vie consacrée (Gembloux-Paris, 1968).

Visage d'Évangile des instituts religieux (Gembloux-Paris, 1968).

"La cristologia nella 'Sacrosanctum Concilium," *Notitiae. Sacra Congregatio pro Sacramentis et Cultu Divino*, 20 (1983), 305–319.

Karl Heinz Neufeld, S.J.

"Die Bibel—Weg zur Einheit?" *Stimmen der Zeit*, 183 (1969), 421–424.

"Abendmahlsgemeinschaft—Für und Wider," *Entschluss*, 24 (1969), 421–424.

"Examen nachkonziliarer Frömmigkeit," *Entschluss*, 26 (1971), 500–504.

"Dienst und Herrschaft," *Die Sendung* 26/4 (1973), 13–16.

"Berufung auf die Basis?" *Entschluss*, 28 (1973), 274–279.

"Christliche Erfahrung und theologische Reflexion," *Stimmen der Zeit*, 193 (1975), 269–278.

"Kircheneinigung—soziologisch," *Catholica*, 31 (1977), 39–50.

"Luterani e Cattolici in dialogo sull'Eucaristia," *La Civiltà Cattolica*, 130/3 (1979), 460–472.

"Von der Last des Katholischen," *Theologisch-Praktische Quartalschrift*, 128 (1980), 221–230.

"Wirksame Ökumene—Kardinal Beas Einsatz für die Einigung der Christen," *Catholica*, 35 (1981), 189–210.

"Dialog der Kirchen," *Stimmen der Zeit*, 201 (1983), 62–65.

"Theologen und Konzil. Karl Rahners Beitrag zum Zweiten Vatikanischen Konzil," *Stimmen der Zeit*, 202 (1984), 156–166.

"Kirche und Kardinal. Zum Kirchenbild Henri de Lubac," *Stimmen der Zeit*, 203 (1985), 859–861.

"Henri de Lubac S.J. als Konzilstheologe," *Theologisch-Praktische Quartalschrift*, 134 (1986), 149–159.

Gerald O'Collins, S.J.

"Divine Revelation," *Month*, 35 (1966), 332–336.

Theology and Revelation (Cork, 1968).

Foundations of Theology (Chicago, 1971).

Fundamental Theology (New York-London, 1981).

"At the Origins of 'Dei Verbum,' " *The Heythrop Journal*, 26 (1985), 5–13.

James Swetnam, S.J.

"Hermeneutical Challenge" in "A Symposium on Changes in the Church Since Vatican II," *Catholic Mind*, 78 (1980), 56–58.

"Pakistani Catholics and the Bible," *The Bible Today*, 19 (1981), 127–131.

"Pontifical Biblical Institute: International Center of Study and Research," *The Bible Today*, 19 (1981), 248–254.

"Japanese Catholics and the Bible," *The Bible Today*, 19 (1981), 388–393.

"Haitian Catholics and the Bible," *The Bible Today*, 20 (1982), 171–175.

"Indian Catholics and the Bible," *The Bible Today*, 21 (1983), 268–271.

"Italian Catholics and the Bible," *The Bible Today*, 21 (1983), 294–298.

"Nigerian Catholics and the Bible," *The Bible Today*, 22 (1984), 181–185.

"Brazilian Catholics and the Bible," *The Bible Today*, 22 (1984), 376–380.

"French Catholics and the Bible," *The Bible Today*, 23 (1985), 111–115.

"South Korean Catholics and the Bible," *The Bible Today*, 23 (1985), 262–265.

"Mexican Catholics and the Bible," *The Bible Today*, 24 (1986), 108–111.

"Philippine Catholics and the Bible," *The Bible Today*, 24 (1986), 310–313.

Contents
of All Three Volumes

PART III

The Church, Sacrament of Salvation

Volume Two

PART IV

Liturgy and Sacraments

PART VI

The View of Humanity

Volume Three

PART VII

The Consecrated Life

63. The Decree on the Means of Social
    Communication: Success or Failure of the Council?
    André Ruszkowski

64. Mass Media and Culture in Contemporary
    Catholicism: The Significance of Vatican II
    Robert White, S.J.